LAWRENCE HENRY GIPSON

AUTHOR

JARED INGERSOLL: A STUDY OF AMERICAN LOYALISM IN RELATION TO BRITISH COLONIAL GOVERNMENT

STUDIES IN CONNECTICUT COLONIAL TAXATION

THE MORAVIAN INDIAN MISSION ON WHITE RIVER

LEWIS EVANS

THE COMING OF THE REVOLUTION, 1763–1775

THE BRITISH EMPIRE BEFORE THE AMERICAN REVOLUTION

    VOLUME I. THE BRITISH ISLES AND THE AMERICAN COLONIES: GREAT BRITAIN AND IRELAND, 1748–1754

    VOLUME II. THE BRITISH ISLES AND THE AMERICAN COLONIES: THE SOUTHERN PLANTATIONS, 1748–1754

    VOLUME III. THE BRITISH ISLES AND THE AMERICAN COLONIES: THE NORTHERN PLANTATIONS, 1748–1754

    VOLUME IV. ZONES OF INTERNATIONAL FRICTION: NORTH AMERICA, SOUTH OF THE GREAT LAKES REGION, 1748–1754

    VOLUME V. ZONES OF INTERNATIONAL FRICTION: THE GREAT LAKES FRONTIER, CANADA, THE WEST INDIES, INDIA, 1748–1754

    VOLUME VI. THE GREAT WAR FOR THE EMPIRE: THE YEARS OF DEFEAT, 1754–1757

    VOLUME VII. THE GREAT WAR FOR THE EMPIRE: THE VICTORIOUS YEARS, 1758–1760

    VOLUME VIII. THE GREAT WAR FOR THE EMPIRE: THE CULMINATION, 1760–1763

    VOLUME IX. THE TRIUMPHANT EMPIRE: NEW RESPONSIBILITIES WITHIN THE ENLARGED EMPIRE, 1763–1766

    VOLUME X. THE TRIUMPHANT EMPIRE: THUNDER-CLOUDS GATHER IN THE WEST, 1763–1766

    VOLUME XI. THE TRIUMPHANT EMPIRE: THE RUMBLING OF THE COMING STORM, 1766–1770
    (scheduled for publication in 1965)

    VOLUME XII. THE TRIUMPHANT EMPIRE: BRITAIN SAILS INTO THE STORM, 1770–1776
    (scheduled for publication in 1965)

    VOLUME XIII. PART I. THE TRIUMPHANT EMPIRE: BEYOND THE STORM, 1765–1776, and Summary of the Series
               PART II. HISTORIOGRAPHY and BIBLIOGRAPHY
    (in preparation)

"Every considerable library on American and British history will require Mr. Gipson's volumes as an indispensable work of reference, and most readers will be . . . captivated by the lively reports of this intelligent and humane historical surveyor . . ."

SAMUEL ELIOT MORISON

THE BRITISH EMPIRE
BEFORE THE AMERICAN REVOLUTION
VOLUME VI

THE GREAT WAR FOR THE EMPIRE

THE YEARS OF DEFEAT

1754–1757

THE BRITISH EMPIRE
BEFORE THE AMERICAN REVOLUTION
VOLUME VI

THE GREAT WAR FOR THE EMPIRE

THE YEARS OF DEFEAT, 1754–1757

BY

LAWRENCE HENRY GIPSON

MCMLXV
ALFRED A. KNOPF
NEW YORK

L. C. CATALOGUE CARD NUMBER: 58–9670

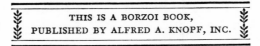

THIS IS A BORZOI BOOK,
PUBLISHED BY ALFRED A. KNOPF, INC.

PUBLISHED FEBRUARY 14, 1946
SECOND PRINTING, MARCH 1959
THIRD PRINTING, APRIL 1965

Manufactured in the United States of America and distributed by Random House, Inc. Published in Canada by Random House of Canada, Limited.

THIS BOOK IS DEDICATED *to the thousands of soldiers from the British Isles who lie buried in unknown graves here in the New World as the result of the Great War for the Empire waged between the years 1754 and 1763. In response to the appeals of the hard-pressed colonials hemmed in to the east of the Appalachian range by the power of France, British regiments were carried across the Atlantic and sent into the American wilderness to bear the brunt of the fighting against French regulars. Suffering heavy casualties, suffering defeats, still they held on with dogged determination — supported on land by the colonial line, on sea by the men of the royal navy, and at home by the continued and heavy financial sacrifices of the people — and thereby, with victory finally achieved, helped to provide a future without parallel for the English-speaking people here on the continent of North America.*

Preface

THIS VOLUME has in the main to do with the activities of small groups of people, both soldiers and non-combatants, in connection with the early years of Anglo-French hostilities that began in 1754 in North America, that in 1756 spread to most of Europe and to the Far East, and that were only to end in 1763 with the Peace of Paris. But let no one suppose that the activities of these small groups during the years in question were unimportant, for the fate of a continent was really at stake. There had previously been other Anglo-French wars involving the New World, but those, even including the War of the Spanish Succession, were in a sense but preliminary sparrings for position. Now Great Britain and France at last faced each other in a struggle that was destined to be so decisive in its outcome as to determine to our own day the main trends of historical development not only in North America but in the subcontinent of India.

The name "The Seven Years' War" as applied to the war the beginnings of which are now to be considered seems to have been employed first in Germany and to have come into general use in Europe during the period between the close of the American Revolution and the beginning of the French Revolution. English chroniclers of it such as John Entick and John Wright, who compiled their histories before the outbreak of the American Revolution, referred to it as "The Late War"; an anonymous writer gives his book, published in London in 1767, the title: *An Impartial History of the Late Glorious War.* Johann Gottlieb Tielke, in his *Beyträge zur Kriegs — Kunst und Geschichte des Krieges von 1756 bis 1763,* illustrates the search for a satisfactory name. In Volume I, published in 1776 at Freiburg, he called the war *"Der 1756 entstandene Krieg"* or *"Krieg von 1756";* such expressions are also used to designate it in subsequent volumes until in Volume VI, published in 1786, he referred in his preface to *"eine eigentliche Geschichte des siebenjahrigen Krieges."*

American historians have realized that the name "The Seven Years' War," appropriately enough used to designate the European war waged between 1756 and 1763, is inapplicable to the contemporary struggle in North America and elsewhere that lasted for nine years. While the two wars were in many respects fused into each other, in many other respects they were quite distinct. Writers therefore have, I believe rightly, sought to give the great war between the British and French empires fought out on land and sea in various parts of the world a distinct name. American historians in the past have, however, generally favoured a title that seems to obscure its real significance and to localize it much more than was actually the case by calling it "The French and Indian War." But there are other objections to this title as being properly descriptive of the war. Among these is the fact that in reality not only were there, as previously intimated, several North American French and Indian wars, but in some of these the natives played a much more important role than in the war in question. The great historian Francis Parkman, interested primarily in the American scene, sought to avoid the obscuration implicit in this title by dropping it in favour of one, more picturesque, it is true, but equally confusing and misleading, for his two volumes that he entitled *Montcalm and Wolfe;* Osgood satisfied himself in the fourth volume of his *American Colonies in the Eighteenth Century* with the very prosaic title "The Fourth Intercolonial War," which leaves much to be desired; Bancroft in his *History of the United States,* which is not a history of the United States, included this war in the Revolutionary War, by calling it *"The American Revolution. Epoch First. The Overthrow of the European Colonial System, 1748–1763"* — an inaccurate title; and John Fiske in his American history series more accurately designates it "The Great War." I have chosen the title "The Great War for the Empire" as the most appropriate for reasons that are set forth with some fullness in the Introduction.

Any historian seeking to write the history of such a war as the one with which this volume is concerned is beset with complexities. First of all, he is faced with various schools of thought and practice among his fellow craftsmen. One of these schools stresses the apportionment of space so that each geographical or political unit will be sure to receive an emphasis that the numerical weight of its population or its economic importance would seem to entitle it to enjoy, irrespective of the significance or lack of significance of developments within its borders; another school demands that a centre of observation be established and that all events be viewed as from this centre for the purpose of providing the basis for a unified narrative and contemporary perspective; still another expects that the chief emphasis shall be placed upon institutional or functional developments in the midst of war, irrespective of questions involving political units or perspective; another requires that major attention be paid to the technique of waging war, with strategical, tactical, and technological problems kept to the forefront at all times; still another insists that a study of the economics of a war should have first place as the most important of all factors in modern warfare; while another finds the answer to history in war as in peace in a study of leaders and leadership; and then, finally, the "climate of opinion" school of the sociological historians demands emphasis upon those factors that condition the attitudes of peoples in a war and thus influence its outcome. It is therefore abundantly clear that no historian could hope to meet the insistent demands made upon him by all the schools.

To me it has seemed not only desirable but necessary that this volume and those to follow should conform closely to the pattern of historical approach established in the first five volumes of this series, irrespective of the demands of the various schools. In the present work one of the motives that dictated the selection of topics and space allotted to each of these has been a desire to emphasize certain important aspects of the history of this conflict that have been, it would seem, especially subject to popular misconceptions and even to serious misinterpretations on the part of many historians and of others who are not. For this reason considerable space has been given to the expulsion of the Acadians — an event held by many writers to be the darkest blot on the history of the activities of the English-speaking people in the New World. Likewise the steps leading to the diplomatic revolution in Europe and the fusing of the Great War for the Empire with the European Seven Years' War have been stressed as matters of major interest. Nevertheless, much effort has been expended to present a well-rounded account of major developments during the early years of the war. It should at the same time be made clear that certain institutional as well as other aspects of the period have been reserved for later detailed analysis — in particular those involving a consideration of wartime finance both imperial and colonial as well as wartime commercial activities.

The amount of material available for use by the student who seeks to master all the details of the history of the Great War for the Empire is almost unlimited in extent. It has therefore been necessary to select with care, and then to rely upon, those sources that appear to be not only the most authentic but the most important. In the writing of history dealing with highly controversial matters, as does this volume, in fairness to the reader it seems desirable whenever possible to quote authority that will be most accessible to him for purposes of checking. For example, copies of many important papers here used are to be found in their original form both in the London Public Record Office and among the Loudoun Papers in the Huntington Library. Some of these have also been collected and printed in particular documentary series to be found in all leading libraries. Without giving the space in the footnotes to indicate the location of all original copies of a document made at the time, the printed source alone is given as a reference when the latter upon examination has proved to be sufficiently accurate. Otherwise reference is given to the location of the original that has been attested; or if more than one copy has been attested, to the depository that logically would be expected to possess it. This applies particularly to such papers as the Dinwiddie Papers; the "fair" copies of the original correspondence sent to London at the time have, as a rule, been used in preference to the printed documents drawn from the Dinwiddie "Letter Books." In this connection it will be noted that, to aid the average reader, quotations from a foreign language are now given in translation. This practice will be followed in subsequent volumes.

In expressing my deep obligation to the many library and archival officials who have aided me in the search for material utilized in the writing of the present volume — a search carried on both before and subsequent to the outbreak of the present war — I must mention in particular those connected with the following research centres: the London Public Record Office, the British Museum, Trinity College Library, Dublin, the Bibliothèque at Vire, in Normandy, the Canadian Archives, the Nova Scotian Archives, the Library of Congress, the Huntington Library, the Clements Library, the Massachusetts State Archives, the Massachusetts Historical Society, the Archives of the State of New York at Albany, the New York Historical Society, the New York Public Library, the Historical Society of Pennsylvania, the Library Company of Philadelphia, the Maryland Historical Society, the Virginia State Library, the Virginia Historical Society, the South Carolina State Historical Commission, and the Library of Lehigh University. The vast collections in the Library of Congress and Canadian Archives of transcriptions of unprinted documents in both English and French, particularly those drawn from France, alone made it possible under the circumstances to round out this study. Once again I must acknowledge my indebtedness likewise to both the Institute of Research of Lehigh University for financial assistance and the university administration for its consistently sympathetic co-operation in this undertaking.

The preparation of this volume has involved far more labour and difficulty in this time of war than was anticipated when work upon it was begun. Nevertheless there are intangible rewards connected with such an enterprise that come in the realization that a specific task of considerable proportions undertaken in high hope has in the face of serious obstacles been carried to completion.

"Rotha"   L. H. G.
Panther Road
Rydal, Pennsylvania
May 12, 1945

Contents

CHAPTER I

INTRODUCTION: THE GREAT WAR FOR THE EMPIRE AND AMERICAN NATIONAL TRADITION

National tradition and the English Common Law compared   3

The power of tradition in a nation   3

American tradition and the Great War for the Empire   4
    The role played by Thomas Paine's *Common Sense*   4
    The responsibility for the outbreak of war in 1754   9
    National tradition and westward American expansion   10
    The national tradition and colonial military prowess   13

The decisive part played by the people of Great Britain in the North American war   15
    Britain's choice of policies in 1754   16

The close of the Great War for the Empire and the movement for independence   18

CHAPTER II

A PALISADO IN THE WILDERNESS

The beginnings of the American conflict   20
    The colonial problem of the French aggressions   21

Washington ordered to the forks of the Ohio   22
    The news of the arrival of the French   23

The decision to march to Redstone Creek   23
    The wisdom of this considered   23
    Dinwiddie's responsibility   24

Dissatisfaction among Washington's forces at the Youhiogheny   29
    Dinwiddie rebukes Washington   29

Washington at Great Meadows   30
  Warnings of the approach of the French   30
  The surprise attack upon Jumonville's force   31
  The arrival of the reinforcements   32

The forward movement to Gist's settlement   34

The Indian conferences   34
  Washington's failure to gain support   35

The council of war   35
  The decision to retreat to Wills Creek   35

De Villiers in pursuit of Washington   36
  His instructions   36
  His march to Great Meadows   36

The fight for Fort Necessity   38
  The unequal battle   38
  The capitulation   40

Washington's return to Wills Creek   42

CHAPTER III

BRITAIN LENDS A HAND

De Villiers returns in triumph to Fort Duquesne   44

The weakness of the colonial position in 1754   44
  Lack of co-operation of the middle and southern colonies   45
  Unwillingness of Pennsylvania to assist Virginia   45
  The New York Independent Companies   45
  The North Carolina reinforcements   46

Dinwiddie plans a new campaign   48
  Colonel Innis to command   48
  The campaign put aside   48
  The critical attitude of Governor Glen   49

Governor Sharpe becomes the new commander-in-chief   50
  Glen's request for a conference refused   50
  A third plan for a campaign   51
  The building of Fort Cumberland   51

The reorganization of the Virginia regiments   51
  Washington resigns his command   52

Collapse of the colonial efforts for a renewed campaign against the
    French   53–4

The Newcastle ministry and colonial defence   54
    Early steps taken to support the colonies   55
    The question of sending regular troops   56
    The appointment of James Braddock   57

The ministerial project for an American campaign   58
    Forces to be placed at the disposal of Braddock   58
    Braddock's "Secret Instructions"   58

Parliament agrees to support the colonies   60

CHAPTER IV

THE DISASTER AT THE MONONGAHELA

The British and French positions respecting the Ohio before
    Braddock leaves for America   62

The Irish regiments   63

American support of the Braddock expedition   64
    Dinwiddie's preparations in Virginia   64
    South Carolina's intransigence   64
    Unpatriotic conduct of New York and Philadelphia merchants   65
    The Pennsylvania Assembly and the war   66

The Alexandria conference   70
    Significance of the failure to summon Governor Glen   70
    The strategy of the year's operations outlined   71
    The failure of the plan for a common fund   71

The route to Fort Duquesne   73
    The Pennsylvania route considered   73

Preparations for the expedition   74
    Failure of Virginia and Maryland to supply transportation   75
    Franklin's contribution to the expedition   75
    Washington joins Braddock's staff   77

Braddock at Wills Creek   77
    Failure of the Southern Indians to join   77
    Conference with the Pennsylvania Indians   77

The expedition an epic in military annals   78

Difficulties of the march to the Monongahela 79
    Readjustments made on June 11 80
    The council of war at Little Meadows 82
    The first division pushes ahead 82

Braddock's leadership 83
    His care of transport facilities 84
    His treatment of his soldiers 85
    His precautions against surprise 85

The third council of war at Salt Lick Creek 85
    The decision to push forward 85

The army arrives at the Monongahela 85

The French preparations to meet Braddock 86
    Troops sent to Canada from France 86
    The gathering of matériel in Canada 87
    The movement of Western Indians against the English 87
    Canadian detachments move to the Ohio 87
    The completion of Fort Duquesne 88
    The construction of Fort Machault 88
    Fort Duquesne and the problem of supply 89
    Efforts to hinder Braddock's march 89

The disaster at the Monongahela 92
    The crossing and recrossing of the river 92
    The line of march on July 9 92
    The lack of Indian support 93
    Colonel Gage's fatal errors 94
    Colonel Halkett's error 95
    Braddock's effort to snatch victory from defeat 95
    Controversies over the battle 95

CHAPTER V

BOSCAWEN MISSES AN ASSIGNMENT

Determination of the French Crown to send reinforcements to
    Canada 99
    Seventy-eight companies of regulars selected 100
    Purpose of these reinforcements 100

The concept of the "line of amity" 100

The British dilemma 101

The Cabinet Council decides to send a fleet to American waters 102
    The fleet to waylay the French reinforcements 102
    Boscawen selected to command 103

The French plan for conveying the reinforcements 103
    The utilization of French ships of the line 104
    Character of eighteenth-century French warships 104
    Factors favourable to the French beyond the "line of amity" 105

The sailing of the French fleet 106
    Convoy of the fleet to the mid-Atlantic 106
    The fleet divided 107

The French fleet off the Grand Bank 107
    The narrow escape of the fleet on June 6 108

Movements of Boscawen 108

The Cabinet Council sends Boscawen a reinforcement 109
    Rear Admiral Holburne's fleet departs 109

The capture of the *Alcide* and the *Lys* 110
    Captain Howe of the *Dunkirk* 111

The movements of the French fleet 113
    De Salvert's squadron reaches Louisbourg 114
    De la Motte's squadron moves into the St. Lawrence 114

Boscawen seeks the remainder of the French fleet 116
    Difficulties encountered by the British fleet 116
    The justification of Boscawen's plan of operations 117

Effect in Europe of the news of the capture of the French ships 117
    Attitude of Newcastle and the British Cabinet Council 117
    Why France did not declare war 118

The return of the French fleet *armés en flûte* 119
    The British efforts to blockade the fleet 119
    De la Motte eludes the enemy 120

De Salvert's escape from Louisbourg 122
    The British blockade of the harbour 122
    The September hurricane season and the British fleet 123
    Failure of the British to overtake de Salvert 123

The *Espérance* seeks to return to France   124
    The capture of the French vessel   125

The achievement of the French navy in carrying reinforcements to
    Canada considered   126

CHAPTER VI

NIAGARA AND CROWN POINT

Aftermath of Braddock's defeat   127
    The terror along the western borders   127
    Colonel Dunbar's leadership in the crisis   127
    Office of commander-in-chief falls to Shirley   129

William Shirley in command   129
    Record of achievement before 1755   129
    Disposition of Dunbar's forces   132

The crisis in western Pennsylvania, Maryland, and Virginia   134
    Steps taken to protect the frontier   134

The campaign against Crown Point   135
    To be linked with the Braddock and Bay of Fundy campaigns   135
    Attitude of New York   136
    William Johnson selected to command   137
    The formulation of the plan   139

The campaign against Niagara   141
    Opposition to Shirley in New York   141
    Problem of the disposition of available forces   142
    The Shirley-Johnson rift   145
    Inadequacy of the forces   147
    Obstacles in approaching Niagara   148
    Preparations at Oswego   149
    Late arrival of Shirley and his regiments at Oswego   150

Shirley's plan for the conquest of Canada   151
    Relation of this plan to Pitt's plan   153

Oswego in the spring of 1755   153
    Condition of the post   153
    Iroquoian neutrality policy and Oswego   154

The Canadian authorities and the British plans of campaign   154
    Fears for the safety of Niagara   155
    Concentration of French troops at Fort Frontenac   156

The defence of Oswego 156
As a factor in the Niagara campaign 156
The decision to build additional forts 157

Postponement of the movement against Niagara 158
The decision to advance upon the French fort 158
The decision to concentrate upon the defences of Oswego 159

Shirley's proposals for the campaign of 1756 160
Inconsistency of these proposals with his instructions 160

CHAPTER VII

THE REPUDIATION OF SHIRLEY

Shirley's return to eastern New York 162
The building of forts at the Great Carrying Place 163

The Crown Point campaign 163
Johnson's preparations for the campaign 163
The construction of Fort Edward 166
Johnson's movement to Lake George 167

The French meet the threat to Crown Point 167
Dieskau takes over command 168
Determination to attack Fort Edward 168

The Battle of Lake George 169
News of movement of the French 169
The defeat of Colonel Williams's detachment 170
The movement of the French against Johnson's camp 171
McGinnis from Fort Edwards drives the French from their
temporary camp 173
Why the French were not pursued 174

Johnson's relations with his army 175
The problem of military discipline 175
Johnson's desire to give up his command 175

Johnson ordered to advance against the French encroachments 176
The colonial commissioners demand action 176
Weather as a factor in the campaign 176

Useless man-power concentrated at Albany   176
Resignation of Johnson as commanding officer   176

Significance of the two campaigns   177

Shirley's council of war in New York   177
Proposals for the campaign of 1756   178
Decisions of the council of war   178

The Cabinet Council and the American war   179
Enlargement of objectives in 1755   180
Determination to supersede Shirley   180

Shirley's difficulties   180
The problem of subsisting Oswego   183
The attitude of Virginia, Maryland, and Pennsylvania   185
Inadequacy of available forces for a Great Lakes campaign in 1756 185
Popularity of the Crown Point campaign in New England   185
The undermining of Shirley   186
Determination of the Cabinet Council to order Shirley to England   187
Shirley's enemies rewarded   188

Lord Loudoun as commander-in-chief   192
Activities of Webb and Abercrombie before Loudoun's arrival   192
The peril to Oswego underestimated   192
Webb in command of the relief   193

The French and Oswego   195
Earlier abortive efforts to seize the post   195
Montcalm charged to capture the forts   196

Colonial defence of Oswego   198
Great delays in strengthening the forts   198
Loss of supremacy on Lake Ontario   198
The French attack   199
The surrender of the post   200

Plans for a second campaign against Crown Point   203
Appointment of John Winslow as commander   203
Agreement for co-operation between Winslow's volunteers and
    the British regulars   204
The New England colonies and the Crown Point expedition   205
The issue over the union of regulars and volunteers   206

Shirley versus Loudoun   209
Shirley blamed for the disastrous turn of events in New York   209
The place of Shirley in British colonial administration   210

CHAPTER VIII

THE TREASON OF THOMAS PICHON

French forts in the Acadian country   212

French claims within the Nova Scotian peninsula   213
   Reports of French plans for continued aggressions   214
   French influence among the Acadians   214
   Weakness of the Nova Scotia defences   215
   Determination of Governor Lawrence to drive the French regular
     troops out of the peninsula   215
   Significance of the French forts in Acadia   216

Thomas Pichon   218
   Warns the British of French plans   218
   Early background in Europe   218
   Activities on Isle Royale   219
   Takes a temporary post at Beauséjour   220
   Becomes alienated from the French administration   221
   Becomes a British spy   224

The movement against Beauséjour   226
   Shirley agrees to raise New England volunteers   226
   Organization of the colonial irregulars   226
   Delay in the sailing of the expedition   227
   The New England regiments in Nova Scotia   228

The defence of Beauséjour   229
   De Vergor's agreement with the Acadians   229
   The weakening of the Acadians   230
   Failure to secure aid from Louisbourg   230
   Pichon works upon the fears of the Acadians   231

De Vergor's capitulation   231
   Concessions to the French troops   232
   Concessions to the Acadians in arms   232
   Was Beauséjour properly defended?   232
   Conduct of the French before the fort was surrendered 233

Pichon's continued activities   233
   His part in the surrender of Fort Gaspereau   233
   Notifies Lawrence of hostile plans of leading Acadians 234
   At Fort Edward   234
   At Halifax   234

In England 235
In Pennsylvania 237
Again in England 237
Efforts to rescue the Acadians in France 238
On the isle of Jersey 239
Pichon and Le Loutre 240

Pichon's last days 241

CHAPTER IX

FAREWELL TO ACADIA

The capture of the French forts in Acadia led to the expulsion of the
    Acadians 243

The Acadians before 1755 243
    Loyalty of the inhabitants to the French Crown 243
    The Acadians as British subjects 243
    Attempt to reconcile allegiance to the Crown of France with
        temporary fidelity to that of Great Britain 244
    Their privileged position within the Empire 244
    Influence upon the inhabitants of the building of the French forts
        in Acadia in 1750 245
    Promise of the Nova Scotia Council that Acadians would not
        have to bear arms 247

The rebellious attitude of the Piziquid Acadians 248
    Abbé Daudin before the Nova Scotia Council 249

Appeal of the Cobequid Acadians to those of Beauséjour 250
    Proposal to attack the English 250

Appeal of the Acadians to the French King 250

Governor Lawrence seeks the advice of the Board of Trade 250
    The Neutral Acadians present a dilemma 251

The reply of the Board of Trade 251
    Recognizes that leniency with the Acadians has failed 251

Le Loutre's efforts to stir up the Neutral Acadians 253
    Proclamations against those supporting Le Loutre 253

The Neutral French and the British attack upon Beauséjour 253
    Acadians of Minas Basin ordered to surrender their arms 253

Determination of the Nova Scotia government to drive out the Acadians loyal to the French Crown 255

Acadian deputies before the Nova Scotia Council 255
 Refusal of the deputies to take the unqualified oath 256
 Decision of the Council respecting Acadians refusing the oath 256

The problem of the disposition of the disloyal Acadians 260
 Various possible destinations for the exiles 260
 The dispersion of the Acadians considered the best means of securing permanent tranquillity in Nova Scotia 261

The decision to send the Neutrals to the older continental colonies 261
 Lands of the exiles to be later distributed to those loyal to the British Crown 263
 Livestock to be forfeited to the Crown 264
 The settlements to be laid waste 264

Preparations for the exile of the Acadians 264
 Chignecto district 264
 Minas Basin district 266
 Annapolis River district 280
 Pubnico district 281

The dispersion 282
 The number of Acadians scattered by the Nova Scotian government 282
 The number of Acadians scattered by the French priests and Le Loutre's Indians 282
 The treatment of the Acadians on shipboard 282
 Extent of responsibility of the Acadians for their own misfortunes 283

CHAPTER X

THE EXILES

The Acadian dispersion in the history of the North American continent 286

The Neutrals carried to colonies being ravished by French, Canadians, and Indians 287
 British refugees from the frontiers and Acadian exiles meet 287
 Intense fear of French-speaking peoples by British colonials 287

The exiles in the continental colonies 287
 In Georgia 287
 In South Carolina 291

In North Carolina   297
In Virginia   299
In Maryland   304
In Pennsylvania   309
In New York   319
In Connecticut   321
In Massachusetts Bay   324

Colonization of Isle Royale and Isle St. Jean by Acadians   336
Precarious condition of the inhabitants in 1758   337
Deportation of the Neutrals to France   337

Fate of the Chaleur Bay refugees   337
Privateering activities of the settlers against the British   337
Captain McKenzie's expedition breaks up the settlements about
the bay   337

Fanatical devotion of the Acadians to the King of France   337
Declaration of the Acadians at Halifax in 1764   338

The Acadians held in England go to France after 1763   338

Disillusionment of the Acadians in France   338
Plans of the King's ministers to send the Acadians to the tropics
or to settle them in France on the land   338
Refusal of the exiles to become French peasants   339
Failure of the social experiment at Châtellerault   339
The Saint-Malo intractables   339
Final permission given in 1784 to return to the New World   342

The scattering of the Acadians a fatal blow to French imperial
ambitions in North America   343

Chapter XI

BRITAIN AND HER CONTINENTAL "SYSTEM"

Europe in the middle of the eighteenth century   345
Leading sovereign powers   345
The Holy Roman German Empire   346

The people of Great Britain   346
Cultural divergencies from the Continent   346
Importance of assets possessed by the nation   347
Weakness of the British as an ally   347
Constitutional position of the King   348

George as an Elector of the Holy Roman German Empire   349
   German possessions of the Elector   349
   His electoral resources   350
   Determined to use his position as King to protect that as a German
     prince   351

Sensitiveness of Britons to developments across the Channel   351
   Interest in the revolt of the Netherlands in the sixteenth century   351
   Relations of England and Holland during the reign of William III
     and Anne   352

Great Britain and the Continental "System," 1715–48   353
   The Barrier Treaty of Antwerp of 1715   353
   Disappearance of Holland as a great European power after 1713   354
   The principle of the European balance of power and the "System"   355
   The "System" in abeyance between 1715 and 1730   355
   The "System" and the Pragmatic Sanction   356

British policy one of limited Continental commitments   357
   Refusal to guarantee Austrian eastern possessions   357
   Refusal to recognize Maria Theresa's unqualified sovereignty of
     the Netherlands   358

Austria moves away from the "System"   358
   Maria Theresa's desire to secure independence of action   358
   The Count of Kaunitz and the court of France   359
   The desire for the recovery of Silesia and a new international
     alignment   360
   The hardening of Austria's attitude toward the "System"   361

British essentials respecting Continental policy   361

The outlook in 1754   362

The Austrian Netherlands and the great European powers   363

Austrian essentials in the maintenance of the Anglo-Dutch defensive
     alliance   364
   The 1755 plan for reciprocal guarantees   365

Holland seeks neutrality in the impending European crisis   366
   Determination in 1755 to repudiate earlier commitments   366

The question of the imperial election   367
   The election and the vitality of the "System"   367

Great Britain and the "System" in 1755   367
   The Hanoverian plan of mutual security   369

Growing British objections to Continental subsidies   369
Efforts to preserve the "System" by a Russian treaty   370

CHAPTER XII

THE RIVALS FIND NEW FRIENDS

France pursues a cautious policy   373
   Mirepoix determines to remain in England after negotiations failed   373
   De Bussy to Hanover   374

Great Britain's attitude toward the French demands   374
   Robinson and the "Exorbitant Pretensions" of France   375

Why France does not declare war upon Great Britain in July 1755   376
   Demand for Spanish assistance   376

Great Britain prepares for open war   377
   Public opinion and a Continental war   377
   The ministry determines to protect the King's German dominions   377

The "System" nears its end   379
   Newcastle favours an entente with Prussia   379
   George II and Holderness hope to revitalize the "System"   379
   Negotiations with Austria end, August 1755   379

The position of Prussia in 1755   380
   Frederick's reputation in Europe   380
   The Prussian defensive alliance with France   380
   Relations with Great Britain   381
   Fear of a great coalition directed by Great Britain   382

Frederick seeks an accommodation with King George   382
   The King of Prussia rebuffed in Hanover   382
   The Duke of Brunswick as intermediary   382
   Frederick offers to arbitrate the Anglo-French issues   384
   Frederick and the Anglo-Russian subsidy treaty   385
   Increased critical attitude toward France   385
   Assurance from Great Britain of peaceful intentions   388
   Determination to act against Saxony   389

Treaty of Westminster, January 16, 1756   390
   Frederick's precarious position   390
   Michell in London authorized to sign a treaty   390
   Terms of the treaty   390
   The termination of disputes   390

Only a potential defensive alliance of limited nature 390
A French move against Hanover blocked 390
Frederick to use the treaty to protect himself in attacking Saxony 391

Prussia and France in 1756 391
Mission of the Duc de Nivernais 391
Convention of Westminster and France 392
Frederick and Nivernais frame a new treaty 393
The recall of Nivernais 393

Prussia and Great Britain after the Westminster Convention 394
Frederick seeks a strong British alliance 394
The British ministry deeply suspicious of Frederick 394

France and Austria, 1755–6 394
Louis XV desires an entente with the Empress-Queen 394
Austria shows her friendship for France 395

The Versailles Convention, May 1, 1756 396
A treaty of union and defensive friendship 396
Specific aid promised by each power 396
Provision for the adhesion of other powers to the convention 396
Disadvantages of this treaty to France 396

CHAPTER XIII

THE LOSS OF MINORCA

Great Britain prepares for defence 398
Resists Frederick's move for an alliance 398
Seeks to motivate the Anglo-Russian treaty 398
Brings foreign troops to England 398
The sending of reinforcements to the colonies 398
Seizure of French merchant ships 399

France shrewdly bides her time 400
Advantages of her great standing armies 400
Advantages of her situation in North America and in India 400
Ability to send reinforcements to Canada 400
Opportunities when the French navy is prepared 400
Naval preparations, 1754–6 401
Squadrons sent to America early in 1756 402

The move against Minorca 402
The justification for a British concentration of naval strength about
the Channel 402
The weakening of the British Mediterranean fleet 402

France gives up plans to invade England in favour of those against
Minorca 403
Weakness of the Minorca garrison 403
French preparations against the island 403
Invasion of the island and the siege of St. Philip's Castle 403

Minorca, an asset or a liability? 404
The population of the island 404
The economic importance of the island 404
The strategic importance of the island 404
Warnings sent to England of an impending French invasion ... 405

Byng to the relief of Minorca 405
Experience and qualifications 405
The scourge of the French merchant marine, 1755 405
Condition of Byng's relief fleet 406
Delays in departure of the fleet 406
Delays in reaching Gibraltar 406
Opposition of Governor Fowke to weakening Gibraltar 406
Difficulties in carrying out his instructions 407

The battle off Minorca, May 20, 1756 408
Byng's futile efforts to communicate with the besieged garrison 408
De la Galissonière's preparations for the British fleet 408
Byng and the Fighting Instructions 409
De la Galissonière's instructions 411
Byng's tactical move to overcome his disadvantages 411
De la Galissonière capitalizes on his advantages 411
The battle technically a British victory but strategically a French
victory 412
The council of war's decision to return to Gibraltar 413

The trial of Byng 414
A miscarriage of justice 414
Reflections upon Byng's attempt to relieve Minorca 415

Great Britain declares war on France, May 18, 1756 416
The surrender of St. Philip's Castle, June 28, 1756 416

CHAPTER XIV

THE AMERICAN CRISIS USHERS IN A WORLD WAR

Austria after the Convention of Versailles 418
Negotiations of de Bernis and Stahremberg 418

Lack of an aggressive alliance with Elizabeth of Russia   419
A European war seemed a remote contingency   419

Frederick plans a war   419
   Protected by the Westminster Convention from Russia   419
   Determines on a sudden move against Saxony and Austria   419
   Secures the right of innocent passage through Saxony   420

The British government and Frederick's aggression   421
   King George's reaction   423
   The ministry and the *fait accompli*   424

The Great War for the Empire now fused with the Seven Years'
   War of Europe   424

Factors in the fall of the Newcastle ministry   425
   The defeat of Braddock   425
   The failure of Boscawen   425
   The failure of Hawke   425
   The loss of Minorca   425
   Frederick's move against Saxony and Austria   425
   The loss of Oswego   425

Achievements of the Newcastle ministry   425
   Emphasis upon the American phase of the war   425
   Emphasis upon the importance of Gibraltar   425
   Great blows against the French merchant marine   426
   The capture of Beauséjour   426
   The removal of the Acadians   426

Newcastle gives way to Pitt   426

Maps and Plans

I. *Canada, Louisiane et Terres Angloises. Par le S^{r.} d'Anville.* (From Richard Waddington's *Louis XV et le Renversement des Alliances*)   Facing page   38

II. The Battle of Great Meadows. (From Jared Sparks's *Writings of Washington*)   Facing page   39

III. Plan of Fort Cumberland, Maryland, 1755, sent to the Board of Trade by Governor Dinwiddie. (From J. Thomas Scharf's *History of Maryland*)   Facing page   50

IV. Braddock's route to the Monongahela. (From Winthrop Sargent's *History of Braddock's Expedition*)   Facing page   51

V. Captain Stobo's map of Fort Duquesne, 1754. (From Winthrop Sargent's *History of Braddock's Expedition*)   Following page   86

VI. The first phase of the Battle of the Monongahela. Mackellar's Map, No. 1, 1755. (From the Duke of Cumberland Manuscripts, Windsor Castle)   Facing page   94

VII. The final phase of the Battle of the Monongahela. Mackellar's Map, No. 2, 1755. (From the Duke of Cumberland Manuscripts, Windsor Castle)   Facing page   95

VIII. A portion of "A New & Accurate Map of the Islands of Newfoundland, Cape Breton, St. John and Anticosta." By Eman. Bowen. (From Bowen's *A Complete Atlas*, 1762)   Following page   110

IX. Map showing the "Military Routes into Canada . . . 1759–60." (From Miles's *History of Canada*)   Facing page   140

X. "Plan of Fort Niagara, with its Environ." (From *A set of plans and forts in America, reduced from actual surveys*, 1763)   Facing page   141

XI. "Plan of Fort Frontenac." (From *A set of plans and forts in America, reduced from actual surveys,* 1763)

Facing page 156

XII. "Plan of Oswego with its Forts," 1755. (From the Duke of Cumberland Manuscripts, Windsor Castle)

Following page 156

XIII. "A Plan of Fort Edward and its environs on Hudsons River." (From Thomas Mante's *History of the Late War,* 1772)

Facing page 168

XIV. The Lake George area in 1755. (From Thomas Mante's *History of the Late War,* 1772) Facing page 169

XV. "Fort Beauséjour and adjacent country, taken possession of by Colonel Monckton, in June, 1755." (From Thomas Mante's *History of the Late War,* 1772) Facing page 244

XVI. *Carte de l'Accadie Dressée sur les Manuscrits du Dépost des Cartes et Plans de la Marine, 1744. Par N. B. Ing^r. et Hyd. de la Marine.* (Public Archives of Canada, Division of Maps) Following page 244

XVII. Thomas Jefferys's Nova Scotia in 1755, indicating the British and Acadian settlements. (From Justin Winsor's *Narrative and Critical History of America*) Facing page 264

XVIII. Captain Charles Morris's survey of the Acadian settlements about the upper part of the Bay of Fundy, 1749, with suggested allotments of lands to English-speaking Protestants. (Public Archives of Canada maps reproduced from the original surveys in the Public Record Office)

Facing page 265

XIX. Captain Charles Morris's survey of the Acadian settlements about Minas Basin, 1749, with suggested allotments of lands to English-speaking Protestants. (Public Archives of Canada maps reproduced from the original surveys in the Public Record Office) Facing page 280

XX. Captain Charles Morris's survey of the Acadian settlements in the region of Annapolis Royal, 1749, with suggested allotments of lands to English-speaking Protestants. (Public Archives of Canada maps reproduced from the original surveys in the Public Record Office)

Facing page 281

XXI. A portion of Nova Scotia in 1829, showing the results of the New England colonization of the peninsula. (From T. E. Haliburton's *An Historical and Statistical Account of Nova Scotia*) Facing page 335

XXII. "An Accurate Map of the North West Part of Germany," indicating the possessions of the Elector of Hanover in 1756. By Eman. Bowen. (From the Map Room, New York Public Library) Following page 348

XXIII. "A Correct Map of the Island of Minorca, 1752." (From John Armstrong's *The History of the Island of Minorca,* 1756) Facing page 406

XXIV. The siege of Fort St. Philip in 1755 indicating the position of the French artillery brought to bear on the fortifications. (From Richard Waddington's *Louis XV et le Renversement des Alliances*) Facing page 407

XXV. The three phases of the naval battle off Minorca. (From A. T. Mahan: *The Influence of Sea Power upon History, 1660–1783*) Facing page 418

XXVI. Germany in the middle of the Eighteenth Century. By T. Jeffery. (From the Map Division, Library of Congress) Following page 418

CHRONOLOGY

1754

April	2	Washington begins his march to the Ohio.
	17	Surrender of Ensign Ward to the French at the forks.
May	24	Washington arrives at Great Meadows.
	28	The death of Jumonville.
June	16	Washington leaves Great Meadows for the Ohio.
	19–21	The Indian conference at Mount Braddock.
	28	De Villiers leaves Fort Duquesne to attack Washington.
	30	Washington begins his retreat to Great Meadows.
July	3	The investment and surrender of Fort Necessity.
	5	Governor Sharpe appointed temporary commander-in-chief of American forces to oppose the French on the Ohio.
Sept.	15	Braddock commissioned commander-in-chief of all regular British forces in North America.
Oct.	19	Conference of the Governors of Virginia, Maryland, and North Carolina over plans to remove the French from their encroachments.

1755

Jan.	15	Braddock sails for America.
Feb.	19	Braddock's arrival in Virginia.
March	25	The British Cabinet Council decides to attempt to waylay the French transports bound for America.
April	14	The Alexandria, Virginia, Governors' Conference.
	27	Admiral Boscawen sails for America.
May	3	The French fleet leaves Brest for Canada.
	11	Rear Admiral Holburne's fleet sails to reinforce Boscawen.
	26	The expedition against Fort Beauséjour leaves Boston.
	30	Braddock's advance upon Fort Duquesne from Wills Creek.
June	2	The arrival of the New England expedition at Fort Lawrence, Nova Scotia.

June	8	Boscawen captures the *Alcide* and the *Lys*.
	14	New England troops bombard Fort Beauséjour.
	16	The surrender of Beauséjour.
	18	The surrender of Fort Gaspereau.
	19	Admiral de la Motte sails up the St. Lawrence with his fleet.
	20	The revolting Acadians begin to surrender their arms to Monckton at Fort Cumberland.
	21	Holburne joins Boscawen.
July	3	The Nova Scotia Council determines to exile all Acadians refusing the unrestricted oath.
	8	William Johnson arrives at Albany to command the Crown Point expedition.
	9	Braddock is defeated near the Monongahela.
	25	The Acadians of the Annapolis River through deputies refuse the oath.
	28	The Acadians of Minas Basin also refuse the oath. The decision to send all Acadians to the more southern British colonies.
Aug.	6	The laying waste of Acadian villages about the isthmus of Chignecto begins.
	9	General Johnson leaves Albany to move against Crown Point.
	11	The gathering of the revolted Acadians in Fort Cumberland.
	18	General Shirley arrives at Oswego in his campaign against Fort Niagara.
	19	Colonel Winslow arrives at Grand Pré to collect the Minas Basin Acadians.
	24	De la Motte's fleet begins its return from Canada to France.
Sept.	5	The confinement of the Minas Basin Acadians at Grand Pré and at Piziquid.
	8	The Battle of Lake George.
	10	The "scene of sorrow" at Grand Pré.
	19	Rear Admiral de Salvert leaves Louisbourg for France.
	27	The council of war at Oswego decides to postpone the Niagara campaign until the spring.
Oct.	11	The departure of the transports from Beaubassin with the isthmus of Chignecto exiles.
	23	The Piziquid Acadians embarked.
Nov.	2–7	The laying waste by the New England volunteers of the Minas Basin settlements.
	11	The capture of the *Espérance*.
Dec.	8	The departure of the transports with the Annapolis River exiles.
	12	Shirley's council of war in New York.

1756

Jan.	16	The Convention of Westminster.
March	17	Lord Loudoun is appointed commander-in-chief of all British regular forces in America.
April	7	Admiral Byng sails from England to protect Minorca.
	18	The invasion of Minorca by the French.
May	1	The Convention of Versailles.
	18	Great Britain declares war on France.
	20	The naval battle off Minorca.
June	25	General Shirley is relieved of his command.
	28	The surrender of St. Philip's Castle on Minorca.
July	22	Loudoun arrives in America.
Aug.	4	Montcalm leaves Fort Frontenac to capture Oswego.
	9	Webb leaves Albany for the relief of Oswego.
	14	The surrender of the colonial forces at Oswego.
	20	Maria Theresa assures the King of Prussia of her peaceful intentions.
	29	Frederick II demands free passage through Saxony for his army.
	30	The invasion of Saxony and the beginning of the European Seven Years' War.
Nov.	11	In America General Winslow withdraws his New England volunteers from the Crown Point campaign. In England Newcastle resigns in favour of Pitt.

1757

March	14	The execution of Admiral Byng.

CORRIGENDA

PAGE 5, *last* line: for "make-wright" read "make-weight"

PAGE 58, *note* 50, line 2: for "Edgecombe" read "Edgcumbe"

PAGE 69, *note* 18: for "*Pa. Col. Rev.*" read "*Pa. Col. Rec.*"

PAGE 121, *note* 84, line 2: for "Dugucy" read "du Guay"

PAGE 184, *line* 22: for "potage" read "portage"

PAGE 202, *line* 33: "Abercrombie" — the preferred spelling, used in Volume VII of this series, is General James Abercromby. ("Abercrombie" appears also on pages 205–8 and index pages i, xxxiv, and xxxviii.)

PAGE 203, *line* 18: for "Canadian" read "Canadians"

PAGE 403, *line* 3: for "Edgecumbe" read "Edgcumbe"

PAGE 407, *lines* 8 *and* 29: for "Edgecumbe" read "Edgcumbe"

INDEX, *page viii:* under "Convention of Westminster," for "1755" read "1756"

INDEX, *page xi:* for "Edgecumbe" read "Edgcumbe"

INDEX, *page xxv:* under "Motte," line 3, for "166–7" read "106–7"

INDEX, *page xxx:* under "Pompadour," for "Marquis" read "Marquise"

INDEX, *page xxxvi:* the entry for "Varin, Jean François Victor" should precede that for "Vaudreuil, Pierre . . ."

THE BRITISH EMPIRE
BEFORE THE AMERICAN REVOLUTION
VOLUME VI

THE GREAT WAR FOR THE EMPIRE

THE YEARS OF DEFEAT

1754–1757

CHAPTER I

Introduction
The Great War for the Empire
and American National
Tradition

EVERY GREAT NATION has a great tradition. Like the English Common Law, based upon custom, it is unwritten and it passes from one generation to another in the form of oral information, opinions, and doctrines, even of practices, rites, and customs. Much of it is immemorial; some of it of comparatively recent origin. It is impossible, as in the case of the Common Law, to indicate its limits, to measure with accuracy its volume; also, as in the case of the Common Law, it not only is subject to constant deletion and accretion but likewise is vast in extent. Even so one must not confuse local tradition with national tradition. Just as local custom may not be common custom and so may never become a part of the Common Law, so local tradition or group tradition may not be common tradition and therefore may never become embodied in the national tradition. As to the latter, some portions of it are based, on the one hand, upon indisputable facts of common knowledge that have stood the test of historical criticism and, on the other hand, upon unhistorical foundations, even upon misinterpretations, distortions, and actual suppressions of facts, as shown by the same test. The sum total of the tradition at any one period in the life of a nation, could it be comprehended by the student for purpose of analysis, offers a sure key to the basis for emotional reactions on the part of the inhabitants of a nation-state to both external and internal developments. For the power that tradition exerts upon a nation is always very great. Whether based upon ascertainable verities or upon baseless myth, it may in either case exercise an authority equal to, if it does not become a part of, the deepest religious convictions of a people. This may be illustrated, by way of example, by the Japanese tradition of the divine origin of their emperor. As a supreme article of national faith it is not subject to rational tests that may be freely applied by the Japanese people to other concepts — it is placed beyond question or dispute. The influence of a particular national tradition therefore has no necessary relation to its truth or falsity, but depends simply upon the degree of importance attached to it by nationals by and large and the quality of the sanction meted out to those who would question it. In view of this fusion of fact and fiction in tradition no greater responsibility rests upon modern historical scholarship than testing its validity; for the supreme mission of the historian is to determine the truth of the past — in so far as this is humanly possible — and to do so with detachment. Behind this mission stands the assumption that in so far as tradition has turned its back upon reality, upon historical truth, it cannot be wholly good — and may be wholly bad.

The student who seeks to present the history of the Anglo-French war of the years 1754–63 is brought face to face with the fact not only that American national tradition has in the main determined the lines of its interpretation to each oncoming generation, but that many if not most writers of American history have paid honour to the tradition without too much regard to its credibility, while at the same time striving for accuracy and perfection in details that would not call it into question. The classic example, of course, is the treatment accorded to the war by George Bancroft in Volume IV of his monumental *History of the United States,* which carries the subtitle: *The American Revolution. Epoch First. The Overthrow of the European Colonial System, 1748–1763.* Many other examples could be cited.

American national tradition relating to the war of the years 1754–63 stemmed largely from the attitudes of those labouring under great emotional stresses produced by the Anglo-American crisis of 1774–5 that brought on the Revolutionary War, that prevailed during the course of the latter war, and that survived it for generations. Of all those who were responsible for the creation of this national tradition respecting the war in question none played a more significant role than did Thomas Paine, the author of the truly epoch-making *Common Sense*, which preceded by some six months the Declaration of Independence and which contributed so powerfully to bring about a public state of mind that made the promulgation of the latter imperative, especially in view of military developments and the desire of an alliance with France. Speaking a language of utmost simplicity and directness, with an imagery that peculiarly suited the occasion, it seared the souls of Americans as they had never been seared before, heaping upon them its red-hot embers of scorn against everything that Great Britain as a mother country had done, or had tried to do, or had been. Thousands of copies of the book were scattered about, eagerly read, and discussed by excited groups of Americans in every colony from New Hampshire to Georgia. In the words of a contemporary:

> "Read by almost every American and recommended as a work replete with truth, against which none but the partial and prejudiced can form any objection . . . it satisfied multitudes that it is their true interest immediately to cut the Gordian knot by which the . . . colonists have been bound to Great Britain. . . ."

Indeed, in the words of another contemporary, Dr. Benjamin Rush, a signer of the Declaration of Independence, *Common Sense*

> "burst from the press with an effect that has been rarely produced by types and paper, in any age or country." [1]

In setting forth his thesis, which is the burden of the book, that the connection of Americans with monarchical Great Britain, far from being a blessing, had actually been a curse,[2] he declares without qualification:

> "I have heard it asserted by some that . . . America has flourished under her . . . connection with Great Britain . . . I answer roundly, that America would have flourished as much, and probably much more, had no European power had anything to do with her." [3]

Again he states:

> "It is the true interest of America to steer clear of European contentions, which she never can do, while, by her dependence on Britain, she is made the make-weight in the scale of British politics . . . and,

---

[1] *The Political Works of Thomas Paine* (Chicago and Toronto, 1879), p. 4.
[2] *Ibid.,* pp. 13, 15 *et seq.*
[3] *Ibid.,* p. 21.

whenever a war breaks out between England and any foreign power, the trade of America goes to ruin, *because of her connexion with Britain.*" [4]

And, further, he asserts:

"We have boasted the protection of Great Britain, without considering that her motive was *interest,* not *attachment;* and that she did not protect us from *our enemies* on *our account,* but from *her enemies,* on *her own account.*" [5]

These affirmations, together with other significant pronouncements contained in the remarkable work, found lodgment in the hearts and minds of those to whom it was dedicated and by general acceptance became a part of the new American national tradition. Here in page after page was contrasted in elaborate detail the peace-loving American interested solely in the business of gaining a livelihood with the war-minded, grasping, selfish, corrupt, monarchy-loving Englishman who was forever dragging the former into European wars that had no relation to his real interests in life and that in fact were utterly irreconcilable with these. Especially was this connection of Americans with Great Britain an evil one in relation to France, in the eyes of Paine. For the French had had no quarrel with the Americans nor had the latter had any with them. But Great Britain and France were traditional enemies and therefore American interests had been repeatedly sacrificed to the selfish interests of the mother country.

When the war that is the theme of the present volume began, Paine was a young Englishman but seventeen years of age, a Quaker by religious profession, the son of a London staymaker. Consistent with his religious principles, he looked upon all wars as both bad and unnecessary and, equally consistent with these principles, he refused to permit his very active mind to dwell upon the specific causes that had brought about the one in question. For all wars, so far as he could see as a young eighteenth-century Quaker, were generated not by the people, but by the wicked and selfish ambitions of crowned rulers; and, as between the latter, there was little to choose, for all parties to all wars were, if not equally to blame for them, far from blameless. Broken, disillusioned, and embittered — with his married life a failure and his relations with the public no better — he

---

[4] *Ibid.,* p. 24.
[5] *Ibid.,* p. 22.

came to America in 1774. When early in 1776 he published in Philadelphia his *Common Sense,* he was no longer a Quaker; he had also come to believe in wars, if waged by the people against the objects of his intense hatred — the crowned rulers — and for gaining their freedom from these. He now could distinguish between good wars and bad; and while he ardently favoured the Revolutionary War, he looked upon the war waged during his young manhood as a bad war and consequently upon its author, George II, one of the "crowned ruffians," as a bad ruler who had dragged his American subjects away from their happy, peaceful occupations to fight his battles for him. So he could cry out passionately as a hater of monarchy and a lover of America bowed down as he felt, under the tyranny of the "Royal Brute of Britain":

> "The palaces of Kings are built upon the ruins of the bowers of Paradise!"

Now, as to Paine's general thesis that the connection of the colonials with monarchical Great Britain had been not a blessing but a curse — a thesis to become a part of the new American national tradition — the question may be raised whether any responsible American in any of the colonies could have been found during the years between 1750 and 1760 who would have subscribed to this. Did the Massachusetts Bay Assembly so consider the connection of the province with the mother country when in its petition to the King in 1750 for military aid it affirmed:

> "It is the high sense we have of the Happiness we enjoy as . . . subjects of the Crown of Great Britain, and the Dread which proceeds even from the most distant prospect of being ever subjected to the Yoke, and Tyranny of the French, that induces us in this humble Address to your Majesty, and it is our Constant and devout Prayer to Almighty God, that your Majesty may long continue to Reign over us, and that our Posterity may remain faithful subjects of your Royal House to the end of time"? [6]

Was the attitude of Paine expressed by Governor William Greene of Rhode Island when, in writing to the King's Secretary of State on behalf of the Assembly in 1755, with America now involved in war, he declared:

---

[6] Public Record Office, A. 40, Nova Scotia, 1751, 63:189.

"And as this Colony are fully sensible of their absolute dependency on the Crown of Great Britain for their Safety and Support;
They will therefore at all Times, with the utmost Chearfulness Obey,
and as far as their Power can reach, perform all his Majesty's Commands signified to them; fully trusting that while they continue to do
so, His Majesty's gracious Favour and princely protection will not be
withdrawn from them"? [7]

Did the Connecticut Assembly give evidence of such a feeling when
after Washington's defeat it stated to the world that the people of
the colony

"delight in obedience to, and admire the protection and privileges of,
the laws of England"? [8]

Or were the above statements made with the knowledge of the authors that what they said at the time was plain hypocrisy and not
their truthful sentiments? Again, if Paine was correct in his thesis,
was Governor Lewis Morris of New Jersey also correct when he
boasted in 1746 in the midst of King George's War that those dwelling within the colony

"were the most easie and happy people of any Collony in North
America"? [9]

Is Governor Belcher of the same colony to be believed when he remarked in 1749, at the close of that war, that the inhabitants remained free of all public burdens and that

" 'tis 17 years since any Tax was raised on the people for support of
the Government [of New Jersey]"? [10]

Or is Paine's thesis to be reconciled with a like statement made by
Governor Morris of Pennsylvania when, in writing to Braddock in
1755, also in time of war, he declared:

"We are burthened with no taxes and are not only out of Debt, but
have a Revenue of Seven Thousand a year and Fifteen Thousand in
Bank, all at the Disposal of the House of Assembly"? [11]

---

[7] C.O. 5:15, p. 487.
[8] "The Reasons Considered and Offered, by the Assembly of the Colony of Connecticut, Concerning the Plan of Union," Massachusetts Historical Society Collections, VII,
207–9.
[9] Papers of Governor Lewis Morris, p. 147.
[10] New Jersey Archives (first series), VII, 246.
[11] Pennsylvania Archives (fourth series), II, 272–3.

Or can it be reconciled with the sentiments set forth by a group of Germans settled in Maryland who declared in 1746, likewise in the midst of war, in writing back to their relatives in the fatherland about their happy condition:

> "The Law of the Land is so constituted that every man is secure in the Enjoyment of his Property, the Meanest person is out of reach of Oppression from the most Powerful, nor can anything be taken from him without his securing Satisfaction for it"? [12]

Again, if Paine is to be believed, what is the student to do with the urgent appeals of Virginia for military aid from the mother country against the French in 1754 and the testimony of the English traveller Burnaby, who in passing through Virginia in 1759, also in the midst of war, expressed his amazement, not at the unhappy state of affairs, but at the extravagance and luxurious form of living of the planters? [13] Or can the statement of the Irishman Arthur Dobbs, Governor of North Carolina, be relied upon, who assured the Assembly late in 1754, after Washington's defeat, that while the people of the mother country were

> "loaded with debts and enormous, tho' necessary taxes, [the government of Great Brtiain, nevertheless] hath not only protected these colonies, but indulged them in . . . the easiest taxes (spent for their own support), of any Civilized nation on the globe"? [14]

In other words, either Paine was mistaken in his fundamental thesis that Americans had been cursed by their connections with Great Britain especially in time of war or those who have been quoted above were guilty of great distortions of the truth.

Now, as to the conflict that raged between 1754 and 1762 and that finally ended in the Peace of Paris, one may affirm — in contrast to the historical views of Paine — that this was a war that George II had no part in beginning. On the contrary, it was really begun by the French and directed against American colonial trade and territorial expansion after a force of a thousand soldiers — the nucleus of them regulars brought over from France — moved in their bateaux down the Allegheny River in the spring of 1754 and through force but

[12] Calvert Papers, Orders and Instructions, No. 295, 1121, Maryland Historical Society.

[13] The Reverend Andrew Burnaby, *Travels through the Middle Settlements of North America, 1759–1760*, pp. 11–14.

[14] *North Carolina Colonial Records*, V, 224.

without bloodshed overwhelmed a small party of workmen that the Ohio Company, organized by Virginians, had sent to the forks of the Ohio River to build a fort preparatory to the colonization of lands thereabout. It became a war of violence and bloodshed when young George Washington led his Virginia volunteers into the region near where the French themselves had now built a fort, with the idea of ejecting the latter from lands that the government of Virginia was persuaded were a part of the Old Dominion. Thus in its beginning the war had nothing to do with the old animosities of Europe. It was at the time, in contrast to Paine's thesis, regarded by both contemporary colonials and the people of Great Britain as peculiarly an American issue and conflict. The Duke of Newcastle voiced this view when he said: "Let Americans fight Americans."

Another part of the American national tradition is the idea — transmitted from one generation to another and embodied in the national literature by Bancroft and other writers before and since his day — that the unlimited expanses of North America were predestined to be the heritage of the Americans: that there was no power that would or could deny them this marvellous birthright and that the war in question was but a somewhat incidental thing. It was, in fact, nothing more than one of a series of so-called French and Indian wars, none of too much importance, yet desirable to bring to the attention of pupils and busy people, especially to make clear that as a result of it not only does Washington first emerge as the potential military leader of his people, but Canada is taken from France by Great Britain, and the British Empire becomes a massive, unwieldy thing. In other words, American national tradition treats this war as a mere interlude in the resistless westward march of the American pioneers.

In contrast to the traditional view stands the simple fact that the war was destined to have the most momentous consequences to the American people of any war in which they have been engaged down to our own day — consequences therefore even more momentous than those that flowed from the victorious Revolutionary War or from the Civil War. For it was to determine for centuries to come, if not for all time, what civilization — what governmental institutions, what social and economic patterns — would be paramount in North America. It was to determine likewise whether Americans were to be securely confined, as are the people of Chile today, to a long but narrow ribbon of territory lying between the coastline and a not too distant mountain chain and whether their rivals, the French — then considered to be the greatest military power of the world and in control of the Appalachians — were to remain a permanent and effective barrier to any enjoyment of the vast western interior of the continent. In contrast to the pleasing and inspiring tradition of the inevitability of American expansion westward are the indubitable evidences of the determination of the government of France — as expressed in royal decrees, in the correspondence of the ministers, in instructions to the governors general of New France, in *mémoires* and in other authentic documents as well as in physical acts — to bind the English colonials to the east of the mountains, to harry them from the Great Lakes region, to hold them in awe to the south of the region of Lake George and Lake Champlain, to drive them out of Nova Scotia and eastern Maine, and through these moves to sever them from their great western fur trade and their great northern fisheries off the Nova Scotia coast, thus dooming them to a constricted existence along the Atlantic seaboard. In contrast to the tradition is also the sobering picture of the actual state of affairs presented by one of the most capable, popular, and determined American colonial governors, William Shirley, the chief executive of a colony that was destined to make a larger contribution of men and money to the ultimate winning of the war than any other on the continent. Writing from Boston to Lieutenant Governor de Lancey of New York early in 1755 he declared:

> "It would be needless for me to Observe to you, how his Majesty's Colonies upon this Continent are surrounded with the Incroachments of the French. They have long since mark'd out for themselves a large Empire upon the back of it, extending from Cap [*sic*] Breton to the Gulph of Mexico, and comprehending the Country between the Apalachean Mountains and Pacific Ocean with the numerous, powerful Tribes of Indians inhabiting it; they are now finishing the extreme parts by a communication between Louisbourg to Quebec across the Isthmus of Nova Scotia, & Bay of Funda at one end & a junction of Canada with the Missippi [*sic*] by a line of forts upon the Great Lakes & Rivers at the Other." [15]

Still another part of the American national tradition with relation to this war is that the American colonials themselves were adequately provided in 1754 with the necessary resources for looking out for their own future; that they owed Great Britain nothing and in turn

[15] Shirley to de Lancey, February 24, 1755, C.O. 5:15, p. 463.

expected little or nothing from her; that whatever assistance came from her in connection with hostilities on the continent was gratuitous and was extended for selfish and even cynical reasons, and particularly that the presence of British troops who crossed the Atlantic by the thousands was rather an interference than a help because of the devotion of these troops to European methods of fighting unsuited to the American scene.

It is true that when the war began there was a feeling among the colonials that by reason of their vastly superior numbers and of their vastly superior accumulated wealth and potential natural and industrial resources with respect to New France they were bound to suc-- ceed, without much aid from the mother country, in ejecting the aggressors from the lands that they themselves claimed. But after the defeat of Washington at Fort Necessity there was a rude awakening from the prevailing attitude of complacency, a growing realization of the dangers that faced them and of the extraordinary difficulties that stood in the way of overcoming them. It is also certain that after four years of discouraging reverses in the war the colonials could do little other than realize that all signs pointed to the ultimate triumph in North America of the fleur-de-lis over the Cross of St. George. In fact, it was by no means clear to them that even the approaches to the Appalachians could be secured for them in the peace that some day would end the conflict. As the year 1757 drew to its disheartening close, the colonial "line of defence," it should be noted, was far to the east of these approaches. It now ran southward of Lake George, lost to the colonials with the capture of Fort William Henry and with the massacre of part of its garrison of New England soldiers by the French Indians; it continued through the central part of the Province of New York, with Lake Ontario now also lost to them by the capture of Forts Oswego and Ontario together with the garrisons composed exclusively of colonials of the Shirley, Pepperrell, and New Jersey regiments; in Pennsylvania it sought by means of a chain of forts to protect the middle and lower valley of the Susquehanna River and in Virginia by another chain of forts to protect the western approaches to the valley of the Shenandoah. Indeed, the once bright dream of Virginians, Pennsylvanians, and other American colonials of a great future awaiting them westward had by the beginning of 1758 all but vanished, and also what earlier confidence they had had of their own ability to contend successfully with French regular soldiers.

In contrast to the American national tradition that Americans fighting as Indians were accustomed to do were far superior to British regulars for wilderness operations and that the government of the mother country blundered hopelessly in not entrusting to Americans themselves the responsibility of ejecting the French from the lands in dispute are the facts that at the beginning of the war few colonials had ever had any experience in this method of fighting and also that the local assemblies, which reflected popular opinion, had much greater faith in the performances of troops trained in the regular method of warfare than in irregulars fighting in Indian fashion. In vain General Shirley at the beginning of 1756 besought the assemblies of Virginia, Maryland, and Pennsylvania to gather men together for a third drive upon Fort Duquesne at the forks of the Ohio — after the failures by Washington and Braddock in 1754 and 1755 respectively. He found that the colonies in question considered the task far too formidable for them to undertake. The capture of the fort was a task, they were convinced — in spite of Braddock's defeat — that could be successfully accomplished only by regular troops brought from the mother country. This conviction was likewise shared by all well-informed Americans, who felt that all-out British aid to them was imperative if they were to be saved from irretrievable disaster. For at an early period in the great struggle men pointed to the danger of the French conquest of some of the most flourishing colonies.

Shirley, undoubtedly the best-informed man on American affairs in 1755, in writing to Secretary of State Sir Thomas Robinson early in that year to plead, in harmony with Governor Dinwiddie of Virginia, that regular soldiers be hurried overseas from the British Isles to the colonies, shows the nature of the American problem and reasons for the great weakness of the American colonies with all their potential strength. Not only was New England, he declared, hemmed in by a series of French forts — beginning with the great fortress of Louisbourg on Cape Breton Island and including Fort Beauséjour on the Acadian isthmus, the fort at the mouth of the St. John River, and Fort St. Frédéric at Crown Point — and thus was able to bring little aid to other colonies, but both New York and Pennsylvania might at any time fall into the hands of the French. He affirmed, to quote him again, that

> "those best acquainted with the History of the Behaviour of the People of New York in every War y[th] the People of New England had with the Indians or French, won't scruple to say, that one part of it,

viz: Albany would surrender to the French upon the first Summons, if they could preserve their Trade [with the enemy] by it; & the City of New York itself, it is thought, when they had such an Enemy upon their Backs, might be made an easy Prey to them. . . ." [16]

As to Pennsylvania, he found the government controlled by those

"whose religious Principles hinder them from putting the Country into a proper Posture of Defence against an Enemy" — [17]

for they refused to organize a militia, to build forts, or to engage in any hostilities whatsoever; he also declared that the German-speaking inhabitants, constituting one half of the population of the province, were

"indifferent about changing the English for a French Government, provided they could be eased of their Quit Rents, & have their Grants of Land enlarg'd to them." [18]

He therefore expressed the fear that by another "sudden blow" the French might make themselves masters of Pennsylvania and also of Albany, "if not of the City of New York itself"; and this, he went on to say,

"would give them two fertile Provinces in the Heart of his Majesty's Western Colonies capable of supporting them & their new [Indian] Allies upon the Lakes & Rivers & in the Country adjacent." [19]

Nor could much be expected, he felt, from the colonies to the south of Pennsylvania because of the vast number of

"Negro Slaves capable of bearing Arms. . . . All which would be in great danger of being seduc'd from their Fidelity to their Masters by [French] Promises of liberty, & Lands to settle upon . . . & it is well known, how much those Colonies abound with Roman Catholicks, Jacobites, Indented Servants for long terms, & transported Convicts, who, far from being depended upon against the enemy, would doubtless, many of them instigate the Slaves to rebel, & perhaps join wth them. . . ." [20]

This view of the essential weakness of the South was also expressed the following year by Louis Evans, the Pennsylvania map-maker and

---

[16] Shirley to Robinson, January 24, 1755, C.O. 5:15, pp. 317–40.
[17] Ibid.
[18] Ibid.
[19] Ibid.
[20] Ibid.

political controversialist, and a sharp critic of the Shirley plans of campaign. Evans, addressing himself to those who thought that the Southern militia could go out against the enemy, declared:

> "The Thing is impossible; they have . . . scarce Whites enough to prevent the Defection of their Slaves; and if any considerable Party should happen to be defeated, when abroad, it could be scarce possible to prevent their total Revolt." [21]

To what extent this fear of a slave insurrection influenced the South in the course of war as against other factors cannot be stated with exactness. Nevertheless, after Braddock's defeat Governor Dinwiddie, in writing to the Earl of Halifax about the difficulties of using the militia for frontier defence, declared:

> "I must leave a proper N^o in each Co^{ty} to protect it from the Combinations of the Negro Slaves, who have been very audacious on the Defeat on the Ohio. These poor Creatures imagine the F^r will give them their Freedom. We have too many here, but I hope we shall be able to defeat the Designs of our Enemies and keep these Slaves in proper Subject^n." [22]

The fact indeed remains indisputable that comparatively few Southern free white men were available even for frontier defence, without reference to their availability to operate outside the bounds of their respective colonies.

In spite, therefore, of the American national tradition, if historical evidence to the contrary be accepted, it points to the fact — something doubtless that may hurt national pride — that if America is great today it is because Great Britain made it possible for her to be great. It is because thousands of men recruited into the regular British army from all parts of the British Isles were carried to America to fight and to die in support of the colonies. It is because the royal British navy, in the face of earlier defeats in the war, continued to deliver tremendous blows against French sea power, reducing the latter at last to impotence in its efforts to carry reinforcements to those serving under the fleur-de-lis in North America. And it is also because the British government opened wide its treasury and saddled the people of Great Britain with a debt, enormous for that age, to finance not only its own war effort and that of its allies in Europe but,

---

[21] Geographical, Historical, Political . . . Essays, Number II (Philadelphia, 1756), p. 10.

[22] Dinwiddie to Halifax, July 23, 1755, Dinwiddie Papers, II, 114.

what is of equal importance, that of the American colonials so that the latter might be able to fight to a successful conclusion the war, which was, in reality, their own.

In this connection it is important to note that at the beginning of hostilities in North America a theoretical choice existed for Great Britain between two sharply divergent lines of action. One of these lines dictated following a cautious policy based upon purely mercantilistic principles — in harmony with the Dutch policy of the seventeenth century. This demanded that the government measure carefully the possible costs of military operations overseas with anticipated financial benefits or losses to be secured or sustained in the way of trade. If the cost seemed too high when it came to the defence of territorial claims in the New World, then only a token resistance to a powerful enemy would be made, as in the case of the Dutch defence of Brazil or of the New Netherlands. An excellent case could have been made for this policy in Great Britain in 1754. Give the French, in spite of the claims and desires of the colonials, what they demanded of North America. The profits of trade would not lessen, even if the colonials were deprived of their opportunities for westward expansion and deprived of their vast Great Lakes and trans-Appalachian fur trade and of their Canso fisheries — the latter, after all, competing with the English Newfoundland fisheries. For Frenchmen in the New World would still be dependent upon England as in the past for supplying all those articles of Indian trade that France herself could not produce successfully in spite of great efforts to do so; the best of the furs of the Great Lakes region would still flow into Albany. This policy would protect the financial interest of taxpayers at home as well as the lives of Britons and would permit the good work of reducing the national debt to continue. It would also mean that the American colonials would never become too powerful and would therefore continue to maintain an attitude of dependency upon the mother country. It was the safe way of the mercantilist.

The alternative line of action demanded a decisive break with the cautious canons of orthodox seventeenth-century mercantilism, with its emphasis upon immediate financial returns from overseas possessions and equal emphasis upon the idea that colonies were only to be valued as feeders for the wealth of the mother country. In contrast, this line of action would be based upon newer eighteenth-century conceptions of colonialism — foreshadowed in the colonization of Georgia in 1734 and fully implemented in that of Nova Scotia in 1749. These conceptions brought into focus the idea that the older, established colonies as a part of overseas Britain were entitled to the fullest measure of support against outside interference, so that in safety they might grow and expand. The maintenance of both Georgia, based upon the Spanish borderland, and Nova Scotia, based upon that of New France, as buffer, semi-military colonies to guard the older colonies lying between them, was as a result held to be a proper charge upon the home treasury in default of revenues from either one of the two. These newer conceptions of colonialism were symbolized in the concept that wherever a Briton was living under the Cross of St. George, he was thereby entitled to its protection against any foreign power, whatever might be the cost to the mother country. That the British ministry and that Parliament adopted this alternative line of action without hesitation — in spite of the unwillingness of George II at first to see troops sent to America — is not surprising in view of the depth of feeling aroused in all parts of Great Britain among all groups of people in 1754 that France must not be permitted to carry out her aggressive policy against the American colonials. It is not without significance, as evidence of this feeling, that men in Great Britain volunteered between the years 1755 and 1762 for service in America to fight the French,[23] but were reluctant to do so between the years 1775 and 1780 to fight in America those they regarded as their own countrymen, men of their own blood.

There was no place in the new American national tradition, born in the fiery heat of revolt, for anything so inconsistent with the major premises of it as the recognition that the people and government of Great Britain had done well, even generously, by the colonials in their great crisis of the years 1754–62. To George Bancroft, who brought this tradition to full flower, the Anglo-French New World crisis was chiefly significant in making clear to Americans the utter unworthiness of the British Crown and Parliament to preside longer over their destinies, and in laying the foundations for the ultimate political separation of the two peoples. But Bancroft or others who before his day or subsequent to it exerted themselves to buttress this tradition never permitted themselves to face this simple question: Is it at all likely, in spite of inevitable irritations and sometimes very vocal colonial rumblings over overseas control, that there would ever

---

[23] The regiments sent to America in 1757 "to relieve their distressed countrymen" received the command to go very "chearfully," according to London Advices to the *Pennsylvania Gazette*, April 14, 1757.

have been either an American revolt or an independent American nation had Great Britain faltered in her duty to the colonies and permitted the French to remain entrenched along the Appalachian range as well as in control of the Great Lakes region and what is now a part of northern New York and northern and eastern New England? What future could possibly await Americans thus hemmed in, their energies thus stifled, outside of sharing in the benefits implicit in continued connection with the British Empire?

In fact, it would seem that the very magnitude of the victory won by the British in the course of this war, as will be subsequently set forth at large in another volume, laid the sure foundation for future American independence — and yet for reasons not stressed by those who have adhered closely to the American national tradition. Mistakes of ministers, mistakes of Parliament, mistakes of royal governors there were, no doubt, that irritated Americans — who since becoming a distinct nation have often been irritated with their government; but behind all mistakes in policy, and of infinitely more importance in setting the stage for independence, it may be suggested, was the grandeur of the conceptions of the mission of a free people inherited by Americans. These conceptions were not drawn from continental Europe but from eighteenth-century England, whose alert people after the long struggles of the seventeenth century against despotism fairly sniffed the air to detect the slightest odour of tyrannical government or encroachment on their liberties. The men of British America who had felled the forests, who had built hundreds of flourishing towns and cities, who had created a great merchant marine, who had laid under tribute millions of acres of fertile land, who had established great metallurgical and shipbuilding industries, were with the dawning of the Peace of 1763 brought to realize their political as well as their economic and social maturity. For no other colonial people in the New World had ever dreamed of enjoying such immunities and liberties. Now, at last freed from the age-long menace of foreign foes along their borders, these men — speaking many languages, having many fatherlands, enjoying many faiths, but united together by common bonds that the vast American wilderness had forged — were stirred with the vision of a great future on the North American continent and of a high mission that must not be denied them. And yet it could not easily be realized, they felt, under the restrictions of an overseas governmental system that, while it had in its day served them well in the main, was at the same time too inflexible to meet the exigencies of a situation that spread unparalleled opportunities before them. They were therefore not slow in making clear to all the world that as a sign of this maturity they were now determined to draw fully upon the vast reservoirs of both their natural and their inherited rights claimed as free Englishmen, and as equally determined to brook no interference — be it from royal governors, from Parliament, or from the King — that might restrain them; nor would they permit themselves to be held back even by a sense of common loyalties or by gratitude for the immeasurable past benefits and favours received. America was once more bravely on the march and by 1776 was well prepared to proclaim Paine's *Common Sense* as her new evangel. Yet it is well to remember, in fidelity to historic truth as against American national tradition, that that march would never have been resumed without the successful termination of a cruel, bitterly fought, nine years' war that may appropriately be called Britain's Great War for the Empire.

CHAPTER II

A Palisado in the Wilderness

THE GREAT WAR for the Empire that was begun in 1754 by North American British colonials against the French in defence of lands that they had long exploited and regarded as a part of the imperial dominion, might not have involved either the royal fleet or the regular army had the colonies, as was emphasized in the preceding chapter, been prepared to meet the emergency with their own decided predominance over New France of man-power and material resources. It is certain, in view of the advantages they enjoyed at the beginning of the struggle, that George II displayed "an utter aversion" [1] to sending troops from the British Isles to the New World, hoping perhaps to localize the conflict. It is equally certain that the people of Great Britain at the beginning of 1754 had little desire to lay down their lives or those of their sons in military operations in distant North America or to be loaded down with additional financial burdens that would come with involvement in a new war — only six years after the rejoicing at the establishment of peace with France in 1748. Both Governor Morris of Pennsylvania and Governor Glen of South Carolina saw the struggle that was opening up in the Ohio Valley — and was ultimately to spread over the world — as peculiarly an "American" affair. The former in this connection was not at all sure that the mother country would permit herself to be involved,[2] while the latter was just as sure that she should not be.[3]

---

[1] Newcastle Papers, Additional Manuscripts, British Museum, 32736:591.

[2] Robert Hunter Morris to Thomas Penn, October 26, 1754, Penn Official Correspondence, 6:231, Historical Society of Pennsylvania.

[3] James Glen to Robert Dinwiddie, March 14, 1754, Public Record Office, C.O. 14:295–8.

Yet both Governor Shirley of Massachusetts Bay and Governor Dinwiddie of Virginia, each supported by his colonial advisers, while readily agreeing that the issue with their neighbours, the French, was essentially a matter affecting the New World, at the same time were persuaded that Great Britain must be induced to come to the aid of the colonies.[4] Their line of argument was simple and direct and may here be summarized from their correspondence.

British colonials were obviously prepared to deal with any menace to their welfare presented by French colonials without making appeals for outside assistance, but unaided they could not contend with the might of the greatest military power in the world. For France herself, they saw clearly, had taken over the contest with them over disputed regions and had therefore placed them in a position of such dangerous inferiority in the waging of war in North America that this could only be redressed by direct British assistance — with all that was implied in the probability of the spread of hostilities to other continents as well. Nevertheless, direct intervention on land and sea was only to take place when the colonial effort to relieve the situation on the Ohio had really collapsed.

It should be borne in mind that British colonials, whether rightly or wrongly, felt in 1754 that they were face to face along their critical borders with a dangerous and aggressive power. This is not to imply that most of them were convinced at the moment that North America, with its endless expanses beyond the regions of Spanish control, was too small to permit both the French and the English to carve out areas where each might dwell and prosper in peace. For, by and large, they seem to have recognized that the French had rights superior to their own in most of the valley of the St. Lawrence, in the upper Great Lakes region, in the Illinois country, and along the Mississippi — rights acquired not merely by traversing the heart of the continent or by fabulous charter grants, but by the recognized titles of long-continued trade exploitation and, best of all, actual settlement. For international law of that day recognized these modes of establishing territorial claims, as well as by conquest and treaty cession, as it does today. What they demanded was that they themselves enjoy the same freedom as did French colonials with respect to the utilization of lands unoccupied and unexploited by any other civilized power; what they also demanded was the fulfilment by their

---

[4] C.O. 217:40, Nova Scotia, 1751, 63:189; Private Papers of Dinwiddie, p. 102 (Virginia State Library transcriptions) and Dinwiddie Papers (ed. Brock), I, 280.

French neighbours of treaty terms and obligations. In place of this, after the Treaty of Aix-la-Chapelle and in time of peace they witnessed the movement of French troops — in what they felt was patent violation of treaty rights — into the peninsula of Nova Scotia and the establishment of Fort Beauséjour and other forts; they witnessed the successful efforts of the French to stir the Acadians dwelling in the heart of that peninsula into open resistance to the British Crown, under the dominion of which most of them had been born and reared. After the peace they also witnessed the French movement along the waters of the Allegheny and upper Ohio — the coming of Céloron de Blainville in 1749 with his proclamation of French ownership of all the Ohio Valley and then the establishment of Forts Presqu'Isle and Le Bœuf on lands conquered in 1656 by the Five Nations from the Erie — long before the Treaty of Utrecht, which had specifically placed the Confederation under the jurisdiction of the Crown of Great Britain. They witnessed the driving of hundreds of their traders from well-established trading centres in the upper Ohio Valley, where previously they had operated without ever facing competition from the French. They witnessed, finally, the movement of a large force of French troops to the forks of the Ohio and the capture of the English post in process of construction there on land far removed from any region where the French had either settled or engaged in trade.

While the movement of the French into the region of the Bay of Fundy was carefully watched by the authorities of both Nova Scotia and Massachusetts Bay and plans were being laid for co-ordinated action against this at the appropriate time, actual hostilities commenced in the region drained by the Monongahela. And it will be desirable to turn our attention first to developments there.

The circumstances under which Lieutenant Colonel George Washington was ordered by Governor Dinwiddie to the Ohio with a force of two hundred men have already been considered.[5] He was, it may here be noted, commissioned "to protect and assist those already there in building the Fort." [6] Leaving Alexandria on April 2, he was moving up the south branch of the Potomac with his small force —

---

[5] See Volume IV of this series, pages 299–306. Washington was promoted from the rank of major to that of lieutenant colonel on March 15, 1754 (*Dinwiddie Papers*, I, 107, and *George Washington's Diaries*, ed. Fitzpatrick, I, 73). The Washington diary covering the period between March 31 and June 27 fell into the hands of the French and by them was translated and published. It must therefore be used with caution.

[6] Dinwiddie to the Board of Trade, January 29, 1754, C.O. 5:1328, pp. 97–100.

actually only one hundred and fifty-nine men — when, on April 20, the news arrived that Contrecœur had three days earlier descended the Allegheny with a thousand troops and with eighteen pieces of cannon and had forced Ensign Ward and his some forty frontiersmen to surrender the unfinished fort.[7] Continuing his march to Wills Creek, where the Ohio Company had constructed a storehouse, Washington thereupon proceeded to hold a council of war, at which it was agreed to advance to the mouth of Redstone Creek, only some thirty miles distant from the forks of the Ohio, where stood the second supply house of the Ohio Company, but recently erected. This, it was felt, was the first "convenient place" on the Monongahela along the path from the settled part of Virginia where the ammunition could be placed, together with the ten four-pounder guns sent by the Ordnance Board to Virginia and destined for the frontier. From this point it was thought that an attack could be launched against the French in their new position on the Ohio. Meanwhile the soldiers could be "preserved from inaction" if on the Redstone, and the Indian allies about the Ohio encouraged to remain in the British interest.[8]

The wisdom of this decision may be questioned in view of the weakness of Washington's force and the strength of the French. Writing to Dinwiddie, however, the inexperienced commander stated with confidence:

> "I doubt not that we can maintain a possession there, till we are reinforced, unless the rising of the waters shall admit the enemy's cannon to be conveyed up in canoes, and then I flatter myself we shall not be so destitute of intelligence, as not to get timely notice of it, and make a good retreat." [9]

It is true that he also urged the necessity of having,

> "as soon as our forces are collected, a number of cannon, some of heavy metal, with mortars and grenadoes to attack the French, and put us on an equal footing with them,"

and the advisability of summoning the Cherokee, Catawba, and Chickasaw to Wills Creek to make peace with the Six Nations and to support the expedition.[10] But neither the cannon nor the Southern

---

[7] Washington's Diaries, I, 75.

[8] Ibid., I, 77.

[9] Letter of April 25, 1754, Writings of Washington (ed. Fitzpatrick), I, 41.

[10] Ibid.

Indians were destined to arrive to assist him in an enterprise that was so involved in hazards that today it would be considered an act little short of bravado.

In present-day military parlance, a task force designed to move effectively against an opponent entrenched and supported with artillery should not only possess a numerical superiority of at least two or three to one of really experienced soldiers, but be aided by guns the fire-power of which surpasses that of the opposing force. These canons of aggressive warfare are held to be fundamental in all sound strategic movements, and only in case of the possibility of surprise attack against a determined and capable enemy may they be disregarded by any commanding officer without danger of disaster. Toward such an enemy, thoroughly on the alert, Washington now prepared to move through a country so broken by the Laurel range of mountains and the precipitous Youghiogheny that an effective means of bringing up the heavy guns could not, with the inadequate means at his disposal, be easily devised. It may be justly pointed out that Governor Dinwiddie and the Virginia Council were by no means free of responsibility for this precipitate action, in spite of the decision of the council of war to proceed. Ensign Ward was sent from Wills Creek to Williamsburg posthaste to give in person the news of the coming of the French in force; all the essential factors of the problem were therefore at the disposal of the Governor, who, it is now clear, as the commander-in-chief should have ordered Washington to delay a forward movement until an adequate force had been assembled at Wills Creek.

Unfortunately, Dinwiddie, with all his splendid energy, was not a military man, nor did he possess competent military advisers. He was also confronted with extraordinary difficulties as he faced the great trans-Appalachian crisis. His Assembly, after much debate, voted but a paltry £10,000 in February for the defence of the frontiers; there was in fact shocking indifference on the part of most of the inhabitants of the Old Dominion to the fate of the back country. The militia did not feel that they were obligated to march to the Ohio, and men were reluctant to enlist; many of those who did so as private soldiers brought dismay to Washington.[11] The Pennsylvania Assembly, dominated by the Quakers, was coldly indifferent to the events to the westward, and the Maryland Assembly excused itself from becoming involved in an issue that it felt did not directly con-

11 *Ibid.*, I, 32.

cern the Province. North Carolina, it is true, agreed to send a regiment of men; also two of the Independent Companies of New York and one of the Independent Companies of South Carolina were promised by the Earl of Holderness. Of these expected reinforcements only the last-named arrived — a well-equipped, small body of men — some two weeks before the final test. This was not all with respect to the inadequacies of the expedition. A military movement, in a wilderness region heavily wooded and marked by dense undergrowth, demanded a force of Indian auxiliaries for scouting and reconnaissance as well as for the mobile, open-formation type of warfare best suited to the terrain. No adequate provision was made for this. Dinwiddie, most optimistically, thought that he could bring up from South Carolina the Catawba and the Cherokee, and even the Chickasaws from the lower Mississippi basin.[12] Had the one thousand Southern warriors arrived, such as he thought he could secure, and had suitable provision been made for them, it not only would have offset the defection of the Shawnee and the Delawares that now occurred, but would doubtless have held the two in line, especially in view of the cordial relations then existing between the Shawnee and the Cherokee.[13] This would have provided Washington with proper Indian support.

But the Governor was guilty in this connection of inexcusable bungling. These Indian groups were directly the concern of the government of South Carolina, and that government jealously scrutinized every attempt on the part of other colonial authorities to interfere with them.[14] Instead of working with Governor Glen, Dinwiddie, to all intents and purposes, ignored his special responsibilities for these Indians — given to him "under the King's royal sign manual" — by entering into direct negotiations with the tribes. As a result, instead of aiding the Virginia Governor, Glen viewed this move with undisguised hostility and finally wrote bitingly to Dinwiddie:

> "The Government of Virginia knows little of our Indians, and can have no great knowledge in any Indian affairs; they have nevertheless busied themselves extreamly for these three or four years past, with all the Indians contiguous to and in alliance with this Province which has been a matter of great Concern to every Member of this

---

[12] See his letters to the Catawba and to the Cherokee of February 4, 1754, as well as those of April 19 (*Dinwiddie Papers*, I, 60–1, 131–3).

[13] For this relation see Volume IV, page 75 of the present series.

[14] See Governor Glen's letter of September 18, 1751 to the President of the Virginia Council, *ibid.*, IV, 73.

Community, as they are sensible how dangerous it may be when matters of so great delicacy are handled by Gentlemen that can have no
great experience in them.

"The person who has often been sent from that Government [15] to
the Cherokees and Catawabas, to invite (and I must add to press)
them to go thither to get Presents, has spoken very disrespectfully of
this Province to the Indians, telling them that they will not be treated
there with old cloaths, alluding to the Presents sent by His Majesty to
be distributed to them by us, and has endeavoured to bring this
Province into Contempt. . . ." [16]

Dinwiddie's excuse for acting as he did was the urgency of the
situation on the Ohio, which led him to take "the more dispatchfull
Method" of communicating with these Indians.[17] Yet he did not take
the South Carolina Governor fully into his confidence as he should
have done, which led the latter, not unreasonably, to write critically
to the Earl of Holderness on March 30:

"Mr. Dinwiddie is not so Kind as to communicate to me his Intentions, or any scheme for the Service of his Province, neither does he
invite me or any of the Neighbouring Governors to meet in order to
concert any plan of operations for material assistance, and the Common Weal of all the Colonies. . . ." [18]

Glen, in fact, had thought in terms of bringing about the fullest measure of co-operation of the colonies principally affected by the French
movement and to that end, on March 14, after getting the support
of the South Carolina Assembly, had proposed to Dinwiddie a conference of colonial governors to that end.[19] But his urgent recommendation that the Virginia Governor should "invite the other Governments to an Interview" without waiting for further orders from the
home government [20] was coldly received and put aside upon very

---

[15] Abraham Smith, of Augusta County, was an Indian interpreter and captain in the
Virginia militia. Yet Governor Glen had a low opinion of Dinwiddie's agent and accused
him of being a horse-thief (C.O. 5:14, p. 493).

[16] Letter of August 15, 1754. C.O. 5:14, p. 475.

[17] His letters dated January 29, 1754 (see *Dinwiddie Papers*, I, 61–3) was received
by Glen at the end of February.

[18] C.O. 5:14, p. 275.

[19] The Committee of Conference of the two houses of the Assembly recommended
that South Carolina in conjunction with the other interested colonies should provide
"proportionable assistance to dislodge or repel any invasion upon his Majesty's Territorys"
as "may be hereafter settled and adjusted" (C.O. 5:14, pp. 291–4).

[20] In this connection Glen wrote: "I think we should not . . . be always a Burthen
to Britain, let us exert our own strength . . ." (C.O. 5:14, p. 296).

flimsy grounds — at least with respect to a consultation of the more southern governments most concerned with developments west of the Appalachians, which could have embraced those of Pennsylvania, Maryland, Virginia, North Carolina, and South Carolina.[21] The last province now became recalcitrant.

As a result, when Dinwiddie finally went to Winchester with his presents for his anticipated great Indian conference, only a handful of natives arrived during the period of sixteen days that he waited there.[22] The Indians on the Ohio who were still loyal to the English were too much concerned with the protection of their wives and children at this critical juncture to go, and the Southern Indians upon whose support he had placed so much confidence, failed to put in an appearance, with the exception of a few stragglers, for reasons that are not hard to determine. It may be that Dinwiddie then recalled the words of the Governor of South Carolina:

> "I again entreat you to be persuaded that the readiest and surest way to have any effectual Assistance from the Catawabas or Cherokees is by the Intervention of this Government; they have been under our direction for upwards of thirty years, and there is not a Headman or warrior of any Note among them that I do not personally know." [23]

While it must be admitted that the co-operation of the more southern colonies in a common enterprise had up to this period never been realized — outside of that between South Carolina and Georgia in the recent war — and was difficult to secure in view of the intense particularism of the inhabitants; yet it may at the same time be affirmed that a gathering along the lines suggested by Glen, with the assemblies likewise represented by commissioners, as at the Albany Conference, would doubtless have strengthened the English western line of defence, possibly very greatly. But South Carolina, as has been suggested, was deeply dissatisfied with a one-sided arrangement for this defence that placed in the hands of the Governor of Virginia all discretion and direction in the use of the common resources. In fact Governor Glen at last became so disgusted with what he and his Council felt was the utter mismanagement that characterized the defensive measures along the western frontier that on June 1 he wrote

---

[21] *Dinwiddie Papers*, I, 128–9.
[22] Dinwiddie to Sir Thomas Robinson, June 18, 1754, *Dinwiddie Papers*, I, 201–5; J. R. Alden, *The Southern Colonial Frontier*, p. 43.
[23] Glen to Dinwiddie, March 14, 1754, C.O. 5:14, p. 297.

sharply to Dinwiddie requesting the return of the South Carolina Independent Company that had arrived in Virginia and was then actually proceeding toward Wills Creek. This was a pretty kettle of fish! The unhappy results of this blundering on the part of Dinwiddie were, moreover, to be felt not only in the western campaign now under way but in that of the following year; for Glen was the only governor who could command the services of a powerful band of warlike Indians in alliance with the English.

But let us now turn to the activities of the youthful Lieutenant Colonel of the Virginia militia,[24] who with his officers, as a result of the conference of war, had determined to advance to the Redstone. The Nemacolin Trail — blazed between Wills Creek on the Potomac and the Youghiogheny in 1751 for the Ohio Company, a distance of some eighty miles — which he must now traverse, was quite unsuited for the movement of supply wagons and the artillery train that was to follow. Washington was therefore compelled to put his men to work "to make and amend the Road." By May 7 his force had reached Little Meadows, having with "great difficulty and labour" traversed a distance of twenty miles at an average of three miles a day. Writing to Dinwiddie on the 9th, he informed him with manifest disappointment that he had seen nothing of the Southern Indians, "tho' this is the time we mostly need their assistance," and then admitted that, in view of the reports that the French troops at the forks of the Ohio had been reinforced by eight hundred men, he could count on only an inadequate force of one hundred and sixty effectives by reason of the fact that he was compelled to discharge Captain Trent's detachment, whose presence was "rather injurious to the other men, than Serviceable to the Exp[edition]. . . ."[25] On May 12, however, he was heartened by an express that brought news not only that Colonel Fry, his superior, with at least a hundred of the other Virginia volunteers had reached Winchester, but that three hundred and fifty North Carolina troops under Colonel James Innes were marching westward to support him, that Maryland would raise two hundred troops, and that Pennsylvania had made an appropri-

---

[24] Washington was in his twenty-third year.

[25] *Writings of Washington*, I, 46. Trent's men were deeply dissatisfied with their pay, which was set by the Virginia Assembly committee at eightpence a day for the enlisted private. Captain Trent, without authorization, had previously promised them two shillings.

ation equal to that of Virginia to finance the expedition.[26] By the 17th he had reached the Great Crossing of the Youghiogheny, where he received the additional news that one of the Independent Companies of South Carolina had arrived in Virginia and would march westward and that two of the New York Independent Companies would soon land.

The information regarding the anticipated arrival of the three companies of colonial regulars seems to have had in one respect a most disturbing effect upon Washington and his fellow officers. For it is at this juncture that he and his staff display a sense of deep grievance over the matter of their pay. One may therefore surmise that this was largely due to the fact that the officers of the Independent Companies were all on the British establishment and in receipt of the pay so provided and would be in a favoured position financially. In writing to Dinwiddie the young commander frankly admitted that his officers were so dissatisfied that nothing would prevent their throwing up their commissions but

> "the approaching danger, which has too far engaged their honour to recede till other officers are sent in their room or an alteration made in their pay, during which they will assist with their best endeavours voluntarily." [27]

Replying to such "ill-timed Complaints," as were voiced in Washington's letters and also in a paper signed by his officers, Dinwiddie pointed out:

> "The first Object^n to the Pay, if made at all, sh^d have been made before engaging in the Service. The Gentlemen well knew the terms on wch they were to serve . . . nor c^d they be ignorant of the Numbers that as well as themselves, and to whom they were prefer'd, approved

---

[26] *Diaries of Washington*, I, 81. For the fate of the Pennsylvania bill for appropriating ten thousand pounds to His Majesty's use see *Pennsylvania Archives* (eighth series), V, 3702–22.

[27] *Writings of Washington*, I, 49. In a letter written later at Great Meadows Washington made clear to Dinwiddie his own position: "I dare say your Honour remembers the first Estimation allow'd to a Lieut. Colo. 15s., and Maj'r 12s.6d. which I then complain'd very much off [*sic*] till your Honour assur'd me that we were to be furnish'd with proper necessary, and offer'd that as a reason why the pay was Less than British; after this . . . you . . . acquainted me that I was to have but 12s.6d. This with some other Reasons, indused me to acquaint Colo. Fairfax with my intention of Resigning, which . . . he dissuaded me from and promised to represent the trifling pay to your Honour . . . to have it enlarg'd" (*Dinwiddie Papers*, I, 176–7).

of the terms. . . . And as to the Canada Expedition [in the preceding war], it is, I believe, a Mistake to say that those who served in it were found with Wine and Beer at the Public Expence, and that their wages were higher, or even as high as Yours." [28]

The issue now raised respecting equal pay of colonial officers with those on the British establishment, as well as that involving the recognition of equal rank, was not to be easily settled, as will be noted in the progress of this work.

While still at the Great Crossing, Washington received reports from both traders and Indians that the forty miles still to be covered to the Redstone post on the Monongahela could hardly be traversed by wagons "over almost impassable Roads and Mountains." He therefore determined to investigate in person the possibility of transporting the expedition part way, at least, by boat on the Youghiogheny. This, however, proved not to be feasible because of the obstructions in the river. He therefore moved slowly forward overland and by the 24th had reached a region called Great Meadows, to the west of the main ridge of the Alleghenies. Here he now hurriedly fortified himself, after receiving a report from the Mingo Chief Tanacharisson, known as the Half-King, that the French had sent out a detachment to meet him. His report to Dinwiddie, in spite of his dangerous situation, was optimistic:

"We have, with nature's assistance, made a good Intrenchment, and by clearing ye Bushes out of these Meadows, prepar'd a charming field for an Encounter." [29]

After a second warning from the Half-King that a party of Frenchmen was watching his movements from "a low obscure place" in this mountainous, heavily wooded region stretching beyond the Meadows off toward Laurel Mountain (also called Laurel Hill) to the west, Washington determined to eliminate this menace. Detaching some of his men to guard the ammunition against a surprise attack, he set forth with forty soldiers on the 27th in a heavy rain, "in a night as dark as pitch, along a path scarce broad enough for one man," with the determination to reach the Half-King's camp — some six miles distant on the mountain at a site since known as Washington's Spring — and then, supported by the Indians, to attack the French hide-out.

28 *Dinwiddie Papers*, I, 171–2.
29 Washington to Dinwiddie, May 27, 1754, *ibid.*, I, 174–5.

Arriving at the Indian camp at sunrise, without delay he thereupon, supported by Tanacharisson and his warriors, moved in the direction of the enemy — encamped in a rocky ravine — hoping to encircle and attack them on all sides unexpectedly, but he was discovered. An engagement ensued. In the fighting the French commanding officer, Ensign Coulon de Jumonville, and nine other Frenchmen were slain, one was wounded, and twenty-one were taken prisoner, with the loss of but one man killed and two or three wounded. Only one fugitive escaped to carry the news to Fort Duquesne.[30]

After so much deliberation in the Old World and so many strategic movements of both the French and the British here in the New, blood had at last been spilled in an armed encounter between military forces. This is the episode heralded throughout Europe as the "assassination" of Jumonville by George Washington while the former was proceeding to Washington's camp "on an Embassy" to deliver a summons.[31]

The young lieutenant colonel's defence of his conduct, however, was complete — and adequate. Moving as he was under proper orders with troops against an enemy that had appeared in time of peace at the forks of the Ohio and that had by show of overwhelming force and hostile threats compelled the immediate surrender of the newly constructed Virginia fort by its garrison, the safety of his command demanded decisive action when it was reported that a body of French soldiers had been hovering under cover some two or three days upon his flanks. Writing to Dinwiddie he stated:

---

[30] Writings of Washington (ed. Fitzpatrick), I, 65–6. It would appear, according to a report brought by the Indian trader Davidson (Davison) to Conrad Weiser, that the Indians took sharp issue with Washington's plan of attack but nevertheless played a leading part in the skirmish: "Col. Washington and the Half-King differed much in judgement, and on the Colonel's refusing to take his advice, the English and Indians separated. After which the Indians discovered the French in a hollow and hid themselves, lying on their bellies behind a hill; afterwards they discovered Col. Washington on the opposite side of the hollow in the gray of the morning, and when the English came out of their cover and closed with the French they [the Indians] killed them with their tomahawks, on which the French surrendered" (Washington's Writings, ed. Ford, I, 124). For an excellent description of the region where the engagement took place see A. B. Hulbert's Washington's Road (Nemacolin's Path), pp. 141–7.

[31] The "summons made by order of Monsieur de Contrecœur" is to be found in C.O. 5:14, pp. 361–4 and also pp. 405–8. The instructions to Jumonville are in ibid., 5:14, pp. 401–4. The French official account of the engagement sent to the French court declared that Jumonville was assassinated when, after the English consented to parley, he started to read his summons to them (Mémoires et Documents, Amérique, 10. I: 92–6). For a recent study of this episode see G. F. Leduc's Washington and "the Murder of Jumonville" (La Société Historique Franco-Américaine).

". . . And instead of coming as an Embassador, publicly, and in an open manner, they came secretly, and sought after the most hidden retreats . . . encamped there and remained hidden for whole days together, at a distance of not more than five miles from us; they sent spies to reconnoiter our camp; the whole body turned back two miles; they sent two messengers mentioned in the instructions to inform M. de Contreçœur of the place where we were, and of our disposition, that he might send his detachments to enforce the summons as soon as it should be given." [32]

The Great War for the British Empire had now begun. Started in peace-time with an insignificant encounter between the English and the French in an isolated mountain ravine on the western slopes of the Alleghenies and within a region void of settled inhabitants, yet claimed not only by France but also by both the provinces of Virginia and Pennsylvania, like the feeble beginnings of a Western forest fire it spread its flames, slowly at first and then more rapidly, carrying in its wake terror and destruction. But unlike a forest fire that is ultimately confined by natural obstacles to a particular geographical area, it was destined to leap over oceans, to illuminate continents, and to end by reducing to ashes the bright dreams of Frenchmen of a great future in the New World.

In spite of this victory, Washington was not unaware of his peril and proceeded to send a messenger to Colonel Fry calling for immediate reinforcements. The latter, unfortunately, had already died at Wills Creek as the result of a fall from his horse, and the colonelcy of the Virginia regiment now went to Washington, while chief command of the expedition devolved on Colonel James Innes, a personal friend of Dinwiddie's, with previous military experience, who commanded the North Carolina contingent.[33] While waiting for the anticipated support before taking the next move toward the Redstone,

---

[32] Writings of Washington (ed. Fitzpatrick), I, 57. As to the question of the peaceable disposition of the French detachment, Washington denied this: "They say they called us as soon as they had discovered us; which is an absolute falsehood for I was then marching at the head of the company going toward them and can positively affirm, that, when they saw us, they ran to their arms, without calling; as I must have heard them had they so done" (ibid., I, 58). For an excellent account of this incident the student is referred to C. H. Ambler's George Washington and the West, pp. 64–72. Rupert Hughes's George Washington, the Human Being and the Hero, 1732–1762, Chapter X, stresses the French version of the engagement.

[33] Dinwiddie explained to Fox, Secretary at War, that he gave the chief command to Innes, "who was a Capt. in the American regim't on the Expedit'n to Carthegena (in the late war) and is an experienc'd Officer" (Dinwiddie Papers, I, 246).

the little force at Great Meadows — still further depleted by reason of the detachment sent back to Winchester with the French prisoners — felt under the necessity of strengthening its position. By June 3 Washington was able to write:

> "We have just finish'd a small palisado'd Fort, in which with my small numbers, I shall not fear the attack of 500 men." [34]

Further, the Indians who had accompanied the Half-King from the Ohio, some eighty in all, including women and children, now joined the troops. Messengers were also sent to various other friendly groups of Indians, calling on them to gather at the Redstone in anticipation of the arrival of the English. The problem of the scarcity of supplies, however, kept Washington from moving forward immediately, but his men continued to work on the road.

On the 9th of June the remainder of the Virginia regiment arrived, in number some two hundred under Lieutenant Colonel George Muse, and on the 12th there appeared the South Carolina Independent Company of regulars commanded by Captain James MacKay (McKay). But Washington was beset with new difficulties. The newly arrived regulars would not accept orders from him since their officers had their appointments directly from the King. After MacKay had established a separate camp and had refused to require his troops without additional compensation to labour on the road leading to the Redstone or even to accept Washington's parole and countersign, the latter came to feel that the absence of that officer "would tend to the public advantage." [35] Further, the Virginia commissary, Major John Carlyle, failed miserably in his duty to forward to the troops either adequate food supplies or ammunition, although forty head of cattle appeared with MacKay's contingent. At the same time ominous reports came from the Ohio that both the Shawnee and the Delawares had taken up the hatchet against the English and that the French fort on the Ohio, now strongly constructed, was receiving eleven hundred additional troops, in two contingents, to reinforce the five hundred stationed there.[36] In view of all these facts it is hard to under-

---

[34] *Writings of Washington* (ed. Fitzpatrick), I, 73.

[35] *Ibid.*, I, 76–84. In an attempt to deal with this problem Dinwiddie appointed Captain Clarke of the New York Independent Company and Captain MacKay brevet lieutenant colonels. Writing to Colonel Innes on June 27, the Governor indicated that he thought that his powers under his commission from the King gave him superiority over MacKay and therefore that he could command the latter and also could appoint someone with the power to do so (*Dinwiddie Papers*, I, 218, 223).

[36] *Ibid.*

stand Washington's motives for ordering the Virginia regiment to give up the protection of the newly constructed fort and to advance to the Monongahela into a trap, if there ever was one. However, on the 16th, leaving the South Carolina regulars behind to their own devices, he moved forward with nine swivel guns over such difficult mountain roads that the supply wagons broke "very often."

The region that Washington now traversed, so changed today, was then one of almost "interminable forests," of giant black walnut, oak, cherry, locust, and other deciduous trees, some of them five feet in diameter,[37] with branches in many cases hopelessly intertwined. The late Professor Hulbert writes:

> "Who but one acquainted with primeval forests can picture the straggling branches of the giant trees reaching out into the etherial battle ground to a last death grapple with . . . hoary rivals . . . weighted down by luxuriant masses of moss and tangled vine?" [38]

One may also add that whoever is not acquainted with such a forest can easily picture its forbidding gloom, its pungent odours, its tangle of fallen monarchs, its masses of decaying vegetation, and its dankishness in inclement weather. Through this forest the Indians and wild beasts moved, following traces worn from time immemorial. Such was the famous Catawba or Cherokee Trail blazed from the Carolinas to the Monongahela, where at Redstone Creek it wound northeasterly to the Youghiogheny and then up the Allegheny; such also was Nemacolin's Path, which at its westward extremity joined the former at the eminence later called Mount Braddock and only branched off from it after many miles. Along the latter the little force proceeded, clearing away obstructions and widening the trail.

The regiment had hardly arrived on the 18th at Gist's settlement — located near Mount Braddock, and not much more than two days' travel without encumbrances from Fort Duquesne [39] — when a band of Ohio Indians made up of Shawnee, Delawares, and Mingos put in their appearance and requested a conference. For three days, between

---

[37] James Veech, *The Monongahela of Old*, pp. 17–18; *History of Fayette County* (ed. Franklin Ellis), pp. 18–21. Washington saw trees on the Great Kanawha with a diameter of over fourteen feet (A. B. Hulbert, *Washington's Road (Nemacolin's Path)*, p. 41.

[38] *Ibid.*

[39] Washington on January 1, in returning from Fort Le Bœuf, left John Fraser's home — later the scene of Braddock's defeat — which was "Eight or Ten Miles up Monangahela" from the forks, and arrived at Gist's the following day, moving along the Cherokee Path (*Diaries of Washington*, I, 67).

the 19th and the 21st, Washington, aided by the Half-King, who also arrived on the scene, exercised all his talents to persuade these Indians and their fellow tribesmen to hold to the English alliance and to support him; but at length he had to acknowledge failure and also that the savages, who thereupon disappeared, had really come as enemy spies to inform the French of the strength and movements of the English.[40] Still bent on reaching the Redstone, some of the men of the regiment as late as the 28th were busy clearing a road and they seem to have covered eight of the remaining sixteen miles from Gist's.[41] On that day reports reached Washington that a large force of French and Indians was advancing. A council of war was called. At first it was agreed to make a stand behind the entrenchment that had been hurriedly thrown up. Then, according to Captain Stephen's account, with the sudden arrival of Captain MacKay and his regulars from Fort Necessity, another consultation was held on the evening of the 29th. Apparently for the first time the folly of attempting to give battle under such adverse conditions to a powerful, well-trained foe was fully recognized and it was sensibly decided to retreat to Wills Creek, giving up even the palisaded fort at Great Meadows.[42] There had been frightful waste of horses and wagons in the advance to Mount Braddock — few of either had survived. As a consequence, in the hurried retreat the troops were placed under the greatest strain in extricating with their own efforts their baggage and precious swivel guns.[43] By July 1 the exhausted soldiers on continuous march had reached Fort Necessity. Unable to proceed farther, they doubtless hoped there to find a measure of safety until reinforcements could reach them.

The advance of the English from the settled part of Virginia westward, meanwhile, had been represented to the French as a formidable movement of a corps of five thousand troops. This rumour impelled Governor General Duquesne to take appropriate measures to protect his position on La Belle Rivière, as the French called the Ohio.[44] With the news of the dispersion of Jumonville's detachment, he commis-

[40] Ibid., I, 93–101.

[41] A. B. Hulbert, op. cit., p. 153.

[42] Maryland Gazette, August 29, 1754.

[43] According to Captain Stephen, the conduct of the South Carolina regulars was most reprehensible: "The Independents refused to lend a Hand to draw the Guns, or help off with the Ammunition; nor would they do Duty as Pioneers, which had an unhappy Effect on our Men . . ." (Ibid.).

[44] Mém. et Doc., Amérique, 10. I: 92–6 (Canadian Archives transcriptions).

sioned the Jumonville's brother, Captain Coulon de Villiers, a veteran of the late war in America, to gather a body of Indians of the tribes in alliance with the French and to hurry to Fort Duquesne. Arriving there with his savages on June 26, de Villiers found that Contrecœur had already formed a detachment of five hundred soldiers, supported by a small body of Indian scouts, which was about to proceed against Washington under the Chevalier le Mercier, a military engineer. Pleading his seniority, his special command of the Northern Indians, and the fact that his own brother had been "assassinated (*assassiné*)," de Villiers was now preferred above le Mercier.[45]

The following day a council of war was held, conforming to orders given by Duquesne on May 29 with reference to measures that should be taken to avenge the death of Jumonville. At this it was agreed that as many soldiers and Indians as could be spared should be sent to chastise the English for the crime of having "violated the most sacred laws of civilized nations." However, as the King desired to maintain harmony between the two Crowns, it was likewise agreed that as soon as the blow was struck and the English force had been chased from His Most Christian Majesty's domains, one of the prisoners to be taken in the course of the campaign should be sent to the commander of the nearest Virginia post to inform him of the determination of the French authorities to sustain the summons Jumonville had carried and of the desire of the French to live in peace with the English, provided that the latter retired peacefully from the lands of the former and consented to a mutual exchange of prisoners. Finally, it was determined that should de Villiers find in advancing that the English had retired from the King's lands, he should nevertheless continue his march into the region of their settlements and proceed to destroy the habitations and to treat them as enemies until he had secured ample satisfaction and a change of conduct on their part.[46] In other words, reprisals were to be made even to the extent of ravishing the English frontier settlements.

Departing from Fort Duquesne on the 28th with the troops and with his band of Indians spreading out so as to avoid surprise, de Villiers purposely diverged from the route that at first he had intended to follow — the most direct along Cherokee Trail. After a conference with the Indians, however, he decided to continue up

45 Mém. et Doc., Amérique, 10. I: 97.
46 Mém. et Doc., Amérique, 10. I: 110–13.

the Monongahela to the mouth of the Redstone, where was located the Ohio Company storehouse, called by the French the *"hangard"* [47] — a small structure built of logs, one upon another, well notched in, about thirty feet in length and twenty in breadth.[48] Arriving there by means of *pirogues,* he again took counsel with the Indians as to the precautions that should be taken to protect the boats and supplies, and then on July 1, having left a guard at the Redstone, he pushed forward over the wooded, mountainous region lying between the Monongahela and Mount Braddock. Although footprints appeared earlier in the day, it was not until three o'clock in the afternoon that his Indian scouts reported that they had reached the road that the English had been building. They had seen no one, however, and it appeared that the enemy had left the region some three days earlier. The march was then continued. Setting off again at break of day on the 2nd before the scouts had returned, de Villiers soon became apprehensive and determined not to move forward until he had positive news of the enemy. At this juncture a party of Indians who had remained at the Redstone appeared with an English deserter. Under threats the latter divulged the information that Washington's forces had retreated from the entrenchment at Mount Braddock, dragging their cannon. Moving on now to the late English camp, de Villiers, as soon as he arrived, sent his scouts out in all directions; although they could not detect the presence of any of the enemy, they did uncover several caches of implements and other utensils, which were appropriated.

After spending the night at Mount Braddock in a downpour, during which the English deserter was again questioned and the Indians were assured that they were not going to be rashly exposed to danger, early on the 3rd the French commander again moved forward over the road so recently constructed by the enemy — with the Indians fanning out as a protective measure. Although it continued to rain, de Villiers felt under necessity to speed his movements in order to give the English no time to throw up new entrenchments.[49] He did turn aside, however, to pause at the place where his brother had met his death, where he saw the bodies of Frenchmen still lying.[50] Having

---

[47] *Hangar* in French means "outhouse."

[48] Mém. et Doc., Amérique, 10. I: 97–109.

[49] *Ibid.*

[50] It is certainly surprising that after the engagement Washington did not provide for the interment of the bodies of the Frenchmen killed there. It would indicate either a certain indifference on his part, which is difficult to accept, or, what is more likely, the

arrived within three quarters of a league of Fort Necessity about eleven o'clock in the morning, he divided his force into detachments and, after ordering them to assume a formation suited to the wooded nature of the terrain, moved forward.

The Great Meadows is a level bottom, through which a small creek, Great Meadows Run, meanders, and is surrounded by hills of moderate size, then heavily wooded. At the point where Fort Necessity was located on firm ground in the centre of the swale, the distance between the hills is about two hundred and fifty yards although at one point the high ground encroached to within sixty yards of the fort. This was apparently built in the form of an irregular square with one side provided with three bastioned gates and another expanded into a triangle so as to include a small tributary of the run with its water supply. The palisades of upright logs were probably reinforced by earth banked on either side of them. Within the enclosure, comprehending about a third of an acre, there was doubtless a log structure, characteristic of all frontier forts, that could serve as headquarters and for the protection of the powder and other matériel; without, trenches and rifle pits had been hastily constructed.[51]

According to de Villiers's version of the fight that ensued, he discovered as he neared the fort that his scouts had misdirected him; some of the troops were therefore deployed to cover an exposed flank that Washington's force had already begun to fire upon with cannon.[52] Soon the English, drawn up in front of the fort in battle formation, began advancing on his right side as though they were about to attack. In the midst of Indian war-cries and shouts of the French

fact that the Frenchmen were really destroyed by the allied Indians rather than by his own troops, and that after being scalped, the bodies, according to Indian custom, were left exposed as symbols of the vengeance of the red men.

[51] For a detailed discussion of Fort Necessity see A. B. Hulbert, op. cit., pp. 173–87. There is now a replica of the fort upon its site. For a photograph of this see C. H. Ambler, op. cit., opposite page 87.

[52] According to the account of the engagement given by Washington and MacKay to Dinwiddie upon their arrival in Williamsburg and printed in the Virginia Gazette of July 19, at nine o'clock in the morning intelligence was brought to the fort of the approaching French and about eleven o'clock the sentinel gave notice of their appearance "by fireing his Piece, which he did at the Enemy, and as we learned afterwards killed three of their men, on which they began to fire upon us, at about 600 yards distance, but without any Effect. . . ." Washington in later years denied that the English fired first. Referring to de Villiers's account as "not less erroneous than inconsistent," he writes: "He says the French received the first fire. It is well known, that we received it at six hundred paces' distance" (Writings of Washington, ed. Sparks, II, 463). The memory of an elderly man is not always to be relied upon.

(From Richard Waddington's *Louis XV et le Renversement des Alliances*.)

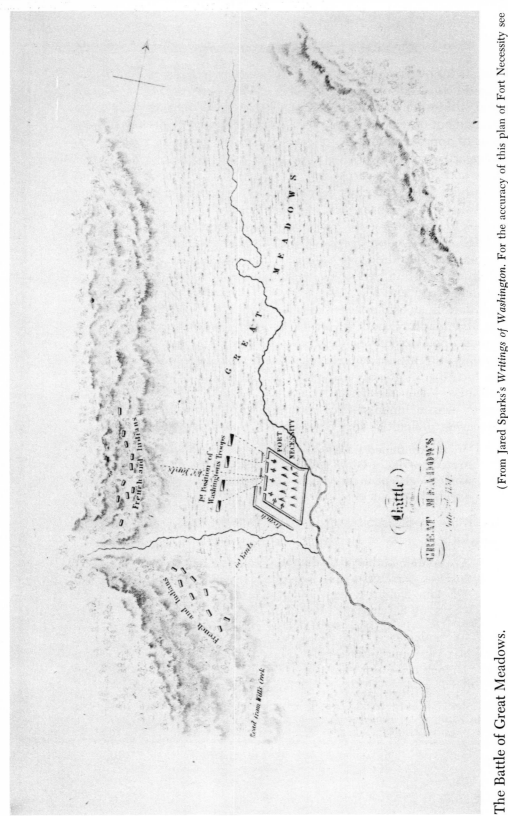

The Battle of Great Meadows.

(From Jared Sparks's *Writings of Washington.* For the accuracy of this plan of Fort Necessity see A. B. Hulbert's extended discussion in his *Historic Highways of America*, III, Chapter V.)

soldiers his own force now pressed forward to give battle; but before it could come close enough to discharge its weapons the English retired within the entrenchments that surrounded the fort, which was situated out of musket range of his troops. He now manœuvred them so as to approach more closely under cover of the trees without unnecessarily exposing his men and established himself at a point of the woods but sixty yards distant. Sharp firing thereupon occurred from both sides, the chief result of which was the silencing of the English cannon. During this engagement, which lasted until eight o'clock in the evening, the rain continued to fall without intermission.

Washington's entire force, now reduced as the result of desertions to some four hundred, was also greatly weakened by the incapacity of almost one hundred of the men. For days the soldiers had been without bread and they had arrived at the Meadows from Mount Braddock in an exhausted condition, as has been indicated. Washington and MacKay, both aware of their dangerous situation, having agreed upon defensive measures, set to work on July 2. While the regulars dug an entrenchment along the exposed southern side of the fort, the Virginians made rifle pits and embankments about the palisades. When the fighting began, the soldiers had to take to the watery entrenchments. The sporadic firing went on, but under ever increasing difficulties for the English. Captain Stephen writes:

> "By the continued Rains and Water in the Trenches, the most of our Arms were out of Order, and we had only a Couple of Screws in the whole Regiment to clean them. But what was still worse, it was no sooner dark, than one-half of our Men got drunk." [53]

According to the report rendered by Washington and MacKay to Dinwiddie:

> "We continued this unequal Fight, with an Enemy sheltered behind the trees, ourselves without shelter, in trenches full of water, in a settled Rain, and the Enemy galling us on all Sides incessantly from the woods, till 8 o'clock at Night. . . ." [54]

De Villiers declared that the French, having taken steps to ensure their own positions and to enclose the English within their fort, about eight o'clock cried out that if the English desired to negotiate they

---

[53] *Maryland Gazette*, August 29, 1754. It is ironical that Stephen, who wrote the above, should in later years, as a major general, have been dismissed for drunkenness during the Battle of Germantown.

[54] *Virginia Gazette*, July 19, 1754.

would cease firing.[55] The latter — after some hesitation, apparently fearing a ruse, and after the French offer of a solemn pledge of safety for one of the officers to come to them — agreed to send Captain Van Braam and Adjutant Peyronie to de Villiers.[56] De Villiers received at least Van Braam in the open meadow and thereupon stated that, since there was no war, he desired to offer the English grace and to avoid exposing them to the cruelty of the savages; but he warned that if they persisted in their resistance he would be obliged to take away this hope. He also made clear that the French had only come against them to avenge the assassination of his own brother and to compel them to move off of lands on the King's domain and then proceeded to hand to Van Braam the terms of the capitulation that he expected them to accept.[57]

Under the terms of this capitulation the commander of the fort was permitted to return to his own country with his entire garrison excepting two captains (Captains Van Braam and Stobo), who were to be held as hostages for the return under escort of the French prisoners made at the time of the "assassination" of the Sieur de Jumonville. The exchange should occur within a period of two and one half months.[58] The cannon, alone of the matériel, was to be reserved and permission was given not only to place in hiding such stores as could not be removed immediately owing to the lack of draught animals but to leave a guard to protect these under stipulation that the English

> "would give their word of honour not to construct any establishment either in this region or on this side of the mountains for the period of a year to begin with this day."

Here, then, was the capitulation, brought to the fort by Van Braam, that was finally accepted. Captain Stephen gives a vivid picture of the deliberations that took place respecting the proffered terms:

---

[55] Mém. et Doc., Amérique, 10. I: 97–109.

[56] Virginia Gazette, July 19, 1754.

[57] For these terms see C.O. 5:14, pp. 427–30; they are to be found in French in Washington's Writings (ed. W. C. Ford), I, 120–1; also in his Writings (ed. Sparks), II, 459–60, and in the Pennsylvania Colonial Records, VI, 52–3. The document in the French Archives (Mém. et Doc., Amérique, 10. I: 114–21) is a translation back into French of the English translation printed in the Pennsylvania Journal under date of July 25.

[58] De Villiers explained his failure to hold the entire English garrison by saying that it was not natural in time of peace to make the soldiers of another country prisoners of war (Mém. et Doc., Amérique, 10. I:97–109).

"It rained so heavily that he [Van Braam] Could not give us a written Translation of them; we could scarcely keep the Candle light to read them; they were wrote in a bad Hand, on wet and blotted Paper so that no Person could read them but Van Braam who had heard them from the mouth of the French Officer. Every Officer then present is willing to declare, that there was no such word as Assassination mentioned; the Terms expressed to us were 'the death of Jumonville.'" [59]

It was at four o'clock in the morning of July 4 when a French detachment appeared at the fort to take possession and the garrison filed out "with Drums beating and our Colours flying," according to Washington and MacKay. De Villiers declared that in spite of his resentment at the death of his brother, the number of the English dead and wounded excited his pity.[60] Nevertheless, it was reported by the Indian trader Robert Callender that no sooner had the English delivered up the fort

"than the Indians got in and pillaged them of all their baggage and provisions, shot down all their cows and horses and in short took everything from them but their powder, which they destroyed themselves by throwing it in the ditch that surrounds the Camp; they [the Indians] also killed two of the wounded and Scalped them, and also three of the Soldiers who happened to get drunk and were asleep. Col. Washington upon this complained of the treatment they received, so contrary to the conditions agreed upon and the French Commander pretending to put a stop to it, ran in among the Indians with his Sword drawn, but instead of persuading them from it, he commended them for their courage, and the treatment they had given the English. The number of the French was 900 and 200 Indians and what is most severe upon us, is that they were all our own Indians, Shawnesses, Delawares and Mingos . . . for many of the English knew them, and called to them by their name to Spare their Goods,

---

[59] *Maryland Gazette*, August 29, 1754. It may be surmised that Van Braam in translating the terms of the capitulation did not use the word "assassination." According to Stephen, Peyronie, who was appointed to accompany Van Braam and was a master of the French language, was dangerously wounded and his services were lost for this occasion (*ibid.*).

[60] Mém. et Doc., Amérique, 10. I: 97–109. In the engagement the South Carolina Independent Company seems to have suffered more severely than did the Virginia regiment. The latter had twelve killed and forty-six wounded out of three hundred, whereas the former apparently had eighteen killed and twenty-four wounded out of one hundred (*Dinwiddie Papers*, I, 241).

but all the answer they got was calling them the worst name their Langūge admits of. . . ." [61]

In view of the massacre of a number of the New England troops by the Indians in 1757 after the surrender of Fort William Henry and in spite of the most solemn engagements, the treatment of Washington's little army by the savages, bad as it was, was mild. This doubtless can be attributed to one circumstance. At Fort William Henry the Indians got at the supply of rum left at the fort by the defeated English, while at Fort Necessity de Villiers took the precaution to stave in the casks still remaining when Washington delivered it up. He also seems to have sought to carry out other parts of the agreement, whatever may have been his leniency with respect to the plundering of the Indians, who simply would not be denied some booty. For it appears that when the Indians had rounded up ten of the straggling English soldiers and had made them prisoner, he set them free and sent them off with another Indian — doubtless one who previously had known the English.[62] His own description of the effect of the Indian outburst of pillage upon Washington's army may have been somewhat exaggerated when he declared that

> "the English now petrified with fright took flight, leaving behind their standard and one of their flags." [63]

Nevertheless, it was doubtless at this juncture a frightened, demoralized little army that sought to save itself by hasty retreat. Only those who are unacquainted with warfare would be inclined to doubt that the morale of this force — which had previously exhibited a good deal of bravery, but which had taxed itself beyond endurance without adequate food, rest, or shelter for days — dropped to a low level as it began its weary retreat to Wills Creek. But the army did not take panic and held together. The first day only three miles were covered, for the force was encumbered by seventy wounded men; then making camp and giving the exhausted troops their first real rest in some days, broken only by the fending off of a party of Indians still bent on loot, Washington proceeded by slow stages to the creek, where on July 9 he and Captain MacKay held an inspection and drew up reports.

---

[61] This report is contained in a letter written by a resident of Paxton to the Governor of Pennsylvania on July 16, 1754 (Penn Official Correspondence, 6:203, Historical Society of Pennsylvania).

[62] Mém. et Doc., Amérique, 10. I:97–109.

[63] Ibid.

The campaign now brought to a close was faulty in both its planning and its execution. The chief justification for the inadequately organized, hurried movement into the valley of the Monongahela was to protect and support the Indian allies of Virginia, allies that in the final test were nonexistent — not a single Indian supported Washington's defence of Fort Necessity. The chief responsibility for the debacle that followed would seem to lie at the door of the Governor of Virginia.[64] Dinwiddie, taking upon his shoulders the duties of commander-in-chief, attempted to settle — without proper consultation and agreement between himself and the neighbouring governments on a *modus operandi* — a grave international issue that directly affected the security and welfare of every colony with trans-Appalachian claims. In view therefore of the orders received from him to march to the Redstone and to fortify himself at that point, Washington's rashness in pushing his three hundred raw recruits with inadequate supplies as far as Mount Braddock and into the neighbourhood of a hostile force of overwhelming superiority, commanded by officers experienced in wilderness warfare and buttressed by fortifications with cannon, must be somewhat condoned, though violating, as this move did, all sound military principles. After all, the Virginia colonel was a very young man, in his twenty-third year, who was still to learn the art of warfare. To his credit, he had shown courage of a high order, ability to stand the ordeals of campaigning under the most adverse conditions, and those qualities of leadership that left him the respect of his fellow Virginia officers and men, even in defeat. That is not a little for a soldier in the making.

[64] For a contrary point of view the student should consult Dr. L. K. Koontz's recent and interesting volume *Robert Dinwiddie*, particularly the chapters entitled "Military Aspirations" and "Undeclared Warfare."

CHAPTER III

Britain Lends a Hand

THE FIRST English campaign in the undeclared war that began in North America in 1754 had ended in failure and the surrender of Lieutenant Colonel George Washington's forces. The mild terms of the capitulation may be explained by the fact that the French force not only was concerned with limited objectives, as has been made clear in the preceding chapter, but was in no way equipped to remain in possession of Fort Necessity had it so desired — marching as it did with a minimum of supplies in order that its movements might not be impeded. In fact, having demolished the fort and broken the cannon, de Villiers, on the same day that the English departed, began slowly to retrace his steps, carrying his wounded men on stretchers. The following morning he arrived at Mount Braddock and, after destroying the entrenchments thrown up by Washington and the homes previously established there and in its vicinity by Gist and his friends, proceeded to the mouth of the Redstone. Here he burned the Ohio Company storehouse — the hangard — appropriated some caches of supplies left by the company, and then took to his *pirogues*. Descending the Monongahela, he arrived at Fort Duquesne the afternoon of the 7th of July, having fully accomplished his mission [1] — he had struck the English and they had now retreated to the east of the Alleghenies.

To the Anglo-Americans this inglorious campaign indicated some of the basic weaknesses in the colonial position now that war had come to the western frontier. The New England colonies had learned

---

[1] His "Journal" is in Affaires Étrangères, Mémoires et Documents: Amérique, 10. I: 97–109.

how to co-operate on occasion in measures designed to protect their vital interests, but not those to the southward. Intercolonial jealousies and friction could not easily be laid aside even in the face of impending danger and disaster. The people of New York showed undisguised hostility to the efforts of those of Pennsylvania to meddle in the affairs of the Six Nations, who claimed to control the western reaches of the latter province; those of Pennsylvania and of South Carolina were not less hostile to the attempts of the Virginians to interfere with Indian tribes customarily visited by their own traders. Whereas in New France there was a unified Indian policy, with the Governor General speaking to the natives in the name of all Frenchmen, this was not true of England overseas, in spite of the efforts of those at the Albany Congress to lend an air of unanimity in the presence of representatives of the Iroquoian Confederation. As a consequence, in this first contest between the French and the English in the new war now commencing, the French were able to rely not only upon the support of their Canadian Indians but even on that of their late enemies the Mingos, the Shawnee, and the Delawares, who now came over to them and sought to harass Washington's retreating army, left without any Indian support.[2]

Again, there was a woeful lack of co-ordination between the colonial governments in connection with the campaign, in spite of the efforts of the Earl of Holderness to rally to Governor Dinwiddie the support of the other colonies to the south of New England. The Quaker Assembly of Pennsylvania was much more interested in its quarrel with the Proprietors than it was in the ominous clouds gathering on its own frontiers, and the Maryland Assembly was reluctant to act, preferring to await developments. Neither had made any preparations for war. The Governor of New York had been ordered by the Earl of Holderness on January 18 to send two of the province's four Independent Companies to the aid of Virginia and, after unaccountable delays, he complied; but these, when they arrived about the middle of June, were found to be but skeleton companies burdened

---

[2] According to the report of the Indian trader Robert Callender, "The English had not one Indian to fight for them; the half king when he heard of the French being on their march, set of [sic] with about twenty Indians, to convoy their women into the Inhabitants, and Andrew Montour with the Indians he had with him to watch the motions of the French did not come upp, 'till after the engagement. By Coll. Washington's account there is only about sixty Indians declared in our favour" (Letter written from Paxton to the Governor of Pennsylvania, July 16, 1754, Penn Official Correspondence, Hist. Soc. of Pa.).

with incompetents and women and devoid of campaigning equipment.[3] Dinwiddie waxed eloquent in making clear to de Lancey his disappointment with them:

> "Your two Companies are at last arrived, after ten Weeks daily expecting them; but they are not agreeable to the Order from Home . . . they are not Compleat in Numbers; many of them old that cannot undergo a March of 200 Miles from Alexandria, and burthen'd with thirty Women and Children; and to complete the Whole, no Provisions . . . no Tents . . . or any Blankets, etc; in short, much worse than new rais'd forces. This Conduct, I acknowledge I am supris'd at. . . ."[4]

The New York companies were still at Alexandria when the blow fell upon Washington at Fort Necessity.[5] Captain Clark, their senior commanding officer, it seems, became ill and he held them there until he could recover.[6]

As to the support of the campaign by North Carolina, the Assembly showed commendable activity in voting in March £12,000 Proclamation money.[7] It was anticipated that with this sum a regiment of seven hundred and fifty effective men could be raised and it was assumed at the time that these troops, once they had reached Virginia, would be maintained by that province. When President Matthew Rowan of the Council was notified by Dinwiddie that each colony would be expected to maintain its own troops, the number of men enlisted was reduced to four hundred and fifty.[8] However, this number was impressive in view of the fact that it exceeded by one hundred and fifty the number recruited from Virginia

---

[3] According to the testimony given to de Lancey by Lieutenants Lewis Pavy and William Ogilvie, the two companies, with headquarters in New York City, were actually mustered but twice a year, in April and in August, when the men appeared to sign the rolls. These officers testified that "the whole Duty is done by one Serjeant, one Corporal, one Drum, & Twelve private Centinels of each Company. . . ." Each company, it is true, also had a sergeant and five privates in the Indian country. The same situation existed with respect to the two other companies at Albany, of which Hubert Marshall and Thomas Clark were captains, with the exception that these companies each had on duty forty-six men whereas the two former had on duty but twenty and twenty-one men respectively (C.O. 5:14, pp. 176–9).

[4] *Dinwiddie Papers*, I, 616–17.

[5] For Sir John St. Clair's biting comment on these soldiers see *Military Affairs in North America, 1748–1765* (ed. Stanley M. Pargellis), p. 62.

[6] *Dinwiddie Papers*, I, 271.

[7] *Colonial Records of North Carolina* (ed. W. L. Saunders), V, 108–9.

[8] *Ibid.*, V, 123–4.

"when it was Virginia soil that was invaded, and when Virginia had three times as many whites as North Carolina." [9]

Unfortunately, the enlisted men were promised three shillings a day as against eightpence, the pay of the Virginia volunteers, and this exorbitant rate of pay could not be maintained by North Carolina. Further, the money of the province had fallen into disrepute and would not pass in Virginia and in other provinces.[10] As a consequence, when the regiment finally moved into Virginia, poorly disciplined and even poorly armed,[11] it was obliged to bring along droves of beef cattle and hogs which it was hoped might be sold to advantage and with the sound currency thus acquired the soldiers' needs could be met. But hopeless confusion dogged the steps of the regiment. Its movements were indescribably slow; the £12,000 in North Carolina currency was soon paid out; disorderly, defiant of their officers, the soldiers mutinied at Augusta Court House; demanding their pay and in need of clothing and other necessaries, they deserted one after another; the hogs, as the result of the long drive, were in poor condition to be sold; and credit, for a time extended by the Virginia commissary, Major Carlyle, and even by Governor Dinwiddie, could no longer be found. Even before the troops had reached Winchester, late in July, Colonel Innes was obliged to contemplate disbanding them, and on August 11 the thoroughly disorganized regiment, now reduced to three hundred and fifty soldiers, was broken and the men turned loose to find their way home as best they could.[12]

[9] *Ibid.*, V, Preface xi.

[10] A. S. Ashe (*History of North Carolina*, I, 283) points out that the Assembly that voted to issue the currency to support the expedition was not recognized as legal in the northern counties of the province and consequently the inhabitants living there would not pay the taxes to maintain the value of the bills of credit, issued at a face value of four shillings to three shillings sterling. What was most serious, and was not mentioned by this writer, was that those who had incurred debts in sterling were permitted to discharge them at the above rate without regard to the value of the bills of credit as these passed from hand to hand. This applied also to the bills of credit issued in 1749. In fact, these bills of credit, not properly supported, depreciated rapidly in value, in spite of the fact that the holders were supposed to be entitled to pay their sterling debts at the above rates with them. This legislation was in 1759 denounced by the Board of Trade as "a Notorious Breach of public Faith . . . since no Man can trust any Property in a Country where such laws are subsisting" (*Acts of the Privy Council, Col., 1754-1766*, pp. 414-15).

[11] Governor Glen of South Carolina referred to the North Carolina regiment as "Neither disciplined nor Armed. Coll. Innes the Gentleman who commands . . . told me . . . that what few arms they had were of very different calibers — some wide bores, some small bores; but a great part had no Arms at all . . ." (C.O. 5:14, p. 502).

[12] *Dinwiddie Papers*, I, 232-3, 270, 304. Dinwiddie, writing to Governor Sharpe of Maryland on September 5, was very caustic in dealing with this situation. He declared

Infatuated with the idea that the French could easily be ejected from the Ohio county, the Governor of Virginia, before the disbanding of the North Carolina regiment, was already contemplating a new campaign in the autumn to retrieve the defeat at Fort Necessity. As to the defeat, he sought to attribute it to a lack of knowledge of the French reinforcements at Fort Duquesne "till the Day before they [the English] were taken on a surprise," as well as to the "dillatoryness" of the New York companies.[13] Preparatory to this new campaign, on July 20 he ordered the building at Wills Creek of a log fort and a magazine capable of receiving provisions for a six months' period for a force of twelve to fourteen hundred men.[14] With the approbation of the council he planned thereupon to send the nine hundred or more troops at his disposal [15] across the Alleghenies, supported by six small swivel guns and under Colonel Innes, who should endeavour during the remaining three months of campaigning weather to capture Fort Duquesne. If not successful, Innes was to build a fort either at the Redstone in the neighbourhood of the French or at "any other Place proper that may be determin'd by a Council of War" [16] — another madcap proposal! [17]

The refusal of the officers of the Independent Companies of New York and South Carolina to obey the commands of Innes, the new commander-in-chief, and the mutinous conduct of the Virginia regiment, with desertions that brought it down to a mere fraction of the two hundred that were at Fort Necessity, compelled Dinwiddie, most fortunately, to lay aside this project for the moment.[18] In fact, he had begun to think that effective voluntary colonial co-operation could not be secured and that the only hope of recovering the trans-Appalachian lands from the French was by determined action on the part of the mother country. This, he felt, should be expressed by

that the disbanding of the North Carolina troops "was occasioned by a monstrous mismanagem't of them from the Beginning; they raised 12,000 [£]. The Presid't of y't Colony gave the private men 3s. Proclam'n Money per Day, and the officers in Proportion, so that their Money was wholly expended before they joined the other Forces, and [the men] w'd serve no longer with't Assurance of the above Pay. This is monstrous ill conduct, and more so, because I wrote the Presid't the Establishm't of the Pay of our regim't" (ibid.).

13 Ibid., I, 271.
14 Ibid., I, 233.
15 Ibid., I, 257.
16 Ibid., I, 255–6.
17 For Glen's lengthy criticism of this move see C.O. 5:14, p. 504.
18 Dinwiddie Papers, I, 268, 287–8.

sending over to Virginia two regiments of regular soldiers furnished with proper siege artillery for reducing Fort Duquesne and by providing an adequate fund in America for the waging of war, to be secured through an act of Parliament placing a poll tax of two shillings and sixpence on all living within the English continental colonies.[19]

But while the two regiments were destined to be sent, the home government was not prepared to throw down a challenge to the colonies in the form of taxation by Parliament, strong as the arguments were that could be advanced in its favour in view of the reluctance of most of the colonies, even in face of the extraordinary crisis, to put forth any real effort to check the aggressive movements of the French.

Meanwhile the Governor of South Carolina, who was of the "opinion that every single step that has been taken is wrong" and who continued to resent bitterly Dinwiddie's efforts to establish direct control of the Southern Indians, ignoring South Carolina's responsibilities for relations with them, continued very logically to press for a meeting of the governors. In place of his earlier suggestion that the Governor of Massachusetts Bay should be included, he now thought it proper to limit this gathering to the representatives of those colonies most directly affected by the French advance in the Ohio Valley country: that is, of Virginia, North and South Carolina, Maryland, Pennsylvania, and New York. At this proposed gathering he thought that the real nature and extent of the encroachments of the French should be re-examined, redress from them demanded, and if this were not forthcoming, then a proper plan of military operations should be concerted, with an agreement as to quotas of men and money that the respective colonies should furnish. He was convinced that:

> "such a Confederacy . . . could either prevent any Controversies between the French and us or soon finish them. Whereas the present management is likely to cherish & protract them, and to feed the flame, a few men raised in One Province this month, a small sum squeezed out of another the next, the men die or desert, the money gone, and nothing done effectually. . . ." [20]

---

[19] These recommendations were made as early as July 24 to the Board of Trade, to Secretary Robinson, and to Secretary Fox as well as to others. For Dinwiddie's letters see *ibid.*, I, 239–51.

[20] Glen to Robinson, August 15, 1754, C.O. 5:14, pp. 469–84.

The gravity of the crisis developing in North America was meanwhile brought home to the mother country as the result of the flood of reports reaching London. In July it was agreed to send to Virginia £10,000 in specie, with credit for an equal amount and two thousand small arms. Further, it was determined to displace Dinwiddie by putting the colonial troops under Governor Horatio Sharpe of Maryland as the commander-in-chief "to oppose the Hostile Attempts Committed by the French in Different parts of his Majestys Dominions." [21] Sharpe, having received his commission on October 7, on the 19th arrived at Williamsburg for a conference of colonial governors.[22] In spite of Governor Glen's offer to Dinwiddie to leave for Virginia at a week's notice [23] for such a conference, he was not invited to attend. In fact, the almost studied neglect of the South Carolina government by Dinwiddie from the very beginning of this crisis had, as has already been emphasized, thoroughly disgusted the popular Governor as well as the Assembly, which at first had been most eager to co-operate with Virginia but now was equally determined to do nothing.[24] This was a great misfortune.

It may be pointed out that South Carolina was the only province to the south of New England that possessed anything approaching a real military establishment. Whereas Virginia, "a great Rich and well settled Province," was without independent companies and men of military training and experience and even lacked, according to Glen, an armoury that was well supplied with small arms,[25] there were not only the professional Independent Companies in South Carolina, but also an armoury with a reserve of two thousand muskets provided with bayonets and equal to those used by the King's troops, and a bombproof magazine containing a reserve of many thousand pounds' weight of powder, with another powder magazine in course of construction. Further than that, every person in the province capable of bearing arms was likewise already furnished with a good gun.[26] Moreover, in view of the fact that the South Carolina Independent Company still stationed in Virginia was now in a sense the backbone for the organized defence of that province, because of the demoral-

[21] Robinson to Sharpe, July 5, 1754, *Maryland Archives*, XXXI, 52–3.

[22] *Ibid.*, VI (*Correspondence of Governor Sharpe*), 103.

[23] In his letter of August 26 (C.O. 5:14, pp. 503–4).

[24] *Dinwiddie Papers*, I, 378.

[25] The Williamsburg magazine did, from time to time, contain a considerable supply of arms (*ibid.*, II, 8, *passim*).

[26] C.O. 5:14, pp. 503–4.

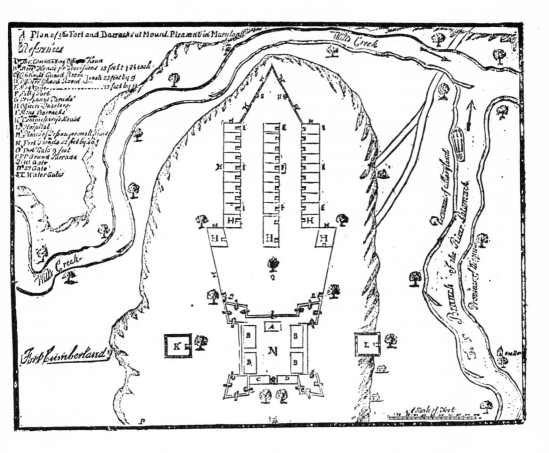

Plan of Fort Cumberland, Maryland, 1755, sent to the Board of Trade by Governor Dinwiddie.

(From J. Thomas Scharf's *History of Maryland.*)

Braddock's Route

A.D. 1755.

Drawn by Middleton

Roads ————
Braddock's Road ········
Scale of miles

(Middleton's map of Braddock's route to the Monongahela. (From Walker-Sargent, *History of Braddock's Expedition.*)

ized state of the Virginia regiment and of the New York Independent Companies, the failure to invite Governor Glen to the conference that met for the purpose of formulating plans for a new western campaign was nothing less than a glaring affront.[27] Sharpe, Dinwiddie, and the newly appointed and newly arrived Governor of North Carolina, Arthur Dobbs, representing Maryland, Virginia, and North Carolina respectively, made up the group and alone sought to determine the lines of action that would involve the interests of every colony with trans-Appalachian interests.

It was proposed at this meeting of the governors that a thousand men, including the Independent Companies of New York and South Carolina, should be assembled and that the new commander-in-chief — a man without military experience — should, unless "the Winter sets in too severely very shortly," attempt to capture Fort Duquesne before it could be reinforced in the spring. This, it was felt, together with the building of a fort opposite to it "on an Island in the Ohio," was all Sharpe could "entertain very sanguine Hopes of being able to execute with so small a Number of Men," unless aided from England. It was agreed, however, that should these moves prove successful, he was further to make an attempt "with our American Strength, on the Forts w'ch the French have built near Lake Erie, up the River Buffaloe [Rivière aux Bœufs]." [28]

But, most providentially, Sharpe was not permitted to cross the mountain barrier on this suicidal mission and had to content himself with the more humble and feasible task of building Fort Mount Pleasant at Wills Creek.[29] In fact, the military situation in Virginia remained chaotic during the rest of 1754.

Dinwiddie in October determined to transform the Virginia regiment into independent companies, following the example of South Carolina and New York. This he doubtless felt would put an end to the interminable friction between his own officers and those of companies on the royal establishment stationed in Virginia. He also, it is clear, decided to deprive Washington of his colonelcy by recalling all the higher commissions granted him and others and by offering them captaincies instead. But so doing meant that the captains of the new companies would be subordinate to those who held com-

27 For Secretary of State Robinson's instructions to Sharpe see *Maryland Archives*, XXXI, 52–3.

28 "The Plan of Military Operations" is to be found in the *Dinwiddie Papers*, I, 351.

29 The name was subsequently changed to Fort Cumberland.

missions of the same rank directly from the King, until they could be brought to an equality by orders of the Crown.[30]

The proposal, under the circumstances, was reasonable and highly desirable. Although Virginia was at war, it was impossible to apply the type of discipline to volunteers that would automatically apply to soldiers who became regulars on the establishment and were thereupon subject to all laws governing these. No longer could the soldiers with impunity trail off home with their guns when conditions were not satisfactory in camp and no longer would the problem of their pay raise continual vexations.[31] Among the staff officers of the regiment, Washington alone refused to continue in service under the proposed reorganization plan. Therefore his resignation was accepted by Dinwiddie, apparently without regret. In fact, it would seem that the only thing the Governor regretted was, not the resignation, but that he had ever entrusted the chief command of the Virginia regiment to one so young in years and so inexperienced in military affairs — who, from his point of view, had made a good deal of a mess of the late campaign by his movement beyond Fort Necessity before he had made that place sufficiently defensible to hold with the forces at his command in case of retreat. It is clear that Dinwiddie did not feel that Washington was sufficiently qualified to assume any post beyond that of captain in the contemplated professional military establishment. On the other hand, he expressed the desire that Colonel Innes, a veteran of the Carthagena campaign, should become one of the two majors in the new regiment and suggested himself for the colonelcy of the same.[32] It doubtless had become abundantly clear to him that the officers of the three Independent Companies were very uneasy and dissatisfied and would remain so as long as the young Virginia lieutenant colonel was placed over them. Nevertheless Governor Sharpe, now in command of the expedition, sought to retain Washington's service as titular colonel. But the latter refused to hold a commission that had "neither rank nor emolument annexed it" and charged that the so-called "peremptory Orders" from England for reducing the volunteer regiments to independent companies "were generated, hatched and brought from Wills Creek." [33] He thereupon

---

[30] Ibid., I, 403.

[31] On the fewness of desertions from the regular British regiments see J. S. Corbett, England in the Seven Years' War, I, 34.

[32] Ibid., I, 355, 410.

[33] Washington to Colonel William Fitzhugh, November 15, 1754, Writings of Washington (ed. Fitzpatrick), I, I, 104–7).

retired to private life. In doing so he deprived the colony and the forces being concentrated at Wills Creek of the services of a courageous and energetic young man who had gained some valuable experience in wilderness campaigning; but he also, it must be added, by resigning relieved a most embarrassing situation.[34]

It is clear that Washington not only was unpopular with the regular officers of the Independent Companies, but had come to be disliked and even distrusted by the Indian allies of the English and had therefore disqualified himself for taking a leading role in the immediate future in military activities that would involve their co-operation. This last point requires some clarification.

In a conference that Colonel Innes had with a band of Ohio Valley Indians in the fall of 1754, the latter did not hide the grudge that they had against Washington, whom they called "fool-hardy." The resentment of the Indians against the young colonel as well as their lack of confidence in him was based not only upon what they considered his poor judgment as a soldier, but upon other grounds: first, his "desertion" of those among their number who went with him to Fort Le Bœuf in 1753; second, his disregard of them by failing to return from that mission to Logtown to report the outcome of it to their council, affecting their vital interests as it did; third, his unwillingness, in connection with his late unsuccessful campaign, to take into his confidence those among them who had come to aid him. They declared:

> "He never consulted with us nor yet [would] take our Advice . . . we wanted a place of security or Fort for our Wives and Children that they might not be left and exposed [something that he did not provide] which was no Satisfaction to us at all. . . ."

Finally, they resented what they considered to be his desertion of the frontier after his defeat,

> "leaving all this thin settled country to be protected by a few Strangers [that is, protected by the Independent Companies of New York and South Carolina at Wills Creek while he was recruiting at Alexandria]. Col. Washington's conduct [they asserted, in summarizing their grievances against him] we greatly blame, for not concerting matters properly. . . ."[35]

It was high time for Britain to lend a hand. Virginia, with an estimated population of 230,000 inhabitants, including blacks, and with

---

[34] *Dinwiddie Papers*, I, 462–3.
[35] "Indian Treaty at Mount Pleasant," C.O. 5:15, pp. 389–96).

a militia numbering 27,000, according to Dinwiddie's report drawn up the latter part of the year 1754,[36] was able after many months of recruiting the new companies in Virginia to furnish only some 600 men and these were secured in the face of desertion and seditious conduct of the recruits and anti-recruiting riots at both Petersburg and Fredericksburg.[37] Maryland, with an estimated population of 154,188 and a militia numbering 16,500 — "undisciplined as well as badly armed" — finally recruited a company of 100 men, who were sent to Wills Creek to join the Virginia troops — now reduced, as has already been noted, to 200 through death and desertion [38] — and the three Independent Companies, whose commanders still refused to obey officers appointed in the colonies.[39] The Pennsylvania and New Jersey assemblies continued indifferent as they had been to frontier developments; North Carolina under its new Governor seemed disposed to furnish a company of 100 men and voted £5,000 in good money; South Carolina, however, turned its attention to the plan of building a fort in the Cherokee country and continued to display hostility toward the frontier activities of the government of Virginia. It is therefore not surprising that Dinwiddie and Sharpe no longer toyed with the fantastic idea of marching a handful of raw levies through the mountains against the French stronghold on the Ohio. Indeed, they were now fearful of a sudden and successful attack against their weak outpost at Wills Creek, which was given the name Fort Cumberland.

This, then, was the situation in the middle and southern colonies as the year 1754 drew to its gloomy close. The only break in the overhanging clouds was the news that England was planning to send really seasoned troops and an experienced general to Virginia. For, irrespective of the self-confident attitude assumed by the colonials after the termination of the war, there was at this juncture no voice raised in America to declare that the people were in no need of aid from the mother country, but, on the contrary, were quite prepared to rely upon their own material resources and the prowess of their own troops in defending their own vital interests.

Whatever may have been the shortcomings of the Duke of Newcastle, who was at the time directing the British government, he and

---

36 *Dinwiddie Papers*, I, 387.
37 For the difficulties in recruiting men see *Ibid.*, I, 414, 462, 465, 471.
38 *Maryland Archives*, VI, 116, 353.
39 *Dinwiddie Papers*, I, 401.

his fellow ministers, in view of the alarming news of French activities in the Ohio Valley, saw clearly the necessity of coming to the support of the colonies.[40] Writing on June 29 to Horatio Walpole as to the resolutions adopted by the Cabinet Council, Newcastle declared:

> "The first point we have laid down is, that the colonies must not be abandoned, that our rights and possessions in North America must be maintained and the French obliged to desist from their hostile attempts to dispossess us." [41]

The first step in implementing this plan was the appointment of Governor Sharpe on July 5 temporary commander-in-chief of the American forces and the appropriation of £20,000 to support an expedition to the Ohio, as has already been mentioned. With the news of Washington's defeat, which reached London early in September, it was realized that something more must be done. Dinwiddie had made an appeal to send a regiment or two,[42] but Britain and France were at peace and no one in the government wanted war. It was therefore suggested, apparently by the Earl of Granville, that assistance to the colonies should be limited to the sending of an adequate supply of munitions and also officers who could train the colonials in the art of war.[43] When Newcastle waited upon the King to urge the necessity of supporting the colonies at this highly critical juncture, he found that His Majesty, although agreeable to the idea of providing a general officer to take command of the colonial forces, manifested "an utter aversion . . . to send any Regiment from hence." [44]

If it was not clear to the Cabinet Council just how under the circumstances the colonies could be most effectively supported to ward off the French aggressions, it was nevertheless clear that they must be aided, unless a purely mercantilistic policy toward them was to be adopted, in connection with which considerations of present commercial profits of British business men would be permitted to triumph over those involving the present and future interests of British colonials. Happily for the English-speaking people in North America, when the government, for their protection, had embarked in 1749 upon the costly experiment of the colonization of Nova Scotia,

---

40 Minute of the Cabinet Council of June 26, 1754, British Museum, Newcastle Papers, Additional Manuscripts, 33,029: 124.

41 B.M., Add. Mss., 32,735: 597.

42 *Dinwiddie Papers*, I, 238, 246.

43 William Murray to Newcastle, September 7, 1754, B.M., Add. Mss., 32,736: 438 and 515.

44 Newcastle to Murray, September 28, 1754, B.M., Add. Mss., 32,736: 591.

it had, as indicated in the Introduction, definitively turned its back upon the canons of orthodox mercantilism, and in 1754 it was, as a consequence, already committed to a program that was in harmony with new conceptions of colonialism, with emphasis upon the support of interests that Americans had greatly at heart. Little as it would mean in material benefits to the average Englishman or Scot in his lifetime to see the right of Virginia to control the forks of the Ohio vindicated, that right was to be upheld whatever the cost to Englishmen and Scots in wealth as well as in lives. Such were some of the financial as well as military implications of the new colonialism.

It has already been suggested that aid to the colonials by the mother country could have taken at the time several forms. At one extreme this aid could have been limited to the gift of ordnance to them; under the circumstances the colonials would have been expected to do all their own fighting with their own men and money. At the other extreme this aid could have been all-out, with the colonials called upon at most for incidental support and with the mother country carrying the burden of supplying money, matériel, and the fighting forces. Between these extremes there were various modifications, all of which had their merits as well as their drawbacks.[45]

It was at this point that William Augustus, Duke of Cumberland and captain general of the British army, the soldier son of the King, enters the picture. As the commander-in-chief of the allied forces he had fought with skill against the great Marshal Saxe on the Continent in 1745, and in 1746 he had crushed rebellion in the Highlands in the decisive Battle of Culloden and in the severe measures that followed it — measures reminiscent of those employed in Ireland by Cromwell. In Europe in 1747 he again as commander of the allies suffered defeat at the hands of Saxe at Lauffeld. Denounced by many in civil life as a brutal martinet, he won the praise of such soldiers as Sir John Ligonier and James Wolfe and was generally recognized as Britain's leading military man, although only thirty-three years of age. When his advice was sought by the ministers of the King,[46] he pro-

---

[45] For an admirable discussion of various plans of military aid see S. M. Pargellis, *Lord Loudoun in North America*, Chapter I, "Colonial Defense before 1756."

[46] "I desir'd the King," wrote Newcastle to Murray, "that he would Send Sir T. Robinson to wait upon the Duke. That, produc't the Conferences mention'd in Sir T. Robinson's letter. I afterward desir'd the King, that His Servants might attend His Royal Highness upon this Question; & Accordingly, My Ld Chancellor, My Lord President, the two Secretarys, my Ld Anson and My Self attended the Duke, on Thursday last, and then it was determin'd after much debate, to send *forthwith* two Irish Regiments to Virginia . . ." (*ibid.*).

ceeded to outline the broad lines of strategy that should be undertaken to secure the English position in the New World. These included the ejection of the French not only from the Ohio but from
the Lake Champlain region and from the Nova Scotian peninsula. In
this connection he strongly supported the idea of sending a general
officer to America and as strongly opposed the King's view that British troops should not be made available for the task in hand. His influence with George II on military affairs was so great that the latter
was at last led to waive his previous objections to taking a step that
he feared might imperil the peace and agreed to honour Dinwiddie's
request for two regiments.[47]

The man recommended by Cumberland as best qualified to undertake the great responsibility of restoring English prestige in North
America was Major General Edward Braddock.[48] The son of a soldier
who had after long years of service attained the rank of major general
in the famous Coldstream Guards, Braddock became an ensign in the
Guards in 1710 at an early age and in the course of years was promoted from one rank to another; in 1743 as a lieutenant colonel in
the line his regiment fought brilliantly at Dettingen in the presence
of the King and the Duke of Cumberland, and also in 1745 at Fontenoy against Marshal Saxe; in 1746 he served under Cumberland in
the campaign against Prince Charles Edward in Scotland and then
on the Continent until peace was declared. After forty-three years'
service in the Guards he accepted in 1753 the colonelcy of the 14th
regiment of foot, stationed at Gibraltar, where, according to Horace
Walpole, "he made himself adored" by the garrison,[49] and early in the
following year was gazetted a major general. Known as a rigid disci-
plinarian, he was doubtless felt to be the type of soldier needed to
whip into shape the raw, insubordinate colonial levies; he had also

---

[47] See Robinson to Newcastle, September 23, 1754, Add. Mss., 32,736: 569. The
student is referred to the thoughtful introductory essay by Dr. Stanley M. Pargellis in
his volume of documents selected from the Cumberland Papers and published under the
title: *Military Affairs in North America, 1748–1765.* In this (pp. ix–xi) he indicates the
basis of the very great influence exercised by Cumberland.

[48] Writing to Lord Holderness on July 11, 1755, Newcastle indicated the difficulties
of his position, incidentally pointing out that he had no part in the appointment of Braddock: "In all Administrations Somebody must be the *Butt.* I am very undeservedly . . .
at present. If Braddock, or Boscawen are beat, I must answer for it, who had no Hand
in appointing Either of them, but extreamly approving the latter; I must find Money to
pay all their Expenses, & these Expenses cannot by the Nature of Things be directed or
govern'd by me" (B.M., Add Mss., 32,857: 53).

[49] *Correspondence,* III, 145.

campaigned in the wild glens of northern Scotland and therefore knew something of fighting in a mountainous country. The King, moreover, had a good opinion of his "Sense and Bravery" and also mentioned that he had "heard he is become very *stayed*." Therefore, in spite of his age, he seemed to be an excellent choice. He was ordered to report in London for his new assignment.[50]

The plan adopted by the Cabinet Council visualized not only the appointment of a commander-in-chief for all British forces in the New World and the sending out of two British regiments, but also the recruiting of these to full strength upon their arrival in Virginia and the raising of two additional regiments in America to be placed on the British establishment by reviving the Shirley and Pepperell regiments that had been broken in 1748 even before they had been recruited. Further, the plan called for colonial support: the furnishing of available colonial levies, as well as provisions and wagons and, in line with the Board of Trade's recommendations, the setting up of a common fund to pay the cost of recruiting troops — a fund that would be available as needed by the commander-in-chief.[51] All this was in line with the idea of distributing the burdens of the military operations. It was finally agreed that Braddock should carry to America two of the regiments of foot soldiers stationed in Ireland: the 44th under Sir Peter Halkett and the 48th under Colonel Thomas Dunbar, with proper matériel, including ordnance as well as other supplies; that the two new regiments to be raised in North America should be recruited up to one thousand men each; and that a proper person should be sent to the Northern Indians and another to the Southern Indians to engage these groups to join in the military operations.[52] As to the broad strategy involved in the projected campaign, this was embodied in the "Secret Instructions" issued to Braddock on November 25.

Braddock was ordered to carry his regiments to Virginia to begin operations, "as the season will allow Our Troops to take the field

---

[50] Although Braddock was commissioned on September 24, 1754, he was at the time on board ship in the Mediterranean making his way with Commodore Edgcumbe from Gibraltar to Marseille, a trip that took forty days. He did not arrive in London until the second week in November and thereupon learned for the first time why he had been requested in the name of the public service to hasten to England (Shelburne Papers, 36: 64 and 68, Clements Library).

[51] S. M. Pargellis, *Lord Loudoun*, pp. 33–4.

[52] B.M., Add. Mss., 35,909: 196; *Military Affairs in North America, 1748–1764* (ed. Pargellis), pp. 34–6.

much sooner, in the southern parts, than in any other parts of our Colonies." Concentrating his forces at Wills Creek, he was to move against the French on the Ohio and, after driving the intruders from their posts, build there "a good and sufficient Fort, on the most convenient pass upon the said River." Leaving at the new fort a strong garrison, consisting of the Independent Companies stationed in Virginia supported by provincial troops, he was then to undertake the next service "of the greatest importance" — the dislodging of the French from the Niagara River. Should the new regiments under Shirley and Pepperell be prepared to move before the Ohio River campaign had been terminated, these could be directed against Fort Niagara and also against Crown Point on Lake Champlain; otherwise, he was to move his regiments of regulars against Niagara while the two colonial regiments concentrated upon Crown Point. With the reduction of both these French forts, the "last and most material service" that he could perform would be the destruction of the French fort at Beauséjour in Nova Scotia, working to that end in co-operation with Governor Lawrence in command of the Nova Scotian forces and the artillery companies of Newfoundland and Nova Scotia. Finally, he was ordered to send to France prisoners that might be taken, since that country and Great Britain were not at war.[53]

The above strategy envisioned the methodical rolling back of the French, starting with the Virginia frontier and ending with the isthmus of Chignecto, with the limited objectives of using force to compel the aggressors to give up their hold upon those lands only that were considered to be embraced within the respective limits of the provinces of Virginia, New York, and Nova Scotia.

Unhappily, the plan of operations was fundamentally unsound in view of the existence of certain unfavourable geographical factors that were not at the time sufficiently appreciated by the ministers. In this connection it is quite clear that the influence exercised by Lieutenant Governor Dinwiddie was most unfortunate. In his correspondence that led up to the expedition he either ignored or tended to minimize, if not falsify, the enormous difficulties of an effective campaign against Fort Duquesne by way of Wills Creek, the Youghiogheny River, Laurel Mountain, and the Monongahela. The presence of two British regiments would, he represented, in itself all but guarantee the capture of the French fort with a minimum of effort. The earlier plans of campaign against it that he had assisted in projecting

[53] *N. Y. Col. Doc.*, VI, 920–2

were likewise characterized by the same utter lack of realism — a dangerous thing in the waging of even an undeclared war. When, therefore, the Duke of Newcastle, Lord Holderness, Lord Chancellor Hardwicke, and Sir Thomas Robinson — upon whom the decision really rested, in consultation with the Duke of Cumberland — agreed to follow the recommendations of the Virginia Governor, a fatal decision was made without adequate information that should have been furnished and could have been made available. Instead they were apparently led to rely upon a distorted picture of conditions for campaigning in the Virginia back country.[54] In doing so they at the same time turned their backs upon the urgent as well as sound recommendations of the Earl of Halifax, President of the Board of Trade, presented on November 7, which dealt clearly with the advantages and disadvantages of various possible lines of action against the French in North America.[55]

In setting forth the difficulties of approaching the French forts by way of Virginia, Halifax gave as his opinion — most prophetic in view of the course of events — that so long as the line of communication remained open between these forts and Canada, twelve hundred French troops supported by their Indian allies would be able to defend them against four times as many English, and that

> "as all Convoys of Provision . . . as well as the Artillery, must be brought . . . thro' a Country full of Woods, it is sufficiently obvious how liable they would be to be interupted."

Rather, he urged, attention should be directed against the French on the Niagara and at Crown Point, particularly in the first-named region. Not only were the approaches to Fort Niagara easier for troops and artillery, but such a step would swing the Five Nations into line and tend to restore English influence among the Ohio Valley Indians. Once having broken the Niagara link that connected Canada with the Ohio, the French, he contended, would be in no position to maintain themselves in their outlying forts, and their "present undertaking" could then be dealt with by the power of a combined attack delivered by Virginia, Maryland, and Pennsylvania.

Once the decision had been made to come to the aid of the American plantations, it was agreed that this should not be done with a

---

[54] See *Military Affairs in North America, 1748–1754*, pp. 32–3.

[55] This is entitled "Methods of Disappointing the French in North America, delivered by Lord Halifax, November 7, 1754" (B.M., Add. Mss., 33,129: 138–42).

niggardly band. On November 14 the King opened Parliament with a speech that, while observing all the formal amenities of peaceful purposes, nevertheless indicated the resolution to protect the colonies. Parliament, after passing the addresses unanimously, proceeded to vote a million pounds to strengthen the army and navy and on the 28th voted an additional fifty thousand pounds specifically to meet the charges of raising the two new regiments in America and of providing for the pay of Braddock's officers.[56] By the beginning of the following year the government had committed itself to support the British colonials to the limit. As a result Secretary at War Fox on January 2 wrote to the Board of Trade:

> "The King has commanded me to Signify to Your Lordships that you do forthwith Acquaint me with what Sum of Money it may be proper to ask of Parliament for the Assistance of His Majesty's Subjects in North America." [57]

When the estimates for supporting them in a war came in, these, as will be indicated in a subsequent chapter, ran to six million pounds. There was no hesitation, however. Thus what in the spring of 1754 had been Virginia's little private war, as viewed by Governor Glen of South Carolina, was by the following spring becoming Britain's Great War for the Empire.

---

[56] Winthrop Sargent, op. cit., p. iii. Writing to the Earl of Albemarle in Paris on November 21, Robinson declared:"It gives me the Opportunity of observing to you, that as these Addresses passed unanimously in both Houses, the Court of France will see, that the wise Measures which His Majesty is pursuing for the Vindication of His just Rights and Possessions . . . are universally applauded" (Shelburne Papers, 36:85, Clements Library).

[57] C.O. 323:13, O, 133.

CHAPTER IV

The Disaster at the Monongahela

"The imminent Danger with which the Peace and safety of the British Settlements were thus threatened, made His Majesty think it necessary, in the Month of November, to order Two Regiments of Foot of 500 Men each, under Command of Major Gen¹ Braddock, convoyed by two Ships of the Line, and two Frigates, under that of Commodor Keppel, to proceed, without Loss of Time, to North America, for the Protection of the rights & Possessions of the Crown; the Instructions given to the General, to the Commodore, & to the Governors of the Several Colonies, were to maintain and defend His Majesty's rights, & if necessary to repell Force by Force, but were free from any Design to give just Alarm to any Power whatsoever, or to do any Thing, that might be construed an Infraction of the General Peace; a Fact, which indeed is almost self evident from the Nature & Extent of the Armaments themselves." [1]

ERE WE HAVE set forth the formal position of the ministry at the close of 1754 respecting British designs in North America. When rumours of the intended embarkation of troops in England reached the French Minister, Rouillé, Comte de Jouy, in October, he sharply questioned the British Ambassador, the Earl of Albemarle. The latter freely admitted that troops were being sent "to prevent the progress of the French Arms, in that part of the world," and then went on to remind Rouillé that the French "had been for many years sending Ships, Men, Arms and Ammunition to Their American

---

[1] "Narrative of the Hostilities committed by the French upon the Ohio in No. America & of the Negociations with M° de Merepoix" (B.M., Add. Mss., 33,029: 278).

Settlements," which the Minister was obliged to admit was true. If the French had done so without protest from the British, upon what grounds could the French now justly protest when the British adopted similar measures? To Rouillé's assertion that the French on the Ohio

"only retook Possession of their own, and endeavoured to confine Us to Our Limits, since We had encroached on Their's, so far as the above mentioned River,"

Albemarle asked

"in virtue of what Principle They [the French] took upon Them to prescribe Our Limits to Us, when I understood that both Crowns had named Commissaries to settle those Points, and that during Their Negotiations, nothing was to be attempted on either Side. . . ." [2]

Later, when the news of British military preparations on a large scale reached France, Rouillé, now deeply apprehensive, asked Albemarle if there was no peaceful means of settling the urgent issue of rival claims to the Ohio. The Ambassador replied that, although uninstructed on the point, he would recommend that His Most Christian Majesty

"sho^d order his Troops who had made such rapid Encroachm^{ts} to return behind the Ohio, leave everything on the English side of that River in the State it was in before, after wch if France had any Compl^{ts} to make or proposals to offer they wo^d be rece^d wth the just Attention that wo^d be due them." [3]

But His Most Christian Majesty was not prepared to take any such backward step, involving a loss of prestige in the eyes of his ministers, and the British government therefore proceeded with its plans for a relief expedition.

As each of the two regiments of foot on the Irish establishment fell short of the complement of five hundred, steps were taken to supply the deficiency from other regiments stationed in Ireland and in England.[4] The Royal Regiment of Artillery also detached a company,

---

[2] Albemarle to Robinson, October 23, 1754, Shelburne Papers, 36: 69, Clements Library.

[3] Albemarle to Robinson, November 27, 1754, B.M., Add. Mss., 33,027: 283.

[4] Regiments stationed in Bristol and Salisbury each supplied one hundred men; the two at Limerick each furnished seventy-eight, and a regiment and a battalion at Galway provided the remainder of the draft (Winthrop Sargent, *The History of an Expedition against Fort Du Quesne, in 1755,* pp. 134–5).

which was provided with four twelve-pounders, six six-pounders, four howitzers, and fifteen cohorn mortars.[5] Tents for eight thousand men and other matériel on the same generous scale were shipped to Cork, where on January 15, 1755 thirteen transports and three ordnance store-ships loaded with troops and military stores lifted anchor and under escort of two men-of-war and two frigates started for the New World.[6] Between March 2 and 15 they moved into Hampton Roads, Virginia, without incident and were thereupon ordered by Braddock, who had arrived the preceding month, to proceed to Alexandria, preparatory to marching to Fort Cumberland.

Braddock, reaching Hampton Roads on February 19, arrived in Williamsburg on the 23rd to confer with Dinwiddie. The latter was able to make clear to him the general situation with respect to the support or lack of support of the expedition on the part of the colonies most concerned. Certainly the indefatigable Governor of Virginia had done everything within his power to bring that province into line and to gain the support of the neighbouring colonies for an enterprise that he had so much at heart.[7] His only serious personal failure — a failure, however, that was to have consequences even more disastrous with respect to the Braddock campaign than to that of the campaign in 1754 — was the feud that, as noted in the preceding chapter, he had permitted to develop with Governor Glen of South Carolina, the origin of which may be charged to his own shortsighted statesmanship.

Glen, soon to depart from the province, enjoyed a high degree of popularity among his people [8] and continued to be strongly supported by his Assembly in his determination not to permit direct interference with the Southern Indians on the part of the government of Virginia — or anyone else not of South Carolina. The powerful Cherokee

---

[5] The cohorn was a small mortar made of brass.

[6] The French Minister of the Marine thought that the British armament might be designed for the seizure of the Neutral Islands of the West Indies rather than for operations on the Virginia frontier (Arch. Nat., Col., B. 99: 11–12).

[7] Dinwiddie could report that his own Assembly had voted £20,000, that almost a thousand troops had been recruited by the province, and that both Maryland and North Carolina were co-operating with at least some men and money.

[8] On November 25, 1749 the Commons House of Assembly declared to Glen: "We acknowledge with gratitude your Excellency's great care for our happiness and your extraordinary Knowledge in our provincial affairs . . ." (Journal, 23: 49, South Carolina Hist. Commission). When in the spring of 1754 the news was received that he was to be recalled, on May 11, a committee of the Commons House framed another laudatory address (Journal, 29: 42–4). It was not until 1756, however, that William Henry Lyttelton displaced Glen.

and the Catawba were certainly available for the campaign — this is clear by their presence later with the Forbes expedition through Pennsylvania — yet they could be brought to co-operate only by the government that long had supported their trade and from whom they were accustomed to receive the King's presents. But Glen, repeatedly snubbed by Dinwiddie, had by 1755 lost interest in the Ohio campaign and was only concerned in building up defences for his own province.[9] His attitude was narrow and unreasonable, but it must not be forgotten that when he determined to let Virginia fight its own wars and drew back from his earlier hearty demand for intercolonial solidarity in the face of the enemy, he felt that he had the best of grounds for so acting. After all, he was the Governor of a province the inhabitants of which were a proud people and not accustomed to treatment that they considered contemptuous, if not underhanded.

Therefore, while Dinwiddie could optimistically hold out to Braddock prospects of support of the campaign by the Southern Indians,[10] but none whatsoever from South Carolina, he simply was not facing the realities of the situation. And, unhappily, this was perhaps the Achilles heel of all the Governor's plans and endeavours to eject the French from the Ohio Valley, which were at last, it seemed, coming to fruition.

As to the notorious misconduct of merchants of New York and Pennsylvania that had been brought to the attention of Braddock, on January 20 Dinwiddie was impelled to write to Secretary of State Robinson:

> "I think it my Duty to Acquaint You that all the Provisions the French have for conducting this unjust Invasion on the Ohio is, as I am credibly informed, by a Supply from New York and Philadelphia. They carry large quantities of Flour, Bread, Pork, Beef, etc. to Lewisbourg . . . where they sell it for Rum, Molasses and Sugar, the Produce of their Islands." [11]

Yet he was obliged to admit to Braddock that, while the French had thus been supplied, he had not been able to secure as yet adequate

---

[9] Glen on January 4, 1754 had requested Dinwiddie to forward to him £7,000 out of the £20,000 cash and credit granted by the home government for the defence of the frontiers. With this he planned to build a fort on the upper Tennessee. Dinwiddie in reply soundly scolded him and sent him only £1,000 (*Dinwiddie Papers*, I, 484–7).

[10] Writing to the Earl of Halifax on February 24, 1755, Dinwiddie declared: "I have good Reason to expect a considerable Number of Catawbas and Cherokees to meet our Forces on the Ohio unless prevented by ill-natured Insinuations" (*ibid.*, I, 514).

[11] C.O. 5:15, pp. 285–8.

provisions for the expedition soon to be launched against Fort Duquesne. He was also doubtless impelled to warn him that Albany,
according to reports, was again involved in its old policy of neutrality
with the French in Canada in time of war — for he had written sharply
to Governor de Lancey of New York the previous month:

> "There is an Affair prevails at the Camp [at Wills Creek] y^t the N.
> York [Indian] Commissioners at Albany have concluded a Neutrality
> with the Caghuawaga [Caughnawaga] Ind^s, the Chief Nat^n in Can-
> ada in the French Int^t, and y^t this is only to support them in their
> trade from Albany with the Fr. If this is true, I think its a sordid Step
> to Trade with our Enemies in any Shape after they have so notori-
> ously broke the Peace by Invading His M$^{y's}$ Lands and taken of his
> Forts, and such Trade at this Time must be very destructive to the
> B^h Int^r and the Affairs we have in View. . . ." [12]

Of all the aggravations that had faced the Virginia Governor, however, the conduct of the Pennsylvania Assembly seemed hardest to
bear. This body, dominated by pacifistic groups, had spent almost
a year, not in laying plans for ejecting the enemy now within the borders of the province, but in disputes that, as one reads them today,
seem to carry more than an air of casuistry to the uninitiated. The
Quakers, in actual control of the Assembly, had consistently borne
their testimony against war under any circumstances and were supported by the Mennonites and the Dunkards, as well as by some of
the other German religious sects in the province. These groups had
cultivated friendly relations with the neighbouring Indians; they
walked soberly, most of them in plain dress, were industrious and
God-fearing, and constantly examined their consciences. Heirs of an
early Christian tradition of pacifism, they lived, on the whole, peaceable lives; although one must hasten to add that the Quakers could
be infinitely disputatious when challenged and had come to place so
high a value on property that they did not hesitate to make war at
least upon crime by legislating the death penalty against robbers,
burglars, and horse-thieves and provided arms for those who would
apprehend them or kill them if they resisted arrest.[13] Consistently
enough, they were bitterly opposed, as is well known, to making ap-
propriations of public money that they as taxpayers had contributed,
for any purpose that they rejected as individuals. But having said

---

[12] *Dinwiddie Papers*, I, 456.

[13] See my article: "Crime and Its Punishment in Provincial Pennsylvania," *Pennsylvania History*, I, 3–16.

this, one must face another inconsistency in their attitude. Most pacifists are not martyrs nor do they long for martyrdom. This was true of the Pennsylvania Quakers. They wanted to live in an orderly society that would protect them, their wealth, and also their right to refuse to protect themselves as well as others, from public enemies.

No commonwealth has ever existed that has not been protected by those willing to preserve it with their lives.[14] The only conditions therefore under which pacifism can survive in any age in a community motivated by conceptions based upon it are that that community shall be but a part of a larger community or commonwealth in which in the last analysis force can and will be applied to subdue internal and external enemies to law and order. Unfortunately, there is no alternative to the application of force for self-preservation in the world in which men have lived within historic times. Pennsylvania under Quaker control down until 1756 was such a subordinate pacifistic community and exemplifies perfectly the principle just enunciated.

The province enjoyed protection and security by reason of the fact that it was a part of a great empire that not only supported a powerful fleet and a small army of professional soldiers, but had at hand inexhaustible material resources for the waging of war — all of which meant security from lawless nations or groups. The arrangement was ideal to the mind of the eighteenth-century Pennsylvania pacifist. Thoroughly convinced that if one bore testimony against war one should not yield any assistance to waging it, he was apparently as thoroughly convinced that if one bore testimony in favour of war, one was under the same solemn obligations to do all things necessary, even to sacrificing wealth and life itself, that war demanded for the protection of those who could not in good conscience support war. Therefore when Deputy Governor Thomas in 1741, in the midst of the maritime war with Spain, pointed out to the Assembly that the province was in danger — destitute as it was of forts, troops, or any

---

[14] Deputy Governor George Thomas, with biting sarcasm, replied as follows in 1740 to the pacifist Pennsylvania Assembly's plea that the constitution of the province would be overthrown and the liberties of the people destroyed if the latter were as a group compelled in violation of conscience to support military measures: "If your Principles will not allow you to pass a Bill for establishing a Militia; if they will not allow you to secure the Navigation of the River, by building a Fort; if they will not allow you to provide Arms for the Defence of the Inhabitants . . . if they will not allow you to raise and appropriate Money to the Uses recommended by his Majesty; it is a Calumny to say, 'That your Principles are inconsistent with the ends of Government . . .'" (Pennsylvania Archives, eighth series, III, 2636).

warlike equipment and hence with itself and its flourishing commerce an easy prey to the enemy — the pacifist deputies blandly replied:

> "Among the many Advantages this Colony, with others enjoy, under our gracious King, that of being protected . . . is One. To this End, there are generally Ships of War stationed at Boston, New York, and Virginia, as Places the most commodiously situated, that whenever Enemies approach, they might, on Notice given them, be in Readiness to scour the Coasts. . . ." [15]

Here, then, is the keynote of the policy supported by the Assembly in 1754 and 1755 as in 1741, with all the tactics of delay and endless argument over such technicalities as the meaning of royal instructions and the force of proprietarial instructions, employed with matchless dexterity and persistence, with the idea of throwing the odium for inaction upon the Governor.[16] Hand in hand with this policy was that of seeking to strip the Governor of all essential authority as the agent of the Proprietors; but the latter project was carefully disguised as an endeavour to maintain the liberties of the people, who were represented as anxious to further the common cause of defence by every means within their power.

In reality, the inhabitants of Pennsylvania, occupying a most privileged position within the Empire — enjoying in abundance what others must defend for them — were as anxious as any privileged group not to surrender a favoured position and therefore quite naturally they struggled to maintain it. In the embarrassed words of Governor Morris, in addressing Braddock, one gets a true picture of the situation:

> "I am, Sir, almost ashamed to tell You that We have in this Province upward of Three Hundred Thousand Inhabitants; that We are blessed with a rich soil and temperate Climate, and besides our own Consumption raise Provisions enough to supply an Army of One Hundred Thousand Men, which is yearly exported from this City, and with other Commodities employs upwards of four hundred Vessels, mostly owned by the Merchants of this Town. . . . And yet

---

[15] Ibid., III, 2685.

[16] "I am sorry to say," wrote Governor Morris to Secretary of State Robinson on January 30, 1755, "that instead of such a Conduct as might reasonably be expected, from the representatives of a Province actually invaded by the French, They [the Assembly] have Industrially entered into a controversy concerning the force of Royal and Proprietary Instructions, which they insist are not binding upon a Governor of this Province, & have taken the Liberty to represent the Issuing such, as destructive of their Libertys and infractions of their Charter" (C.O. 5:15, pp. 263–5).

when their *All* is invaded they refuse to contribute to the necessary Defence of their Country, either by establishing a Militia or furnishing Men, Money, or Provisions." [17]

General Braddock, upon being informed of the refractory attitude of the province, "by far the most populous and most opulent of any upon the Continent" — an attitude that seemed impossible to defend upon any rational grounds in the face of developments of such grave import to every inhabitant of Pennsylvania — on February 28 wrote angrily to Governor Morris

> "expressing the greatest Surprise to find such pusillanimous and improper Behaviour in your Assembly, and to hear of Faction and Opposition where Liberty and Property are invaded, and an absolute Refusal to supply either Men, Money, or Provision for their own Defence while they furnish the Enemy with Provision. . . ." [18]

He even dropped a scarcely veiled threat to winter-quarter his regiments upon the province if the representatives of the people did not mend their ways.

The pacifists, however, were not lacking in astuteness. If they refused to pause at the French menace, expecting others to free them from it, they at least saw the danger that might sweep their majority out of the Assembly should Parliament be impelled to act. After they had been gathered together again in the spring of 1755 and after the Governor had steadfastly refused to violate his instructions by passing a money bill that did this, they sought vindication of their loyalty to the King by "resolving" to set aside fifteen thousand pounds for "victualling the King's Troops" — thereby circumventing the Governor's authority over money "bills." [19]

In commenting upon the unconstitutional nature of this action of the Assembly, Governor Morris wrote to Secretary of State Robinson on April 9:

> "I need not observe to you, Sir, the Danger of such powers in the Hands of any Assembly, and especially of one annually chosen by a People, a great Part, if not a Majority of whom, are Foreigners unattached to an English Government, either by Birth or Education;

---

[17] *Pennsylvania Colonial Records*, VI, 336. No direct taxation existed in Pennsylvania at this period. An abundant revenue was secured on mortgages by the Loan Office and this was supplemented by excises on ardent spirits. For this see Volume III (1st edn.) of the present series, pages 191–2. See also Volume III, revised, p. 174.

[18] *Pa. Col. Rec.*, VI, 307.

[19] *Pennsylvania Archives* (eighth series), V, 3877.

and as none of these Things are warranted by the Proprietary Charter . . . or in the least Countenanced by the Proprietaries themselves, I think them the more extraordinary, and very worthy the
Notice of the Government." [20]

In making his preparations for the Ohio expedition Braddock
therefore had to meet the challenge of the extreme apathy of most of
the colonies and most colonials — outside of New England — toward
the frontier crisis. By his open instructions he had been ordered to
maintain a close correspondence with the colonial governors, and
in accordance with these, and apparently after consulting Dinwiddie,
he sent notices on March 10 to Governors Shirley, de Lancey, Morris,
and Sharpe to meet him in Annapolis, Maryland, early in April for
a conference. It is to be noted that the one man who perhaps more
than any other governor held the key to the success of the Braddock
campaign, James Glen, was not invited to attend and it may be inferred that this neglect came as the result of the fixed determination
of Dinwiddie to see that he was ignored. It will be recalled that when
the South Carolina Governor urged just such a conference, he had
recommended the presence of Shirley, but Dinwiddie had brushed
this suggestion aside upon the grounds that the Governor of Massachusetts Bay was too far removed from Virginia to permit his attendance. Now Shirley was invited at the special request of Secretary of
State Robinson,[21] and Glen, prepared to leave South Carolina for Virginia upon a week's notice, was excluded.

Instruction No. 8 that Braddock received before leaving England
had to do with securing the co-operation of the Southern as well as
the Northern Indians

"to engage them to take part, & act with our forces, in such operations
as you shall think most expedient."

The importance of the role of Indians in wilderness fighting cannot
be overestimated and was therefore rightly emphasized in the instruction. But in vain Washington had looked for the Cherokee and
Catawba that Dinwiddie had promised would support him in his
campaign, and in vain Braddock was to look for that same vital support, which the Governor of Virginia continued to promise but Glen
alone could deliver. In fact, Braddock was woefully misled and finally
trapped to his death by unbelievable stupidity that must be laid pri-

[20] C.O. 5:15, p. 512.
[21] His letter to Shirley under date of November 26, 1754, C.O. 5:211.

marily at the door of Dinwiddie, who for reasons not unrelated to personal ambition, it would seem, had used every resource at his disposal — and his influence was very great indeed both in England and
in America — to place Glen in an unfavourable light.

It was not until April 14 that the conference was held, and then it
took place at Alexandria rather than Annapolis. Not only were all the
above colonial governors present, but also Admiral Keppel, commander-in-chief of His Majesty's Ships in North America, and Colonel
William Johnson from Mount Johnson on the Mohawk, the latter
gentleman called to appear as the result of the recommendations of
Governor Shirley. After General Braddock had referred to his instructions for securing a "common Fund" for carrying on the services
in America and to those for engaging the Indians in His Majesty's interest, he proposed that such a fund be established and that by employing Colonel Johnson and by providing suitable presents to that
end "the five Nations of Indians and their Allies should be gained."
He also acquainted the conference with the plans for attacks on the
French forts at Crown Point and Niagara and asked their opinion as
to the desirability of placing Johnson in charge of operations against
the first-named.[22] These projects were unanimously endorsed, as was
Braddock's plan to strengthen Oswego Post by means of the two Independent Companies still stationed in New York and two companies
from Pepperrell's new regiment, as well as by building vessels on
Lake Ontario. With respect to the establishment of a common fund
out of which the costs of military operations would be paid, the governors were obliged to report that each had made application to his
assembly for this desirable end but had not been able to secure favourable action and gave

> "as their unanimous opinion that such a Fund can never be estab-
> lished in the Colonies without the aid of Parliament." [23]

Nevertheless, it must be recorded that, in spite of the shabby treatment accorded to South Carolina, the government of that province
appropriated six thousand pounds toward this fund. "This was the

[22] As will be indicated in the progress of this narration, Governor Shirley had strongly
recommended a movement against Fort St. Frédéric at Crown Point and had also strongly
recommended William Johnson to command a proposed expedition against it (Shirley
to de Lancey, February 24, 1755, *Correspondence of William Shirley*, ed. C. H. Lincoln,
II, 136).

[23] "Minutes of a Council held at Alexandria," B.M., Add. Mss., 33,092: 175–6. These
have been printed in *The Documentary History of the State of New-York* (ed. E. B.
O'Callaghan), I, 378–9.

only money raised by the Provinces," according to Captain Orme, aide-de-camp to Braddock, "which ever passed through the General's hands."[24] The minutes of the meeting, kept by Governor Shirley, do not indicate that any matter pertaining to the campaign on the Ohio was touched upon. Surprisingly enough, even the instruction for securing the support of the Southern Indians was ignored. It must therefore be assumed that General Braddock had arrived at an understanding with Dinwiddie on this point and as a result was not unduly concerned about the ability of the government of Virginia to bring up this aid at the time when it would be needed.[25]

It should also be mentioned that during the Alexandria conference and in private interviews with Governor Shirley, Braddock not only agreed heartily to the arrangements that the former had concerted with Governor Lawrence of Nova Scotia for expelling the French from the Bay of Fundy but dealt with the proposal already made to Shirley that he lead in person the attack on Fort Niagara. Shirley "express'd the greatest Readiness to engage in it. . . ."[26] Braddock also agreed that the new colonial regiments commanded by Shirley and Pepperell should be placed on a footing of equality with his own with respect to allowances of provisions, taking the position that

> "a Soldier here should have every Advantage, as their Fatigue is very great and their pay not near sufficient in this dear and desolate Country."[27]

With the hope of any large assistance from a common fund to be contributed by the various colonies for their defence now blasted by the unfavourable report of the governors, General Braddock was obliged to rely upon the "Private Instructions" that had been issued to him, in addition to those that were open as well as those designated as "Secret."[28] By these he was authorized, if the colonies refused to

---

[24] Orme's "Journal," Sargent, op. cit., p. 325.

[25] Admiral Keppel wrote to the Admiralty on March 18 from Williamsburg: "It seems to be the Opinion of most People that all the tribes of the Iroquois are gone over to the Interest of the French except the Mohawks, but some have great Expectations that they as well as the Cataboes [Catawba] a warlike Nation . . . and some of the Cheroquies will join us" (Admiralty, In-Letters, 1746–63, 480: 1087, Public Record Office).

[26] Braddock to Robert Napier, April 19, 1755, Stanley M. Pargellis, Military Affairs in North America, 1748–1756, pp. 81–4.

[27] Ibid.

[28] These are dated November 25 and are among the Public Record Office papers under C.O. 5:6 and also among the Secretary's dispatches to be found in the series 211–215 of the same class.

respond, to draw upon the royal paymaster in North America for the charges that would face him in carrying out his private instructions.[29] This he proceeded to do. Great Britain thus with each passing day became more deeply involved financially as well as militarily in lending a hand in the colonial crisis, which most colonials were apparently quite willing to see transformed into a crisis of the mother country. Such it became indeed, without, however, losing its earlier character.

The route that Braddock had been ordered by his secret instructions to take against Fort Duquesne was by way of Wills Creek, and this meant by way of the newly constructed wagon road to Gist's and then on to the fort by way of the Cherokee Trail. In all of Dinwiddie's dispatches to the ministers this route, as was emphasized in the preceding chapter, had been stressed as the logical way of approach, and it must be borne in mind that the advice of only two colonial governors at this period carried great weight with the ministers — that of William Shirley and that of Robert Dinwiddie, who were considered at the time not only the most dynamic but the most capable executives the King had in the New World. In fact, Braddock's whole plan of campaign, as embodied in the instructions, may be ascribed to these two gentlemen. That a most serious error was made in sending Braddock to Virginia has already been pointed out. Even so, Braddock was possessed of the necessary discretion in interpreting his orders to destroy Fort Duquesne to have chosen a different route had this seemed to have offered greater advantages. The route later followed by Forbes is usually suggested as the proper approach to the fort. The advantages of the latter over the route via Wills Creek, Great Meadows, and Gist's Plantation cannot now be denied. In fact, it appears that General St. Clair was strongly considering an approach by way of Pennsylvania, but was discouraged by Governor Morris and by the Pennsylvania surveyor and map-maker Lewis Evans. On February 28 the Pennsylvania Governor declared in answer to St. Clair's inquiries respecting a route to Fort Duquesne by way of Philadelphia:

> "There is an open Waggon Road from this Town to the Mouth of Conegochege [Conocachiague] which I am told is a very good one,

---

[29] Admiral Keppel, who was present at the conference, as was stated, affirmed that all present were unanimously of the opinion "that the King's Service in the Colonies and the carrying on the present Expedition must be at a Stand unless the General should think proper to make use of his Credit upon the Government at home, to defray the Expense of all the Operations under his direction" (Letter of April 30 to the Admiral, P.R.O., Admiralty, In-Letters, 480: 1112).

by which any Quantity of Provisions may be carried and along which the Northern Forces may march and join the Europeans at Winchester with only crossing three small Ferries, but there is no Waggon Road from Carlisle West through the Mountains but only a Horse Path. . . . I send You herewith a Map of that Path from Carlisle to the Shanappin's Town [just to the north of Fort Duquesne on the Allegheny River], where the French Fort now stands, by which you will see the great Difficulty that will attend the making a Waggon Road that Way." [30]

The map to which Morris makes reference was Evans's famous "A General Map of The Middle British Colonies in America," which was just completed. This map was furnished with an elaborate *Analysis,* which supported the thesis that the logical approach from the ocean to Fort Duquesne was by way of the upper Potomac.[31] As to that thesis, Evans wrote the following year when under attack:

"Let any Person look at the Map and he will perceive that this wants no Refutation; because of the Nearness of that Fort to the Sea by that Way, and the vast Distance it is by any other; and none destitute of Woods, Defiles and Indian Enemies. But let him look into the Analysis, and he will find, that there is but about seventy Miles Land Carriage, between Potomack and the Branches of Ohio. This Land Carriage begins at a Place, 'till of late pretty well settled by the English. Potomack, in all the Way from the Falls to Wills Creek . . . has not in all the Way so many bad Rifts as the Mohock's River has, from Skenectady to Fort Hunter." [32]

In light of the position taken by Morris and Evans, it is no wonder that Braddock and St. Clair were persuaded that the Virginia approach was the more desirable, particularly in view of the fact that the Duke of Cumberland, their superior, had permitted himself to be committed to the route via Wills Creek.[33] Having made the toilsome journey to the latter stream by way of Winchester, however, Braddock was made to realize that he had been deceived. Writing to Adjutant General Napier from Fort Cumberland on June 7, he affirmed that the information given to him was "utterly false":

[30] *Pa. Archives* (fourth series), II, 358.

[31] For the map of the "Middle British Colonies" and the *Analysis* the student may consult my *Lewis Evans.*

[32] *Ibid.,* pp. 182–3. A. D. Graeff, however, declares: "Pennsylvania would have been more direct [to Fort Duquesne], shortening the distance by one hundred miles and the time of march by at least six weeks" (Pennsylvania German Society, *Publications* XL, vii, 79).

[33] Colonel Napier to General Braddock, November 24, 1754, Sargent, *op. cit.,* p. 399.

"Nothing can well be worse than the Road I have already pass'd and I have an hundred and ten Miles to march Thro' an uninhabited Wilderness over steep rocky Mountains and almost impassible Morasses. . . . I have order'd a Road of Communication to be cut from Philadelphia to the Crossing of the Youghyanghain [Youghiogheny],[34] which is the Road we ought to have taken, being nearer, and thro' an inhabited and well cultivated Country, and a Road as good as from Harwich to London, to some Miles beyond where [at Shippensburg] they are now opening the new Road." [35]

Once the regular troops were encamped in Virginia and Maryland and the Virginia volunteers had been formed into light horse troops, artificers or carpenters, and rangers, and the New York and South Carolina Independent Companies and the Maryland volunteers had been reviewed, steps were taken to concentrate all these forces — together with the North Carolina company that was destined for the service but had not arrived [36] — at Wills Creek preparatory to the great advance over the mountains. General St. Clair had taken preparatory steps to provide the necessary supply of provisions and wagons and assured Braddock that Virginia and Maryland had agreed to contribute twenty-five hundred horses and two hundred wagons.[37] But the promises that he had received were not fulfilled. Indeed, when Braddock inquired of Governor Sharpe for the promised hundred wagons the latter had agreed to provide, Sharpe had to admit his inability to deliver them; nor had the large quantity of flour ordered from Pennsylvania materialized. Virginia was busy preparing salt meat for the campaign, and salt fish had been ordered from Boston. Ultimately the Philadelphia merchants contracted for abundant provisions and forage, but still the means of transporting these necessaries were lacking.

Deputy Postmaster General Benjamin Franklin, who had agreed to establish a dispatch service between Philadelphia and the general's

---

34 The road was to extend from Shippensburg to the juncture of the Youghiogheny, Laurel Hill Creek, and Castleman's River. This juncture of streams was known as the Turkey Foot.

35 Pargellis, op. cit., pp. 84–92. On May 15 Lieutenant Governor Morris wrote home: "I am opening a Road from Shippensburgh Westward to the Forks of the Yohiogany and [also one] to Fort Cumberland, which I hope to have finished by the time they will be wanted, as there are now a hundred men at work and I have sent Mr. Peters, Secretary of the Province, with orders to employ as many as he thinks necessary" (C.O. 5:15, p. 563).

36 The North Carolina company of seventy-two men arrived at Fort Cumberland under command of Captain Dobbs, son of the Governor.

37 Pargellis, op. cit., p. 85.

headquarters, was now in a position to render an important service. Although strongly favouring strong defensive measures on the part of Pennsylvania and the support of the expedition, he was at the same time a bitter opponent of the Proprietors of the province, and as the official printer for the Assembly and also as a member of that body he was influential with the common people — even with those of pacifistic principles, to whom the Proprietors no longer Quakers were anathema. Braddock, meeting him at Frederick in Maryland, made clear to Franklin his dilemma, which if not resolved seemed destined to thwart the expedition.[38] Thereupon Franklin offered to secure the necessary wagons out of his own province. By means of an advertisement posted in all public places in the populated portions of the Susquehanna Valley, where lived thousands of prosperous German families, he succeeded in getting the required number of wagons, about one hundred and fifty in all, and about five hundred pack-horses, much to the relief of Braddock.[39] It may be mentioned that he accomplished this by exciting, on the one hand, an eagerness for a large profit to the owners of horses and vehicles and, on the other, a deep fear of the enraged soldiers led by St. Clair, "the Hussar," who would appear in the valley and impress these facilities by force if not furnished voluntarily.

But even with the support thus secured from Pennsylvania in the latter part of May under the circumstances related, there came other extraordinary vexations. The beef prepared in Maryland for the march was no sooner brought to camp than after survey it was ordered to be buried; for the dishonest contractors had not tried to pickle it. Horses collected for the expedition, according to Captain Orme, were stolen by an unruly frontier element almost as fast as they could be collected,[40] which led Braddock to refer to them as "a parcel of Banditti who call themselves Indian Traders." [41] In fact, instead of receiving the type of sympathetic support from those his army had come to protect upon appeal for aid, Braddock found that too many of the inhabitants acted more like vultures, thinking only of getting some large personal profit out of the efforts now being put forth by the mother country.

---

[38] "The Autobiography," *The Writings of Benjamin Franklin* (ed. A. H. Smyth), I, 394.

[39] *Pa. Archives* (first series), II 294–6.

[40] "Journal," Sargent, *op. cit.*, pp. 313–14.

[41] Pargellis, *op. cit.*, p. 84.

While the general was busy with the affairs that have been discussed, he added to his staff George Washington, who although still adjutant of the Northern Military District of Virginia had resigned his commission as lieutenant colonel of the Virginia volunteer regiment, as has already been noted.[42] The young Virginian was anxious to serve under an experienced veteran in order to learn the art of war, and Braddock was apparently just as anxious to have at his side one who, if his inexperience and faults had created dissatisfaction among officers on the establishment in 1754, not only enjoyed the respect of other leading Virginians but had acquired valuable knowledge of the route over which the army was to pass and therefore of the conditions under which the campaign must be conducted.[43] Washington's position was that of a volunteer without pay but with his expenses provided for out of the general's chest. That the two soldiers — in spite of differences in view that might have been expected in a task involving enormous difficulties — continued to respect and confide in each other up to the death of the general is not to the discredit of either. Nor, significantly, did Washington after this event join in the chorus of condemnation of Braddock.

With so many problems faced and solved, on April 31 General Braddock left for Winchester, hoping to meet the Indians that Governor Dinwiddie had continued to promise him. But no Indians put in their appearance, much to his disappointment. Moving on to Fort Cumberland at Wills Creek, where he arrived on May 10, he again looked about for his Indian support. Again, of the hundreds of Southern Indians that Dinwiddie was to furnish, not one appeared.[44] Realizing that none of Dinwiddie's glittering promises could any longer be trusted, he now turned to Governor Morris, who, through the aid of the Indian trader George Croghan, was the means of sending to him some fifty warriors. But some of these Indians had been involved

---

[42] That Washington was anxious to secure the post that he had recently enjoyed but of which he had been deprived by Dinwiddie is evident from a letter that he wrote to Speaker Robinson of the Virginia Assembly, "who seem'd to sympathize in my disappointments, and lent . . . friendly Aid to reinstate me in a suitable Command . . ." (*Writings of Washington*, ed. Fitzpatrick, I, 112).

[43] *Ibid.*, I, 109–10.

[44] In fact, so little were the Cherokees being stirred up against the French at this period that Duquesne wrote in October of the preceding year that they voluntarily sent to the French Governor in Louisiana a French slave with these friendly words: "If you recognize the good treatment that he has received, go tell our father that we desire to make a solid peace with him and then come to us with his reply" (Arch. Nat., Coll., C¹¹ A. 99: 290).

in Washington's disastrous campaign, and not only had lost all faith in the young Virginian, as was made clear in the preceding chapter, but were utterly lacking in morale.[45]

It is no wonder that Braddock in addressing Sir Thomas Robinson on June 5 should despondently write:

> "When I arrived in America, I was assured that I might depend upon a great number of Indians from the Southward, but the bad conduct of the Governor of Virginia, has turned them entirely against us; in effect they [the Virginians] behaved to the Indians with so little discretion, and so much unfair dealing, that we must at present be at great expense to regain their confidence, and there is no trusting even those who have embraced our cause." [46]

The general's fears with respect to Indian support were well founded. In fact, the Delawares, the Shawnee, and the Mingos, bound to the English by many treaties of friendship, in company with the Canadian Indians, many of whom had come a thousand miles for such an opportunity, in the end were to sink their tomahawks into heads of the general's soldiers. In the final test of strength, in fact, the British could count but eight Indians, so weak in number and so cowed in spirit that they could not be relied upon for the essential services that should have devolved upon them in a wilderness campaign.

When General Braddock finally moved his army with its siege artillery through the Appalachian barrier over indescribable mountain roads, he performed what one writer had described as the "eighth wonder of the world." [47] I know of no other feat in the annals of the military history of North America that can be compared with it — certainly not Burgoyne's campaign or even Arnold's intrepid and painful expedition up the Kennebec and down the Chaudière in 1775, which may be more nearly likened in difficulty to Washington's movement from Great Meadows to Mount Braddock and then back again

---

[45] In a conference held at Fort Cumberland on May 16 Braddock addressed the Pennsylvania Indians in a tactful speech and gave them a present. In calling upon their young warriors to accompany him he said: "We shall not desire them to do any more than to scout about & give us Notice on the Approach of the French or their Canada Indians & to prevent them killing our Horses & Cattle . . . on our March." He also asked them "to open your Hearts and Minds & give us your best Advice in any Thing you know or can say for the good Success of our Arms & the happy repossession of you & ourselves upon your hunting Grounds on the Ohio" (C.O. 5:15, p. 558).

[46] Braddock to Robinson, June 5, 1755, printed in N. B. Craig, The Olden Time, II, 237–9.

[47] A. B. Hulbert, Braddock's Road, p. 116.

in 1754. It will be noted that when the Ordnance Board sent to Virginia in 1753 a number of four-pounder cannon in place of the small three-pounders requested, the Virginians were dismayed at the possibility of ever getting them over the mountains and finally, after repeated efforts, gave it up as futile. But Braddock brought with him real siege guns in the form of great eight-inch howitzers, large twelve-pounders, as well as six-pounders, and the smaller cohorn mortars. Some of the twelve-pounders, in fact, came from the upper-tier battery of the H.M.S. *Norwich,* in need of new masts and tied up at Alexandria, and were so huge that that old sea-dog Admiral Keppel, who furnished them to Braddock on request, declared in writing to the Admiralty:

> "I have very strong doubts that these additional Guns to the Train will prove so heavy that they [the army] will meet with great, and perhaps, insurmountable difficulties in getting them over the Mountains." [48]

But Braddock was determined that what appeared to be an impossibility should be achieved. He would take this heavy artillery over every obstacle to have it available for pulverizing the French fort. Anticipating the difficulties that would be encountered, he also received from Keppel thirty sailors who could help the army over rivers in floats and boats and who also could make "leeff tackles," [49] by means of which the howitzers and the great guns could be lifted over barriers too precipitous for horses to pull them. [50] These monsters finally appeared, as by a miracle, in the neighbourhood of Fort Duquesne, and, with the smaller cannon, were left behind by the British in the panic that followed the defeat. The French, however, apparently appalled at the time by the problem of transporting them even eight miles over fairly smooth terrain, spiked and dismantled them and then proceeded to take the six-pounders to the fort to strengthen their defences. [51]

---

[48] Letter of March 14, 1755, P.R.O., Admiralty, In-Letters, 1746–63, 480: 1060. On March 18 Keppel wrote: ". . . I own I have my Fears that the heavy Guns must be left off this Side the Hill [Allegheny Mountains]" (*ibid.,* 480: 1085).

[49] A leeff tackle was used to control the weather leech or forward leech of a fore-and-aft sail. It consisted of a double and a single pulley with ropes and hooks so arranged that in lifting a weight, power is multiplied three or four times.

[50] P.R.O., Admiralty, In-Letters, 480: 1061.

[51] Later the big guns were, it is true, taken to Niagara and to Frontenac and some were used against Fort Oswego (Sargent, *op. cit.,* p. 257).

Even after Braddock had stripped his army of all non-essentials, it was stretched out for three or four miles. Now moving along the single road blasted from the mountain sides or blazed through virgin forests of immense white pines and northern cypress and equally immense hardwoods with interlocking branches so dense that, in the words of Sir John St. Clair, a man might go "Twenty Miles without seeing before him ten yards"; [52] then wading through swampy lands filled with venomous snakes that struck and killed or through underbrush alive with wood-ticks that stung like scorpions; again, balancing itself on rocky ledges or worming its way among boulders and the stumps of trees, on and on it moved, ever inching its way with deadly persistence toward its goal. Over Great Savage Mountain it passed; then crept through the Little Shades of Death; traversed Tumblestones and on through the Shades of Death; then it moved over the Great Crossings of the Youghiogheny, on to Great Meadows and the ruins of Fort Necessity, up over a spur of the rocky Laurel Range and down the valley to Stewarts Crossing; then, leaving Chestnut Range on the right, it proceeded on to Mount Pleasant. Horses fell dead in their traces, wagons were racked to pieces, the men became sickly on a diet of salt meat; even Washington, with his iron constitution, was taken down with the bloody flux before he reached the Great Crossings of the Youghiogheny on June 28.[53] While the army, after it left Great Meadows, had some stragglers picked off by the lurking enemy Indians, the latter, under French leaders, at first shrewdly directed their chief attacks against the frontier settlements or isolated families of Maryland and Virginia. This had the effect of placing the people living in this region "in such Frights and Apprehensions" that they fled for security to certain advantageous points. But Braddock was not to be diverted by these acts and marched ahead, very properly leaving to the colonial militia of the two provinces the responsibility of providing protection to their own inhabitants.[54]

In the course of this historic march many adjustments were made. On June 11 at a council of war — after Lieutenant Colonel Burton,

---

[52] Pargellis, op. cit., p. 94.

[53] Writings of Washington (ed. Fitzpatrick), I, 139.

[54] "I don't think the General has sent . . . any parties whatsoever, after those troublesome Indians," wrote Admiral Keppel on July 6 from Hampton Roads; "his not doing it will in all Probability be a disappointment to the French . . . for I cannot help thinking but they have sent the Indians so near, in order to tempt him to weaken his Army, by sending detachments after them" (P.R.O., Admiralty, In-Letters, 480: 1188).

who was with the advanced party, had reported that he was able to make but five miles in two days "on a better road than we were to expect afterwards, occasioned by the extreme faintness and deficiency of the horses" [55] — it was agreed to send back to Fort Cumberland two of the six-pounders and four cohorns and some of the ammunition, as well as all the King's wagons that Braddock had brought with him, since these were found to be too heavy for the task. The lighter country wagons were now substituted for these and the load was limited to fourteen hundred pounds — far short of a ton's weight. To draw each light wagon, four horses were provided; to pull each of the great howitzers, seven of the strongest horses were selected, and five of the strongest for each of the twelve-pounders. Each bat horse was limited to two hundred pounds, a very reasonable pack; but the horses furnished on contract by the Virginians were so defective — "the offcasts of Indian Traders" — that they could hardly carry a hundredweight. Representing to his officers the great need for horses and how important it was therefore to eliminate all but the most essential baggage and to send this back to Fort Cumberland, the general made an appeal to them to surrender their extra mounts. Washington led the way in giving up his best horse; his example was generally followed, with the result that "near a hundred able horses were given to the public service." [56] After two days spent in adjusting loads the army again moved forward over the "excessively mountainous and rocky" road. On the 15th, in passing the summit of Savage Mountain, involving a continuous rocky ascent of almost two miles and in many places extremely steep, one half of the soldiers were detailed to help push the wagons and gun carriages up the grade when the horses became faint and many died; then came the dangerous descent from the summit, described as "very rugged and almost perpendicular," where some of the wagons were dashed to pieces and others shattered. Many horses that survived the ordeal were now mere wrecks. Even before this passage Washington had expressed the fear that unless some of the wagons were eliminated and pack-horses substituted for carrying the stores and provisions, the difficulties of continuing the march might prove insurmountable.[57] Yet he did not despair. Writing to his brother Samuel on the same day — that is, the 14th — he declared that

[55] Orme's "Journal," Sargent, op. cit., p. 331.
[56] Ibid., pp. 331–2.
[57] Writings (ed. Fitzpatrick), I, 140.

". . . we have gone thus far, and shall continue on to Fort Duquesne; where, I hope the dispute will soon be decided. . . ." [58]

From the summit of Savage Mountain other ranges of the Appalachian chain towered to the west before the eyes of the determined leaders. Could the army continue onward? Others than Washington had now come to the conviction that it would be "impossible to proceed with such a number of carriages." [59] At Little Meadows Braddock therefore summoned his second council of war since leaving Fort Cumberland. His high regard for Washington led him to get his private opinion of the expedition before the council was held. Speaking of this informal conference, Washington declared:

> "I urg'd it in the warmest terms I was Master of to push on; if we even did it with a chos'n Detacht. for that purpose, with the Artillery and such other things as were absolutely necessary; leav'g the baggage and other Convoys with the Remainder of the Army, to follow by slow and regular Marches, which they might do safely, while we were advanced in Front." [60]

The advice of Washington was sound and the council of war, acting upon it, determined that a flying column supported by artillery should move ahead at the greatest speed possible in order to arrive at Fort Duquesne before the expected French reinforcements. Twelve hundred troops in all — composed of some of the best of the grenadiers and of the rank and file, with pioneers, artillerymen, the party of seamen, and the light horse — were detailed as a special task force. Each soldier was supplied with a hundred rounds of ammunition. Four of the great howitzers, each with fifty rounds, four of the twelve-pounders, each with eighty rounds, together with some of the six-pounders were also included. On the 18th of June four hundred men supported by six-pounders, under command of Colonel Gage, later of Revolutionary War fame, moved forward with their axes to blaze the way; the following day Halkett's regiment and then the remainder of the selected force plunged into the forest gloom. It seemed that much greater speed could now be attained: the howitzers and their caissons were pulled by nine of the strongest horses instead of seven, the twelve-pounders by seven, and the wagons containing the ammunition and other matériel by six; while great strings of bat horses

---

[58] *Ibid.*, I, 141.
[59] Orme's "Journal," Sargent, *op. cit.*, p. 335.
[60] *Writings*, I, 143.

carried a month's provisions for the entire force.[61] But still there were delays as the army was obliged to wait for the pioneers to prepare the way for the passage of the artillery train and the ammunition wagons — now through swamps and springs, now over mountains, and most of the time through dense forest. To Washington, who had fallen ill and was impatient for action, it was intolerable

> "that instead of pushing on with vigour, without regarding a little rough Road, they were halting to level every Mold [sic] Hill, and to erect Bridges over every Brook; by which means we were 4 Days gett'g 12 Miles. . . ."[62]

But one must feel that the youthful aide-de-camp was wrong. Many, many weary miles lay ahead for man and beast. Far beyond over rough mountainous country was still the great Laurel Range, which the preceding year had taken such a frightful toll of both horses and wagons that when Washington himself had had to retreat from Gist's Plantation, his men were obliged to pull the swivels and carry the supplies on their backs. But now the horses were pulling howitzers and twelve-pounders and other large cannon with the caissons, and wagons loaded with ammunition and other matériel. This demanded the utmost care because of the great dead weight, lest at best the horses should have their shoulders irreparably galled and consequently become useless and at worst should fall dead of overexertion. In explaining the slowness of his progress St. Clair, in charge of the pioneers, records in his Journal:

> "The Roads are either Rocky or full of Boggs, we are obliged to blow the Rocks and lay Bridges every Day."[63]

All this took time, but time well spent.[64] Moreover, the general, to save his precious horses, provided that at very precipitous places the guns and wagons should be handled by his soldiers using the tackle blocks and assisted by the sailors. Again this took time.

In fact, General Braddock, in spite of undeniable faults of charac-

---

[61] Orme's "Journal," Sargent, op. cit., p. 336.
[62] Writings (ed. Fitzpatrick), I, 144.
[63] Pargellis, op. cit., p. 95.
[64] I may perhaps be permitted to state that during the years that I lived in the Far West, where I was reared, I came to have personal knowledge of the serious problems involved in carrying freight over mountain roads by the use of horses and wagons — especially over newly opened roads filled with what one might regard superficially as minor obstructions. A horse is a highly expendable asset.

ter and unmeasured censure later heaped upon him, was not an unworthy leader of so desperate an adventure. Although a man of years,
he pursued his objectives "with a great deal of vigour and Vivacity,"
according to Sir John St. Clair; [65] there was an absence of that brutality which some writers have assumed he possessed; he had even
words of praise for his two Irish regiments, who, he reported,

> "behave well and shew great Spirit and Zeal for the Service, which
> will be a good Example to the rest." [66]

His humaneness is also indicated by the records of the courts-martial,
which he repeatedly overruled by mitigating the severe punishment
decreed against his soldiers.[67] He knew the limits of exertion of those
who marched with packs and of horses dragging loads, and thought-
fully ordered frequent and proper rests. If, on the one hand, he lashed
out against those in America who would not honour their contracts
and acted fraudulently in their transactions with the army, he may
be pardoned since he had a keen sense of the great responsibilities
he had assumed in undertaking so difficult a campaign. On the other
hand, those who had proved to be worthy of his trust and friendship were treated most courteously and generously; some received
almost fatherly consideration. For example, when Washington became violently ill, the general ordered his own physician to attend
him and detailed a body of soldiers to stand guard over him when his
army moved forward. He also promised not to attack the French before his young aide-de-camp could join the advanced detachment,
and he kept his word; then when the battle was joined, he refused
to permit the young man, still weak and suffering from his ailment,
to expose himself unnecessarily to the enemy's fire. Further, as a
good soldier he sought advice and, when it seemed sound, acted upon
it.[68] Personally without fear, he helped to instil confidence in others,

---

[65] Pargellis, op. cit., p. 94.

[66] Ibid., p. 83.

[67] His "Orderly Books" are in the Congressional Library. Among the Ayer Collection
in the Newberry Library is the transcription of a copy of these made by George Washington. These books throw much light upon Braddock's military arrangements. Orme's
"Journal" also repeats many of the orders.

[68] For example, before leaving Wills Creek, Braddock called a council of war of his
leading officers and informed them that "he had formed a plan of march and encampment . . . that he offered it to them for their opinions, in which he desired they would
be very explicit, and make such objections, and offer such amendments, as they should
judge proper, by which some general plan might be formed which would effectually answer the end proposed, of marching and encamping with the greater security" (Orme's
"Journal," Sargent, op. cit., p. 317).

especially the soldiers of his Irish regiments, who at first were deeply apprehensive of the great forest that had swallowed them up. His military conceptions and his tactical arrangements were sound and most errors of judgment in connection with the campaign were committed by others, his military superiors or inferiors; yet his correspondence is remarkably free from any censure of his fellow officers. Finally, an examination of his orders shows that he felt under necessity to take the utmost precautions against surprise attacks, whether on the march or in camp. To illustrate: While in the vicinity of the first branch of the Youghiogheny, as his army was skirting "an immense mountain," reports came of the presence of the enemy; thereupon he ordered a detachment of a hundred men to occupy the eminence until his artillery and baggage train should pass by this dangerous point. Scouting parties, pickets, and sentries he constantly employed; moreover, strong detachments preceded and followed and, when possible, flanked the army as an additional precaution against surprise, especially when rivers had to be crossed.

On June 30 the army passed over the Youghiogheny at Stewarts Crossing and then proceeded on to Salt Lick Creek, now called Jacob's Creek, where Braddock called his third council of war to consider Sir John St. Clair's recommendations that the force should halt there and send back all the horses to bring up the rest of the forces commanded by Colonel Dunbar, who was struggling along with a great wagon train and an utterly inadequate number of horses. After full consideration it was decided that this would involve great delays: it had taken the lighter detachment eleven days to come from the position that Dunbar had attained at Squaw's Creek and his force was much more encumbered with baggage. Washington's advice — given at Little Meadows — in favour of "pushing on" was still favoured by Braddock, and the council agreed to it unanimously.[69] Thereupon the army proceeded, with great precautions observed, in the direction of the Monongahela. On July 7 an attempt was made to pass Turtle Creek some miles before its junction with the Monongahela, but was wisely given up in the face of dangers involved in the precipice that bordered it; instead it was decided to move to the left toward the

---

[69] Washington did not join Braddock until the 8th of July, when he arrived with the supply wagons coming from Dunbar's contingent with additional food supplies, including livestock. Dunbar had remained at Little Meadows until June 2 and then moved forward slowly. He could not transport all his supplies with the available horses without sending them back with their drivers under military escort to the preceding halting-place — a situation that made rapid movement impossible.

main stream. In approaching it through the valley of Long Run on the 8th, great care was taken by means of powerful detachments to secure control of eminences that dominated both the right and the left flanks of the army. Up to the very day of the great disaster so extraordinary had been all the proper precautions, so efficient the means of overcoming the tremendous problem of transport, so confident the once dispirited and even mutinous soldiers through the example set by the general, that no one doubted or had good reason to doubt the happy outcome of this epic campaign in the wilderness.

But Braddock was moving to meet the enemy, and we must now turn to consider developments at Fort Duquesne — and also at Quebec.

The movement of the two British regiments to Virginia and the plans for recruiting two additional regiments in America were known to the French. In fact, one may believe that the instructions relative to strengthening the British arms in the New World were not designed to be hidden from the representative of His Most Christian Majesty in London. Whatever restraining effect of this knowledge upon French activities in North America may have been anticipated by the ministry, the truth is that it led to redoubled efforts on the part of Versailles. For it was thereupon determined to send to America six battalions of the finest troops that France with her great military tradition could afford — the battalions of La Reine, of Artois, of Burgundy, of Guienne, of Languedoc, and of Béarn, making a corps of three thousand regulars of the line to reinforce the twenty-eight companies of regulars already in New France as well as the Canadians, who could provide some twelve thousand trained militia. All these were placed under the command of one of the late Marshal Saxe's most highly esteemed officers, the German Baron de Dieskau.[70] Governor General Duquesne, however, was warned by the Minister in February that these troops, who could not sail from Brest until April, would not arrive in Quebec before the British regiments had reached Virginia, from which colony, it was anticipated correctly, they would march to the Ohio, or La Belle Rivière as the French called it.[71]

That the French anticipated grave developments in the Ohio Valley region — doubtless in view not only of the hostilities that had already occurred there but of the determination of the British min-

---

[70] For his commission and instruction see *New York Colonial Documents*, X, 285–9.
[71] *Ibid.*, X, 276.

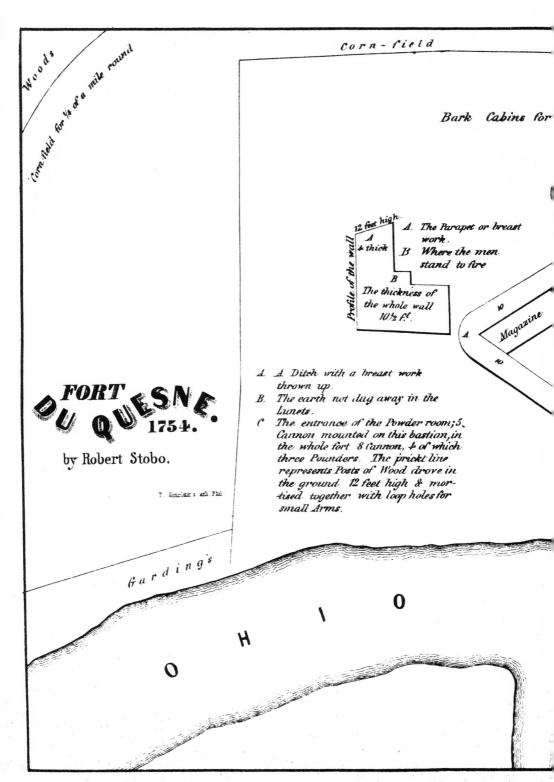

Woods

Corn-field for ¼ of a mile round

Corn-field

Bark Cabins for

Profile of the wall

12 feet high

A
4 thick

B

The thickness of
the whole wall
10½ ft.

A. The Parapet or breast
   work.
B. Where the men
   stand to fire

10

Magazine

A

10

A. A Ditch with a breast work
   thrown up.
B. The earth not dug away in the
   Lunets.
C. The entrance of the Powder room; 5.
   Cannon mounted on this bastion, in
   the whole fort 8 Cannon, 4 of which
   three Pounders. The prickt line
   represents Posts of Wood drove in
   the ground 12 feet high & mor-
   tised together with loop holes for
   small Arms.

**FORT
DU QUESNE.**
1754.

by Robert Stobo.

T. Sinclair's lith. Phil.

Gardings

OHIO

OHIO

Captain Stobo's map of Fort Duquesne, 1754.

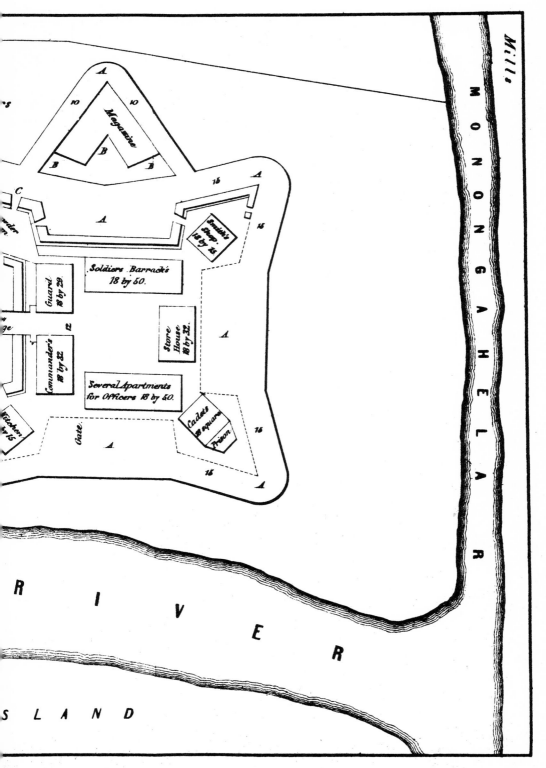

(From Winthrop Sargent's *History of Braddock's Expedition*.)

istry to maintain the rights of the Crown there — is indicated by the elaborate instructions given to acting Intendant Varin. He was ordered to adopt the necessary measures to compel, if need be, those who had either wheat or flour available in Canada to surrender it at a price to be designated; also to secure a large supply of salt pork and other provisions; and, finally, to prepare a sufficient number of bateaux at Quebec and Montreal to transport between two and three thousand men and their equipment to the back country.[72] But the threat to Fort Duquesne was not all that the government of New France had to worry about. Late in February the authorities at Louisbourg received a code letter written the previous month from New York by a Frenchman who went there ostensibly to purchase cattle for the French at Cape Breton. This warned that the British were preparing to send six thousand men against Fort Duquesne, one thousand against Fort St. Frédéric at Crown Point, and two thousand down the branches of the Chaudière to the Indian village of Becancour, near the St. Lawrence and opposite Quebec. This alarming intelligence, partly true and partly false, was sent posthaste to the Marquis de Duquesne.[73]

Doubtless French concern for the safety of the Ohio Valley was moderated somewhat by the news that reached Quebec from that region about the same time as the above alarm, which indicated that the Shawnee, "the strongest nation in that quarter," had taken up the hatchet against the English and were bringing in scalps and prisoners. Duquesne, writing to the Governor of Louisbourg early in March, declared that nothing could be more advantageous under the circumstances and that these Indians must be sustained. To do so, he added that he had ordered a French detachment to leave for the Ohio on the ice and, with the opening up of navigation, would send a "brigade."[74] It should be pointed out in this connection that the number of soldiers kept at Fort Duquesne fluctuated. They came and went. Before the beginning of the winter of 1754 the garrison, upon receipt of news that troops would be sent to Virginia, was reinforced so as to consist of 1,100 Frenchmen and 400 Canadian Indians. Then, with the coming of snow and ice in the mountains, and the accompanying feeling of security, the number was reduced to 250 regulars on account of the difficulties of providing subsistence

[72] Ibid., X, 279.
[73] Ibid., X, 281–4.
[74] Ibid., X, 290.

for a greater number of men. By early spring there were scarcely more than 200 Frenchmen and Indians there.[75] By the summer, however, the garrison had been increased so that it numbered at least 1,600 Frenchmen and Indians.[76]

As to the fort itself, work proceeded in the direction of strengthening it [77] and by May its commander, Contrecœur, was able to report that it was completed, with its bastions, breastworks, and stockade, its powder house, its officers' quarters, and barracks; that six six-pounder cannon and nine of smaller size were mounted, and that neither ammunition nor arms were lacking.[78] To maintain it in supplies, a new fort had been constructed at Venango at the mouth of Rivière aux Bœuf (French Creek) and was named Fort Machault in honour of the Minister of the Marine. It was now possible to go up the St. Lawrence to Lake Ontario, pass to Lake Erie by making the short Niagara River portage around the falls, and then, arriving at Presqu'Isle, to carry the supplies by cart or sled or horseback over a well-constructed road to the head of the Rivière aux Bœuf, where Fort Le Bœuf stood, and when the water was high, float these down to Fort Machault. The trip from Le Bœuf to Machault could be made "safe and sound" in forty-eight hours. How different the journey of the French from Canada to the forks of the Ohio from that of the English from Wills Creek across mountain barriers and precipitous rivers and through endless primeval forests!

Steps likewise were taken to make the fort largely self-sustaining in the matter of food supplies. In 1754 seven hundred *minots* [79] of maize were raised on lands adjacent to it; other lands meanwhile had been cleared, and it was anticipated, according to Duquesne, that two thousand *minots* would be gathered in 1755. Peas also had been sown and livestock provided. Moreover, it was found that forage that made excellent hay was abundant in the neighbourhood of Presqu'Isle.[80] There was every indication that the French were expecting to remain permanently at the forks. And well they had planned, and well might they feel confident, especially after the

---

[75] Duquesne to the Minister, November 3, 1754, Arch. Nat. Col., C¹¹A. 99: 399; and Sargent, *op. cit.*, p. 187.

[76] *N. Y. Col. Doc.*, X, 307.

[77] C.O. 5:15, pp. 281–4.

[78] *N. Y. Col. Doc.*, X, 307.

[79] The *minot*, an old French measure, equalled some 39 litres; the latter amounts to something more than one and three fourths pints.

[80] *N. Y. Col. Doc.*, X, 300–1.

Washington debacle, that the British would never be able to surmount the tremendous difficulties of an overland passage from the
Atlantic seaboard with any force that could be a serious menace.

Nevertheless, as the spring of 1755 passed into early summer, the
defenders of Fort Duquesne had to face problems. The prolonged
drought, with consequent low water in the streams, made it difficult
to use the Rivière aux Bœufs to advantage for the easy transportation
of supplies. Consequently many of the sixteen hundred men concentrated at the fort — including regulars, Canadian militia, and Indians
— had to be employed by Contrecœur for this purpose. Therefore
when the news reached him of the steady progress of Braddock from
Wills Creek through the western wilderness, not many men were
available to form detachments to harass the British troops and no
large force could be spared for a real attack on them. That a larger
number of troops were not hurried to him from Canada may be
ascribed not only to the problem of maintaining any greater number
at the forks but to the alarming news that continued to reach Quebec
in the late spring of other British projects against French positions.

The new Governor General, the Marquis de Vaudreuil, who arrived in Quebec from France on June 26, instead of finding, as anticipated, an easy berth and tranquillity, was filled with dismay.
Writing to the court of Versailles on July 2, he affirmed that not only
was Fort Duquesne threatened, but that Fort Beauséjour within the
Nova Scotian peninsula had actually fallen to a large British force;
that the fort on the St. John River across the Bay of Fundy was also
menaced by the same troops, and Fort St. Frédéric at Crown Point
by another large concentration of soldiers at Albany; that the English had launched two sloops armed with cannon on Lake Ontario,
and that a powerful detachment was moving to attack Forts Niagara
and Frontenac.[81] He had at first contemplated sending most of the
new battalions that had arrived with him into the Great Lakes region
to support Forts Frontenac and Niagara and also Fort Duquesne,
and they were actually proceeding to their destination under Dieskau
when some of them were ordered back to strengthen Fort St. Frédéric. Fort Duquesne was therefore obliged to rely upon what
strength it already possessed in meeting the British threat.

According to the French accounts, from the early part of June one
expedition after another was sent out from Fort Duquesne for the
purpose of turning Braddock aside. On the 6th M. de Normanville

[81] Mém. et Doc., Amérique, 10. I: 155-9.

led a party of French and Indians that penetrated the wilderness to the site of Fort Necessity; on the 18th M. de Neverville left with one hundred and thirty Indians and a small body of French to harass the enemy; on the 26th nineteen Indians left and returned with a scalp; on the 28th it was a party of one hundred and twenty Indians — Hurons and others — with ten Frenchmen under the command of M. Rigoville; M. Roctoyade also was sent out at that time with another mixed party with the same design. Although these detachments succeeded in firing upon the soldiers and killing some of them, the Indians were disappointed and not a little discouraged since they were unable to secure scalps because of the alertness and good order of the British, who proceeded without interruption in their methodical march. Nevertheless, the last-named two parties and others that left on the 30th and on July 5 hung upon the flanks of the advancing army until it was within eight leagues of the forks of the Ohio and then most of them returned on July 7 to report their failure to check its progress.[82] In commenting upon this failure Contrecœur declared that

> "these troops remain so constantly on guard, always marching in battle formation, that all the efforts that our detachments put forth against them are useless."[83]

The conduct of the defenders of Fort Duquesne was at this critical juncture marked by great indecision. For example, on the 6th of July a party of Hurons appeared at the forks with the news that the British were marching forward briskly with their artillery. To secure more accurate information, the Chevalier de la Peyrade was sent the same day with a small party; but after going some three or four leagues, his guide, an Iroquois living at the forks, refused to proceed farther. The Ottawa and the Michilimakinac, who were to have gone out on the 6th to strike the British, were detained by the other Indians for a conference with Contrecœur, at which it was at length decided that all the Indians at the forks would proceed together the following day. But on the 7th nothing happened except that two new parties went out by different routes to observe the British; these on their return amply confirmed the accuracy of the

---

[82] See the Frenchman Godefroy's "Relation" in Relations diverses sur la bataille du Malangueulé, gagné le 9 Juillet, 1755 (ed. J. M. Shea), pp. 9–10; also among the Chatham Manuscripts (Volume XCVIII, folios 12–19) is to be found a most detailed account, translated into English, of activities at Fort Duquesne between the 6th and 12th of July. A transcript of this is in the Canadian Archives.

[83] Pargellis, op. cit., p. 129.

earlier information of their near approach. Again the plan to strike
the enemy was postponed to the 8th, and it was agreed that every
Frenchman and Indian that could be spared from the fort would then
march out. But on the 8th, in spite of the fact that Captain de Beaujeu, a man of energy and determination who had led the reinforcements to the forks in the spring, who possessed great influence with
the Indians, and who had been appointed to lead the expedition,
sang the war-song, the Indians still held back.[84] Now it was the Potawatomi who remained silent on their mats.[85] On the other hand, the
Shawnee and the Mingo, living in the region of the forks — the very
Indians whom Dinwiddie had sought to protect from the French in
sending Washington on his adventure the preceding year and who
had for years been showered with presents by Virginia and Pennsylvania — appeared before Contrecœur and offered to assist him in
opposing the British. He entertained them in a proper manner at the
commandery in order to win over the other natives and complacently
granted all their demands. Armed and equipped, they declared themselves ready to set forth immediately with the French. But Beaujeu
proposed that the expedition be once more postponed, now to the
9th, when he was determined to set forth at daybreak, hoping that
all the Indians would then join him. The French, most of them "in
Indian dress" on that fatal day, to set an example marched two musket-shots from the fort and then halted, for the Indians had not
joined them. There were one hundred and eight regulars — including
Captains Beaujeu, Dumas, and Deligney, four lieutenants, six en-
signs, and twenty-three cadets — and one hundred and forty-six
Canadian militia. Beaujeu thereupon, it is said, dramatically appealed
to the Indians, announcing that if need be he would meet the English
alone:

> "I am determined to go against the enemy! What! Will you allow
> your father to go alone?" [86]

Even the Potawatomi took fire at this display of courage. Loading
themselves with the ammunition from the barrels that had been

---

[84] *Relations diverses sur la bataille du Malangueulé,* p. xi. Beaujeu had commanded
both at Detroit and at Niagara.

[85] On July 5 a party of Potawatomi and Missisauga had gone out to strike the British,
but they returned without accomplishing anything and apparently deeply impressed with
the formidable nature of the invading forces (*ibid.,* p. 10).

[86] "Relation depuis le départ des Trouppes de Quebec, jusqu'au 30 du mois de Sep-
tembre, 1755," Sargent, *op. cit.,* Appendix, p. 411.

placed before the gate of the fort, they now, to the number of over six hundred, raced forward to join the waiting French troops.

The defenders of Fort Duquesne apparently had hoped — when tidings were received that Braddock had avoided what might well have been a trap presented by the more direct approach along the well-established trail that crossed Turtle Creek — to be able to ambuscade the British as they crossed or recrossed the Monongahela. But the General, encamped on the evening of the 8th only two miles from the river, took the precaution to order Lieutenant Colonel Gage, with three hundred and sixty regulars, supported by Captain Gates's New York Independent Company and two six-pounders, to march well before daylight in order to protect the rest of the army as it passed over to the left bank and then back to the right bank below the mouth of Turtle Creek to regain the well-worn trail leading to the forks of the Ohio and Fort Duquesne. Gage, moving about two o'clock in the morning, secured these vital crossings without opposition and for reasons that have been made clear. To the men who made the crossings that morning it must have seemed providential that the enemy had not taken advantage of banks — rising twelve feet perpendicular from the shores — to pour a devastating fire upon those attempting to ford the stream, some three hundred yards in breadth at the points selected. At four o'clock St. Clair's pioneers marched, followed by the rest of the army, which was delayed in getting the heavy artillery across the river and back again. But by early afternoon the whole army was safely back on the right bank and the soldiers, in the words of one of them,

> "hugg's themselves with joy at our Good Luck in having surmounted our greatest Difficultys. . . ." [87]

The taking of Fort Duquesne now seemed assured.

Gage was once again ordered to advance along the trail until three o'clock, when in the more open country to the north — perhaps in one of the areas the French had cleared for field crops — camp would be struck for the day. The trail wound past Frazier's trading house, through a fairly dense growth of trees up along a ridge only some twenty rods in width, into a region which was more open and yet which was flanked on either side by ravines with a dense undergrowth and dominated by a hill likewise covered with underbrush

---

[87] Royal Engineer Harry Gordon, "Journal of Proceedings from Willes's Creek to the Monongahela," Pargellis, *op. cit.*, pp. 105–6.

rising from the ravine on the right.[88] Most of the usual precautions were observed. Scouts moved ahead, followed after an interval of some two hundred yards by the vanguard and then the main body of Gage's command protected by flank guards. After these came the pioneers clearing the way for the artillery carriages and the wagons, followed by the gunners with two six-pounders and the ammunition and tool wagons, likewise protected by rear as well as flank guards. After another interval of a quarter of a mile came the main body of troops, including the general's guard, the heavy artillery, the remainder of the wagons, and a herd of cattle. Here at last but three leagues from Fort Duquesne was the place where the enemy would give battle and here the British need of adequate Indian support became painfully apparent.[89]

Where were the Catawba, so held in dread by the very Indians living about the forks who had gone to Contrecœur only the day before to express their willingness to help the French destroy the approaching army? [90] Where were the Cherokee, who, together with the Catawba, had stealthily passed and repassed this very spot endless times bent on their deadly missions against the Northern Indians — over the trail that, significantly, was called the Catawba-Cherokee Path? One may affirm with confidence that had Dinwiddie been able to provide only half the number of these Southern Indians that he had promised and that were available, the history of this fatal July 9 would have been very different. For they could have been in possession of the very ravines and the commanding eminence from out of

---

[88] One of the most careful studies of the terrain of the battlefield was made by J. K. Lacock in his article "Braddock's Road" (*Pa. Mag. of Hist. and Biog.*, XXXVIII, 1–38). After the most painstaking examination, he wrote that "the contour of the road over which the line of march extended [on the day of the battle] was found to be so much altered that even the slightest traces of its course were not perceptible." We are therefore obliged to rely upon contemporary accounts.

[89] The court of inquiry that reported upon the disaster gives as one of the three causes: "The Want of Indians or other irregulars to give timely Notice of the Enemy's Approach . . ." (*Corresp. of William Shirley*, II, 313). George Croghan, the famous Pennsylvania Indian trader, declared after the defeat that he was "yet of opinion that had we had fifty Indians instead of eight, that we might in a great measure have prevented the surprise, that day of our unhappy defeat" ("Journal to the Ohio," Du Simitiere Mss., Library Company of Philadelphia).

[90] In a letter dated July 29, 1754 Captain Stobo, one of the two hostages that Washington had given to the French at Fort Necessity, wrote from Fort Duquesne to Governor James Hamilton: "I wish a Peace may be made up between the Catawbas and the nations here; they [the Ohio Indians] are much afraid of them [the Catawba]" (*Pa. Col. Rec.*, VI, 141–2).

the mystery of which death spoke alike to British grenadier and Virginia rifleman. Lacking this support, there remained as a protection the maintenance of all those safeguards that had preserved the army thus far from surprise and serious attack on its difficult and dangerous march.

It will be noted that when the army on June 19 passed over the Little Crossings on the upper waters of Castleman's River and was obliged to skirt a high mountain, Colonel Gage, leading the vanguard, on his own responsibility very properly ordered a detachment to occupy it; when Braddock moved up with the main force, he in turn, as has been mentioned already, posted a hundred soldiers on it, who remained there until his artillery train and wagons had safely passed by. On the 8th of July similar precautions were observed, as has been emphasized, when the army moved toward the Monongahela down Long Run. But Gage, after his successful crossing and recrossing of that river, was apparently lulled into a false sense of security. Before the attack took place he passed by a dominating hill without bothering to secure it with his vanguard, as did the pioneers under Sir John St. Clair who followed him. Once the opportunity was missed thus to secure the army, it never returned.

When Beaujeu with his French and Indians moving rapidly along the trail came into view, the advanced British scouts fell back upon the vanguard of grenadiers. The latter formed a skirmish-line and proceeded to open fire. They were soon joined by the gunners with their six-pounders. Beaujeu fell mortally wounded and many of the Canadian militia fled. But Captain Dumas now took over command. In an instant his regular troops and the Indians divided, some racing through the trees to the right and others to the left of the British vanguard. Faced now by a cross-fire delivered under cover of the trees, Gage could have pushed forward and thereby gained the still more open ground and in turn placed the enemy at a serious disadvantage, not only by finding itself ultimately enveloped in the cross-fire of the vanguard and the main body of the British army but by having a force between it and Fort Duquesne. Instead he decided to retreat — his second major error. For in falling back he came within the range of fire of the Indians and French who had poured into the ravines that he had already passed and who also concentrated in force upon the hill that he had also passed without seizing and from which they now "did the greatest Execution on the King's Troops."

But this was not the only serious consequence of Gage's retrograde

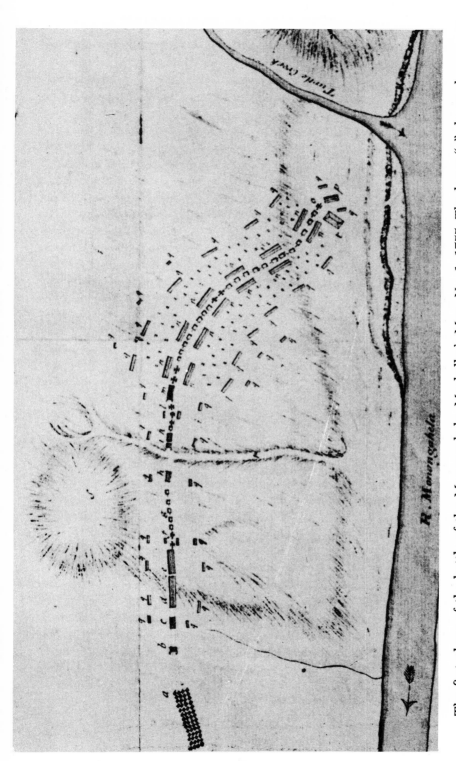

The first phase of the battle of the Monongahela. Mackellar's Map, No. 1, 1755. The letter "a" shows the advancing French and Indians before they swung around the flanks of the British forces moving forward with the artillery and baggage train.

(From the Duke of Cumberland Manuscripts, Windsor Castle.)

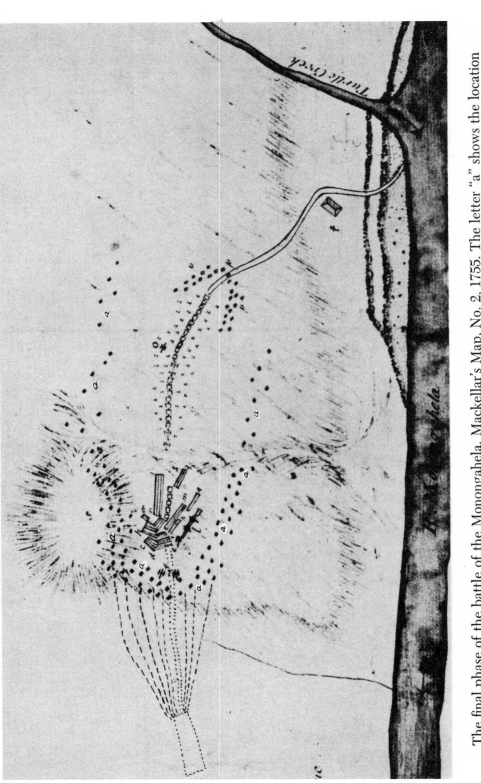

The final phase of the battle of the Monongahela. Mackellar's Map, No. 2, 1755. The letter "a" shows the location of the French and Indians as they fired under cover upon the disorganized British forces.

(From the Duke of Cumberland Manuscripts, Windsor Castle.)

movement; for he helped mightily to throw into confusion the large detachment immediately sent forward by Braddock to support him. According to Orme, when the firing was heard, the general,

> "imagining the advanced parties were very warmly attacked, and being willing to free himself from the incumbrance of the baggage, ordered Lieutenant Colonel Burton to re-enforce them with the vanguard [that is, the vanguard of the main body], and the line to halt. According to this disposition, eight hundred men were detached from the line, free from all embarrassments, and four hundred were left for the defence of the Artillery and baggage, posted in such a manner as to secure them from any attack or insults." [91]

Burton, as he moved forward, sensed the necessity of securing immediate possession of the hill on the right of the road and was making preparations to carry it by assault when the retreating troops of the advance helped to plunge his own command into confusion.[92] This confusion seems to have become hopeless when, in addition to the appearance of the retreating troops, which made proper manœuvring of his own force impossible upon a narrow twelve-foot road already swarming with soldiers, the French and Indians now brought his command also under a galling cross-fire, which was the more deadly in its demoralizing effects in that the enemy was hidden, while his troops were in an exposed position in the roadway running along the ridge. What also added immeasurably to the confusion was the forward movement of the baggage train. This, when a quarter of a mile from the scene of action, was ordered to halt by Braddock.

As the firing continued, Braddock rode forward, leaving Sir Peter Halkett in charge of the convoy. Why Sir Peter permitted the convoy

---

[91] "Orme's Journal," Sargent, op. cit., p. 354.

[92] This was denied in an "Advertisement" printed in the Pennsylvania Gazette of September 4, 1755. Dr. Stanley M. Pargellis in his important article "Braddock's Defeat" (American Historical Review, XLI, 251–9) develops and supports the thesis that the battle was lost not because the soldiers did not fight in frontier fashion, not that they displayed cowardice, but on account of the failure of the officers to measure up to their responsibilities and to apply sound tactical principles already laid down in Bland's Treatise of Military Discipline. His blame is particularly directed against Braddock rather than against Gage. However, on March 27 Braddock issued permanent orders for the conduct of "firings" and platoons in connection with the campaign (Major-General Edward Braddock's Orderly Books from February 26 to June 17, 1755 [Cumberland, Md., 1878], pp. v–vi) that were manifestly based upon Bland's Treatise. Burton, it appears, attempted to carry out these orders in moving forward from the baggage train, but could not execute the required formation on account of the retrograde movement of Gage's troops and those of St. Clair.

to continue along the road in face of a positive command to halt cannot be understood. But when it was brought to a stop, it was planted squarely against Burton's soldiers, who had of course left it in order to be free to manœuvre. Under these trying conditions — with the shrieking of six hundred Indians, the staccato of musketry, the roar of cannon, and the cries of the wounded and dying soldiers all creating a terrifying symphony of death — the only possibility of snatching success from the prospect of total defeat lay in stoically accepting the necessary losses and pushing forward resolutely until the more open country that lay ahead had been reached.[93] This Braddock apparently sought to do, but in vain. For he found himself now in possession of a milling mass of disorganized soldiers firing aimlessly without seeing an enemy. Desperately he tried to drive them back into proper formation with the flat of his sword; desperately he sought to urge them forward. Standards were raised to rally the soldiers; officers responded only to be stricken down as they came out into the open on the flanks. Five horses were shot out from under the general as he recklessly exposed himself before he received his fatal wound and before the battle was lost and the once proud little army with banners flying had become mere hunted fugitives, with most of its officers either dead or wounded.

As to the easy assumption made by many writers in that day and subsequently that the field could have been won had the Virginia and other troops been encouraged to post themselves behind trees and fire at will, this will not bear the test of critical analysis. It would seem that many, if not most, of those who were killed or wounded were shot, not by the enemy that they faced, but by the enemy behind them, who, by their murderous cross-fire, had every advantage in the engagement, which lasted between two and three hours before the British forces fled in wild panic — an engagement that exacted, incidentally, a particularly heavy toll of those who, leaving the ranks, sought under the given conditions to fight in typical backwoodsman style. Of 1,373 non-commissioned officers and privates but 459 were neither killed nor wounded; of 86 officers, but 23.[94] The Virginians, placed as flank guards, were sadly decimated, not only

---

[93] When Lieutenant Colonel Smith was caught by the Minute Men's cross-fire in his retreat from Concord in 1775, in pushing ahead he did the only thing that was practicable under the circumstances. Had he attempted to halt and fight as the colonials were fighting, it is more than likely that his detachment would have been completely decimated.

[94] "A list . . . of those killed and wounded, in the Action on the Banks of the Monongahela, 9 July, 1755," C.O. 5:46.

by the fire of the enemy but also, it would appear, by that of the British regulars, blinded by fear and also by the smoke of battle. In the words of Washington:

> "Our poor Virginians behaved like men, and died like soldiers; for I believe that out of three companies that were there that day, scarce thirty were left alive."

He thereupon asserted:

> "In short the dastardly behavior of the English soldiers exposed all those who were inclined to do their duty to almost certain death. It is imagined (I believe with great justice, too) that two-thirds of both killed and wounded received their shots from our own cowardly dogs of soldiers, who gathered themselves in a body, contrary to orders, ten and twelve deep, would then level, fire, and shoot down the men before them." [95]

Although the movements of the army after the disaster at the Monongahela will be considered in a subsequent chapter, it may here be said that out of the defeat developed many bitter controversies. Such men as Sir John St. Clair and Colonel Dunbar and their supporters cast the chief blame for it upon the general.[96] Their charges involved his decision — taken after securing Washington's advice, which he acted upon — to separate his army and push forward at maximum speed with a picked detachment. Dunbar, left behind with most of the convoy, bitterly resented being placed in this position. He and St. Clair favoured the movement of the whole army in one body; the latter also strongly favoured taking time to build blockhouses and other defences at strategic points, which would have delayed the advance upon Fort Duquesne doubtless until the fall.[97] The strategic move strongly recommended by Washington may have been unsound, but many strong arguments can be advanced in support of it. He himself, after due reflection upon the

[95] C.O. 5:46. The *Public Advertiser* (London) of August 27, 1755 in its account of the battle quotes the following from a letter from Wills Creek on July 10: "It is rumoured that most of the Officers were killed by the European Troops firing upon them when they endeavoured to rally them; and that very few of our Men were killed by the Enemy; in short that a *full* Account of this Action would disclose such a Scene as was never seen before in our nor perhaps in any other Army." Statements of this type must be placed in the same category as those of such men as Fossit and Allison about the shooting of Braddock.

[96] For letters written by St. Clair, Dunbar, and others, including Captain Orme, see Pargellis, *Military Affairs in North America, 1748–1765*, pp. 98–124.

[97] The Forbes expedition did not arrive at the fort until the latter part of November.

disaster, arrived at conclusions that the historian would do well to ponder. Writing from Mount Vernon on August 14, 1755, soon after his return from the scene of the battle, in referring to the difficult position of any commanding officer, but obviously with Braddock in mind, he notes:

". . . how little credit is given to a Commander, who perhaps after a defeat, in relating the cause justly lays the blame on some individual whose cowardly behav'r betray'd the whole to ruin; how little does the World consider the Circumstances, and how apt are Mankind to level their vindictive Censures against the unfortunate Chief, who perhaps merited least of the blame." [98]

[98] *Writings of Washington* (ed. Fitzpatrick), I, 161.

CHAPTER V

Boscawen Misses an Assignment

THE PROLOGUE of the great drama unfolding in North America in the duel between the two most dynamic of the oversea powers was high-lighted, as we have seen, by the two reverses inflicted by the French upon the British in the region of the forks of the Ohio, first upon Washington and then upon Braddock. But the year 1755 witnesses not only Braddock's movement from the British Isles to Virginia and then across the Appalachians, to face disaster in what is now western Pennsylvania, but a steady deterioration elsewhere in the formal peaceful relations of Great Britain and France. This is evident in the sudden turn of events in Nova Scotia and in the equally sudden determination of the British ministry to use its superior sea power to put a check to the sending of French regular troops to Canada, as well as in Continental politics. Each of these developments is of such importance for an understanding of the course of the struggle that was to decide the ultimate fate of the northern half of the Western hemisphere that these must be given distinct and detailed treatment, and preferably in the reverse order of that in which they are mentioned.

The plans for sending the two Irish regiments to Virginia could not be, nor were they designed to be, very secret, however private were the instructions that the British ministry gave to Braddock. What France had continued to do openly, Great Britain manifestly had a right to imitate as openly.[1] It seems quite clear that the French

---

[1] The French Minister of the Marine, writing to Governor General Duquesne on June 30, 1753 (Archives Nationales, Colonies, B. 97: 195), declared, in reply to a request for more troops, that it was not possible to do anything at the present moment.

intelligence did not secure access to the orders that Braddock was called upon to carry out in America when the ministers of His Most Christian Majesty determined to counter the British move.[2] For although the King was persuaded that it was not the intention of His Britannic Majesty to rupture the peace,[3] it was nevertheless now judged proper to send powerful reinforcements to Canada. As a result of this decision, thirteen companies of the Bourgogne battalion, and the same number of those of La Reine, Languedoc, Guienne, and Béarn, and nine companies *"Partout"* — in all, seventy-eight companies,[4] and, incidentally, some of the best-trained in France — were selected to go; and at their head was placed Baron de Dieskau, who on March 25 received instructions to act, under the orders of the Governor General, for the defence of the rights and possessions of the King against English usurpations in North America.[5] These instructions and also the orders given to the Marquis de Duquesne [6] and to the new Governor General, the Marquis de Vaudreuil de Cavagnal,[7] indicate that France was determined by means of this reinforcement not only to hold her advanced positions in Nova Scotia, on Lake Champlain, and on the Ohio — considered by Great Britain as gross usurpations — but even before its arrival to destroy, as a "defensive" measure, Fort Halifax, erected by the government of Massachusetts Bay in 1754 on the upper waters of the Kennebec in Maine.[8] In other words, by the spring of 1755 diplomacy had failed to settle peacefully the issues between the two nations. All that was now left was force. Yet the rival governments, while resolute to protect their respective interests in North America, sought by every means within their power to keep war away from Europe, to give no provocation to each other even in the eastern portion of the Atlantic.

This concept of a limited war — involving not only the legal fiction that there were areas lying beyond the European "line of amity" and that only within this hypothetical line did treaties of amity and the principles of international law have their full application, but also that of "localized hostilities" — had survived from an earlier period

---

[2] Arch. Nat., Col., B. 101: 123–30.

[3] *Ibid.*

[4] Vaudreuil's "Journal," *New York Colonial Documents*, X, 299.

[5] Arch. Nat., Col., B. 101: 140–3.

[6] Arch. Nat., Col., B. 101: 123–30. These instructions were under date of February 17, 1755.

[7] Arch. Nat., Col., B. 101: 163–75.

[8] Arch. Nat., Col., B. 101: 123–30.

and indeed has had its application even in our own day in the distant although serious border clashes of such expanding powers as Russia and Japan in Outer Mongolia, which did not involve the participants either in the termination of treaties or in an all-out war. It is important that the student should take into consideration this concept if he is to comprehend the significance of the steps now taken by the British ministry and the course of events that follow, up to the open declaration of war in May 1756.

The news that the French King was determined to send large reinforcements to Canada — which would more than counterbalance the sending of the two Irish regiments that had been ordered to America by reason of the earlier concentration of French regulars upon the borders of the British colonies — brought the British ministry face to face with a dilemma of the utmost gravity. Should these reinforcements be permitted to reach the New World? If so, then all the well-laid plans to vindicate British-American claims in North America would be likely to come to naught. If not, then there loomed the possibility of another great European war; nay, even the utmost probability that it would break out should the convoy that carried these troops be attacked by the royal navy in European waters. Newcastle, therefore, hurriedly summoned a committee of the Cabinet Council on January 21 to discuss the problem. At this meeting there appeared Lord Chancellor Hardwicke, Lord President Granville, Secretary of State for the Northern Department Holderness, Secretary of State for the Southern Department Robinson, First Lord of the Admiralty Anson and Lieutenant General of the Ordnance Ligonier. What decisions were reached may only be surmised. It is clear that the opinion prevailed that should large French reinforcements be actually sent out in the spring, these should be waylaid by the navy — but, significantly, in American waters. Immediately feverish preparations were entered into to prepare the navy, hitherto on a peace-time footing, for active service.[9]

That there were still some doubts as to the proper course for the British government to follow is indicated by certain notations that Newcastle made preparatory to the meeting of the Cabinet Council committee on March 18. This was held after the final rejection of a proposal for a suspension of arms in North America for a period of two years that the French had proposed,[10] during which period the

---

[9] J. S. Corbett, *England and the Seven Years' War*, I, 36, 40.
[10] B.M., Add. Mss., 32,850: 185.

status quo would be observed along the disputed frontiers, with France in possession of the areas under dispute. The Newcastle memorandum envisioned the likelihood of war on a large scale, with not only Hanover and Flanders invaded by French armies, but even Great Britain; the means to thwart at least some of the designs were also suggested. It reads as follows:

> "Invasion here, Hanover, Flanders. The French will bring war into Europe. The orders to be given to our fleet. To get to sea as soon as possible. Query. Whether to intercept ships and land forces going to North America? To send a squadron to block up Brest. Query. Order to General Braddock to attack Montreal and Quebec. Query. Order to Shirley and Lawrence about Nova Scotia." [11]

After considering the general situation, the Council contented itself with the determination to send a powerful fleet to take post at Tor Bay on the Devon coast — later changed to Plymouth — which from this station would be in position to watch the maritime movements of the French. It was also agreed that should the admiral of this fleet receive intelligence that a number of French ships were sailing to North America, he was to detach a squadron sufficiently strong either to prevent them from landing troops there or even to destroy the hostile fleet in the western waters, depending upon circumstances. It was doubtless felt that either measure, serious as it would be, especially the latter, would still, in view of France's own extreme aggressiveness in the New World, fall short of a proper provocation for a general war, which, however, a blockade of Brest or an attempt to strike at either Quebec or Montreal would surely occasion.

On March 24 Parliament met and the King in a speech from the throne called upon that body to appropriate funds to augment both the land and the sea forces.[12] This was done without delay. On the same day another meeting of the committee of the Cabinet Council took place.[13] At this it was decided that seven ships of the line should be sent to America to cruise off Cape Breton Island for the purpose of "intercepting" the French convoy, which, according to information now received, would sail some time in April. This decision was now referred to a meeting of all the leading ministers, who gathered

---

[11] Corbett, *op. cit.*, p. 42.
[12] *The Parliamentary History of England* (ed. T. C. Hansard), XV, 517–18.
[13] B.M., Add. Mss., 32,996: 57–8.

at Newcastle House on April 10,[14] at which it was agreed that the squadron should

> "cruise off Louisbourg, with instructions to fall upon any French ships of war that shall be attempting to land troops in Nova Scotia or to go to Cape Breton, or through the St. Lawrence to Quebec." [15]

Soon afterward the Honourable Edward Boscawen, Vice Admiral of the Blue, was appointed to this command, and on April 22 all the Lords Justices but two who had been designated by King George to carry on affairs during his prospective absence in Hanover confirmed a decision of the committee of the Cabinet Council to send the admiral immediately to America with eleven rather than seven ships of the line and one fifty-gun frigate.[16] On the 27th he sailed with orders in harmony with the decisions that had been reached; the following day the King set out for Hanover to rebuild his diplomatic fences, to be followed on the 29th by the Earl of Holderness, Secretary of State for the Northern Department. The die had been cast.[17]

When Braddock's regiments, as well as other troops from the British Isles, were sent to the New World to participate in the Great War for the Empire, they were carried, it may be noted, in regular transport ships convoyed by warships. This was logical and proper — that is, for the British with their superior sea power. But the French ministry was now gambling, and for very high stakes, and undoubtedly realized well that at this critical juncture of affairs there were enormous risks involved in sending an army across the Atlantic in a fleet of slow-sailing transports; for it could be unaware neither of British naval supremacy nor of the rising British determination to put a stop to the series of *faits accomplis* that had characterized the past five years of French activity in North America. Here doubtless is the key to the truly amazing game of hazard in which it now engaged. For it determined that in order to increase the chance of the arrival in Canada of the desperately needed troops and supplies, the risk should be run of losing as many as fourteen of the best fighting ships in the

---

[14] B.M., Add. Mss., 32,996: 73–4. At the meeting on March 24 all those who had met on January 21 were present except Sir John Ligonier. On April 10 the meeting was attended by thirteen ministers, or the full Cabinet Council.

[15] *Ibid.*

[16] B.M., Add. Mss., 32,996: 89–90.

[17] Aff. Étrang., Corres. Pol., Ang., 439: 24–6.

already dangerously weak French navy.[18] More specifically, it was determined to remove the heavy batteries from eleven of these ships so that room could be made for the accommodation aboard them of soldiers and munitions. These could thereupon be escorted by the remaining fully armed battleships (*armés en guerre*): the *Entreprenant*, the flagship, Rear Admiral Dubois de la Motte (Mothe), carrying 74 cannon; the *Bizarre*, Rear Admiral de Salvert; and the *Alcide*, Captain Hocquart,[19] both of the latter ships carrying 64 cannon. These were to be accompanied by certain smaller craft.[20] Such was the plan.

In justice to the ministry, it may be said that no better-constructed, better-balanced, better-armed, fleeter, or more easily manœuvred ships existed in the world than the fourteen selected out of the Brest fleet for this tremendously important but dangerous mission.[21] Moreover, it may be affirmed that the ships were each in command of men who showed themselves, when put to the test, alert, resourceful, and in general possessing all those qualities of competence and loyalty that would do honour to any navy. In fact the chief elements of inferiority of the French ships stripped for action when pitted against English ships of the same fire-power was that the latter carried a much larger complement of men, a factor that frequently could determine the outcome of an engagement that was long drawn out or that involved grappling and hand-to-hand fighting.[22] The

---

[18] William Mildmay, a British member of the Anglo-French commission and still in Paris, sent information to England on April 23 that nine ships of the line and eight other ships of the same character "on which for want of cannon on their lower tier they embark their troops and ammunition" had sailed for Louisbourg. According to him, these troops upon arriving there, should war be declared, would be used to attack and take over the new English settlements in Acadia; otherwise they would proceed up the St. Lawrence to reinforce the widely scattered French garrisons ("Private Correspondence," Mildmay Papers, Clements Library).

[19] Arch. Nat., Marine, B⁴68, folios 116–20.

[20] *Ibid.*

[21] For a discussion of French naval architecture see Charnock, *History of Marine Architecture*, III, 158 et seq.; Corbett, op. cit., II, 366–71; and H. W. Hodges, *Select Naval Documents*, p. 122. It should be added, however, and this is a point of great significance, that the English great sails were, according to the testimony of one of the French captains, lighter and the small sails larger than those of the French vessels, which gave the former an advantage in a moderate breeze (Captain Hocquart's "Relation," 1755, Arch. Nat., Marine, B⁴68, folio 158).

[22] The captain of the *Illustre*, Captain Choiseul-Praslin, in writing to the Minister of the Marine on September 21, 1755, declared that he had a crew of but 420 for his sixty-four-gun ship whereas a British ship of fifty guns would have as many as 450 (Arch. Nat., Marine, B⁴68, folio 188).

British sailors were also, as a rule, superior to the French in gunnery and seamanship.[23] It was perhaps these factors, or the natural prestige of the British navy, with a great record of victories already to its credit over the French as well as the Spaniards and the Dutch, or the fact that the French navy was so seldom in a position to move out against the British and give battle and so frequently compelled for the best strategical reasons to avoid combat and flee to the shelter of harbours, or, what is more likely, all of these as well as other factors combined, that unfortunately produced among many of the brave men who helped to man the French navy in 1755 a certain lack of morale; for some of these men seem to have lacked faith in their own ships, in spite of the many outstanding qualities possessed by them.[24]

The ministers, nevertheless, undoubtedly calculated that although this squadron to be sent to America could not be expected to fight one of equal size that Britain might and probably would send against it, at least it would have a very good chance to outmanœuvre and outsail the enemy ships, provided the latter were not given the opportunity to move out in advance to take positions across its pathway. They further calculated, it would seem, that once the fleet had moved west of the "line of amity" — in this case into North American waters in the region of the Banks, where anything might happen in time of peace — it would enjoy the protection of the fogs in seeking to elude the "enemy." Nevertheless, to ensure the utmost safety to these precious ships and even more precious military reinforcements while still in European waters, they determined to give it the protection of a convoying fleet under command of M. de Macnémara, who carried the title of *Lieutenant Général d'Armée Navalle*. This fleet was to accompany it until it could proceed on its way with fair confidence that it would not be attacked by any fleet based on the British Isles.[25]

The French expedition did not get under way as soon as had been planned or anticipated. That it would be permitted to cross the At-

---

[23] Mr. Clerk of Elden in his classical *Essay on Naval Tactics* (1804) stressed the record of this superiority.

[24] Arch. Nat., Marine, B⁴68, folio 223.

[25] How well the British were kept informed of French plans by their secret service is indicated by a letter written on May 10 from Paris which states: "Mr. Macnamara, who commands the whole Fleet, is to escort the Transports and some Frigates, as far as the Azores & then return; the Transports & Frigates to make Their way to Canada (B.M., Add. Mss., 32,855: 153).

lantic without challenge, if it delayed its departure too long, now seemed very unlikely in view of the British naval preparations. In orders issued on April 10 to the two commanding officers, M. de Mac-némara and the Comte Dubois de la Motte, they were warned that if the English should attack, it would be for the purpose of preventing the movement of troops to Canada and of weakening the navy.[26] They were also warned that they must not give the English time to reassemble their naval forces before leaving for Canada and, further, that once having set sail, they were to use every means to avoid an engagement without at the same time dishonouring the flag.

The date of departure of the French fleet had been fixed for the 15th of April. Had it sailed at this time the British fleet could not, under given circumstances, have preceded it into American waters. Its failure to lift anchor on schedule cannot, however, be charged to the negligence or incompetence of its personnel. Apparently realizing all that was at stake for France's North American possessions and also for her navy, those responsible for the preparations for departure had placed the six battalions and the munitions on board well in advance [27] and were ready to leave at the appointed time, but unhappily — according to the Chevalier de Lorgeril, captain of the *Lys*, who had reason to lament when he wrote — strong adverse winds were blowing on that day and they continued for seventeen days. It was not until early on May 3 that the wind shifted, giving the fleet its spread from the northeast.[28] Then it was that out of Brest moved the two squadrons in three columns; the largest, of fourteen ships of the line and four frigates,[29] to cross the Atlantic, the other, of nine, to escort the former beyond European waters and then to turn back. As the great flotilla moved out into the Atlantic and headed southwest, two English frigates cruising off the island of Ushant, to the west of Brest, started to follow it and continued until they finally disappeared on the 7th.[30] Since everything was going along smoothly

---

26 Arch. Nat., Col., B. 102: 135–6.

27 It may be pointed out that on each of nine of the ten converted ships (*armés en flûte*) eight companies of troops were placed; on one other, reserved as a hospital ship, only two companies were placed, with the same number on two of the three fully armed ships (*armés en guerre*). The flagship alone was not used to transport troops (de la Motte's Ship Papers, Arch. Nat., Marine, B⁴68, folio 122).

28 Arch. Nat., Marine, B⁴68, folio 266.

29 Arch. Nat., Marine, B⁴68, folio 122.

30 Captain Faulker in the *Lyme* with a small squadron followed the French from Ushant well out into the Atlantic and kept company until the night of the 7th of May (B.M., Add. Mss., 32,855: 39).

enough and the frigates had given up the trail, du Bois de la Motte gave Macnémara the signal that he now felt safe [31] and on the 8th the two fleets separated.[32] Macnémara turned back now to enter the port of Lisbon while de la Motte headed west-northwest for the Grand Bank. Arriving near it on the 25th of the month the admiral ordered a rendezvous of the vessels and, having opened his own sealed orders, gave in turn sealed orders to each captain respecting his destination, to be opened only in case of separation from the rest of the fleet.[33] Further, Rear Admiral de Salvert of the *Bizarre*, one of France's best fighting ships, was now ordered to convoy into the port of Louisbourg five of the other ships, on which were two full battalions of French troops.[34] The favourable weather that up to then had accompanied the squadron now deserted it. Great winds and fogs scattered the ships; they were also now in the presence of ice-floes and icebergs "of enormous size and height." On the 29th the weather cleared up somewhat and de la Motte, having arrived within some few leagues of Cape Race and having ordered his ships to rally, managed to bring together thirteen out of the nineteen, which now proceeded to sail in three columns. But again the fog returned and the vessels had to battle an adverse wind from the southwest. In addition they became hopelessly scattered in spite of signals.[35]

On June 6 de la Motte, now in the deep waters between the Grand Bank and the Green Bank lying westward, got his first positive intimation of the presence of Boscawen. His flagship, the *Entreprenant*,

---

[31] According to orders given to both de la Motte and Macnémara, the latter was not to return with his fleet until the former judged he was beyond the regions where he might be attacked by enemy forces superior to his own (Arch. Nat., Marine, B⁴68, folio 125). Macnémara was by separate sealed instructions ordered to cruise from August 15 to September 7 in the latitude of Cape Ortegal, Spain, and some forty leagues to the west of that promontory, in order to establish a rendezvous with de la Motte on his return. During this cruising period he was permitted to enter the ports of Lisbon and Cadiz for fresh water and at the end of it, should neither de la Motte's fleet from Canada nor de Salvert's from Louisbourg put in an appearance, he was to make his return to France (Arch. Nat., Col., B. 102: 154–7).

[32] According to Captain Lorgeril the point of separation was at 44° north latitude and 16° 12′ west latitude, Paris meridian (Arch. Nat., Marine, B⁴68, folio 266); according to de la Motte, it was 82 leagues west-northwest [L'O. 1/4. N. O.] of Cape Finisterre (*ibid.*, folio 126).

[33] *Ibid.* For the general instructions to de la Motte see Arch. Nat., Col., B. 102: 139–41; see also *ibid.*, 102: 154–7.

[34] *Ibid.* See also Vaudreuil's "Journal," *N. Y. Col. Doc.*, X, 297–8. The new Governor General was on board the flagship, and this "Journal" covers the voyage.

[35] Arch. Nat., Marine, B⁴68, folios 127, 157, 176, 266.

accompanied by but three vessels — the *Bizarre,* the *Deffenseur* and the *Actif* — on that day noticed with the clearing of the fog the sails of ten ships at a distance. Thinking they might be the scattered ships, though they did not respond to his signal, the admiral advanced a league in their direction in order to recognize them more effectively. It was at last quite evident that they were English warships, which remained up to that moment unaware of the presence of their quarry. Although the wind was unfavourable for the British to approach before the fog enveloped everything again, the signals from the cannon of Boscawen's ships seemed to leave no doubt of their desire to manœuvre in the direction of the French. De la Motte therefore by sound of voice instructed the remnants of his squadron to keep very close to him while the four withdrew eight leagues to the eastward and to temporary safety. Writing of this incident, the rear admiral later declared that it was a most fortunate circumstance that the fleet was at this critical moment widely scattered.[36] Indeed, had the fog not providentially dispersed de la Motte's squadron and intervened to aid his own withdrawal from a position of the utmost danger, the pride of the French navy might that June day have been obliged to lower their flags before an enemy vastly superior in terms of armament. The course of military operations during the next two years in North America might also have unfolded a very different story. It may be added that had but the four vessels to which reference has been made been captured, these would have netted the British not only sixteen of the veteran French companies and four superb vessels, but also Vaudreuil, Governor General of New France, and General Baron Dieskau, who were both on board the *Entreprenant,* besides a certain French officer on the *Bizarre* who carried the name Montcalm de Saint-Véran. Within a year this officer was to show himself in strategical moves in North America to be a military genius of the first order, and in fact was to become the chief instrumentality of the series of extraordinary reverses inflicted upon the British and their colonials by the French regulars, spearheaded by the battalions now on their way to Canada.

Turning now to Vice Admiral Boscawen, it should be pointed out that by his secret instructions [37] he had been expected to establish a rendezvous at some place in the neighbourhood of Louisbourg to be agreed upon after consultation with the most experienced officers

---

[36] Arch. Nat., Marine, B⁴68, folio 128.

[37] For these see C.O. 5:211, pp. 385–402.

of his fleet. To support his enterprise, he had also been given the command of Commodore Keppel's squadron, already in American waters. After having arrived in the New World, he had been ordered to cruise in a manner most likely to meet with the French fleet and had been instructed in the following explicit terms:

> "And in Case you should meet with any French Ships of War, or other Ships, having Troops, or Warlike Stores on board, you shall use your best Endeavours to seize & secure the same; And in Case any opposition shall be made to your so doing, you will use the Means in your Power to take and destroy them. . . ." [38]

Sailing from Portsmouth on April 21, four days later he had moored in Plymouth Sound and had taken on board a detachment of Colonel Yorke's regiment, and thereupon on the 27th, as previously indicated, he had started across the Atlantic with eleven ships of the line and two frigates and with a total complement of about fifty-four hundred men, including seamen, soldiers, and supernumeraries. [39]

After Boscawen's departure the British Cabinet Council anxiously awaited news of the sailing of the French fleet. On May 8 the first intelligence had reached London, sent by the commander of one of the frigates detached to watch the movement of ships out of Brest. It had carried the news that nineteen ships of the line and six frigates had left that port. [40] Were these all destined for Canada? If so, it was realized that Boscawen would face serious obstacles in attempting to execute his orders. It was therefore determined to reinforce him with six additional ships of the line and a frigate all under command of Rear Admiral Holburne. [41] However, before the departure of the latter on May 11, he had been instructed that should he secure knowledge that Macnémara had returned into European waters from escorting de la Motte, he also should return. [42] Boscawen, it was felt, would under these circumstances be in a most favourable position to deal with the French squadron. It was calculated by Anson that he must have had a start over the Frenchmen equal to a hun-

---

[38] C.O. 5:211, pp. 390–1.

[39] "Abstract of the State and Condition of His Majesty's Squadron . . . May 4, 1755," P.R.O., Admiralty, In-Letters, 481.

[40] According to this, eight of the ships of the line and one fifty-gun ship were fully armed (en guerre) and ten ships of the line were partially armed (en flûte). (Newcastle to Holderness, May 9, 1755, B.M., Add. Mss., 32,854: 459.)

[41] B.M., Add. Mss., 32,854: 415.

[42] The "Secret Instructions" and "Most Secret Instructions" to Holburne are to be found in B.M., Add. Mss., 32,854: 417 and 419.

dred leagues, by which advantage he would be able to collect his scattered ships and

> "consequently be able to pick up, & attack, the French squadron, before they can get together at their suppos'd Rendezvous at Louisbourg." [43]

To Newcastle it therefore seemed that "these Transports must fall an immediate sacrifice to the King's fleet in America." [44]

Boscawen had made the crossing of the Atlantic without incident. During the passage at one point he had come upon a French fishing ship from the Banks, but could secure no information from it with respect to the presence of the French fleet, which, it is clear, had sailed from Brest some days after his departure from Plymouth. Touching the eastern shore of Newfoundland, he had then moved down to Cape Race, the southeastern tip of the island, off which he had proceeded to cruise. On June 6 he had been sighted by de la Motte, as has been indicated, although no one in his fleet seems to have observed the four French ships because of lack of alertness or because of atmospheric conditions. It was not until the 7th that the British got the first intimation of the presence of the enemy fleet. On that day Captain Howe reported that an English Banker had informed him that he had seen a large French warship loaded with soldiers.[45]

But if the Frenchmen were not visible to the British, the latter were to the commander of the *Alcide,* a sixty-four-gun ship that, in company with the *Lys* and the *Dauphin Royal,* was sailing west-northwest in the region of Cape Race, with the island of Saint-Pierre lying some leagues to the northwest. For Captain Hocquart that same day, about six o'clock in the evening, detected five or six leagues to the leeward the masts of eleven ships.[46] After lying becalmed during the night, early the next morning he noted that the ships were only three leagues away — now to the south instead of to the east-northeast — and when he signalled to them and they could not respond, he knew that they were British warships, which now at last perceiving the enemy gave chase with a full spread of canvas and a favouring wind. The three French ships in turn fled toward the

---

[43] J. S. Corbett, *op. cit.,* p. 47.

[44] *Ibid.*

[45] Boscawen to the Admiralty, June 22, 1755, P.R.O., Admiralty, In-Letters, 481; C.O. 5:46.

[46] Arch. Nat., Marine, B⁴68, folios 156–7, 266.

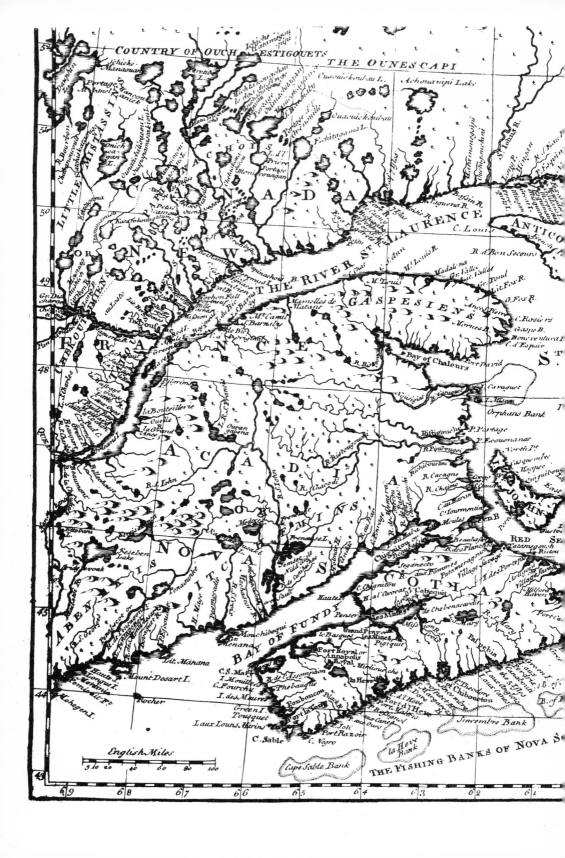

(From Bowen's *A Complete Atlas*, 1762.)

northwest, the *Lys* in advance of and to the leeward of the *Alcide,* and the *Dauphin Royal* in advance of and to the leeward of the *Lys.* Thus this bright morning of the 8th — after days of storm and fog and icebergs almost invisible to the pilots — the French were now fleeing for their lives.

The *Dunkirk,* of sixty guns, one of the fastest of the British ships of the line [47] followed by the flagship, the *Torbay,* and two other ships of the line — began drawing close to the rear French ship, the *Alcide,* whose commander had determined to cover the escape of the other two vessels. [48]

Hocquart's decision was wise. For his own vessel — not employed as a transport and therefore with all his broadside intact — was prepared for action; whereas the *Lys* was burdened with eight companies of regulars and the *Dauphin Royal* with nine, and both were consequently only armed *en flûte* — that is, with only a portion of their guns available for use — the *Lys* with only twenty-two out of sixty-four; the *Dauphin Royal* with only twenty-four out of seventy-four. Between ten and eleven o'clock the chase was so close that the *Alcide* could have fired her four rear cannon to effect had her captain dared to attack. But Hocquart was determined not to begin the fight. By eleven o'clock, with the sea now smooth as a mirror, the *Dunkirk* was cutting athwart the path of the *Alcide* and soon loomed at half pistol-shot. But still Hocquart refused to open fire and also refused to come to. In justifying himself, he wrote that although he could not doubt that he was to be attacked he felt impelled to let the enemy take the initiative since war had not been declared in Europe before his departure. [49] According to his statement, however, he called to the English vessel:

"Are we at peace or at war? "

And at length received the mocking reply from Captain Richard Howe of the *Dunkirk:*

[47] The great speed of the *Dunkirk* is emphasized by Admiral Holburne in a letter without date later written from his station off Louisbourg to Boscawen (P. R. O., Admiralty, In-Letters, 481): "I have thought it right as the *Dunkirk* sails so much better to lett Captn How make the best of his way to you," he wrote. Again, in describing his effort to overtake three French warships, he notes that these "greatly outsaild us, except the *Dunkirk* . . ." (ibid.).

[48] The commander of the *Alcide* explains why the *Dunkirk* was able to overtake him. He notes that there was a gentle breeze from the south, which gave the English ship a great advantage with its lighter and larger sails (Arch. Nat., Marine, B⁴68, folios 158–9).

[49] "*Relation de ce qui s'est passé à la prise de l'Alcide* . . ." Arch. Nat., Marine, B⁴68, folios 158–9.

"At peace, at peace!" [50]

Hocquart was also informed that Boscawen, with whom he was acquainted, commanded the British fleet. But from the *Torbay's* topmast was flying the red pennant — the signal to Howe to begin firing — and the *Dunkirk* immediately delivered her full broadside of chain shot, bar shot, and mitraille of all sorts and a burst of musketry, all with devastating effect, to which the *Alcide* replied.[51] However, with her rigging raked, her masts about to fall, many of her cannon dismounted, and a hundred of her crew killed or wounded by the intensity of the *Dunkirk's* close-range fire, the *Alcide*, after an engagement lasting not much more than a quarter of an hour, now surrounded by hostile ships, was unable to carry on, and her commander surrendered. And thus the maritime war between Britain and France began. This engagement was characterized by Captain Lorgeril of the *Lys* in the following words:

"Behold! a very singular kind of peace, or rather a war declared in a very singular manner." [52]

As for the *Lys*, sailing somewhat ahead and to the leeward of the *Alcide*, she was, in the midst of the combat just described, pursued by the *Defiance* and two other ships. The armament of this once powerful ship, now *armée en flûte*, consisted of but two twenty-four-pounders, ten twelves, and twelve tens. Captain Lorgeril now ordered the two twenty-fours and two of the twelves to be dragged to the stern of the vessel ready to fire upon his adversaries as soon as they might come within range. The weather remained calm, the breeze gentle; and just as the *Alcide* under these conditions had been outsailed by the *Dunkirk*, so the *Lys* found the interval closing, but very slowly, between herself and the *Defiance*.[53] About two

[50] *Ibid.* Thomas Pichon, who became a French traitor, in his *Lettres et Mémoires sur Cap Breton* (p. 248) speaks scornfully of Hocquart's attitude. He declared that the English took the position that when Howe declared that the two nations were at peace, he attached the same meaning that the French themselves had given to this expression in America: "A lie that deceives no one is not a lie, according to many of our French casuists. Mr. Hocquart should not have believed in this banter given in form of reprisal but should have paid attention to the red streamer flying from the topmast of the flagship — supposing that he was disposed to ignore the possibilities of reciprocal hostilities."

[51] Arch. Nat., Marine, B⁴68, folios 159–60, 266; see also Arch. Nat., Mém. et Doc., Amérique, 10. I: 152–5; Corres. Pol., Angleterre, 439: 557–8; and likewise Arch. Nat., Col., K. 1,351.

[52] Arch. Nat., Marine, B⁴68, folio 267.

[53] The *Lys* was considered to be a very speedy vessel in a good breeze (Arch. Nat., Marine B⁴68, folio 223).

o'clock in the afternoon, with the latter now within range, Lorgeril gave the order to open fire. This running fight continued until between five and six o'clock, when the *Defiance*, at last in position to cut athwart the stern of the *Lys* at two musket-shots' distance, now brought her broadside into play without the latter being able to reply. It is true that the guns were hurried from the stern and placed in the battery, but without effect. The *Defiance* — carefully avoiding the hull — concentrated her deadly fire against the masts and rigging of the French ship so effectively as to deprive her of the ability to manœuvre. At this juncture the second British ship appeared, the *Fougueux*,[54] of sixty-four cannon, and opened fire, and the third also began drawing close. Lorgeril was in a hopeless position. Had the British ships come within range of musketry fire the French regulars who crowded the deck of the *Lys* could have been used to some effect; but they did not. With her sails drooping, as it were in sign of mourning (*"toutes nos voiles en pantène"*); with no hope of rescue by the returning of the fog, the King's flag was at last lowered at half past six of that memorable day.[55]

The *Dauphin Royal* at the beginning of the chase was sailing, as has been stated, in front and to the leeward of the *Lys*. With the exception of the *Deffenseur* she was perhaps the fleetest of the great ships of the French navy.[56] On that day her speed stood her in good stead; Captain de Montalais unreefed every inch of her sails as she fled with the wind. In vain one of the ships following hard after the *Lys* moved off in pursuit of her, but finding that it could not gain upon her, gave up the chase. As a result, on June 11, with the enemy now far removed, she sailed, in accordance with her orders, into the harbour of Louisbourg.[57]

On June 8, therefore, two out of the three French ships encountered by Boscawen fell into his grasp. On that same day the *Entre-*

---

[54] The *Fougueux* (that is, the *Impetuous*) was a French-built ship captured by the English in the late war (Arch. Nat., Marine, B⁴68, folio 267).

[55] *Ibid.* The news that reached France late in July was that the *Alcide* had been taken, but that the *Lys* and *Dauphin Royal* "both got away" (secret advices from France, July 26, 1755, B.M., Add. Mss., 32,858: 53).

[56] According to Boscawen the *Dauphin Royal* was called by the French "the best Saylor in France" (C.O. 5:46). Rear Admiral Periet de Salvert of the *Bizarre*, however, had a chance in the fall of 1755 to test the speed of his ship with that of the *Dauphin Royal* and the *Deffenseur*. He found the last-named vessel even speedier than the *Dauphin Royal* (Arch. Nat., Marine, B⁴68, folio 230).

[57] Captain de Montalais to the Minister, June 12, 1755, Arch. Nat., Marine, B⁴68, folios 273–5.

prenant, the *Bizarre*, the *Deffenseur*, and the *Actif* were to the east of him in the vicinity of Cape Race and the island of Saint-Pierre and still in great danger.[58] At eight o'clock in the evening the commander of the *Bizarre*, Rear Admiral de Salvert, who had been ordered to conduct a portion of the fleet into Louisbourg harbour, notified de la Motte that he would leave him early the next day and head westward for his destination; the *Deffenseur* was to accompany him. But in the midst of fog and a violent wind the vessels were separated. The *Bizarre* proceeded on its way, certainly passing in the neighbour-hood of the British fleet without detection, and on June 12 entered Louisbourg harbour, where de Salvert found, to his joy, not only the *Dauphin Royal* riding at anchor, but the *Espérance*, the *Aquilon*, and the frigate *Comette*, none of which he had seen since May 31; the following day the *Deffenseur* also appeared. As a result, he was able to report the safe arrival of all the vessels destined for this port, and also of the two battalions, those of Artois and of Bourgogne, which he declared were in as good condition as they would have been if moved from garrison on land.[59]

As for Rear Admiral de la Motte, on the 9th he found that his ship was now quite alone as the result of the great storm the preceding night. Avoiding the dangers that lurked about Saint-Pierre, he moved southwest and then northwest; on that day a vessel was seen at a distance, but was soon lost from view; on the 11th, with the weather clear and beautiful, the pilot of the *Entreprenant*, reconnoitring the land that appeared in the distance, discovered at six o'clock in the evening that it was the isle of St. Paul, north of Cape Breton. The flagship was therefore now at the entrance of the Gulf of St. Lawrence and out of danger. By noon of the 13th she was off the Gaspé Peninsula and the following day met the frigate *Sirenne*, which reported the arrival in this region of the *Algonkin*, the *Opiniâtre*, the *Illustre*, and the *Léopard*.[60] The first two named, having made the signals off Cape Rosier agreed upon and having received no reply from the frigate *Fidelle* — which, according to de la Motte's instructions,[61] was to have brought to the cape experienced pilots from Quebec to assist the fleet up the St. Lawrence — entered Gaspé Bay on the 11th and, not finding the frigate, secured pilots from the fish-

---

[58] Arch. Nat., Marine, B⁴68, folios 128, 221.
[59] *Ibid.*
[60] Arch. Nat., Marine, B⁴68, folio 128.
[61] Arch. Nat., Col., B. 102, 139–41.

ing vessels there and left to go up the river. The two other vessels, also in search of pilots, were still in the bay when de la Motte appeared off the peninsula. He thereupon ordered the *Sirenne* to enter the bay with orders to the two captains to leave it immediately and join him, for any moment they might otherwise find their escape blocked by the British. That same day the *Apollon* joined the admiral, who, without waiting for the two ships to unite with him, moved up the gulf and into the mouth of the river, arriving at the island of Bic, another rendezvous provided for in the instructions, on the 17th. There he found the frigate *Dianne* and his two store-ships and also two bateaux full of experienced pilots for the river navigation who had arrived from Quebec, and there also he learned that the *Algonkin* and the *Opiniâtre* were already proceeding up the river. Joined by the *Illustre* and the *Léopard* the following day, on the 19th de la Motte ordered the remainder of the squadron to move up the St. Lawrence. All but the *Entreprenant* passed the great whirlpool and other obstructions to reach the capital of New France; but de la Motte, always cautious, would not risk his great ship and remained moored to an island just below the whirlpool — the Isle aux Coudres — until he later dropped down to Bic, where there was safer anchorage.[62] Thus the squadron destined for Quebec, with the exception of the *Alcide* and the *Lys*, arrived intact. Boscawen, therefore, failed in his assignment. Of the seventy-eight companies of regulars that he sought to lay his hands on, only ten were secured by the capture of the *Lys* and the *Alcide*.

It would appear that most of the French vessels bound for the St. Lawrence followed the traditional and well-defined route of the deep waters between the Grand Bank and the Green Bank, and then moved into Cabot's Strait. It is clear, however, that the *Illustre*, fearing the danger of capture after it had been separated from the *Léopard* and the *Sirenne* on June 3, hugged the southern shore of Newfoundland. Captain Choiseul-Praslin came to the determination to

---

[62] Duquesne took the position that no ship of more than sixty-four guns should attempt to pass the whirlpool. The *Algonkin*, a seventy-four, was, however, permitted to ascend the river to Quebec in order to repair her bowsprit when Bigot represented that this could be done much better at Quebec (Arch. Nat., Marine, B⁴68, folio 130). De la Motte, by his instructions, was ordered to take all his vessels up to Quebec unless he should judge it would be running too much risk to attempt to ascend the river to this city with the largest ships. Under these circumstances he would provide anchorage for them at some convenient place (Arch. Nat., Col., B. 102: 139–40).

do this in face of the protests of his pilots. Creeping westward of Cape St. Mary, on the 6th he skirted the shores of Saint-Pierre; from there he continued to move along those of Newfoundland with the idea that the English, if they had the design of preventing the arrival of reinforcements in Canada, would be cruising about the Banks rather than in the dangerous waters close to the island.[63] On the 9th, upon taking his bearings, he found that he was only ten leagues to the east of Cape Ray. Still cautiously hugging the shore, always against the protests of his pilots, he now sailed into the gulf and headed for Cape Rosier.[64]

After the capture of the *Alcide* and the *Lys* on the 8th, Boscawen continued to search the waters between the Great and the Green Banks while moving in the direction of Cabot Strait. But "fogs and hard gales" hindered his movements, and the other French ships that he so eagerly sought were thus enabled to elude him. While on the 11th the master of a Massachusetts Bay schooner observed the British fleet "stretching after the French Squadron," [65] in fact three of his ships together with the two captured ships became quite separated from the rest of the fleet as he scoured the waters. It was not until over a week after the separation that four of the missing ships joined him — on the 18th. As for the *Lys*, loaded with French troops and with only one hundred British seamen on board, she quite lost touch with the other ships and therefore proceeded directly to Halifax.[66] One cannot refrain from suggesting that had the *Lys* fallen across the path of the *Entreprenant* and as a result been picked up by de la Motte while he was still to the south of Newfoundland, Boscawen would doubtless have hardly survived the criticism that would have found expression in Great Britain — great as it was in some quarters when the meagre results of his expedition became known.

On the 20th and the 21st the fleet was reinforced by that of Holburne, and the combined force now appeared at the entrance of the harbour of Louisbourg, where four large ships and two frigates were riding at anchor. But no orders existed that would permit an attack

---

[63] Arch. Nat., Marine, B⁴68, folio 180.

[64] The theory cautiously advanced by Corbett (*op. cit.*, I, 56–7) that de la Motte was able to save most of his squadron by moving east of Newfoundland and entering the gulf by way of the Strait of Belle Isle must of course be rejected. None of the ships entered the gulf by that route.

[65] C.O. 5:15, p. 655.

[66] P.R.O., Admiralty, In-Letters, 481.

upon this fortified place had Boscawen felt in a position to do so with hope of success. In fact, the crews of his own ships had become very sickly and he was therefore compelled to go to Halifax for them to recuperate, while Holburne was left to establish a none too effective blockade of Louisbourg and the entrance of the St. Lawrence.[67]

In considering the strategic move that Boscawen was ordered to carry out, no serious fault can be found with his effort to execute it. In cruising off Cape Race he was in position to move against the French fleet in case it should make for the Strait of Belle Isle to the northward or Cabot Strait to the west. All the odds seemed to favour the latter, not only because of the presence of Louisbourg — where it was thought the entire French fleet would anchor at least temporarily — but also because of the risks involved in the former. Nevertheless, instead of moving as far west as Cape Breton and Cabot Strait, Boscawen continued in his strategic position, searching the waters about the Grand Bank. De la Motte, passing over the Grand Bank, actually moved westward, as Boscawen surmised he would do.[68] Only very unfavourable weather conditions, therefore, prevented the English admiral, who was thoroughly on the alert, from achieving a larger measure of success than he did.[69] He, in fact, faithfully carried out his instructions that if he should meet with "any French Ships of War," after taking position in American waters in the region of Louisbourg, he was to attempt to seize them and, in case of resistance, to use the means that he possessed "to take and destroy Them."

The news of his ill success, nevertheless, had a disturbing effect upon the ministers. Writing to the Duke of Newcastle on July 14, Hardwicke declared:

> "What we have done is either too little or too much. The Disappointm[t] gives me great Concern. The Account is to me confus'd, but

---

[67] Boscawen to the Admiralty, June 22 and July 4, 1755, P.R.O., Admiralty, In-Letters, 481; Holburne to Robinson, June 28, 1755, C.O. 5:46.

[68] Vaudreuil's "Journal," N. Y. Col. Doc., X, 298.

[69] Corbett, one of the most eminent authorities on naval strategy, severely blames Boscawen for having "struck at a couple of ships without first making sure it was possible to attain the object of his mission with the rest" (op. cit., I, 59, passim). Taking all things into consideration, however, it would seem that had the admiral permitted all the ships to slip through his fingers because of his inability to strike them all at once, scattered as they actually were by the fog after May 31, he would have been seriously blamed for negligence. In striking for the three ships that he chased on June 8, he doubtless reasoned that these might be the vanguard of the main fleet, which would soon appear.

I understand by it that we have taken only two french Ships and that our Ships are very sickly & we talk of coming home." [70]

Newcastle, however, was prepared to accept the full consequences of the strategic move that had achieved so little in the way of favourable results and, on the other hand, had brought the undeclared war much closer to Europe.

It was now for the Lords Justices to come to a decision as to the next move that should be made; for in their hands, with the departure of the King to Hanover, rested full discretionary power. Preparatory to their meeting, the Duke, in writing to Holderness on July 15 showed great resoluteness of purpose. Supported by Hardwicke,[71] he had now come to the decision that it was more than ever necessary for Vice Admiral Hawke to challenge the enemy in European waters:

"That the French may see, that His Majesty is both able & determin'd to support What He has done." [72]

The orders to be issued, he felt, should be

"to attack any Number of Men of War, or Merchantmen; But that He should not begin Hostilities in Europe for the sake of a single Ship. The preventing the Juncture of the Toulon & Brest Squadrons, the taking M[or] Du Gray's squadron, or a Martinico Fleet of Merchantmen crowded with good Sailors are Objects. And the Protection of our own Trade, which may now be fallen upon, is a necessary Service." [73]

But the Lords Justices at their meeting, while reaching the decision to send Hawke out "with the greatest part of the Fleet," were apparently not prepared at the moment to take any such decisive step as Newcastle contemplated. As a result the vice admiral was directed "to sail forthwith to the Westward & lie off Torbay 'till further Orders." [74] It is quite clear that the Justices were waiting to see the nature of the French reaction to the capture of the *Alcide* and the *Lys*.

That France did not declare war immediately after the news of

---

[70] B.M., Add. Mss., 32,857: 91.

[71] Hardwicke had on July 14 raised the question as to "whether Hawke should not put to sea now" (*ibid.*).

[72] B.M., Add. Mss., 32,857: 109.

[73] *Ibid.*

[74] B.M., Add. Mss., 32,857: 182–3.

Boscawen's attack on her fleet was received is quite understandable. She was not ready for an all-out war nor, in view of her record of bad faith and hostile measures against her great rival in the New World since the Peace of Aix-la-Chapelle, could she reasonably expect that Great Britain would now retreat from her determination, which could no longer be disguised, to use force without limit if war were once declared and in doing so to employ every one of the great advantages that she indubitably enjoyed both on the high seas and in the New World in any sustained period of hostilities.[75]

But the story of the great French expedition for the purpose of bringing reinforcements to New France is not concluded. While the British fleet had failed to capture the French veteran companies and the great supplies that accompanied them — outside of those contained in the *Alcide* and the *Lys* — it now had from every appearance the flower of the French navy at its mercy. For of all these great ships but two were fully armed (*armés en guerre*) — the *Entreprenant*, flagship of de la Motte, resting in the St. Lawrence, and the *Bizarre*, under command of Rear Admiral Perier de Salvert, anchored at Louisbourg. The other warships (*armés en flûte*) were only protected, in one case, by the treacherous waters of the St. Lawrence and, in the other, by the great batteries of Louisbourg. It is clear that a sufficiently effective blockade of the entrance of the St. Lawrence and of Louisbourg could immobilize these ships. Boscawen thereupon proceeded to make the necessary tactical disposition of his forces to carry out the sound strategical principle that in naval warfare a fleet commander must seek either to destroy or to immobilize the ships of the enemy: if the first cannot be done unless at too great a cost or risk, the second must be attempted.

The British fleet was divided into three squadrons of eight, seven, and six vessels respectively.[76] One kept a rigid and constant patrol of the waters about Louisbourg, cruising from Cape Canso up to the island of Scatary; another patrolled Cabot Strait, ranging from Ingonish on Cape Breton to Cape Ray, Newfoundland, and ascended

---

[75] The people of London were apparently not at all dismayed by the course of events and were behind their government. "I hear, in general, the People of the City are very much pleased with what has pass'd in No. America," wrote Newcastle to Holderness on July 18, "And that the Vice Adm¹ Boscawen has not had all the Successes, He had Reason to expect, His Orders, however, appear now to have been Such, as they approve. They are extremely for action . . . and therefore will much approve the Sending out Vice Adm¹ Hawke. They wish mightly for the King's Return" (B.M., Add. Mss., 32,857: 185).

[76] Arch. Nat., Marine, B⁴68, folio 226.

into the gulf; the third was in position to relieve either of the other two — so essential at times — and to range about the area of the Great and Green Banks.[77] De la Motte, in writing to the Minister on September 21, 1755 from the lower St. Lawrence at Bic, declared that, from information he had received, fourteen British vessels were waiting for him when he attempted to leave the gulf; what is more, the Gaspé fishermen had reported a very great number of British warships were ranging in the region of Cape Rosier at the very entrance to the mouth of the St. Lawence.[78] As for the rear admiral, in addition to his flagship, the *Entreprenant*, he had under his charge, he declared, seven of the best vessels of the King, all without defence, which must be brought back to France at the earliest possible moment, both for the protection of the country and its commerce and to avoid the winter season in the river.[79] But before de la Motte departed from the river, Captain Frager L'Équille in the frigate *Dianne*, a dispatch vessel not attached to his squadron,[80] anticipated the daring step he would take in order to keep his ships out of the clutches of Boscawen and Holburne and return them safely to France. Leaving Quebec on August 5 with former Governor General Duquesne and dispatches on board, L'Équille, on the recommendation of de la Motte,[81] determined to do something that no commander of one of the King's ships had up to that time ever attempted — to traverse the perilous Strait of Belle Isle.[82] The *Dianne* therefore sailed to the north of Newfoundland, passing beyond the strait on August 19, and for eighty leagues thereafter was continuously surrounded by icebergs and ice-floes.

On August 23 de la Motte, still moored at Bic, gave orders to his ships to leave two at a time, one following the lead of the other. The *Algonkin* moved out on the morning of the 24th, followed the same

[77] *Ibid.* Later in the cruising season the three squadrons were reported patrolling the general area from Cape Breton south to Sable Island and east to Saint-Pierre (*ibid.*, folio 214).

[78] Arch. Nat., Marine, B⁴68, folio 140.

[79] *Ibid.*

[80] The *Dianne* left France for Louisbourg at the end of March and arrived on April 30; on May 11 she left for Quebec, arriving there on the 23rd; she carried the pilots for de la Motte's fleet down the river early in June and then returned up the river with the new Governor General, Vaudreuil, on board, who transferred from the *Entreprenant* (Arch. Nat., Marine, B⁴68, folio 218).

[81] Arch. Nat., Marine, B⁴68, folio 140.

[82] L'Équille, writing to the ministry in September, when referring to his passing through the Strait of Belle Isle says: "My vessel was the first of the King's ships to make the passage" (Arch. Nat., Marine, B⁴68, folio 215).

day by the *Opiniâtre;* early on the 25th the *Actif* left, followed by the *Léopard;* at four o'clock in the afternoon of the same day, after the two vessels were out of sight, the *Illustre,* the *Apollon,* and the *Entreprenant* moved down the river, separated by a proper interval for fear that in fog and contrary winds they might interfere with and run foul of one another. Leaving the mouth of the river, they sailed to the north of Anticosti, where they again united for a final conference. Each of the captains having received his orders, the vessels now separated with the understanding that each would move through the Strait of Belle Isle. Because of hard gales it was not until the night of September 1 that the *Entreprenant* entered the strait — the first of the squadron. The other ships proceeded to follow carefully the lead of the flagship, guided by lights on its stern and the mast, which were repeated by each vessel moving in column. Although the night was foggy, an experienced pilot, a M. Pélegrin, Lieutenant of the Port of Quebec, by the aid of charts, guided the great ship, which was also encouraged on its way by a favourable current. By eight o'clock the next morning de la Motte had brought his squadron through the strait.[83]

Beyond Belle Isle the fleet now moved through a field of enormous icebergs. When safely beyond these, four of the seven vessels separated by agreement with the admiral, each making for the coast of France, while two of them, the *Illustre* and the *Apollon,* were taken under convoy for the crossing by the *Entreprenant,* which lost touch, however, with the *Apollon.* On September 21 de la Motte arrived at Brest, having still in charge the *Illustre.* There he found the *Léopard,* and the same day the *Actif* appeared. He was also informed that three of his other vessels were moored near Belle-Ile-en-Mer farther down the coast. He had thus eluded the British and brought back his squadron, except for the *Alcide* and the *Lys.*[84]

---

[83] Arch. Nat., Marine, B⁴68, folio 141.

[84] According to information furnished on July 26, 1755 by the British secret service installed in France, a fleet of six ships of the line and three frigates under M. du Guay had been ordered "to stay so many days at Lisbon, then so many at Cadiz, & then to Cruise off Cape Finister so many Days to convoy the Transport Men of War of de la Motte's Fleet, expected home from Canada: and not meeting or falling in with them to return back without them: which it seems will be her fate since the Fleet is blocked up by the English Admirals" (B.M., Add. Mss., 32,858: 53). This is not far from the secret instruction furnished to Macnémara on May 25 (Arch. Nat., Col., B. 102: 154–7). De la Motte did not, of course, seek to gain contact with the latter, who, as he knew, had been ordered to return from the rendezvous agreed upon forty leagues west of Cape Ortegal if by September 5 he had not been joined by one of the squadrons sent to the New World.

But the French squadron of Rear Admiral de Salvert was still in Louisbourg when de la Motte moved with his own down the St. Lawrence and north of Anticosti and through the Strait of Belle-Isle — still immobilized by the constant patrol of the British blockading fleet.

> "For a long time I have been awaiting with impatience a favourable moment,"

wrote de Salvert on August 7.[85] But he was to see midsummer pass into fall before that favourable moment arrived for moving out of the harbour with any of his great ships.[86] During the early part of the summer the blockade of Louisbourg was only one of limited nature and objective, effective as it was. Until the beginning of August the fishing craft and most coasting trade moved in and out of the port almost without molestation. Ships that came from the West Indies were stopped and inspected and then permitted to make their way to Isle Royale. It may be added, however, that the captains of these small craft were warned by the British that they would not be permitted to pass if their ships were loaded with munitions of war or other military supplies or with troops.[87] But even small dispatch vessels were permitted to proceed by the British after the dispatches had been surrendered.[88]

As week after week passed by with no word that the Louisbourg squadron had sailed, the French Minister of the Marine became more and more anxious.[89] By September his attitude had become one of the greatest impatience. In spite of the fact that every movement of de Salvert at Louisbourg was more closely scrutinized than ever by Boscawen's ships, on August 31 he sent out the frigate *Comette* to make its way to France.[90] Sailing at night through the fog and manœuvring between two British squadrons, the frigate carried dispatches indicating that de Salvert himself in his flagship, the *Bizarre*, would

---

[85] Arch. Nat., Marine, B⁴68, folios 226–7.

[86] It is true that small ships that could creep along the coast were able to elude the British blockading fleet. De le Jonquière, commander of the frigate *Fidelle*, brought needed supplies to Louisbourg from Quebec and returned to Quebec during the summer, accompanied by a merchant ship which had on board most of the garrisons that had surrendered at Beauséjour and at Gaspereau. These ships followed the practice of sailing during a time of deep fog (*ibid.*).

[87] *Ibid.*

[88] *N. Y. Col. Doc.*, X, 315.

[89] See Machault's letter of September 5 to de Drucourt and Prévost, *ibid.*, X, 314–16.

[90] De Salvert to the Minister of the Marine, August 31, 1755, Arch. Nat., Marine, B⁴68, folio 228; also *ibid.*, folio 232.

plan to leave Louisbourg between the 15th and 20th of the following month in company with two of the great seventy-fours reduced to twenty-four cannon, the *Deffenseur* and the *Dauphin Royal;* and that the third seventy-four, the *Espérance,* and the frigate *Aquilon,* a forty reduced to twelve cannon to serve as a hospital ship would leave later.

It should be indicated that as the blockade of de Salvert's squadron at Louisbourg continued with ever greater vigilance, the more it assumed the proportions of a general blockade of the port. By the end of August many merchant ships coming from France to Isle Royale and Canada, as well as fishing ships and coastal craft, were taken and held by Boscawen.[91] Cabot Strait and the approaches to Louisbourg were constantly under his scrutiny. Nevertheless two small coastal craft managed to slip into Louisbourg on September 10 bringing news that de la Motte had left the New World with his squadron by way of the Strait of Belle Isle. In order to mislead the British into feeling that the squadron would remain in the harbour to the end of October, de Salvert ordered that final preparations should be made most quietly.

The month of September brought with it a period of bad weather and violent gales from the southeast. This compelled the British fleet for safety to hold itself at least ten leagues from the land; the vessels were also driven somewhat to the northward of Louisbourg. On September 16 the two British squadrons, each of nine ships, were observed by a Basque fishing vessel to be well north of Louisbourg — in fact, in the waters off the island of Scatari.[92] The next two days the wind blew so very violently as to indicate that the British squadron had been forced even farther north and to the east. Here at last was the moment for which de Salvert had prayed. Early on the 19th his three vessels therefore set sail.

Clearing the harbour before noon, they struck southward; then after some hours altered the direction so as to avoid treacherous Sable Island. Not until five o'clock the following morning, when more than twenty-one leagues to the southeast of Isle Royale, was there any evidence of enemy ships. Then five of them — a part of Holburne's squadron — loomed at a distance to the leeward and in front of them. In the words of de Salvert:

---

[91] Referring to the English fleet, de Salvert wrote in his letter of August 31 that it had taken many French merchantmen and had also attacked fishing and coastal vessels (*ibid.*).

[92] De Salvert's "Journal," Arch. Nat., Marine, B⁴68, folio 233.

"We were, one might say, all mixed together, when we discovered them." [93]

With great decision the course of the vessels was altered. As they already had a full spread of canvas, they succeeded in gaining at least a league, making a total of a league and a half, before the British vessels could unfurl. Again the sailing qualities of the French vessels were put to a supreme test, and the two seventy-fours showed the excellence of their design and construction: the *Deffenseur* drew ahead of the other two French ships as well as from the pursuing vessels; the *Dauphin Royal* also drew away, and de Montalais thereupon sent a message to de Salvert that he was separating. Until three in the afternoon the British ships doggedly held to the pursuit, the *Bizarre* compelling the enemy to take her waters [94] — a great advantage in the days of sailing ships. Apparently only the speedy *Dunkirk*, which had overtaken the *Alcide*, was at all able to press de Salvert.[95] But after ten hours of racing it was evident that the French ships were still beyond the British grasp, and Holburne gave the signal to cease the chase. Thus again, and in spite of almost superhuman efforts in carrying on a blockade of Louisbourg day and night, in fair and foul weather, and in patrolling the waters about the Banks, three of France's finest ships reached the mid-Atlantic and subsequent safety. On October 10 de Salvert was able to write to the Minister from the port of Brest giving the details of the escape.

Of the great ships that came to the New World under convoy, only the *Espérance* remained in the harbour of Louisbourg. She was the last of the seventy-fours that had been reduced to twenty-four canon. It was not until October 17, the day after the departure of the frigate *Aquilon* from the same port, that she moved out under cover of favourable weather conditions. There she sailed without incident until the 25th. On that day a sudden squall carried away her great sail and cut to shreds her main topsail and her mizzen-topgallant sail; [96] two days later her rudder bar was broken in another storm; and then on November 8 a third storm snapped her main-yard. As the state of the weather made it impossible to repair it, Captain Bouville was obliged

---

[93] *Ibid.*

[94] De Salvert to the Minister of the Marine, October 10, 1755, Arch. Nat., Marine, B⁴68, folio 230.

[95] *Ibid.* See also the letter of Holburne to Boscawen, without date, P.R.O., Admiralty, In-Letters, 481.

[96] Captain de Bouville to the Minister of the Marine, November 30, 1755, Arch. Nat., Marine, B⁴68, folio 285.

to depend upon his now defective main-top and main-topgallant sails. He was now between one hundred and one hundred and twenty leagues from France. Three days later in the morning he noticed a vessel some three leagues toward the northeast and then three other vessels a little farther distant. Upon signalling these ships he was made to realize that he had encountered a British squadron. Fleeing with all the sail he could spread, he directed his vessel toward the southeast, hoping to gain the coast of Spain.[97] Only after a race lasting six hours, at about four o'clock in the afternoon, was the nearest of the pursuing ships — the *Oxford*, a "seventy" ship of the line — at last in position to check the progress of the *Espérance*, handicapped as she was. The British ship, now within half cannon-shot distance, fired a warning shot and raised her flag; de Bouville responded; and the combat began. The *Espérance* had as a lower broadside only six eighteen-pounders and four eights loaded with bar-shot and grape-shot, but she was also supported by musketry fire, which became effective as the *Oxford* soon closed in to within half musketry-shot distance.

For an hour and a half the unequal running combat continued, with the *Espérance*, while tacking, still headed toward the distant Spanish coast; then her main-tack was cut and it was possible for Captain Stevens of the *Oxford* to manœuvre so as to plant his repeated broadsides most effectively. Later the other three British ships — including the *Buckingham*, the flagship of Rear Admiral Temple West, who commanded the squadron — appeared on the scene and joined in the fight. But de Bouville was unwilling to surrender even against such hopeless odds, and now in the moonlight the battle continued with unabated fury. Only at nine o'clock, after the *Espérance* was filling with water, with seventeen great holes smashed in her sides at or under the water-line, with her rigging cut to pieces, her decks piled with the bodies of her brave defenders, and 270 of her crew of 450 either dead or incapacitated from wounds, did he at length call to the Admiral — to whom alone he was determined to surrender — to cease firing. In his report he declared, not without pardonable pride, that for three hours, with but twenty-two guns he fought a seventy-gun ship.[98]

When the gallant Frenchman was brought to the deck of West's

---

[97] His position at the time was 18° west longitude, Paris meridian, and 47° 12′ north latitude — still far distant from Spain (*ibid.*).

[98] *Ibid.*

flagship and offered his sword to the latter, he returned it saying with a gallantry equal to that of de Bouville, that he did not know what it was to take the sword of a man so worthy to carry it and that the glory that the commander of the *Espérance* had acquired in the glorious defence that he had made ought in some fashion to console him.[99] As for the surrendered ship, stricken to death the superb vessel had made her last voyage and had fought her last fight. Since it was found to be impossible to bring her to port, the following day — after having removed from her all who were still alive — the torch was set and as she slowly settled beneath the waves her blazing timbers served as the funeral pyre for those men of France who had given their all for her glory and for the honour of her navy.[100]

Thus with the loss of three ships had been accomplished the task of bringing powerful aid to New France, for her defence and for French enterprises along her borders. While the true significance of the support thus received will be made clear in the chapters to follow, one may nevertheless, in bringing to conclusion the account of the hazardous undertaking, quote the measured statement rendered to Machault by de la Motte on his return to Brest:

> "I have the honour to represent to you, sir, that your enterprise of sending powerful support to Canada was dangerous and particularly so for those charged with its execution. But I myself now know that it was absolutely necessary to save the colony — about to be attacked on all sides by the English. Our arrival with troops, provisions, and munitions has without doubt disconcerted the enemy and has given all possible encouragement to the King's troops, to the inhabitants, and even to the Indians." [101]

---

[99] *Ibid.*, folio 287.

[100] *Ibid.* The report sent from London under date of November 18 and printed in the *Boston Weekly News-Letter*, under date of February 5, 1756 shows how defective news despatches can be. It reads as follows: "Yesterday in the afternoon came Advice that Captain Stevens in . . . the Oxford [of 70 Guns] fell in with the Esperance, a French Man-of-War of 74 Guns, which was going from Rochfort to Brest, and after a short Engagement took her, and sent her to Plymouth." It well may be that the London writer confused the capture of the ship-of-the-line *Espérance* with that of the packet boat *Espérance*, a *goelette* which carried despatches from Louisbourg to Bayonne arriving at the latter port late in July (Minister of the Marine to de Drucourt and Prevost, July 29, 1755, Archives des Colonies, B. 101, page 225). The *Pennsylvania Gazette* of February 12, 1756, gives a more accurate account of the engagement in its London despatch of November 20. It, however, stated that the *Espérance* was "quite in fighting Order, in thorough Repair" and that only twenty-six men on her were killed. Nevertheless, the latter account stresses the strong defence of the ship by de Bouville, who was later presented with two thousand crowns by King Louis for his valiant conduct (*ibid.*, April 22, 1756).

[101] Arch. Nat., Marine, B⁴68, folio 141.

CHAPTER VI

Niagara and Crown Point

THE DEATH OF Major General Braddock, the utter demoralization of his proud little army as the result of the crushing defeat of its vanguard and centre in the Battle of the Monongahela, and the success of the ministers of His Most Christian Majesty in getting badly needed reinforcements and supplies into New France in the spring of 1755 combined together to alter profoundly not only the whole plan of strategy of the British in North America but even the prospects of an early ejection of the French from most of those regions where they were considered by the British to be intruders and aggressors. What is more, now that hostilities on a fairly large scale had taken place along the western frontiers with the drawing into these regions of so many of the enemy, the peoples of the populous colonies of Pennsylvania, Maryland, and Virginia — in place of their previous absorption in the business of seeing what profits could be secured from British army contractors for furnishing supplies, good, bad, and indifferent — were brought face to face with the stern reality that no effective barrier to the utter devastation of their undefended frontier settlements any longer existed. In terror the inhabitants of these settlements now began to flee eastward.

Colonel Thomas Dunbar, who had taken over the command of the British forces in the Ohio Valley from the dying Braddock, was, unhappily, utterly incapable of measuring up to any high military standard of resoluteness and resourcefulness, although previously he himself had been very critical of Braddock's handling of the campaign against Fort Duquesne. With twelve hundred regulars under him — an army referred to by one of the officers as " still the finest ever seen in America "[1] — and possessed of an impressive numerical superiority of soldiers over the French; with great reserves of food and munitions and a considerable reserve of ordnance still intact; with the really formidable obstacles of terrain well to his rear and not still to face him, thanks to the exertions of St. Clair's pioneers; and, finally, with more than one favourable place available for establishing a fortified camp and for making a stand until fresh reinforcements could be sent up from the colonies, he threw away every advantage. Using as a flimsy pretext, to hide his own lack of leadership, the orders of a mortally wounded superior whose mind was clouded, he proceeded feverishly to destroy or to wreck every bit of matériel that could not easily be taken away.[2] He determined to seek immediately the shelter of Fort Cumberland and also, with four months of good campaigning weather still ahead — it was only July — to go from that place into winter quarters in Philadelphia.[3] Under the circumstances that have previously been considered, the defeat of Braddock was no disgrace to British arms, and this may be affirmed against the prevailing views of contemporaries; but what can be said of Dunbar's resolve and of his actions in carrying it out? Indeed, it would be hard to point to a less courageous act in British military annals.[4] Fortunately, upon the death of Braddock the office of com-

---

[1] Quoted in a letter from P. V. B. Livingston to William Alexander, July 3, 1755, William Alexander Papers, I, 42, New York Historical Society.

[2] Governor Dinwiddie in his letter of July 29, 1755 to Major General Shirley (*Correspondence of William Shirley*, ed. C. H. Lincoln, II, 213) writes: "I think if Col. Dunbar had made a Stand at the Meadows, the Enemy wou'd not have attack'd us in an open Field; But I hear that he destroyed every thing that was there, Provisions and all, and marched into Fort Cumberland." Later some of Dunbar's field officers condemned the destruction of the matériel (see Shirley to Robinson, November 5, 1755, *ibid.*, II, 231). In order to accelerate the flight of the army, enormous quantities of provisions that Dunbar's contingent of the army had been carrying were destroyed. This was carried out to such an extent that the colonel "was actually obliged to send for thirty horse loads" of food supplies stored at Fort Cumberland before his troops could reach that place (*Review of Military Operations in North America, 1753–1756*, Mass. Hist. Soc. *Coll.*, first series, VII, 94).

[3] Shirley to Dunbar, August 6, 1755, *Corresp. of Shirley*, II, 215. "Yesterday the Post came in By which we learn all the General's Papers were taken. That our Army arrived at Wills Creek the 21st and a finer Army Capt. Rutherfurd [sic] says you shall not see in America notwithstanding all that has happened. I perceive he is much chagrin'd . . ." (Goldsbrow Banyar to William Johnson, July 30, 1755, *Sir William Johnson Papers*, I, 793).

[4] How some British soldiers felt about this is indicated by a letter of August 12 from John Shirley to Governor Morris of Pennsylvania (*Pennsylvania Archives*, first series, II, 387): "I have little of News to add since my father's last letter to You, inclosing Copies of his Orders to Col. Dunbarr, whose Retreat is tho't by many here to be a greater Mis-

mander-in-chief of the British forces in North America did not revert even temporarily to Dunbar. That honour and responsibility fell upon the shoulders of Major General William Shirley, Governor of Massachusetts Bay.[5] The question therefore should be raised as to his qualifications for the post.

William Shirley, one may assert with confidence, was undoubtedly the most dynamic and resourceful and also the best-informed and, all in all, the most capable of the governors in British North America in the eighteenth century. In the course of his governorship, extending over a period of fifteen years, he had succeeded to a remarkable degree in winning the loyal co-operation of the General Assembly of the most aggressively inclined of the British plantations. Again, when the Empire had become involved in King George's War, he had formulated broadly the outlines of the strategy for the conquest of Cape Breton Island, had thereupon tactfully won the support of the four New England colonies to implement it, and also had taken a leading part in the working out of the tactical details of the campaign of 1747 that ensued and that met with such resounding success under the direct leadership of William Pepperrell; further, he had been most instrumental in securing for the participating colonies the reimbursement of the expenses incurred by them in connection with the expedition, which added to his prestige as a leader. Before the war had terminated he had moreover developed a project for the conquest of Canada, and when peace came he had put this aside to urge the colonization of Nova Scotia by the British government. He also had made a careful study of the respective rights of Great Britain and France to the regions to the south of the St. Lawrence and had enlightened the Board of Trade and the Secretary of State for the Southern Department as to his views, in a series of extensive reports in the form of letters. It was therefore not unnatural that he had been designated by the ministry in 1750 as one of the two "commissaries" to support His Majesty's New World territorial claims in Paris. In spite of the differences that arose between him and his British colleagues, which

fortune than the late Genl Braddock's unhappy Defeat. What Dishonour is thereby reflected upon the British Army!"

⁵ Robert Orme, Braddock's aide-de-camp, writing to Shirley from Fort Cumberland at Wills Creek on July 18, says (*Corresp. of Shirley*, II, 209): "I should be extremely happy to have your Directions. . . . As Col. Dunbar seems to think that he has an Independent Command, and as it was always imagin'd that in case of any Accident the whole Command on the Continent devolv'd on you, I shall not part with any Papers 'till I receive your instructions . . ." (see also Dinwiddie to Shirley, July 29, 1755, *ibid.*, II, 211–12).

led to his recall to London, his views on the vexed international issues and his detailed knowledge had been so highly valued by the Board of Trade — busied with the preparation of memorials — that his return to Massachusetts Bay had been held up for over a year.[6] Again arriving in America in the fall of 1753, for the second time he had given his efforts to promoting intercolonial co-operation against the French, and, looking toward the establishment of an effective colonial union, in the spring of 1754 he had secured for the Massachusetts Bay commissioners to the Albany Congress the most liberal set of instructions possessed by any of the delegations to this conference. This was not all.

At the very time that the Congress was gathering and deliberating, Shirley had led a force of seven hundred Massachusetts Bay volunteers to the mouth of the Kennebec River and in a series of treaty conferences with the Norridgewalk Indians had successfully overcome the influences of their French Catholic missionaries. Thereupon ascending the river to its upper tributaries and the high ground of the divide, he had proceeded to construct and to garrison Fort Halifax to serve as a barrier against French aggressions within Maine. Then upon his return to Boston he had engaged in a correspondence with Governor Lawrence of Nova Scotia looking to the capture of the French forts located within the limits of the peninsula and came to an agreement to raise two thousand New England volunteers to that end. He also brought the British government to agree to the enterprise. All this enhanced his influence immensely with the people of New England and Nova Scotia.[7] William Clarke, who dedicated to him his *Observations on the late and present Conduct of the French,* published in Boston in 1755, wrote:

"You will permit me, Sir, to say that it is very much to your Representations, that the Interest of these Plantations is made the great

---

[6] The author of *A Review of Military Operations in North America,* writing in 1756 and evidently possessed of precise information, refers thus to Shirley's activities in France and England during the years 1750–3: "Amidst all the splendors and delicacies of Versailles, he forgot neither OUR interest, nor HIS duty. As a proof of his integrity and diligence, during that fruitless embassy, one need only peruse these judicious and laborious memorials, in support of his Majesty's right to Nova-Scotia, which were principally framed by him, and lately published by order of the Lords of Trade, as a full exhibit of our title to that part of America" (Mass. Hist. Soc. *Coll.,* first series, VII, 70).

[7] Lawrence, the Governor of Nova Scotia, in writing to Shirley on November 5, 1754 declared (P.R.O., N.S., 1754, A. 56): "Your Excellency was the first mover of the undertaking the settlement of this province by way of Barrier to the eastern parts of New England. . . ."

Object of the Attention of their Mother Country, and that Spirit raised, which so happily prevails in Great-Britain for their Preservation from the destructive schemes of the French."

When early in the winter of 1754–5 Shirley projected additional plans for the capture of Fort St. Frédéric at Crown Point and submitted them to the New England assemblies, they once again fell into line with his views, agreeing to support the project, and showed their further confidence in the Governor by requesting him to appoint the commander-in-chief to lead it rather than to have the appointment become a matter of dispute.[8] Having thus secured their co-operation and also that of New York and New Jersey to this end, he thereupon, as noted in an earlier chapter, had journeyed to Alexandria, Virginia, to participate in the governors' conference called by General Braddock after arriving in the New World. As a result he was able to secure Braddock's approval of the plans for the Nova Scotian and Crown Point campaigns along the lines already agreed upon and, what was of equal importance, to confer with him respecting an expedition against Fort Niagara that the general had already signified to him by letter he was anxious for him to command.[9] The troops for the expedition, according to Braddock's proposal, were to be the new Shirley and Pepperrell regiments of regulars enlisted in the colonies and provided for by the King's commissions issued the preceding fall.[10]

Carrying now the chief burden of launching the three northern campaigns, the Massachusetts Bay Governor before returning to Boston had conferred along the way with various colonial leaders.

---

[8] With reference to the resolves of the Massachusetts Bay Assembly, Shirley wrote to Sir Thomas Robinson on February 18, 1755 (C.O. 5:14, p. 430): "The Assembly's Request to me to appoint a Commander in Chief for the propos'd Expedition is a Circumstance, I could have been content on more Accounts than one to have omitted in their Resolves: But I could not decline complying with it, without occasioning such a general Dissatisfaction, and Jealousy, as might have hurt his Majesty's Service at this Conjuncture."

[9] This is made clear in Shirley's letter to Sir Thomas Robinson of March 24, 1755, *Corresp. of Shirley*, II, 145–6.

[10] It is of interest that Shirley in the extended proposals that he made to Sir Thomas Robinson on January 24 (C.O. 5:14, pp. 320–1) had not visualized a campaign against Fort Niagara separate and distinct from that against Fort Duquesne. In fact, in his letter he assumes that his regiment of regulars and that given to Pepperrell either would be employed in Nova Scotia or would be a part of the force that Braddock would command. In February he had indicated to the Massachusetts Bay Assembly that he desired that his regiment should be employed in the Crown Point expedition to be commanded by William Johnson (C.O. 5:14, p. 439).

Soon after he had seen the flotilla move out of Boston Bay bound for Nova Scotia and had been relieved of this responsibility, he had left for Albany, and it was there, busy with the preparations for the two other expeditions, that the news reached him of the disaster on the Monongahela. Shirley had now reached the high point in his career of distinguished achievement. A contemporary — William Livingston, it would appear — in his *Review of Military Operations in North America* (1756),[11] all in all justly characterizes him and his public activities:

> "Of all our plantation governors . . . Mr. Shirley is the most distinguished for his singular abilities. . . . He is a gentleman of great political sagacity, deep penetration, and indefatigable industry. With respect to the wisdom and equity of his administration, he can boast the suffrage of a wise, free, jealous, and moral people. Though not bred to arms, he is eminently possessed of these important military virtues: An extent of capacity to form and execute great designs; profound secrecy; love of regularity and discipline; a frugal and laborious manner of living; with the art of conciliating the affections. . . . In the first of these great qualities, Mr. Shirley is universally acknowledged to shine; and it is, in reality, more estimable, than all other military endowments without it. . . . But, whether it arises from his being so far advanced in years, or from his constitutional disposition and make, he has not, in my opinion, that activity and alertness so conducive to warlike expedition; and on which the success of an enterprise frequently depends. This was one of the characteristics of Braddock; a commander, vigorous in execution, as Mr. Shirley, judicious in contriving a plan . . . and 'tis easier . . . to find active hands, than able heads."[12]

In assuming the chief command of the British troops in North America Shirley's first task was to make some proper disposition of the two regiments of British regulars commanded by Dunbar. Clearly these must not be permitted to go into winter quarters with so much still to be done. As a result of this decision, on August 6 he ordered Dunbar to proceed to New York so as to make his forces available for the campaigns on the borders of that province.[13] But after an express had left bearing his order, another arrived from Governor Dinwiddie

---

[11] For a brief discussion of the authorship of this work see my *Lewis Evans*, p. 75. Livingston later became the first Governor of the state of New Jersey.

[12] *Mass. Hist. Soc. Coll.* (first series), VII, 69–70.

[13] Shirley to Dunbar, August 6, 1755, *Corresp. of Shirley*, II, 215–16.

that emphasized the importance of making still another effort against Fort Duquesne that year and indicated the readiness of Virginia to provide Dunbar with a reinforcement of between four hundred and five hundred men should Shirley approve of a new attempt at this time.[14] Shirley, delighted with the prospect now held out of reviving the British offensive against the forts of the Ohio, proceeded to write to Dunbar countermanding his orders and enclosing new ones to the effect that in co-operation with the governments of Pennsylvania, Maryland, and Virginia he should seek "to retrieve the Loss" by marching again to besiege the French fort.[15] But if he failed to take this place he was to dispose of his troops so as to guard such frontier settlements as Shippensburg, Carlisle, and McDowell's Mill in Pennsylvania. In view of the possibility that these forces might be too demoralized to be employed in any independent capacity, Shirley even qualified the latter order by making clear that if it was impracticable to put the foregoing orders into execution, his order of August 6 should be followed.[16] As Dunbar and his military advisers after holding a council of war did not think it desirable to attempt to bring the dispirited regiments into action again without effective support,[17] they, together with the two New York Independent Companies — in all, some sixteen hundred men, it was asserted — with four six-pounders and as many cohorns, marched slowly to Philadelphia[18] and then as slowly through New Jersey to Perth Amboy, where they were placed on transports that in the fall brought them to Albany for winter quarters. There it was that on October 21 the officers presented a report, after holding a court of inquiry into "the Causes and Circumstances of the bad Behaviour of the Kings' Troops" under their command.[19] In forwarding this to Sir Thomas Robinson, Shirley did

---

[14] Dinwiddie to Shirley, July 29, 1755, ibid., II, 211–13. Writing to Dunbar on July 26, Dinwiddie asks: "Is there no Method left to retrieve the dishonour done to the British Arms? . . . You must still have remaining 1600 men." He pointed out that Virginia would furnish additional troops, that large quantities of food were still in reserve, and that at Winchester there were four twelve-pounder cannon with necessary appurtenances. He finally argued that with Shirley attacking Fort Niagara, and Johnson Fort St. Frédéric, the French would be obliged to draw away the defenders of Fort Duquesne (C.O. 5:46).

[15] Shirley to Dunbar, August 12, 1755, C.O. 5:46; Shirley's orders of the same date are printed in the Corresp. of Shirley, II, 231–4.

[16] Ibid.

[17] At this council of war Dunbar, Gage, St. Clair, Major Chapman, Major Sparks, and Governor Sharpe of Maryland agreed that Governor Dinwiddie's scheme of a renewed offensive was impracticable (Mass. Hist. Soc. Coll. [first series], VII, 100).

[18] Ibid.

[19] For this report, signed by Dunbar and Gage, see Corresp. of Shirley, II, 311–13.

not fail to make clear that some of the officers themselves were far from blameless for the defeat.[20]

With the disappearance of the British regulars from this region the three provinces of Pennsylvania, Maryland, and Virginia were presented with the greatest crisis in their history up to that date. Referring to the movements of the French and their Indian allies within western Pennsylvania, Governor Robert Hunter Morris, writing to Shirley early in November declared:

> "Their scheme seems by their motion to be to take Possession of the Susquehannah, which we shall not be able to pass without great difficulty, and they will be in that case perfectly at Liberty to destroy all the rich country beyond the River, where there are many thousands of familys seated. . . . The Inhabitants in general are in great consternation, but being undisciplined and mostly without arms, they can do very little good. . . ."[21]

Virginia was equally open to the enemy. Lewis Evans, in referring to the orders that Colonel Dunbar received toward the end of September to proceed to Albany, wrote in December:

> "It was also about a Month after *all* the Frontiers of Virginia had been reduced to one universal Waste by the Burning, Murdering and Scalping committed by the Indians. In Virginia the Enemy was fetched to the Door and left there, without any body to oppose him; there no Forces were left to cover the Militia, while they formed themselves into an Army for their own Defence."[22]

In an effort to provide additional safety for the people in the western part of Virginia, four companies of rangers were ordered out and the thoroughly alarmed Assembly voted £40,000 for furnishing a thousand men for frontier defence against the flying parties of the enemy that plundered, burned, and murdered.[23] In this connection Dinwiddie later in the year applied to Shirley for a colonel's commis-

---

[20] *Ibid.*, II, 317–23. In November of this year Dunbar was superseded in the command of his regiment and was permanently retired from active service. Nevertheless, he seems to have had influence at court; he was first sent to Gibraltar as Lieutenant Governor; then at the beginning of 1758 was promoted to the rank of major general and toward the end of 1760 to that of lieutenant general (Winthrop Sargent, *An Expedition against Fort Du Quesne*, p. 267).

[21] *Corresp. of Shirley*, II, 322.

[22] *Geographical, Historical, Political . . . Essays*, No. II (1756), p. 8.

[23] *Review of Military Operations, 1753–1756*, Mass. Hist. Soc. Coll. (first series), VII, 100–1.

sion for George Washington, who was now placed at the head of the provincial forces.[24] But very little was done to furnish any proper protection to the western settlements of either Pennsylvania or Virginia until the following year. Even then many of these — particularly the very exposed communities in Pennsylvania — were drenched in blood. Manifestly, one way to ease the pressure of the enemy upon this region, extending north and south hundreds of miles to the east of the Appalachians, was to apply even greater pressure to such vital links in the French system of defence as Niagara and Crown Point. We must therefore turn to a consideration of the problems that arose in connection with the campaigns launched in 1755 for the capture of these strongholds.

When Governor Shirley on February 24 communicated to Lieutenant Governor de Lancey of New York his proposal to erect near Crown Point a stronghold such "as may command the French Fort there, and curb the Citty of Montreal itself" by means of the combined efforts of New England, New York, and New Jersey troops,[25] this was to be but one of three simultaneous expeditions directed against the French encroachments in North America. For it was settled that Braddock should proceed with two thousand troops against Fort Duquesne by way of the upper Potomac, and that Colonel Robert Monckton was to head an expedition of two thousand New England volunteers to sail from Boston and move up the Bay of Fundy against Fort Beauséjour.

In making this proposal for launching a third campaign — that against Crown Point — Shirley did not fail to make clear that the man he himself considered best qualified to have charge of it was the New Yorker Colonel William Johnson, member of the Provincial Council and great friend of the Six Nations. While the government of New York could not easily hesitate to support an undertaking so manifestly advantageous to itself as the clearing of its northern borders of the French intruders, and particularly one that took so fully into account its own great sensitiveness to any intrusion of the governments or peoples of neighbouring colonies either in its affairs or upon

---

[24] Dinwiddie to Shirley, November 4, 1755, *Dinwiddie Papers*, II, 261. It is clear that Washington, in view of his embarrassment during and after his campaign in 1754, wanted something more than a commission from the Governor of Virginia.

[25] A copy of this letter is in C.O. 5:14, pp. 463–9; see also the *Sir William Johnson Papers* (ed. James Sullivan), I, 447. Pennsylvania was also urged, but unsuccessfully, to co-operate in the Crown Point enterprise (Shirley to Morris, February 24, 1755, Penn Papers, Official Correspondence, 7: 7).

the lands that it claimed, yet there is evidence that de Lancey was rather unhappy to find himself the tail of the Shirley kite and did not at first give the proposal support. It was asserted that only when members of the Assembly were approached by Thomas Pownall, who carried Shirley's letter to New York as the latter's official representative and actively promoted among the legislators a sentiment in favour of the expedition, did the Lieutenant Governor fall into line with the views of the majority in the Assembly.[26] Nevertheless, it was asserted by one writer that de Lancey was still able to use his influence with the Assemblymen to save his own dignity:

> "Out of pique . . . to Mr. Shirley, to whom this expedition was solely committed, he prevailed upon them to suspend the execution of their vote, until General Braddock's approbation was obtained: and by this artifice occasioned a considerable delay in the operations."[27]

However, the New York leaders in the government were openly opposed to one phase of the projected triple assault against the French encroachments: the plan that provided that Braddock should launch his own attack against Fort Duquesne rather than against Fort Niagara. This opposition was effectively set forth by Colonel Johnson:

> "It is my own and the opinion of every one I converse with, that should the General begin the attack at Niagara (leaving a few Men toward the Ohio to keep the French in Expectation of a Visit there) it would be the speediest Method to deprive them of their Encroachments on the Ohio which they would soon find themselves under a Necessity even to abandon if we take [and] keep Possession of that important Pass."[28]

What is more, this highly influential person attended the conference called by Braddock at Alexandria and, it would seem, pressed the view of the New York leaders upon the general.

---

[26] P.R.O., Nova Scotia, A. 56:503.

[27] Mass. Hist. Soc. Coll. (first series), VII, 89. Writing to Sir Thomas Robinson on April 3, de Lancey says, with reference to the Crown Point project (C.O. 5:14, pp. 497–8): "I also laid before them [the Assembly] a Plan of Mr. Shirleys for attacking Crown Point. The result of their short Meeting (from Tuesday to Saturday) is contained in their Votes. . . . They agree to Mr. Shirley's Plan and will bear their part, provided the General [that is, Braddock] approves of it being carried into Execution; All which appears from the Papers enclosed, which being short I take the Liberty of troubling you with." By this statement it is clear that the Lieutenant Governor showed no great enthusiasm for the project although it meant much to New York.

[28] Johnson to Shirley, March 17, 1755, Johnson Papers, I, 458–9.

"Here it appeared, that through misrepresentations from Virginia, the general was enjoined to proceed immediately to Fort Du Queene. Those, who were well acquainted with the country, could not help observing . . . that the vicinity of New-York to Canada, its fort of Oswego on Lake Ontario, together with the advantages of water carriage, rendered that province by far the fittest theatre of action." [29]

Johnson, at this time, was favoured not only with Braddock's commission "to have the sole management & direction of the Affairs of the Six Nations of Indians & their Allies" [30] but with Braddock's approval of the Shirley nomination to have him command the volunteer forces to be raised by the more northern colonies for the reduction of Fort St. Frédéric. The colonel, it also appears, gave his hearty support to Braddock's plan to have Shirley attack Fort Niagara by using against it the newly recruited Shirley and Pepperrell regiments.

In view of later developments involving weird political entanglements and bitter estrangements in connection with the effort to put into motion the two New York campaigns, it is well to bear in mind that William Shirley was the originator of the Crown Point campaign and that he not only urged upon the other colonial governments the appointment of William Johnson to command it but went so far as to say to the Massachusetts Bay Assembly in recommending this undertaking on February 13:

"It will require no small Force, Gentlemen, to execute with Success the Attempt I propose; And so far as it depends upon me, you may rely upon the Assistance at least of my Regiment to do it." [31]

On the other hand, Johnson was undoubtedly — in the light of his previously expressed views — most enthusiastic in supporting at Alexandria, as was suggested, the proposed Niagara campaign and the plan to place in charge of it his warm friend and admirer. Neither individual sought the post of great responsibility that, as it were, fell upon him and that ultimately seemed destined to crush him; each in the beginning, in fact, more strongly favoured the campaign that he was not chosen to direct rather than the one that he did; yet before either campaign could be fully launched, each of these powerful, talented men had become convinced that the other was working to defeat his efforts to make his own a success.

[29] Mass. Hist. Soc. Coll. (first series), VII, 90.
[30] For this commission see *Johnson Papers*, I, 465–6.
[31] C.O. 5:14, p. 439.

Johnson's appointment for the Crown Point expedition certainly seemed a most happy one. He was powerfully entrenched in the government of New York and was popular and respected. In the preceding war he had campaigned in the direction of Lake Champlain with his Indians; he would be able now to rally them again to form a strong escort for his colonial levies, which were expected to carry the brunt of the fighting against the French within their citadel. Everything at first appeared to be most favourable for him. He had received while at Alexandria not only his commission from Braddock as sole superintendent of the Six Nations, as noted, but also, at the close of the conference there, a commission issued by Shirley — in the name of the New England governments concerned in his campaign and with the approbation of Braddock — appointing him "Major General and Commander in Chief of the Forces . . . for the Service of the aforesaid Expedition." [32] The commission read in part as follows:

> "You are therefore to take upon you the Command of the said Forces, and diligently to execute the Duty . . . according to such Instructions as you shall receive from me bearing even date with these Presents: and to follow such further Orders as you shall from time to time receive from me or any your superior Officers herein. . . ."

At the same time he received from Shirley his instructions,[33] which were generously framed. Later, it is important to point out, he received a separate commission and also instructions from Lieutenant Governor de Lancey which, while holding in the main to the language of those issued by Shirley, failed to include the reference to "such further Orders as you shall from time to time receive from me [Shirley] or any your superior Officers herein. . . ." [34]

In both sets of instructions he was specifically called upon to take command of the forces of New England and New York designed for the Crown Point expedition; to engage as many of the members of the Six Nations as possible to participate in the campaign and thereupon to move from Albany to Crown Point, clearing a "practicable Road" as he passed along, over which his artillery train and ordnance stores could be moved and along which "Strong Houses" for the se-

---

[32] For this commission, dated April 16, 1755, see *Documentary History of New York* (ed. E. B. O'Callaghan), II, 380–1.

[33] For these instructions see the *Johnson Papers*, I, 472–7.

[34] The commission from de Lancey, without date, is to be found in the *Documentary History of New York*, II, 381–2; the instructions are printed in the *Johnson Papers*, I, 468–71. These were not sent to Johnson until June 24 (*ibid.*, I, 649).

curity of the supplies should be erected wherever needed; to proceed, upon his arrival in the vicinity of the French fort, to erect batteries on the eminence that dominated the fort and, in case of opposition from its garrison, to use force; to summon and compel, if need be, the commandant to retire with his soldiers from the French encroachments in this region and to break up all settlements made there on lands of the Six Nations in violation of the Treaty of Utrecht; then, after a council of war, either to occupy and strengthen Fort St. Frédéric or to erect at some other place an adequate stronghold, which should be garrisoned; and, finally, to acquaint his Indian allies of His Britannic Majesty's intention to recover their lands at Niagara and on the Ohio from the French, and to engage some of them to meet Governor Shirley at Oswego to assist in his service. As in the case of the two commissions, only in one respect, as has been indicated, did the instructions that he received from the Governor of Massachusetts Bay and those from the Governor of New York present any important divergence: in the former it was indicated that he might receive from time to time "particular Instructions" in addition to those contained in the general instructions; in the latter he was permitted to exercise his discretion, by means of a council of war composed of his principal officers, in all matters not covered by the general instructions; in other words, in the first instance he could not enjoy — under General Braddock's broad supervision — an independent command, but would be subject to the orders of Shirley as his immediate superior officer in the field; in the second instance he could. The lack of agreement on this point proved to be a determining factor in the disappointing turn of the New York military operations for the year 1755.[35]

Upon returning to New York Johnson proceeded, apparently after preliminary consultations with Shirley, to lay down the requirements for a successful campaign. While his instructions had not referred to movement by water, it is clear that he became convinced that the proper course of procedure was to move from Albany up the Hudson to the Great Carrying Place with eight hundred bateaux, each large enough to accommodate five men. There at the site of the trading

[35] "Our Govr. has Mr. Shirley's Instructions sent him; but not your Commission," wrote Deputy Secretary Bangar of New York to Johnson on May 19 and added: "He is determined to give you a Commission; he has no objection to your Instructions but that instead of following such other Instructions as you may receive from Mr. Shirley, which Mr. De Lancey says is putting the entire Direction of the Troops under him, It must be to act (in such Matters as your Instructions are silent in) by advice of a Council of War" (Johnson Papers, I, 520).

house of Lydius he would establish his first fort; then portaging his
boats from this point to Lake George, over a road to be constructed
— a distance of some twenty miles — he was to construct a second
fort and also an armed galley of forty tons; thereupon, taking to the
water, his flotilla was to move up Lake George to the Narrow, where
a third fort at Point Ticonderoga should be erected, aptly called by
him

> "a verry Dangerous, & important place, & to be secured at all Events,
> as it will then command the only two passes they [the French] have
> to our Country. . . ." [36]

With some four thousand colonial levies, supported by from two to
three hundred of his Indians, it seemed that he would then be in a
position to move into Lake Champlain and seize the eminence that
dominated Fort St. Frédéric and thereby place that fort at his mercy
by using the heavy guns that would be a part of his equipment.

Johnson's plan of operation was undoubtedly sound. Avoiding a
long and very treacherous land route to Fort St. Frédéric in favour
of an "amphibious" operation,[37] he felt it desirable to protect his line
of communication by constructing strong places at certain "important and dangerous Passes." These could serve as depots for his supplies and as security centres in case of the necessity of retreat. The
point should be emphasized, however, that the success of the operation depended upon speed — speed in gathering and equipping his
contingents from the colonies and from the Six Nations committed
to participation in the campaign, speed in moving these to Albany,
speed in the construction of the large number of bateaux and the
armed galley, speed in building in each instance a fort sufficiently
strong to fulfil its purpose.[38] For it can be appreciated that, were time
allowed, there was danger that the French would in turn take the
initiative and by means of other avenues than those designated by
Johnson, and supported by flying detachments of their Indian allies,

---

[36] Johnson to Shirley, May 1, 1755, ibid., I, 483–4. See also Johnson's estimates of
his needs (ibid., I, 476–82).

[37] The operation was very properly described at this period by the above term.

[38] The same necessity for speed faced Braddock in his march against Fort Duquesne
in order to arrive there before the expected French reinforcements. Braddock, as has been
emphasized, committed himself to this tactical move and overruled Sir John St. Clair and
others who recommended a more leisurely progress that comprehended the construction
of a fortification and the concentration of the army at Great Lick, which would have
caused considerable delay.

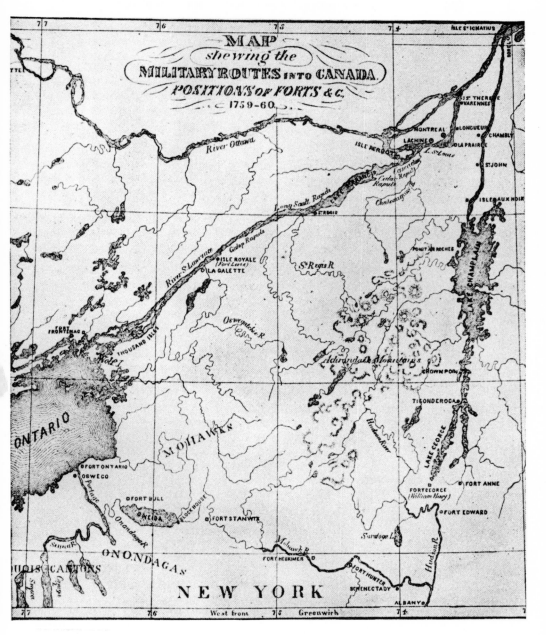

(From Miles's *History of Canada.*)

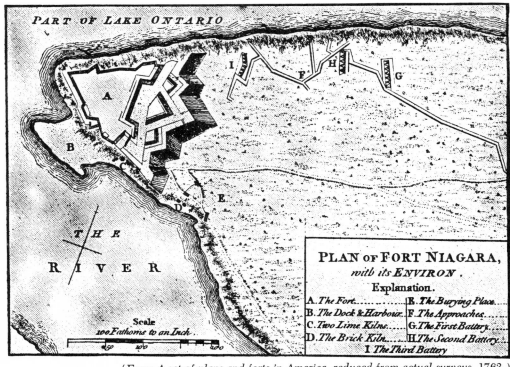

PART OF LAKE ONTARIO

A

B

C

D E

T H E

R I V E R

I

F H G

PLAN of FORT NIAGARA,
with its ENVIRON.
Explanation.

A. *The Fort*............. E. *The Burying Place*......
B. *The Dock & Harbour*. F. *The Approaches*.....
C. *Two Lime Kilns*...... G. *The First Battery*.....
D. *The Brick Kiln*...... H. *The Second Battery*....
I *The Third Battery*

Scale
100 Fathoms to an Inch .

(From *A set of plans and forts in America, reduced from actual surveys,* 1763.)

move to the rear of the Great Carrying Place or between it and Lake George and by ambuscading operations inflict a terrifying defeat upon the British colonials. In view of this fact Lieutenant Governor de Lancey's dilatory procedure during the early months of 1755 was worthy of the censure that it received from his critics.

But important as was the operation to be undertaken by Johnson, that against Fort Niagara was even more so.[39] In the minds of New Yorkers, the safety of Oswego was a matter of prime consideration and, as has been noted, they were without exception convinced that Braddock should strike against Niagara, by way of the Mohawk and Oswego, rather than against Fort Duquesne. When they found that he was committed to a campaign against the latter but that he had commissioned Shirley to move against Niagara with the two regiments of colonial regulars, it might be thought that this campaign that they previously had had so much at heart would have received their most enthusiastic support. But, unfortunately, Shirley was faced by obstructionist tactics almost from the beginning. He had to deal not only with de Lancey, whose jealousy gradually changed into scarcely veiled hostility, but also with Johnson, who — once he had received his commission from Braddock as sole superintendent of the Six Nations and that from the five colonies as commanding officer of the Crown Point expedition — now seemed to lose all interest in the Niagara campaign.

On the other hand it is clear from the surviving correspondence that Shirley continued to have deeply at heart the success of the two campaigns.[40] In fact, when Johnson first wrote to Braddock, on May 17, outlining the problems that faced him, he expressed fear that the Six Nations could not be brought to open hostilities against the French and that the colonies engaged to support his expedition would not act "with that Vigorous & generous Spirit so very necessary toward its Success," but voiced no word of criticism of Shirley — unless it was his tactful statement that the

---

[39] For Braddock's instructions to Shirley, dated April 16, 1755, see C.O. 5:14, pp. 615–18.

[40] See, for example, Shirley's letter to Johnson dated May 7, 1755 (*Johnson Papers*, I, 491–3); see also Goldsbrow Banyar to Johnson, May 16, 1755, and Johnson to de Lancey and also Johnson to Shirley of the same date (*ibid.*, I, 498–507). In writing to Secretary Willard of Massachusetts Bay on July 22 with reference to the Braddock defeat, Shirley observed: "I think it a strong Reason for pushing on the Prosecution of the Expedition against Crown Point, which must proceed at all Events; Otherwise the Indians of the Six Nations, as well as others upon the Continent must be given up for lost to the English" (New York Historical Society Manuscripts).

"500 men from Jersey under Col. Schuyler are I understand to go to Niagara, not a Company yet marching this way that I hear of . . . nor have I any Account of what progress they [the colonies concerned] are making. . . . I dread those Delays & those Provincial Desputes about Quotas. . . ." [41]

And, as to his last statement, he might have added that the government of New York was the chief offender in this respect. It was also responsible for making clear to Johnson at this juncture that it was opposed to his taking orders from Shirley, next in command to Braddock and the latter's successor, as has been emphasized, if anything should happen to the general. This came in the form of a letter from the Secretary of the province, Goldsbrow Banyar.[42] Four days later the Secretary confided to Johnson that Shirley had sent a communication to de Lancey "full of sly insinuations" and indicated that the latter was "a little displeased at Mr. Shirley's Treatment of him." [43]

However much the Governor of Massachusetts Bay might have disliked the attitude shown by de Lancey when the latter sought not only to relieve New York of much of its burden by trying to get the major portion of its quota of troops from Connecticut but also to prevent him from making use of certain artillery for the Niagara campaign, he was certainly very much in earnest over the success of the Crown Point expedition. With Johnson showing signs of discouragement over delays, he wrote from Boston on May 24 a letter full of confidence in the New Yorker's success and his own good wishes. He did mention, however, that while he could answer for a proper response from the New England colonies with troops and funds and in other ways, he could not speak for New York.[44] Again on June 1 he addressed Johnson to make plain why he had been forced to divert some of the troops from the Crown Point expedition to that of Niagara, particularly the 505 furnished by New Jersey, and 500 out of 2,000 that were being raised in Massachusetts Bay. He also made clear in this connection that under the quotas that had been fixed — with Massachusetts Bay providing 1,500 troops for Johnson, Connecticut 1,000, New Hampshire 500, and Rhode Island 400 — the New

---

[41] *Johnson Papers*, I, 512–16. Later, writing to Robert Orme, Braddock's aide-decamp, he declared: ". . . I dread Confusion, want of Money, & that my hands will be too much tied up. . . . Govr. Shirleys Attack is happily not upon Provincial Funds, & I hope therefore it will be carried on with Vigor & Success" (*ibid.*, I, 522).

[42] This is under date of May 19, 1755 (*ibid.*, I, 520).

[43] *Ibid.*, I, 534–5.

[44] *Ibid.*, I, 540–2; *Corresp. of Shirley*, II, 174–6.

England contingent, together with the anticipated contribution by New York of 800, would provide a total larger than it had seemed necessary to raise when the Crown Point expedition had first been proposed. He also stressed the fact that the drive against Niagara, together with that against Duquesne, would inevitably have the effect of compelling the French to direct against the region of the Great Lakes and the Ohio Valley, much of the strength that otherwise would be available to support Crown Point; and to the extent that this took place Johnson's task would be lightened. Finally, regarding his own expedition, he did not fail to point out that there was danger that even the expanded force intended for Niagara might be obliged to face one twice its size, especially if the French were led to retreat from Fort Duquesne and to concentrate upon that strategic river, the vital link for all the upper Great Lakes trade; for the enemy, if obliged to make a choice, would not hesitate to sacrifice Crown Point to save Niagara.[45]

The Niagara expedition, in fact, under the altered disposition of available troops, could depend upon only the two recently recruited regiments of regulars, who were not veterans, the raw New Jersey regiment, and the levy of Massachusetts Bay, both of which were volunteers — a total of but 2,400 men as against at least 3,700, without including Johnson's Indians, for that against Crown Point.[46] It would therefore seem, in weighing all factors, strategic and tactical, involved in the twofold New York campaign, that Johnson, in spite of the weakness of his forces, could not justly complain of bad treatment at the hands of his superior.

The growing rift between Shirley and the New York authorities, with such serious consequences for the Niagara campaign, was undoubtedly not unrelated to the extreme friction, involving violence, that had developed between inhabitants of the two provinces of New York and Massachusetts Bay over lands claimed by both the manor of Livingston and the town of Westenhook.[47] In vain Shirley sought in the spring of 1755 to bring an end to the dispute, so unfortunate at this time, in a proposal to de Lancey that the boundary between the two provinces be determined by "disinterested referees"; this offer was declined by the latter.[48] In fact, out of this friction there

---

[45] *Ibid.*, II, 179–82; *Johnson Papers*, I, 551–5.

[46] Shirley to Robinson, June 20, 1755, *New York Colonial Documents*, VI, 955.

[47] For treatment of this conflict see pages 113–15 of Volume III of this series.

[48] William Smith, *History of the Late Province of New York* (New York Hist. Soc. *Coll.*, V), II, 210–11.

developed deep animosities between the two colonies, which greatly disturbed Shirley, who, thinking in terms of close intercolonial cooperation at this critical juncture, rose above local issues.[49] Unfortunately, de Lancey did not possess the same attitude of detachment.[50] He therefore undoubtedly resented a letter addressed to him by Shirley on May 25, which, after giving excerpts from communications received from New York as evidence, declared:

> "Your Honour will think that it is absolutely necessary for your Government to take some immediate step for preventing the mischievous effects of the pernicious intercourse between the French Indians and Albany at this juncture; from whence it can't be doubted but that the French of Canada have constant intelligence given them by the latter of every motion of the English, than which nothing can have a greater tendency to disappoint his Majesty's service in every part of the present Expedition. . . ."[51]

The very questionable part that de Lancey himself had played in the preceding war in supporting the old Albany-Canada neutrality and the connection of the de Lancey family with the vast contraband trade that flourished in war and peace between Albany and Montreal may be only mentioned in passing.[52] Much of his influence in political life in fact depended upon the support of those who profited by this lawless traffic. When Shirley struck at this trade, he struck the Lieutenant Governor in a very vital part. Further, on June 1 he again addressed de Lancey respecting the refusal of the latter to permit certain artillery belonging to New York to be used in the Niagara campaign and de Lancey's insistence that the forces originally designed for Crown Point should not be weakened and his equal insistence that a mere five hundred soldiers could reduce Fort Niagara, unless the French should throw up new works about it and reinforce its garrison — a contingency that seemed unlikely to de Lancey. Shirley not only dealt with these points in rather crisp terms, but expressed his objections to the efforts of New York to recruit Connecticut men rather than its own to fill its modest quota of 800.[53]

---

[49] *Documentary History of New York*, III, 739, 754, 774.

[50] *Ibid.*, III, 789, 801–3.

[51] *Johnson Papers*, I, 543.

[52] For this point see page 130 of Volume III of the present series. Writing to Johnson on June 7, de Lancey raises the question "How far it may be prudent to make them [the French Indians] our Enemies at this time . . ." (*Johnson Papers*, I, 568).

[53] *Corresp. of Shirley*, II, 182–8.

There was no love lost between the two men, it is clear; it is equally clear that de Lancey had even less to thank Shirley for when the latter refused to give de Lancey's brother Oliver the contract for provisioning the Niagara campaign.[54]

At first Johnson did not appear to share de Lancey's intense jealousy and dislike of Shirley. In fact, he himself had for long been in opposition to the Lieutenant Governor and his group.[55] But as he became more deeply involved in the complexities of the preparations for the Crown Point campaign, he became more and more susceptible to the suggestions coming to him from de Lancey's supporters that Shirley was sacrificing him for his own glorification. Then on June 15 Shirley, preparatory to his arrival at Albany to begin operations up the Mohawk, sent a request to Johnson to provide him with Indian escorts for the march. As the student today considers this request — in the light of what ultimately took place about Niagara in the war, and in particular the destruction in 1759 of the French forces under such experienced leaders as Marin, Aubry, and Legneris by Johnson supported by his Indians — it seems so proper and necessary that one is surprised that it was not met with alacrity. In fact, one may affirm that Johnson himself would never have dreamed of venturing on the Niagara campaign in 1755 without powerful Indian support; it is clear that when he later participated in the movement against Fort Niagara, under the superior direction of General Prideaux, he enlisted for support every Indian that he could prevail upon to accompany him. But, in contrast, this request of Shirley's had the effect, it would appear, of fully identifying him now with the de Lancey group, a group bent upon obstructing in every way the Niagara campaign — incredible as this may be, with so much at stake for New York in it.

There can be no doubt that after Shirley arrived in New York early in July and sought to obtain the desired Indian support, this was not forthcoming; on the contrary he had to face the determined opposition of Johnson. The latter at a great Indian conference denounced as a "Snake" the man appointed by Shirley to lead the anticipated Indian patrols to Oswego, Colonel Lydius; [56] and he indicated to

---

[54] William Smith, *History of the late Province of New York*, II, 213.

[55] Johnson had strongly supported Governor Clinton during King George's War while the latter was under attack by the de Lancey faction.

[56] Although Lydius had been selected by the Connecticut people of the Susquehanna Company to negotiate the purchase of lands in what is now and was then northern Penn-

Shirley himself that the commission received from Braddock to act as superintendent of the Six Nations precluded any interference with them on the part of anyone else. This led to Shirley's reply that it was inconsistent for Johnson to take this position when, to quote him:

> "I don't understand, that you have yet endeavoured, or now design to engage any Indians to go wth me." [57]

Nor was this all. The author of *A Review of Military Operations in North-America* bluntly asserted that both de Lancey and Johnson sought to obstruct the Shirley campaign and in "support of a charge so heavy as this" affirmed that not one Indian joined Shirley at Schenectady, despite the general's orders to Johnson, nor did any of the natives as he passed from this place through the Six Nations country to Oswego. Further, the writer charged that upon reaching the great trading post the general was actually waited upon by an Indian delegation from Onondaga which brought a belt that its members claimed had been sent to all the Six Nations by Johnson with a request that none of them serve with the troops designed for the Niagara campaign — a message confirmed by Indians of the Seneca, Oneida, and Cayuga cantons, who also had arrived at this great trading centre.[58]

Nor did the fact that Shirley succeeded to the authority of Braddock as commander-in-chief of the British forces in North America even before he ascended the Mohawk bring about any fundamental change in the attitude of de Lancey and Johnson.[59] Moreover, they were joined by Thomas Pownall, who had been sent by Shirley to New York, as previously noted, as his commissioner to promote the Crown Point campaign and had now as Lieutenant Governor of New Jersey turned against him.[60] It is therefore not surprising to find

---

sylvania, he was not a happy choice to carry out an assignment in 1755 with Johnson in opposition to Shirley. Yet as a member of the Tortoise (Turtle) clan he was the most influential man with the Indians that was available to Shirley.

[57] Shirley to Johnson, July 17, 1755, *Johnson Papers*, I, 733–6.

[58] *Mass. Hist. Soc. Coll.* (first series), VII, 99. It is true, however, that Shirley, in spite of all hindrances, prevailed upon a hundred Indians to meet him at Oswego to participate in the Niagara campaign.

[59] *Johnson Papers*, I, 805.

[60] Pownall, who went without invitation to Alexandria, Virginia, at the time of the conference called there by General Braddock, is said to have taken deep offence that Shirley, who introduced him courteously to the general, did not also feel free to press the general to admit him to the conference (*Mass. Hist. Soc. Coll.*, first series, VII, 134–6). Lord Loudoun later was impelled to write very plainly to England regarding Pownall's defects of character, especially his unbounded egotism (*Military Affairs in North America, 1748–1764*, ed. S. M. Pargellis, p. 404).

Johnson not only preparing a case against Shirley, with the aid of Wraxall, to be submitted to the Board of Trade by Pownall, who was returning to England, but writing on July 30 to de Lancey about his own opposition to the "Pernicious Schemes" of Shirley "to turn the Indians from the Crown Point to the Niagara expedition." [61] This cry of anguish from the distressed Johnson, who did not want to see his campaign subordinated to that against Niagara, much as he had personally at stake at Oswego in the way of business ventures, has been repeated by leaders in later wars and even today in the midst of the Great World War it has come from field commanders. This human weakness in the case of Johnson was combined with insubordination. That his resistance to Shirley's efforts to secure an Indian escort was unreasonable and even reprehensible is indicated by the fact that at the Great Carrying Place to the east of Oneida Lake a detachment of soldiers and the stores concentrated there were destroyed in April by a party of five hundred French Indians.[62] But we must now turn to the Niagara campaign.

The force for attacking Fort Niagara that Major General Shirley succeeded in gathering late in July after so much effort and controversy was — it is clear to one writing today from the vantage point of having knowledge of facts necessarily hidden from the general — quite insufficient to carry out its tactical assignment. Further, taking into consideration the logistics of the campaign — the factors of transport and supply — this force was even more inadequate when it came to the inclusion of a sufficient number of men capable of dealing efficiently with the problem of conveying from Albany to Niagara — by whatever means were most feasible in an amphibious operation — the artillery and matériel for the investment of the French fort and supplies for the troops. It was inadequate also in that it lacked trained artillerymen, nor did it include a really efficient military engineer

---

[61] *Johnson Papers*, I, 795. On August 1 Johnson also wrote to Robert Orme about his difficulties with Shirley, avowing: "Govr. Shirley grew Jealous & Distrustful of me & he was peremptory that he would have Indians to escort him to Oswego." Johnson then went on to say that he did not feel that Shirley needed any such protection to that place. As to the Indians affording it, he declared: "I am well assured [that they] would have declined it had I proposed it upon 'em." However, farther on in the same letter he makes an admission not in all respects consistent with the statement just given: "Since the unfortunate Turn of Affairs [on the Ohio] . . . I am sensible it will increase the utility of Mr. Shirleys having more Indians with him at Oswego"; and then hastens to add: "And without Indians it would be madness to undertake the expedition to Crown Point" (*ibid.*, I, 814–15).

[62] James Pitcher to Henry Fox, New York, April 29, 1755, C.O. 5:46.

capable of laying out proper defences for Oswego. The difficulties of launching a successful campaign against Crown Point in the summer of 1755 were sufficiently great; they were perhaps even greater against Niagara. In fact, had Shirley succeeded in capturing this fort under given conditions during the summer or fall of the year mentioned, it would have been little short of a miracle. The task was a formidable one, so formidable, indeed, that when it was once agreed upon, the projected Crown Point campaign should have been made subordinate to it in all respects. In other words, for its success it was a matter of vital importance to have a sufficiently large force to cover both Albany and the line of supply between that city and Lake Ontario. The chief danger to these was from attempts that might be made against them on the part of the French by way of Lake George or Wood Creek to the east, which flows north into Lake Champlain. It is certain that the forces not required for this purely defensive holding operation should have been used to strengthen the position of Oswego and support the attack against Niagara. Had this been done, while it is by no means certain that even then success would have accompanied the undertaking, the chances of its capture would have been enormously increased. This, of course, does not take into account other factors that would necessarily enter into the problem of carrying the campaign to its logical culmination, which must be considered at the proper time.

But first of all let us attempt to visualize more clearly the nature of the physical obstacles to be overcome before the troops arriving by ship at Albany could appear before Fort Niagara. Between Albany and Oswego, by following the waterways and portages, there lay some two hundred and fifty miles; between Oswego and Fort Niagara some hundred and fifty more by way of the waters of Lake Ontario. From Albany to Schenectady there was an excellent wagon road. At that point the Mohawk River became the highway, unimpeded by obstructions for sixty-five miles, except by a rapid current in high water or rifts in low water, until Little Falls was reached; over this stretch, therefore, bateaux, capable of carrying fifteen hundredweight and propelled by two bateau-men with paddles and setting poles, could move. At Little Falls there was a portage of about a mile over marshy ground; as a result the bateaux were placed on sleds by the Germans living in the neighbourhood and dragged by horse to the navigable water; then sixty miles farther up the same river, which must be ascended against a still swifter current than below Little Falls, brought one to the Great Carrying Place, where sleds again were used for some six miles of portage to the narrow stream called Wood Creek, which flows into Oneida Lake some forty miles distant. The creek, its banks covered with thick woods, was obstructed here and there by logs and fallen trees, but was not otherwise especially dangerous, and Oneida Lake offered at least in good weather safe transport for thirty miles. At the western extremity of the lake its waters empty into a branch of the Oswego River. Down this stream the bateaux raced. Swept forward and into the Oswego by a rapid current, they now faced the greatest hazards of the whole trip to Lake Ontario; for the river abounded in rifts and protruding rocks, and also, twelve miles from Oswego and its mouth, come the sheer drop of the falls — scene of many a tragedy — and the last of the portages.[63] From Oswego to Fort Niagara there stretched the waters of Lake Ontario, placid enough as a rule in summer, but turbulent and dangerous for bateaux and other small craft at other times of the year. But even in good weather no flotilla of bateaux could now safely venture to move across the lake unless protected by large armed vessels; for the French, it was well known, had one or more sloops that were used between Niagara and Fort Frontenac or Fort La Galette (Picquet's Presentation) on St. Lawrence. Thus, bateaux must be supplemented by schooners, and the latter could only be constructed on the shore of the lake, by shipwrights brought there for that purpose. The military operation demanded, as has been emphasized, an adequate force trained in the tasks that it entailed, with adequate matériel and a steady flow of provisions for those all along the line contributing to it; finally, it had to be timed so that full advantage could be taken of the summer weather.

To do justice to Shirley, it should be pointed out that for this service he engaged all available bateau-men in Albany County as well as a vast number of bateaux previously used in the trade to Oswego.[64] The garrison of the fort there had been increased so that late in the spring one hundred men were there under command of Captain King; late in May Captain Bradstreet of the regular army arrived to take command, with two hundred more — two companies from Pepperrell's regulars — together with a group of workmen to begin construction of the vessels agreed upon at the conference at Alexandria;

---

[63] A Review of Military Operations, op. cit., p. 95.
[64] Ibid., p. 96.

and on June 7 the Boston shipwrights appeared, so that there were then some three hundred and twenty men available for ship-construction. Late in June the first of these vessels, an undecked forty-foot, twenty-ton galley mounting twelve swivels and furnished with fourteen oars, was launched — the first British vessel ever to float upon the waters of the Great Lakes.[65] But it was the middle of September before the three other vessels — another undecked galley armed with fourteen swivels, a decked schooner of sixty tons with eight four-pounders and twenty-eight swivels, and a decked sloop also of sixty tons with eight four-pounders and thirty swivels — were ready.

It was the beginning of July before Colonel Schuyler's New Jersey regiment, having arrived at Schenectady, began to ascend the Mohawk in bateaux, and the latter part of the month before it arrived at Oswego; meanwhile the waters of the Mohawk and Wood Creek were falling rapidly, and this increased the difficulties of transport, especially that of the artillery; added to this, when the bateau-men heard of Braddock's defeat and also did not get their pay on time — for there were delays in the payment of the troops and workmen — about half of them "dispersed themselves into the Country, and fled to their respective habitations." [66] Shirley, seriously impeded by the disappearance of the bateau-men and the desertion of soldiers and also concerned in attempting to rally the Indians to aid him, was still at the Great Carrying Place as late as August 11. Writing to Sir Thomas Robinson on that date, he pointed out that the total force at his disposal for the attempt on Niagara was now only seventeen hundred, including fifty Albany scouts and one hundred Indians whom he had managed, in spite of Johnson, to enlist. He therefore stated that

> ". . . whether . . . they are now sufficient for the Reduction of Virginia [Niagara] will depend upon the Intelligence, I shall receive on my Arrival at Oswego (where I hope to be by the 16th or 17th Instant) of the Strength of the French at that place."

He nevertheless expressed confidence that should the expected intelligence reveal that the French were too powerful to be attacked this season with his available troops, he would at least be able to strengthen Oswego and by means of the naval force on Lake Ontario

---

[65] Lewis Evans, *Geographical, Historical, Political . . . Essays*, Number II (1756), p. 18.
[66] *Ibid.*, p. 20; *Review of Military Operations*, op. cit., p. 96.

"to cut off the Return of the French from their Forts on the Ohio as well as at Niagara this year as also from being supply'd with Provisions from Montreal, and so starving their Garrisons there this Winter. . . ." [67]

It was not until August 17 that Shirley at length appeared at Oswego, and not until the 31st that Colonel Mercer arrived with the artillery and September 2 that the last of the eight divisions of the troops entered the post.

In accounting for the late arrival in the campaigning season of most of the troops and their commanding officers, Shirley offered a partial explanation in communicating with the Secretary of State for the Southern Department soon after he reached Oswego. He pointed out, first of all, that he was prevented from leaving Boston with his regiment until May 21 on account of the failure of the deputy paymaster to arrive there with funds for the expedition, which was to be carried out at the expense of the Crown; thereupon twenty-two days were consumed in conveying the soldiers, their baggage and stores, and the artillery to Schenectady; then came the "difficult Navigation of about 215 Miles" to Oswego, which could only be carried out by dividing the troops into eight divisions on account of the lack of bateau-men and horses at the portages, where all supplies had to be unloaded.[68] This took over two months.[69] He might also have added that while the painful process of pushing his soldiers upstream was going on, he was also concerned with the problem not only of recruiting Indians, but of preventing all the bateau-men from leaving and his soldiers from deserting; inexperienced with river navigation, they were, according to Lewis Evans, "terrified" and

> "thought it less Risk of hanging for Desertion, and leaving the Battoes and Lading than of drowning, by running down the several Rifts and Falls." [70]

By the time Shirley had made his way to Oswego he had, in spite of his accumulated difficulties, already projected plans for the capture not only of Fort Niagara but of Fort Frontenac, lying on the

---

[67] *Corresp. of Shirley*, II, pp. 219–20.

[68] *Ibid.*, II, 229.

[69] Twenty days was the time ordinarily allotted under favourable conditions for a bateau to go from Schenectady to Oswego and return, according to Lewis Evans (*op. cit.*, p. 15).

[70] *Ibid.*, p. 13.

northern shore of Lake Ontario not far distant from the entrance to the St. Lawrence.[71] What is more, he also came back to his favourite theme: the conquest of Canada. He had insistently advocated this step in the course of the preceding war after the fall of Louisbourg and had won tentative approval of the idea from the ministry. Upon his recall from Paris, where he served as commissaire, and before he returned to his post in Massachusetts Bay in 1753, he again turned to this idea in proposals made to Pelham, who was then at the head of the ministry, but, we are told, "was silenced by the pacific and economical maxims of that minister, and ordered out to his government, from whence he never ceased . . . to excite the administration to some vigorous exertions." [72] On August 15 in addressing Robinson, just before he left Oneida Lake for Oswego, he tactfully ventured, "in case the plan for the Conquest of Canada devised in the late War be renewed," to offer some modifications to it.[73] As the relationship of Shirley's plan of 1755 has so close a relationship to that finally approved by Pitt and carried into execution, it must not be dismissed without a word of comment.

In the preceding war, when the British government, as previously indicated, was playing with the idea of the conquest of Canada, the plan before it urged by Shirley comprehended the sending of a powerful fleet and five or six regiments from England and the raising of seven thousand colonials, with which a general attack would be delivered upon the French province. Shirley now recommended certain changes in this plan, particularly with respect to the quota of troops that each colony would be expected to raise, so that by including the regular regiments now in America, the figure would reach 17,400 troops; to these there would be added four or five regiments sent from England and also a British fleet. These regular forces from home and the fleet would ascend the St. Lawrence to fall upon Quebec, while 3,000 of the troops in America would march up the Kennebec to Fort Halifax and then down the Chaudière to assist the British regiments before the capital of New France. At the same time 3,000 troops would move from Oswego across Lake Ontario and descend upon Montreal, while 11,400 would proceed against the

---

[71] This is outlined in his letter of August 12 to Robinson (Corresp. of Shirley, II, 221–31). While, according to this, he would hold Niagara, he would destroy Fort Frontenac — as Bradstreet did in 1758.

[72] William Smith, History of New York, op. cit., V, 206.

[73] C.O. 5:46.

same city by way of Lake Champlain, "in which March the strongest Opposition is to be expected." Upon the capture of Montreal, reinforcements from the lines around the city would move down to support the besiegers before Quebec, thus sealing the doom of French Canada.

But all such grand strategy had to await an open declaration of war and the coming of William Pitt to power. It may be noted, however, that the ultimate conquest of Canada followed with a good deal of faithfulness the broad strategy laid down by Shirley, with one exception: the failure to utilize the Kennebec-Chaudière approach by a force to supplement the efforts of the British regiments convoyed up the St. Lawrence by the fleet — an approach that Arnold took in the fall of 1775, when he was aided without avail by Montgomery in the siege of Quebec after Montgomery had captured Montreal.

Oswego, perhaps the greatest Indian trading centre possessed by the British in North America and the envy of all New France, was a place difficult if not impossible to defend against serious attack, dominated as it was by eminences to the northeast and to the west. The dilapidated fort, built by Governor Burnet in 1728 on the west bank of the Oswego "next to the Lake," may be described as a large blockhouse surrounded by a masonry wall some six hundred feet in circumference and three and a half feet thick, which was flanked with two bastions. The wall was so defective by 1755 that some of the seven three-pounders and the two fours protruding from it could only be fired at the risk of bringing it crumbling down on the heads of the defenders.[74] Close beside the fort, used also as a magazine for trading supplies, and stretching up the river, there were two lines of some seventy traders' "huts," each facing the single street.[75] Three days after Captain John Bradstreet arrived at the post with his two companies of regulars to take command, he wrote to Sir Thomas Robinson:

> ". . . I find the Fort, or Trading House So trifling & the Situation so bad that any additional Works would be throwing Money away,

---

[74] *Corresp. of Shirley*, II, 262; Patrick Mackellar's Report to James Montresor, May 25, 1756, C.O. 5:47.

[75] Thomas Pownall, *A Topographical Description . . . of North America*, Appendix No. 1. As the cabins were only designed for summer use, they were open to the weather. John Shirley, son of the general, declared they really were nothing but sheds (*Corresp. of Shirley*, II, 250).

therefore have determined to do nothing more, until I shall hear from Colonel Shirley, than to throw Some Palisades round back of it . . . and to cut down & clear the Woods round us, which are Thick, & close to the Fort. We have already cleared for the Distance of a Musket Shot round, [and] cut all the Palisades necessary for the Work intended."

Bradstreet also pointed out in this letter the grave irregularities of the Indian trade at the post and its political implications when he added:

"But it is with concern that I tell You, Sir, that nothing can be more Scandalous than the Manner in which the Trade is now carried on here & I am really Surprized the Indians have not long since destroyed the Traders, & plundered the Place. . . ." [76]

The safety of this post previous to the coming of Shirley's troops, in fact, depended almost entirely upon the maintenance of the old understanding insisted upon by the Six Nations as to its exemption from hostile attack from the French, as was Niagara from the British. Before the arrival of Bradstreet hundreds of French troops bound for Niagara and the Ohio country had moved across the waters of Lake Ontario in sight of Fort George without making the slightest effort to take it. It is true that early in July a force of Frenchmen, estimated to be five hundred, supported by two hundred Great Lakes Indians, landed at a point some four miles to the east of Oswego, whether to attack or simply to reconnoitre is not clear. It is of interest to note, however, that the resourceful Bradstreet sent a warning message to these Indians that if they supported the French their families would not be safe. This had the effect of causing them to desert in a body, and the French thereupon embarked in their bateaux and proceeded in the direction of Niagara.[77]

It must not be supposed that while all the preparations for the dual New York campaigns against Niagara and Crown Point were being perfected and the troops were in movement the French were not made perfectly aware of all that was going on by means of loyal Indians engaged in the Albany contraband trade. Writing to M. Machault on July 10, the Marquis de Vaudreuil, the new Governor General, declared respecting the preparations for these campaigns:

---

[76] Bradstreet to Robinson, May 30, 1755, C.O. 5:46.
[77] Bradstreet to Robinson, July 10, 1755, C.O. 5:46.

"We had confirmation of this intelligence from some reliable Indians belonging to different villages, who have given us pretty strong assurances of it, not admitting of a doubt."

He then went on to state that the English were sending four thousand to Oswego — called by the French Choueguen or Choueguin — and that the Five Nations would form the wings of this army; also that another army of five thousand encamped outside Orange (Albany) was to march against Fort St. Frédéric. The objectives of the first army, he indicated, were the seizure of Forts Niagara and Frontenac, and for this purpose six hundred bateaux had been built at Albany. In this connection he made the following interesting comment:

"The preservation of Niagara is what interests us most. Were our enemies masters of it, and to retain Choueguin the upper Countries would be lost to us, and we should have no further communication with the river Oyo" (Ohio).[78]

Again on July 25, still ignorant of the disaster to English arms on the Monongahela, Vaudreuil, in communicating with the Minister of the Marine, expressed grave fears for the safety of Niagara:

"In regard to Niagara, 'tis certain that, should the English once attack it, 'tis theirs. I am informed that the fort is so dilapidated, that 'tis impossible to put a peg in it without causing it to crumble; stanchions have been obliged to be set up against it to support it. Its garrison consists of thirty men without any muskets. Sieur de Villiers has been detached with about 200 men, to form a camp of observation there. . . . The expedition against Choueguin, which at all times would have been easy, is now unfortunately very difficult, and that (I cannot but repeat) because the English have experienced no impediment to their labors and ambitions." [79]

Fortunately for the British colonials, the reports that came to the French of the concentration of a large number of troops at Oswego were greatly exaggerated. According to M. Bréard, assistant to Intendant Bigot, writing on August 13 from Quebec, the last advices from that post stated that

---

[78] N. Y. Col. Doc., X, 305.

[79] Ibid., X, 307–8. As to Fort Niagara, its weakened condition was emphasized by Governor General Duquesne in his mémoire of July 6, 1755. He states: "The site of Fort Niagara is to be changed, as it is undermined by the lake and crumbling in every direction" (ibid., X, 301).

"there are nearly 6000 men to guard it, and to oppose the designs of the French in that quarter. They do not want for artillery; they have some cannon even on board their sloops that navigate Lake Ontario, on which they have likewise a number of bateaux." [80]

But he also added that the greater part of the French army formed at Montreal, numbering 5,000 men had proceeded to Niagara. As a matter of fact, some 1,200 troops were actually at Fort Frontenac when he wrote, "all ready to march against Chouaguen."

In other words, by the time of Shirley's arrival at Oswego on August 18 the French had gathered a large force at Fort Frontenac and had available another considerable body of soldiers concentrated on the Allegheny River and at Presqu'Isle on Lake Erie to cover Niagara in case of danger. What is more, the troops at Frontenac, as was intimated by Vaudreuil's letter, were sent there for the express purpose of moving against Oswego. [81] It had been expected that they would be commanded by Baron Dieskau, who had lately arrived in New France with his veteran battalions eager for action. These were ordered to Montreal to form the nucleus of the army that would strike against the English post. Although Dieskau was recalled with a portion of his infantry while en route to Frontenac, a reinforcement of some six hundred had arrived, so that the troops gathered there, some twelve hundred in number, as stated, were therefore quite adequate not only to protect the fort from possible attack, but with the aid of armed sloops to keep the waters of the lake open for communication and supplies destined for Niagara and beyond.

Before reaching Oswego Shirley had indicated the necessity of providing adequate defences for that place. The possibility, in other words, of seeing his troops, while advancing upon Niagara, some hundred and fifty miles distant from that place, suddenly cut off from all means of help by a powerful and successful thrust against it from Frontenac, only fifty miles distant, determined him to make this the first order of business. In doing so he was observing sound canons of military science. In this connection it seemed imperative not only to strengthen old Fort George but to erect works on the two hills that dominated it. As Shirley was under direct orders, through the instructions given by Braddock, not to build any fort of

---

[80] *Ibid.*, X, 310.

[81] Dieskau to Doriel, August 16, 1755, *ibid.*, X, 312; see also Duquesne to the Minister of the Marine, July 1755, *ibid.*, X, 306.

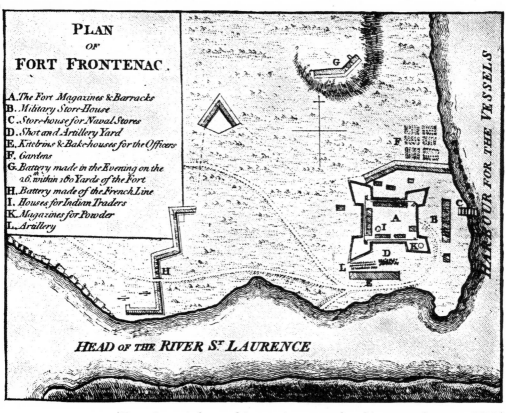

PLAN
OF
FORT FRONTENAC.

A. The Fort Magazines & Barracks
B. Military Store-House
C. Store-house for Naval Stores
D. Shot and Artillery Yard
E. Kitchins & Bake-houses for the Officers
F. Gardens
G. Battery made in the Evening on the
  26.th within 160 Yards of the Fort
H. Battery made of the French Line
I. Houses for Indian Traders
K. Magazines for Powder
L. Artillery

HARBOUR FOR THE VESSELS

HEAD OF THE RIVER ST. LAURENCE

(From *A set of plans and forts in America, reduced from actual surveys,* 1763.)

Plan of Oswego with its Forts, 1755.

(From the Duke of Cumberland Manuscripts, Windsor Castle.)

great expense without approbation from home and, even had this been permitted, was determined to provide without delay protection for his army, he decided to construct on the eminence to the northeast across the river

> "a Logg palisadoed Fort built, according to the enclos'd Plan of one I had erected upon the River Kennebeck the last year, capable of mounting large Cannon upon the middle Block House, and containing Barracks for 300 men; and which I apprehend will, with a Garrison of that Strength, and from the Dimensions of it's Loggs, be defensible against small Cannon: and if it should be judg'd requisite to have a Strong, regular Fortification built round it another year, may be of Service, not only whilst the new work shall be erecting, but after it is finish'd." [82]

To what extent the plan of Fort Halifax on the Kennebec was ultimately altered with the consent of Shirley in the building of Fort Ontario, as the new fort was called, is not clear. Some alterations were certainly made. The individual charged with the construction of the new fort, a Mr. George Demler, in his report drawn up the following year declared that he was ordered to mark the ground on the hill

> "in the figure of a Star with a Block house and four Cavaliers, designed by Messrs. Alexander and Bradstreet. . . ."

He then went on to say:

> "I made great Objections at the insufficiency and Construction of the plan . . . but Mr. Alexander ordered to have the plan executed according to the draught, and that I had nothing further to do, than follow his Orders which the General Confirmed." [83]

Unfortunately, Fort Ontario, designed in a hurry for temporary purposes, was found to be seriously defective when viewed the following year by a competent military engineer, Patrick Mackellar.[84] Nor did the efforts to strengthen Fort George and the beginnings of Fort

---

[82] Shirley to Robinson, September 19, 1755, C.O. 5:46.

[83] Demler's "Report" of May 28, 1756, C.O. 5:47.

[84] Mackellar criticized the star shape of the palisade with the main gate placed in an angle and "so flanked on neither side, which must be the Case of a Star as all the Angles are dead"; he found no banquettes, nor loopholes except for the cannon; he further discovered that there was a great loss of fire-power from the gallery at the top of the palisade because of the fact that the barracks were mostly built against the latter (C.O. 5:47; a copy of this found among the Cumberland Papers is printed in *Military Affairs in North America, 1748–1765*, ed. S. M. Pargellis, pp. 189–93).

Oswego on the hill to the west of the river escape his serious criticism.[85]

While the construction work on the forts was proceeding, Shirley came to the resolution to make his attack upon Fort Niagara with a portion of his troops. While still at Oneida Lake he had sent to the French fort two Indians, who had stayed there two days and had then returned with an encouraging report. At the time they were there the place was guarded, they declared, by a garrison of only some sixty Frenchmen and a hundred Indians.[86] As the weather was settled, it certainly seemed the logical time to strike at it, whether or not it could be held when captured. At a council of war summoned on September 18 the general set forth his plan to take six hundred regular troops, besides the Albany scouts, the Indians, and, for battering and investment purposes, an eighteen-pounder and four twelves, a mortar, and other smaller guns, leaving behind at Oswego seven hundred effective troops, supported by twelve cannon — nines, sixes, and three-pounders. All the officers agreed that the intended force against Niagara was sufficient; most of them also thought that seven hundred soldiers could guard Oswego; two thought they could if the redoubt on the eminence to the west were built; finally, all agreed that the construction of this was necessary and should be hurried. When Shirley also raised the question as to the desirability of "making a feint at Cadaraqui" (where Fort Frontenac stood), it was thought not to be expedient.[87] This decision may have been taken in view of the fact that the general reported that large reinforcements of both French and Indians were expected at Frontenac.

Preparations for the attack were now hurried. Artillery and ordnance were sent aboard the sloop *Ontario;* the *Oswego,* the other sailing vessel, was loaded with part of the provisions, and the rest

---

85 Mackellar discovered many defects in the construction of the old fort and in the work done to improve it. He declared that the new hornwork and the ravelin in front of it were badly laid out, the latter being built so high as to obstruct the fire of the flanks of the half-bastions and of the curtain; that the flanks of the old half-bastions did not properly defend the opposite faces and that the wings of these were really "enfiladed from end to end"; and that the powder magazine, sunk deep in the ground, was so very damp as to endanger the powder supply within it. As for Fort Oswego — never more than partially completed — consisting of some stockading and low wattle walls, he found it filled with soldiers' huts, and a thoroughly untenable place (*ibid.*).

86 This information was doubtless correct, as the number of French soldiers at Niagara fluctuated at this period almost from week to week in their movements to and from the upper Great Lakes posts and the Allegheny.

87 For the minutes of this council of war see C.O. 5:46.

were put in readiness to place on board the two galleys, as well as on the eight whaleboats that had also been built at Oswego and some of the bateaux reserved for this purpose. It was also determined that four hundred of the men would go in bateaux. But Shirley was destined never to set eyes on Niagara. Writing on September 28 to Sir Thomas Robinson, he stated that during the preceding thirteen days immoderate rains had fallen and tempestuous weather had prevailed on the lake, and as a result soldiers without proper shelter had fallen ill, work on the fortifications had been stopped, needed provisions had not arrived, and the Indians who had previously agreed to join in the expedition had now declared that the season was too late for it; some even had already started for their homes. Their opinion, he indicated, was supported by the Albany scouts, who knew the lake so well; he also declared that uneasiness about its present feasibility had taken the place of earlier optimism even among his officers.[88] In fact, at a council of war held on the 27th it was pointed out by Lieutenant Holland, who for three years had resided at Oswego, that the English bateaux were not adapted to the lake during this season of wind and swells.[89] Major Bradstreet, Shirley's best officer, who was later to win high distinction in the war as the destroyer of Frontenac, also warned that, by his own observation, over sixteen hundred French soldiers in the early summer had passed Oswego on their way to the Ohio and must for want of provisions be on their return to Montreal, as well as the traders from the upper Great Lakes region, and all must now be in the vicinity of Niagara; he further affirmed that soldiers could not handle the bateaux in rough water. The officers agreed, moreover, that nothing should be done until the anticipated provisions, the movement of which had been delayed by the storms, had come down the Oswego, and, further, that it was absolutely necessary to erect barracks for the soldiers, whose condition was becoming serious under constant exposure. It was also their opinion that this construction work, together with that on the two new

---

[88] *Corresp. of Shirley*, II, 289–301, and "Minutes of the Council of War," September 27, 1755, C.O. 5:46.

[89] As indicative of the difference between the English and the French bateaux, Lewis Evans (*op. cit.*, pp. 18–19) refers to the passing of the French bateaux close to Oswego on May 29: "But though our Forces and Workmen exceeded Three Hundred, we could not venture to attack them, as they were near four Miles in the Offing, had large Batteaux, wherein the Soldiers could stand to fire without Danger of oversetting; whereas ours, intended for smaller Streams, will not hold above six or seven Men, and are so ticklish, that an inadvertent Motion of one Man will overset them."

forts, would absorb the strength of all the soldiers before the winter set in and that, since Fort Niagara if now taken could not be held, it would be better to attack the place early in the spring, when it might be retained.[90]

But while the present campaign against Niagara was thus perforce laid aside, Shirley affirmed that he would

"be answerable that every part of his Majesty's Service requisite . . . for securing the whole Western and Southern Country, as far as the Mississippi, together with the Indian Trade, might with 6000 men . . . be effected the next year." [91]

He therefore now proposed to the ministry the following ambitious campaign to be undertaken the following spring from Oswego: first of all, the reduction of Fort Frontenac and the securing of the Lake Ontario entrance to the St. Lawrence by means of a force of four or five thousand men in two hundred whaleboats supported by a proper train of artillery and two hundred Indians; after this the capture in turn of Fort Rouillé at Toronto, west of Frontenac, of Fort Niagara, of Fort Presqu'Isle, of Fort "Pourchartrain" (Pontchartrain) at Detroit, and, lastly, of Fort Michilimakinac on Lake Huron, together with "securing the several Harbours and passes upon these Lakes and Straits." [92] Thus in one sweep he would exclude the French from the Great Lakes and upper Ohio Valley regions. As to retaining this great acquisition, he thought that one thousand men could hold Fort Frontenac and the entrance to the St. Lawrence, provided that the works there were strengthened; and that eight hundred additional troops distributed about the other posts and a somewhat expanded naval force on Lake Ontario would be adequate.[93] But this comprehensive plan was to wait four years for even partial fulfilment.

Again Shirley was right, from a purely military point of view, in placing first in importance in the Great Lakes campaign, once it really was launched, not the capture of Fort Niagara but that of Fort Frontenac and the sealing off of the St. Lawrence. But it must be emphasized that in making these the first and prime objectives, as well as in his plans for striking at Detroit and Michilimakinac later, he was departing fundamentally from the policy of the British min-

---

90 C.O. 5:46; Pennsylvania Archives (first series), II, 427–19.
91 Corresp. of Shirley, II, 292–3.
92 Ibid.
93 Ibid., II, 294–5.

istry as expressed in orders given in 1755 to him as well as to Braddock and to Governor Lawrence of Nova Scotia. These orders make
clear that British forces in North America should be employed simply to remove French encroachments upon lands that Britain claimed
for the colonies upon the basis of the Treaty of Utrecht. Forts Duquesne, Le Bœuf, Presqu'Isle, and Niagara in the west, Crown Point
on Lake Champlain south of the St. Lawrence, and Beauséjour, Gas-
perau, and St. John in the region of the Bay of Fundy and across the
narrow isthmus connecting the peninsula of Nova Scotia with the
mainland were in this category. But the British had never put forth
a claim to Cadaraqui, where Fort Frontenac stood, or to Toronto, the
site of Fort Rouillé, or to the Detroit strait, with its populous French
settlement, or to Mackinac Island, where stood Fort Michilimakinac.

Here now was a British general demanding a war of conquest
as a reply to French encroachments at a time when the ministry was
appealing to the courts of all Europe that what it was doing in North
America — even in sending out Boscawen with his fleet — was solely
to protect rightful national interests. There had been no declaration
of war nor would there be until the following year; theoretically,
therefore, and upon the basis of international law as then understood,
the two empires were still at peace. Yet in his letter of September 28
to the Secretary of State for the Southern Department, Shirley declared without qualifications:

> ". . . I am determin'd to begin the Operations of the next Year with
> attempting the Reduction of Fort Frontenac." [94]

Would the ministry permit the American commander-in-chief to
carry out his plans?

---

[94] *Ibid.*, II, 296.

CHAPTER VII

The Repudiation of Shirley

NOW THAT THE STROKE against Fort Niagara had been given up for the year, Major General Shirley gave his chief immediate attention to preparations for placing in winter quarters his troops encamped on the shore of Lake Ontario. He determined to keep his own regiment and Pepperrell's at Oswego for an early spring drive and to send back the New Jersey regiment, either to Schenectady or to Albany, where the two regiments of British regulars that had come and had campaigned with Braddock would also be quartered. He therefore used his entire military strength on the Oswego in an effort to rush to completion barracks and a hospital for the two regiments as well as the two new forts. As his presence was urgently required in eastern New York and later in Massachusetts Bay, however, he determined to leave the post on October 20. Upon going down the Mohawk he would be in a position to see that the three other regiments were properly cared for and could confer with Johnson respecting the Crown Point campaign; and in proceeding to New York City he could hold a council of war with the governors of New York, Maryland, and Pennsylvania, and later, in going into New England, with those of Connecticut and Rhode Island, "upon the general plan of service for both the Eastern and Western Colonies next year." [1] Further, he could meet his own Assembly early in the winter and make all preparations needful for his return to Albany in April, should he be continued in his command.

As Shirley passed eastward the latter part of October, he stopped to make arrangements for the building of Fort Williams and Wood

---

[1] Correspondence of William Shirley (ed. C. H. Lincoln), II, 297.

Creek Fort at either end of the Great Carrying Place between the Mohawk and Wood Creek. At Albany he acknowledged the receipt not only of a commission from the ministry to act temporarily as the commander-in-chief of all the British forces in North America "in the same manner and with the same powers as the late General Braddock had it," but also of copies of all orders and instructions given to the latter.[2] With this express affirmation of his authority by the Crown he was now at last in a position to deal effectively with the recalcitrance of Major General Johnson.

From Albany he proceeded to New York, where about the middle of December he held an important council of war. But before taking the work of this council up for consideration it will be necessary to follow the fortunes of the Crown Point campaign, which was as much the subject of consideration of this gathering as was that of Niagara.

Just as in the case of Shirley's expedition, there were great delays in the movement of the troops commanded by Johnson. These were caused by the slowness with which colonial levies and the essential matériel were concentrated at Albany and by the fact that the major general during the early part of the summer was deeply involved in an Indian conference at Mount Johnson, which took place between June 24 and July 4 with over a thousand Indians present, including the representatives of nine nations — the Six Nations and their allies. As a result of this, however, Johnson felt that he had secured the support of the Confederation for his campaign. Writing to General Braddock on June 27 in the midst of the conference, he made clear the state of preparation for this:

> "I have been spurring the several Gov[ts.] to forward their Levies & the necessaries for the Crown Point Expedition. Several Companies within these few days are arrived in Albany. The Artillery W[ch] has been too much neglected is now getting ready. The Quotas of Men are all Compleat as the Gov[rs] write me except this Province[.] They have hired 300 Men from Connecticut, three hundred more are raised by officers in this County, but the other Two Companies I hear nothing of. The several Quotas of Expence are not yet settled, and I much fear this Point will cause some Provincial Debates." [3]

In this connection he did not fail to stress the fact that he greatly regretted that Shirley was diverting a thousand men from the Crown

[2] *Ibid.*, II, 315–25.
[3] *The Papers of Sir William Johnson* (ed. James Sullivan), I, 664–5.

Point service to that for Niagara: "Crown Point is known to be the strongest Fortification of all the French Encroachments & they can in 6 days send all the powers in Canada to its relief." He nevertheless hastened to add: "However tho not pleased, I will do my Duty & serve my Country to the utmost of my abilities." [4]

As Connecticut had contributed heavily in men to the expedition and therefore demanded recognition, the second place of command in it was accorded to Phineas Lyman with the same rank as that enjoyed by Johnson — that of major general.[5] Although Lyman arrived on June 30 at Albany, where workmen were busy building bateaux and also gun carriages for the large cannon,[6] it was not until July 8 that Johnson was able to reach the point of concentration after having wound up his Indian conference and not until after the middle of the month that Lyman was ordered to lead the advance up the Hudson from Albany to the Great Carrying Place, about fifty miles to the north, with about a thousand men and two field pieces.[7] In advancing he was to open a proper road and construct bridges and, having arrived in the neighbourhood of the Lydius trading house at the beginning of the portage, to erect log magazines for the reception and protection of the supplies. By the 25th Johnson was able to write that Lyman had left with his division, that a second would follow in a few days — some twelve hundred soldiers with the battering train and field pieces — and that soon after he himself would move forward with the remainder.[8]

But Johnson's constant activities seemed to be affecting his health

---

[4] *Ibid.* Among the Johnson Papers are the "Reasons against Reducing the Forces" (*ibid.*, I, 677–80), which present twelve reasons advanced by Johnson for not taking from him five hundred of the Massachusetts Bay troops in order to strengthen Shirley. This does not seem to have been sent to Braddock.

[5] A native of Durham, Connecticut, and a graduate of Yale, Lyman had attained prominence in New England affairs as a lawyer and legislator before his appointment on Johnson's staff. He served later under Abercrombie and then under Amherst in the Lake Champlain area and was well regarded by his superiors. With the conclusion of hostilities in North America he participated in the successful Havana expedition and then turned his attention to a project for establishing a colony on the Mississippi.

[6] The Connecticut troops, to be forehanded, had brought their own bateaux, but these were found to be so small that they would not do; moreover, their number was inadequate. It was therefore necessary to construct a sufficient number at Albany so that the entire army could be supplied (Captain Eyre to William Johnson, June 30, 1755, *ibid.*, I, 670–1).

[7] His instructions, dated July 17, 1755, are published in *ibid.*, I, 730–2.

[8] *Ibid.*, I, 770; Captain Eyre to Robert Napier, July 27, 1755, *Military Affairs in North America, 1748–1765* (ed. S. M. Pargellis), p. 128.

and his equanimity, as his rather extraordinary letter of July 30 to Lieutenant Governor de Lancey indicates:

". . . I have been so very much engaged in settling various Points relative to the Crown Point Expedition with General Shirley, & obliged to go up to Mount Johnson to meet & fit out Parties of Indians, these joined to the duties of my Command of the Provincial Forces have not left me sufficient time either for Meals or for Sleep & have hurt my health for I am very far from being well."

He then referred to the efforts of Shirley's agents "working with Money and by every kind of Artifice to destroy my Influence . . . & to turn the Indians from the Crown Point to the Niagara Expedition. . . ."[9] It may be added that when this letter in a deleted form was submitted to the Council and then to the Assembly, the effect of it was to divide the latter body. As the Deputy Provincial Secretary made clear to Johnson:

"It was highly disapproved of . . . and 'tis now mentioned to your disadvantage by some, who seem rather affected to the Niagara than the Crown Point Expedition, for I assure you that's a Kind of Party Matter; and by some who were not formerly your Friends. . . ."[10]

Johnson at length left Albany on August 9,[11] and on the 15th, having arrived at the Carrying Place, he held his first council of war, at which it was determined to request a reinforcement of a thousand men from Massachusetts Bay and Connecticut.[12] The army numbered some thirty-five hundred men, called by Captain Eyre of the regular army "raw and undisciplined Troops." It was provided with a train of heavy cannon — six eighteen-pounders, each weighing some fifty-two hundredweight, two thirty-twos, eight sixes, together with mor-

---

[9] *Johnson Papers*, I, 794–5. Johnson also wrote on August 8 to de Lancey that his character and conduct had been vilified to the Indians without regard to "Fact or Truth" (*ibid.*, I, 841).

[10] Goldsbrow Banyar to Johnson, August 5(?), 1755, *ibid.*, I, 832.

[11] On August 4 Banyar wrote a somewhat critical letter to Johnson, who he thought was paying too much attention to his Indians and not enough to the problem of transport of his heavy cannon: "Your other Occupations will not admit of your attending to Matters of less Moment, tho very material to your Success. I mean the employing proper Carpenters, Smiths & other Persons as well to repair the Carriages in Case of accident on the Way as to facilitate the Carrying of the Train. I deel [sic] plainly with you. . . . See every thing necessary about the Train: It is even as necessary as Indians" (*ibid.*, I, 830).

[12] See Johnson's letter of August 15 to the several governors, urging a reinforcement (*Doc. History of N. Y.*, II, 678–80). The minutes of the council of war are printed in *ibid.*, II, 680–1.

tars — and yet it could count only one man trained as a military engineer, who had been sent by Braddock to aid Johnson, and few who knew anything about the use of artillery.[13] The call for a reinforcement was certainly justified, in spite of the fact that the New Hampshire regiment of five hundred would soon arrive, and both of the New England colonies applied to seem to have responded — Massachusetts Bay by raising eight hundred additional men;[14] Connecticut by responding loyally as well. Governor Fitch in reply to the appeal wrote on August 29:

> ". . . the Assembly as well as the Colony in General are Spirited to Exert themselves to the utmost in Supporting you and the Troops under your Command . . . the Assembly have Resolved to Raise fifteen Hundred Men over and above the five Hundred which are now Raising being in the whole Two Thousand Men to Reinforce the Troops in the Crown Point Expedition. . . ."[15]

On the 18th, at another council of war held at the Carrying Place, it was agreed to erect there a fort such as could be completed "without any Delay to the Expedition."[16] This was at first known as Fort Lyman, but the name was soon changed to Fort Edward in honour of Edward Duke of York. Situated on an eminence close to the Hudson, where a large island divided the river, and built about the log house of Lydius, it took, when completed, the form of a work of three bastions and a half-bastion, with parapet and ditch, between which was also a strong palisade.[17] On the same day that the war council agreed to erect Fort Lyman it also came to the decision to send forward toward Lake Champlain a division of fifteen hundred men "to cut a Road from this Place to South Bay" and unanimously agreed that Major General Lyman was the most proper person to command it.[18] However, it appears that when Johnson's Indians came flocking

---

[13] *Military Affairs in North America, 1748–1765*, p. 128.

[14] *Ibid.*, p. 132; *Johnson Papers*, I, 884–5.

[15] *Ibid.*, I, 888; *Connecticut Historical Society Collections*, I, 265–9.

[16] *Johnson Papers*, I, 861.

[17] Harry Gordon's "Remarks" (1756), *Military Affairs in North America, 1748–1765*, p. 179. The original plan of the fort laid down by Captain Eyre, a competent military engineer, was modified. Johnson, writing to Pownall on August 24, declared: "Cap^n Eyre has laid out a p^n of fortification here round Lydius's Log House, which if finished, would be very Serviceable in case of a retreat, but as it is thought too large by most of the officers, & Cannot be finished before we go, It gives so Great Uneasiness, that they propose to Apply to me About it, I understand this day" (*Johnson Papers*, I, 883).

[18] *Ibid.*, I, 860–1.

to the camp in such unexpected numbers that the major general felt
that he would have some four hundred at his disposal,[19] it seemed
best to utilize this support in the advanced division, and as a result
it was determined that Johnson himself should take command of it
and that Lyman should remain with the rest of the soldiers at the
Carrying Place.[20] It was also determined, instead of opening up a
road to South Bay, to open one to the southern shore of Lake Sacrament.

The distance between Lydius's cabin and Lake Sacrament was
only some fifteen miles and on August 28 Johnson arrived at the lake
without incident. The land about it was "all a thick Wood." Immediately the soldiers were ordered to clear a suitable place for an encampment and also for a fort. It was at this juncture of affairs that
the beautiful, island-dotted lake on the edge of which the British
forces had now appeared received a change in name. In the words
of Peter Wraxall:

> "The French call it Lake St. Sacrament, but the General gave it the
> Name of Lake *George*, thereby further to ascertain His Majesty's un-
> doubted Right to it." [21]

With the clearing of the land, temporary storehouses were erected
with the available timber, and Johnson, having selected a spot with
the aid of Captain Eyre, started to erect a fort.

There was need of haste if anything of importance was to be accomplished during the remainder of the season suitable for campaigning. For already before August 24 reports had reached Major General Johnson through his Indians that there was great activity among
the French to the north of Crown Point, with the road that led from
La Prairie on the St. Lawrence to Fort St. Jean at the head of Lake
Champlain filled with wagons conveying stores and provisions and
also with men marching southward, "coming in such parties that the
French would be Superior to us, Not only in the Number of Troops,
but also of Indians." Moreover, these reports had stressed the fact

> "That the French are making Several New Works at Crown Point,
> and that if our Army Marched by Wood Creek they intended to for-
> tifie themselves and Oppose us at So^h [South] Bay, if we marched by
> Lake St. Sacrament, at Tiecondaroga." [22]

---

[19] *Ibid.*, I, 879.
[20] *Ibid.*, I, 881. For Johnson's order to Lyman see *ibid.*, I, 887–8.
[21] *Military Affairs in North America, 1748–1765*, p. 138.
[22] "Extracts from the Council of War," *Johnson Papers*, I, 883.

Writing to Shirley on September 1, Johnson also indicated that other Indian scouts had just returned from the upper end of the lake, where they had noticed a party of French and Indians at Ticonderoga, but no fortifications. In this communication he expressed his great impatience to get a number of his bateaux over the portage and put into shape so that he could proceed with a party [23] to that place, where, as he had previously indicated, he would construct a third fort before moving beyond the Narrows to Crown Point.[24]

The French authorities at Quebec, as has been emphasized in the preceding chapter, had been made fully aware of the general purpose of the expedition under Johnson through information furnished by their Indian allies engaged in the contraband Albany trade. They were by no means disposed to await his arrival at Crown Point. The Marquis de Vaudreuil had therefore directed Baron Dieskau, in command of all French forces in Canada, to turn back from his contemplated campaign against Oswego and to move down to Lake Champlain with two of his veteran battalions, supported by some sixteen hundred Canadians and almost seven hundred Indians, to reinforce the Crown Point garrison.[25]

Soon after the 1st of September thirty-five hundred Frenchmen and Indians under the personal command of Dieskau moved southward in bateaux to still unfortified Ticonderoga, leaving only two hundred and fifty soldiers to guard the fort. There a British prisoner gave the French general a very misleading account of the true situation of the enemy. For he indicated that all but five hundred troops had retreated to Albany and that the remainder were guarding the British fort at the Great Carrying Place. Dieskau thereupon determined to make for Fort Edward by the shortest route with fourteen hundred of his troops.[26] This seemed to be provided by moving south-

---

[23] Johnson expected to take with him a thousand men according to Wraxall (*Military Affairs in North America, 1748–1765*, p. 138).

[24] *Johnson Papers*, I, 893–4. Wraxall in describing Lake George to Henry Fox writes: "It is navigable for Boats for about 36 Miles, when It grows very Narrow, and has a perpendicular Fall, which stops all Navigation; there the small Boats & Canoes in use here are carried over the Land for about a Mile, and launched into the Lake again. . . . This Fall is about 18 Miles from Crown Point . . . & a little beyond it, is another grand Pass called Tionderogo, which commands all the Water Passage between Crown Point, and these Parts" (*Military Affairs in North America, 1748–1765*, p. 138).

[25] "État de l'Armée française," *Johnson Papers*, II, 18.

[26] "Examination of French Prisoners, September 9, 1755," *ibid.*, II, 26–7; Dieskau to d'Argenson, September 14, 1755, *N. Y. Col. Doc.*, X, 316; Vaudreuil to Michault, September 25, 1755, *ibid.*, X, 319.

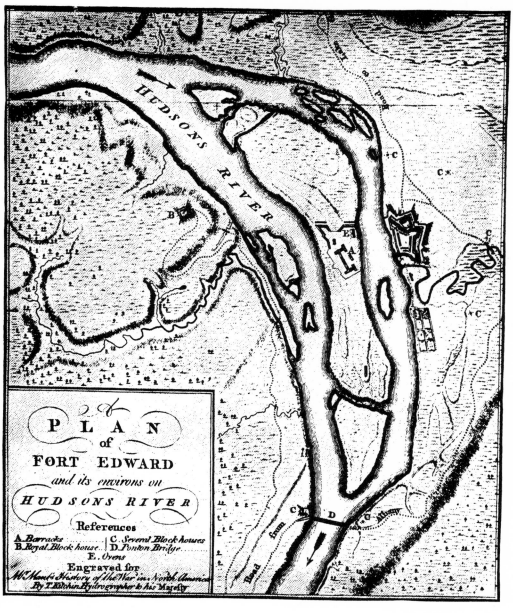

(From Thomas Mante's *History of the Late War*, 1772.)

The Lake George area in 1755.

(From Thomas Mante's *History of the Late War,* 1772.)

ward to South Bay, midway between Wood Creek to the east and Lake George to the west. In a day and a half the party covered this distance in their bateaux. Leaving these at South Bay, they then moved southward over the Indian trail in the direction of the Great Carrying Place. Besides Dieskau's force it appears that a fairly large number of French Indians with Canadian irregulars were also operating in the vicinity of the two British forts; a Connecticut soldier was scalped and another was taken prisoner in the vicinity of Fort Edward, while Johnson's Indians, fanning out from the Lake George encampment on September 3, came upon the tracks made about a week earlier by as many as a hundred and fifty of the enemy which led off in the direction of Schenectady.[27]

Even as late as September 5 — just three days before the Battle of Lake George — Johnson and his officers in a council of war held at the encampment were so little apprehensive of the grave danger that threatened that they came to the following decision:

> "The Opinion of this Council is that a Capt 2 Subs & 100 Men will be sufft. to be left to Garrison the Fort at the Camp at the Great Carrying Place." [28]

In other words, they were unwittingly prepared to make almost a gift of Fort Edward — where some of the heavy artillery and most of the other matériel were still concentrated — to the French, who by taking possession of it could have cut Johnson's army of colonials off from its only safe retreat, thereby opening up the possibility of a British disaster still greater than that visited upon Braddock's army.

On the 7th, which was Sunday, another council of war agreed to the plans prepared by Captain Eyre for "a good defensible Fort" at Lake George, and that same evening still another was suddenly called as the result of the return of Indian scouts who were sent to reconnoitre in the direction of Crown Point. The scouts reported finding the fresh tracks of a very great body of men moving southward from South Bay in the direction of the Great Carrying Place and they judged that an attack upon the fort there either was in progress or would begin that very night. The council thereupon came to the decision to send a warning by two different expresses to Colonel Blanchard of the New Hampshire regiment, who was in command there, and to send out scouts from each of the units of the encampment to gather additional information. The guards were doubled also and

[27] *Johnson Papers*, II, 8.
[28] *Ibid.*, II, 13.

the men slept on their arms.[29] About midnight some of the scouts returned with the report that they had ascertained that the French forces were about four miles to the north of the Great Carrying Place.[30] But Dieskau, who was fortunate to capture one of the expresses riding to warn Blanchard of his peril, found in questioning him that most of the British troops had not retreated to Albany — as reported by the British prisoner at Ticonderoga — but were encamped near Lake George without the support of a fort. As the French Indians very strongly favoured a move against the latter place rather than against the defences of Fort Edward, it was determined in a council of war held just two miles distant from the fort to alter the direction of the march.[31]

Now as to the forces encamped at the lake. At first it was determined to send out against the French by different routes two contingents of five hundred to attack it. To this Chief Hendrick objected and his position was sustained, with the result that a thousand men were placed under command of Colonel Ephraim Williams of Boston, called "a brave officer" and certainly one highly respected by his associates, who marched out of the encampment and within four miles came in contact with the enemy.

It has been the pastime of American writers in the past to speak derisively of Braddock, untutored in the American manner of fighting, for falling into an ambuscade laid by the enemy; and also, when he had fallen into one, for not using this American method of fighting. But in the first Battle of Lake George the American colonial levies, with the warning of Braddock's defeat still ringing in their ears, were ambushed by a French commander fresh from Europe who had never fought in the American way.[32] In the words of Johnson's secretary, Wraxall:

---

[29] *Ibid.*, II, 17. Blanchard with two hundred and fifty men of his New Hampshire regiment had arrived on September 5 at Fort Edward, where were posted five companies of the New York regiment. The rest of the forces were now at Lake George.

[30] Dieskau charged that on the march his Iroquois (the Caughnawagas) treacherously misled him (*N. Y. Col. Doc.*, X, 817).

[31] *A Review of Military Operations in North America, 1753–1756*, Mass. Hist. Soc. *Coll.* (first series), VII, 106.

[32] Baron Dieskau, writing later of the movement toward him of the force under Williams, says: "I immediately made my arrangements, ordered the Indians to throw themselves into the woods, to allow the enemy to pass, so as to attack them in the rear, whilst the Canadians took them on the flank, and I should wait for them in front with the regular troops. This was the moment of treachery. The Iroquois [Caughnawagas], who were on the left, showed themselves before the time and did not fire. The Abenakis, who oc-

"The Party in the Morning, with the Indians, & the sustaining Party sent out upon Our hearing the first Fire, were equal, if not superior in Number to the Enemy. Our people were surprised, by neglecting to have advanced & flank, Guards. Only the Indians, & some of the foremost of Our men stood the Attack; among both those there was a great slaughter: The rest did not advance, or make any Motions to sustain the Front, upon which They were beat back, a Panick took Place, & the whole fled in a disorderly Manner toward the Camp. The Enemy pursued, and kept firing upon the nearest Fugitives. Our People run into Camp with all the Marks of Horror & Fear in their Countenances, exagerating the Number of the Enemy, this infected the Troops in Camp." [33]

The engagement itself was no reflection upon American bravery or fighting ability; it reflects only on the inability of raw, undisciplined troops commanded by inexperienced officers to act up to the role of battle-seasoned veterans under battle-seasoned officers.

Fortunately for the horrified fugitives, the Lake George camp had been selected with some care for its defensibility, with the protection of "a low, thick-wooded swamp" on the flanks.[34] Trees had also been felled by the order of Johnson to form a breastwork of some fashion; but, in the words of a contemporary: "This was all his cover against an attack, having hitherto strangely delayed the proper retrenchments." [35] The general, however, soon after the detachment of a thousand had left, had seen that the cannon, located some five hundred yards to the rear, were brought forward and manned, and that some eminences on the left flank of the encampment were occupied in force. With the fugitives streaming into the rude enclosure, the French army under Dieskau made its appearance late in the morning marching in regular formation along the road directly upon Johnson's centre. When about one hundred and fifty yards distant from the breastworks, the enemy halted as a result of "some Disputes among their Indians." [36] Again in the words of Captain Wraxall, who was encouraging the colonial line to fight,

---

cupied the right, seeing themselves discovered, alone with a few Canadians attacked the enemy in front and put them to flight. I immediately prepared to join them, in order to accompany the fugitives into their camp, though still more than a league off" (Dieskau to d'Argenson, September 14, 1755, N. Y. Col. Doc. X, 317).

[33] *Military Affairs in North America, 1748–1765*, p. 139.

[34] *Review of Military Operations in North America, 1753–1756*, op. cit., VII, 107.

[35] *Ibid.*

[36] *Corresp. of Shirley*, II, 255.

"this happy Halt, in all Probability saved Us, or the French General would have continued his Pursuit & I am afraid entered with the last of our flying Men, before our Troops recovered their Consternation. Great numbers of our Men hid themselves during the Engagement, and many pretended Sickness. I did all in my Power to drive several out to the Breast Work, but for the most Part in vain." [37]

Nevertheless, some seventeen hundred Americans on that Monday morning in September did gather themselves together to resist.

When the veteran French grenadiers of the La Reine and Langue-doc battalions again marched forward along the road, their burnished fixed bayonets gleaming in the sunlight, and firing by platoons, while the Canadians and the Indians "squatted and dispersed on our flanks," the British artillery — fortunately having arrived in time from Fort Edward, and under the competent direction of Captain Eyre — began playing upon them, and to this was soon joined the musketry of the foot soldiers, now pretty well protected behind the fallen trees. Thus, while most of the balls from the French muskets were stopped short of their objectives by the makeshift breastwork, those from the British colonial muskets and the cannon began striking home. The Canadians and Indians, not liking the warm reception that they had unexpectedly received, now, melting away, "skulked into the swamps, took to trees, and maintained a scattered fire upon our flanks. . . ." [38] The French regulars, bearing with them the military reputation and traditions of Europe's greatest military power, "kept their ground and order for some time with great resolution and good conduct. . . ." [39] But even their high morale was affected by the

[37] *Military Affairs in North America, 1748–1765,* p. 139. Dieskau explains the delay so fatal to his hopes thus: "Meanwhile the Iroquois [Caughnawagas] collected on a hill, unwilling to advance. Some of them even wanted to force the Abenakis to release three Mohawks whom they had captured at the first encounter . . . but the Abenakis, seeing the Iroquois immovable, halted also, and the Canadians, seeing the retreat of the one and the other, were thereby intimidated" (Dieskau to d'Argenson, September 17, 1755, *N. Y. Col. Doc.,* X, 317).

[38] *Review of Military Operations in North America, 1753–1756,* op. cit., 107.

[39] Johnson to Shirley, September 9, 1755, *Corresp. of Shirley,* II, 255. Vaudreuil, in reporting on the action to Machault, gives an opinion unfavourable to Dieskau: "I cannot help having the honor to represent to you that had he followed . . . his instructions, and marched with his entire army . . . his center column should have consisted of 1000 regulars . . . he could have stationed 2000 Canadians and Indians on the heights, whence they might have fired with advantage on the enemy, and diminished the latter's fire on our regulars, who . . . might have charged with the bayonet and forced the intrench-ments, over which the Canadians and Indians would have leapt with equal intrepidity, and massacred the English" (*N. Y. Col. Doc.,* X, 324).

play of artillery and musketry upon them, which seems to have made havoc especially among their officers. Nevertheless, when ordered to shift to the right of the encampment and attack the colonial troops stationed on the eminences there, they responded and for an hour continued firing still ineffectively upon the new position, when, at last deserted by the Canadian militia and the Indians, with most of their leaders stricken, they were ordered to withdraw. As to what then happened, we had best let Captain Wraxall speak:

> "When the Enemy was beat off and flying, a Trial was made to pursue, but Men & several Officers were backward. However, I don't know but a Pursuit might have been dangerous to Us. The Day was declining — The Rout of the Enemy not certain, — The Country all a Wood, — our Men greatly fatigued, provided neither with Bayonets or Swords, undisciplined, & not very high spirited." [40]

Of much more importance than the loss of French regulars in the engagement was the fact that their leader, Baron Dieskau, commander-in-chief of all the King's troops in Canada, with a wound in the leg, which impeded his movement, found himself, as a result of a sortie of the English out of their breastworks and the dispersing of his soldiers, quite alone. In fact, when the enemy arrived, the general, according to a contemporary, was

> "resting on a stump utterly abandoned and destitute of succour. Feeling for his watch, to surrender it, one of our men suspecting him in search of a pistol, poured a charge through his hips; of which wound he is not yet recovered." [41]

The discomfited French and Indian allies, after retreating some four miles, reassembled at the very place where they had early in the morning inflicted their defeat upon Colonel Williams, with the loss of his life as well as that of other brave officers. The Indians were bent on securing the scalps of all the slain, and the French on refreshing themselves after the day's exertions and consulting on the possibilities of retrieving the defeat. Suddenly, at about eight o'clock in the evening they were struck by Captain M'Ginnis (McGinnis) leading a force of some two hundred New Hampshire and New York troops from Fort Edward, coming to the relief of Johnson. This, the

---

[40] *Military Affairs in North America, 1748–1765*, p. 139. Johnson's circular letter to the colonial governors (*Corresp. of Shirley*, II, 255) leaves the impression that there was a real pursuit and that in this his soldiers "slaughtered numbers" of the enemy.

[41] *Review of Military Operations in North America, 1753–1756, op. cit.*, VII, 107–8.

third engagement on that autumn day, was "the only considerable Honor on our Side." [42] Although greatly outnumbered, the British colonials, in spite of a mortal wound received by M'Ginnis, drove the surprised Frenchmen and Indians from their ground, seized their baggage, and slaughtered many of them. Thus the French, although they won the first engagement, were checked in the second, and lost the third, in the Battle of Lake George; yet their total loss was but 100 killed and 130 wounded as against 262 British casualties.[43] Why were they not pursued after their defeat, which came after their demoralizing check about the British encampment? [44]

Major General Johnson, it may be pointed out, was wounded in the thigh early in the engagement at the encampment, with the result that actually "the defence was conducted by General Lyman of Connecticut," next ranking officer.[45] It was asserted that although the latter in a council of war held the next day urged "with great warmth" the pursuit of the enemy, Johnson and most of the field officers showed "an equal disinclination." [46] The minutes of the council held on the 9th disclose only the unanimous decisions to inform immediately by express the colonial governments that furnished troops as to the outcome of the engagement and to employ "all our time in securing ourselves here in the best manner possible." [47] In fact, the Crown Point campaign of 1755 really ended on the shores of Lake George with the building, after much discussion, of Fort William Henry.[48] Yet, while falling far short of its objective, it was not a failure.

---

[42] *Military Affairs in North America, 1748–1765*, p. 140. See also Thomas Pownall to the Board of Trade, September 20, 1755, *N. Y. Col. Doc.*, VI, 1008.

[43] Vaudreuil to Machault, September 25, 1755, *ibid.*, VI, 1006–7, and X, 324.

[44] The author of *A Review of Military Operations in North America, 1753–1756* (*op. cit.*, VII, 108), writes: "Why the enemy was not pursued, when their retreat became general, no tolerable reason has ever been assigned; and Mr. Johnson, in his letter, seems very artfully to evade it."

[45] William Smith, *op. cit.*, p. 220. Timothy Dwight emphasizes the opinion of New Englanders (*Travels*, III, 367–70) that Lyman was the real hero of the Battle of Lake George. Charging that a systematic effort was made on the part of Johnson's friends to build him up at the expense of others, the author of *A Review of Military Operations in North America, 1753–1756*, affirms (*op. cit.*, VII, 109–10) that General Johnson himself, "two days after the action, frankly acknowledged, in his tent, that to Lyman was chiefly to be ascribed the honour of the victory."

[46] *Ibid.*, VII, 108.

[47] *Johnson Papers*, II, 24–5.

[48] Johnson wrote to Shirley on November 7 (*ibid.*, II, 279): "the Fort finishing here . . . I have named William Henry after two of the Royal Family." It was named in honour of William Duke of Gloucester and Henry Duke of Cumberland; just as Fort Edward honoured Edward Duke of York.

In turning to the aftermath of the battle, it is important to point out that not only had Johnson, as indicated, been wounded and remained rather incapacitated for some time after the engagement, but his relations with most of his field officers and the commanders of the colonial contingents, it is clear, became very strained. In fact, one may say that for all practical purposes he lost command of his army. Even his great friend and admirer Goldsbrow Banyar early in October pointed out to him, in referring to the rebellious attitude of the soldiers supposedly under him:

> "These are the blessed Effects of that unbounded Liberty we boast of & value ourselves for. Every Man with you thinks himself as at home, & that he's a right to be directed by his own Sentiments." [49]

Many soldiers had refused to engage in construction work on the forts and scows unless given extra pay, and their officers made little effort to see that orders were obeyed; even courts-martial had proved to be ineffective.[50] A month later Banyar, with reports continuing to reach New York of almost universal insubordination at Lake George — with the Connecticut troops, for example, refusing "to do any Duty either to work at the Fort or to mount Guard" unless their demands regarding rations were met [51] — emphasized one of the basic weaknesses of Johnson as the commanding officer:

> "You were certainly right to consult in all occasions, but perhaps it had been better for the Common Cause if you had been guided by Y^r own Judgment, or at least have try'd your authority early." [52]

No one realized this more fully than did the major general. It is therefore not surprising that he should write to Shirley on November 9 that he felt that the time had come when he should give his entire attention to the Indian problem:

> "Thus Sittuated, the public Good & My Duty to His Majesty seems to require that I should surrender the honor conferred on me in the Command of this Army, and under these Considerations I am willing

---

[49] Letter of October 11, *ibid.*, II, 181.

[50] Banyar in writing to Johnson makes the following interesting comment: "That you should be reduced to the necessity of abandoning the Work on the Scows, that the Fort might go on & that the latter will take a month still to finish is what cannot, I think, be accounted for, but by the officers and Men being disobedient to orders, and where the whole are so, there's no Punishing" (*ibid.*).

[51] They demanded more bread and flour and also "a Sauce to Their Meat wch they are used to & cannot live without it," wrote Johnson to Shirley on November 9 (*ibid.*, II, 284).

[52] Letter of November 11, *ibid.*, II, 286.

to relinquish my Military to attend to my Indian Department in w[h.] I apprehend I shall be able more effectually to serve My King & Country." [53]

But the governments that had commissioned Johnson were reluctant to have him resign until he had made one substantial effort to dislodge the French at least from Ticonderoga. On November 17 a council of commissioners representing Massachusetts Bay, Connecticut, and New York, at which both Shirley and Governor Hardy of New York [54] were present, met in Albany and came to the decision that Johnson's army should advance against the enemy and attempt to remove them from their encroachments "as far as they are able this Season." [55] But the season was too far advanced, Lake George was now not to be trusted, the enlistments of the New England troops at the forts were running out and the soldiers were determined to go home. Likewise the problem of conveying to Lake George supplies from Albany and hundreds of bateaux still at the Great Carrying Place over almost impassable roads made this thrust impossible to realize. But it is of interest to note that the New England colonies, after the defeat of Dieskau, poured reinforcements into New York so that Johnson had available in the late fall of 1755 almost eight thousand fresh troops. Could these have been utilized effectively, something might have been accomplished over and beyond what was achieved. But they could not, and remained something of an embarrassment at Albany.

So little confidence did Johnson have in the officers of the provincial contingents — among which were Israel Putnam, John Stark, and Seth Pomeroy, all of later Revolutionary War fame, and also Major General Lyman — that, when considering the problem of garrisoning the forts for the winter, he wrote to Governor Hardy that

". . . in my own private Opinion, from my Experience & Conversation amongst their Officers, I should not think it prudent to leave these Forts wholly in their hands." [56]

It is not without significance that in bringing the campaign to a formal conclusion, with the discharge late in November of all the

---

[53] *Ibid.*, II, 283.

[54] Sir Charles Hardy arrived in New York on September 2 with a governor's commission and thereupon took over the administration of the province, displacing Lieutenant Governor de Lancey, who took up his duties again as Chief Justice of the provincial superior court.

[55] "Minutes of Council of Provincial Officers," *Johnson Papers*, II, 305.

[56] *Ibid.*, II, 257.

provincial troops under his command except the number that the colonies concerned in it agreed should remain at Forts William Henry and Edward for garrison duty, he should have mentioned for commendation by name in his circular letter to the colonial governors only three men, all on the royal establishment as members of the regular forces.[57] This doubtless was a factor, if not a most important factor, in arousing that bitterness displayed the following year by the officers of the colonial line against those of the regular army which came to a head upon the arrival of Lord Loudoun in North America.

Thus the Shirley and Johnson campaigns had both bogged down. Nevertheless each had served a purpose. The arrival of Shirley's regulars at Oswego, with the strengthening of the defences, undoubtedly saved that place temporarily — once it was clear that the Six Nations could no longer guarantee the "neutrality" of the British and French posts on Lake Ontario in time of hostility. Likewise the arrival of Johnson's provincial volunteers at the Carrying Place on the upper Hudson — a most strategic spot — and its fortification, had raised a barrier against the French who otherwise under Dieskau would have been in a position to fall upon Albany and Schenectady — like Oswego, no longer protected by the old neutrality. Further, Johnson, with the opening of a road to Lake George, had planted British forces upon its shore-line in a position to observe the movements of the enemy, if not to dislodge them from Crown Point.

On December 12, after Johnson had given up his command, Shirley's projected council of war was held to perfect the plans for the western campaign to be instituted in the spring. At this meeting there were present the following governors, in addition to the general, who was also Governor of Massachusetts Bay: Hardy of New York, Sharpe of Maryland, Morris of Pennylvania, and Fitch of Connecticut. Among other military men in attendance were Colonel Dunbar and Sir John St. Clair both of Braddock's ill-fated army.[58] In opening the conference Shirley presented Braddock's instructions for

---

[57] He commended by name his secretary and aide-de-camp Wraxall, his military engineer Eyre, and Adjutant General Beamsly Glazier (Johnson to the Colonial Governors, December 2, 1755, *ibid.*, II, 361–5).

[58] Shirley under his instructions received from home was called upon to follow those given to Braddock. The latter was ordered by Instruction No. 7 to seek in all "Emergencies and Occurrences" the assistance of a council of war consisting of the commander-in-chief of any British fleet available for it, all governors of colonies, and such colonels and field officers "as shall happen to be at a Convenient Distance from our General and Commander of our Forces." This instruction has already been emphasized in Chapter III of this volume.

carrying on the Niagara and Crown Point expeditions. He then made clear that, from all information that he could gather, the French at Niagara, on the Ohio, about Lake Erie, and as far west as Michilimakinac were wholly supported from Montreal; it therefore followed that by dislodging them from Fort Frontenac and by barring their entrance to Lake Ontario all their forts in the areas described would be cut off. This, he stated, might be accomplished by assembling five thousand troops at Oswego by the end of April, by building larger vessels on Lake Ontario, and by throwing four thousand men first against Fort La Galette on the upper St. Lawrence at the mouth of the Oswegatchie — where Abbé Piquet had built his famous La Présentation mission in 1747 — leaving at the same time a thousand soldiers to protect Oswego from attack. He proposed that after La Galette had been secured, Forts Frontenac, Niagara, Presqu'Isle, and other places, each in turn, should be attacked and occupied. He recommended that while this campaign was proceeding above the Great Lakes, three thousand troops retrace the Braddock road to the Monongahela and strike at Fort Duquesne; that six thousand move against Crown Point; and, finally, that two thousand ascend the Kennebec, proceed to break up the French settlements on the Chaudière, and make a feint against Quebec from the mouth of that river, only three miles distant on the opposite bank of the St. Lawrence. By these simultaneous movements he would keep the French from concentrating against any one point.[59]

Taking into consideration these recommendations, the council of war, after some discussion, was unanimous in favouring the building of the larger vessels on Lake Ontario, the assembling of six thousand men, rather than five, at Oswego, and the concentration of ten thousand men, rather than six, against Crown Point. As for a second attempt against Fort Duquesne, it also supported this and at the same time emphasized particularly the importance of securing the active aid of the friendly Southern Indians and of preventing, if possible, the Northern Indians in alliance with the French from acting in opposition to those concerned in the Ohio expedition. Finally, it was agreeable to the idea of a feint against Quebec by way of the Chaudière, provided that this could be done without prejudice to other parts of the service.[60] Shirley, however, did not have it quite all his own way at the council; it would appear that Governor Hardy took

---

[59] For these recommendations see the New Hampshire Provincial Papers, VI, 463–5.
[60] Ibid., VI, 465–7.

the position that the attack of the force concentrated in the Lake Ontario region should be directed against Niagara and not against Cadaraqui — a position consistent with the secret instructions given to Braddock, which Shirley, one should point out, was still bound to observe.

As has been previously emphasized, an attack upon Fort Frontenac or any French position not identified with the encroachments undertaken by the enemy after the Peace of Aix-la-Chapelle had not been contemplated by the ministry when Braddock's instructions, which had not been altered, were issued. But military necessity pointed directly toward the closing of the upper St. Lawrence, and Shirley now boldly advanced the thesis that the occupation of Cadaraqui by the French in 1672 and the subsequent building of Fort Frontenac there were as clear an encroachment upon Iroquois lands as was the occupation of Niagara, and he pointed to what to him were the plain implications of the treaties of Ryswick of 1697 and of Utrecht of 1713 and to the fact that the region where this fort was built was marked upon "French Charts of the best Authority" as *"païs des Iroquois du Nord* [country of the Iroquois of the North]," just as on the same maps the upper St. Lawrence was called *"le fleuve des Iroquois* [the Iroquois River]." [61] He was determined therefore to act with the support of the council of war in expelling the French from the upper St. Lawrence unless he received His Majesty's orders to the contrary, and to be sure of his position he submitted his proposal, supported with arguments, to the Secretary of State for the Southern Department. [62]

While it is clear that the official attitude of the British government had been expressed in the secret instructions given to Braddock, and that in transferring the supreme command in America to Shirley no change was made in them, it is equally clear that at least by the summer of 1755 the Cabinet Council had come to feel that, with attainment of the objectives outlined in these instructions, the next cam-

---

[61] Shirley to Robinson, December 19, 1755, C.O. 5:46.

[62] *Ibid.*, II, 343–54. At this period there arose the bitter controversy over the question of the validity of the French claims to the region where Fort Frontenac stood. Although Shirley denied the validity of these claims in writing to Robinson (*Corresp. of Shirley*, II, 349–50), Lewis Evans, the Pennsylvania map-maker, in his famous *A General Map of the Middle British Colonies* (1755) and in his elaborate *Analysis No. 1.* designed to accompany it, defended them (p. 14). When Evans's position was criticized by the friends of Shirley, Evans replied in his *Analysis No. 2* (1756), which was a bitter attack on Shirley and his military strategy. Evans seems to have been aided by his friend Thomas Pownall (see my *Lewis Evans*, pp. 75–6, 181–218).

paign must be directed against Montreal, Quebec, and Louisbourg.[63] Therefore it is not likely that the proposal of the council of war to strike against Fort Frontenac would in itself have brought repudiation from the ministers. But by the time that Shirley's letter, written after the New York meeting, had reached London, the decision had been reached to supersede him in his command and to recall him to England. Both Governor Dinwiddie of Virginia, who had viewed with dismay the transfer of Braddock's regulars away from the Virginia frontier, to Albany, and Governor Hardy of New York had strongly recommended the sending from England of an experienced military man to take over the supreme command. The latter had declared to the Earl of Halifax that the command of the British forces in America was

> "a Task far beyond our present General's abilities. . . . I had many Conversations with Mr. Shirley . . . and I must beg leave to say I never met his Equal to transact Business with."

Before closing his letter Hardy did not fail, however, to admit something manifest to all American colonials in public life:

> "Mr. Shirley has made a very able Governor of the Massachusetts, and I beg leave to offer as my opinion, that he is much more able to do His Majesty Service in that Department, than at the Head of his Armies." [64]

Major General Shirley, although not a trained field officer, had nevertheless, without soliciting the direct command of an army, been asked by Braddock to lead the expedition against Niagara and was the latter's choice to succeed him in command of the American forces in case any accident should befall him. The question may be asked, in view of Hardy's criticism, whether Braddock was on sound ground in choosing Shirley. Was there anyone else in America better qualified to receive this mark of confidence?

Among the colonial governors the only men with military ambitions and inclinations besides Shirley were Glen of South Carolina,

---

[63] Among the Hardwicke Papers (B.M., Add. Mss., 35,909: 208–11) under date of August 11, 1755 is the interesting "Project for next Year's Campaign in North America" — apparently the work of the Duke of Cumberland — which called for the use of fifty thousand troops in a suggested campaign for the year 1756 against Canada and Cape Breton.

[64] Letter of November 25, 1755, *Military Affairs in North America, 1748–1765*, pp. 151–2.

Dinwiddie of Virginia, and Sharpe of Maryland, and none of them could begin to compare with him in combining certain qualities and advantages essential to successful leadership in a colonial venture such as the move against the French upon the borders of New York. Nor was there any other man stationed in America in either public or private life, including Pepperrell, the hero of Louisbourg, but now suffering from lameness, who could match him. At the beginning of this momentous struggle only Shirley had the prestige to tap the military potentialities of the only really militant part of British North America — New England. New Englanders associated successful achievement with him; not only had he shown himself to be a prudent, honest, and exceedingly able Governor, but his determination to defend the interests of his people in the regions of Nova Scotia and Maine, his success connected with the New England Louisbourg campaign of 1745, and his equal success in the Kennebec expedition of 1754, in which he directly participated, gave him a great following among all groups, high and low, in the Northern colonies. Therefore, when in 1755 he called upon New England men to volunteer for the campaign for the reduction of Fort Beauséjour up the Bay of Fundy, they responded; they also agreed to support his plans to reduce Crown Point. In fact, by September of that year, under the influence of his effective leadership, almost eight thousand Massachusetts Bay men were under arms and in active service against the enemy.[65] In an address to His Majesty by the Assembly of the province, dated the 26th of the same month, it was stated:

> "We have supplied for the general Good many more men than all the other Colonies together . . . when some of them exceed this [province] in numbers. . . ."[66]

It is thus clear that no fault could be found with Shirley in failing to enlist in the struggle the interest of the people under him. What is more, his proved sagacity as a strategist and his talents as a leader had led the Cabinet Council upon the death of Braddock to give him a temporary commission as commander-in-chief of the American forces, which they apparently expected to make permanent. Writ-

---

[65] C.O. 5:754, p. 50. Of the 2,000 men enlisted for the Nova Scotian expedition there were about 1,500 from Massachusetts Bay; about 1,000 others enlisted in the Shirley and Pepperrell regiments; 4,300 were in, or raised for, the army under Johnson; over 500 were in garrisons at the frontier forts; and, finally, 600 more were employed in scouting parties ("A Representation of the Case of . . . Massachusetts Bay," C.O. 5:754, p. 50).

[66] C.O. 5:754, p. 52.

ing to Sir Benjamin Keene in Madrid on August 25, Newcastle declared:

> "We have appointed Shirley Commander in Chief, for the present; And I hope, We shall, for the future, give more attention to those, Who always thought & said that the Business in *America*, must be done by *Americans*.[67]

Also in a letter written the following day to the Earl of Holderness in Hanover, the Duke went so far as to declare that he thought "it doubtful whether Anybody can be found, Who will do so well, as Shirley. . . . You know *Who* recommended Braddock. . . ."[68]

The indictment of Shirley in his role as commanding officer in North America of the military forces by Governor Hardy, therefore, brings one back again to the Niagara campaign, for which the major general was directly responsible. In making his final preparations for this it had been his great misfortune to run afoul of Major General Johnson over the issue of Indian support; but the blame for this check must rest squarely upon the shoulders of the latter, who, it is clear, should have seen the vital necessity of Indian aid and should have used all his personal influence with the Six Nations to effect it instead of bitterly opposing it as he did.[69] He also had the misfortune to run afoul of the New York authorities, who, in spite of the small contribution of the province to either the Niagara or the Crown Point campaigns, sought to exert a controlling influence, especially with respect to the expedition against the latter place. It is equally clear that on the issues that arose between them and himself he was on solid ground. Nevertheless, it may be said that had Braddock been permitted in the spring of the year to make Niagara his objective, he doubtless would have succeeded where Shirley failed. Johnson, de Lancey, and Pownall would not have dared to combine to destroy him; in fact, there is every reason to believe that, with his royal commission and unchallengeable authority, he would have secured their support; he certainly would have received that of Shirley — and that meant of New England. In coming to Albany he would have had a staff skilled in the peculiar procedures controlling the use of funds by military agencies, and, what is of much more importance, a well-

---

[67] B.M., Add. Mss., 32,858: 318.

[68] B.M., Add. Mss., 32,858: 292.

[69] To Johnson the importance of retaining his personal influence with the Iroquois seems to have transcended public interest on more than one occasion (*Pa. Col. Rec.*, V, 642–7; *N. Y. Col. Doc.*, VI, 795–9).

filled military chest; whereas Shirley had neither and was plagued by problems arising out of this lack and even accused, upon unjust grounds, of grave misconduct in financial matters.[70] If the hundreds of bateau-men — essential to move the army and matériel from Schenectady to Oswego — had been paid their wages promptly, they would probably not have deserted as they did, thus prolonging for two months the movement of the troops in small divisions. Shipwrights and carpenters at Oswego would also have been paid, and with supplies of all sorts arriving from the east and the troops poised for action in July rather than in September, the doom of Niagara might well have been sealed during the summer of 1755.

But under radically different circumstances, with all the delays, which can hardly be fairly charged against Shirley, everything had to await the spring of 1756, and this meant that most of the invasion troops would have to remain at Oswego to be ready for an early campaign. They therefore had to be housed and fed there during the winter, and many of them suffered cruelly. Their ranks were also depleted by death, in spite of everything that Lieutenant Colonel Mercer, who was left in charge of Oswego with the departure of Shirley for New York and Boston, could do.[71] By the latter part of January they were on short allowance of provisions and soon after this their condition grew really serious. Shirley — loaded down meanwhile with a multitude of responsibilities involving not only the new plans for the Niagara expedition and that for Crown Point but problems confronting him that grew out of the Nova Scotia expedition — seems to have been compelled to trust too largely to others to see that even the troops of his own regiment at Oswego had proper care. In fact, Mercer came to feel that he and his men, with scurvy at last sweeping the camp, were forgotten by the general.[72] By February he was in

---

[70] Shirley had to depend upon funds made available by the Deputy Paymaster of the Northern District, Abraham Mortier, and by the Deputy Paymaster of the Southern District, Samuel Johnston. But they might or might not have funds on hand to answer his warrants. For example, a warrant drawn on June 20, 1755, two on July 4, one on September 6, and another an September 25 were not paid by Mortier until July 4, 1756 ("His Excellency William Shirley, Esq. his Account Current," Loudoun Papers, Huntington Library). Some other warrants were paid by driblets; for example, the warrant of September 6 for £10,000 (ibid.). Imagine the confusion inevitably arising out of this situation!

[71] One cause of dissatisfaction and dark whisperings among the troops was that in the fort were stored trading goods. But Shirley, it is important to note, sought to retain the loyalty of the Western Indians by means of these goods (Corresp. of Shirley, II, 355–6).

[72] Mercer's correspondence with Captain Williams at the Oneida Carrying Place is revealing. Writing on January 24, 1756, he says: "At the Generals Departure from this Place he left us only 40 Days Bread, two Months Meat, & 3 Weeks Spirits. It has been

such straits that he determined to abandon the fort unless aid arrived by March 25. Fortunately, on March 24, the day before that set for the departure of the garrison, the first relief arrived from Fort Williams at Oneida Carrying Place.[73] Other smaller reliefs came until in May Lieutenant Colonel Bradstreet arrived with large supplies of provisions and naval stores.[74]

Shirley, it is now clear, far from forgetting Oswego, had come to realize that the earlier method of supplying the troops there was highly defective and in the fall of 1755 he had placed the energetic John Bradstreet in charge of this important task. On January 19 of the new year he had issued a proclamation calling on all bateau-men to enlist in the service and on March 17 had sent to Bradstreet instructions for organizing them into companies of fifty each; in the same instructions Bradstreet was placed in charge of whaleboat- and bateau-construction and was also given full responsibility for providing wagons at the portages and for all other matters pertaining to the work of transport.[75] Bradstreet, on his part, set diligently to work at the assigned tasks without delay; he enlisted two thousand bateau-men and began the construction of whaleboats and bateaux by the hundreds. Further, Shirley sent orders to Fort Williams to have the obstructions removed from the upper reaches of Wood Creek so as to reduce the portage at the Great Carrying Place from eight miles to one. This likewise was carried out in the spring of the year. With the purchase of large supplies by Livingston and Morris, Shirley's agents, provisions began moving to Oswego in quantity by the late spring. The difficult problem of transportation thus seemed to have been solved. Moreover, the garrison, sorely depleted by death during the tragic winter, was reinforced and once again placed in fit condition.

---

my constant employ ever since, to remind him & his Secretary of our Wants. It would appear, that in the Multitude of other Business we have been entirely forgot, as neither of them has taken the least Notice of our Necessity" (C.O. 5:47). On February 22 he sent word that the garrison was "sorely afflicted with inveterate and obstinate Scurvy, the Consequence of Salt & unwholesome food"; he also declared that the regiments had not been paid since October 24 (ibid.). Then on March 14 he wrote in desperation: ". . . a few Days more will put an End to all we have here. . . . Scurvy prevails to a great degree . . . our sole Reliance is on You, exert Yourself to save this Garrison" (ibid.).

[73] James Reade, assistant commissary at Fort Williams, led the relief party. Loading fourteen bateaux with provisions, he took these down Wood Creek to Oneida Lake, which was frozen; rolling the barrels over the ice and dragging the bateaux, he thus crossed the lake to its outlet and then went down the Oswego to the fort, where he was received with great joy ("Examination of James Reade," September 17, 1756, C.O. 5:47).

[74] Mackellar's "Journal," *Military Affairs in North America, 1748–1765*, p. 187.

[75] For his instructions see *Corresp. of Shirley*, II, 419–22.

Further, with Johnson no longer responsible for the Crown Point expedition, he and Shirley reached a harmonious agreement with respect to Indian policy and Indian support at Oswego.

Nevertheless, the comprehensive plans for the campaign of 1756 faced insuperable difficulties and were destined never to see fruition. Virginia, Maryland, and Pennsylvania were unwilling to undertake a second attempt against Fort Duquesne and equally unwilling to support that against Crown Point and they turned to purely defensive measures. Writing to Secretary at War Fox early in March, Shirley indicated that as a result of such measures, from New York extending down through New Jersey, and along the western frontiers of Pennsylvania and Virginia, a line of forts and blockhouses to cover the frontier for a distance of five hundred miles was being constructed and garrisoned; and that patrols and rangers from these were operating so that there was room to feel that a check had been placed upon the incursions of the Indians into the middle colonies.[76]

Something more than a purely defensive posture was required, however. It was vitally important that the French should be ejected from Niagara. This, according to the plan for the campaign of 1756, was to be the responsibility largely of troops on the royal establishment. But the four regiments of regulars now under Shirley's command — his own, Pepperrell's, and the two brought from Ireland — were sadly depleted and needed to be brought up to one thousand men each; further, it was necessary to recruit men for a fifth, the Royal Americans. Yet bitter resentment was developed in Maryland, Pennsylvania, New Jersey, and New York when officers sent into these colonies accepted the enlistment of indentured servants.[77] Others did not readily volunteer. Shirley also faced other problems. New England, while strongly committed to continuing its support of the Crown Point campaign, did not feel that it was in a position to provide the necessary increment of troops to bring the Oswego forces up to the agreed six-thousand mark, with which the major general could proceed to undertake the reduction of all French strong places in the Great Lakes region. The Niagara campaign, therefore, had to be laid aside.

But one should not infer from the reluctance of New England to go beyond its Crown Point objective, which it had greatly at heart, that Shirley had lost his popularity among the New Englanders as

[76] *Ibid.*, II, 415–16.
[77] *Ibid.*, II, 413–14.

the result of his failure to carry to completion the Niagara campaign in 1755. On the contrary, when he returned to Boston early in the following year — after the council of war held in New York — the citizens of that great seaport gave him a welcome such as one would hardly have supposed likely on the part of these people of steady and rather sober ways, a welcome also such as no other royal governor had ever received or would in the future ever receive. It was indeed a day long to be remembered, when the major general and Governor-in-Chief of Massachusetts Bay was greeted with gun salutes, a reception, a parade, a great banquet, and illuminations, with members of the Great and General Court, administrative officials, great merchants, and small shopkeepers vying with one another to show him their respect and good wishes.[78]

Still holding the confidence of the people of his own province, Shirley persuaded the Assembly to go far beyond the quota of troops agreed upon at the New York council of war to be provided by Massachusetts Bay for the new Crown Point expedition, and to increase the number from 1,750 to 3,500 men, when it was realized that the colonies of New Jersey, Pennsylvania, Maryland, and Virginia would not support it.[79] Encouraged by this example, the other New England colonies fell into line, each increasing its quota, and were followed by New York, which had perhaps most to gain from the expedition's successful termination.[80]

But Shirley's leadership in American affairs was drawing to a close. His enemies in America had done their work well. Johnson, upon the advice of Pownall, had written in his own hand to the Board of Trade, under date of September 3, a letter of bitter complaint against the general relating to his interference with the Six Nations.[81] This he had sent to Pownall for perusal before it was forwarded. He also took the occasion to write to Pownall in terms of the most undisguised hostility to Shirley, and in terms that showed a remarkable lack of understanding of the general, whom he denounced as "a bad Man abandoned to passion & enslaved by resentment." [82] For John-

---

[78] For a detailed account of this celebration see the Boston Weekly News-Letter, February 5, 1756; see also the Pennsylvania Gazette, February 12, 1756.

[79] Shirley to Fox, May 6, 1756, Corresp. of Shirley, II, 433–8; see also Shirley's letter of March 8 relative to the support of the Crown Point expedition (C.O. 5:46).

[80] Ibid.

[81] For this letter see the Documentary History of New York, II, 684–9; also N. Y. Col. Doc., VI, 993–7.

[82] Johnson Papers, II, 10.

son was tormented lest Shirley was writing home against him and undermining his influence there — which, incidentally, Shirley did not do.[83] This explains the famous meeting in Johnson's room in a New York hotel attended by Shirley's most implacable enemies: Lieutenant Governor Thomas Pownall of New Jersey, Lieutenant Governor de Lancey of New York, Deputy Secretary of New York Banyar, John Watts of the New York Council, Peter Wraxall, and Daniel Claus, the last two Johnson's aides.[84] At this gathering the groundwork was laid for the ruin of Shirley. And Thomas Pownall, about to return to England, eagerly accepted the responsibility not only of rebutting at home the general's anticipated attack upon Johnson but of carrying on the attack against Shirley. How well these men succeeded has become a matter of history.

On January 7, 1756 the Earl of Halifax transmitted a paper to the Cabinet Council from the Board of Trade, after the latter had considered Johnson's letter of September 3 attacking Shirley, that among other things represented the impropriety of Shirley's continuing in command since his policy had, it appeared, alienated the Indians. The Earl therefore concluded that "no Harmony nor Union in the Conduct of our Affairs is to be expected, but by a General to be sent from Home as soon as possible. . . ."[85] As to Johnson, Halifax recommended that he be given a royal commission as colonel of the Indians, thus placing him outside the jurisdiction of an American commander except in so far as the commission and instructions accompanying it required his acceptance of the commander's authority. These representations, with others, were considered by the ministers on January 20 at a meeting in the Duke of Newcastle's apartments, with the Duke of Cumberland present. Already strongly committed to the idea of sending to America another British general, the royal captain general found no difficulty in bringing the ministers to an

---

[83] For Shirley's mild criticism of Johnson's campaign see the Shirley Correspondence, II, 310.

[84] Proceedings of the meeting are given in detail in the Narrative of Daniel Claus, published by the Society of Colonial Wars (New York, 1904); see also Arthur Pound, Johnson of the Mohawks (New York, 1930), pp. 226–9.

[85] "Lord Halifax's Paper," B.M., Add. Mss., 32,996: 352. As early as November 27, 1755 the Board of Trade sent to Henry Fox, the new Secretary of State, a copy of Johnson's letter of September 3 with its bitter complaints against Shirley. The Lords Commissioners, in transferring it, wrote (C.O. 5:1129, pp. 42–4): "As this unhappy misunderstanding between Persons in so high Command may be attended with Consequences very fatal to the Publick Service, We think it Our duty, altho We have not yet received any letter from Mr. Shirley on this Subject to transmit to you a Copy of the said Letter."

agreement on the point of accepting the Board's recommendations.[86] Cumberland also urged as Shirley's successor John Campbell, Earl of Loudoun, a man long experienced in military matters who had fought at Dettingen under the King and in the Highlands during the days of the Scottish Rebellion of 1745. This nomination was accepted.

It was not until March 17 that Loudoun's commission as commander-in-chief under the Great Seal was issued.[87] Meanwhile, on March 13, Henry Fox, who had succeeded Robinson as Secretary of State for the Southern Department, wrote to Shirley to break the news that Colonel Daniel Webb — acting with the rank of major general while in America — had been appointed temporary commander of the forces in North America; also that a decision had been reached to lay aside the Niagara campaign for the time being; and, finally, that Shirley himself would probably be transferred from the governorship of Massachusetts Bay to that of Jamaica.[88] But not until April 16 was the news of the decisions received by the major general from his supporters in England,[89] and not until June — almost three months after it was written — did Fox's letter finally reach him, officially confirming what had by this time become common knowledge. This letter and another, most ominous in tone, written by the Secretary on March 31, calling upon him to "repair to England with all possible Expedition, having first deliver'd to Col. Webb all such papers as relate to the King's Service," [90] were brought by Webb.[91]

The truth is that Shirley's enemies had succeeded almost beyond their wildest expectations. Thomas Pownall had returned to England and, with his brother John occupying a key position in the powerful Board of Trade, had been most strategically situated not only to strike fatal blows at the general but to see that the latter's enemies in America were rewarded.[92] He had proceeded to do both.

It was in the midst of this hostility so skilfully generated against

---

[86] B.M., Add. Mss., 32,996: 352.

[87] S. M. Pargellis, Lord Loudoun in North America, p. 60.

[88] C.O. 5:212; also N. Y. Col. Doc., VII, 75.

[89] Shirley to Governor Morris, April 18, 1756, Corresp. of Shirley, II, 428.

[90] Shirley to Fox, June 13, 1756, ibid., II, 461.

[91] Ibid., II, 425.

[92] For the comment of William Johnson of Connecticut on the influence of Pownall, see the quotation in S. M. Pargellis, Lord Loudoun in North America, p. 54.

the general, with his conduct "universally condemned in England," [93] that there arose the furor in London over the famous so-called "Intercepted Letters." [94] These letters, addressed by some unknown person in Pennsylvania to the Duc de Mirepoix, French Ambassador in London, indicated that a great Indian uprising against the English was being planned. It now was actually suspected by some in London — so blackened had Shirley's character been by his enemies — that he was a party to it, or at least that people serving under him and in his confidence were.[95] Fox, with his mind full of suspicion of a devilish plot, wrote:

> "I don't suspect Shirley of Treachery, but I have no doubt of his having great Schemes, and that he Trusts the execution to Traitors, and that he ought not to stay in North America." [96]

As for Cumberland, he favoured having the Governor sent home a prisoner, but Hardwicke, not so easily swayed by such fantastic evidence, was opposed to any such drastic step. The Cabinet Council, nevertheless, determined upon his immediate recall to England.[97] This agreement was reached on March 29, with the result that two days later Fox framed the brusque letter of recall referred to above. All idea of rewarding Shirley with the governorship of Jamaica or in any way was put aside. He was, if anything was done, to be brought before a court-martial.

---

[93] Goldsbrow Banyar to Sir William Johnson, April 20, 1756, *Johnson Papers*, II, 441.

[94] For these letters see the American Historical Association *Report*, 1896, I, 660–703. Colonel Lydius was suspected, without evidence of guilt.

[95] On December 22 Governor Morris of Pennsylvania, who was in New York City, addressed a letter to Shirley about "the Continuance of the Ravages of the Indians in the Province of Pensilvania" and about the unhappy condition of the people living in that colony (*Corresp. of Shirley*, II, 366). Two days later Shirley, who was also in the city, sent an instruction to Major General Johnson calling upon him to engage the Six Nations to take up the hatchet against the French and Indians operating in Pennsylvania. The instructions then read as follows: "That they be requested immediately to proceed to Pensilvania where the[y] will find a large force actually in readiness, and there concert the best measures for carrying on the War" (*ibid.*, II, 367). A copy of this instruction was sent to the Board of Trade in Johnson's letter of December 18, 1755 (*N. Y. Col. Doc.*, VI, 1923–4). This arrived on March 17. The ministers, now deeply suspicious of the Governor of Massachusetts Bay and doubtless putting two and two together, saw a diabolical connection between Shirley's orders for the sending of Johnson's Indians into Pennsylvania and the plans for the Indian uprising within that colony.

[96] S. M. Pargellis, *Lord Loudoun in North America*, p. 76.

[97] *Ibid.*, pp. 76–7.

In building up Johnson at the same time that Shirley was pulled down, it had not been difficult for those committed to this project not only to enlarge upon the really important work that the former had done in seeking to perpetuate the old alliance between the English and the Six Nations but also to embroider a good deal his victory at Lake George. His great financial sacrifices in connection with his Indian relations had likewise been stressed, with little or nothing said of the even greater rewards in Indian lands and trade that had already made him a very wealthy man. The first impressive testimony of ministerial support and royal favour had been the issuance from the office of the Privy Seal on November 27, 1755 of a patent making Johnson a baronet, a "Degree of Hereditary Dignity between the Degree of a Baron and the Degree of a Knight." This signal honour, according to the patent, was not for his skilful management of Indian affairs, nor for commanding the army that checked the French, but because the said

> "William Johnson of Our Colony of New York in America Esquire (a Man Eminent for ffamily Inheritance Estate and Integrity of Manners) . . . generously and freely Gave and ffurnished to Us an Ayd and Supply large enough to Maintain and Support Thirty Men in Our ffoot Companies in Our said Kingdom of Ireland to continue for three whole Years for the Defence of our said Kingdom and Especially for the Security of the Plantation of our said Province of Ulster. . . ." [98]

Then came the vote in Parliament of five thousand pounds as a gift from the nation and as a mark of appreciation of his services in America. This was followed on February 17, 1756 by a commission from the King appointing him colonel of the Six United Nations and their Confederates and also "Our Sole Agent and Superintendent of the said Indians and their Affairs with the Annual Salary of Six hundred Pounds Sterling." [99] The same day that Fox wrote his letter depriving Shirley of his command he wrote to Johnson of the parliamentary grant and of the royal commission. [100]

As for that able and ambitious man Pownall, whose influence had been so potent in bringing about the revolution in American affairs, he was by no means forgotten. Robert Hunter Morris, a great friend and supporter of Shirley, who as Governor of Pennsylvania had been

---

[98] This patent is reproduced in the *Johnson Papers*, II, 343–50.
[99] *Ibid.*, II, 434–5.
[100] Fox to Johnson, March 13, 1756, *N. Y. Col. Doc.*, VII, 76–7.

fighting the Proprietors' battles with the Assembly and had been seeking to put that populous colony in a position to defend itself, was now slated for recall. Thomas Penn, realizing that his province was then under bitter attack both within and outside of Parliament for failure of the Quaker-dominated Assembly properly to support the Crown in its efforts to dislodge the enemy from the western frontiers, had determined upon this step and offered Morris's post to Pownall. This the latter declined.[101] Instead he chose to become Shirley's successor as Governor of Massachusetts Bay.

When Governor Morris in the spring of 1756 had received news of Shirley's probable transfer to the governorship of Jamaica — the best-paying office in the New World — and before he was made to realize the insecurity of his own position, he had written to Shirley:

> "I congratulate you on the King's Determination . . . but sure I am that this change, tho' possibly more profitable to yourself, will not be agreeable to those who wish well to the Northern Colonies as it must be universally acknowledged that You understand their Interests and Connections perfectly well. . . ." [102]

This statement is prophetic of the regret that many leading colonials were to feel in the passing of Shirley from the colonial scene. Even Benjamin Franklin, a bitter opponent of Morris in Pennsylvania politics and closely associated with Pownall before the latter left America for England early in 1756, was impelled to admit later that the recall of Shirley from his command of the American troops and the appointment of Loudoun was a great mistake:

> "He [Shirley] would in my opinion, if continued in place, have made a much better campaign than that of Loudon, which was frivolous, expensive, and disgraceful to our nation beyond conception. For though Shirley was not bred a soldier, he was sensible and sagacious in himself, and attentive to good advice from others, capable of forming judicious plans, and quick and active in carrying them into execution." [103]

In view of the complete miscarriage of the campaign of 1756 and the disaster connected with that of 1757 it is hard to escape the feeling that Franklin was right.

---

[101] For Pownall's reasons for declining the governorship see the *Pennsylvania Magazine of History and Biography*, XIII, 441–6.

[102] Morris to Shirley, April 25, 1756, *Corresp. of Shirley*, II, 432.

[103] *Works of Franklin* (ed. J. Sparks), I, 220–1.

Shirley was ordered to hand over his command to Major General Daniel Webb, who brought Fox's letters of recall from England, as previously stated. Webb in turn, upon the arrival of Major General James Abercromby, was to turn the command over to him; Abercromby was thereupon to remain in control until the arrival of the Earl of Loudoun. Unhappily, these men, supposed to possess superior qualities of leadership and certainly possessed of far superior training in military techniques than the Governor of Massachusetts Bay, were themselves to lose whatever reputation as commanding officers they had gained before coming to America. Between 1754 and 1758, in fact, the New World became the graveyard of British military reputations.

Webb landed at New York on June 7 and thereupon sent off Fox's letters to Shirley. Instead of going up the Hudson without delay to take over the command, as anticipated, he awaited the arrival of Abercromby, which took place on the 16th; then after a brief delay the two left for Albany and on the 25th Abercromby relieved Shirley of his command.[104] To Abercromby and Webb, both of the regular army, Shirley doubtless appeared to have been but an amateur bungler in his late role as major general and commander-in-chief of the British forces in North America. It certainly was to be found when his accounts were later examined that there was much confusion. For the drive against Ticonderoga and Crown Point, however, he had collected a provincial army of some seven thousand men at Forts Edward and William Henry under the immediate command of Major General John Winslow, with whom for years he had been closely associated and whose abilities he had tested. He also had at Oswego most of the troops of the two regiments on the establishment, his own and Pepperrell's, and most of the New Jersey regiment — numbering in all over a thousand men, under Colonel James Mercer — now held there with nothing more immediate in mind than protecting that immensely important post while the Lake Champlain campaign was in progress. In reporting quite fully to Abercromby on June 27 as to the general military situation in New York, he made clear the dangers to Oswego because of the difficulty of keeping open the communications with Albany, and in this connection he reported the failure of Sir William Johnson to persuade the Six Nations to keep scouting parties out and also the judgment of the latter that unless companies of rangers were sent out, he *"despair'd of the Com-*

---

[104] S. M. Pargellis, *Lord Loudoun in North America*, p. 83.

munication to Oswego being secur'd."[105] Shortly after submitting this survey he also turned over to the military engineer James Montrésor, to carry to Abercromby, a report on the conditions of the forts at Oswego made by Patrick Mackellar, who had been sent to the post early in the spring to study their defences and to make the necessary additions or alterations. This was apparently placed in the hands of the new commander-in-chief.[105]

As Mackellar's report indicated the weakness of the temporary forts against possible attack, it pointed to the necessity of action, as did Johnson's warning to Shirley respecting the danger to the communications. Again on July 10 Bradstreet arrived with the bateaux at Schenectady from Oswego, after having carried to the latter place six months' supplies for five thousand men and a great quantity of military stores. He brought ominous news of the movement of a large French force against the place. Still Abercromby was not stirred into action, although as the result of a council of war held on the 20th General Webb was ordered to hold the 44th regiment (Halkett's old regiment) in readiness to march to its defence. This paralysis at headquarters may perhaps be attributed to the fact that the major general doubtless hesitated to commit himself to a movement of troops until the arrival of Loudoun, who was expected in New York and who would then assume control. The latter, appointed commander-in-chief in January, did not leave England for America until May 20, and it was not until July 22 that H.M.S. *Nightingale*, bearing him and his personal staff, among the members of which was Thomas Pownall in the role of "Secretary Extraordinary," cast anchor off Sandy Hook.[107] In New York City the Earl met Shirley, who "insinuated," according to Loudoun, that "I would find every thing prepared, and had nothing to do but to pull Laurels. . . ."[108]

On July 28 the general arrived at Albany, where he found not only the paymaster's funds exhausted[109] but also a "Multiplicity of Warrants" granted by Shirley to those who had been directed to provide things for the army and who made clear to the new commander-in-chief that there were still great sums due them. Other demands against the paymaster were likewise coming in constantly. What

---

[105] Shirley to Abercromby, June 27, 1756, *Corresp. of Shirley*, II, 476. The italics are in the original and showed Shirley's concern over the safety of Oswego as early as June 27.

[106] Shirley to Montrésor, September 6, 1756, C.O. 5:47.

[107] S. M. Pargellis, *Lord Loudoun in North America*, pp. 81–2.

[108] Loudoun to Fox, August 19, 1756, C.O. 5:47.

[109] For the explanation of this see the *Correspondence of Shirley*, II, 518.

especially horrified Loudoun, as one committed to observing army procedures with the utmost care, was that many of those who set forth claims produced neither their contracts nor their accounts and that, as he indicated in writing to Fox,

> "every branch of the Service has been taken out of the hands of proper Officers for Executing them, and in general, put into the hands of private Agents of whom we have no Accounts. . . ." [110]

He was also made aware of "the defenceless state of the fortifications" as set forth by the Mackellar report on Oswego and the situation of the garrison, according to letters sent by Colonel Mercer.[111] He therefore agreed to the decision of the council of war held on the 20th, before his arrival, that Webb, with one of the Braddock regiments, should be sent forward to reinforce the Oswego garrison. But evidence is lacking that either he or Abercromby was unduly alarmed over the situation. Webb, in fact, was to move slowly: reviewing troops along the way, inspecting the condition of the forts, and making arrangements for additional storehouses.[112] It was not until August 9 that the regiment left Albany for Schenectady to embark on the bateaux and not until the 12th that it began the ascent of the Mohawk.[113] Webb was at German Flatts on the night of August

---

[110] Loudoun to Fox, August 19, 1756, C.O. 5:47.

[111] Ibid. On August 29, after the capture of Oswego by the French, Loudoun accused Shirley of concealing from Abercromby the Mackellar report of May 25 on the weakness of the Oswego fortifications (Corresp. of Shirley, II, 522). This will hardly bear the test of critical investigation. The report, addressed to James Montrésor, the military engineer, was turned over to Shirley, who, very soon after the arrival of Abercromby at Albany, returned it to Montrésor to be given to the new commanding general. In writing to Montrésor on September 7 regarding this charge, which, he stated, gave him "no small surprize and Concern," Shirley declared that "you told me that you did so [that is, turned the report over to Abercromby] either the same or next day after I delivered it to you" (C.O. 5:47). Loudoun, already bitterly hostile to Shirley even before his arrival in the New World and seeking a case against him (see S. M. Pargellis, op. cit., pp. 81–2), did not, it is interesting to note, accuse him in the letter to Fox referred to above of concealing either the Mackellar report or Colonel Mercer's letters from Oswego. It is clear that had there been an attempt at concealment, the Earl would have made the most of it in communicating with the British Minister.

[112] Ibid., p. 164.

[113] Why the relief for Oswego did not leave until a month had elapsed after the arrival of Bradstreet with his alarming report became a matter of dispute. Shirley's enemies accused him, as previously indicated, not only of holding back information but of failing to provide both provisions and entrenching tools. But these latter charges are no better founded, it would appear, than the charge of concealment and should be considered in light of the statements contained in the "State of the Dispute Concerning the true cause of the Delay of its Embarcation" enclosed in Shirley's letter to Fox of September 16 (C.O. 5:46). This indicates that, on orders from Shirley, Livingston and Morris in December

17 when the news was brought by an Indian that the French in force had surrounded the forts at Oswego.[114] That same day Captain John Parker of the New Jersey regiment sent word to Major Craven at the Great Carrying Place that Oswego had been taken and the garrisons of the forts made prisoner.[115] This information was carried down to Webb the next day by a soldier of Shirley's regiment who had escaped from the fallen place. At last stung into energetic action, Webb notified Loudoun that he had ordered the regiment and over a hundred soldiers of the Independent Companies to march to the Great Carrying Place and there to entrench themselves.[116] He arrived there with them two days later, but only remained for some twelve days and then hastily retreated down the river, after obstructing with logs Wood Creek, which Shirley had had cleared in the spring of that year, and after burning the forts that had been erected at either end of the portage.[117] Thus all the western portion of New York fell into the hands of the French and their Indian allies.

The French, it is clear, had had their eyes on Oswego ever since the construction of the English fort there in 1727 by the New York authorities. As it grew in importance with each passing year, its possession became the preoccupation of a succession of governors general of New France. However, in spite of royal orders and the deep desire of Galissonière to lay his hands upon it, it had remained undisturbed during King George's War as the result of the determination of the Six Nations that neither it nor Fort Niagara should be molested. But with the outbreak of Anglo-French hostilities in 1754, the Iroquoian no longer possessed sufficient influence to guarantee the safety of either stronghold. Shirley's abortive drive against Niagara

1755 purchased large quantities of supplies for Oswego and the forts along the way and that much of these, before the arrival of Abercromby and his own contractor, Christopher Kilby, in Albany, had been sent up to the posts, while the remainder had been delivered to the King's commissary general at Albany and was ready for supplying the 44th regiment. According to an affidavit of a Mr. John Murray, Webb, until a considerable period of time had elapsed and circumstances at length forced him to do so, refused to take any provisions but those furnished by Kilby.

[114] Webb to Loudoun, August 17, 1756, C.O. 5:47.

[115] Parker to Craven, August 17, 1756, C.O. 5:47.

[116] Webb to Loudoun, August 18, 1756, C.O. 5:47.

[117] On August 20 Loudoun replied to Webb's letter of the 18th relating to the latter's decision to go up the Mohawk from German Flatts to the Great Carrying Place. In approving this movement he also made clear that Webb's position was a dangerous one and that if it was found necessary to retreat he should destroy the forts there before leaving (C.O. 5:47). Webb not only did this but in his panic and without authorization had trees cut down to obstruct Wood Creek.

in 1755 had halted at the mouth of the Oswego, where his troops proceeded to entrench themselves behind the new works erected about the old fort or in its neighbourhood. But the plans of the English against Niagara were well known to the authorities of New France, who for a time were much disturbed at the prospect of the loss of that strategic place and, turning to counter-measures, concentrated at Fort Frontenac as many of the French battalions that had come with Baron Dieskau in the spring of 1755 as could be spared from the Lake George operations. This hapless general, as already noted, had thought that he would be privileged as the commander-in-chief of the forces in New France to lead his regulars against the English post, but instead had been ordered by Vaudreuil to attack first of all the English provincials who were threatening Crown Point; and in leading the attack against Fort William Henry he had been wounded and captured. His place was now filled by the capable and dashing Marquis de Montcalm.

Early in the new year the Marquis, who had returned from Louisbourg, where he had gone with the transports under de Salvert, was commissioned a brigadier general (*maréchal de camp*) and nominated to command the French troops in Canada.[118] He was ordered to proceed to Canada at the earliest possible moment, accompanied by two other very able officers, Brigadier François de Lévis-Leran and Colonel Bourlamaque (Boulamaque), a military engineer, together with two new battalions of troops — the La Sarre and Royal Roussillon — and a considerable body of recruits to fill up the ranks of the battalions already stationed in New France. Early in March six merchant vessels — loaded with provisions and six hundred troops and apparently moving as separate units to avoid capture — left France for Canada, and early the following month Montcalm and his staff, with the remainder of the troops, departed from Brest on three ships of the line, the *Illustre*, the *Léopard*, and the *Héros*, and three frigates, all sailing doubtless *en flûte* and certainly in three divisions, with a frigate attached to each capital ship. This impressive reinforcement of men and supplies arrived in the St. Lawrence in May, having successfully eluded the British fleet, as had most of the transports under de la Motte the preceding year.[119]

---

[118] D'Argenson to Doreil, February 29, 1756, *N. Y. Col. Doc.*, X, 393. For Montcalm's commission, dated March 1, 1756, see *ibid.*, X, pp. 394–5; for his instructions, he was to follow those given to Dieskau in every particular (*ibid.*).

[119] Montcalm to d'Argenson, June 12, 1756, *ibid.*, X, 413–16.

Once in Canada, Montcalm threw himself with infinite zest into the great task that lay ahead of him, which was not only to perpare for the defence of Canada but to act aggressively against Oswego. Realizing the importance of gaining the friendship of the Indians, he spent the better part of a month in Montreal with them, receiving and returning compliments.[120] He was delighted with the high morale of the French regular troops and even observed in writing to d'Argenson that they were paid too much money. It is clear that he felt that all depended upon the battalions that he had brought with him and those that had arrived in 1755. The sentiments expressed by his adjutant general, de Montreuil — that only regulars should be relied on in an expedition, but Canadians and Indians to harass the enemy [121] — were also undoubtedly those of Montcalm. With these regulars, supported by Canadians and Indians, it had been agreed for him to strike at Oswego. But before going to Fort Frontenac to prepare for the assault, he hurried to Fort Ticonderoga to see that all was in condition to ward off blows against that place by the British forces that had again gathered at Lake George.

On July 16, leaving the Chevalier de Lévis in charge, he returned to Montreal and on the 21st began his journey up the St. Lawrence. Already at Fort Frontenac two battalions had been concentrated: that of Guienne, which had been brought to Canada by de la Motte, and that of La Sarre, which had been sent out with him. Already Boulamaque was busy erecting entrenchments for the camp near the fort; already some eight hundred Canadians and a great body of Indians under the Sieur de Villiers had established a camp at Niaouré Bay (now Sackett's Harbor) on Lake Ontario, just fifteen leagues above Oswego, and were busy falling upon parties moving to and from that post. To Niaouré Bay at this critical juncture of affairs was sent the Béarn battalion, which early in the spring had been rushed to the defence of Fort Niagara, where it had greatly strengthened the fortifications. Arriving at Frontenac on the 29th, Montcalm found all in readiness for the great adventure. On August 4, after having sent out two armed vessels to establish a blockade of Oswego and to prevent interference with his plans by the British troops, he moved with the two battalions posted at Frontenac and with four pieces of cannon to join the Béarn battalion and the irregulars at the bay and arrived there on the 6th. That same day he sent out his vanguard to

---

120 Ibid.
121 M. de Montreuil to ——, June 12, 1756, ibid., X, 419.

take position three leagues from Oswego and on the 10th the invest-ment of Fort Ontario began.[122] Meanwhile what were the British do-ing at Oswego?

The capture of Fort Bull in the early spring of 1756 at the Great Crossing was but one of many ominous occurrences that pointed to the danger to Oswego. When the military engineer Patrick Mackellar arrived at Lake Ontario on May 16 with Bradstreet, who came with his convoy of bateaux carrying provisions and naval stores, he found that the woods about the place were so infested with enemy Indians that only large parties under military escort could venture into them to secure timber for building the additional lake craft ordered by Shirley.[123] After surveying the condition of the forts, as requested by the general, to which reference has already been made, he applied to Colonel Mercer for men to strengthen them; but a council of war on May 17 took the position that men could not be spared at the time from the work of shipping-construction. Not until a month later was the task of clearing the woods about the forts for added protection begun. On June 10, after Mackellar's report was received in Albany by the chief engineer, Montrésor, both the latter and Shirley directed him to proceed immediately with the completion of the works ac-cording to his recommendations.[124] Not until June 17, however, was any work done to remedy the defects in the forts. Even then work proceeded slowly, by reason of the painful shortage of men and the lack of encouragement to them with no money in sight. It is there-fore to be understood why Bradstreet's urgent request that men be spared to build a fort at Three Rivers to protect his convoys was re-fused. Moreover, in spite of the emphasis placed upon the building of shipping, Captain Broadley of the royal navy, in charge of the British naval forces on Lake Ontario, was obliged to report on June 27 that he "judged the Enemy considerably superior to them in force."[125] Even the launching of a brigantine and a sloop on July 3 did not change fundamentally this unfavourable position on the lake; nor did the subsequent launching of another sloop and a schooner do so; for these vessels before the attack were never equipped to

---

[122] "Journal of the Siege of Oswego," ibid., X, 457–61.

[123] "Mackellar's Journal," Military Affairs in North America, 1748–1765, p. 188.

[124] Shirley assured Mackellar that payment for the work would be prompt, but cau-tioned him that in settling with the carpenters it was important that they be paid in "a Regular Way, so as to be good Vouchers to annex to the Warrants that shall be drawn . . ." (ibid., p. 197).

[125] Ibid., p. 199.

fight for the supremacy of the lake, which had definitely gone to the French.

A new blow to the hopes of Mercer and his men came early in July with the receipt of word from Shirley's secretary of the change of command and the consequent unwillingness of Shirley to assume further responsibility for providing funds for payment of the work on the fortifications. As a result a council of war assembled by Mercer on July 5 agreed to the necessity of suspending these vitally necessary operations. Not until the 23rd were arrangements made to continue this work, which then went on after a fashion at all three forts without interruption until the very day of the attack.[126] When this was delivered, there were 1,134 officers and men of the three regiments and of the Royal Artillery at Oswego. The rest of the troops of these regiments were posted at the Great Carrying Place and at other passes between Oswego and Schenectady.[127]

On August 9 a French camp located on the lake shore about a mile from Fort Ontario was discovered; the next day two of the British sloops venturing near it were fired upon; and the day following, French irregulars and Indians began firing on the fort from the tops of trees.[128] The night of the 12th trenches were opened within pistol-shot of the fort, and early in the afternoon of the 13th the garrison — some three hundred of Pepperrell's regiment — having suffered three killed and one wounded, retired across the Oswego to the old fort, after spiking the cannon. Colonel Mercer, in command, thereupon determined to reinforce Colonel Schuyler of the New Jersey regiment, who with a detachment was at new Fort Oswego on the hill to the southwest dominating Fort George, by sending him the entire Pepperrell regiment and some of the troops from Shirley's. That night the French, in possession of Fort Ontario, proceeded to erect a battery in front of it that could play upon the defences of the old fort. In the morning of the 14th they began firing on the fort and sent a force across the river just out of cannon range of it.

Mercer, unfortunately, was killed by a cannon-shot early in the

---

126 Mackellar in his "Journal" included tables showing the nature of the work done on the forts from June 17 to August 13 and the number of men employed in each instance out of the three regiments (*ibid.*, pp. 214–16).

127 "An Account of the Strength of the Garrison & State of the Works at Oswego . . . in August 1756," *ibid.*, pp. 218–21.

128 Testimony of Peter Tilly and others given to General Webb on August 21, 1756, C.O. 5:47.

engagement on the 14th. The command now fell upon Lieutenant Colonel Littlehales of Shirley's regiment, who thereupon ordered Colonel Schuyler to march his troops to the old fort for a concentration of British forces. The enemy proceeded to occupy Fort Oswego, and the troops were now completely trapped, with the lake as well as two of the three forts in control of the enemy. After about four hours of cannonading, with the guns in Fort George replying ineffectively to those of the French battery, Littlehales, who had lost only some twelve or fourteen men,[129] decided to call a council of war. The officers now felt that the outlook was hopeless and, fearing a massacre if they continued to resist, decided to ask for terms. It had been hoped that Montcalm would accord the British troops the honours of war and permit them to march away from the fort. Instead they were made prisoners and were transported to Fort Frontenac and then down the St. Lawrence to Montreal after the French general had destroyed the forts and the habitations at Oswego.

The fall of the great trading emporium, contemptible in appearance as it was, had its reverberations on both sides of the Atlantic. The Western Indians, who, on Shirley's invitation to establish a council fire at this post, had expressed a desire to gather there, now turned against the British. In the words of one of them, who appeared in Montreal to set his eyes on Montcalm:

> "We wanted to see this famous man who tramples the English under his feet. But you are a little man, my father. It is when we look into your eyes that we see the greatness of the pine-tree and the fire of the eagle." [130]

In England, still suffering the deep humiliation of the recent capture of Minorca in the Mediterranean by the French, the news produced a profound sensation. Men spoke of Oswego as "ten times more important" than the island even with its great harbour of Port Mahon and its elaborate fortress of St. Philip.[131]

The question may now be raised: Was Oswego a doomed place in the summer of 1756? Would even the arrival of the 44th regiment and

---

129 In his brief report of the battle from Montreal, where he was carried a prisoner, Littlehales, in addressing Loudoun on August 30 (C.O. 5:47), declared that the loss of soldiers in the engagement itself did not exceed twelve or fourteen, but that after the capitulation "some of them having got in Liquor fell into Wrangling with the Indians & Several of them were Kill'd. . . ."

130 Bougainville's *Journal* (Parkman: *Montcalm and Wolfe*, I, 475).

131 Walpole's *Memoirs*, III, 41.

the New York Independent Companies under Webb before the siege have guaranteed its safety? While it is impossible to answer these questions categorically, it is quite evident that the presence of these reinforcements, which had the preceding year suffered so disastrous a defeat on the banks of the Monongahela, might not have given the British a sufficient margin of strength to stave off defeat. The colonial troops of the Shirley and Pepperrell regiments, although on the royal establishment, were no more battle-seasoned veterans than were those of Schuyler's regiment of New Jersey irregulars — nor were they more inspirited or eager to fight to the bitter end. Would these reinforcements, then, have given those already at Oswego what was demanded for success?

It should be made clear that certain factors that aided the French in the defence of Fort Duquesne in 1755 were present to aid them in the conquest of Oswego in 1756. For example, in neither instance were the British able to call upon their Indian allies for effective assistance. On the contrary, they were operating in each case in a wilderness region swarming with French Indians, supported by Canadian irregulars, and this was especially true of the approaches to Oswego. The dangers facing any force whose communications with the outside world can be cut are axiomatic in military science. The cutting of these communications was a part of the French strategy in 1756. It is true that had the Six Nations thrown their full strength in June or July against the cloud of Great Lakes Indians and the Canadians operating with them, the way might have been kept open. But Sir William Johnson could not undo in a day the evil he had wrought when in the spring of 1755 he had turned the minds of the Six Nations away from the defence of Oswego. Again, other factors favoured the French in 1756. The full measure of significance of the success of the French naval commanders in eluding the British fleets in the spring of 1755 and of 1756 while carrying to Canada the battalions of regulars was now clear. These soldiers, among the finest in a nation of soldiers, showed themselves superbly adapted to warfare even under wilderness conditions and were full of fire and eager enthusiasm for battle. Unfortunately for the English, the French were pitted at Oswego against colonials distinctly lacking in morale. Not one of the British leaders in North America seems to have realized that the presence of these newly arrived French battalions — to be compared in size to the British regiments — had altered profoundly the strategical and even the tactical situation in North America as it existed in the spring of 1755 before their coming, and that the scales were now tipped heavily in favour of the French. This also brings up the question of leadership. What had the British at Oswego to pit against the fiery, contagious enthusiasm and dash of Montcalm? Could Webb have supplied these qualities had he reached the post? Did he know his soldiers, and, what is even more important, did they know him? Did he not, when in command, whether at the Great Carrying Place or later at Fort Edward, manifest an incurable timidity and lack of decisiveness in aggressive action?

In retrospect it seems quite evident that Shirley's proposal at the council of war held in New York on December 12 and 13, 1755 — which was to send in the spring a force of some five thousand men to Oswego to bring about the destruction of the French forts in the region of Lake Ontario and to get firm control of that lake — held out the best prospect of English success in the Great Lakes area in 1756. In this connection it is equally evident that the campaign against Crown Point should have been suspended and that the colonial effort in that direction should have been limited to the strengthening of Fort Edward and Fort William Henry and the protection of Albany and Schenectady from French thrusts and to keeping open the communications between Schenectady and Oswego. Unfortunately, not only were the New England colonies and New York, as previously noted, now determined to confine their efforts to prosecuting the Crown Point campaign as of more immediate interest to them, but the southern colonies, which had so much to gain by the destruction of French power in the Great Lakes region, were unwilling, except for North Carolina, to support any movement up the Mohawk. Wars are not won under such handicaps, nor would this war be won until responsibility for all strategic moves was centred in London.

It is barely possible that had Shirley continued as commander-in-chief, events at Oswego might have taken a different turn. At least we can be sure that he would not have disbanded, as Abercromby did, most of the two thousand bateau-men whom Major Bradstreet had enlisted as irregulars and organized in companies of fifty men each. These rough, undisciplined men had the merit of knowing well the wilderness country between Schenectady and Oswego, in which they had lived for years; they were doubtless dissipated, but at the same time they were brave and had shown their ability to beat back the powerful Indian attack upon the convoy returning from

Oswego in July. They were especially well adapted to perform the vitally important service of keeping open the supply lines. Again, Shirley would also undoubtedly have sent without long delay a powerful relief to the post when the news was brought by Bradstreet of the establishment of a large French encampment only thirty-two miles from that place preparatory to attacking it. He had intended the 44th and 48th regiments for service in the Lake Ontario area, according to the plans submitted to the council of war in January, and although it had been agreed tentatively to divert them to the Crown Point campaign in the later council of war in May, the information of the danger to Oswego and, incidentally, to his own regiment, his confidence in Bradstreet as a soldier, and reliance upon the latter's judgment of military necessity would, it is quite evident, have influenced his own decisions. Colonel Mercer might therefore have found himself in possession of enough power and also of enough freedom and mobility of action, by using the bateau-men in large parties to scour the woods under the direction of their enterprising leader, to have discouraged the French Indians and the Canadians. Without the aid of the last-named groups, and facing continuous and heavy fire from some five regiments in prepared defences, it is also possible that the French regulars in assaulting the forts might have been sent reeling back, as happened in the Battle of Lake George the preceding year. We are dealing, however, with a hypothetical situation.

Let us now turn to the Crown Point campaign. When Johnson, after showing his inability to secure the confidence or co-operation of the New England troops, had resigned his command and retired to Mount Johnson and his Indians, it was necessary to find someone who would be likely to succeed where he had failed — especially in view of the fact that the colonies concerned had so much at heart the prosecution of this campaign early in the spring of 1756. Shirley at first had thought of giving the command to the conqueror of Louisbourg in the late war, Sir William Pepperrell, the President of the Massachusetts Bay Council. But he was lame and was manifestly ageing. The general then turned to Colonel John Winslow, who had been in charge of the troops that had ascended the Kennebec with him in 1754 and who, as will be noted in the chapter to follow, had been commissioned by him to command one of the two regiments of New England irregulars sent to Nova Scotia the following year to operate against the French. Winslow had acquitted himself on these occasions in a manner highly satisfactory to the government of Massachusetts Bay; he also enjoyed the confidence of his soldiers; he was, in fact, held to be the most experienced and capable officer in New England — and doubtless was. Therefore, while still in Nova Scotia, he was offered in March the command of the Crown Point expeditionary forces and accepted it.[132]

Returning to Massachusetts Bay, he set to work in close co-operation with Shirley, and with the hearty support of the New England governments, to gather the various contingents that would make up his army of irregulars and then moved on to Albany and thence to Lake George to make his arrangements for the advance against Ticonderoga and Crown Point. It was now determined that most of the forces would move along the west shore of Lake George while the artillery and other heavy matériel would be transported by sloops, barges, and bateaux up the lake to a point agreed upon.

Although the New England colonies and New York had agreed to raise some 8,800 troops, as late as the latter part of May the number that had actually arrived for the operations had fallen short of this by some 1,800. As a result Shirley on the 25th at a council of war, at which Colonels Gage and Burton, Quartermaster General Sir John St. Clair, and other regular officers were present, raised the question of employing on the expedition the two regiments that had come with Braddock, which had been again recruited up to strength. The council of war gave its unanimous opinion that

> "the 44th and 48th Regiments with the Provincial Troops appear to be, from the Intelligence of the Enemy's Strength, a sufficient Force to attempt the Reduction of the French Forts at Ticonderoga and Crown point . . . and that immediate Preparations be made for joining them with the Provincials. . . ."[133]

It also agreed to Shirley's recommendation that Fort Edward at the Carrying Place be strengthened and that a fort be constructed at "South Bay in the Way to Crown point" to prevent the French from again approaching by that route, employed the preceding year by Baron Dieskau. The decision to strengthen the provincials with the regiments of regulars was communicated by Shirley to General Winslow and also to Governor Hardy of New York under the cloak of absolute secrecy, but to no other colonial governor. It is clear that an

---

[132] Winslow to Fox, December 30, 1756, C.O. 5:46.
[133] Corresp. of Shirley, II, 459.

understanding had been reached by General Shirley that comprehended, on the one hand, Winslow and his provincial officers and, on the other, Lieutenant Colonel Gage of the 44th regiment and Lieutenant Colonel Burton of the 48th. It is just as clear that that understanding involved, for the good of the cause in hand, a winking at the regulations then in force respecting the loss of rank of provincial staff officers when serving with regularly commissioned officers,[134] just as these regulations had been ignored at Oswego, where the officers of the New Jersey irregulars took their places with those of the two regiments on the establishment, without any evident friction. General Winslow and his staff would therefore have continued in command of the provincials, with the regulars operating under their own officers and all under the ultimate authority of Shirley — duly commissioned by His Majesty not only as the commander-in-chief of the British forces in North America but also as the Governor of the province that had furnished by far the largest proportion of the provincial troops serving under Winslow.

The displacing of Shirley as the commander-in-chief of the British forces in North America, first by Abercromby and then by Loudoun, threw into inextricable confusion the whole Crown Point campaign. These British officers knew their "Rules and Articles of War" thoroughly and expected to follow them without deviation. Under them General Winslow and his staff would lose all significance; further, the provincial forces, if serving with the regulars, would be subject to the severe provisions of military law under the terms of the Mutiny Act, such as were applied in the British army in time of war. But an impediment existed to either Abercromby's or Loudoun's displacing from command General Winslow and his officers as the result of the action of the New England assemblies earlier in the year. For the conditions of service of the contingents that made up the provincial army were clear and definite in each case; in volunteering it had been agreed that they were to be concerned with the Crown Point campaign alone and were bound to obey only the orders of Winslow.[135]

---

134 Article 2 of Section 19 of the Rules and Articles of War.

135 Winslow received his commission from Shirley and was "confirmed in this appointment by the other governors." For example, on March 26 Governor Fitch at the request of the Assembly commissioned Winslow as major general and commander-in-chief of the forces raised by that colony. The commission declared that ". . . you are to observe and Follow such Orders and Instructions as you shall from time to time receive from me or the Commander in Chief of the Said Colony for the time being . . ." (C.O. 5:47).

The explanation for the insertion of these conditions of service by the assemblies harks back to the extreme friction that developed at Lake George between Major General Johnson and the New England troops in 1755 and also to the situation of the New England irregulars in Nova Scotia serving under Colonel Robert Monckton of the regular army during that year. In the course of the campaign against Fort Beauséjour and particularly at its conclusion — during the period that the Acadians were being deported — serious animosities were engendered as the result not only of charges of favouritism shown by Monckton to his regulars as against the provincials but also of efforts on his part to recruit as many of the latter into Nova Scotia regiments as possible, in spite of the fact that their terms of service had been expressly limited to one year. In fact, the Massachusetts Bay Assembly angrily requested Shirley to demand the return of all the troops, including those who had accepted this service.[136]

When Winslow, who was deeply involved in the controversy with Monckton and who was persuaded that although he was the second in command of the forces against Beauséjour, he had suffered many humiliations at Monckton's hands, took over the Crown Point expedition in the spring of 1756, it is more than likely that he saw fit to secure from the New England assemblies a certain protection against interference from officers on the regular establishment — a protection they were delighted to give. Therefore when Loudoun and Abercromby sought to incorporate his troops into the regulars and to place them in consequence under their orders, there was trouble. In other words, under the Shirley plan — a plan that ignored the army regulations — the regulars were to co-operate with the provincials; but under the regulations that bound all British generals — and that in truth bound Shirley — this relationship was not possible. Major Bradstreet, writing to Shirley on July 24 after the latter had left Albany but before the arrival of the Earl of Loudoun, grasped the essentials of the situation:

[136] Writing to Fox on June 14, Shirley set forth the situation tactfully and succinctly (*Corresp. of Shirley*, II, 464–5): "Soon after the Surrender of Beau Sejour, some small Animosities happen'd, as I have been inform'd, between the Commanding Officer of the Expedition and the principal Officers of the Irregulars which were afterwards increas'd by an Order given in Nova Scotia, whilst the New England Regiment subsisted as a Corps, for inlisting such of the Soldiers of it into the King's Regiments, as could be got to do it. . . ."

"The French are certainly in great Numbers toward Crown point, and our Affairs that Way seem to wear a gloomy Aspect; this would not have happen'd had your Excellency continu'd here, and taken the Command upon you, as in that Case they [the provincials] would have consented to the Regulars joining them." [137]

At first it appeared that the difficulty would not be too great to surmount. When Abercromby arrived in Albany the latter part of June, at a conference that he held with Shirley, Webb, and Winslow it seemed to be agreed that the provincials would proceed against Ticonderoga as planned and that the regulars would then occupy the provincial camp at Half Moon, ten miles above Albany and Forts Edward and William Henry. Under the impression that all was settled, Winslow returned to his camp and on July 15 started to move forward with the artillery and ordnance stores. After proceeding a short distance he was ordered by Abercromby to return to Albany. In obeying the command, however, he in turn ordered General Lyman to proceed with the train to Fort Edward. When he appeared before Abercromby, the latter asked Winslow his opinion of the effect that a junction of the regulars with the provincials would have upon the expedition. The comamnder-in-chief of the provincials replied that he would be "Extreamly well pleased" if such a junction could be made, but apprehended that if this would cause the provincial officers to lose their commands it would cause universal discontent among the troops.[138] The officers who were with him likewise agreed that this would be the case. Again Winslow returned to his post and on July 20 reached Fort Edward with the main body of his troops. From there he ordered Colonel Bagley at Fort William Henry to get ready all the sloops, lighters, and bateaux to proceed to the neighbourhood of Ticonderoga and he himself began the movement of his matériel to Lake George and on the 28th arrived there. Busy with his preparations, on August 3 he learned of the arrival in Albany of Lord Loudoun and sent congratulations to him and an account of the situation. But that same day he was again ordered to Albany and instructed to bring with him his principal field officers.

Upon arriving in the city Winslow and his officers were requested by the Earl to state in writing whether the troops raised by the colonies and furnished with His Majesty's arms would in obedience to

[137] *Ibid.*, II, 488.
[138] Winslow to Fox, December 30, 1756, C.O. 5:46.

His Majesty's commands act in conjunction with His Majesty's troops and under his commander-in-chief in North America. The officers replied that they themselves would submit in all dutiful obedience to act as desired, but pointed out that since the troops had been raised "on particular terms," which had been observed up to that time, it would be a favour to the provincials to be permitted to act separately "in so far as it is consistent with His Majesty's Service." [139] Under the impression that all was now satisfactorily explained, Winslow and his staff returned to Lake George, and on August 19 orders were given to start the bateaux with the military stores to the place of rendezvous, which was to be some five miles to the south of Ticonderoga. But the expedition was not to take place, for the next day a letter came from Loudoun announcing the loss of Oswego and pointing out to Winslow that if, in attacking Ticonderoga, the troops "should meet with any Misfortune," it would be out of his power to stop the enemy from overrunning the whole country. The general therefore directed that for the present the provincials should hold themselves on the defensive, especially so as to guard against an attack by way of South Bay or Wood Creek. To accomplish this purpose Winslow marked out a "strong camp" that lay between the bay and Fort Edward and by arming the sloops on the lake came into control of it. During the months of September and October all was therefore in readiness for the expected attack by Montcalm. But none came. Since the New England troops still persisted in refusing to be brigaded with the regulars or to be controlled by orders of officers of the latter, as Loudoun and Abercromby desired, and since they held firmly to the terms of their enlistments, it was at length determined to disband them. As a result, on November 11, after receiving orders from Abercromby to decamp, Winslow gave over his command to Major Eyre and led the first contingent of the New England provincials from Lake George to Albany. He was followed on the 17th by General Lyman with the remainder of the troops, except the sick and a number who were carpenters or masons and who continued to work on Fort Edward. Upon reaching Albany the troops were discharged from service.[140] So faded away for the second time in the Great War for the Empire the hopes of the northern colonies to be freed from the menace of Crown Point, to which was now added that of Ticonderoga.

---

139 *Ibid.*
140 *Ibid.*

The blame for the loss of Oswego was fastened upon Shirley by the Earl of Loudoun,[141] as was also the blame for the refusal of the New England troops to be incorporated with the regulars in connection with the Crown Point campaign. Neither charge, it would seem, can be effectively supported upon the basis of existing evidence. In fact, Shirley did not hesitate to send General Winslow a stinging rebuke after Loudoun had reported to him that the provincial commander and his officers had acted in a mutinous manner. Writing to Winslow on July 26 from New York, he said:

> "Yesterday the Earl of Loudon acquainted me that he had been informed, that you and the other Officers of the Provincial Troops under your command have declared that in case you should be joined by Regular Troops in your March to Ticonderoga for the Reduction of that Fort and Crown point, you would withdraw your Troops and return home, or to that Effect. I don't think it possible for yourself, or any Officer that has the least Sense of Honour and his Duty to make so mutinous a Declaration as this, or even to entertain so criminal a thought. . . ." [142]

Loudoun was also under the conviction that Shirley was "raising parties to support himself" and to oppose the new commander-in-chief and that he was doing this by two methods: first, by enriching his friends through "lavishing the Public Treasure," and, second, by attempting to impress the people that he was "the only Man entrusted in American Affairs, by the King or his Servants." [143] This charge appears likewise to be baseless. In answer to it Shirley declared in writing to the Earl on September 13:

> "What parties, My Lord? Surely Your Lordship Can't mean parties to Obstruct His Majestys Service, either under Your Lordship's Command, or in the Civil Department, within this Government [Massachusetts Bay], in the hands of my Successor; A long Series of Faithful

---

141 Dr. Stanley M. Pargellis in his *Lord Loudoun in North America* is critical of Shirley as a commander and yet he shows clearly the difficulties that Shirley faced in his work. For an interpretation of the history of Shirley's activities that is in some respects in opposition to mine, the student should therefore read with care Chapter V of this scholarly study.

142 *Corresp. of Shirley*, II, 492. Winslow in reply to Shirley made clear that the above was not a true statement of the attitude of the provincial officers, and since their attitude was expressed in writing and only in writing to Abercromby, he sent Shirley a copy of the statement they had signed. This emphasized the peculiar conditions of service attached to the raising of the New England troops for the Crown Point campaign (*ibid.*, II, 495–8).

143 Loudoun's comments on Shirley's letter to him, dated September 13, 1756, *ibid.*, II, 557.

Services to His Majesty, and my Establish'd Character founded on 'em will protect me, I doubt not from so injurious a Charge; let it come from what Quarter it will." [144]

In fact, one may affirm that Shirley himself had become the victim of a "party" raised up against him by Pownall, de Lancey, and Johnson. It had been so successful in achieving its objectives in England and, enjoying the complete confidence of Lord Loudoun, had so poisoned the latter's mind against his predecessor that he saw in every step that Shirley took, no matter how praiseworthy, some sinister effort to obstruct his work. How completely the Earl misjudged Shirley, how little he appreciated the notable and patriotic role that the Governor of Massachusetts Bay had played in American affairs for over a decade in advancing the cause of the Empire, is indicated by the fact that he actually contemplated sending this distinguished man home a prisoner for high crimes and misdemeanours in connection with the Oswego campaign. In forwarding to Secretary of State Fox the letter of explanation that Shirley had sent him, referred to above, he declared:

"My own Opinion was, that on the Information I send you, of his Management last year and this at Oswego, I am entitled to send him home Prisoner; but other People thought this would appear Violent. . . ." [145]

When Shirley finally left his government in the fall of 1756 to render an account of his stewardship to his hostile superiors at home, he was the symbol of something that disappeared from British continental America never to return. For never again would a royal governor in any colony be able to harmonize to the same extent as Shirley the interests of the mother country — imperial in nature — with those of the vigorous corporate colonies — local in nature. Never again would a native Englishman enjoy in eighteenth-century America the vast prestige that came through the exercise of superior capacities directed to the enlistment of the voluntary support of the colonials for certain common and important ends. Doubtless the secret of his power lay in the fact not only that his spacious and disinterested views on American affairs appealed to most colonials but also that he understood Americans, he respected them, and was inclined to support them whenever possible against the claims of superiority of

---

[144] *Ibid.*, II, 557–8.
[145] *Ibid.*, II, 558.

his fellow Englishmen, and even to cut administrative red tape in doing so. This last point may be illustrated by his decision in 1756 in favour of Colonel George Washington as against the claims to superiority of Captain Dagworthy, in charge of Fort Cumberland in Maryland, and by his entire management of his military office — and this did not endear him to the British officers. What was true of his military office was equally true of his civil administration in New England. While Loudoun with superior military training and experience in military affairs could take over his post of commander-in-chief of the American forces, while Pownall, a capable man possessed of an active mind and powerfully entrenched at home, could occupy his old civil seat in Boston, in each case a void existed that neither could possibly fill and that never was filled by any man before the old Empire finally disintegrated in the throes of internal strife. For Shirley displayed something little short of genius in making the creaking colonial system work. This is indicated in the striking tribute to his services that came from the Massachusetts Bay Assembly in August 1756:

> "The Affection that we bear to your Excellency's Person, & your Regard for the Interests of the Province, cause this in us. . . . Yet Justice as well as Gratitude would oblige us to bear our Testimony to the World that the affairs of this Province have been so wisely conducted by your Excellency that your Name ought to be ever Dear to the Inhabitants: & there have been so many Instances of your Excellency's great Regard to the general Interests of these colonies that your Memory ought forever be respected by them, and your Administration distinguished as a happy Period by them." [146]

Little did they realize how soon the name of Shirley would sink almost into oblivion, under a wave of anti-British sentiment whipped up against his successors in office.

The gloom cast by events taking place in northern and western New York and along the Pennsylvania, Maryland, and Virginia borders during the years 1755 and 1756 was only partially lifted as the result of striking successes in the region of the Bay of Fundy during the same period. Here, and here alone, the British were able to make headway against their French rivals. To describe these events we must now pass from the older continental British colonies to the newest of them.

---

[146] Mass. Bay General Court Records, 21: 242-3.

CHAPTER VIII

The Treason of Thomas Pichon

IN THE CHAPTER entitled "Land of the Acadians" in the preceding volume, an effort was made to illustrate the nature of the discouragements that faced the government of Nova Scotia from 1713 to 1754 in its efforts to make loyal subjects of the French-speaking Acadians living about the Bay of Fundy and numbering some ten to fifteen thousand by the latter date. The present chapter is concerned with the unfolding of events in this region precipitated by the establishment of a number of French forts in the midst of Acadian settlements and by the determination of the servants of His Most Christian Majesty to employ whatever means were necessary to draw the inhabitants away from the allegiance that they owed to the British Crown.

As the year 1754 drew to its close, the picture presented in old Acadia was a confused one. French regular troops were in control of the narrow isthmus of Chignecto, connecting the peninsula with the mainland, and of lands lying to the east and south of it well within the peninsula; they were also in control of the St. John River, which empties into the Bay of Fundy. Wherever they had appeared, forts and posts had likewise made their appearance. There were Fort Beauséjour on the Missaquash River, which flows into what was then Beaubassin, toward the head of the Bay of Fundy; the fort on the St. John; a post at Shepody between the two and also near the head of bay, as was Beauséjour, but on the mainland; Fort de Gaspereau on the northern shore of the narrow isthmus facing Baye Verte; a post at Village de la Baye Verte, on the road between Gaspereau and Beauséjour; with still another at Remstreque on the coast, some

twelve leagues southeast of Baye Verte and on the line of communication between it and the Acadian settlements about Cobequid Bay,
which lies on the eastern extremity of Minas Basin.[1] Some were mere
stockades sheltering only a few soldiers, others were of masonry containing a strong contingent; but all had flying above them the fleur-
de-lis as sign of possession of the lands by the King of France.

This was not all. The claims of France extended into the very heart
of the peninsula itself. Governor Shirley of Massachusetts Bay, in
pointing out this fact to Secretary of State Robinson, declared:

> "When I had the Honour to be employed as one of his Majesty's
> Commissaries at Paris . . . for settling the limits of Nova Scotia, the
> state of the limits assign'd by the French Commissaries stood thus:
> They allowed the Sea Coast upon the Atlantick Ocean between Cap
> Canso & Cap Sables to be the Country of Nova Scotia; how far the In-
> land limits extended they could not be brought to ascertain, other-
> wise than they did not extend to the City of Annapolis Royal, w^ch
> they say thô it was ceded in Express Terms to Great Britain by the
> Treaty of Utrecht, Yet it is not by the Terms of the Treaty ceded as
> part of Nova Scotia, but as a place not included within the Antient
> limits of that Province, so that the French Commissaries exclude the
> three Districts of Annapolis River (except the spot upon which the
> City of Annapolis stands), Minas, and Chiegnecto out of the limits."[2]

In drawing up the instructions for the new Governor General of New
France, the Marquis de Vaudreuil, in the spring of 1755, the Minister, in referring to the position taken by the French commissaries,
re-emphasized the fact that the latter in dealing with the cession of
Acadia in 1713 held rigidly to the position that this involved only a
portion of the peninsula and consequently that the British were intruders upon French soil in attempting to control the whole of it —
without reference to the larger British claims:

> "They [the French commissaries] have taken the view that the ces-
> sion of Acadia should be understood to comprehend only a part of
> the peninsula."[3]

In view of the position taken by the French after 1750 that all those
districts where the Acadians were living were not in ancient Acadia

---

[1] "State of the English and French Forts, Garrisons & Militia in Nova Scotia, 1754,"
C.O. 5:15, p. 69; B.M., Add. Mss., 33,029: 324-9.

[2] Shirley to Robinson, December 8, 1754, C.O. 5.15, p. 63.

[3] "A specific instruction for M. de Vaudreuil as to his relations with the English,"
April 1, 1755, Arch. Nat., Col., B. 101: 163-75.

but rightfully within the bounds of New France,[4] it is not surprising that Colonel Lawrence, Governor of Nova Scotia, should warn Shirley in November 1754 that he had received intelligence

> "that the French have designs of encroaching still further upon His Majesty's Rights in this Province and that they propose the moment they have repair'd the Fortifications of Louisbourg to attack our Fort at Chignectou. . . ."[5]

The strength of the position of the French in Nova Scotia at this critical juncture of affairs cannot be questioned. Although the number of regular soldiers posted there in the early winter of 1754 was only three hundred and fifty, they were able to look forward to powerful reinforcements from France in the coming spring and also aid from the French forces at Louisbourg, which in 1752 numbered twelve hundred. As has been made clear, a thousand of the most seasoned French veterans — made up of the battalions of Artois and Burgundy — were diverted from the troops destined for Quebec and sent in 1755 to Louisbourg. Further, the Acadians that had openly declared for the French — some 1,280 families — were estimated to number 1,650 fighting men; added to these were at least 400 Abenaki and Micmac Indians fully under the control of the famous French fighting priest Abbé Le Loutre. Finally, within the districts of Minas Basin and Annapolis River, among the Acadians who had not as yet openly declared for the French and were called "Neutrals," it was estimated that there were 2,500 fighting men, all "under the influence of French Jesuit Priests," who would not fail to welcome a successful move of a French force into their midst.[6] As against this potential hostile force the government of Nova Scotia could count on 1,560 regular troops and rangers and 1,350 militia; but at least one half of the latter were stated to be "of suspected faith to the King's

---

[4] There is hopeless confusion and inconsistency on the part of many French writers regarding the position of the Acadians in 1755. For example, Abbé H. R. Casgrain in his "Coup d'Œil sur l'Acadie avant la Dispersion de la Colonie française" (Le Canada-Français, I, 114–34) by the very title of his article gives away the French case, to wit: that the region where the Acadians were living was not really surrendered Acadia but New France.

[5] C.O. 5:15, p. 81. The warning of the proposed attack on Fort Lawrence was contained in a communication forwarded by Thomas Pichon, the French spy serving the British, entitled "Reflexious sur le mémoire concerning l'établissement de Beauséjour, (Pichon Papers, E, Nova Scotia Archives; a translation of this is contained in J. C. Webster's Thomas Pichon: The Spy of Beauséjour, pp. 33–7). Referring to the proposed attack, the communication reads: "Finally, this enterprise ought not to take place until the fortifications of Louisbourg have been repaired."

[6] C.O. 5:15, pp. 59–60.

Government." [7] Again, the weakness of the British position in the northern and western portions of the peninsula is shown by the fact that at Fort Lawrence, across the Missaquash from Fort Beauséjour, there was a garrison of but some 350 troops in a hostile region quite dependent upon outside assistance by water; at Fort Edward at Piziquid, southeast of Minas Basin, there were only 160; and at Annapolis Royal, 120. Further, with respect to the defence of Nova Scotia in its entirety against attack, it was asserted by Shirley

> "that the English have not one fort there except that of Annapolis Royal, which could stand out one day against an attack with a few Peices [sic] of Cannon; that the Garrisons therefore would in such case be under the necessity either of Surrendring at Discretion, or issuing out & engaging the Enemy at all Events; and Annapolis Royal itself could not hold out long, being in a very ruinous condition; and but weakly Garrison'd." [8]

In view of the fact that in 1749 the French had advanced into a region that in the seventeenth century, and up to the very signing of the treaty of cession of Utrecht in the eighteenth, they had consistently maintained was a part of old Acadia and had thereupon fortified; in view also of the sweeping claims they had put forth after that date, as indicated by Shirley's statement, which would have limited the British rights in ceded Acadia simply to the eastern littoral of the peninsula and to the town of Annapolis Royal — and backed by ever increasing pressure upon the Acadians to obey only the orders of the French King — it is not difficult to appreciate the infinite embarrassments faced by Governor Lawrence in attempting to maintain an orderly government of the province of Nova Scotia and his final determination in 1754, with the support of the home government, to rid the peninsula of the intruders before they could make new advances.[9] In communicating his definite proposal to Governor Shirley on November 5 he wrote:

---

[7] C.O. 5:15, p. 60.

[8] C.O. 5:15, p. 48. Lieutenant John Waite, in communicating with Edward Weston on June 18, 1752 from Fort Lawrence, declared, in referring to the French at Beauséjour (Weston Papers, Hist. Mss. Com., Tenth Report, p. 308): "We have let them build a Very large strong Fort, in which at this Time they say they have forty pieces of Canon, & two thirteen Inch Mortars; any Day they please they may drive us out of this Fort, its only pitching two or three of their Bombs amongst us and it will be impossible to stay in our Wooden Houses."

[9] Governor Shirley on May 8, 1754 wrote to Secretary of State Robinson that he had information of a proposed Indian attack on the English east of the Kennebec, instigated

"I think it high time to make some effort to drive them [the French troops] from the North side of the Bay of Fundy; but as it is impossible for me to collect Men enough to execute this design without weakening the Metropolis and exposing the Settlers in this part of the Province to the insults of the French and Indians, I have sent the Bearer, Lieut. Colonel Monckton, to sollicit your assistance and to advise with your Excellency how such an undertaking might be carry'd on with the greatest Privacy and Effect. . . ." [10]

Lawrence thereupon proposed that New England should raise two thousand volunteers,[11] which, added to the regulars that he could supply from the Nova Scotia posts, would, he thought, be sufficient to perform the task that he had in mind the coming spring. This enterprise, he further indicated, would be wholly at the expense of his own province [12] and depended for its success upon secrecy and on its consummation "before the Shipps of War are arrived at Louisbourg from France. . . ." [13]

There has been a disposition on the part of historians to treat the project of the conquest of the French forts established in the region of the Bay of Fundy and Bay Verte as incidents of some interest but not of major importance with respect to the larger issue of the respective positions to be assigned to the French and English in North America as the result of an appeal to arms. It is certain that this was not the point of view of those responsible for the growth in importance, as well as for the defence, of Canada. To them it was clear that there could never be a great and prosperous New France capable of protecting all its potential as well as existent vital interests from interference by its powerful southern neighbour without control of the western and northern shore-lines of the Bay of Fundy and of the region stretching south of the St. Lawrence and including the river

---

by the French, and that he had been assured by Governor Lawrence that with the assistance of one thousand men from New England the position of the French and their Indians about the isthmus of Chignecto could be made untenable. The Governor of Massachusetts Bay indicated to Robinson that he endorsed Lawrence's proposal to drive the French from their Nova Scotia encroachments (*Nova Scotia Documents*, I, 382–3).

[10] C.O. 5:15, p. 81; see also another letter of the same date, of much the same tenor, in P.R.O., N.S., A. 56: 33.

[11] In his first suggestion to Shirley earlier in the year he had given one thousand New England men as a sufficient complement to enable him to remove the French forts.

[12] "I have given Colonel Monckton an unlimited Credit upon Messrs. Apthorp & Hancock," stated Lawrence in a second letter to Shirley under date of November 5 (*ibid.*).

[13] *Ibid.*

systems of the St. John and the Richelieu. While Quebec was rightly regarded as the great bastion of defence of Canada, Louisbourg, another bastion, was only of second importance, guarding as it did the one feasible approach to the Gulf of St. Lawrence by a hostile fleet. But in isolation Louisbourg on Isle Royale, or Cape Breton Island, was in a dangerous position in time of war and needed the support of a hinterland by which it would be firmly supported and as firmly linked to Quebec. French military strategy had by 1755 succeeded in binding Quebec and New Orleans together by means of a chain of forts including Montreal, Frontenac, Niagara, Rouillé, Detroit, Presqu'Isle, Le Bœuf, Duquesne, Vincennes, St. Joseph, and Chartres. This same strategy had also dictated the equal importance of Beauséjour, Gaspereau, the fort on the lower St. John, and St. Frédéric on Lake Champlain, which, taken together with the western chain, provided an impressive system extending over two thousand miles from the cold waters that washed Cape Breton to the warm waters of the Gulf of Mexico. If this system could be supported intact, the heart of the North American continent was destined to be French; but any breaching of it at a vital point imperilled the whole. That the narrow isthmus of Chignecto was conceived to be such a point is clear from the great efforts and expenditures made to protect it, and from the determined attitude taken by the representatives of the French Crown both in Paris and in London during the protracted period of negotiations from 1750 to 1755 to make no concessions respecting it. Rightly they felt that the fate of their North American empire would to a great extent depend upon its fate and that of the mainland south of the St. Lawrence.

This was not all. The French positions about the Bay of Fundy, taken together with their stronghold at Louisbourg, threatened the entire province of Nova Scotia, which Governor Shirley called "the Key of all the eastern colonies upon the Northern Continent." [14] The loss of this colony — with its commodious harbours capable of sheltering large squadrons, and its soil capable of producing provisions of all sorts — would inevitably attract a large French immigration; its loss would also mean, he was convinced, the relinquishment to the French of the most eastern portions of New England, from which the royal navy was being supplied with almost all of its masts, yards, and bowsprits, and of the New England cod fisheries carried on in the region of Nova Scotia, in which so many thousands of men from

[14] Shirley to Robinson, March 24, 1755, *Correspondence of William Shirley*, II, 149.

Massachusetts Bay had earned a livelihood. With these advantages consolidated and in the enjoyment of others, the French in time, he feared, especially in time of war, as the result of their peculiar form of government and their influence with the Indian nations on the continent, would come to threaten the continued existence of the older British colonies and perhaps even "accomplish the reduction of every one of them." [15]

But while French statesmen, soldiers, and priests were putting forth their best efforts to consolidate their position in the upper reaches of the Bay of Fundy, the Frenchman Thomas Pichon was just as busily working to undermine it and at least as early as the fall of 1754 was strongly advising the British to attack Fort Beauséjour before the French would be ready to proceed against Fort Lawrence.[16] In fact, it is quite clear that Governor Lawrence arrived at his determination not to delay the contemplated stroke largely as the result of warnings that came to him and his lieutenants from Pichon. It is also quite clear that the contribution that Pichon made to the final collapse of the French strategy in the upper region of the Bay of Fundy was by no means trivial. For while the important military victories of the British there were to be attributed solely to military action by those charged with the application of force, it is by no means certain that the striking success of this action was not in reality dependent upon the collaboration of one entrenched in so strategic a position as was Pichon at Beauséjour.[17]

Thomas Pichon was of Normandy, born at Vire in 1700 of Jean-Pichon, a merchant, and Marie Esnault.[18] He seems to have studied both medicine and law at Paris,[19] where he also, incidentally, became

---

[15] *Ibid.*

[16] Writing to Captain Scott at Fort Lawrence on September 17, he referred to a *mémoire* relating to Fort Beauséjour — also forwarded to Scott — that he had assisted Captain de Surlaville in drawing up "at a time when I did not expect either to see you or to be of service to you." He then went on to say: "May it not offend you nor any one else; but having read it, do you not think that it is more than ever important to forestall the French next spring?" (Webster, *op. cit.*, p. 38.)

[17] A similar question is presented in our own day as to the degree of importance of the underground work that was carried on in French North Africa by the United Nations in connection with the success of the assaults finally launched against it.

[18] The most important study of the life of Pichon is J. C. Webster's *Thomas Pichon: The Spy of Beauséjour* (1937), to which reference has already been made. The life, as distinct from the documents, covers only the first twenty-seven pages. The Reverend Albert David, Missionaire du Saint-Esprit, also published in 1934 his *Le Judas de l'Acadie.*

[19] That he practised law in France with honour, as he claimed in one of his letters, referred to in the footnote that follows, is considered false by Webster (*op. cit.*, p. 2).

a party to intrigues involving more than one young woman. In 1741, through the influence of his patron, the Marquis de Breteuil, Minister of War, he received a post in the hospital service of the army and during the War of the Austrian Succession rendered other services "in different sections of the army" and "always performed the duties assigned to him with the greatest efficiency, winning for himself distinction as well as approbation" — in the words of testimony of the Comte de Raymond, who had observed his conduct in Europe for a period of nine years.[20] The Comte, in fact, was so favourably impressed with him that he was invited to go to Louisbourg to act in the most confidential capacity as secretary when Raymond became Governor of the colony of Isle Royale in 1751. Pichon was also given expectations of advancement. That he bore a reputation for integrity and efficiency is indicated by the fact that in November 1751 the Governor, desiring to put an end to the notorious smuggling of contraband supplies into and out of the island, recommended him strongly for the office of the King's Attorney General in Admiralty of the colony (*Procureur du Roy de l'Amirauté de cette colonie*), as one highly qualified to fill it with distinction.[21] But the appointment was not made nor was he later offered the post of attorney general (*Procureur Général au Conseil Supérieur*) of the colony — to take the place of Sieur Seguin, who had offered his resignation — which Raymond apparently desired to secure for him. The explanation for the failure of the Comte to be able to advance his old acquaintance seemed to be not in any lack of desire to serve him but in the fact that all matters relating to law-enforcement pertained more directly to the administration of the office of the Ordonnateur of the colony than to that of the Governor. M. Prévost's preferences rather than those of Raymond therefore carried weight with the Minister, especially in view of the peculiar "constitution governing the administra-

---

[20] For this testimony and recommendation by the Comte de Raymond see Pichon Papers, Nova Scotia Archives, No. B. This is translated by Webster (*op. cit.*, p. 29). Pichon made numerous written statements about his earlier career, to be found among the papers just cited and those in the Canadian Archives and the British Museum. The only statement that manifestly contains falsehoods, so far as I have been able to determine, is in the form of a letter written to Madame de Beaumont that was patently designed to play upon the lady's sympathies at the time the Frenchman was paying court to her. Dr. Webster has printed this letter.

[21] Comte de Raymond's words are: "Mr. Pichon is quite capable of filling this post with distinction. He has moreover an established probity. This position would make it possible for him to secure a perfect knowledge of all that the ships bring into the port and carry away from it. He would thus place me in a position in which I could do away with every abuse" (Arch. Nat., Col., C[11] 31: 47).

iton of the colonies"; and the two did not see eye to eye.[22] The Minister of the Marine was nevertheless favourably disposed toward Pichon and expressed himself as prepared to do something for him should he desire to remain at Isle Royale after the Comte had returned to France.[23]

The cordial relations existing between the Governor and Pichon seem to have been marred in 1753 by an incident involving a crumpled memorandum in the handwriting of the latter which was found in a waste-basket in Raymond's office after Pichon had resigned his post as secretary. The Comte had become convinced in the spring of that year that Governor Shirley of Massachusetts had been receiving accurate information relative to Louisbourg from someone, and this paper caused him to suspect that Pichon might be the guilty party. But Pichon was apparently able to convince the Governor that had he been guilty of such misconduct he certainly would not have left any incriminating evidence in so accessible a place, but would have destroyed it.[24] At least in October of that year the Comte gave to Pichon a recommendation referring to his work as secretary with high praise. It affirms that

> "he [Pichon] has performed the duties of this office with intelligence, probity, fidelity, exactitude and all possible disinterestedness, not only to our satisfaction but to that of all others. In witness of which we have subscribed the present certificate at Louisbourg on Isle Royale October 10, 1753." [25]

In that same month he also received a letter from Le Loutre, established at Beauséjour, in which the Abbé indicated that he had

---

[22] This is made clear in a letter from the Minister of the Marine to Raymond, of July 13, 1753 (Arch. Nat. Col., B. 97: 274–6).

[23] *Ibid.*

[24] A translation of this letter is given by Webster, *op. cit.*, pp. 4–5. No evidence has been uncovered that would indicate that at this period Pichon was contemplating entering the services of the British and was in touch with Shirley. What he was then busily engaged in doing, it is quite clear, was the preparation of his well-known and critical *Lettres et Mémoires pour servir à l'Histoire Naturelle, Civile et Politique de Cap-Breton.* It is quite possible that some portion of this volume — perhaps a part of his able essay, composed at this period, entitled "Reflections or Conjectures on Isle Royale; a Project for making Louisbourg Impregnable. Plans and Means Proposed to the Court of France by the Comte de Raymond" (Letter No. XV) — may have been tossed into the waste-basket.

[25] Pichon Papers, No. B., Nova Scotia Archives. Pichon's attitude toward the Comte was not consistent and, in fact, was very temperamental. On the one hand he insisted that Raymond was stupid and had grossly deceived him, and on the other he told the Comte: "People I like are held in almost the same veneration as the things I adore" (Webster, *op. cit.*, p. 5).

written to Ordonnateur Prévost at Louisbourg making clear that the commandant of the fort was very infirm and entreating him to send Pichon to act *ad interim* at Beauséjour under the elderly La Martinière, who also desired to utilize his services.[26]

Now without a post, Pichon accepted the opportunity for temporary employment and in November arrived at Fort Beauséjour, where he seems to have taken charge of the commissariat and also to have fulfilled the duties of secretary for the commandant and for Le Loutre. While he therefore performed the functions of commissaire, ordonnateur, and subdelegate of the Intendant at this post, according to his own statements, which seem to be correct, he was carrying on *ad interim* without a royal appointment. In view of his previous disappointments and rebuffs at the hands of his government, he had now apparently become thoroughly disillusioned respecting its desire to recognize and reward his services; he also had doubtless become convinced that men of lesser talents had continued to avail themselves of his training and abilities for their own advancement and had thereupon proceeded to forget him, all of which must have embittered him, particularly as he saw some of these men plundering without any sense of shame.[27] But beyond this there was the fact that Pichon had come to question the validity and good faith of the entire French status with respect to Nova Scotia; for he had been in a position to follow closely the course of events. On September 17, 1751 the Comte de Raymond had written to the Minister of the Marine that he had summoned the Micmacs of Isle Royale and near by and had engaged them to send one of their number to the Indians of Acadia to engage them to break the peace which the latter had made with the English.[28] Such unneutral conduct as this, and the exhortations of the priests to the Indians to fall upon the English in times of peace "in the name of religion," [29] caused him to observe that "if the quarrel with the English is not based upon equity and justice, all this will be too much against us." [30]

---

[26] For this letter to Pichon, which is in the Vire Collection, see *ibid.*, p. 6.

[27] In writing to M. de Surlaville on November 12, 1754 (*ibid.*, pp. 133–4) he remarked respecting the conduct of de Martinière, late commandant at Fort Beauséjour, and that of his successor, M. de Vergor: "The former, although bed-ridden, has managed to accumulate and take away more than 80,000 livres. His successor, without even knowing how to read, will take away even more."

[28] Arch. Nat., Col., Col., C¹¹C. 31: 62.

[29] See Pichon's "The Indian War against the English," Letter XVI in his *Lettres et Mémoires.*

[30] *Ibid.*

But justice and equity Pichon could not find on the side of his own country. In a series of lengthy and very carefully developed essays in the form of letters from one Frenchman to another, conceived in the bantering mood of Voltaire, whom he seems greatly to have admired — the earliest of which were manifestly written at Louisbourg with the aid of the Governor's correspondence and other official data and before Pichon had decided to enter, or even contemplated entering, the service of the British,[31] and which were later brought together and published under title: *Lettres et Mémoires pour servir à l'Histoire Naturelle, Civile & Politique de Cap-Breton* — he probes into questions involving international morality, setting down side by side for contrast and comparison the conduct of the French and the British in North America, with particular reference to the unfolding of events in Acadia. In one of these he prays that no one may be able to accuse his countrymen of the treachery of driving the Indians into making war upon the English, with whom his nation is at peace. Yet in quoting the words of one of the French commanders of the Indians, he asks:

> "Is it possible to interpret these words so as to cleanse us of this blot?"[32]

In another, in dealing with the Treaty of Utrecht, the inconvenient articles of which he finds his fellow Frenchmen now determined to put aside, he observes:

> "I repeat again. Consternation and despair dictated the Treaty of Utrecht; prudence on our part did not determine the character of its articles, and it is to be doubted if good faith signed them."

He goes on to observe, however, that for a country to interpret a treaty according to its own interest, even quite clearly to break it, may not be a matter of embarrassment for the stronger party but is very dangerous for the weaker; but that there is another method employed by those now determined to undo the treaty, which is

---

[31] The first eighteen of these essays or expositions would seem to have been composed while he was still on Isle Royale. Letters XII, XIV, and XV are concerned, as has been made clear, with the commerce and defence of Isle Royale; Letters XVI, XVII, and XVIII probe searchingly into the validity of the conduct of the French in Acadia during the years 1749–52, in which Pichon utilized materials that were not available at Beauséjour and was especially critical of the views of the Comte de Raymond on these developments, which views he quoted extensively.

[32] In his letter on "The Indian War against the English," *ibid.*, pp. 200–10.

"to expand their objectives, to gain land without, however, admitting the design to do so and in protesting the candor of their intentions, and to continue this move without hesitation up to the moment that they are sufficiently strong to tear away the veil of constraint." [33]

To Pichon France's record in Acadia was therefore one of bad faith, and by implication he placed the responsibility for this not so much on his fellow countrymen as on the Crown, in the service of which "obedience to duty and necessity excuses everything." [34]

In view of the circumstances, it would not have been surprising had Pichon determined to sever his connections with France. In a communication directed apparently to Governor Lawrence and written at Halifax on July 26, 1755 — after he had taken this step — he stated that, when he had found that he had been deceived by the Comte de Raymond in accompanying him from France to Isle Royale with promises of advancement, he came to a resolution. In his own words:

"I then determined to retire to a nation that I love and know to be the most reasonable, the most generous of all those in either hemisphere." [35]

Therefore, before going to Fort Beauséjour, if his statement is correct, Pichon had determined to avail himself of an opportunity to join the English. This presented itself soon after his arrival when Captain Scott, who was commanding at Fort Lawrence, hard by across the little Missaquash, and who had made Pichon's acquaintance at Louisbourg, sent him his compliments and invited him to make a friendly call at the English fort.[36] Such a proceeding at this juncture was not unusual, in view of the temporary good understanding that then existed between the two garrisons,[37] and Pichon accepted the invitation.

The first conversations, according to him, revolved about the respective interests of the two Crowns in America.[38] One may believe that the Frenchman, in view of his sentiments, was not hesitant in

[33] In his letter entitled: "Reflections on the Origin of the Present War," ibid., pp. 210–18.

[34] This is fully developed in No. XVIII of the letters, ibid., pp. 218–32.

[35] This letter is among the Dr. Andrew Brown Manuscripts in the British Museum (Add. Mss., 19,073: 21).

[36] Ibid.

[37] Dr. Webster (op. cit., pp. 7–8) illustrates these not unfriendly relations during the governorship of La Martinière at Beauséjour during the year 1753.

[38] B.M., Add. Mss., 19,074: 21.

making clear how reprehensible, he felt, had been the conduct of his own country on this continent since the late treaty of peace. When Captain Scott therefore finally came to the point of proposing that Pichon should enter the service of the British, he did not have to undertake the unpleasant task of corrupting him. For Pichon, it is quite clear, was seeking the opportunity to change his allegiance and only stipulated that Scott should be able to fulfil his promise, freely made, to see that he lacked nothing (*que rien ne manqueroit à ma satisfaction*).[39] As a result he now became a British spy in the French service, and in doing so repudiated his obligations to the French Crown. In his own words: "I gave myself completely to do everything that was desired of me."[40]

In spite of the dangerous nature of the assignment that he accepted, there is no evidence that Pichon ever regretted his decision. On the contrary, the *mémoires* that he prepared after this event, which were subsequently published with his earlier *mémoires,* are ample proof that he was convinced that he had now enlisted in a good cause in contrast to an earlier bad one. For example, his *mémoire* on the causes of the Anglo-French hostilities that began in 1754,[41] written after the news reached him of Washington's defeat at Fort Necessity and before the Braddock campaign, is by far the most capable contemporary presentation of the British case in North America that has come to my attention. Under the calm surface of philosophical discourse can be detected an almost passionate devotion to the justice of the British position in his contention that the French Crown in adopting a policy of aggression in North America against its neighbour had thrown to the winds every sound principle of international comity and good faith. When still later the news reached him of the capture of the *Alcide* and the *Lys*, he probed to the foundation in another *mémoire* the basis for Boscawen's attack on the French fleet, bringing into view at the same time the facts relative to the capture of Fort Beauséjour. His four other *mémoires* dealing with subsequent events of the war and included in his volume give additional evidence that he continued resolute in his position and that his mind was at peace.

Pichon, however, was guilty of treachery.

To the student of history it is difficult to justify a casuistry that

---

[39] *Ibid.*
[40] *Ibid.*
[41] This is Letter No. XIX of the series.

very properly would denounce his treachery but refuse at the same time to denounce that of the Comte de Raymond, of Bigot, and of Abbé Le Loutre in secretly and treacherously sending the Micmacs, furnished with French arms, into a region that France freely admitted was a part of the British domain, to fall upon, kill, and scalp the inhabitants in a time of profound peace and to reward them as secretly for their horrid deeds.

Pichon also committed treason.

As this chapter was being written, France was undoubtedly filled with men who were traitors to the Vichy government of that country, who were using their official positions secretly to bring destruction upon that government. De Gaulle and his followers were openly traitors to it and would have suffered as such if apprehended. The Hitler regime in Germany was also the legal government, but hundreds of Germans had turned traitor to it. Some had been apprehended and had been executed before firing squads; others had fled and had placed their services as well as official documents at the disposal of the open enemies of that government. Here again one is inevitably led to raise the question: Can anything justify treason? In other words, if treason under certain circumstances may be justified, what is to be the nature of the justification for it and who is clothed with the responsibility of determining when it is permissible and when it is not? Should the grave decision of the act of treason, as also its moral justification, rest solely with the individual's discretion and conscience? Is there a higher law that resolves all such questions?

With the utmost zeal M. Pichon, after the understanding with Captain Scott, set to work: he prepared maps; he made copies of official correspondence and the letters of Le Loutre; he indicated the disposition of French troops and supplies and the weaknesses in the French position; he warned of contemplated moves; and he suggested the most practicable methods for reducing the French forts erected within the disputed area of Acadia.[42] When the British were prepared to act against Fort Beauséjour, therefore, they were able to do so with full knowledge of every important factor involved in the problem of striking at one of the key positions in France's overseas

---

[42] The earliest communications of Pichon have not survived. The collection of Pichon Papers in the Public Archives of Nova Scotia gives as the earliest of his letters that to Captain Scott dated September 17, 1754. The documents in the Public Archives of Canada show that Pichon at least furnished copies of documents drawn up much earlier. For example, No. 41 of this collection offers a survey of the defences of the isthmus as of June 17, 1753.

empire. The Earl of Halifax, in referring to Pichon's contribution to this end, unhesitatingly declared that "upon his Information the Successful Operations of the last Summer's Campaign were formed." [43]

Of the two officers who were sent by Governor Lawrence to Boston in the early winter of 1754–5 to solicit help from Governor Shirley for the projected campaign — Lieutenant Colonel Robert Monckton and Captain George Scott — each had acted as commandant at Fort Lawrence; one had also, as has been noted, established the most confidential relations with Pichon. Further to persuade the government of the powerful New England colony to act, Lawrence early in December sent another urgent letter to Shirley recommending action without waiting to hear further from England and enclosing certain papers respecting the French designs so highly confidential in nature that he begged him not to communicate these to anyone — except to his own representatives still in Boston — "as the person [undoubtedly Pichon] I had them of may otherwise run great risque of being discovered." [44]

Shirley did not need to be persuaded as to the necessity of the contemplated step for protecting British interests in North America and fell fully into line with Lawrence, supporting the latter's position in a series of lengthy letters to Sir Thomas Robinson. On January 24 he wrote that preparations for the expedition were moving ahead in Boston "consistent wth the Secrecy requisite in this Case" and stated that

". . . a few days hence I shall open the matter to the Assembly of this Province, & the Governours of the three other colonies of New England, & begin to raise the Men; and I think there is an exceeding fair prospect of the levies being compleated, & imbark'd with Great Artillery, Ammunition & Stores of all Kinds provided here; (good Firelocks excepted, which I shall be in hopes of having sent in time from England) before the last week in March, or by the latter end of it at furthest." [45]

On February 18 he was able to report that two thousand "irregulars" — that is, rangers — were being raised in the province for the attempt against the French encroachments in Nova Scotia, and that Governor de Lancey of New York had contributed to this end ten "battering

[43] Halifax to Newcastle, July 6, 1756, B.M., Add. Mss., 32,866: 49–54.
[44] Letter of December 12, 1754, C.O. 5:15, pp. 350–6.
[45] C.O. 5:15, p. 320.

peices [*sic*] of 18^{lb} ball," to which he himself would add four twenty-four-pounders from Castle William; further, that an abundance of mortars and shells were available at Halifax. He also noted that measures had been taken to keep the destination of the irregulars as secret as possible. To this end all French subjects in Boston were placed under restraint, and with the consent of the Assembly all ships that might be suspected of seeking to carry information were detained for a period of four months and all masters of other outward-bound vessels were placed under strict bond to prevent the carrying of provisions and military stores to the French.[46]

John Winslow, a descendant of Governor Edward Winslow of Plymouth, one of the Pilgrim Fathers, was given the chief responsibility for the recruiting of the New England volunteers. He had had military experience in the preceding war and, as has been already noted, had been employed in 1754 to lead the Massachusetts Bay troops that ascended the Kennebec and constructed Fort Halifax on its upper waters. This work of enlisting was done with secrecy and efficiency.[47] As the men were paid out of the Nova Scotia parliamentary fund, Governor Lawrence first forwarded £6,000 for recruiting purposes and then an equal sum late in March.[48] The recruits upon volunteering were enrolled for a period of one year [49] in a corps or regiment, one battalion of which was commanded by Winslow and the other by an officer of the regular army, George Scott (the friend of Pichon), each with the temporary rank of lieutenant colonel of the New England volunteers. Lieutenant Colonel Robert Monckton, also of the regular army, was designated by Lawrence, with the approval of Shirley, to command the expedition. While it had been planned that the regiments should sail for Nova Scotia as early as possible in the spring of 1755, there were delays after the troops had

---

[46] C.O. 5:15, pp. 431–6.

[47] A most important source of information for this expedition is to be found in the "Journal of Colonel John Winslow of the Provincial Troops, which engaged in the siege of Fort Beauséjour in the Summer and Autumn of 1755." The manuscript, possessed by the Massachusetts Historical Society, was published in Volume IV of the Nova Scotia Historical Society *Collections*. It shows (*ibid.*, pp. 119–24) that Winslow experienced some difficulties in recruiting in both New Hampshire and Connecticut as the result of the opposition of the governments of those colonies to the activities of his recruiting officers. This caused him to make clear to both Governor Wentworth and Governor Fitch the critical nature of the service the New England irregulars would perform and the limited nature of it.

[48] Lawrence to Monckton, March 28, 1755, Mass. Hist. Soc. *Coll.* (fourth series), IX, 214–21.

[49] *Corresp. of Shirley*, II, 464.

been raised and brought to Boston on account of the lack of powder and small arms.[50] It was not until May 26 that the fleet left its moorings at Deer Island in Boston Bay and then sailed for Annapolis Royal for the concentration of the forces.[51] There were in all some thirty-three transports and store-ships under escort of three frigates.[52] Arriving at Annapolis on the 27th, the fleet was joined by other vessels bringing an artillery train and additional supplies from Halifax and then set sail for Fort Lawrence, where the force arrived on June 2 under cover of a thick fog.[53]

On the 4th of June the two thousand New England troops and two hundred and fifty regulars, supported by four six-pounders dragged by soldiers for want of horses, left the British fort and, marching eastward and then northward, crossed the Missaquash at the Pont à Buot and reached the road that connected Fort Beauséjour with Fort Gaspereau, thus cutting the main line of communication between the two. Thereupon the force moved westward in the direction of the French fort. In executing this manœuvre it was necessary in rebuilding a bridge over the Missaquash to confront a blockhouse with fascine entrenchments that the enemy had erected on the opposite bank, where were concentrated several hundred soldiers and Indians who fired upon the troops with swivel guns and muskets. But the fire was returned, with the result that the occupants retreated after the six-inch guns came into action, but not until they had set fire to the log fort and the neighbouring village.[54] The following day the main camp of the volunteers was established at a distance of about a mile east of the main French fort.[55] On the 6th large fires were noted — the Acadians round about had begun to burn their homes; [56] the village of Beauséjour outside the fort and Le Loutre's newly completed church now went up in flames. On the 8th a strong contingent of

---

[50] Mass. Hist. Soc. Coll. (fourth series), IX, 214–21. On June 1 the regiment was listed with a total strength of 1,950 (Winslow's "Journal," Nova Scotia Hist. Soc. Coll., IV, 144).

[51] Monckton at first apparently decided to concentrate within Minas Basin, but Lawrence recommended Annapolis Royal (Mass. Hist. Soc. Coll., fourth series, IX, 214–21).

[52] "Diary" of John Thomas (Journals of Beauséjour, ed. J. C. Webster, p. 13; Winslow's "Journal," N. S. Hist. Soc. Coll., IV, 134–5; Monckton's "Journal," in the Appendix of Dr. Webster's The Forts of Chignecto, p. 110.

[53] Monckton's "Journal," ibid., pp. 110–11.

[54] Winslow's "Journal," Nova Scotia Hist. Soc. Coll., IV, 146.

[55] At the Butte à Mirande, called today Mount Whatley (Journals of Beauséjour, ed. J. C. Webster, pp. 15 and 35).

[56] John Thomas "Diary," ibid., p. 15.

volunteers under Winslow marched to an eminence some nine hundred yards northeast of Beauséjour known as the Butte à Charles, where a sharp engagement took place, with the French retreating to their fort. At the Butte entrenchments were dug and mortars and guns were brought up, and on the 14th occurred the first bombardment of the besieged place.

But let us turn to trace developments at Fort Beauséjour. The commandant, Louis du Pont du Chambon de Vergor, was taken completely by surprise by the sudden appearance of the transports and frigates on the upper Bay of Fundy. Awakened early in morning of June 2 by messengers who brought the news, he sent out orders to all the Acadians able to bear arms who were living at the upper end of the bay — numbering some twelve or fifteen hundred — to report immediately at the fort. As a result it would appear that most of those of Shepody, Petitcodiac, Memramcook, Aulac, Ouekad (Westcock), Pont à Buot, and La Coupe responded and indicated their willingness to fight the English; but, significantly, they would take up arms only on condition that, to guarantee their safety in case of defeat, Vergor would issue an order to the effect that they must help defend the fort under pain of dire punishment if they disobeyed.[57] For their situation, they realized, would indeed be precarious in case of defeat — born as practically all of them had been within the dominions of the King of Great Britain and therefore his subjects. The order was issued to their satisfaction. After this was done the settlers departed to conceal their families in the woods and backlands and then returned to the fort and placed their services fully at the command of Vergor.[58]

A sturdy defence of Fort Beauséjour now seemed assured. The hundreds of hardy Acadians formed into companies under militia captains were in a position to give effective aid to the French regulars of the marine regiments who comprised the garrison. Moreover, Vergor sent off couriers to the Chevalier de Drucour, Governor of Louisbourg, and to the Marquis de Duquesne, the Governor General of New France, calling for additional help; he also ordered the ships at Baye Verte to sail immediately for Canada to bring relief. As all provisions for the fort were housed outside of the walls, he ordered

---

[57] "Journal of Louis de Courville," Journals of Beauséjour (ed. J. C. Webster), p. 46. The agreement with Vergor doubtless saved many of them later from being hanged as rebels, for they were able when captured to plead compulsion in taking up arms.

[58] Ibid.

these to be brought within them and directed the Acadians to aid the soldiers in digging trenches outside the fort. Then, with the successful movement of the enemy across the Missaquash and the scattering of resistance at the crossing of the stream, he and Le Loutre came to a decision: to destroy the settlement that had grown up about the walls of the fort. In spite of some protests, orders were given to set fire to all the houses and barns, and even to the church. This was done, as has already been noted. The real desolation of old Acadia had now begun.[59]

Here, at last, was war in earnest. But, unhappily for the defence of Fort Beauséjour, with the beginning of reverses and the approach of the enemy from the east, many of the Acadians lost all desire to fight; they faltered at the defence work and at last began to desert to their families. In response to Vergor's pleas to return to their duty they complained that they did not want to perish from fire and plague within the fort.[60] Nevertheless some hundreds of them continued there, and, to provide them with fairly good protection from cannon-fire and bombs, the supplies were taken from the casemates. As it was evident by the 8th that the enemy could not be kept from approaching the fort, there followed the demolition of the combustible roofs of all the structures within it. On the 14th, the day of the first bombardment, unwelcome news was received by the defenders. In reply to Vergor's plea for immediate aid, Drucour wrote from Louisbourg that it would be impossible to send it, as a fleet of the enemy was cruising about the coasts of Isle Royale. While this gloomy information was conveyed only to the officers of the fort, the demoralization of the defenders was rapidly developing; on the day following, with the bombardment continuing, the most resolute of the Acadians made clear to the commandant that they no longer were willing to remain in the fort and asked to be permitted to depart before it was completely invested; and on the 16th — after a large bomb had broken through a casemate and had killed the occupants,

---

[59] Ibid., p. 47, and Pichon's "Journal," in Webster, Thomas Pichon, p. 101. Le Loutre, in his Autobiographie (Nova Francia, VI, 29–30), takes the responsibility for the beginning of the laying waste of Acadia. He writes: "The missionary, who with five hundred inhabitants of the country had retired to the fort, as soon as he saw the English approaching his church — which was so beautiful and which had cost so much — gave orders to some of the inhabitants to put the torch to it and here began the entire desolation of the country."

[60] Courville's "Journal" (ed. J. C. Webster), p. 47.

most of whom were French officers — the defenders became completely demoralized.[61] Vergor was therefore obliged to capitulate.

As may well be appreciated, Thomas Pichon within the fort used every means in his power to put an end to French resistance. In a letter written a little over a month following the termination of the siege, he declared that before this attack took place he succeeded in retarding the defensive preparations at both Beauséjour and Gaspereau with assurances that there was no danger of an attack in the immediate future, and when Beauséjour was invested he worked upon the fears of the defending Acadians. Referring to its surrender, he declared that the inhabitants to the number of more than five hundred, who had been enclosed in the fort to defend it, as the result of his advice forced the commandant to request a capitulation, which he insisted greatly shortened the siege.[62] Further, that Abbé Le Loutre, who was in the fort and who was eagerly sought by the English, succeeded in escaping at the time of the capitulation cannot be charged to any lack of desire on Pichon's part to see him apprehended; for by the time he was in a position to disclose the hiding-place of the priest, it was too late.[63]

In submitting propositions for the capitulation, Vergor requested an armistice of forty-eight hours, after which the garrison should be permitted to leave the fort with full honours of war and to take with it six of the largest cannon and a mortar, with fifty charges for each piece. He further requested that he should be furnished with the necessary vehicles to transport his troops and the artillery to Baye Verte, at which place the garrison would embark on ships to go wherever it seemed best to him.[64] As for the Acadians, he asked that they should not be harmed for taking up arms, inasmuch as they had been forced to do so on pain of death; and that they should continue to enjoy their religion and have their priests; further, that permission should be given to those among them who so desired to retire to the lands of the King of France with their movable effects and that they should have a year of grace to do so.[65]

---

[61] Pichon's "Journal," op. cit., p. 104.

[62] Th. Tyrell to ——, July 26, 1755, B.M., Add. Mss., 19,073: 21.

[63] Ibid.

[64] C.O. 5:15, pp. 647–50.

[65] Ibid. Here Vergor acknowledges, by implication, that Beauséjour and the Acadian settlements were not located on the lands of the King of France as the French authorities contended they were.

Although Monckton quite properly refused to grant a relatively lengthy armistice — during which much damage could have been done to the fort and the supplies inside it — and demanded the acceptance of his own terms within a period of two hours, he nevertheless permitted the garrison to leave the fort with the honours of war — since Washington had been permitted to do so at Fort Necessity the preceding year — and to take with it its small arms and baggage. However, it was specified that the French regulars should be taken directly to Louisbourg by sea at the expense of the King of Great Britain and furnished with provisions sufficient for the passage, with the understanding that for a period of six months they would not carry arms in America. With respect to the Acadians, it was simply agreed that since it had been made clear by the commandant of the fort that they had been forced to take up arms on pain of death — which of course was not true — they would be pardoned for the part they had taken in its defence.[66] With these preliminaries completed, the British forces entered the fort and in place of the fleur-de-lis the Union Jack was hoisted over it and its name was changed to Fort Cumberland.

Even recognizing the great contribution that Pichon made to the above end, it is still a matter of surprise that Beauséjour fell so easily. The fort was not a mere group of blockhouses connected with palisades, as was Fort Le Bœuf, but a real fortress covering some two and a half acres of ground. Built in the form of a pentagon on elevated ground overlooking the marsh, it was a work of masonry, provided with palisades, glacis, moat, banquettes, and ramparts. From its embrasures bristled the muzzles of twenty-four cannon; within its walls were magazines, barracks, and officers' quarters and abundant supplies of provisions and ammunition. Enjoying all these advantages, its garrison should have held the enemy at bay for many days if not weeks. It doubtless would have done so had all possessed the determination of Abbé Le Loutre, who, when the question of surrender was raised, declared vehemently that it would be far better to be buried in the fort than to surrender it. But few felt as he did. Colonel Monckton, indeed, was greatly surprised to receive the request for a truce almost at the beginning of what seemed destined to be a protracted siege. But the kind of men supporting the King of

---

[66] C.O. 5:15, pp. 643–6 and Monckton's "Journal," op. cit., p. 113. As will be made clear in the chapter to follow, this pardon did not extend to the conduct in general of the revolting Acadians toward the government of Nova Scotia.

France's cause at Beauséjour is indicated by the fact that from ten o'clock in the morning, when the flag of truce was sent to the British camp, till late in the evening most of the officers, according to Louis de Courville, the King's notary, were occupied only in pillaging the King's stores.[67] According to Pichon, the officers and their servants made up large bundles of merchandise for themselves. Commandant Vergor, he asserted, had his loot removed by some of the inhabitants who were related to him and by his valet, St. Germain.[68] He apparently had taken to heart the advice of Intendant Bigot given the previous summer upon sailing for Europe:

> "Profit by your place, my dear Vergor; clip and cut — you are free to do what you please — so that you can come soon to join me in France and buy an estate near me." [69]

But Pichon's work was not completed. Fort Gaspereau across the isthmus, lying near Baye Verte, still stood and if powerfully reinforced from Canada could serve the French effectively in any effort that might be made to recapture Fort Beauséjour. Pichon not only assisted Colonel Monckton in framing a letter to its commandant, M. de Villeray, which was sent to him by one of the Acadians, together with a copy of the terms of capitulation of Beauséjour, but also through a separate message carried by the same inhabitant personally urged Villeray not to attempt any resistance.[70] As a result, when Colonel Winslow appeared at Baye Verte with a force, no resistance was made and the small garrison of this fort in capitulating was accorded terms comparable to those granted at Beauséjour.

The reduction of the two French forts located in one of the most strategic positions in North America — accomplished with a minimum of effort and sacrifice of life — was a greater blow to France's New World empire than most contemporaries at the time realized. Louisbourg had now been isolated from the remainder of the Empire except by water, and the value of the great fortress as an outlying defence of it thereby greatly reduced. The only significance now of

---

[67] "Journal," op. cit., p. 50.

[68] "Journal," Life of Pichon, p. 104.

[69] "Mémoires sur le Canada, 1749–1760," quoted by Parkman, Montcalm and Wolfe, I, 242.

[70] In recounting his services the following year, Pichon affirmed that as a result of his advice the commandant of Fort Gaspereau agreed to surrender simply upon the basis of a letter carried to him by an inhabitant from Colonel Monckton — a letter that Pichon helped to dictate (Military Affairs in North America, 1748–1765, ed. S. Pargellis, p. 182).

the rather barren Isle Royale was that it protected Cabot Strait and was still a fisheries centre. But its continued existence and usefulness even for these limited purposes, important as they were, depended on continuous relief by sea. For a vital link in the Empire had now been broken — and Pichon had helped to break it. In considering the downfall of Beauséjour Shirley places its importance even higher than that of the campaigns against Crown Point, Niagara, and Duquesne. Writing to the Earl of Halifax after this event he declared: "I look upon this Blow as the most important one that we were in Expectation of the Issue of."[71]

As for the Acadians, after the last of them had left Fort Beauséjour, just before the entrance of the British troops, the more warlike, especially those of Petitcodiac, determined to withdraw to the St. John and, in company with the Abenaki Indians, continue to war upon the enemy. Having been informed of this, Pichon proceeded to convey the information to Monckton, with the result that means were taken to prevent the movement, and the leaders, members of the influential Beausoleil family, were seized. He was also able to furnish to Monckton plans of the forts on the St. John and other useful information respecting this region.[72]

But even this was not the last of his services. Having been made a prisoner at his own request, he was taken to Fort Edward on the Piziquid in the heart of old Acadia, where he sought to influence the inhabitants who came to consult him to give up their resistance to the government that had so long been established over them. He tactfully counselled them, without avail, to think of the future of their families and to make a comparison of the nature of the English domination on the one hand and of that of the French on the other and pointed out that the former was infinitely to be preferred to the latter.[73]

Thereupon, transferred to Halifax, still in the guise of a prisoner, he joined in confinement the French officers captured on the *Alcide* and the *Lys.* One of them, François-Pierre de Rigaud, the Governor of Trois Rivières and brother of the newly appointed Governor General of New France, was led to turn over to him the famous *"savonnette"* (ball of soap) in which was secreted a plan of Halifax and the daring proposal for its capture by surprise the following winter, with the burning of the fleet stationed there — a project prepared, accord-

---

[71] Quoted in Halifax to Newcastle, July 27, 1755, B.M., Add. Mss., 32,857: 305.
[72] B.M., Add. Mss., 19,073: 21.
[73] *Ibid.*

ing to Pichon, by Captain Hocquart of the *Alcide* and three French engineers.[74] The discovery of this paper, it may be added, was considered to be of such importance as to call for a day of thanksgiving in Halifax.[75] Pichon also came into possession of a large collection of French documents, among them all the correspondence and other private papers of the Marquis de Vaudreuil, gathered while acting as Governor of Louisiana and entrusted to Rigaud on the *Alcide*. These priceless materials the Frenchman carried to England and placed at the disposal of Lord Loudoun, who had been appointed, as was made clear in the preceding chapter, commander-in-chief of the British forces in North America in place of Shirley and who was about to sail for the New World.[76]

In going to England Pichon was not unmindful of all that he had done for the cause that he had embraced with such ardour and did not fail to support his claims to recognition. That his services were held to be of the highest importance can be gathered from the fact that both Vice Admiral Boscawen and Governor Lawrence strongly recommended them to the consideration of the government.[77] As a result, he was granted a sum to provide for a proper establishment and a pension of two hundred pounds a year.[78]

Soon after his arrival in Great Britain he sought without success to bring over to the British side two French officers serving in the New World with whom he was acquainted and who were apparently at the time deeply dissatisfied with the treatment that they had received. One was Captain Dumas, who led the French and

---

[74] Admiral Boscawen, writing to John Cleveland of the Admiralty Board on November 15, 1755 (P.R.O., Admiralty, In-Letters, 481), stated that he was sending to the Admiralty "A Plan of Halifax with a Scheme of attacking it from Canada taken out of a Wash Ball that was in a French Officer's Chest, going to Louisbourg, this Plan I apprehend to be the Invention of Mon^r Vaudreuil, Governour of the Three Rivers, he is taken in the Alcide, is brother to the Vice Admiral of that name, the Governour of Canada. . . ."

[75] *Military Affairs in North America, 1748–1765* (ed. S. M. Pargellis), pp. 180–4. According to the *New-York Mercury* of November 10, 1755, the plan, secreted in the ball of soap, called for an expedition the following winter against Halifax on the part of Canadians, Indians, and regulars, who "when they had taken the Town . . . were to fire the Batteries upon the ships; the Inhabitants all to be shut up in the Church, and Fire put to it, and the troops . . . all put to the Sword without Quarter."

[76] B.M., Add. Mss., 32,866: 49–54. These Vaudreuil papers, embodied in the Loudoun Manuscripts, are now in the Huntington Library, San Marino, California. For confirmation of the Vaudreuil correspondence in the hands of Pichon see Loudoun to "My Lord," August 16–October 17, 1757, Parkman Papers, Vol. 42, p. 195, Massachusetts Historical Society.

[77] Halifax to Newcastle, July 6, 1756, B.M., Add. Mss., 32,866: 51.

[78] *Ibid.*

Indians against Braddock in the Battle of the Monongahela; the other was a relative of de Vergor, the military engineer Lieutenant Jacau de Fiedmont, who had been placed by de Vergor in charge of the defences of Fort Beauséjour.[79] The two Frenchmen were not to be reached, however, and in the course of time each received generous recognition from the King.[80] That Pichon also sought that same year to influence some of the officers commanding at Fort St. Frédéric at Crown Point to desert to the English is quite clear from a letter that the President of the French Navy Board wrote to M. Rouillé on January 2, 1757. In this it was stated that he was seeking to carry on a correspondence with persons at the fort and that he was "an object of suspicion"; at the same time it was pointed out that his effort to correspond with those stationed there was "less important than his knowledge of Louisbourg and the relations he may have maintained there." As the purpose of his attempted correspondence was not clear and since it was desirable to fathom it, the President of the Board recommended that it would be well "to accept the offer made by the one who gave the information."[81]

Pichon, for his own part, seems to have come now to the realization that his desire to win over other Frenchmen to the cause that he had embraced was not destined to bear fruit. At least no evidence that he continued to seek to influence them has been uncovered. He doubtless became convinced of the truth: that he had become an object of deep suspicion among his former fellow countrymen. He did succeed, however, in attracting to himself an accom-

[79] It would appear that Pichon wrote to Lord Loudoun, soon after the latter, on February 20, 1756, had been appointed general and commander-in-chief of all His Majesty's forces in North America, making clear that he was seeking to win over to the British services the officers referred to above. He also seems to have entrusted to Loudoun a letter addressed to de Fiedmont, doubtless hoping that the general would find means through the secret services to place it in the hands of the Frenchman. An opportunity to do so does not seem to have developed. These letters are in the Loudoun Collection in the Huntington Library and have been reproduced in Dr. Webster's *Thomas Pichon*, pp. 118–19.

[80] Dumas in 1756 received the Cross of St. Louis; in the following year he became major of Quebec and in 1759, Major-General Inspector of Troops. In 1757 Fiedmont was promoted to the rank of captain, and in 1765 to that of commandant general of Guiana.

[81] The extent of the suspicions that Pichon had aroused within the French government is evident in the following statement embodied in the above letter: "This Pichon, the man in question, was in reality the secretary of M. le Comte de Raymond at Louisburg. It is equally certain that he was at Beauséjour at the time of the capture of that fort, and the circumstances connected with his special treatment by the English during his retention by them in Acadia, together with his present sojourn in England certainly tend to render him an object of suspicion" (*Canadian Archives Report* [1905], I, Part 6, p. 246).

plished French lady, Marie-Barbe Le Prince, Madame de Beaumont, author and educator, who had established a girls' school in London. This alliance, short of marriage, was maintained for three years; then Madame de Beaumont retired to Savoy and once again took up her career as teacher and writer and, incidentally, sought repeatedly without success to prevail upon Pichon to join her.[82]

The year 1757 — the year that Pichon made his connection with Madame de Beaumont — saw him in the New World again, it would appear, on a special assignment. It may be noted that while at Beauséjour he had expressed to Captain Scott the desire to go to Pennsylvania in order to find a permanent abode. That he secretly arrived there in the spring and remained there for a brief sojourn, living, we are told, in the guise of a needy French officer who had been made prisoner,[83] seems quite clear, according to information contained in one of Lord Loudoun's letters to Pitt.[84] Here he continued to render service to the British cause. Mixing with the exiled Acadians sent to this province, he gave information to Loudoun of a plan that they were projecting whereby the men, leaving behind them their women and children, would go as a body "to join the French in the back country" — presumably at Fort Duquesne.[85] This information led to the arrest of five of their leaders, who were temporarily removed from the colony, with the result, as will be noted in a subsequent chapter, that these unhappy people became much less refractory than they had been.

How long Pichon continued in the New World has not been ascertained. His stay could not have been protracted. We know that he was back in London in 1758, for in that year he addressed his friend John Cleland, writer and Celtic scholar, about his affair with Madame

---

[82] For two of Madame Beaumont's letters to Pichon see J. C. Webster, *op. cit.*, pp. 125–35.

[83] Emile Lauvrière, *La Tragédie d'un peuple*, II, 120.

[84] Writing to Pitt on April 25, 1757 from New York, Loudoun declared: "Captain Cotterell, who is Secretary for the Province of Nova Scotia, and is in this Country for the recovery of his health, found among those Neutrals [sent to Pennsylvania] one who had been a Spie of Colonel Cornwallis and afterwards of Governor Lawrence, who tells me [that he] had behaved well both in giving accounts of what those people were doing and in bringing them intelligence of the situation and strength of the French forts and in particular of Beauséjour; by this man I learnt that there were five principal men among them who stir up all the disturbance these people [the Acadian exiles] make in Pennsilvania, and who persuade them to go and join the enemy and who prevent them from submitting to any regulations made in the country, and to allow their children to be put out to work" (Hist. Soc. of Pa. Memoirs, VI, 305–6).

[85] *Ibid.*, VI, 305.

de Beaumont.[86] In 1760 his volume on Cape Breton Island appeared both in French and in English, and after that date for some years he continued his literary labours and, it would seem, enjoyed a rather quiet existence, which included a correspondence with a limited circle of acquaintances.

But in 1767 his life received a new motivation. For in October of that year an acquaintance brought to his apartment on Woodstock Street — Madame de Beaumont's former apartment — two Acadians who represented the great body of exiles that were living in or about Saint-Malo in France. These people, who had given their all in loyalty to His Most Christian Majesty and for years now had been living on his bounty, had, it seems, at last come to the realization that they had made a tragic mistake in refusing while in their beloved Acadia to recognize properly the authority of the King of England. According to the report of the two emissaries, at least five hundred and probably a thousand of them were anxious to return to their old abodes and, to gain this privilege, were now quite prepared to take the unqualified oath of allegiance that they previously had refused. The two exiles had therefore sought out Pichon, now living under the name of Tyrrell, who agreed to aid them.

The following January he addressed a letter to John Pownall, Secretary of the Board of Trade, which began:

"Sir:
"You have known my attachment for Great Britain. I have given my proofs of this and you are better situated than any one else to appreciate the solidity of these." [87]

In this letter he made a powerful plea that the exiles, who had at first accepted so eagerly allegiance to the French King, should now be permitted to return again to the country of their nativity. He argued that these good people, living under an administration as tranquil as that which had brought happiness to the English colonies, would become without question very affectionate as well as very useful subjects. Born in Acadia and accustomed to life there, they would be in a position to instruct the new settlers that the government was sending there and to encourage the work of the latter as the result of their own experience and greater expertness in the necessary labours. The Saint-Malo exiles, he also pointed out in a post-

---

[86] For this letter see J. C. Webster, op. cit., pp. 21–2.
[87] Canadian Archives Report (1905), II, Appendix J, pp. 250–1.

script, had entered into secret agreements and measures with some of the inhabitants of the near-by English island of Jersey, to which place they were prepared to flee from the French jurisdiction until the way was open for a return to what they called their native land. He also forwarded with his letter a memorial to the King of England that the two Acadians had prepared in the name of the group, showing their complete spirit of submission.[88]

While the story of the wanderings and trials of the Acadians has been reserved for separate treatment in this volume, it may be pointed out that once again Thomas Pichon and Abbé Le Loutre found themselves opposed to each other and once again the struggle had to do with the fate of the Acadians. Apparently in order to further more conveniently the plans for the proposed flight of the Saint-Malo exiles to Jersey, preparatory to sending them back to old Acadia to be settled within what are now the bounds of the province of New Brunswick, Pichon shifted his place of residence some time after 1769 from London to St. Helier on that island.[89] His activities there are obscure, but he seems to have worked with such Jerseymen as Philippe Robin (or was it Pichon using this nom de plume?), who in 1772 was carrying on a secret correspondence with the Saint-Malo group and whose letter to a leading Acadian living there was waylaid and brought to the attention of the Minister of the Marine. However that may be, as a result of the exposure of this correspondence orders were issued by the Minister to watch the activities of all ships resorting to the Channel Islands. Further, this effort — "to debauch the Acadiens and to drag them into the English colonies" [90] — was called to the attention of Abbé Le Loutre, Pichon's old Beauséjour acquaintance, now in France after spending some years as an English prisoner at Castle Elizabeth in Jersey.[91]

---

[88] For this see *ibid.*, pp. 251–2.

[89] J. C. Webster, *op. cit.*, p. 24.

[90] *Canadian Archives Report* (1905), I, Part VI, p. 405.

[91] Le Loutre, as was noted, escaped from Fort Beauséjour; he thereupon fled to Quebec through the woods; thence he went to Louisbourg, preparatory to returning to France, and there took passage on the *Embuscade*. His vessel had the misfortune to be captured by Admiral Hawke on September 15, 1755. Recognized by the admiral, he was sent to the port of Plymouth, where he remained under guard on the *Oxford*. Transferred to Portsmouth early in November, he was detained there for over a month on the *Royal George*; then in December the sloop *Swan* carried him to the island of Jersey, where he was incarcerated in Elizabeth Castle for eight years. It was not until October 30, 1763, "after having made any number of requests" and also after the Treaty of Paris, that he was finally set at liberty and permitted to go to France ("*Une Autobiographie de l'Abbé Le Loutre,*" *Nova Francia*, VI, No. 1, pp. 30–1).

Le Loutre, always a man of action, was at this juncture using all his powers of persuasion to reconcile the dissatisfied Acadians to become French cultivators of the soil.[92] It was perhaps fitting that in the same year that he was informed of the plot to help the Acadians back to America he should have died (on September 30) in the midst of a valiant, if vain, effort to bring the rebellious Saint-Malo Acadians to agree to settle in the old province of Poitou in southwestern France. As for Pichon, it is clear that, as one highly suspected by the French government, he could not openly act in any relationship with these exiles who still continued to long for America, although most of them, torn by indecision, lingered on many years at Saint-Malo. It is nevertheless true that he had an opportunity to welcome a small group to the island in 1773, who were then transferred to America, and that he remained at St. Helier until his death in 1781, doubtless as earnest in his desire to aid them to return to their Acadia as he had been in 1768.

It may here be suggested that these two men, Le Loutre and Pichon, cleric and layman, offer a striking contrast and comparison: one fanatically of the robe, the other wantonly of the world; one clinging to the past, a child of the Middle Ages, was ruthless with the present; the other scorning the past, a child of the age of rationalism, was all-absorbed in the significant present; one a Frenchman who saw the *summum bonum* in concepts that would subordinate all mankind to the autocratic rule and will of both church and state authorities, the other a Frenchman who saw it in concepts that would subordinate the church and state to the inherent natural rights and general will of mankind. Each with good reason may be accused of a record of treacherous conduct; yet each seems to have been fully convinced of the correctness and moral justification of the course that he took. Each contributed mightily, although working at cross-purposes, to the destruction of the old French Empire; each also held to a large degree the welfare and the fate of the inhabitants of Acadia in his keeping. The priest assumed the grave responsibility of refusing to recognize that, so far as Acadia was concerned, the past was irrevocable; the layman an equal responsibility in affirming that it was. The guilt of each lies in the manner of the implementation of his conviction. But to keep the record clear it must be pointed out that of the two Le Loutre bears not only a greater responsibility but a greater guilt in that his treachery in driving his Indians into action,

---

[92] Ernest Martin, *Les Exiles acadiens en France au XVIII° siècle*, pp. 90–3.

in a time of open peace between England and France, against the British settlers at Halifax and even against all Acadians in Nova Scotia who would co-operate with them, began that chain of tragic events which led directly to the uprooting of the thousands of these betrayed people. Pichon, doubtless already strongly inclined toward anticlericalism, was made bitterly so by the conduct of the priest and other missionaries who supported the fatal Indian policy noted above and found himself, if we may believe statements made before his treason, at last completely estranged from a system that supported such practices; and therefore he apparently determined, in repudiating this system, to lend himself to fight treachery with its own weapon. As a result, one of the two kept faith with the past and died, as he had lived, a devoted servant of the church of his ancestors and an equally devoted servant and pensioner of His Most Christian Majesty; the other during his lifetime broke violently with the past and, after turning his back upon both his ancestral church and the King whom he had served for many years with some distinction, died a devoted servant and pensioner of His Britannic Majesty. Each, the unconscious instrument of so much injury to the Acadians, gave as an act of expiation as it were, all be it unwittingly, his last best public services — each in his own way and again working at cross-purposes — to restore to some of these deluded and now bitterly disillusioned people at least a portion of the values of purposeful living that had been snatched from them with their dispersion.

But Pichon's life in Jersey does not seem to have been a happy one. After his settlement at Saint Helier he found himself faced with growing physical infirmities; he also now became introspective, fearing the end. Yet he could, in his reflections, write in 1778 to a friend:

> "I have always conducted myself according to the laws of honour; I have loyally kept my promises; I never wronged or injured any one. In short, I have adhered to the principles of nature. Do they not suffice to govern our lives?"

He then answered his own question:

> "Reason, then, has deceived me; it was, doubtless, incapable of directing my life, since it was too weak to defend me against the terrors of death. . . . Moral probity which I made my idol was but the shadow of the obligation I failed to fulfil, for, alas, what is honour without piety?" [93]

---

[93] For this English translation of the letter of 1778 written in French and in the Vire collection see J. C. Webster, op. cit., pp. 25–6.

Firm in his anticlericalism, he had renounced the Roman Catholic faith and become a Protestant.[94] He passed away at St. Helier on November 22, 1781. In his will he avowed his Christian fellowship and faith "by the special grace of God . . ." and also declared in a spirit of humility:

> "I have studied long to find out very late how little I had learned; science has added nothing to my fortunes. I have been of great usefulness in many circumstances in France, Germany, America, and England. I must consider myself fortunate that I only lost the recompense due to my success, and that scorn was not added to calumny and ingratitude." [95]

He requested a funeral like that of the poorest inhabitant of Jersey, and left a small bequest for the poor of his parish. But his estate, including his library and manuscripts, he desired should go to the town of his nativity. In leaving his manuscripts intact to be transferred to Vire in France he apparently decided that he was quite willing to leave his case to the judgment of posterity. So it rests.

In bringing this chapter to a conclusion one might raise the question whether there is in existence any other body of documents that sets forth in such faithful detail as do the Pichon manuscripts the workings of the mind of one who laid himself open to the charge of high treason. One may further ask whether, in modern times at least, there was ever committed another treason that more materially and effectively advanced certain vital interests of the nation that was the beneficiary of it and more fatally handicapped those equally vital of the nation against which it was directed.

---

[94] There were apparently a good many French Protestants on the island of Jersey. One hundred and eighty of these Huguenot refugees from France escaped to this place in 1750 (B.T., N.S., 9: F 143. Canadian Archives transcriptions).

[95] Webster, *op. cit.*, p. 26.

CHAPTER IX

Farewell to Acadia

THE CAPTURE OF the French forts on the isthmus of Chignecto by the British colonial forces, the account of which has been given in the preceding chapter, led directly to the expulsion of the major portion of the so-called "French Neutrals" from old Acadia. This action has been the subject of so much attention on the part of writers, uninformed as well as informed respecting the problem faced by the government of Nova Scotia in 1755, that it merits careful consideration at this point in surveying the course of the Great War for the Empire in North America.

In the chapter on "The Land of the Acadians" in the preceding volume of the present series attention was given to the relations of the settlers with the English after the Treaty of Utrecht had provided for the cession to the Crown of Great Britain of Acadia, or Nova Scotia, with its ancient limits. The loyalty of the inhabitants to the throne of France in 1714, it was suggested, apparently surpassed their attachment to their homes and it appears that they were prepared to leave *en masse* to take refuge on Isle Royale, or Cape Breton as the English called the island, but were discouraged in their determination as the result of the lack of facilities for transporting all their effects and also their desire to be permitted the time necessary to dispose of their non-movables; the specific terms in the treaty gave them but a year and a day in which to leave, if they were not to be considered British subjects. The years between 1714 and 1749 constituted a period of temporizing with the problem of reconciling the inhabitants to their legal status as British subjects. It is clear that while those who had been the heads of families in 1714 had gradually passed away and their places had been taken by a new generation, and that while through the process of natural increase their numbers had multiplied many-fold and their settlements had spread to new places, they remained Frenchmen at heart, although born and reared on English soil. They were little affected by the weak authority of the Governor of the garrison at Annapolis Royal, but profoundly influenced by the ministrations of their spiritual guides, who, trained in the French seminaries and supported by pensions granted by the Crown of France, shared their simple life either as parish priests or as missionaries to the neighbouring and friendly Indian tribes, with whom the Acadians had intermarried. It is equally clear that the inhabitants sought not only to reconcile two utterly irreconcilable conceptions: ultimate allegiance to the Crown of France and temporary fidelity to that of Great Britain, but at the same time to continue to live in security in a region that — with the growing rivalry between these two great colonial powers and the development of the crisis over the disputed ancient boundaries of Acadia — was destined to become one of the most insecure in all North America.

Indeed, within the British domain the position of the Acadians in 1749 was unique and in opposition to every accepted conception then and today of the obligations resting upon those living within the bounds of the authority of a state. They refused absolutely to take the oath of allegiance that could be demanded of any British subject — although most of them agreed to take in 1727 a highly qualified and unauthorized oath of fidelity — and therefore insisted on a privileged position within the Empire. It may be noted in this connection that when New Sweden was obliged to submit to the New Netherlands in 1655, those Swedes who desired to remain on the Delaware were expected to give an oath of unqualified allegiance to the new authority; likewise when in turn the New Netherlands was obliged to submit to the English in 1664, the Dutch about the Hudson and elsewhere were also expected to do so, should they desire to remain beyond the period of a year. The rule, in fact, has had in international law its broadest application and was applied not only to the French in Canada after 1763 but to those in Louisiana after its cession to the United States in 1803 and to the Mexicans in northern Mexico after the treaty of cession in 1847.

Further, the Acadians in 1749, while refusing allegiance and denying that they were "natural-born subjects" — although under English law all born within the English dominion were held to be so — demanded rights that were denied to aliens; for under the terms of a statute passed in the eighth year of the reign of William III, relating

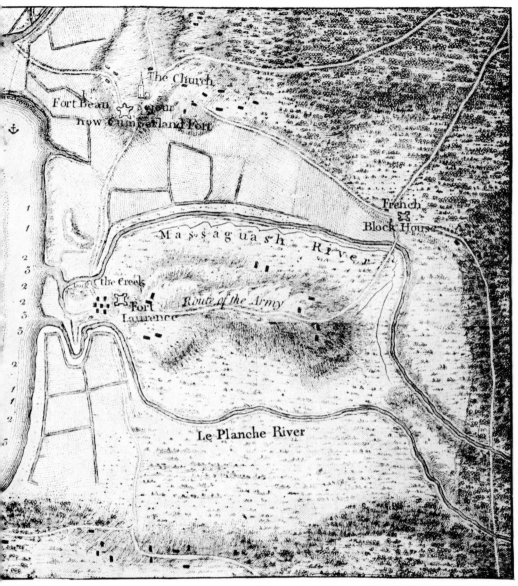

Fort Beauséjour and adjacent country, taken possession of by Colonel Monckton, June, 1755.

(From Thomas Mante's *History of the Late War,* 1772.)

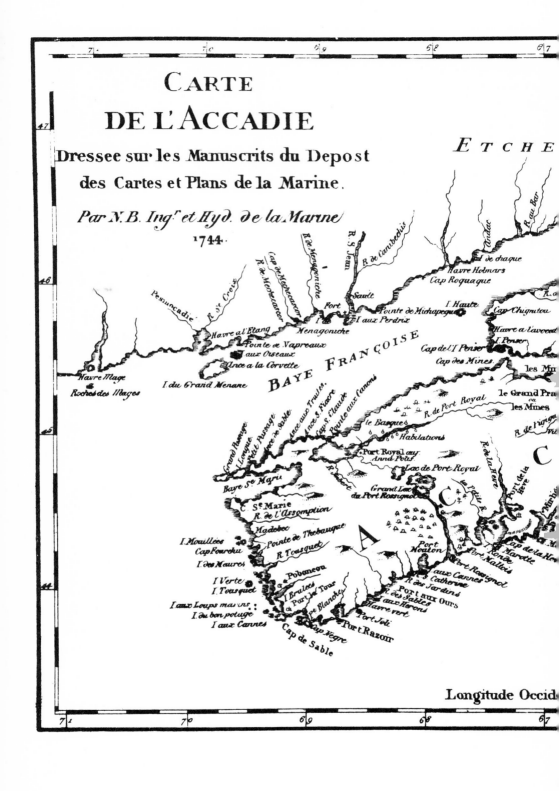

CARTE
DE L'ACCADIE

Dressée sur les Manuscrits du Depost
des Cartes et Plans de la Marine.

Par N.B. Ing.ʳ et Hyd. de la Marine
1744.

ETCHE

R. au Bar.

de Chaque
Havre Holmars
Cap Roguaque

R. o

R. de Menagonteché
R. S Jean
R. de Canibechis
Sault
Pointe de Michapegu
I. Haute
Cap Chignitou

R. de Mechcarton
Port
I. aux Perdrix
Havre a l'avocat
I. Poure

Cap de Mehcaron
Pesuncadie
R. de Croix
Havre a l'Etang
Menagoniche
Pointe de Napreaux
aux Oiseaux
Ance a la Corvette

Cap de l'I Perse
Cap des Mines
les Mi

Havre Mage
Roches des Mages
I. du Grand Menane

BAYE FRANÇOISE

le Grand Pra
ou
les Mines

R. de l'rigou

Grand Passage
Longue
Petit Passage
Terre de Sable
Ance aux Trutes
Lac S Frere
Log S Claude
Pointe aux Canons
le Basques
Habitations
R. de Port Royal
R. de la Here
Port de la
Here

C

Port Royal ou
Anna Polis
Lac de Port Royal

R. Dibet

Baye Se Marie

Grand Lac
du Port Rossignol
la Petite R.

C

St Marie
R. de l'Assomption
Madobec
Pointe de Thebauque
R. Toasquet

A

Cap de la He

I. Mouillées
Cap Fourchu
I. des Maures

I. Verte
I. Tousquet
I. aux Loups ma: ns:
I. du bon potage
I. aux Cannes

Pobaneou
I. Brutes
Port de Tour
Cap Blanche
Cap Negre
Port Joli
Port Razoir
Cap de Sable

Port
Moaton
Port Rossignol
aux Cannes
R. ste Catherine
Port aux Ours
R. des Jardins
R. des Sables
aux Herons
Havre vert

Ronde
Port Mattois

Longitude Occid

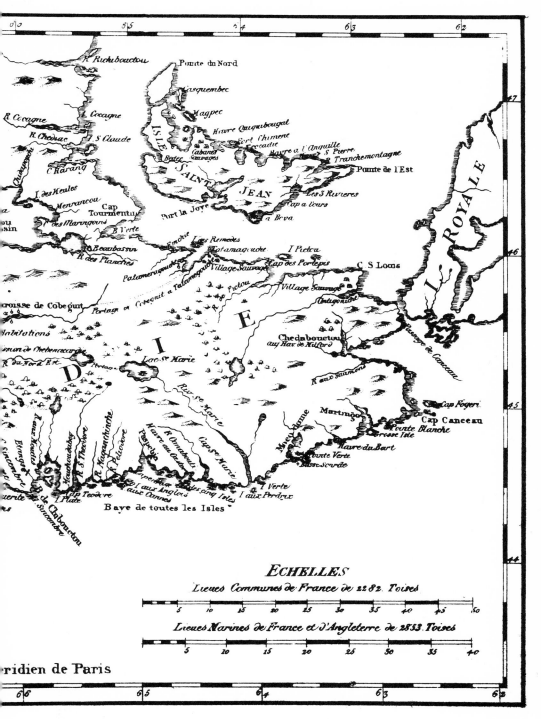

to the acquisition of land by any alien within any portion of the English dominion, no such acquisition was legal without express consent of the Crown.[1] Yet from time to time after 1714, on their own initiative, they sought out and occupied and thereupon claimed to possess lands about the Bay of Fundy and beyond, wherever these seemed to be adapted to their needs. In this connection numerous disputes arose among them over respective rights to these lands, which, however, could not be settled by any of the established processes of law, since they did not consider that they were bound by the laws applicable to all subjects of the Crown; and as persons who had refused the unrestricted oath of allegiance, they were moreover not entitled to the benefit of legal processes for adjudicating such disputes.[2] All in all, the position of the Acadians within the Empire was anomalous, to say the least.

It had been hoped that with the passing of years and the coming of new generations — all born beyond the dominion of the King of France — they would, from pure self-interest if for no other reason, be prepared at last to do what the Swedes and the Dutch to the south had in the preceding century felt impelled to do. That hope would without doubt have been easily realized had it not been for the constant, active influence of the men of God, their parish priests, by and large ardent French patriots, whose only connection was with France and who, understandably enough, looked forward to the time when the heretical English should give place once again to those who upheld not only the true faith but the fleur-de-lis. Therefore, when Governor Cornwallis in 1749 brought to Nova Scotia the first English settlers and a royal instruction requiring at last after so much temporizing an unqualified oath of allegiance of all the inhabitants of the province, he was met by firm resistance. This might not have been so serious in itself, in spite of the thousands of the Acadians, had it not been for the implications that it involved. For to have ordered the French Neutrals from the province upon their refusal would have been a welcome thing to those guiding French Canadian policy. This would have given them an accession of strength in Canada far beyond that indicated by the mere numbers of the Acadians. In carrying out their plan for the reconquest of Acadia it would have

---

[1] 7 and 8 William III, c. 22, Par. 16.

[2] Public Record Office, Nova Scotia, A. 54: 221–3. (This reference will be indicated hereafter by the letters P.R.O., N.S.) See also Nova Scotia Documents (ed. T. B. Akins), I, 207–8.

presented to them a body of people — according to some authorities some twelve to fifteen thousand in number — all inflamed with a deep sense of injury, who with their Indian allies and in many cases Indian kinsmen knew almost every foot of the peninsula and who from the dense woods could have, with proper supplies of food and munitions, so harassed the English that successful settlement of any portion of the province — without reference to any of the lands claimed by the Acadians — would have been out of the question. Again there was temporizing. Then in 1750 came the building of the French forts on the St. John and at Beauséjour and Gaspereau within the peninsula and the intensified efforts of the French to draw the Acadians behind their lines to put new lands into cultivation and to work upon the fortifications. With this French intrusion came not only the destruction of the flourishing town of Beaubassin at the hands of its own inhabitants, incited by Le Loutre, and the Micmacs, stirred to action by this missionary, but the desertion of hundreds of the Acadians to the French, who thereupon cast aside all pretence of neutrality and took an unqualified oath of allegiance to the French monarch.[3]

But most of the French Neutrals did not resort to such drastic action as has been described. Dwelling in the interior of the province, they hesitated. Nevertheless, only under duress would they render aid to the British settlement at Halifax, while at the same time they eagerly seized every opportunity to send needed supplies of grain and cattle by unfrequented paths to the French garrisons at Louisbourg, Beauséjour, and Gaspereau — even in the face of strict prohibitions. They seem to have lived in a state of alternating fear and hope: fear of retribution at the hands of the British government should they openly resist it and openly consort with its enemies; hope of the reunion with other Frenchmen in the success of French arms in North America. Their prudent course of conduct seemed to have been vindicated when in the fall of 1753 many of the so-called "deserted Frenchmen" — those who had fled to the French forts — now disillusioned and impoverished,[4] sought to return to their homes

---

[3] For the part taken by Le Loutre in bringing the Acadians to take an unqualified oath of allegiance to the French King see "Une Autobiographie de l'Abbé Le Loutre," Nova Francia, VI, No. 1, p. 20.

[4] According to Le Loutre, all the inhabitants in that region behind the French lines, refugee and non-refugee, to the number of 3,700 would have starved during the winter of 1752–3 had he not purchased wheat from the English shipmasters, doubtless from those colonials who resorted to Louisbourg (ibid., pp. 23–4).

and fertile lands and, to gain permission, approached the commander of Fort Lawrence on the Missaquash. Although they had but recently taken the oath of allegiance to the French King,[5] they now declared in their petition their entire willingness to take the old qualified oath of fidelity to the King of Great Britain that had been administered to their fathers without authorization in 1727, provided that all the exemptions as to the bearing of arms and freedom of religion accorded at that time should be granted in writing to them and to their descendants. In addition they specified that they were to have as many apostolic priests as were necessary, who should not be compelled to take an oath of allegiance; further, that they were to have the entire enjoyment of their property "without being disturbed by any one in the world"; and that the lands at Fort Lawrence occupied by the English should be restored to those to whom they formerly had belonged.[6] The Nova Scotia Council in its reply to this petition was clear: that while the refugees could look forward to having a proper number of priests and all the lands restored to them except those upon which Fort Lawrence itself was located, it would be quite necessary for them to take the new unqualified oath [7] — a position that was strongly and properly supported by the Board of Trade in view of the attitude of those who treated the old oath so lightly.[8] It was not until the following June that the petitioners replied that they would not return unless they were assured that they would be given the confirmed status of neutrals — a status that was absolutely denied them within the French lines.[9]

While the Council had no power to make any such formal exemption to the oath of allegiance to the Crown as the refugees desired, it had already made clear through its secretary that it was prepared to give them a solemn verbal assurance that they would not be expected to bear arms, especially since "the nature of our constitution makes it both unsafe & unprecedented to trust our cause in the Hands of people of their [religious] persuasion. . . ."[10] The Council, there-

---

[5] La Jonquière to the Minister, May 1, 1751, Arch. Nat., Col., C¹¹A. 97: 16.

[6] Minutes of the Nova Scotia Council, September 27, 1753, *Nova Scotia Doc.*, I, 203–5.

[7] *Ibid.*, I, 207–8.

[8] Board of Trade to President Lawrence, March 4, 1754, *ibid.*, I, 207–8.

[9] Arch. Nat., Col., C¹¹A. 97: 16.

[10] Secretary William Cotterell to Captain Scott, April 12, 1754, *Nova Scotia Doc.*, I, 208–9. The disarming of the Catholic Highlands in Scotland after 1746 showed the attitude of the Crown toward the carrying of arms by members of the Catholic faith.

fore, determined on June 21 that it could not go beyond its concessions made in September of the preceding year.[11]

These refugees were now in the unenviable position of having
sworn allegiance to His Most Christian Majesty and were thus as his
subjects quite deprived of any claim to neutrality; but, unable to
make a living on inhospitable lands, they longed deeply to return
to their old abodes about the ruins of Beaubassin within the British
lines. Yet this could not be accomplished. For they could not or
would not accept the terms, certainly generous enough, of the government of Nova Scotia. They claimed, in this connection, that were
they to agree to do so, their old friends the Indians "threatened them
that they would every day run the risque of having their throats cut
and their cattle destroyed. . . ."[12]

The fate or salvation of these unhappy people, there can be little
doubt, rested in the hands of one man, Le Loutre, England's most
implacable enemy and chief missionary to the Micmacs, who, established now at Beauséjour, had become the most powerful person in
all Acadia. The Abbé, having set his Indians in 1749 to threaten their
old friends and neighbours should they show any friendship for the
English, was not at all disposed to call them off in 1754. In fact, he
still thought in terms of drawing all the Acadians from the peninsula
and succeeded late in the spring of that year in persuading hundreds
of them from about Annapolis Royal, Minas Basin, and the Piziquid
River to defy the orders of the government of the province and to go
to Beauséjour in order to spend the summer season assisting the
French at the fort in reclaiming lands for cultivation.[13]

To suggest that the Acadians — refusing profitable work offered
by the government of the province and resorting to the French fort
in defiance of orders — showed any respect for the restricted oath
of fidelity to the King of Great Britain that they freely admitted they
and the other Acadians had once taken and as freely asserted that
they themselves were now prepared to maintain can be given little
credence; nor can credence be given to the contention of their actual
neutrality. However, Colonel Lawrence made clear at this juncture
that all who had taken even the old defective oath must realize that

---

[11] Minutes of the Council, June 21, 1754, ibid., I, 211–12.

[12] Ibid.

[13] Ibid. The Acadians were brought to Beaubassin by Le Loutre to build a great dike
there. This was designed to drain lands sufficient for the needs not only of the refugee
Acadians but of all those within the peninsula, according to the priest ("Autobiographie,"
Nova Francia, VI, No. 1, 25–6).

it was still in force; that no one could annul it without permission of the King; and, as a consequence, should any be taken in arms against him, they would be punished for this high crime.[14] Moreover, in a further effort to put an end to the practice of the Acadians, as well as some unscrupulous English colonials, of carrying the abundant food supplies produced about Minas Basin to the French forts at Beauséjour and Gaspereau on the peninsula and to Louisbourg on Cape Breton rather than to Halifax, early in the month of September he issued a proclamation warning all those who took corn out of the province without permission of the commander-in-chief that they would be liable to a penalty of fifty pounds.[15] Again, later in the month, he instructed Captain Murray — now acting as commander of the English Fort Edward on the Piziquid River and in general charge of the Minas Bay district — to refuse passes to all inhabitants who sought to go to Fort Beauséjour, on pain of forfeiting their lands for violating the order, and to acquaint them that they were not to pay the least regard to

"any Declaration or orders whatsoever from Mr. Le Loutre or any person Civil, Military, or Ecclesiastical, except such as go forth from his Majesty's Government under which they live. . . ."[16]

It may be noted that only once during this period, in the month of August, was there a slight break in the recalcitrant front of the Acadians. Some twenty-five of them who had gone to Cape Breton, where they had vainly sought to gain a living on the barren soil, now in a starving condition escaped to Halifax and freely took the unqualified oath of allegiance. They were given provisions, tools, and lands to cultivate in the eastern part of the province, beyond the effective range of the influence of Le Loutre.[17]

But at Piziquid Captain Murray was obliged to report that the priest Daudin, who had been brought to the province in 1753 by Le

---

[14] Minutes of the Council, September 9, 1754, *Nova Scotia Doc.*, I, 215–19.

[15] Proclamation of September 17, 1754, *ibid.*, I, 219–20. In this connection it was made clear that no one would be constrained to sell his corn to any particular individual or at any fixed price, but that the pressing needs of the province must first be supplied before this commodity could be permitted to leave it. Lawrence also pointed out that it was the general practice of nations to hinder the exportation of corn until the nation itself was supplied; this was true of France and even of England, with its corn laws favouring the export only of surplus corn (*ibid.*, I, 221–2).

[16] Secretary Cotterell to Captain Murray, September 23, 1754, *ibid.*, I, 221.

[17] Secretary Cotterell to Colonel Sutherland, August 24, 1754, *ibid.*, I, 214.

Loutre and well instructed by him,[18] was "very busy with the inhabitants."[19] Brought before the Council at Halifax, Daudin was charged with stirring up the Acadians and it was pointed out to him that when he was at Annapolis he had also created among the people there much

> "uneasiness and discontent, also that the Inhabitants of Piziquid who were very quiet and obedient in his Absence, grew immediately refractory and disobedient upon his return to them."[20]

Only by threat of expelling the priest from the province were the Acadians of Piziquid once more brought under some semblance of control. It seems to be quite clear, however, that at this juncture those of Cobequid, resenting the fact that their arms were demanded and some of their leaders were taken into custody — including their fiery curé, M. Girard — sent a memorial to their fellow refugees at Beauséjour which called upon them to aid the rest of the Acadians to escape from the English and repair to French territory. These revolted Acadians were asked to attack the English of Cobequid; after driving Lieutenant Gorham from the parish, they would join, according to the plan, to expel the English from Piziquid, Grand Pré, and Port Royal, the people of which would not fail to unite to escape the slavery that threatened them.[21] Another memorial on the part of the "French Acadians" was directed to His Most Christian Majesty, appealing to him, rather than the King of Great Britain, as their natural protector, to support them in their privileged position and asking him

> "to graciously give orders that they be granted concessions in the neighbouring French territory of Acadia, with the same privileges that His Majesty accorded to the settlers of Isle Royale."[22]

Writing to the Board of Trade in August, Lawrence made clear the dilemma that was facing the government of the province. In referring to the Neutral French he declared:

---

[18] Abbé d'Isle-Dieu to the Minister, March 21, 1753, Arch. Nat., Col., C¹¹A. 99: 152–206.

[19] Captain Murray to President Lawrence, September 22, 1754, *Nova Scotia Doc.,* I, 221.

[20] Minutes of the Council, October 3, 1754, *ibid.,* I, 226–7.

[21] "Pichon Papers," No. 12, Nova Scotia State Archives.

[22] *Nova Scotia Doc.,* I, 231–4; J. C. Webster: *Thomas Pichon,* pp. 61–3. This communication and the one above are in the handwriting of Abbé Le Loutre.

"I believe they have at present laid aside all thoughts of taking the oaths voluntarily . . . and . . . while they . . . have Incendiary French Priests among them there are no Hopes of their Amendment . . . and tho I would be very far from attempting such a step without your Lordships approbation, yet I cannot help being of the opinion that it would be much better, if they refuse the oaths, that they were away.

"The only ill consequence that can attend their going would be their taking up arms and joining with the Indians to distress our settlements, as they are numerous and our troops are divided. . . ." [23]

The Lords Commissioners made a reply that should be studied with care:

"We were in hopes that the Lenity which has been shown to those People by indulging them in the free exercise of their Religion and the quiet Possession of their Lands would by degrees [have] gained their Friendship and Assistance and weaned their Affections from the French; but we are sorry to find that this Lenity has had so little Effect, that they still hold the same Conduct with respect to them and Us, that they did before the Settlement of the Province, furnishing them with Labour, Provisions, and Intelligence, and concealing their [that is, the French] Designs from Us."

They then went on to make clear that, by the Treaty of Utrecht, an express condition of the continuance of the Acadians within the province, after the expiration of a year, was that they should become subjects of Great Britain, "which We Apprehend they cannot be but by taking the Oaths required of Subjects." They thereupon raised the question whether the Acadians' refusal to take these oaths would not operate to invalidate the titles to their Lands and then stated:

". . . it is a question, however, which we will not take upon ourselves absolutely to determine, but would wish that you would consult the Chief Justice upon this Point, and take his Opinion, which may serve as a foundation of any future measure it may be thought advisable to pursue with regard to the Inhabitants in general."

However, they indicated to Lawrence that, should the Chief Justice take the position that the Acadians of the district of Chignecto, by deserting their lands and actually going over to the French in a body, had forfeited their title to the lands, he should take proper measures to carry out such forfeiture by legal process to the end that these lands might be granted to persons desirous of settling there,

[23] P.R.O., N.S., A. 55: 192–4.

where "a Settlement would be of great utility, if it could be effected." In this connection they made clear that Governor Shirley of Massachusetts Bay had already expressed the opinion that it would be possible to get "a considerable number of People from New England" for colonizing that district and they therefore recommended to the Lieutenant Governor that he consult with Shirley on this point. But before closing they warned him that it appeared to them

> "that every Idea of an English Settlement at this place [the District of Chignecto] would be absurd but upon the supposition that the French Forts Beau Sejour, Bay Verte, etc. are destroyed, the Indians forced from their Settlements, and the French driven to seek such an Asylum as they can find in the barren Islands of Cape Breton and St. Johns [St. Jean, now Prince Edward Island] and in Canada." [24]

The Board of Trade, in other words, indicated to Lawrence that the Acadians were to be considered either British or French subjects; if the former, they must take the oaths all British subjects were expected to take when required; if the latter — should the Chief Justice of the province give as his opinion that a continued refusal of the oaths invalidated the claims of the inhabitants to the lands that they occupied — then their possessions within the province were liable to forfeiture and might be granted to those who might desire to settle them.[25] But they indicated that three measures would be necessary to make any settlement of these lands safe: the French forts within the province must be destroyed, the hostile Indians ejected from their abodes, and, finally, those holding allegiance to the French Crown driven out of the province.

[24] Board of Trade to Lieutenant Governor Lawrence, October 29, 1754, Nova Scotia Doc., I, 325–7.

[25] Chief Justice Belcher in his opinion dated July 28, 1755 — that is, after the Acadians had repeatedly refused to take the unqualified oath of allegiance — declared: "I esteem it my duty to offer my reasons against receiving any of the French Inhabitants [now] to take the oaths and for their not being permitted to remain in the province." He lists five reasons for this position: (1) the conduct of the Acadians from the time of the Treaty of Utrecht to the present showed them in no other light than that of "rebels to his Majesty," whose subjects they became; (2) that to look upon them otherwise would be against Governor Lawrence's instructions regarding the oath of allegiance and would incur the displeasure of the Crown and Parliament; (3) that this would defeat the intent of the late expedition against Fort Beauséjour; (4) that it would put a total stop to the progress of the settlement of the province and disappoint the expectations of Great Britain in incurring vast expense in the province; and (5) that these inhabitants on the removal of the troops — shortly to return to New England — would return to what he called their "perfidy and Treacheries" and yet the province would then be in no condition to drive them out. (Belcher to the Board of Trade, July 28, 1755, P.R.O., N.S., A. 58: 38–48.)

While it is clear that the Lords Commissioners lacked power to direct, they were specifically authorized to advise. One may therefore state that the government of Nova Scotia accepted the advice of the Board — advice that envisioned the ultimate expulsion of the Neutral French unless they took the unqualified oath — as a legal basis of future action. But the expulsion had to wait upon the plans now projected between Lawrence and Shirley for the reduction of the French forts and their execution — an account of which has been given in the preceding chapter. It may be pointed out, however, that the following spring, in the light of information that reached Lawrence that efforts were being made by French emissaries to lead the inhabitants of Minas Basin to take up arms in aid of the French, he was impelled to write to Captain Murray at Fort Edward instructing him to

> "acquaint the Deputies [of the Acadians] that their Happiness and future welfare depends very much on their present behaviour & that . . . if any Inhabitant either old or Young shou'd offer to go to Beauséjour, or to take arms or to induce others to commit any Act of Hostility upon the English, or make any Declaration in favour of the French, they will be treated as Rebels, their Estates and Families undergo immediate Military Execution and their persons if apprehended . . . suffer the utmost Rigour of the Law. . . ." [26]

That Le Loutre at Beauséjour was again busy stirring up the inhabitants within the peninsula, and with some success, is indicated in the same letter; for Lawrence ordered Murray to publish a proclamation offering a reward of twenty pounds sterling for the apprehension of those who on May 5 carried letters to the priest from Cobequid, Minas, and Piziquid.[27] He also ordered that boats should patrol the basin to cut off communication with the French fort.

On June 3 came the landing at Beaubassin of the expedition of New England volunteers under command of Colonel Monckton of the regulars for the purpose of capturing Fort Beauséjour; on the following day Captain Murray at Fort Edward published an order to the inhabitants of Minas Basin to bring all their guns and pistols to

---

[26] Lawrence to Murray, May 13, 1755, *Nova Scotia Doc.*, I, 241–2.

[27] Le Loutre in his *"Autobiographie"* (*Nova Francia*, VI, No. 1, p. 24) declared that "although the inhabitants of the different places within the peninsula were located on lands that the Englishman had secured, they nevertheless refused to regard themselves as his subjects but on the contrary were hoping to be able to leave as soon as the missionary would furnish them the means; further, that they constantly maintained a security correspondence with him."

the fort. Some of the Acadians responded, but most of them held back. Instead, on the 10th, twenty-five of their leaders signed a memorial to the Lieutenant Governor stating that it would be dangerous to obey the order because of the beasts of the forest that attacked their cattle, and the Indians who would threaten them were they to do so; on the contrary, they requested that the arms already handed in should be returned to their owners as their rightful property; they also requested that they be permitted to use their *canots* as formerly — the use of which had been prohibited to cut off intercourse with the French forts about the Bay of Fundy and the isthmus of Chignecto. Much was said in the memorial about the loyalty with which they had kept their oath to the King of Great Britain, and Lawrence was assured:

> "We have today, Sir, the purest and most sincere desire as formerly to prove in every circumstance an attested fidelity to His Majesty, should he permit us to continue to enjoy the same liberties as he has accorded to us." [28]

This was delivered to Captain Murray, commander of the district, who sent it to Lawrence. The commander took occasion to point out that, for a considerable period of time before this was delivered, the inhabitants had behaved "with greater submission and obedience to government than usual," but that at the time of its delivery they treated him "with great Indecency and Insolence." [29] He indicated that this was perhaps due to the fact that a rumour — proved later to be false — had reached the Acadians that a French fleet had appeared in the Bay of Fundy, and this had emboldened them. Far from being a French fleet, the ships — probably seen at a distance by some of the Acadians — were in fact those of the New England convoy carrying the troops for the reduction of Fort Beauséjour.

With the surrender of the fort after a weak defence on the part of the French garrison aided by several hundred of the Acadians — the deserted French and others living about the upper reaches of the Bay of Fundy — Lawrence wrote to Secretary of State Robinson:

> "The deserted French inhabitants are delivering up their arms. I have given him (Col. Monckton) orders to drive them out of the country." [30]

---

[28] Council Minutes, July 3, 1755, P.R.O., N.S., B. 7: 159–207.
[29] *Ibid.*
[30] Lawrence to Robinson, June 28, 1755, *Nova Scotia Doc.*, I, 243.

By this statement it will be noted that the Governor and his Council had not as yet formulated any plan for exiling to the continental colonies even those Acadians who had gone over to the French and had aided them in arms. These were simply to be driven out of the province.

With the news carried to the Acadian settlements about Minas Bay that the French fort had capitulated, there was searching of hearts. The people may well have realized that their situation was now dangerous: the memorial of their leaders to the Governor — perhaps inspired, as has been suggested, by the hope of a successful French invasion by way of the Bay of Fundy — had contained many doubtful statements, and moreover most of them had not handed in their arms as ordered. As a result, on June 24 forty-five of the inhabitants of the Minas Bay district, speaking for all their compatriots, in a second memorial to the Governor referred somewhat apologetically to the first and desired to explain their true intentions, if, perchance, there was found to be "some fault or some lack of respect to the government." [31] In fact Governor Lawrence had already summoned to Halifax the signers of the first memorial, which, when read to the Council, was voted "an Insult upon His Majesty's Authority and Government and deserved the highest Resentment." [32]

The signers of the first memorial, brought before the Provincial Council, found themselves in the uncomfortable position of having it read to them paragraph by paragraph and the truth of each statement discussed. They were reminded

> "That they had enjoyed more Privileges than English Subjects, and had been indulged in the Free Exercise of their Religion . . . had been protected in their Trade and Fishery, and had been for many years permitted to possess their Lands . . . tho' they had not complied with the Terms, on which the Lands were granted, by Taking the Oath of Allegiance to the Crown."

Asked if they could produce an instance of any privilege denied them or any hardships imposed upon them, they acknowledged the justice and leniency of the government.

As to their own conduct, which they had described as "their unshaken fidelity to his Majesty," they were charged with a

> "constant disposition to Assist His Majesty's Enemies, and to distress his Subjects. That they had not only furnished the Enemy with Pro-

[31] P.R.O., N.S., B. 7: 159–207.
[32] Minutes of the Council, July 3, 1755, ibid.

visions and Ammunition, but had refused to supply the Inhabitants, or Government, with Provisions, and when they did Supply, they have exacted three times the Price for which they are sold in other Markets." [33]

Asked thereupon if they could mention a single instance of rendering any service to the government, they were unable to make any reply. As to their refusal to surrender their firearms, it was denied that it was necessary to carry them as a protection against the wild beasts: those who had at first voluntarily brought in their arms did not pretend that they were needed for the safety of their cattle; and as to the use of their *canots,* it was charged that they really wanted to employ them to carry provisions to the enemy.

Then the Council declared to the deputies its intention of testing their claims of fidelity to the King and called upon them to take "the oath of fidelity in the common form." It was explained to them that His Majesty had disapproved of the manner of the taking of the oath before by the Acadians, nor could the Council "accept their taking the oath in any other way than as all other His Majesty's Subjects were obliged by Law to do when called upon. . . ." This, however, they steadfastly refused to do, although they were given another day to make their final determination. Thereupon the Council informed them that it

> "could no longer look on them as Subjects of His Britannick Majesty, but as Subjects of the King of France, and as such they must hereafter be Treated. . . ." [34]

They then were ordered to withdraw. After they had done so, the Council, upon further deliberation, came to the determination that the Acadians throughout the peninsula should be requested to choose new deputies and to instruct them when chosen as to "the General Resolution of the said Inhabitants in regard to Taking the Oath." These deputies were to come to Halifax to report the final decision of the people. The Council also decided that should it then be found that the inhabitants were averse to taking the common oath,

> "none of them should for the future be admitted to take it after having once refused so to do, but that effectual Measures ought to be taken to remove all such Recusants out of the Province." [35]

---

[33] Minutes of the Council, July 3, 1755, *ibid.*
[34] *Ibid.*
[35] *Ibid.*

The resolution was drastic. But the crisis confronting the province seemed to call for drastic measures. The two French forts had fallen, it is true; but France, the greatest military power in the world, was still to be reckoned with: her aggressiveness in North America during the past six years had destroyed every bit of the old complacency of the English authorities in the New World; her troops might again appear, this time in real force, on the northern borders of the province, or be directed against Halifax in a sudden descent upon the metropolis of the colony. Should this happen it was quite clear that no Neutral Frenchman would raise a hand to protect the province from invasion, and many of them would not hesitate to assist the enemy as hundreds had done at Beauséjour. Moreover, the colony could not support any large body of troops for police purposes. New England volunteers had had to be brought in to reduce the forts, but under solemn agreement that their term of service should not extend beyond a year. When they departed, what then?

It is easy for writers, in the security of their studies, to describe the resolution as inhuman and quite unnecessary. Doubtless few of them, had they been living in Nova Scotia in 1755, would have felt so, in view not only of the extreme weakness of the English settlements in the eastern part of the peninsula, but of the fixed determination of the Neutral French, much more numerous and much more permanently established than were the English, to do everything possible to keep them weak. In this connection there is little doubt that the Acadians gave every secret aid within their power to Le Loutre's Indians, who ceaselessly ravaged these settlements.[36]

Here then was the rule of action adopted by the provincial government that led to the expulsion of the Acadians from Nova Scotia. Its first application was directed against those who had come to Halifax upon summons and had repeatedly refused the oath. Called before the Council for the last time, they were now informed of the decision. These inhabitants, we are told, brought face to face with the fact that the authorities, at last putting to one side "Lenity and

---

[36] Le Loutre in his "Autobiographie" (*Nova Francia*, VI, No. 1, p. 27) has the following to say about the Indian hostilities: "While the court of France had charged the missionary [Le Loutre] that he should seek to establish the Acadian families (who continually arrived from regions under English control to throw themselves into his arms), the Indians did not cease to make incursions from all sides against the English, who were daily increasing their claims — in spite of the infinite number of people killed by the natives for which the English blamed the missionary."

persuasion," would no longer permit them to take the required oath, now

> "Offered to take the Oath, but were informed that as there was no reason to hope their proposed Compliance proceeded from an honest Mind, and could be esteemed only the Effect of Compulsion and Force and is contrary to . . . an Act of Parliament . . . whereby Persons who have once refused to Take the Oaths cannot be afterwards permitted to Take them [37]. . . Therefore they could not now be indulged with such Permission. . . ." [38]

They were thereupon ordered into confinement as enemies of the province.

Having now determined to require all the Acadians to face at last the issue of accepting allegiance to the Crown under penalty of forcible removal from the province for refusal to do so, the Council, doubtless realizing the gravity of the step, decided, upon recommendation of the Lieutenant Governor, to request the presence of Vice Admiral Boscawen and Rear Admiral Mostyn — both then in Halifax — "to consider measures of safety to the Province." [39] At a meeting held on July 15 it laid before them the late proceedings. The admirals strongly approved of these and gave as their opinion "that now was the properest time to oblige the said Inhabitants to take the Oath of allegiance or to quit the country." [40]

On July 25 a memorial from the inhabitants of the Annapolis River, signed by over two hundred of them, was read. In it they stated that they had agreed to deliver up their arms, which they never desired to use against the government, and then declared:

> "We cannot reproach ourselves on this subject nor with respect to the fidelity that we owe to the government of His Majesty, since, Sir, we can assure your Excellency that many of us have risked life itself to give to the government intelligence of the enemy."

They also stated that they had selected thirty of their number to proceed to Halifax, but warned the Council that

> "we have enjoined them to agree to no new oath; we are resolved and determined to hold to that oath which we have given and to which we have been faithful in so far as circumstances required."

[37] 1 George II, c. 13.
[38] Nova Scotia Doc., I, 256.
[39] P.R.O., N.S., B. 8: 188.
[40] Minutes of the Council, July 15, 1755, P.R.O., N.S., B. 7: 159–207.

These deputies, when summoned before the Council, stated that they spoke for all those living on Annapolis River and that they were unanimously agreed that, rather than take any other oaths or take up arms, they would quit their lands; but in the latter case they asked for a period of time that they would consider convenient for making their departure. When asked by the Council to give a single instance of the inhabitants giving intelligence that had been of aid to the government, the deputies were unable to do so. It was then charged not only that the Acadians of that region had

> "always omitted to give timely intelligence when they had it in their power and might have saved the lives of Many of his Majestys Subjects but that they had always secretly aided the Indians and many had appeared in Arms against His Majesty." [41]

The deputies were then informed that the people must now resolve to take the oath without reserve or quit their lands. It was pointed out that

> "Affairs were in such a Crisis in America that no delay could be admitted, that the French had obliged us to take up Arms in our Defence against their Incroachments, and it was unknown what steps they [the French] might take further; for which Reason if they (the Inhabitants) could not become Subjects to all Intents and purposes, they could not be suffered to remain in the Country."

In spite of the warning that, once they and their fellow inhabitants refused to take the prescribed oath, they would not be permitted to take it subsequently and would lose their possessions, the deputies remained firm in their refusal to do so. [42]

On the 28th the memorials of the people of the Minas Basin district were considered by the Council. That from Piziquid, signed by one hundred and three of them in the name of all, declared that they had taken the oath of fidelity in good faith and could take no other and requested the release of their neighbours detained at Halifax.

---

[41] Minutes of the Council of July 25, 1755, *ibid.* In this connection it should be pointed out that one of these Acadians, Louis Rochibeau, who with the rest refused to take the specified oath and was exiled to Massachusetts Bay, in a petition to the Governor and Assembly of this province on September 10, 1756, declared that he had assisted in repairing the fort at Annapolis and further stated that "some of my family gave intelligence of Du Vivier's coming to attack the Fort, of which they would otherwise have had no timely notice . . ." and also rendered other services to the English (*Canadian Archives, Report* [1905], II, Appendix I, p. 197).

[42] *Nova Scotia Doc.,* I, 260–4.

That from Minas, the River Canards, and other places, signed by two hundred and three, likewise in the name of all, pointed out they were unable to take

> "an oath of obedience that conforms in any respect that taken by natu-
> ral subjects of His Majesty. . . . We shall never commit the incon-
> sistency of taking an oath that in whatever degree, it may be, changes
> the conditions and privileges secured for us by our sovereigns and
> our fathers in times past."

This made clear that these Acadians expected to enjoy immunities not given to "natural subjects" and that they held that "their sovereigns" — whether French or British is not clear — had secured for them this privileged and unique position within the British Empire.

When the deputies from the various districts of the province were brought before the Council and for the last time refused the oath, they joined those who had previously come from Piziquid and had been placed in confinement. As it had already been decided by the vote of the Council of July 3 — endorsed by the admirals on July 15 — that the Acadians under the given circumstances should be sent out of the province, all that remained to be done was to agree upon what measures would be taken "to send them away, and where they should be sent to." [43]

There were at least four possible solutions of the problem, each of which presented serious embarrassments: to send them to Canada, or to England, or to France, or, finally, to other English colonies. It was clear that sending them to Canada would have been presenting the French authorities with no small army of enraged frontiersmen, skilled in the use of arms, who with the Indians, their allies and kinsmen, could easily, with proper support, as has been already suggested, make the orderly colonization of Nova Scotia almost if not quite an impossibility; for it seemed quite sure they would return to join the Indians who at this time were harassing the English settlers without mercy. It was equally clear that moving ten thousand Acadian Catholics to England would have been an arduous and expensive undertaking and would have given the mother country an unwelcome burden with little prospect of the exiles being able to make any useful contribution to their own happiness or to the life of the nation. As to deporting them to France, the same problems of transport existed as to England; moreover, nothing could have pre-

---

[43] Minutes of the Council, July 28, 1755, P.R.O., N.S., B. 7: 195–207.

vented the French authorities from returning them in the next convoy to Canada, especially in view of the attachment of the people to the New World. Finally, as to scattering them in the more southern English colonies, while this was sure to bring great inconveniences and hardships, yet it seemed to offer the best solution of a pressing problem.[44] Far removed from their old haunts and their old Indian allies and, equally important, from the influence of the ecclesiastics of France and Canada, they could, it seemed reasonable to believe, start a new life on new lands — as thousands of newcomers, Catholics as well as Protestants from the British Isles and Europe, were doing in these colonies — with the hope that in time, under changed conditions, they could become loyal British subjects.

Governor William Shirley of Massachusetts Bay, after the massacre at Grand Pré of the New England troops by the French in 1747 in the course of King George's War, had recommended to the Duke of Newcastle that two thousand New England troops should be sent to the isthmus of Chignecto to drive out the French regulars stationed there and that the Acadians of this region, who had shown every disposition to aid the French and consistent hostility to the English control, should be deported to New England, and the lands upon which they were seated without permission or authority should be divided among the families of these troops. He thought that, as a consequence, in the course of time intermarriages might take place between the English settlers there and the Acadians of the peninsula neighbouring this region, and that after three or four generations the perplexing Acadian problem would thus disappear, and most of the inhabitants become Protestants.[45] But Newcastle saw great difficulty for the success of this plan; moreover, before Shirley wrote his letter a rumour had spread among the Acadians that they were to be deprived of their lands, and, as a result of the unrest that it created, the Duke in a dispatch dated June 10 had ordered the Governor to contradict the rumour in the most solemn manner. In his reply to Shirley he did say, however, that

> "His Majesty begs you to consider how such a project could be executed in suitable times and what precautions should be taken to prevent . . . inconveniences. . . ."[46]

---

[44] *Nova Scotia Doc.*, I, 260–4.
[45] Shirley to Newcastle, July 8/19, 1747, C.O. 5:901, p. 136.
[46] Newcastle to Shirley, October 3/14, 1747, C.O. 5:901, p. 157.

But instead of the Shirley solution, English colonization of the peninsula without expulsion had been tried in 1749, with the two groups widely separated by the wilderness, which continued to remain the haunt of the Micmacs and the terror of the English settlers. Could tranquillity be maintained, it had been felt that the colony would ultimately prosper; but Le Loutre and the authorities of Isle Royale saw to it that there was no tranquillity, bitterly resenting as they did the presence of Englishmen on the peninsula although it had been fully ceded by France to Britain. Only by means of the constant use of detachments of regular troops had it been possible for the new settlers to be protected in any measure from the Indians, who for years were ceaselessly sent on the warpath.[47] Even in 1755 the British settlements, which were clustered along the eastern coast of the province, were still an experiment — and a very costly one at that. To maintain Nova Scotia under these adverse conditions, with its population numbering, besides the Acadians, scarcely five thousand, cost in that year over forty thousand pounds sterling [48] — some eight times the annual charge of running the government of populous Connecticut [49] and vastly more than that of the wealthiest of all the colonies, Virginia, with an estimated white population of some two hundred thousand.[50] Further, the province, serving as a buffer for other colonies, was commercially unprofitable and between 1751 and 1758 was able to send to the mother country commodities valued at only £550.13.11; on the other hand its imports from England for the same period amounted to £96,735.2.4 — all at the King's expense.[51]

The crux of the problem, as has been suggested, clearly lay in removing the hostile French influences that stifled all enterprise and compelled the government to support the settlers. That the Acadian

[47] The Micmacs of Nova Scotia were of course kept in the field as the result of a fixed French policy and were supplied with all the means necessary for harrying the English settlements. Drucour, the Governor of Isle Royale and its "dependencies," was instructed by the Minister of the Marine on May 12, 1754 in his duty to these Indians, especially that of supporting them (Arch. Nat., Col., B. 99: 175–90).

[48] "Estimate of the Charges of Supporting and Maintaining the Settlement of His Majesty's Colony of Nova Scotia for the Year 1755," Canadian Archives, transcriptions. This estimate did not include the great charge involved in bringing in the New England volunteers.

[49] American Historical Review, XXXVI, 729–30.

[50] Boston Weekly News-Letter, January 15, 1756.

[51] "A Sketch of the Trade to and from England . . . Nova Scotia," Shelburne Papers (Clements Library), Vol. CII, folio 14.

settlements, as well as the other congregating places of the Indians, were all centres of such influences, even after the capture of the French forts, no one could seriously question. But with the removal of the French Neutrals and with it much of the source of subsistence to the natives, the way would at last, it appeared, be open for effective control of the Indians and the coming of tranquillity.

Such was the background of the dramatic scenes that were to follow as the blow fell upon the heads of the hapless Acadians. Uprooted, dispossessed, even the remnants of the thousands who once proudly and in quiet and sullen defiance ignored so long the government of the province in keeping their bodies within it while their hearts and souls were in France, could still after nine years of travail declare in 1764 to the government of Nova Scotia that they themselves acknowledged "no other sovereign but the King of France" and only begged to be permitted

> "to prove to their prince how devoted they are to his service, and how ready they are to sacrifice, not only their own lives but the lives of their women and children, to testify their zeal and love for their country." [52]

Unhappily, they had been led to idealize a King who was utterly unworthy of such high devotion and who was in fact quite incapable of grasping the inner meaning of anything so fine. It is true that so long as they were useful to him and his ministers in working out the pattern of French expansion in North America, they were encouraged and supported; but once that had vanished with the loss of Canada, the Earl of Halifax was able to report that the ministers of His Most Christian Majesty had shown themselves quite ready to acquiesce in the right of the King of Great Britain "to dispose of those People as He sees proper, and do not pretend, in any Degree, to interfere in their Behalf." [53]

Thus on July 28 the Provincial Council of Nova Scotia, after mature consideration, unanimously agreed that to prevent their return to molest those who might later be settled upon their confiscated lands the most proper step to take was to distribute the great body of the Acadian French among the several colonies on the continent and to that end a sufficient number of vessels were to be hired without

[52] Memorial of the Acadian French to Governor Wilmot, May 12, 1764, *Nova Scotia Doc.*, I, 347.
[53] Halifax to Governor Wilmot, February 11, 1764, *ibid.*, I, 342-3.

delay.[54] To pay the expense of their removal, it was also agreed that their cattle and the crops, as well as their lands, should be forfeited to the Crown and that they should be allowed to carry away only their ready money, their personal effects, and their household furniture.[55] Finally, to remove, in so far as was possible, every inducement to return, it was determined that their settlements should be laid waste.

These were, in truth, warlike measures — just as were those involved in the driving of hundreds of Pennsylvania traders from their trading establishments in the Ohio Valley in 1753 by the French, with the loss of all their effects and some of their lives. In the instance under consideration, the above measures were to be directed against those who — on the one hand, by refusing to act as good subjects and, on the other, by giving aid and comfort to the enemy with whom violent blows were being exchanged on land and sea — were now considered to be irrevocably hostile to the colony of which they had been from their earliest years a reluctant part and, in consequence, to have forfeited any further claims to clemency and forbearance.

With the extension of hostilities now already begun in North America to include the Acadian French, the ruses and stratagems of war were employed to deal with the problem of their removal in the most effective manner, and particularly to prevent their escape into the wilds of Canada with their cattle, by means of which they could continue to subsist. Writing on July 31 to Colonel Monckton, established at Beauséjour, Governor Lawrence reported the decision of the Council and also made clear that it was desirable to make a beginning with the inhabitants of the district of Chignecto who had lately been in arms against the government and whose lives — which, as those of rebels, could have been forfeited — had been spared. Monckton was cautioned that it would be necessary to keep the plan as secret as possible, for the reasons already given,

> "and the better to effect this you will endeavour to fall upon some stratagem to get the men, both young and old (especially the heads of families) into your power and detain them till the transports shall arrive." [56]

It was on June 17 that the French regulars had marched out of Fort Beauséjour and had turned that stronghold over to Colonel

---

[54] Ibid., I, 266.
[55] Lawrence to Monckton, July 31, 1755, ibid., I, 267–9.
[56] Ibid.

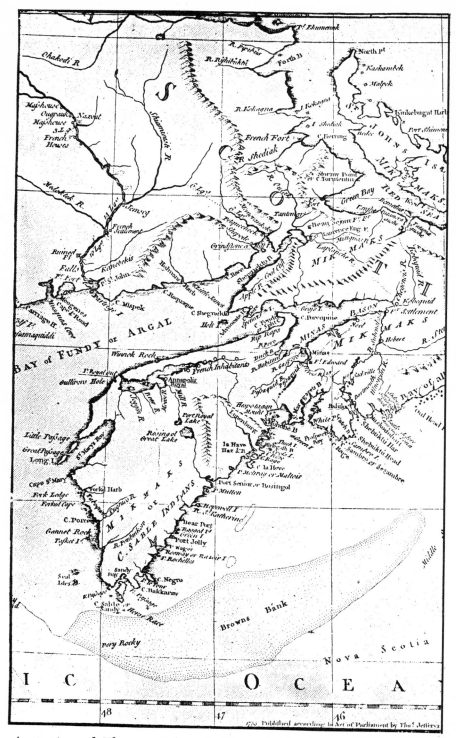

A portion of Thomas Jefferys's Nova Scotia, 1755, indicating the British and Acadian settlements.

(From Justin Winsor's *Narrative and Critical History of America*.)

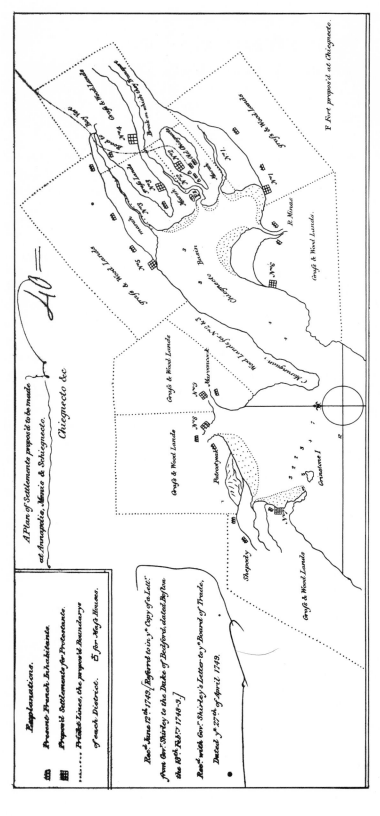

—Captain Charles Morris's survey of the Acadian settlements about the upper part of the Bay of Fundy, 1749, with suggested allotments of lands to English-speaking Protestants.

(Public Archives of Canada maps reproduced from the original surveys in the Public Record Office.)

Monckton and on that day it had been given a new name, Fort Cumberland. The following day orders had been issued for the Acadians of the district of the Chignecto peninsula to bring in their arms. On the 20th three hundred of them had responded and on the 25th still others had surrendered their weapons. On August 5 the orders referred to above were received by Moncton from Lawrence for the sending off of the inhabitants and, as a result, the following day a body of colonial troops under Captains Willard and Lewis were ordered to burn the villages of Cobequid, Tatamgouch, Ramsack, and others lying east of the isthmus and in the direction of the northern coast.[57] This was done as a precaution to prevent the movement of the Acadians *en masse* with their livestock either to Isle Royale or to the Isle St. Jean. These villages therefore now took their place with once flourishing Beaubassin, destroyed by fire by Le Loutre and its inhabitants when the English under Major Lawrence appeared before it in 1750, and the villages about Fort Beauséjour, also destroyed by the priest and the French in June of the year under consideration when the British colonials under Monckton and Winslow were about to gain possession of them. Smitten by friend and foe alike, the inhabitants, wherever they had established themselves in what had been their own beloved Acadia, were destined to witness — before they themselves were scattered to the four winds — all the fruits of the toil of generations reduced to smoke and ashes. Surely these simple-hearted, bewildered people deserved a better fate than to be ground between the upper and nether millstones of French-British rivalry in North America! But, unfortunately for them, they had placed their trust and with it their lives in the keeping of those who in the final analysis were the paid emissaries of one who could use them for his purposes but was utterly unable to protect them from misfortune.

On August 6 Colonel Monckton notified Lieutenant Colonel Winslow, in command of one of the New England regiments at Beauséjour, that he was to go with a part of his troops to Minas Basin "to Consult about Settling part of the Country by New England men." [58] Winslow was also informed that it had been determined to remove all the French inhabitants out of the province. On the 11th the heads of families living within the region of Chignecto peninsula were

---

[57] "Journal of Lieutenant-Colonel Monckton, 1755," in J. C. Webster's *The Forts of Chignecto*, Appendix, pp. 113–15.

[58] Winslow's "Journal," Nova Scotia Historical Society *Collections*, IV, 221.

summoned to Fort Cumberland to have read to them the orders of the Governor and Council of the province. Some four hundred having assembled, they were thereupon notified that, although their lives had been spared, their property was forfeited to the Crown for their late rebellion, and they themselves were to remain in detention — to be transported with their families out of the province.[59] Ten days later H.M.S. *Syren,* mothering nine transports, appeared at Beaubassin to take away the inhabitants. But the work of collecting them was still only partially executed. On the 28th Major Fry of the New England troops was ordered to the mainland to burn the villages of Shepody, Petitcodiac, and Memramcook, all at the head of the Bay of Fundy, and to bring in the settlers. While they destroyed some three hundred houses, they were able to secure but a handful of women and children. The rest of the Acadians escaped to the woods and, joined by their Indian allies, now turned upon the New England volunteers and caused them to retreat to their ships after severe losses.[60] It was not until September 10 that Monckton began to fill up his transports with those he had succeeded in securing; this work was continued for over a month. In the midst of it, on October 1, eighty of those detained at Fort Lawrence made their escape by night after tunnelling for thirty feet under the stockade of the fort. But on October 13 the transports, with eleven hundred Acadians on board lifted anchor and, escorted by two men-of-war, headed down the Bay of Fundy.[61] Yet only a fraction of the inhabitants of the upper portion of the bay had been apprehended; [62] the efforts therefore to complete the task of rounding them up before winter set in were continued. Sheltered in the deep woods and aided by the Indians, the refugees, however, were comparatively safe. But their deserted villages, in a region that hitherto had escaped destruction, now went up in flames.[63]

Meanwhile Lieutenant Colonel Winslow on August 16 left Fort Cumberland with somewhat over three hundred troops — four of the companies out of his New England regiment — and proceeded by

---

[59] *Ibid.,* IV, 227; Monckton's "Journal," *Forts of Chignecto,* p. 115.
[60] *Ibid.*
[61] *Ibid.,* p. 116; John Thomas notes in his diary on October 13 that but 960 French prisoners were carried away (*Diary of John Thomas,* ed. J. C. Webster, p. 26).
[62] *Canadian Archives, Report* (1905), II, Appendix A, Part III, p. xv.
[63] Monckton's "Journal," *op. cit.,* p. 116.

ship to Minas Basin.[64] Arriving at Fort Edward on the Piziquid, where Captain Murray commanded, he was handed the instructions that had been prepared for him by Governor Lawrence and the Nova Scotia Council. By these he was called upon with the aid of Murray "to send away such bad subjects as the French inhabitants" from the region of the basin; for this purpose vessels for carrying off one thousand of them would arrive from Boston — estimating one ton for each two persons placed aboard and it was also indicated that some of the transports that had gone to Beaubassin could be spared after Colonel Monckton had completed his work there. As to the problem of collecting the people, Winslow was instructed that

"if fair means will not do . . . you must proceed with the most vigorous measures possible not only in compelling them to embark but in depriving those who shall escape of all means of shelter or support by burning their houses, and by destroying everything that may afford them the means of subsistence in the country." [65]

It may be added that similar instructions were at the same time sent to Major John Handfield, commanding at Annapolis Royal.[66]

But nothing as yet could be done. No transports for the purpose in mind had arrived. As a result, the responsibilities of Winslow and Murray for the present were limited to keeping the inhabitants from escaping out of the country with their effects. Indeed, the Acadians were ordered to proceed with their harvest as though they were to remain in the country, but were also warned that should their Indian allies attack the troops, a life for a life would be taken at their own expense.[67]

On August 19 Winslow arrived with his New England troops at Grand Pré on Minas Basin to establish his headquarters. Governor Lawrence had recommended that, as a measure of safety, he should take possession of the church. Before doing so, however, he sent for the elders "to remove all sacred things to prevent their being defiled

---

[64] Winslow's "Journal," N.S. Hist. Soc. Coll., IV, 241.

[65] Winslow's Instructions, Council Minutes, August 11, 1755, Nova Scotia Doc., I, 271–4.

[66] For these see ibid., I, 274–6.

[67] Memorandum for Captain Murray, August 9, 1755, N.S. Hist. Soc. Coll., IV, 241–2.

by Herriticks." [68] He then threw a picket about the churchyard and established himself in the home of the curé.[69]

It was not until the latter part of August that the first Boston transports appeared in the basin. Immediately upon their arrival Winslow and Captain Murray conferred on the best method for securing the male inhabitants. It was agreed that all those settled at Grand Pré, at Minas, and on the rivers Canard and Gaspereau should be summoned by Winslow to appear at the Grand Pré church on September 5 to hear the King's orders and that on the same day those of Pizi-quid and the other villages lying about Fort Edward should likewise be summoned by Murray to the fort for the same purpose.[70] After swearing his captains to secrecy, Winslow confided to them his instructions from the Governor with respect to the disposition of the Acadians and also the terms of his agreement with Captain Murray. How well the secret was kept is indicated by the fact that some of the inhabitants visited the transports to inquire their errand and were told by the masters simply that they had come to attend Winslow and his troops. By September 1 three more transports moved into the bay and brought news that eleven more would leave Boston in a few days.[71] In a final conference between the two commanders a statement was prepared to the "inhabitants of both districts," which was translated into French by the Swiss merchant Beauchamp of Pizi-quid. That for the Minas district, according to Winslow's Journal and following his peculiar orthography, reads as follows:

> "Whereas his Excellency the Governor has Instructed us of his last resolution Respecting the maters Proposd Lately to the Inhabitants and has ordered us to Communicate the same to the Inhabitants in General in Person, his Excellency is desirous that each of them should be fully Satisfyed of his Majesty's Intention which he has also ordered us to Communicate to you Such as they have been Given him.
>
> "I therefore order and strictly Injoin by these presents to all Inhabitants . . . both old men and young men as well as all the Lads ten years of age to attend at the Church at Grand Pré on Friday the 5th Instant at Three . . . in the afternoon that we may Impart to

---

[68] Winslow's "Journal," ibid., IV, 243.

[69] The Abbé Chauvreux of this parish was placed under arrest on August 4; on the 6th Abbé Daudin, now of the Annapolis parish, was also arrested; and on the 10th the Abbé Lemaire of Rivière aux Canards surrendered to Captain Murray (Canadian Archives, Report [1905], II, Appendix A, Part III, p. vii).

[70] Winslow's "Journal," N.S. Hist. Soc. Coll., III, 87.

[71] Winslow to Murray, September 1, 1755, ibid., III, 89.

them what we are ordered to Communicate to them: Declaring that no Excuse will be admitted of on any Pretence whatsoever on Pain of Forfitting Goods and Chattels on Default." [72]

Everywhere the Acadians were busy with their harvests before the fatal day in September; for the weather was perfect. Captain Adams and a party returned from the Rivière aux Canards to the west of Grand Pré and reported the country full of people, who had a beautiful church and "abundance of Ye Goods of the World. Provisions of all Kinds in great Plenty." [73] Everywhere the inhabitants were quiet, very quiet indeed. No longer were there meetings and the drawing of resolutions. They must of course have heard what was taking place at Beaubassin and silently feared. But, after all, their brethren of that region had taken up arms, while they — at least most of them — about Minas Basin had remained at home. Yet all was not right; their own deputies — many of their leading men who had gone to Halifax were in confinement. They themselves as a body had already come to the resolution never to take the oath to the King, such as natural subjects would take, and had thus defied the government. That was something now to think about. Then there were the transports lying in the basin — now eight in all — and the soldiers garrisoned in their midst at Grand Pré. But what was to take place no man could say. Soldiers had been at Grand Pré before; a body of them — also New England men — had been massacred there by the French in the late war and guided at night to the village by some of the inhabitants. Yet nothing had happened to them then and perhaps nothing would now happen. Nevertheless, all was not right; for now they were summoned — even the boys — to Grand Pré to hear His Majesty's intentions toward them.

Silently the inhabitants filed into the church at the appointed hour — "418 of Their Best Men." Through interpreters Winslow delivered the following message:

> "Gentlemen. I have Received from his Excellency, Governor Lawrence, The King's Commission which I have in my hand and by whose orders you are convened together to manifest to you his Majesty's Final resolution to the French Inhabitants of this his Province of Nova Scotia, who for almost half a Centry [Century] have had more Indulgences Granted them, then [than] any of his Subjects in

---

[72] *Ibid.*, III, 90.
[73] *Ibid.*, III, 91.

any part of his Dominions. What use you have made of them you Your Self Best Know.

"The Part of Duty I am now upon . . . is very Disagreeable to my natural make & Temper as I know it must be Grevious to you who are of the same specie."

He thereupon came to his orders:

"That Your Lands & Tennements, Cattle of all Kinds and Live Stock of all Sortes are Forfitted to the Crown with all other your Effects Saving your money and Household Goods and you yourselves to be removed from this his Province. . . . I shall do Everything in my Power that all Those Goods be Secured to you and that you are not molested in carrying of them of [off] and also that whole Familys Shall go in the same Vessel and make this remove which I am Sensible must give you a great Deal of Trouble as Easy as his Majesty's Service will admit and hope that in what ever part of the world you may Fall you may be Faithful Subjects, a Peasable & happy People.

"I must also Inform you That it is his Majesty's Pleasure that you remain in Security under the Inspection & Direction of the Troops." [74]

It is clear that Lieutenant Colonel Winslow and Captain Murray in their addresses and orders to the inhabitants of Minas Basin and Piziquid carried out strictly the intentions of the government of Nova Scotia; it is equally clear that Governor Lawrence never received from His Majesty, through his Secretary of State, express orders for the removal of the Neutral French from Nova Scotia — at best only advice from the Board of Trade that this might be necessary. In fact, when Sir Thomas Robinson received Lawrence's letter after the fall of Fort Beauséjour indicating that he planned to drive "the deserted French Inhabitants at all Events, out of the Country," he was disturbed and immediately posted a message to the Governor to find out more clearly his intentions. In this connection he wrote:

"Let your Intention have been what it will, it is not doubted, but that you will have acted upon a strict Principle of immediate and indispensable Security to your Government, and not without having considered the pernicious consequences that may arise from any alarm, which may have been given the whole body of French Neutrals and how suddenly an insurrection may follow from Disputes: Or what an additional Number of useful subjects may be given by their Flight, to the French King: It cannot therefore, be too much

---

[74] *Ibid.*, III, 94–5.

recommended to you to use the greatest caution and prudence in your conduct toward these Neutrals, and to assure such of them, as may be trusted, especially upon their taking the Oaths to His Majesty, and His Government, That they may remain in quiet Possession of Their Settlements, under proper Regulations." [75]

It is therefore quite evident that Lawrence, in speaking in the name of His Majesty to the Acadians of Nova Scotia, not only leaned upon the advice of the Board of Trade but fell back upon the discretionary powers that all those appointed as His Majesty's representatives under the Great Seal were entitled to exercise — but, may it be added, at their own risk. It is commonplace to all students of British colonial history that colonial governors in their proclamations and other communications spoke in the name of the King and indicated that they were so doing, whether or not they had been particularly instructed so to do. The principle that Lawrence acted upon was the one stated in Robinson's letter: that "of immediate and indispensable Security to your Government." Robinson himself laid down a specific condition for assuring the French Neutrals who had not taken up arms that they might remain in quiet possession of their settlements: "their taking the Oaths to His Majesty, and His Government." But this they had refused to do. All that any governor under such circumstances could do, failing express instructions from the Crown, was to exercise, after consultation with his constitutional advisers, his best judgment. This Lawrence did. In his reply to the Secretary of State there was therefore no word of apology. After dealing with the question of the treatment of those inhabitants who had deserted to the French he then stated that

> "when we found the French Inhabitants who had not deserted their lands entertained the same disloyal sentiments with those who had, and positively rejected the Oath of Allegiance, we thought it high time to resolve . . . that the whole French Inhabitants, as well those who had not deserted as well as those who had, should be embarked on Transports to be sent out of the Province." [76]

In fairness to the government of Nova Scotia it should be stressed that its view of the necessity of freeing the colony of the Acadians was shared by that of Massachusetts Bay, which had long been vitally interested in the Nova Scotian fisheries. Not only did the Assembly

---

[75] Robinson to Lawrence, August 11, 1755, *Nova Scotia Doc.*, I, 278–80.
[76] Lawrence to Robinson, November 30, 1755, *ibid.*, I, 283–5.

of that province agree that the step was absolutely necessary but Lieutenant Governor Phips, before hearing of the decision to take it, wrote to Lawrence as follows:

> "I must also propose to your Consideration whether the danger with which his Majesty's Interest is now threatened [in North America] will not remove any scruples which may heretofore have subsisted with regard to the French neutrals as they are termed and render it just and necessary that they should be removed unless some more effectual security can be given for their fidelity than the common obligation of an oath; for by the principles of their Religion this may easily be dispensed with and although they expose themselves to be treated as Rebels, yet what confidence can ever be placed in Subjects who are inclined to revolt whenever they can do it with safety?" [77]

The chief direct responsibility for carrying out the orders of the Nova Scotia government for the removal of the great body of the French Neutrals now fell upon the shoulders of John Winslow. Descended from a leading religious refugee who had come to America in the *Mayflower* in 1620, and bearing his family name, Winslow had established his position as a highly respected citizen of Massachusetts Bay before turning to the profession of arms. "He hath the best reputation as a military man of any officer in this province," declared Governor Shirley, who went on to say that "his character in every respect stands high with the Governmt. and people and he is particularly well esteemed and belov'd by the soldiery . . . and I flatter myself he will not dishonour his command. . . ." [78] It may also be pointed out that under his immediate command at Grand Pré were the New England volunteers; many if not most of them with strong family ties; men to be sharply distinguished from the hardened professional soldier type — really farmer boys and town mechanics, who, although in the spirit of adventure quite willing to break away for a brief expedition against Louisbourg in 1745, or up the Kennebec in 1754, or again against Fort Beauséjour in 1755, would turn eagerly again to the ways of peace in their home communities. [79]

---

[77] Phips to Lawrence, without date, *ibid.*, I, 409–10.

[78] Shirley to Lawrence, January 5, 1755, *ibid.*, I, 396.

[79] Shirley writing to Lawrence in February 1756 refers to those among the New England volunteers with parents, children, or near relatives in Massachusetts Bay (*ibid.*, I, 423).

To think that none of the Acadians who came to Grand Pré on September 5 anticipated being retained would tax one's credulity, in view of the retention of their deputies in Halifax, who in July had answered the summons to attend the Governor and Council, and more particularly in view of the fact that Winslow and Murray followed the same general procedure employed by Monckton on August 11, almost a month earlier, who in summoning all the males among the deserted French of the Chignecto district to Fort Cumberland thereupon confined them. Nevertheless, common humanity, if nothing else, demanded that the families of those detained at Grand Pré be properly notified. Therefore when the prisoners who declared, with the appearance of "incredulity and astonishment,

> "that it was a Great Grief to them, that they had Incurd his Majesty's Displeasure and that they were Fearful that the surprise of their Detention . . . would quite overcome their Familys,"

and prayed Winslow that most of them be permitted to go home, leaving the rest as hostages, he agreed to allow them to select twenty of their number to acquaint the various families how matters stood and to assure the women and children that they would be perfectly safe in their habitations.[80]

Among those confined were quite a few men of property beyond that of the rest and also those with substantial families — such men, for example, as Charle Granger, of Granger village, father of six boys and five daughters and owner of many oxen, cows, sheep, and hogs and of a span of horses; Charle Terriot of Jean Terriot village, possessed of two sons and eight daughters and an abundance of livestock; and Pierre Landry of Grand Pré, with four sons and three daughters, and also blessed with many fat kine and other barnyard animals. According to an enumeration prepared by François Landry (Landrée), within the region of Grand Pré and Rivière aux Canards, a total of 2,743 people were living, settled in a large number of communities, most of which bore the name of one of them. Of these, 483 were men, 387 women, 1,105 children or young people, and 820 old and infirm.[81] While all of the men had not appeared at the summons, most of them, if not all, finally gave themselves up.

Winslow's success at Grand Pré was equalled by Captain Murray

---

[80] Winslow's "Journal," N.S. Hist. Soc. Coll., III, 95.

[81] For a list of the names of those confined, their place of residence, the number of their children and of their various grazing animals and hogs see ibid., III, 114–22.

at Fort Edward, where 183 men — almost all the able-bodied — were secured. However, Major Handfield, at Annapolis Royal, who sought late in August to secure the heads of families living about the Annapolis River, found that the men with their wives and children — doubtless rendered suspicious by the appearance of the transports — had left their villages and with their bedding had retired into the woods.[82] He was nevertheless able to report to Winslow on September 7 that all the French inhabitants on the river had returned to their homes and had promised to submit to the King's orders.[83] Captain Murray also reported the following day from Piziquid that the Acadians were

> "more patient than I could have expected for People in their Circumstances and [that] which Stil Supprises me more is the Indifference of the Women who really are or Seem Quite unconcerned." [84]

Winslow also found the people at first generally submissive: several men who had failed for some reason to appear at the church on September 5 came in voluntarily; in fact, Réné Le Blanc, who had acted as notary public among his people, and his son were marked out for commendation for preventing some of the young men from disappearing into the woods. As a result, the millers were permitted to attend to their mills, and ten men from Grand Pré and ten from Rivière aux Canards were each day given leave in order to provide for the rest.[85] But by the 10th the Acadians confined within the churchyard began to show uncommon signs of activity. It was therefore deemed prudent to send the younger men to the transports without delay.

François Landry, already mentioned, one of their most influential men, who spoke English, was notified that two hundred and fifty would be selected to go that day and was requested to tell the other Acadians that they were to form in six ranks with the younger men on the left. He reluctantly obeyed. But the young men, when ordered to march, "answered they would not go without their fathers." Only when the soldiers were ordered to fix their bayonets and to advance upon them could they be put into motion. Then they went off slowly, in the words of the "'Journal":

---

[82] Handfield to Winslow, September 1, 1755, *ibid.*, III, 96.
[83] *Ibid.*, III, 103.
[84] *Ibid.*, III, 107–8.
[85] *Ibid.*, III, 104.

"Praying, Singing & Crying, being Met by the Women & Children all the way (which is 1½ Miles) with Great Lamentations upon their Knees praying etc." [86]

After these had departed, Winslow permitted the remaining Neutrals to select about a hundred married men — to make up the total — to follow the younger people on board. They readily complied and those chosen were marched to the shore, where boats were waiting to receive them. Thus ended a day that Winslow describes in his "Journal" as the "scene of sorrow." To make conditions on board the transports as favourable as possible for the new arrivals, he gave those confined the choice of having the King's provisions — provisions designed for the crews — or having their food brought to them by their relatives and friends, with the added concession that as many of the latter would be permitted to visit them each day as the ships' boats would hold. Further, to put an end to misconduct on the part of some of his soldiers, he posted an order on September 13 forbidding any to leave the camp at Grand Pré after the calling of the roll at sunset. In doing so he stated that "many bad thing[s] have been done Lately, in the night Season to the Distressing the Distressed French Inhabitants in this neighbourhood." [87] On the 15th he showed his determination to enforce these measures of protection for the people by ordering a court-martial of two soldiers "for stealing from the French Last night Twenty-one Dunghil Fowles." [88] They were sentenced to thirty lashes apiece.

At this period the deputies of the various Acadian villages were sent back under guard from Halifax, where they had been held on St. George's Island. In forwarding the twenty-seven from Annapolis to Major Handfield on September 9, Winslow referred sadly in his letter to "this Troublesome affair which is more Grevious to me than any Service I was ever Employed in." [89] By September 29, three hundred and thirty men had been placed on the transports. But other vessels than those now in the basin were needed for the whole population living about the streams flowing into it. This brought additional delay.

Although Winslow had been commanded by Lawrence not to regard any petitions and remonstrances from the inhabitants, he wrote

---

[86] *Ibid.,* III, 108–10.
[87] *Ibid.,* III, 110–13.
[88] *Ibid.,* III, 123.
[89] *Ibid.,* III, 134.

to the Governor on the day referred to above that, in spite of the fact
that he had been plied with many which he had refused, he was
making an exception: "I Shant Trouble your Excellency but with
one which they So Importune with me to Send that I Could not put
them off." [90] He also made clear to the Governor's secretary the difficulty that faced him in honouring a requisition for some of the forfeited livestock to be sent from the Acadian villages to the new
Lunenburg settlements:

> ". . . they Stil Look upon them as their Property and make heavy
> Complaints when Ever we Meddle . . . it hurts me to hear their
> weeping & wailing and Nashing of Teeth."

After the people were gone, he declared, it would be easier to furnish five hundred of their confiscated cattle than the one hundred
requested, and in ending his letter he prayed soon to be "rid of the
worst peace of Service Y^t Ever I was in. . . ." [91] But the necessity
for cattle was great in another quarter. Most of the crews of the ships
of the royal navy under Boscawen at Halifax, almost three thousand
of the sailors, were suffering from illness, one half from the dread
scurvy, as was made clear in an earlier chapter; and fresh meat was
absolutely required to restore their health. [92] Captain Murray at Piziquid had rounded up forty-five cattle for this purpose and called upon
Winthrop to complete the requisition. [93] Even this urgent demand
he failed to comply with until he had got many of the families on
board the transports.

On October 6 a plan of embarkation was agreed upon: the people
were to be placed on board the ships according to their villages and
so that whole families would go together; and orders were sent to
the several families to hold themselves in readiness to leave with
their household goods and other personal possessions. In spite of all
preparations for their removal — with all the active men already on
board the transports — Winslow recorded that he "Even now Could
not Persuade the People I was in Earnest." [94] He had intended the
general embarkation for the 7th, but delayed it on account of rain.
That night twenty-five young men escaped from two of the ships, although each ship was well guarded. The following day two of the

[90] *Ibid.*, III, 155.
[91] Winslow to Hensheldwood, September 29, 1755, *ibid.*, III, 157.
[92] Deschamps to Winslow, October 7, 1755, *ibid.*, III, 165.
[93] Murray to Winslow, October 7, 1755, *ibid.*
[94] *Ibid.*, III, 164.

transports were filled with eighty families. Winslow's "Journal" gives the story of the embarkation succinctly:

"Oct. 8. Began to Embark the Inhabitants who went of [off] Very . . . unwillingly, the Women in Great Destress Carrying off Their Children in their arms. Others Carrying their Decript Parents in their Carts and all their Goods Moving in Great Confusion & appeard a Scene of Woe & Destres." [95]

But with all his natural sympathy and kindness Winslow was a soldier, and when it was found that one of the Acadians, a François Herbert, was involved in the escape of the young men, Herbert was ordered ashore and taken to his house; thereupon it and his barn were burned before his eyes. The colonel also served notice upon the relatives of those who had escaped that they would be treated in the same manner and their household goods confiscated if the fugitives did not surrender themselves in two days. He also threatened the summary execution of the latter should they later fall into the hands of the soldiers. Since the Acadians as a body had previously solemnly agreed not to countenance any plan of escape, in return for the privilege of visiting their menfolks on board ship, François Landry offered to bring about the return of the men if Winslow would agree not to punish them. Winslow gave his word of honour and as a result twenty-three of them returned — after the remaining two had been shot by the soldiers when, upon being discovered, they sought to flee.

As Major Handfield at Annapolis meanwhile had been meeting with extraordinary difficulties in collecting his people, seven of the transports assigned to him had been ordered into Minas Basin. These arrived on October 10 and three of them were assigned to Captain Murray at Piziquid. On October 13 nine of the transports loaded with their precious cargoes of unhappy people — those of Grand Pré and of the Gaspereau River — dropped down the basin with orders to seek convoy of H.M.S. *Nightingale* to their respective destinations: two were bound for Pennsylvania, the *Hannah*, Captain Adams, and the *Swan*, Captain Hazlum (Haslam); two for Maryland, the *Leopard*, Captain Church, and the *Elizabeth*, Captain Milbury; and five for Virginia, the *Sally and Molly*, Captain Parrington (Purrington), the *Mary*, Captain Dunning, the *Prosperous*, Captain Bragdon (Bragdton), the *Endeavour*, Captain Stout, and the *Industry*, Captain Goodwin. Each contained from one hundred and forty to one

[95] *Ibid.*, III, 166.

hundred and eighty-six passengers and all were within the quota assignments of two passengers per ton.[96] The commander of each was ordered to issue provisions regularly to the people, to be watchful against any attempts at seizure of the vessel and therefore to allow at one time only a limited number of the Acadians on deck at any time, and to proceed under convoy to his destination. Upon arrival he was to get in touch immediately with the governor of the colony, to deliver a packet consigned to him, and then to make all possible dispatch in disembarking his passengers.[97]

Winslow still had five hundred people living upon the rivers aux Canards and Habitant to embark after the transports had received their sailing orders. These, therefore, had to await the arrival of more ships.

At Fort Edward at Piziquid Captain Murray also faced a shortage of ships and was deeply disturbed at the situation. Writing on October 14, he stated that he was embarking his people on two sloops — the third that had arrived had cast an anchor — and would need additional vessels. He indicated that even with the arrival of another sloop to be sent by Winslow the people would be "Stowed in Bulk but if I have no more Vessels I will put them aboard let the consequences be what they will." At the time of writing, Murray had nine hundred and twenty people. The two sloops at hand, with a combined tonnage of 154 tons, and the sloop to arrive, of 90 tons, would provide a total of only 246 tons — not enough for five hundred people. He ended his letter emphatically: "That can not do!"[98] Winslow, having been promised three additional transports by Monckton at Fort Cumberland, who, as has been noted, was meeting with great disappointments in getting in the people of the Chignecto district, sent still another vessel to Murray. The latter was thereupon able on October 23 to embark all of the inhabitants about Piziquid, numbering at least over one thousand. Unhappily, we must assume the vessels were overloaded.[99]

---

[96] *Ibid.*, III, 178. These ships were provided on contract by Apthorp and Hancock of Boston. The charge per month for them was from £40 to £48. See "Accounts Transmitted by Apthorp and Hancock, 1755," *Nova Scotia Doc.*, I, 285–9.

[97] This packet contained a copy of Governor Lawrence's circular letter to the governors on the continent written on August 11, 1755. A copy of this is to be found in P.R.O., N.S., A. 58.

[98] Murray to Winslow, October 14, 1755, N.S. Hist. Soc. *Coll.*, III, 173.

[99] From the accounts transmitted by Apthorp and Hancock, it is clear that a number of the transports that left Nova Scotia were overloaded. For example the *Neptune*, Wil-

As for the disposition of the rest of the inhabitants dwelling on the rivers aux Canards and Habitant, Winslow left Grand Pré on October 19 to supervise their embarkation. Great was his disappointment when he found that the vessels promised by Monckton had not arrived; nevertheless he proceeded to fill up what transports were at hand. Writing to Lawrence, he declared:

"And Altho' I put in more than Two to a Tun & the People greatly Crowded yet remains Upon my Hands for want of Transports the whole Vilages of Antoine & Laundry & some of Cannard Amounting to 98 Familys & upwards of Six Hundred Souls. All which I removed from Budro [Budrot's] Pointe to Grand Pré, Where I have at Present Set them down in Houses Nearest the Camp and Permit them to be with their Familys upon their word of being at any Call ready to Imbark and answering to their names upon the Roll Caled at Sun Set in the Camp." [100]

Winslow was now nearing the end of his distressing task. On October 27 he was ordered by Lawrence to send a contingent of soldiers to Major Handfield, still faced with the problem of collecting the people about Annapolis Royal for transportation, and also, as soon as the situation warranted, to march with the rest of his troops to Halifax.

But there was still unfinished business about Minas Basin; for Winslow had to carry out his instructions to burn the settlements. The sight of this destruction he had spared most of the inhabitants, who were now on the high seas to be scattered in the English colonies to the southward. On November 2 the homes, barns and outhouses of the inhabitants of the Gaspereau went up in flames; on the 5th, 6th, and 7th those of aux Canards and the Habitant and in between. In all about seven hundred structures, including eleven grist-

---

liam Fort master, bound for Virginia, carried a total of 207 Neutrals, twenty-seven more than her complement; the *Three Friends*, Thomas Curtis master, bound for Philadelphia, had an excess of eighteen; the *Ranger*, Francis Piercy master, bound for Maryland, carried eighty-one persons in excess of its quota, with a total of 208; the *Dolphin*, Zebad Forman master, also bound for Maryland, had an excess of fifty-six, with a total of 230; and the *Elizabeth*, likewise bound for Maryland, with an excess of fifty-two persons, carried 242 (*Nova Scotia Doc.*, I, 285–292). The government of Nova Scotia adopted a policy respecting the transportation of the people that, had it not been for miscalculations and the failure of the contractors, would have made it unnecessary for Winslow, Murray, and Handfield to overcrowd any of the ships as, with the winter approaching, they did in order to expedite the departure of the people.

[100] Winslow to Lawrence, October 27, 1755, N.S. Hist. Soc. *Coll.*, III, 179.

mills and one "Mass House," disappeared.[101] Only Grand Pré — where the six hundred Acadians brought from the region of aux Canards were being sheltered — was temporarily spared. It appears that these people — enjoying their own provisions and living in the warm houses of those already exiled — fared better than did the New England soldiers in garrison there. At least Winslow, writing to Major Handfield on November 13 — a time of early winter in Nova Scotia — was obliged to point out the hardships of his men. He observed:

> "Could do if we had bread, butter and molasses and we really have neither pay, barracks, beds, provisions, and clothes." [102]

It was not until the latter part of December that transports were available to take away the last of the Minas Bay Acadians.[103] When the time came for their departure — they had been free on parole — they "appeared without great difficulty according to the number given by Monsr. Landree [Landry] and . . . embarked," taking with them as much of their effects as could be placed aboard the transports, and were carried to Boston, Connecticut, and Virginia.[104] A grand total of some thirty-two hundred Acadians were apparently removed from the regions of Minas Basin and Piziquid — not including the Cobequid district, the inhabitants of which fled at the approach of the soldiers.[105]

At Annapolis Royal, Major Handfield was busy from August until the early part of December in gathering up the inhabitants living about the Annapolis River. The transports arrived there long before the Acadians could be brought together and as a consequence were sent early in October to Minas Basin, as has been pointed out, where they were put to immediate use. Handfield, with inadequate forces, could not control the movements of the Neutrals, many of whom lived miles up the river and would dive into the woods upon the approach of the English soldiers. Late in October Governor Law-

---

101 "1755. Buildings Burned by Lieut. Colonel Winslow in Minas," *ibid.*, III, 185.

102 *Ibid.*, III, 184–5.

103 On December 13, 114 Acadians were carried to Connecticut on the sloop *Dove*, Samuel Forbes master, and 236 to Boston on the brigantine *Swallow*, William Hayes master; on the 20th, 120 left also for Boston on the *Racehorse*, John Banks master, and 112 for Virginia, on the *Ranger*, Nathan Murrow master (*ibid.*, III, 188, 192–3). This completed the removal.

104 *Ibid.* In Winslow's original instructions, which were subsequently modified, he was to send five hundred of the Acadians to Maryland and North Carolina and a thousand to Virginia, among those living in the Minas Basin region.

105 Winslow to Monckton, November 3, 1755, *ibid.*, III, 182–3.

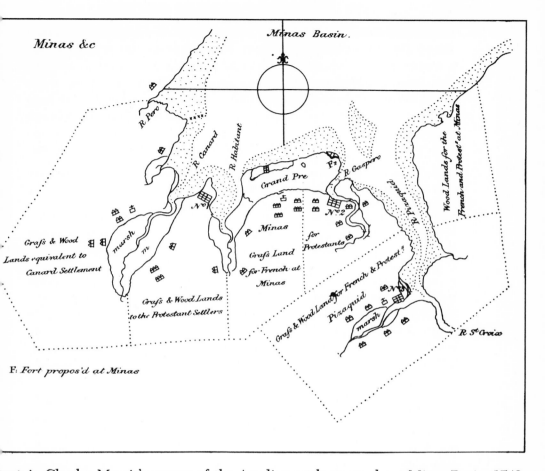

Minas &c

Minas Basin.

R Pero

R Canard

R Habitant

Grand Pre

F*

R Gaspro

Pizaquid

Wood Lands for the
French and Protes⁴ at Minas

N° I

marsh

m

Minas

Grafs & Wood
Lands equivalent to
Canard Settlement

N° 2

for
Protestants

Grafs Land
for French at
Minas

Grafs & Wood Lands
to the Protestant Settlers

Grafs & Wood Land for French & Protest⁴

Pizaquid

N°

marsh

R S⁴ Croix

F: Fort propos'd at Minas

Captain Charles Morris's survey of the Acadian settlements about Minas Basin, 1749,
ith suggested allotments of lands to English-speaking Protestants.

(Public Archives of Canada maps reproduced from the original surveys in the Public Record Office.)

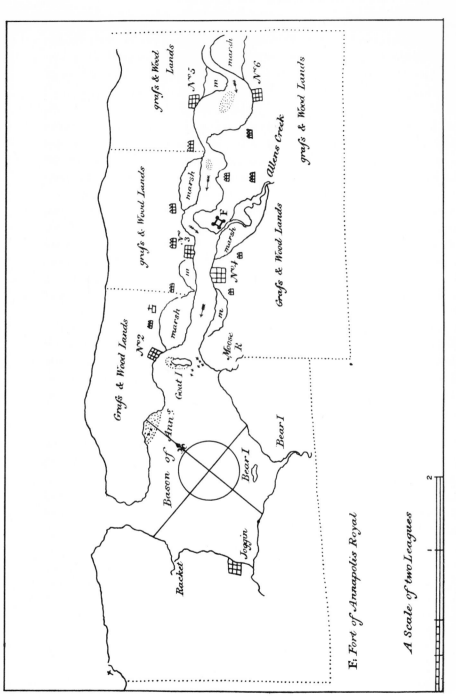

Captain Charles Morris's survey of the Acadian settlements in the region of Annapolis Royal, 1749, with suggested allotments of lands to English-speaking Protestants.

rence issued orders to Winslow to send eighty soldiers to aid him; by the time this contingent had arrived at Annapolis, at the beginning of December, most of the inhabitants were prepared to accept their fate: hunger and exposure in the woods and the destruction of their homes had done their work. As a result 1,664 persons were placed on board two ships, three snows, and one brigantine and on December 8 left Goat Island under convoy of the sloop of war *Baltimore*. All the ships seem to have been greatly overloaded — with an average number of passengers of 278 as against an average of 167 carried off from Minas Basin in October — with a total of 1,503 from the last-named region accommodated in nine ships.

Handfield was ordered to send these unfortunates to the northern colonies in such proportions, for example, as three hundred to Connecticut and two hundred to Boston.[106] In January of the following year he dispatched two hundred more, destined for North Carolina, but the bold spirits on board overwhelmed the crew and carried the vessel, the *Pembroke*, across the Bay of Fundy to the St. John — and to freedom.

Later in the spring of 1756 the New England troops fell upon the Acadian settlement at Pubnico in southern Nova Scotia and carried to Boston a number of these people, incorrectly called Cape Sable Acadians. In fact, the work of rounding up the inhabitants who had escaped deportation continued through the duration of the war and even after hostilities had ceased, as will be indicated in the chapter to follow. In this unhappy work of freeing the province of the Neutrals there was only one aspect that gave Governor Lawrence satisfaction: their places could ultimately be taken by those prepared to make important contributions to the strengthening of Nova Scotia, against the thousands of internal enemies who had previously worked to weaken it. Writing to the Lords Commissioners for Trade and Plantations on October 18 he declared:

> "As soon as the French are gone, I shall use my best Endeavours to encourage People to come from the Continent to settle their Lands, and if I succeed in this point, we shall soon be in a condition of supplying ourselves with provisions. . . . This was one of the happy effects I proposed to myself, from driving the French off the Isthmus, and the additional circumstances of the Inhabitants evacuating the Country, will, I flatter myself, greatly hasten this event; as it furnishes us with a large quantity of good land ready for immediate cul-

---

[106] "Instructions to Major John Hanfield," *ibid.*, III, 274–6.

tivation, renders it difficult for the Indians, who cannot as formerly be supplied with provisions & intelligence, to make incursions upon our settlers, and I believe the French will not be so sanguine in their Hopes of possessing a province that they have hitherto looked upon as ready peopled for them the moment they could get the better of the English." [107]

It may be said that at the most conservative estimate over six thousand people were carried out of Nova Scotia on the orders of its government.[108] But this does not take into account the thousands who were so wrought upon by their "incendiary priests" or so terrified by the threats of Le Loutre's Indians that they fled from their settlements within the peninsula before Lawrence and the Council had determined upon their dispersion and established themselves either on Isle St. Jean or Cape Breton or on the mainland in the direction of Chaleur Bay. In all some twelve to fifteen thousand Acadians were apparently involved in the various dispersions, if one also includes the scattering of the Acadians of Petitcodiac, Memramcook, and Shepody living northwest of the Bay of Fundy.

With respect to those Acadians sent away by the government of Nova Scotia, very great hardships were suffered by many if not most of them, with overcrowding and a record of deaths on some of the transports; indeed, as will be indicated in the following chapter, some of the ships were sunk as the result of storms with the tragic loss of all on board. It may nevertheless be said that the mortality and suffering even on the vessels that were overburdened could not be compared to that on the slavers making the "middle passage" — that is, the trip from Africa to the New World — or to that on many of the emigrant ships that brought the German redemptioners from Rotterdam to Philadelphia before the passing in 1750 of the Pennsylvania statute to prevent not only overcrowding by shipmasters but the development of conditions on many vessels so shocking as to be almost indescribable.[109] However, many of these uprooted people were stricken with ship fever and in want of food and adequate clothing when they arrived at the ports of debarkation. They were miserably

---

[107] Governor Lawrence to the Board of Trade, October 18, 1755, P.R.O., N.S., A. 58: 84–100.

[108] D. L. Le Blanc estimated (*The True Story of the Acadians*, p. 44) that a total of 7,250 were exiled to the southern colonies. Some of his figures are subject to correction.

[109] *Pennsylvania Statutes at Large*, IV, 382–8. For conditions on emigrant ships see Volume III of the present series, pages 167–8.

unhappy and many of them, in spite of serious efforts to keep families together, were separated from their loved ones. In a petition to the King on the part of those landed at Philadelphia it was stated:

"Parents were separated from children, and husbands from wives, some of whom have not to this day met again; and we were so crowded on the transport vessels, that we had not room even for all our bodies to lay down at once, and consequently were prevented from carrying with us proper necessaries. . . . And even those among us who had suffered . . . on account of their attachment to your Majesty's Government, were equally involved in the common calamity, of which Réné Leblanc, the notary public . . . is a remarkable instance. He was seized, confined, and brought away among the rest of the people, and his family, consisting of twenty children, and about one hundred and fifty grand children, were scattered in different colonies, so that he was put on shore at New York, with only his wife and two youngest children, in an infirm state of health, from where he joined three more of his children at Philadelphia, where he died without any more notice being taken of him than any of us. . . ." [110]

The story of this great dispersion, with the wanderings of these unhappy people, is of such importance to an understanding of certain aspects of British colonial history that it must be reserved for separate treatment. Nevertheless, before turning to this, one final comment must be made.

Accepting the fact that the policies of France in the New World dictated the use of every influence — civil, ecclesiastical, and military — to alienate the French-speaking inhabitants of Nova Scotia from the government under which they were born and to which they owed their allegiance by every sound concept of public law and by the most solemn of international covenants, and that these influences were unceasingly applied without regard to the present or future welfare of these people, the people themselves cannot stand blameless for the unhappy fate that at last awaited them. They permitted the propaganda of their priests and missionaries — all without exception, as has been emphasized, trained in France and supported by funds out of the public treasury of that country — to lead them not only to

---

[110] This long petition is printed in full in T. C. Haliburton's *An Historical and Statistical Account of Nova Scotia*, I, 183–95. Three hundred of these exiles to Pennsylvania came from Annapolis, and the ships leaving that port were greatly overcrowded, as has been indicated.

forget that no people in America had been so favoured, so privileged, as they themselves had been, but to refuse to become reconciled to the government that had extended to them these favours and privileges. In fact, they went beyond this and in the words of Waddington, the leading French authority on the war that had now begun, they were in truth, as a result of the influences that played upon their daily lives,

> "French in heart and in language, detesting the English with a hatred that nourished their fervent attachment to the Catholic faith and were much more obedient to their priests than to the British officers." [111]

Even members of their own faith and language, even men of the robe, then and since, have recognized — in spite of the flood of literature that has tended to obscure the essential facts and has made the exiles the martyrs and victims of brutal British policy — that the chief blame for their misfortunes cannot justly be placed upon the shoulders either of the government of Great Britain or of that of Nova Scotia. [112] Bishop Briand — a native of Brittany and a priest in Canada before its conquest, who became Vicar General of Quebec in 1760 and six years later Bishop of Quebec — on August 16, 1766 in his pastoral letter to those Acadians who, after their exile in the southern colonies had painfully found their way back to Canada, declared:

---

[111] Richard Waddington, *Louis XV et le renversement des alliances*, pp. 9–10. Earnest Martin in his *Les Exiles Acadiens en France au XVIII⁰ siècle*, in referring to the refusal of the unqualified oath by the Acadians before their expulsion, says (p. 21) that "the French inhabitants were resolved to refuse any new oath of allegiance that would be a constant menace to their Catholic religion and their national ties."

[112] Governor Lawrence is especially singled out by writers for violent attack as the source of all the unhappiness that fell upon the Acadians; it is charged that he was a plunderer and a friend of plunderers and organized the exile for the opportunity of plunder (see, for example, D. L. Le Blanc, *op. cit.*, pp. 22–3). This charge seems to be unjust. When the Nova Scotia legislature was informed in 1760 that he had died, it was voted to erect a monument to his memory: "From a grateful sense of the many important services which the Province has received from him during a continued course of zealous and indefatigable endeavour for the public good, and a wise, upright and disinterested administration" (N.S. Hist. Soc. *Coll.*, XII, 57). The funeral, placed in charge of the Masonic Lodge, was magnificent and at the expense of the province. Although in 1754 Lawrence inherited £10,000, he died poor; for he generously paid out of his own purse half the expense of erecting the new government house and he also furnished it. Of all the governors of Nova Scotia from Cornwallis to Wentworth, according to a modern writer, "the one who stands proudly eminent above the rest in intellect, courage and executive ability, head and shoulders over them all, is Lawrence. As an administrator he combined all their good points without a shadow of their weaknesses" (*ibid.*, XII, 58).

"Would to God, that you never had disregarded the wise and Christian instructions as to your submission to your superiors. Then we would now have the pleasure to visit you in your quiet and happy homes. You could now have priests among you and you would still enjoy the possession of all the temporal goods you had been blessed with during the many years, when you were living as true Christians under the rule of your conquerors." [113]

Indeed, one may say with confidence that had the Acadians determinedly followed the example and wise counsel of such worthy and venerable priests among them as Fathers Desenclaves (Deseuclaves) and Chauvreux, rather than the exhortations to desperate measures of Le Loutre and his pupil Daudin, misfortunes would never have been heaped upon them. But unhappily they did not.

---

[113] This translation from the French is to be found in the American Catholic Historical Society of Philadelphia Records, XXXI, 162–73. The sentiments expressed by Briand in 1766 are echoed by Abbé Auguste Gosselin, the distinguished church historian, in his L'Eglise du Canada après la Conquête (pp. 306–21).

CHAPTER X

The Exiles

THE SCATTERING of the Acadians by the thousands from their abodes about the Bay of Fundy represents the greatest forcible dispersion of people of European extraction in the history of the New World and therefore merits much greater attention than has generally been accorded it by American colonial historians.[1] George Bancroft says of this historic episode: "I know not if the annals of the human race keep the record of sorrows so wantonly inflicted, so bitter and so perennial, as fell upon the French inhabitants of Acadia."[2] French-Canadian writers, particularly those of Acadian extraction, go even farther in denouncing the action as an atrocious crime.[3] The Reverend Andrew Brown, a Scotsman, in agreeing, classed it as an atrocity with the massacre of St. Bartholomew's Day;[4] while another writer, the New Englander William Lincoln, called it "the darkest blot on our history."[5] Unhappily, there are no sound grounds for questioning the necessity of the step if the expulsion is viewed as simply a phase of the tremendous Anglo-French struggle for dominance on the North American continent. As Edward Channing has wisely pointed out, it was the great misfortune

[1] The late Professor Osgood, for example, gives but two brief sentences to the Acadian dispersion in his monumental American Colonies in the Eighteenth Century; John Fiske ignores the exile in his series.

[2] History of the United States (edition of 1853), IV, 206.

[3] For example, Claude Gaudet in his Le Grand Dérangement, in placing responsibility upon Governor Lawrence for the Acadian dispersion, refers (p. 20) "to his crime . . . an action so barbarous, so atrocious . . ."; Professor Emile Lauvrière in his La Tragédie d'un peuple (II, 140), denominates the project of the expulsion "Lawrence's diabolical plan."

[4] Justin Winsor, Narrative and Critical History of America, V, 458.

[5] History of Worcester, Massachusetts, p. 61.

of the Acadians not to have been settled one hundred miles to the southward of the Bay of Fundy; [6] for had they been, it is quite unlikely that they would ever have been molested either by the French or by the English, and therefore they would have been permitted to abide in peace.

In recounting the fate of these unhappy people who were at length put ashore from the transports to find themselves in a strange and even hostile environment, it must not be forgotten that this occurred at a time when the western settlements of southern and middle British colonies were being ravished by parties of French regulars, Canadian militia, and their Indian allies. These faced little resistance after the defeat of Braddock on the Monongahela, as terrified frontier families fled from the bloody tomahawk and the blazing torch. At the very time of the arrival of the Acadians fugitives were pouring into the eastern seaboard counties with their tales of horror, which did not fail to impress those more safely established in the thickly populated regions. Everywhere there was the most intense fear of Frenchmen — and, it may be added, of Roman Catholics. Even the people of Georgia who had escaped the fury were not unaffected; for the colony was weak and even in a declining condition. Moreover, it was at the mercy of powerful Indian tribes, particularly the Creeks; and among the Upper Creeks the French had long been entrenched at Fort Toulouse.

It appears that the Acadians intended for Georgia and South Carolina sailed from the isthmus of Chignecto late in October in twelve transports under convoy of three men-of-war. [7] They first proceeded to Minas Bay and, having been joined by the loaded transports awaiting them there, again took up the southward voyage. About the middle of November one of the accompanying warships, the *Nightingale*, Captain Dudley Diggs, put into New York harbour, having, as the result of a storm, been separated from the convoy; the latter, however, pushed southward under escort of the two remaining ships of war. [8] Early in December one of the two transports destined for Georgia arrived at Tybee Island at the mouth of the Savannah, under convoy of H.M.S. *Syren*, with one hundred and twenty exiles, mostly women and children. [9] Upon receiving the news at Savannah Governor

---

[6] *History of the United States*, II, 576.

[7] *Boston Weekly News-Letter*, October 30, 1755.

[8] *New-York Mercury*, November 17, 1755.

[9] The *New-York Mercury*, November 27, 1755, says that on November 19 the Syren and the transport passed the bar off Charleston.

Reynolds issued an order to the chief pilot "forbidding him at his peril to bring any more such people into the Province . . ." [10] and then departed for Augusta to keep an appointment with the Indians. The order, however, was not executed, with the result that the second transport, carrying two hundred and eighty Acadians, mostly men who had borne arms against the English at Beauséjour, put in its appearance.[11] Although the Governor upon his return to Savannah attempted to elude the problem of caring for the exiles by ordering the ships away, Captain Trattles of the *Prince Frederick* absolutely refused to move without having his vessel victualled and before he himself was indemnified.

The matter was brought before the Provincial Council on December 14, which after discussion — and doubtless not oblivious of the great financial assistance still coming to the colony from Great Britain and therefore unprepared to act in a manner that would merit rebuke from the government at home — voted that the passengers should be allowed to land; it was also agreed that a pound of rice for ten days should be given to each person and, further, that some of the exiles should be taken to Frederica on the Altamaha, and others to Midway and the Great Ogeechee and the Little Ogeechee settlements.[12] But difficulties arose. Some of these settlements were menaced by hostile Indians and were soon deserted. It is not clear, therefore, how many of the Acadians left Savannah.[13] Early in January a petition from them was presented to the Council indicating their languishing condition and praying for assistance. As a result a week's provisions were allowed those who were sick and in need.[14] The following month an attempt was made to secure legislative action that would determine the fate of the exiles, but the two houses of the Assembly were at loggerheads over certain other issues and it was therefore not until the latter part of November — almost a year after the appearance of the first transport — that a bill was finally passed.[15]

[10] John Reynolds to the Board of Trade, April 16, 1758, Public Record Office, Board of Trade Papers, Georgia, Vol. 27. This reference in the future will be B. T. Georgia.

[11] *Ibid.*

[12] *Colonial Records of Georgia*, VII, 301–2.

[13] Stevens asserts that the exiles were distributed in small parties about the province and maintained there until spring (*History of Georgia*, I, 417). Governor Reynolds in defending his management of this affair in 1758 is very indefinite in his statements (Reynolds to the Board of Trade, April 16, 1758, B. T. Georgia, 27).

[14] *Ga. Col. Rec.*, VII, 304.

[15] *Ibid.*, XVI, 115–17. The act was entitled "An Act for Providing for and Disposing of the Acadians now in this Province."

Meanwhile, many of the Neutral French themselves were determined to return to their homeland and were apparently assisted to that end by Reynolds and the Council. Ten boats were constructed, purchased or contributed — the facts are obscure [16] — in which some two hundred men, women, and children left Georgia early in the spring of 1756 and began coasting northward. The latter part of March they appeared off the coast of South Carolina and, arriving at Port Royal, were convoyed by one of the South Carolina scout boats.[17] But they had no idea of lingering after securing refreshment, and eight days later they had reached Wilmington on the Cape Fear River in North Carolina, with passes from the governors of both Georgia and South Carolina. Tidewater North Carolina was an isolated region — both from the rest of the English coastal settlements and from the dangers of the western frontier — and was sparsely settled. Here the French Neutrals were welcome to grants of land where they could build their own French settlements and live in peace. However, when Governor Arthur Dobbs made this generous offer to them on condition that they take the oath of loyalty,

> "they absolutely Refused saying they would not stay in this Colony and that they took the Oath of Alegiance before and could not take it again." [18]

Having received, in addition to other incidental supplies, "one steer and ten bushels of corn," they were dismissed "without any further expense to this Province." [19] The survivors, apparently joined by some of their fellows from South Carolina, continued up the coast. In May the captain of a sloop arriving in Virginia reported he saw " 300 of 'em from Georgia coast⁵ along the shore in Canoes." [20] By the latter part of June they were in New Jersey, where it was reported that

---

[16] Governor Dinwiddie of Virginia repeatedly accused the authorities of Georgia and South Carolina of providing vessels for the exiles (Dinwiddie Papers, II, 478, 538, 544). Governor Reynolds, facing charges of maladministration by the Board of Trade, made the following statement respecting the French exiles: "That many of them built boats for themselves & left the Colony this Respondent knows is true; for having no orders to receive or detain them or funds to support them your Respondent felt it was best to let them go as they were all Papists & enemies of our religion and government and unfit to be suffered to remain in so weak a province" (Reynolds to the Board of Trade, April 16, 1756, B. T. Georgia, 27).

[17] Charles Town advices, April 1, Boston Weekly News-Letter, April 22, 1756.

[18] Colonial Records of North Carolina, V, 655.

[19] Ibid.

[20] Dinwiddie to Fox, May 24, 1756, Dinwiddie Papers, II, 412.

> "a great number of French Neutrals, some say seven Boat Loads, who were permitted to leave Georgia and South-Carolina are arrived and stopt in Monmouth County, somewhere near Shrewsbury . . . and a Council called at Elizabeth-Town about them." [21]

They were permitted to proceed northward, however, and were doubtless encouraged on their way. They then arrived in New York,[22] and, having received a pass from the Governor, kept on — now but ninety of them in seven boats — until they arrived within the bounds of Massachusetts Bay. There they and their boats were ordered to be secured by Lieutenant Governor Phips, since it was felt that it would be unsafe to permit them to proceed farther — back to Nova Scotia, to take revenge. Writing to Governor Lawrence of the latter province, Phips declared:

> "What appeared pretty extraordinary was, that these People had been furnished with a Passport from the Governors of Georgia, South Carolina, and New York. . . ." [23]

Thus for almost five months these hardy, determined people braved the Atlantic in open boats with one fixed purpose: to return to the region of high tides and swamps and deep forests that to them was home; and, after so great exertion and hazard, they were defeated — at least temporarily — in their plan.

But there were others — some two hundred — left in Georgia who were not then prepared for such an adventure. Nevertheless, of this number half had disappeared by the next spring. For Henry Ellis, who had by that time become Governor, writing to the Board of Trade from Savannah, declared:

> "Upon this occasion I cannot help expressing my surprise that the Acadians which were sent here were not better disposed of than to be suffered to leave the Province. Out of near 400 that arrived only about 100 remain, some of which are dispersed among the plantations & others have built themselves huts near this Town & are very useful to the Colony as they employ themselves in making Oars, hand spikes & other implements for sea craft that are immediately bought up & sent to the Islands where they meet with a good market." [24]

---

[21] *New Jersey Archives*, XX, 42–3.

[22] Two of the boats were filled with six men and sixty women and children, all under the leadership of Jacques Maurice (*Journal of Southern History*, IV, 202–3).

[23] *Selections from the Public Documents of the Province of Nova Scotia* (ed. T. B. Akins), I, 301–2.

[24] Governor Ellis to the Board of Trade, March 11, 1757, B. T. Georgia, 27.

Yet it appears that most of these French people were reduced to distressing circumstances.[25] The Governor after inspecting their situation early in April 1757 appeared before his Council and declared that he was

> "very much affected to see such a number of distressed People surrounded with large Families of helpless Infants. . . ."

He thereupon proposed that land be allotted to them for a "Garden" by means of which they would be able to gain a more comfortable support.[26] This was agreed to by the Board. In the course of time it appears that few of these families remained. Some seemed to have found their way to the French West Indies and others to Louisiana.

The Acadians sent to South Carolina,[27] like those sent to Georgia, came from the isthmus of Chignecto and had borne arms against the English. The first group arrived in November 1755 and the second in January of the following year, making a total of nine hundred and forty-two received into the province by certificates carried by the shipmasters. As to the first contingent, which appeared on November 19, there has survived a rather vivid account of their coming by a Charleston correspondent writing on the 20th:

> "On Saturday arrived here, under Convoy of His Majesty's ship Syren, Charles Proby, Esq. Commander, from the Bay of Fundy in Nova Scotia, a Ship, a Brigantine, and a Sloop, having on board 471 of the Neutral French, viz. the Ship 210, the Brigantine, 137, and the Sloop, 124; and we hear that several Children have been born in the Passage on board each Vessel."

He later adds this item to the occurrences on November 19:

> "The same Day [yesterday] arrived here another sloop with 127 Neutral French from Nova Scotia, but last from Boston." [28]

Apparently the same correspondent, writing from Charleston on November 25, in referring to these new arrivals, declared, with some display of feeling, that

---

[25] Emile Lauvrière in *La Tragédie d'un peuple* (II, 108) asserts that the Georgia planters treated the Acadians as a commodity: "These British planters sold them like slaves."

[26] *Col. Rec. of Ga.*, VII, 506–7.

[27] Two recent studies on this topic have appeared: that by Ruth A. Hudnut and H. Baker-Crothers, "Acadian Transcients in South Carolina," *American Historical Review*, XLIII, 500–13; and that by Marguerite B. Hamer entitled "The Fate of the Exiled Acadians in South Carolina," *Journal of Southern History*, IV, 199–208.

[28] *New-York Mercury*, November 27, 1755.

". . . they are insolent Rascals, [who] talk in a high strain, call themselves Subjects of the French King, own they were Neutrals, and
that they took up Arms against us. . . . They say they'll settle here,
if we'll allow them such Privileges as they require, particularly the
public exercise of their Religion, with their Priests. . . . They will
not even upon any Terms take the Oaths of Allegiance — By this we
may judge what a pernicious dangerous Gang they were in Nova
Scotia." [29]

In view of the aggressiveness of these Frenchmen from about Beaubassin it is not difficult to conclude that in sending them to South
Carolina it was desired to remove them as far as possible from the
scene of their late activities.

Those French Neutrals who were brought to South Carolina, it is
interesting to note, came among the most important group, numerically, of Huguenots in the New World. Thus two groups of French-
speaking exiles were face to face — one exiled from their homelands
for refusing to repudiate the King of France in favour of the King
of Great Britain; the other for refusing to repudiate Calvinism in
favour of Roman Catholicism. Each had suffered loss and persecution
for their loyalty to an ideal; but as between the two there are few
students who would venture to deny that the trials faced by the
Huguenots were much more terrifying than those faced by the Acadians, grievous as these were. Some four hundred thousand of the
former, after the Revocation of the Edict of Nantes, were outlawed
for their faith and hunted out of France. No longer possessed of a
civil status, should they venture to assemble for divine worship the
men ran the risk of spending the rest of their lives in the galleys, and
the pastors of being hanged. Nor was this, unhappily, an idle threat.[30]
So it was that men and women fled from France by the thousands —
and hundreds of thousands. Those who came to South Carolina by
and large prospered, and yet many doubtless remembered the ter-
rible days of the dragonnades and all associated the Roman Catholic
church with heartless persecution. It will therefore be understood
why the new arrivals, as "bigoted Papists," did not get a warm wel-

---

29 Extract of a letter in the New-York Mercury, December 15, 1755.

30 For descriptions of the attacks of French dragoons upon unarmed Huguenot con-
gregations in the middle of the eighteenth century, with the shooting down of the defenceless and the consigning of the leaders to the galleys, see Gibbon's Sympathy with our
Suffering Brethren . . . Occasioned by the Cruel Oppressions of the Protestants in
France . . . (London, 1755). For the legal status of Protestants in France see Cambridge Modern History, VIII, 56.

come from any group, whether Huguenot, Anglican, or Baptist, especially when it was learned from the mouths of the Acadians themselves that the men among them before being deported from Nova Scotia had actually been in arms against the King. The idea of permitting such people to settle in the province — where they might stir up the Negro slaves, who outnumbered the whites almost two to one, and the Indians, still more powerful, lying westward of the settlements — was utterly repugnant to the people.

Nevertheless, a sense of common humanity would not permit the government to refuse to permit them to land and to provide them with sustenance. On December 3 the Assembly came to an agreement that those who could be trusted should be put to work under indentures and those who could not should be held in the Charleston workhouse; but all were to be temporarily under guard.[31]

Then came, as has been mentioned, the next consignment of three hundred and forty-two exiles the middle of January. Although the Commons House of Assembly was absolutely opposed to this new landing of exiles,[32] and the Governor was disposed to support their position, the captain of the ship was still more determined not to leave the port until his passengers had been placed on shore. He also called upon the government to take proper steps to preserve the lives of these unfortunates. Again, a sense of humanity finally triumphed over less worthy sentiments — but not until the newcomers had remained on board ship for twenty days.[33] Still no definite policy had been evolved for the establishment of the Acadians. The Carolinians, however, showed real determination in one respect in dealing with them: to prevent their escape into the back country, where they might be the means of stirring up the Indian tribes against the English. When two parties of the Acadians late in February sought to escape to the interior, posses were therefore sent in pursuit of them and brought all but thirty of them back.[34] Early in March a small group of these fugitives appeared at a plantation on the Santee and, having rifled the house of arms, clothes, and money, escaped into the swamps and apparently headed for Fort Duquesne.[35]

It is clear that the provincial government had one thought upper-

---

[31] House Journal, for December 3, 1755, C.O. 5:472, Library of Congress microfilm series.

[32] House Journal, for January 16, 1756, C.O. 5:472.

[33] House Journal, for February 4, 1756, C.O. 5:472.

[34] Charles Town advices, February 12, *Boston Weekly News-Letter*, March 11, 1756.

[35] *Ibid.*

most in mind in dealing with the Acadian problem in the spring of 1756: placing the burden and responsibility for the care of the French upon other shoulders than those of the inhabitants. Some of the exiles were allowed to go to England, probably on board merchant ships that left the province in the spring; [36] they may have been men who could be useful as crew members or who were in a position to pay their passage, and the matter was therefore quietly passed over. At least it is clear that, once in England, they were left stranded there, with no means of getting to France such as they doubtless hoped to find. The great bulk of the exiles, however, could not be disposed of in this simple manner. Then a bright idea dawned upon some members of the Assembly and, as a result, in April that body resolved to purchase two vessels and supplies so that the unwanted strangers could depart for whatever place they saw fit; and twelve thousand pounds was raised by subscription to that end. [37] The ships, such as they were, were bought and were provisioned after a fashion, and the exiles were invited to leave. But with the Bay of Fundy and treacherous intervening coasts in mind, the exiles demanded that they be furnished with pilots by the government. The leaders of the Assembly sensed that the granting of this request — which would really mean conveying the exiles back to their old abodes by the government itself — would lay the province open to a charge of sheer defiance of the mother country and dared not grant it. However, the Acadians now drew back from their demand and the ships, described by the French as "two ancient vessels," together with "a small quantity of bad provisions," were turned over to them with full permission to go in them wherever they desired. [38]

Into these vessels crowded an undisclosed number of Frenchmen — apparently those "able and stout" exiles from whom the Assembly feared the greatest danger and whom it was most anxious to see away [39] — and began their return to Nova Scotia. But new perils faced them: the rotten vessels soon began shipping water from all sides.

---

[36] The Board of Trade in writing to Governor Lawrence on July 8, 1756 mentions the arrival in England of several hundred Acadians sent from Virginia and also "several from South Carolina" (*Nova Scotia Doc.*, I, 300–1). Governor Glen, in fact, gave permits to at least two former residents of Beaubassin to go to England, for which he was rebuked by Secretary at War Fox (South Carolina, House Journal, June 2, 1756, C.O. 5:472).

[37] *Dinwiddie Papers*, II, 410.

[38] "Mémoire sur les Acadiens," 1763, *Canadian Archives*, Report (1905), II, Appendix F, p. 151.

[39] House Journal, April 9, 1756, C.O. 5:472.

To save their lives the exiles, according to a *mémoire* prepared in 1763, were obliged to run for shore and beached their rickety craft near the port of Hampton in Virginia.[40] At their first appearance they were thought to be French privateersmen come to pillage; then they were judged to be pirates; and when the truth was finally ascertained, they were considered to be dangerous guests who must be got rid of without delay. Since they could not get away in their water-filled vessels, and since their one desire was to sail northward, they were now forced to buy a ship that would carry off all of them. This was done by pooling their wealth, to the amount of four hundred Spanish pieces of eight. But the craft after they had set sail proved to be even less trustworthy than the vessels they had deserted.[41] Again they were obliged to seek safety on the coast of Maryland and for two months they laboured to make their wreck seaworthy.

At length succeeding in their efforts, for the third time they put to sea and, to their joy, finally reached the mouth of the St. John in the Bay of Fundy. Having made a union with the French forces under Boishébert, these sturdy, determined men, who had thus returned in the face of perils and great hardships, afterward found themselves in possession of an armed privateer, in which they preyed with great zest upon the English vessels in the bay.[42] In other words, they were no more neutral than when they had sent their families to the woods and entered Fort Beauséjour the preceding year to help defend it from the English colonial forces.

Such was the outcome of the South Carolina government's blithe manner of escaping imperial responsibility. Yet after these Frenchmen had disappeared, most of the nine hundred and nine exiles remained. To care for them the Assembly decided to follow the Georgia plan of scattering them about the province. Quotas were assigned to each parish; those refusing to accept gainful employment were bound out — for three years if over eighteen, and until twenty-one if under that age.[43] But the plan had its drawbacks, as was found in Georgia,

---

[40] "*Mémoire sur les Acadiens*," *op. cit.*, p. 151.

[41] The *mémoire* has the following to say about this incident: "It would be unfair to fail to mention at this point that one of the Virginia magistrates having learned of the perfidy that had been shown to these unhappy people took steps to punish the inhabitants of Hampton and sent a boat after the Acadians to bring about their return and to make clear to them the condition of their ship." It appears, however, that the ship was wrecked before it could return (*ibid.*).

[42] *Ibid.* See also Vaudreuil's report on this (*New York Colonial Documents*, X, 518–19, 540).

[43] *Amer. Hist. Rev.*, XLIII, 506–7.

and numbers continued to drift away to follow their brethren back to old Acadia. By the month of June 1756 between two and three hundred in all had disappeared.[44] Writing to Secretary at War Fox on July 24, 1756 from Williamsburg, Governor Dinwiddie threw some light upon this when he declared that

> "many hun[ds] of 'em have been seen on the sea coast. . . . They were those sent to So. Caro. and Georgia. It appears that those Gov[ts] gave 'em small Vessels to go where they pleas'd." [45]

It must therefore be inferred that many others succeeded in reaching the Bay of Fundy besides those who left in the spring in the two ships.

Governor Glen, although seeking to rid his province of these unwanted people, seems to have come to the conclusion that it was hardly showing due loyalty to the Crown to continue the practice of speeding these unneutral "Neutrals" back to their homeland. He therefore in the month of May hit upon the brilliant idea of dumping some of these people on the shores of Virginia. Fifty of them, perhaps the more dangerous characters, were placed on board a sloop and carried up to the Old Dominion. But Dinwiddie and the Assembly had not the slightest idea of receiving them; accordingly, the master of the ship was ordered to return them to South Carolina. Instead of doing so, however, he continued northward.[46] Whether he actually carried the exiles into the Bay of Fundy and then unloaded them is not clear; but I have uncovered no evidence that he placed these people ashore in any of the colonies to the south of Nova Scotia. We may be sure that if they were returned to the region of their old habitations this fact was carefully hidden from the authorities in Nova Scotia and in England.

The remainder of the exiles were either those with large families or the infirm, and for years to come they remained the objects of charity. Some twenty-five thousand pounds were expended upon them between the years 1755 and 1760.[47] Under the terms of a law

---

[44] Ibid., XLIII, 508.

[45] Dinwiddie Papers, II, 462.

[46] Ibid., II, 412. In writing in protest to Governor Glen on June 12, Dinwiddie made clear why Virginia could not entertain the new arrivals and then added significantly: "They are gone to the No'w'd (ibid., II, 444).

[47] Amer. Hist. Rev., XLIII, 506–7. According to Lauvrière (La Tragédie d'un peuple, II, 110), four hundred of the exiles incapable of work were maintained at the charge of the parish of St. Philippe of Charleston.

passed on July 6, 1756, most of them were scattered among the parishes with those capable of working and under the age of twenty-one, indentured to the owners of plantations.[48] In other words, little or no effort was made to keep the families intact. And as to wages, they were limited to food and clothing.[49] That there was resistance to this new dispersion is indicated by the fact that it was necessary to handcuff and fetter many of them before it was possible to scatter them broadcast.[50] Unfortunately, disease took a heavy toll among them — particularly the smallpox — and doubtless many pined away in this inhospitable country. From almost a thousand the number of the exiles, through either dispersion or death, dwindled to scarcely over two hundred by 1760, of whom only forty-five of the survivors were men. Even most of these disappeared in the course of the next few years, some making their way to their fellow Frenchmen in the West Indies, and others, it would appear, to those in Louisiana. However, one family at least, the Lanneau, did remain and, accepting the Protestant religion, contributed two very capable and devoted ministers to the Presbyterian church.[51]

It may be noted in passing that in 1760 the South Carolina Assembly strongly favoured sending to Great Britain the remnants of the Acadians planted in their midst. This was not done. In fact, it was made clear to the Assembly by Lieutenant Governor Bull that such a step was sure to incur the royal displeasure and would be a direct violation of orders that had been received by his predecessor, Governor Lyttelton.[52] Those orders were sent to South Carolina doubtless as the result not only of the permits given by Governor Glen early in 1756 to some of the exiles to go to England, but of the comfortable solution of the problem of the disposition of those consigned to Virginia by its government at the expense of the people of the mother country.

The only English plantation ready and even anxious to receive a good many of the Acadians was the province of North Carolina. Yet, through fortuitous circumstances, most of those destined for this colony never arrived. The transport *Pembroke*, with two hundred and thirty-two exiles, sailed for the province in January 1756 from

---

[48] *Journal of Modern History*, IV, 204–5.
[49] *Ibid.*
[50] *Ibid.*, p. 206.
[51] A. G. Doughty, *The Acadian Exiles*, p. 142.
[52] House Journal, August 4, 1760, C.O. 5:472.

Annapolis Royal. Through lack of vigilance, however, the crew was overpowered by the French on board, who thereupon carried the vessel first to St. Mary's Bay, Newfoundland, and then to the St. John in the Bay of Fundy. After delivering the crew to the mercy of the Indians, the Acadians placed themselves under the leadership of Boishébert, French commandant of the fort on this river, and engaged in active hostilities against the English.[53]

Again an effort was made to send a shipload of "Cape Sable" Acadians to the colony. In the month of April 1756, when the New England troops under command of General Preble were en route from Halifax to Boston, they stopped off at Pubnico in southeastern Nova Scotia and seized over seventy of them. Conveyed to Boston with the troops under convoy, the exiles were apparently not at first permitted to land.[54] Then, when the information spread among them that they were to be shipped to North Carolina,[55] they were dismayed and even enraged. In the words of Captain Church of the *Leopard:* [56]

> "there arose a Great Dissention among s^d French, & they all arose, Forc'd their way on shore with their Baggage and it was not in my power to proceed . . . as they said they would sooner suffer the pains of Death upon the Wharff in Boston than be carried to North Carolina, but were very Desirous . . . to be sent to the Northward, or stay in this Province & work for their Living. . . ." [57]

The Massachusetts Bay Council — after hearing the facts in the case and Thomas Hancock's recommendation that the exiles be permitted to remain in Boston for fourteen days, after which, should it be the mind of the Council that they should be sent out of the province, he could provide a vessel for their transportation without any charge to the government — agreed to permit them to remain for a two-week

---

53 *Boston Weekly News-Letter,* March 11 and 18, 1756; John Knox, *Historical Journal,* I, 85.

54 Apthorp and Hancock to Captain Church, May 8, 1756, *New England Historical and Genealogical Register,* XXX, 19. They are here inaccurately called Cape Sable Acadians.

55 Governor Lawrence on April 9 had written to Shirley of his plans to send the Cape Sable Acadians to Boston. He went on to say that should there be difficulty in accommodating them there, they would be willingly received by North Carolina (*Nova Scotia Documents,* I, 299).

56 The *Leopard* was used by Winslow the preceding year to transport Grand Pré Acadians to Maryland.

57 *New England Hist. and Geneal. Register,* XXX, 18.

period, with the added proviso that Hancock would assume all liability for their support.[58] These Acadians, according to a petition that
was now presented to the Governor and Council of Massachusetts
Bay, were all fishermen and naturally desired to remain in a region
where they could carry on their old activities and not be obliged to
turn to the cultivation of the land. They therefore begged

> "to be received into this Province where they can be employed in
> their old way of Business, and where . . . as in all the fishing Towns
> they shall find Persons with whom they have been acquainted and
> between whom and themselves offices of Friendship have often
> passed." [59]

That their prayer was finally granted is indicated by the presence
of members of this group later in Massachusetts Bay.[60]

North Carolina, however, did apparently receive some fifty of the
exiles. According to the financial accounts submitted by Apthorp
and Hancock, these people were carried there from Halifax in the
sloop *Providence*, John Campbell master.[61] It is certain that in the
spring of 1757 a body of Acadians was settled in the region of Albemarle Sound; for in November of that year, it may be noted, the Council voted

> "that a Sufficient Sum be allowed and paid to the Neutral French in
> and about Chowan County toward their Subsistence." [62]

That these exiles ever were able to promote the development of the
province, so much desired by Governor Dobbs, is hardly likely.

The first group of Acadians to reach Virginia arrived in Hampton
Roads on November 16, 1755 in two sloops.[63] An express sent from
that port to Dinwiddie at Williamsburg made clear that four more
ships were daily expected from Nova Scotia.[64] This unwelcome infor-

---

58 *Ibid.*, XXX, 19.

59 *Canadian Archives, Report* (1905), II, Appendix A, Part III, p. 105.

60 For this see *ibid.*, pp. 113–15, 124, 126.

61 Among the financial records of the dispersion is the following: "To John Campbell. To the freight of fifty French people brought from Halifax to North Carolina, in
sloop Providence, per. certif. at 12s 6d. . . . £31.5.0" (*Nova Scotia Documents*, I, 289).

62 *N. Car. Col. Rec.*, V, 894.

63 Clifford Millard in "The Acadians in Virginia" (*Virginia Magazine of History*, XL,
241–58) raises certain questions as to the proofs that the Acadians appeared in Virginia.

64 The express was sent by a Mr. Balfour of Hampton who advised Dinwiddie that
the two vessels that had arrived contained three hundred and ninety French Neutrals
"and that four sail more are hourly expected, who, it is presumed, will bring in upwards
of six hundred more" (Minutes of the Council, November 13, 1755, *Virginia Magazine*

mation seems to have come as a complete surprise to the Governor, in spite of intimations already appearing in the colonial newspapers that the Acadians were to be distributed among the colonies. In a letter to Secretary of State Robinson he also made clear the public reaction to it, declaring:

> "It is very disagreeable to the People to have imported, to rest among us, a No. of French People, when many of that Nat'n join'd with Ind's are now murder'g and scalp'g our frontier Settlers." [65]

He added, however, that he would consult the Council as to their disposition. At a meeting of this body on November 22 it was agreed that the exiles on one of the five ships that had already appeared should be carried up the James to Richmond, that those on two others should be landed at Norfolk, and that those on the remaining two should be held at Hampton. [66] Provision for their housing and sustenance was also made. [67] They numbered, according to Dinwiddie, over a thousand. [68]

Although the exiles were now temporarily provided for, Dinwiddie was not at all happy. "I wish You had given me previous Notice

---

of History, VI, 386). The names of the vessels that came to Virginia were the *Sally & Molly*, Captain Purrington, the *Mary*, Captain Dunning, the *Prosperous*, Captain Bragdon, the *Endeavour*, Captain Stone, the *Industry*, Captain Goodwin, and the *Neptune*, Captain Ford. The first five took on board 831 Neutrals, with an average complement of 167 passengers; the last-named had 207 upon its arrival — twenty-seven more than its proper complement (*Canadian Archives, Report* [1905], II, Appendix A, Part III, p. 34, and *Nova Scotia Doc.*, I, 285–9).

[65] *Dinwiddie Papers*, II, 268.

[66] At a meeting of the Council on November 20 Philip Ludwell and the commissary, Dr. William Dawson, were appointed as a committee to visit the transports in order to secure information as to the number of families and their circumstances; they were also instructed to learn if the exiles "were willing to take the oath of Allegiance . . . without any Reservation . . ." (*Va. Mag. of History*, VI, 387). At the next meeting of the Council they presented a paper signed by the French "importing their submission and adherence to His Majesty and promising fidelity to him" (*ibid.*).

[67] *Ibid.* The weekly allowance of food was four pounds of flour and two pounds of beef or pork per person. Mr. Balfour of Hampton and Mr. Stewart of Norfolk were ordered to provide the exiles with "Houses."

[68] Dinwiddie to Arthur Dobbs, November 22, 1755, *North Carolina Colonial Records*, V, 446. This figure must, however, have included the exiles carried in the sixth ship, that did not arrive until later — apparently some time in December. A letter written from Williamsburg on November 28, and appearing in the edition of the *Boston Weekly News-Letter* published January 15, 1756, referred to the arrival of the five vessels with "near 900 Souls. . . ." The writer of it mentions the fact that the ship sent to Richmond had 170 people, and that the two ships sent to Norfolk had "about the same quantity each." These ships were in the first convoy that left Minas Basin.

of their coming," he wrote protestingly to Governor Lawrence of Nova Scotia. At the same time, he made clear the embarrassments that he faced in carrying out his own views of their proper disposition:

> "I shall endeavour to appropriate them some Lands to set down upon, tho' this will be attended with some Difficulties, as the Lands in the lower Parts are all taken up, and [are] private property, and it will be by no means proper to send them to our Frontiers." [69]

While the Council seems to have agreed that as a temporary measure the Acadians should be given leave "to hire themselves as Labourers or to any other Employments," [70] the latter determined, rather inconsistently with the spirit of submission they first manifested, to consider themselves as prisoners of war, and as a consequence could not be "prevail'd on to work." Maintained at the expense of the fund raised through the two shillings on every hogshead of tobacco exported out of the province, they lived in idleness. Late in December the Governor, although apparently still toying with the project of attempting to settle them on the land, wrote to Sir Thomas Robinson:

> "The Council desir'd me to write for leave to send 'em to Brit'n, or some other Place. . . ." [71]

The following month the sixth transport appeared with more Acadians.[72]

It was not until March 25 that, with the meeting of the House of Burgesses, Dinwiddie appeared before the General Assembly of the province to ask that some definite policy be adopted respecting the exiles. In this connection he pointed out that the "Two Shillings" fund [73] was almost exhausted and recommended that the legislators

> "provide for the future disposit'n of those People, and . . . put them under such Regulations and Restrict'ns as may keep them in a due

---

[69] *Dinwiddie Papers*, II, 293–4. This letter refers to "5000 People sent to Ye Dom'n so late in the year" — the figure "5" is manifestly a copyist's error.

[70] Williamsburg advices, November 28, 1755, *Boston Weekly News-Letter*, January 15, 1756.

[71] *Dinwiddie Papers*, II, 306.

[72] Dinwiddie to Dobbs, February 5, 1756, *Col. Rec. of N. Car.*, V, 562. He mentions the fact that "We have had 1150 neutral French imported here from N. Scotia." The transport seems to have been the *Ranger* which left Minas Bay on December 20 for Virginia. According to Winslow, however, this ship had only 112 passengers (N.S. Hist. Soc. *Coll.*, III, 192–3). Others were evidently placed on board at the last moment.

[73] *Dinwiddie Papers*, II, 363.

> Submiss'n to our Constitut'n, and from being burthensome to the different Parishes, and probably they may become useful Members of this Community." [74]

The Governor's recommendations point to the fact that he himself still continued to cling to the idea of retaining the Acadians in Virginia. As further indication of this, in February he had written to Governor Morris of Pennsylvania to find out what policy had been adopted for dealing with those consigned to that province; early in March the Pennsylvania Assembly provided by statute for the scattering of the Acadians throughout the older townships. Dinwiddie, therefore, may well have thought that some similar plan could be worked out in Virginia. But he was utterly unable to convince his Assembly to adopt any such views. In fact, on the 29th the House of Burgesses adopted resolutions in the form of an address which stressed

> "the Danger we apprehend from such a Number of Neutral French Roman Catholics, being suffered to continue amongst us at this Time, and to desire that his Honor will be pleased to order them to be immediately shipped to Great Britain to be disposed of as His Majesty shall think proper. . . ." [75]

The address also added that the House "will chearfully pay the expense of their Transportation." When Dinwiddie submitted this to his Council for its advice, the latter concurred in "the necessity of transporting them . . ." but, perhaps in self-defence, did not mention England as the destination.[76]

The Governor was now faced by a dilemma: should he act in opposition to the Assembly and refuse to send away the exiles, his usefulness would be over in Virginia, so bitter was the opposition of the people at this critical juncture to the presence of these Roman Catholic Frenchmen; but should he act in direct opposition to the interests of the Crown he would face recall. In his reply to the address, therefore, he was impelled to place the responsibility for the proposed removal upon the shoulders of the Burgesses. Pointing out that the deported Acadians were divided among the colonies by the

---

[74] *Ibid.*, and *Journal of the House of Burgesses, 1752–1758*, p. 337. In his address Dinwiddie refers to "upw'ds of 1,100"; in writing to Lord Halifax on February 24 he gave the figure as 1,140 (*Papers*, II, 347); early in February he mentioned to Dobbs, as indicated in the preceding footnote, that there were 1,150; he also indicated that they were "very sickly."

[75] *Journals of the House of Burgesses, 1752–1758*, p. 345.

[76] *Dinwiddie Papers*, II, 380.

Nova Scotia Council, assisted by Admirals Boscawen and Mostyn, and that there were reasons to believe that this policy was agreeable to instructions that Governor Lawrence had received from His Majesty, he also made clear that he himself had no orders for retransporting the exiles to Great Britain. Nevertheless, he indicated his willingness to comply with the Assembly's request in view of the fact that this body was of the opinion that the presence of these people constituted a real danger to the government. He therefore on March 31 called upon it to provide ships and subsistence for the voyage.[77]

It was not until the second week in May that the first contingent of the exiles left Hampton Roads, when three hundred set sail on the *Bobby Goodrich* bound for Portsmouth. Writing to Secretary at War Fox on May 10, Dinwiddie again emphasized that his own desire had been to settle these people on the land "in the different counties," but that the opposition of the Virginians to this was too strong. In justice to the latter he pointed out that the Neutral French "behav'd here very mutinously and were tamper'g with the Negroe Slaves," while at the same time the French and Indians were invading the country from the west; finally, he made clear that had the Acadians been permitted to scatter about the province, many of them would doubtless have joined the French forces on the Ohio.[78] By the middle of June most of them had been carried away "at the Expense of £5000 to the Country" and by August the rest had followed.[79]

As might have been anticipated, the sending of the Acadians to England from Virginia did not awaken any sentiments of gratitude on the part of His Majesty's government. In reply to Dinwiddie's letter Fox wrote on August 10 in stern reproof; and to this the Governor made answer in November:

> "It gives me very great Concern to hear his Majesty's Displeasure and Disapprobation of send'g the neuter French (that were sent here from N. Scotia) to Great Britain."

[77] *Ibid.*, II, 381; *Journals, 1752–1758*, p. 351. On April 1 a bill was presented to the Burgesses for the removal of the Acadians, and on April 15 the same, approved by the Council, received the Governor's signature. It is entitled "An act to enable certain Persons to contract for the Transportation of the Neutral French to Great Britain" (*Statutes at Large of Virginia*, ed. W. W. Hening, VII, 39–40).

[78] *Dinwiddie Papers*, II, 408. Writing to Major General Shirley on April 28, Dinwiddie mentioned the capture of three Neutral French on their way from South Carolina to Fort Duquesne (*ibid.*, II, 396).

[79] *Ibid.*, II, 444, 479.

He then went on to state:

> "It is what I could by no means evade." [80]

If Virginia, South Carolina, and Georgia were disposed to shove the Acadian exiles sent to them upon others, not so Maryland or the other colonies lying north of that province.[81] In fact, in some of the more northern colonies there was a much more understanding and sympathetic attitude toward these people. This may be illustrated in the case of Maryland by an announcement that appeared in the *Maryland Gazette* of December 4, 1755:

> "Sunday last (Nov. 30) arrived here the two last of the vessels from Nova Scotia with French Neutrals for this Place, which makes four within this Fortnight who have brought upwards of Nine Hundred of them. . . . As the poor people have been deprived of their Settlements in Nova Scotia, and sent here (for some very Political Reasons) bare and destitute, Christian Charity, nay, Common Humanity, call on every one according to his ability to lend assistance and to help these objects of compassion."

In all, five transports, bearing some nine hundred and thirteen people, ascended Chesapeake Bay to Annapolis, most of them overcrowded and with their burden of sick people.[82] As Governor Sharpe was away attending a governors' conference in New York, it devolved on the Council to take immediate action. One of the first things done was to disperse the Neutrals by sending one of the ships to Somerset and Wicomico counties on the lower bay, another to Oxford in Talbot County, another to the Patuxent River on the lower

---

[80] *Ibid.*, II, 538.

[81] For the exiles in Maryland see Basil Sollers, "The Acadians (French Neutrals) Transported to Maryland," *Maryland Historical Magazine*, III, 1–21.

[82] The *Elizabeth*, Captain Milbury, carried 242 exiles, fifty-two more than the complement of two persons to the ton; the *Dolphin*, Captain Forman, arrived in Maryland with 230, fifty-six more than the agreed complement; and the *Ranger*, Captain Piercy, evidently a smaller vessel than either of the other two, arrived with 208, eighty-one persons beyond the proper complement (*Nova Scotia Doc.*, I, 42–4). These people had inhabited the region about Minas Basin — 493 from Piziquid and 420 from Grand Pré (Lauvrière, *La Tragédie d'un peuple*, II, 103). Two of the shiploads, those of the *Dolphin* and the *Ranger*, which sought temporary shelter in Boston as the result of a storm that lashed them after leaving Minas Basin in October, were found to be in a sickly condition. On the *Dolphin* sickness was occasioned by her overcrowded condition; forty people were obliged to sleep on the deck. On the *Ranger* the water was found to be "very bad" (*Canadian Archives, Report* (1905), II, Appendix A, Part III, E, p. 81). After these conditions had been remedied by the Massachusetts Bay authorities the vessels sailed southward.

Eastern Shore, and a fourth to Baltimore; the fifth was permitted to land its passengers, about one hundred and seventy, at the provincial capital.[83] Although it cannot be denied that there was much hostility to Roman Catholics in this province — originally established as a refuge for those of that faith — with numerous petitions at this period calling upon the government to enforce rigidly the numerous harsh persecuting statutes against them passed by the Assembly in the early part of the century; yet, on the other hand, there was little disposition on the part of the authorities to do so, and Catholics lived quietly and prospered.[84] In fact, it was estimated one out of every twelve people in Maryland was of that faith.[85]

While it was reported that the Acadians landed in Somerset County were obliged "to betake themselves for shelter to the swamps, now and a long time full of snow, where they sicken and die," [86] nevertheless a resident of that section, Henry Lowes, came to their rescue with supplies. Those that were landed at Oxford were aided by the merchant Henry Callister, called a "skeptic and a Whig," and the Reverend Thomas Bacon, pastor of the Oxford Anglican church, who were both deeply touched with sympathy for the sorry plight of their fellow beings and who, in spite of "potent opposition and much difficulty," succeeded in placing most of the Oxford French families in good homes for the winter.[87] But the exiles there remained a dead weight upon the generosity of a few people. As a result, early in 1757, the freeholders of Talbot County framed an address to their deputies in the Assembly

---

[83] Annapolis advices, December 11, 1755, *Boston Weekly News-Letter*, January 15, 1756; see also J. T. Scharf, *History of Maryland*, p. 475, and James Johnsongurd to Henry Callister, Callister Papers, New York Public Library photostats.

[84] For example, in the spring of 1756 a petition was received from Calvert County reflecting upon the great danger to the government "by the Increase of Popish Recusants and . . . the great Resort of Jesuits to this country who are daily endeavouring to seduce his Majesty's good Subjects from their Religion and Allegiance and . . . accumulating great wealth, and enjoying some of the best estates in the Province, contrary to Law, and . . . requesting of his Excellency the execution of the Penal Laws of England against the Papists . . ." (*Archives of Maryland*, XXXI, 122).

[85] *Ibid.*, VI, 497.

[86] Henry Callister to Anthony Bacon, December 25, 1755, quoted in J. T. Scharf, *History of Maryland*, p. 476.

[87] *Ibid.* Callister was apparently so generous in using his personal means to supply the pressing needs of the Acadians that he found himself somewhat financially embarrassed. It may be added that when he and Henry Lowes presented bills to the Assembly for supplies furnished the Neutrals, these were disallowed (*Archives of Maryland*, LII, 346).

"to have this pest removed from among us, after the example of the people of Virginia or Carolina, at their own expense, as they request, or otherwise, as the Assembly shall, in their own wisdom, think fit." [88]

It may be well to point out that as the result of an order of the Council the burden of entertaining the Acadians fell upon Protestant householders, for none of the exiles could be received into the home of a Roman Catholic.[89] Further, one influential member of the Council, Colonel Edward Lloyd, seems to have shown strong opposition to making any legal provision for them.[90] What complicated the problem was that the exiles were confused in their own minds as to their status. Those who were landed at Annapolis, for example, declared themselves French prisoners of war and expected to be treated as such; while those in Talbot County, in a memorial addressed to His Majesty, described themselves as faithful subjects who had been unfairly deprived of their estates in Acadia.[91] But all were deeply resentful, whether they regarded themselves as French or as British subjects. For they felt that — in the words of Henry Callister — they had been

"rob'd by us or for us, of their Lands, their Estates & Liberties. . . ."

This good man made clear his own deep sympathies for them in declaring:

"I, an inhabitant of the world, a human creature with all its weaknesses am apt to think them better entitled to an immediate support than any poor . . . already provided for by the constitution of the Country." [92]

The most fortunate of all these Acadians were those sent to Baltimore, where they were temporarily lodged either in private homes or in a large, empty residence deserted by its Irish owner, who had subsequently passed away. In this structure they soon consecrated a

---

[88] Printed in Scharf's *Maryland*, p. 478.

[89] *Ibid.*, p. 477.

[90] Henry Callister to Governor Sharpe, January 7, 1756, printed in *ibid.*, pp. 476–7. At first the Neutrals were supported almost entirely by private generosity, it would appear from the complaint of Daniel Dulany late in the year 1755. He writes: "They have almost eaten us up; as there is no provision for them, they have been supported by private subscription" (*Pa. Magazine of History and Biography*, III, 147).

[91] Scharf, *op. cit.*, pp. 476–7.

[92] Callister to the Reverend Thomas Bacon, November 17, 1756, Callister Papers, New York Public Library photostats.

little chapel and there the priest living at Charles Carroll's manor, not far distant, came to minister to their spiritual needs. In the course of time these Baltimore exiles constructed simple homes in a section of the town that came to be known as "French town."

As to the final disposition of the French Neutrals, it should be pointed out that with the return of Governor Sharpe from New York further steps were taken to scatter most of the Acadian families in the various parishes except within the frontier county of Frederick. At the same time the Governor issued an order that they should be warned

> "against Stragling from the Plantations where they may be settled and let them know that Orders are given the Troops on the Western Frontiers to destroy without hesitation any of them that may be seen in that Part of the Province and that the Attempt of any one to make off will deprive the Rest of the Liberty they will otherwise be permitted to enjoy." [93]

Committed strongly to the policy of supporting Governor Lawrence, Sharpe was able to write to the latter in August assuring him

> "that none of the French who were imported into this Province last year from Nova Scotia have been suffered either by Land or Water to return again thither." [94]

In fact, there seems to have been no disposition, even on the part of the most charitably inclined Marylanders, to question the wisdom of their removal from Nova Scotia. Their greatest defender and supporter, Henry Callister, in writing to Governor Sharpe on their behalf declared:

> "A good point gained it certainly is, that they are removed and dispersed; and it certainly would be bad to restore them." [95]

For some months there was hesitancy regarding the formulation of a plan for the more regular care of the exiles. On April 19 the Governor, in reminding the Assembly of the plight of these people sent that body a copy of an act passed by the Pennsylvania legislature. As a result the deputies finally passed a comprehensive statute which, in providing for an equitable distribution of the Acadian families

---

[93] *Archives of Maryland*, XXX, 103. Sharpe in this letter, addressed apparently to the vestry of Upper Marlboro in Prince George's County, does not say that the families to be distributed are Neutral French, but the inference is too strong to leave one in doubt.

[94] Letter of August 24, 1756, *ibid.*, VI, 471.

[95] Letter of January 7, 1756, in Scharf, *op. cit.*, p. 477.

among the various hundreds, at the same time required the justices of the peace of the several counties to care for those who were real objects of charity upon the same basis as the other poor. To this extent the law followed that of Pennsylvania of March 5, 1756, as will be noted; it went beyond this statute, however, in providing not only that the children of those unable or unwilling to work should be bound out, but that Neutrals who were inclined "to wander and loiter" or who refused employment should be jailed. Finally it stated that no exile should, without express permission of the magistrates, go more than ten miles from the place where he should be settled.[96] Here we have established a rather rigid location policy. In practice, however, the authorities were disposed to aid those among the exiles seeking relatives from whom they were separated in the dispersion, and as a result some scattered families were reunited.[97]

In 1763, with the coming of peace, there were in all some eight hundred and ten Acadians living within the province, including those who had survived and the newly born.[98] Although these exiles as a group undoubtedly longed to find themselves once again among those whom they regarded as their fellow countrymen, it was not until 1767 that some two hundred of them left by boat for the Mississippi to join others who were drifting into the region thereabouts from the other southern colonies.[99]

One final comment may be made on the Acadians in Maryland. In coming into this province they found themselves in the midst of many other Roman Catholics. One of their expressed fears before their exile — as was indicated in the preceding chapter of this volume — had been that should they take an oath of allegiance to His Majesty, they would be obliged to bear arms against their French brethren and the Indians. That this fear had been baseless must now have become apparent to them. For, as had been pointed out to them before the orders for expulsion were issued, the bearing of arms by

96 For this law see *Archives of Maryland*, XL, 542–4.

97 Governor Morris of Pennsylvania wrote to Sharpe on February 2, 1756 that there were two Neutrals, one brought to New York and the other to Pennsylvania, who had obtained leave to go to Annapolis in search of their families, which, they thought, had been carried to Maryland. Arriving in Maryland, one of them found his family at Annapolis and the other went to look for his "in a distant part of the Province" (*ibid.*, VI, 343, 345).

98 They were distributed as follows: 169 at Oxford, 157 at Port Tobacco, 78 at Annapolis, 77 at Baltimore, 68 at Georgetown and also at Snow Hill, 58 in Upper Marlboro, 44 at a place called Newton, 33 at Princess Ann, and 26 in Lower Marlboro (Affaires Étrangères, Angleterre, 450, folio 436).

99 *Maryland Magazine of History*, III, 20.

Roman Catholics within the Empire was neither desired nor encouraged, and in harmony with this they found that all those in Maryland of this faith, in spite of their oaths of allegiance, were "excused from attending Musters as Militia (a Privilege which they enjoy in common with the Magistrates). . . ."[100]

The authorities of Maryland, in passing the law of May 22, 1756 relating to the French Neutrals, had followed in some respects, as was indicated, the pattern provided by the Assembly of Pennsylvania in its statute of March 5 of that year.[101] For to the latter province came three transports between November 18 and 20, 1755 from Minas Bay, bringing in all four hundred and fifty-four exiles.[102] It appears that a fourth was also destined for the same colony but never arrived; unhappily, it is recorded that in the midst of a hurricane the ship disappeared with all on board.[103]

As was the case with Virginia and Maryland, the defeat of Braddock in July had left the frontiers of Pennsylvania exposed; these frontiers were also in the case of the Quaker colony quite undefended. The inhabitants of the outer settlements west of the Susquehanna were, at the very time of the arrival of the exiles, fleeing in terror from bands of French and Indians engaged in their destructive work. Only a week before this event came the massacre and destruction of Tulpehocken, located only sixty miles from Philadelphia — a settlement described as "one of the finest of this Province."[104] On November 24 the Mayor and Council of Philadelphia in a memorial to the Assembly declared:

---

[100] *Archives of Maryland*, VI, 419–20.

[101] For the exiles in Pennsylvania see William B. Reed, "The Acadian Exiles, or French Neutrals in Pennsylvania," *Memoirs of the Historical Society of Pennsylvania*, VI, 285–316; W. P. Ledet, "Acadian Exiles in Pennsylvania," *Pennsylvania History*, IX, 118–28; and also *American Catholic Historical Researches*, Vols. IX, XVIII, and VII (new series), and the American Catholic Historical Society of Philadelphia *Records*, Vols. I, II, V, and XXXI for many original records of the Acadians.

[102] *Pennsylvania Gazette*, November 20, 1755. These were the *Three Friends*, the *Hannah*, and the *Swan* (*Nova Scotia Doc.*, I, 287–8).

[103] A "Mémoire sur les Acadiens" (1763) has the following comment: "The Acadians on the fourth transport destined for Pennsylvania suffered less than those of whom we have spoken; a hurricane, having engulfed their ship, suddenly put an end to the miseries that awaited them" (*Canadian Archives, Report* (1905), II, Appendix G, 151). Governor Morris also was notified of the coming of a fourth vessel. Writing to the Proprietors on November 22, he stated: "Yesterday and to-day three vessels are arrived from Nova Scotia, and a fourth is coming with Neutral French that Governor Lawrence has sent to remain in this Province" (*Pennsylvania Archives*, fourth series, II, 554).

[104] *Pa. Archives* (first series), II, 501.

"Scarce a day has passed wherein you have not heard of the inhuman slaughter of your Fellow Subjects . . . and the melancholy prospect of having far greater numbers of the unhappy back settlers driven in upon us from their Habitations." [105]

And now several hundred potential, if not active, enemies had arrived to be quartered in the very heart of the colony! Governor Morris, uncertain of his grounds but fearing that "under our present Circumstances" it was not safe to permit the French exiles to land, took the advice of his Council and thereupon ordered the transports that were near or in the port of Philadelphia to drop down the Delaware.[106] Provisions were given to those on board and a guard was placed to watch their movements.[107] The feeling of most of the inhabitants of the province toward these unfortunates was doubtless expressed by the Governor, who, in writing to Major General Shirley, pointed out the new dangers that now seemed to threaten from having thrust upon them "such a Number of People of their Principles . . . at this time." [108] On November 24 Morris in an address to the Assembly made clear what steps had been taken respecting them and the necessity of providing for their wants, now encamped as they were on Province Island.[109]

Fortunately for the Acadians, they found a true friend in the person of the Quaker Anthony Benezet. Although of Huguenot descent, unlike those Huguenots of South Carolina he was filled with compassion, and his services on behalf of the exiles are worthy to be recorded beside those of the freethinker Henry Callister of Maryland. Without awaiting official authorization, he proceeded to minister to their needs, as did the latter, providing them with additional clothing and other necessaries. It is pleasant to record that his solicitude for their welfare was properly recognized by the government; for although Callister's bills were rejected by the Assembly of Maryland, Benezet was apparently promptly reimbursed by that of Pennsylvania. Further, he was also entrusted with the responsibility of seeing that the exiles suffered no lack until a permanent disposition was

---

[105] *Pennsylvania Colonial Records*, VI, 734-5.

[106] "Some vessels are in the River from Halifax with French Neutrals, one of which came up to Town on Tuesday Night, but is since ordered down again," wrote a correspondent from Philadelphia on November 20 (*New-York Mercury*, November 27, 1755).

[107] *Pa. Col. Rec.*, VI, 711-14.

[108] *Pa. Archives* (eighth series), V, 4150.

[109] *Ibid.* (fourth series), II, 549-600, and *ibid.* (eighth series), V, 4150-9.

made of them.[110] For many years to come he was to remain their chief adviser and wise counsellor. His spirit of charity was supported substantially by other members of the Society of Friends. Writing in later years to the Frenchman Gérard, he made clear the extent of the efforts of his group to watch over the welfare of the Neutrals in Pennsylvania:

> "Testify the thousands and thousands of francs which we raised among ourselves to aid the poor Acadians . . . and the pleadings which we presented in their favor to the Assembly of Pennsylvania, to the Governor of Acadia, and to the King of England himself, by the hand of our Proprietor, Thomas Penn." [111]

It was not until early in February that the Assembly, having met again after its adjournment on December 3, took up the problem of the disposition of the Acadians. The exiles seem to have felt that their situation, while unhappy enough, was, on the whole, fortunate in that they were carried to Pennsylvania. At least one of them, Jean Baptiste Galerm (Galerme), in a memorial to the Assembly, dated February 11, after giving a history of the trials of his fellows in Nova Scotia, was led, in speaking for the group, to declare:

> "Yet, blessed be God, that it was our Lot to be sent to *Pennsylvania,* where our wants have been relieved, and we have in every Respect been received with Christian Benevolence and Charity." [112]

At the same time the memorial laid bare the tragic misconception that all the Acadians laboured under while still a free people in Nova Scotia — a misconception, already stressed in this chapter, which undoubtedly was instilled into their minds by Le Loutre and other Frenchmen — that were they to have taken the required oaths, they would have been required to take up arms against their kinsmen who had become the enemies of Great Britain:

> "Deprived of our substance, [we were] banished from our native country, and reduced to live by Charity in a strange Land; and this for refusing to take an Oath, which we are firmly persuaded Chris-

---

[110] *Ibid.,* V, 4161.

[111] *American Catholic Historical Researches,* XXXI, 228.

[112] *Pa. Archives* (eighth series), V, 4192. This memorial and subsequent memorials seem to have been put into literary English by Benezet. At least when Robert Walsh, Jr., in his *Appeal from the Judgment of Great Britain respecting the United States,* printed one of the memorials of the exiles, he stated (p. 437) that it was from a draft in the handwriting of Benezet; see also Justin Winsor's *Narrative and Critical History of America* V, 462.

tianity absolutely forbids us to violate, had we once taken it, and yet an Oath, which we could not comply with, without being exposed to plunge our swords in the Breasts of our near Friends and Relatives." [113]

It was clear to the Assembly that it was highly undesirable to keep the Neutral French in idleness in the port of Philadelphia. After some debate it was agreed that a committee headed by James Pemberton, a leading Quaker, should prepare a bill for dispersing them in the townships of the three old river counties and those of Lancaster County. The bill, having passed the various readings, was finally approved on March 5. This statute, the model for the Maryland law of May 22, as has been indicated, sought by means of dispersing the people to make it possible for the industrious to support "their numerous families" by their own labour. Commissioners were appointed for each of the four counties with power to apportion the exiles among the townships of the same, with the proviso that not more than one family should be allotted to the care of the overseers of the poor in any township. As most of the Acadians were bred to the management of farms, the law contemplated their re-establishment on the land. It provided that the commissioners should be empowered to rent plantations for them, so that they might "by their honest labor and industry procure a subsistence for themselves and families," and also to purchase the stock and utensils necessary for their settlements. It was provided that those who were unable to work, as the result of sickness or other misfortune, should be supported by the overseers of the poor.[114]

What was undoubtedly expected to be a happy solution of the problem of disposing of the Neutrals was not in practice realized. It is true that the dispersion was at least partially carried out. Nevertheless it is clear that in Philadelphia County some of the townships were unwilling to receive their contingents; nor did the exiles desire to leave the city except to depart from the province. As a result, on April 16 the commissioners of this county sought the advice of the Assembly [115] and on August 27 that body received another memorial from the Acadians in which they stressed the fact that they were in truth, and wanted only to be, French nationals and prayed

---

[113] *Pa. Archives* (eighth series), V, 4192.
[114] *Statutes at Large of Pennsylvania*, V, 215–19.
[115] *Pa. Archives* (eighth series), V, 4216, 4226.

"that you would extend your Goodness so far as to give us Leave to depart from hence, or be pleased to send us to our Nation; or any where, to join our Country People." [116]

In view of this frank acknowledgment that they were loyal Frenchmen and not loyal subjects of His Britannic Majesty, as they had previously claimed to be, it is perhaps not surprising that they should have been equally frank in making clear their unwillingness to avail themselves of the bounty of the Assembly:

> "It is true, you have been so good as to offer us some Assistance towards procuring ourselves a Living, such as Cows, Gardens, etc. which we have refused. . . . Our refusing to accept the Assistance offered to us . . . arose from an Opinion which we entertained, that being Prisoners, we were not obliged to make settlements against our Inclination. And . . . we shall never freely consent to settle in this Province." [117]

The Assembly was now faced by a dilemma. The exiles had determined to insist that as loyal Frenchmen they must be treated as prisoners of war and as such were entitled to support until exchanged. But this involved not only British imperial policy, but the British laws relating to nationality and in this connection the established principles of international law based upon *jus soli*. Could one born on British or on French soil rid himself of his nationality and of its obligations by simply announcing that he had decided to adhere to another nation? This was what the Acadians as a body were now seeking to do. In perplexity the legislators sought the advice of the new Governor, William Denny. The latter, after going over the correspondence having to do with the exiles and after submitting the issue to his Council, declared that it was the unanimous opinion of the Council and himself that these people could not be considered prisoners of war and were therefore not entitled to be treated as such; he further recommended to the Assembly that "they should be more generally dispersed and settled as far from the Frontiers as possible." [118]

Doubtless the open avowal of the Acadians that they were at heart Frenchmen and that they only sought to join their French brethren did not encourage the Pennsylvanians — living as they were at the time under great emotional strain because of continuing bloody in-

[116] *Ibid.*, V, 4294.
[117] *Ibid.*
[118] *Ibid.*, V, 4307, 4309.

cursions by the French and Indians — to make use of the services of those among them who were willing to work.[119] With a number of the townships absolutely refusing to provide for their support, many remained congregated in Philadelphia and, facing actual starvation, were impelled "to pilfer and steal for the support of Life." [120] In October they petitioned the Governor for relief, and he in turn referred their unfortunate situation to the Assembly. Although a committee was appointed to draft a bill early in November, it was not until early in January of the following year that a law could be passed agreeable to both the Assembly and the Governor. The "Act for Binding Out and Settling such of the Inhabitants of Nova Scotia Imported into this Province as are Under Age, and for Maintaining the Aged, Sick and Maimed at the Charge of the Province," [121] must have come as a great shock to the exiles. For it provided that those unable to work should be supported at the expense of the province by the overseers of the poor, and that the children of those incapable of providing for them should be bound out, the males until twenty-one years of age and the females until eighteen — "thereby they might become reputable inhabitants entitled to the rights of British subjects." To the end that these children might become loyal subjects they were to be taught to read and write the English language and at the expiration of their indentures were to be regarded as "legally settled" in the city or township where they had been held. In other words, families now were to be broken up — and some were broken up. Children were scattered about in the homes of Protestant families, all to the inexpressible grief of the parents.

In a memorial to the King, penned, it would appear, at this juncture, by their friend Benezet, the Acadians recounted their sufferings in Pennsylvania. They declared that

"most of us have been prevented, by sickness, from procuring the necessary subsistence for our families; and therefore are threatened with that which we esteem the greatest aggravation of all our sufferings, even of having our children forced from us, and bound out to strangers. . . . We have already seen in this Province of Pennsylvania two hundred and fifty of our people, which is more than half the number that were landed here, perish through misery and vari-

---

119 The "Remonstrance" of William Griffith of Philadelphia of October 28 emphasized the "general Dislike in the Inhabitants of this Province against employing the Neutrals in their service . . ." (ibid., VI, 4408).

120 Ibid. Their numbers were reduced as the result of an epidemic of smallpox.

121 Statutes at Large, V, 278–80.

ous diseases. In this great distress and misery, we have, under God, none but your majesty to look to with hopes of relief and redress. . . ." [122]

Unhappily for these exiles, the accumulated afflictions that came upon them were, one must affirm, largely self-inflicted. Whenever it was open for them to choose between a wise and an unwise course of action, they had consistently chosen the latter — doubtless as the result of bad advice. They would never have been disturbed in their Acadian homes had they not refused to do what ultimately all those hundreds that returned to Nova Scotia and Canada were at length impelled to do: take the oath of allegiance. They would never have been separated from other members of their immediate families and could have escaped the pestilential dangers of an eighteenth-century seaport had they not refused to accept the offer, certainly generous enough, to settle as families on the land and to be provided with implements and livestock to improve it at the expense of the provincial government. But instead of accepting the opportunity thus provided, they spread alarm of themselves by affirming loyalty to their French nationality, when most if not all of them had been born on British soil and were therefore, under the law, held to be British subjects — although, in this instance, "bad subjects." [123]

It is doubtless not surprising — in view of the determination of the Assembly, and in spite of all petitions to the contrary from the Acadians, to apply the law for binding out their children — that some of the exiles should have been led into violence of speech and action. As a result, when the Earl of Loudoun, commander-in-chief of all the British forces in North America, came to Philadelphia in the spring of 1757, information against some of them was lodged with him. Writing to Pitt on April 25 of that year, he stated:

> "When I was at Pensilvania, I found that the French Neutrals there had been very mutinous, and had threatened to leave the women and children and go over to join the French in the back country; they sent me a Memorial in French setting forth their grievances. I re-

[122] This memorial is printed in T. C. Haliburton's An Historical and Statistical Account of Nova Scotia, pp. 185–95.

[123] The bewilderment of these exiles is well expressed by their pathetic appeal to the Assembly on February 8, 1757, in which they cried out: "O merciful Gentlemen, what Crime have these innocent Creatures been guilty of that you should thus separate them from those who, after God, are Authors of their Lives? Being deprived of that substance which God had granted us, permit us at least to live or die with our Children, and those of our deceased Brethren" (Pa. Archives, eighth series, VI, 4509).

turned it and said I could receive no memorial from the King's subjects but in English, on which they had a general meeting at which they determined they would give no memorial but in French, and I am informed they came to this resolution from looking on themselves entirely as French subjects. . . . I learnt that there were five principal leading men among them who stir up all the disturbance these people make in Pensilvania, and who persuade them from submitting to any regulations made in the country, and to allow their children to be put out to work." [124]

Loudoun requested a warrant for the apprehension of these five ringleaders, each of whom was declared to have uttered at various times "menacing speeches against His Majesty and his liege subjects and [to] behave in a very disorderly Manner." [125] They were therefore by order of Governor Denny put under arrest, placed for safekeeping on H.M.S. *Sutherland,* and carried away from the colony. Ultimately, and apparently after promising to mend their ways, they were released and found their way back to Philadelphia in 1758.[126] This firm action put an end to the disorderly conduct of the Neutrals. It may also be added that in practice the law for binding out the young Acadians does not seem to have been very rigidly enforced.

---

[124] *Memoirs of the Historical Society of Pennsylvania,* VI, 305–6. It should not escape the notice of students that the earlier petitions and memorials of the exiles in Pennsylvania, as well as the memorial of 1760 to the King of Great Britain, were all in English.

[125] *Pa. Col. Rec.,* VII, 446. The warrant is to be found in the *Pennsylvania Archives* (fourth series), II, 785.

[126] S. M. Sener, "The Catholic Church at Lancaster," American Catholic Historical Society of Philadelphia *Records,* V, 314. The names of these Neutrals were Jean Baptiste Galerm, Charles Le Blanc, both settled in Philadelphia, Philip Melançon of Frankford township, Paul Bujauld of Chester, and Jean Landy (Landry?) of Derby. The first-named, it is of interest to note, had been the author of the first memorial to the Assembly of February 1756, in which, for the group, he had thanked God that it had been their lot to be sent to Pennsylvania "where our wants have been relieved, and we have in every Respect been received with Christian Benevolence and Charity." It may also be added that a namesake of Le Blanc in time became a great figure in the commercial life of Philadelphia.

With respect to this episode of the arrest of the Acadian leaders, Loudoun's letter to Pitt of April 27, 1757 (*Memoirs of the Historical Society of Pennsylvania,* VI, 305–6) throws additional light upon the activities of the British spy Thomas Pichon. As indicated in an earlier chapter, it was he who supplied Loudoun with the evidence that the exiles were being stirred to revolt by the five leaders. Professor Lauvrière has the following comment to make upon this (*La Tragédie d'un peuple,* II, 120): "What is worse: upon the denunciation of the infamous Pichon, the traitor of Beauséjour, who is again found living here on the fruits of his new treasons (passing among his compatriots in the guise of a poor French officer made prisoner as were they), the five last-named Acadian notables were arrested and placed on board the ships serving as convict prisons."

Industrious parents found that they were able to make a livelihood and keep their children with them; and many others, unable to provide for their dependents, were apparently permitted to keep them. At least in 1761 some families were rebuked for opposing the operations of the law and making their children public burdens, especially in time of sickness. But the committee of the Assembly appointed in that year to investigate their condition was able to report

> "that there are amongst them Numbers of industrious labouring Men, who have been, during the late Scarcity of Labourers, of great service in the Neighbourhood of this City" (Philadelphia).[127]

As to the exiles themselves, their conduct with respect to their allegiance continued to be contradictory. In 1760 they addressed a long memorial in English to the new King, George III, asking for permission either to return to Acadia or to go to France. In recounting their manifold sufferings, they stated:

> "Thus we, our ancient parents and grand parents, (men of great integrity and approved fidelity to your Majesty), and our innocent wives and children, became the unhappy victims to . . . groundless fears. . . ."[128]

Yet in 1763, just three years later, three hundred and eighty-three of them in a memorial in French directed to the French King's representative in London, the Duc de Nivernais, expressed their great desire to be carried either to France or to some French colony, and in this the French King was referred to as *"notre souverain."*[129]

---

[127] Pa. Archives (eighth series), VI, 5206–8.

[128] T. C. Haliburton, Historical and Statistical Account of Nova Scotia, I, 194. Most of the memorial is to be found here (pp. 183–95); for this see also American Catholic Historical Researches, Volume XVIII.

[129] Lauvrière, op. cit., II, 121. It will be noted that the number who supported the petition of 1763 was three hundred and eighty-three; in 1760 the English memorial of the exiles stated: "We have already seen in this Province of Pennsylvania two hundred and fifty of our people, which is more than half the number that were landed here, perish through misery and various diseases." In spite of this assertion the number 383 seems to be correct as it is contained in an enumeration of the exiles in the various English colonies under date November 22, 1763 (Aff. Étrang., Corresp. Pol., Angle., 452 f. 203). All authorities agree that most of those exiles who died of disease, such as smallpox, were living in Philadelphia. The records of burials of members of the Catholic faith in that city between the years 1755 and 1759 show that there were one hundred and ten burials, including the Acadians buried in the Potter's Field as well as all other Catholics, who outnumbered the Acadians (American Catholic Historical Researches, XVIII, 47). To reconcile the figures, if it is possible, one must conclude that there was a surprising number of births among those unhappy and distressed people.

Neither of the memorials referred to above brought any relief to the Neutrals. Nevertheless, as time passed, the circumstances of many of these unfortunate people were eased, particularly as the result of the efforts of the benevolent Benezet and other members of the Society of Friends. A number at length seemed to have given up all thought of leaving the province, where they had won not a few sympathetic friends. Free to practice their religion, freely associating with British subjects of the same profession, and ministered unto in Philadelphia by Fathers Harding and Farmer of St. Joseph's Chapel, they at length seem to have become — as it was hoped that all of them would — quite reconciled to the new way of life now opened to them.[130] A number of their children were privately instructed by Benezet; others entered private schools. It is pleasing to record that one of them, Charles Le Blanc, a youth of seventeen upon his arrival and apparently the son and namesake of one of the five Acadians imprisoned for seditious conduct and grandson of René Le Blanc, who had acted in Nova Scotia as the King's notary public before his exile, ultimately turned to commerce and became a very wealthy man, amassing, we are told, before his death in 1816, "an enormous fortune," including large estates not only in the old English colonies but also in Canada.[131] But most others seem to have found difficulty in making a good living, particularly in Philadelphia, where in 1771 the overseers of the poor stated that about one half of the seventy-eight living there were in need of relief as the result of sickness or infirmity.[132] That there was any concerted migration of the survivors out of the colony at any one time is not clear.[133] As late as 1779 they were apparently still the object of solicitude of Benezet and other Friends.[134]

---

[130] The marriage records kept by Father Farmer of St. Joseph's, covering the years 1758–86, indicate the presence of Acadians in Philadelphia at least down to the period of the American Revolution. They also indicate the marriage of Acadians with other Catholics. (American Catholic Historical Society Records, II, 277–315). S. M. Sener, in his "Catholic Church at Lancaster, Pa." (Amer. Cath. Hist. Soc. Records, V) shows the continued presence of these people in Lancaster County as late as 1798.

[131] A. G. Doughty, The Acadian Exiles, p. 145.

[132] American Catholic Historical Researches, XVIII, 140–2.

[133] J. F. Watson (Annals of Philadelphia, p. 536) indicates that the exiles in Pennsylvania left in a body to settle in Louisiana near New Orleans.

[134] "We have obtained," declared Benezet, "a considerable subscription to pay a lawyer to plead their cause at the council of the King" (Benezet to Conrad Alexander Gérard, October 17, 1779, Amer. Cath. Hist. Soc. Records, XXXI, 228). It is difficult to interpret this statement as having application to the year in which Benezet wrote, unless reference is to the King of France.

New Jersey did not have to face the problem of receiving any of the French Neutrals. In fact, Governor Belcher was not at all backward in indicating the nature of the reception that would have awaited them in this province. Writing to Governor Morris of Pennsylvania on November 29, 1755, he declared:

> "I am, Sir, truly surprised how it cou'd ever enter into the Thoughts of those, who had the ordering of the French Neutrals, or rather Traitors & Rebels to the Crown of Great Britain, to direct any of them into these Provinces, where we have already too great a Number of Foreigners for our own good and safety. I think they shou'd have been transported directly to old France. I entirely coincide with Your Honour, that these People wou'd readily join with the Irish Papists, etc. to the Ruin and Destruction of the King's Colonies, & should any of the [them] attempt to land here, I shou'd think in Duty to the King & His good People, under my care to do all in my Power to crush an Attempt." [135]

New York, it appears, received two shiploads of Acadians, as well as a body of exiles that were sent to Georgia, but were detained when upon their return to Nova Scotia they reached Long Island.

On April 28, 1756 a schooner, Captain Dunning, arrived in New York harbour with a number of exiles who were said to be from Cape Sable.[136] On May 6 there were listed ninety-four of them within the province, all located in the southern counties.[137] The latter part of May the brigantine *Experiment*, Captain Stoddard, also appeared. She had left Annapolis Royal in December 1755 with thirty families. Caught in hurricanes, the vessel was swept so far to the southward of its objective that it was compelled to take on additional supplies at St. Christopher in the West Indies [138] and to go to the neighbouring island of Antigua to refit after braving the storms for six weeks.[139] During the process of refitting, a number of the Acadians escaped to the French islands. It also appears that the mortality on the ship was heavy before the *Experiment* finally, after five months, reached New

---

[135] *Pa. Archives* (first series), II, 513–14.

[136] Emile Lauvrière, *op. cit.*, II, 113. In fact, most of the so-called Cape Sable Acadian exiles came from the region about Pubnico.

[137] *Ibid.* On April 30 it was voted by the Council to locate these people on Long Island and Staten Island and in Westchester County (*Sir William Johnson Papers*, II, 459–60).

[138] *Nova Scotia Documents*, II, 292.

[139] Charles Town advices, February 12, *Boston Weekly News-Letter*, March 11, 1756.

York under convoy of a warship. There are indications that the total number taken on board was some two hundred and fifty; according to one report, by the time the brigantine anchored at Antigua the figure had been reduced to two hundred.[140] Of the thirty families that began the voyage, but twenty-one reached New York.[141]

The passengers, we are told, upon their arrival were "poor, naked, and destitute of every convenience and support of Life. . . ."[142] To make proper provision for them and also for the earlier arrivals — now totalling some three hundred and thirty-two — the Assembly in July passed a statute that followed largely the pattern laid down by Maryland some six weeks earlier. Under the terms of this law the justices of the peace were required to bind out with respectable families those among the exiles who had not arrived at the age of twenty-one years; the indentures were to run "for such a space of time as they (the justices of the peace) may think proper." [143] It was stipulated in the act, however, that should any be found within this age limit who were "already become useful subjects and able to support themselves by their Labour," they should not be bound out. Significantly, the counties designated in the act to receive the exiles were, with the exception of Westchester on the mainland, located either on Long Island or Staten Island — Suffolk, Queens, Kings, and Richmond — and therefore as far removed as possible from the Canadian frontier.[144]

The third contingent of Acadians that reached New York came from Georgia in bateaux and were headed for Nova Scotia carrying passports given by the governors of Georgia and South Carolina. Reaching Long Island on August 22, they were detained by Governor Hardy, who distributed them "in the most remote and secure parts of this Colony." [145] In practice the young, healthy Acadians seem to have been indentured, with the hope that this would make

---

[140] *Ibid.* The period for which the *Experiment* was employed by Apthorpe and Hancock as a transport in this work was from October 10, 1755 to May 27, 1756 (*Nova Scotia Doc.*, I, 292).

[141] *William Johnson Papers*, II, 459–60.

[142] *Colonial Laws of New York*, IV, 945.

[143] *Ibid.*

[144] However, a number of Acadians were also sent to Orange County. The following distributions of the exiles took place after the law was passed: Westchester received 141; Orange, 81; both Suffolk and Queens, 44; Richmond, 13; and Kings, 9 (Lauvrière, *op. cit.*, II, 114).

[145] *N. Y. Col. Doc.*, VII, 125.

them useful citizens.[146] For example, on August 29, 1756 one hundred and ten of them, fifty-six of whom were girls, were put out to service.[147] A number of those consigned to Westchester County fled to seek refuge and liberty with the French at Crown Point in 1757, but in July were stopped near Fort Edward and returned.[148] As a result of disorders among them, the following month most of them seem to have been placed in temporary confinement.[149] That few of them succeeded in escaping from control is indicated by the fact that in October 1763 the French ministry was informed that there were three hundred of them still within the province living "in the very greatest misery." Most of them, with the establishment of peace, seem to have gone to St. Domingue, and many of these, leaving the West Indies, ultimately found their way to Louisiana.[150]

However unfortunate was the lot of the Acadians placed in the colonies south of New England, it has been asserted — whether justly or not the reader will be able to determine — that the most unhappy of all the exiles were those sent to the latter region.[151] It will therefore be well to examine with some care the nature of the treatment accorded to them by the more northern colonies. In Connecticut the Assembly at its fall session ending in November 1755 — long before the arrival of the Acadians, but in anticipation of their coming — authorized the Governor to issue the necessary orders for receiving and disposing of those exiles that should be allotted to it.[152] Further, the little commonwealth in so acting took the position that the safety of the other colonies was bound up with the safety of Nova Scotia, stating that steps that were being taken "for evacuating the Province of Nova Scotia of its French inhabitants and removing or dispersing them to other places" were measures "consistent with the safety of his Majesty's American dominions." [153] On January 21 the *Elizabeth*,

---

[146] *Ibid.*

[147] Lauvrière, *op. cit.*, II, 114.

[148] *Ibid.*

[149] *Ibid.*

[150] *Ibid.*, p. 175; *Canadian Archives, Report* (1905), I, Part VI, p. 340; Earnest Martin, *Les Exiles Acadiens en France au XVIIIᵒ siècle*, p. 53. It may be pointed out that in an enumeration made of the Acadians in New York under date of November 22, 1763 the number is given as two hundred and forty-nine (Aff. Étrang., Corresp. Pol., Angle., 452 f. 203).

[151] Lauvrière, *op. cit.*, II, 123.

[152] *Connecticut Colonial Records*, X, 425.

[153] *Ibid.*

Captain Rockwell, from Annapolis Royal moved into New London harbour with 277 exiles out of 280 originally embarked upon her.[154] The following day a sloop, Captain Wooster, from Minas Basin bearing 173 more arrived at the same port.[155] Apparently not until the latter part of May did a third transport put in its appearance, the snow *Edward,* Captain Cook, which, as in the case of the *Experiment,* destined for New York, was driven by great storms off her course as far south as the distant Leeward Islands in the West Indies. In leaving Annapolis Royal, she carried 278 of the Neutrals; [156] after being knocked about for six weeks in a turbulent ocean she succeeded in entering an Antigua port on January 19 — undoubtedly English Harbour, the only port then in the British West Indies where vessels could be refitted — with her passenger list now reduced to 260 Acadians; [157] this number was further sharply reduced before her arrival in New London on May 22, for it is recorded that smallpox was raging aboard her and many people were dying.[158]

The very day that the *Elizabeth,* the first of the transports, put in her appearance, the Assembly met on special order of the Governor and an act was passed almost immediately after the news had reached New Haven of her arrival at New London.[159] This statute made disposition once and for all of the Acadians. Each of fifty towns designated in it was made responsible for a certain number of them based

---

[154] *New-York Mercury,* February 2, 1756. Another vessel named the *Elizabeth,* Captain Milbury, carried exiles to Maryland (*Nova Scotia Doc.,* I, 292). These latter were from Grand Pré.

[155] New London advices, January 22, in the *Boston Weekly News-Letter,* January 29, 1756; see also the *New-York Mercury,* February 2, 1756.

[156] There were forty-one men, forty-two women, eighty-six boys, and one hundred and nine girls (John Knox, *Historical Journal,* I, 85).

[157] *Boston Weekly News-Letter,* March 11, 1756.

[158] Francis M. Caulkins, *History of New London,* pp. 469–70. It is possible that it was the *Edward* that entered a Rhode Island port about the middle of January "with about 250 of the French inhabitants of Nova Scotia." The vessel in question, it was stated, was bound for Connecticut and sought shelter on account of contrary winds (*Boston Weekly News-Letter,* January 22, 1756). If it was not the *Edward,* then it is clear that a fourth transport was sent to Connecticut. The sloop *Dove,* Captain Forbes, it is true, sailed from Grand Pré on December 13 with one hundred and fourteen exiles for Connecticut, but her destination seems to have been changed (Winslow's "Journal," Nova Scotia Hist. Soc. *Coll.,* III, 188).

[159] The act was passed before the news came from New London of the actual arrival of the second transport, which entered the New London harbour the day following the appearance of the *Elizabeth.* The preamble states: "Whereas, there is a number of French people sent by Governor Lawrence into this colony, and more daily expected, to be disposed of here, supposed to be about four hundred in the whole . . ." (*Conn. Col. Rec.,* X, 452); actually the two transports brought four hundred and fifty people.

on an estimate of some four hundred to arrive, "or as near as may be a like proportion of the whole number whether greater or less." The two most populous towns, Norwich and New Haven, were each to receive nineteen or in proportion; Fairfield, seventeen; Middletown, sixteen; Farmington and Stratford, each fourteen; Hartford, thirteen; and so down the list until Tolland, Voluntown, Ashford, Haddam, Bolton, and Enfield were each liable for only three. The distribution was placed in charge of a committee of the Assembly, and the selectmen of each town were required "to take care of, manage and support" the exiles, "as tho' they were inhabitants of such town, according to the laws of this Colony." [160] The committee was at the same time charged "to take care in distributing said people, that no one family of them be separated and sent into two or more towns." As to the disposition of the sick or those unable because of age or infirmity to travel, they were to be cared for at the charge of the colony; and those inclined to wander away without written permission from the town designated as their place of residence were to be returned and placed in confinement.[161]

The regulations thus laid down were adhered to apparently without much alteration. New London, however, in addition to the twelve that were its proportion, seems to have entertained others, such as the incapacitated, who, however, were cared for, as stated, at the charge not of the town but of the colony.[162] Some of these exiles, it would appear, finally became contented settlers in the Puritan colony.[163] However, it is quite clear that in 1763 in the month of August six hundred and sixty-six of them — doubtless practically all the sur-

---

[160] The manner of handling the exiles sent to Guilford was doubtless rather typical. On April 12, 1756 the selectmen were directed by the town meeting "to put out to service so many of the French family, which is amongst us, as they can dispose of, without expense to the town, to free it from charge" (B. C. Steiner, *History of Menun Katuck and of the Original Town of Guilford*, p. 233).

[161] *Conn. Col. Rec.*, X, 452–3.

[162] The orderly administration of the regulations is well illustrated in the case of Woodbury. This town was required to care for nine French Neutrals. Two additional families of three persons each arrived there from Maryland in 1757. The selectmen thereupon memorialized the Assembly asking that some disposition be made of the newcomers. The Assembly resolved that one of the families be sent to Litchfield and the other to New Milford (*ibid.*, X, 615).

[163] William Cothren in writing his *History of Ancient Woodbury* in 1854 stated (p. 165) that descendants of the Acadians sent to this town were still living there. In Guilford on April 13, 1772 the town meeting, on petition of "the old Frenchman" who desired to go to Canada, decided that "2 pounds be given to the person who appears to carry him and his family to Albany" (B. C. Steiner, *op. cit.*, p. 233).

vivors — drew up a memorial that indicated the fervency of their attachment to France and her King. In this

> "they implored the protection of the Duc de Nivernais to make it possible for them to return to France in obeisance to His Most Christian Majesty." [164]

While the petition to the Duc de Nivernais did not bring results, in line with this at least some thirty-three of the Neutrals living in New London County managed to reach Cape St. Nicholas in the French West Indian island of St. Domingue,[165] and in the year 1767 — approximately eleven years after their arrival in Connecticut — two hundred and forty left with their priest for Canada on board the brig *Pitt*, Captain Leffingwell.[166] Undoubtedly the secret of the success of Connecticut's administration of its imperial trust was that the authorities came to an early determination to co-operate fully with Nova Scotia and hit upon a plan that was, all in all, just to all parties — including the Acadians themselves — and carried it out with a good deal of consistency and firmness.

The only other colony to the south of Nova Scotia that received the dispersed Acadians was Massachusetts Bay.[167] This colony not only was obliged to assume responsibility, at least for a time, for twice as many of these exiles as any other colony but experienced by far the greatest difficulty in dealing with them.[168] Governor Lawrence had

---

164 Lauvrière, *op. cit.*, II, 112.

165 *Ibid.*, p. 116.

166 Francis M. Caulkins, *History of Norwich*, p. 310.

167 On November 19, 1755 Lieutenant Governor Phips wrote to Governor Benning Wentworth of New Hampshire that Massachusetts Bay was receiving twice as many French Neutrals as its proportion and asked if New Hampshire would not accommodate some thirty families that had arrived from Chignecto (*New Hampshire Provincial Papers*, VI, 445). Captain William Shirley also wrote to Wentworth on November 24 from on board H.M.S. *Mermaid* in Boston harbour indicating the difficulty of convoying transports southward at this time of year and inquired as to what proportion of two thousand exiles — then in Massachusetts Bay or in transports in its harbours — New Hampshire could accommodate under these circumstances (*ibid.*, VI, 446). These requests were submitted by Wentworth on the 27th to the Assembly, which on December 19 accepted a report of a committee that "it would not be for his Majesty's interest to receive any of the French people into their Government, it being a long Frontier & but thinly inhabited & so near the French & Indian settlements that it would be of a dangerous consequence to this his Majesty's Province" (*ibid.*, VI, 452).

168 Two volumes among the so-called Massachusetts Archives (Vols. XXIII and XXIV) marked "French Neutrals" throw light upon the relations of the government of the province with these exiles. Much of the material in these Archives has been embodied in the *Canadian Archives, Report* (1905); see also Pascal Poirier, "*Des Acadiens déportés*

indicated that the number to be assigned to the province was two hundred families,[169] or, roughly, about a thousand persons. By November 12 one vessel with thirty families had arrived at the port of Boston, and it was indicated that other transports were daily expected.[170] As a result, an advertisement was inserted in the November 13 edition of the *Boston Weekly News-Letter* notifying those inhabitants of the colony who might be inclined to take these people into their service or to accommodate them with settlements that a committee of the General Court had been appointed "to place them out in such manner as shall be most for the interests of the Province."

By November 19 over two thousand exiles had arrived in Massachusetts Bay. They all seem to have come from the isthmus of Chignecto and from Minas Bay.[171] It is evident that most of these transports ultimately were sent southward. Yet other vessels continued to come which discharged their unwilling passengers so that a rather heavy burden continued to rest upon Massachusetts Bay, it would appear, for many years. The first of the groups of exiles to arrive after November 19 appeared later in the same month on the *Seaflower*, Captain Downell, carrying two hundred and six of them from the Piziquid River in the Minas Basin region.[172] Many of them were suffering and ill. They found a friend, fortunately, in the person of Thomas Hutchinson, a member of the Provincial Council and later to become Governor of the province and then to suffer exile himself as a loyalist. His benevolence, humanity, and continued solicitude for these unhappy people entitles his name to appear side by side with those of the Marylander Henry Callister and the Philadelphia Friend, Anthony Benezet. It was Hutchinson who went to the *Seaflower*, discovered the condition of the sick widow Benoit, and brought her tenderly to his own mansion, together with her four sons and a grandson, and who exhausted every means unavailingly to nurse her back to health; it was he who granted the poor woman's dying request to protect her children, and to do so waged a long

---

à Boston, en 1755," Royal Society of Canada, *Proceedings and Transactions* (third series), II, 125–80. The student should also consult "The Records of the General Court" of the province, Vols. XXI–XXII inclusive, for light on policies adopted in relation to the exiles. These volumes are also in the state Archives.

[169] *Boston Weekly News-Letter*, November 13, 1755.

[170] *Ibid.*

[171] Lieutenant Governor Phips to Governor Wentworth, November 19, 1755, *New Hampshire Provincial Papers*, VI, 445.

[172] *Canadian Archives, Report* (1905), II, Appendix A, Part III; Pascal Poirier, *op. cit.*, pp. 127–8.

although unsuccessful contest with his own government for permission to keep them in his home under his guardianship; [173] and he it was also who sought to secure for the Acadians as a body compensation for the loss of their estates. We may quote his own words, written with great modesty:

> "A gentleman who was much affected with their sufferings, prepared a representation proper for them to make to the British government, to be signed by the chief of them in behalf of the rest, praying that they might either have leave to return to their estates, or might receive a compensation; and he offered to put it into the hands of a proper person in England to solicit their cause. They received the proposal thankfully, took the representation to consider of, and, after some days, returned it without having signed it. They were afraid of losing the favour of France, if they should receive or solicit for compensation from England." [174]

Hardly had the occupants of the *Seaflower* been cared for than the *Swallow*, Captain Hayes, appeared on December 13 with one hundred and thirty-six from Minas; [175] on December 26 came a third transport with a "considerable number" of exiles,[176] and then between that date and January 15 four more: the brigantine *Helena* from Annapolis Royal with three hundred and twenty-three Neutrals and another from Halifax with an undisclosed number, both on January 5; and the following week a snow with "a large number of French Inhabitants" from "Malagash" and the schooner *Racehorse*, Captain Banks, from Grand Pré with one hundred and twenty.[177] In May came seventy-two Pubnico Acadians who were intended for North Carolina, but were permitted, after much resistance on the part of these exiles to being sent southward, to remain in the province.[178] Finally, in August ninety of the exiles sent to Georgia landed to the south of Boston on their way back to the Bay of Fundy; they were

---

[173] *Ibid.* The children were, however, permitted at length to be domiciled in Hutchinson's home in Milton (Massachusetts Bay, General Court Records, 21: 280).

[174] Hutchinson, *The History of the Province of Massachusetts Bay from the Year 1750, until June, 1774*, p. 41. A footnote indicates that the author was the person who sought to assist them.

[175] Pascal Poirier, *op. cit.*, p. 128.

[176] *Canadian Archives, Report* (1905), II, Appendix A, Part III, 83–4.

[177] *Boston Weekly News-Letter*, January 9 and 15, 1756; John Knox, *Historical Journal*, I, 85; Pascal Poirier, *op. cit.*, p. 130.

[178] *New England Historical and Genealogical Register*, XXX, 18–19; Emile Lauvrière, *op. cit.*, II, 128.

prevented from continuing their journey and, according to Governor Shirley, were "distributed in the Country Towns and provided for." [179] Even after many of these unfortunate people had undoubtedly quietly fled to the region of the St. John, there were in 1763 over one thousand of them living in Massachusetts Bay. [180]

The Provincial Council early in December — with the arrival of large numbers of the Acadians — resolved that Lieutenant Governor Phips should write to Governor Lawrence acquainting him that while the exiles had been received by the province, it was "in expectation of being indemnified from all charges that might arise on their account, and therefore desire his Excellency (Governor Lawrence) will give orders for defraying all such charges." [181] When Phips's letter and the Council's resolve came before the Nova Scotia Council in January, that body requested Governor Lawrence to write to Phips that it was taking the request into consideration. [182] There is no evidence, however, that anything was done or could be done by Nova Scotia to reimburse any of the other colonies to whom had been presented groups of French Neutrals.

Meanwhile a committee of the Massachusetts Bay Assembly was authorized to dispose of the newly landed people in such manner as would be least inconvenient to the province. This involved scattering them among the towns, where most of them were cared for out of the town treasury, since it was impossible during the winter, which was already at hand, for many of them to provide for their own support. [183] On December 23 an act was passed that made the arrangements for the Neutrals more definite. Power was given to the courts of General Sessions of the Peace, as well as to the individual justices of the peace of the counties and to the overseers of the poor, and the selectmen of the towns,

> "to employ, bind out or support said Inhabitants of Nova Scotia, in like manner as by law they would have been impowered to do were they the Inhabitants of this Province." [184]

---

[179] Shirley to the Earl of Halifax, September 4, 1756, *Correspondence of William Shirley*, II, 534. One group of Georgia exiles, as previously indicated, was held in New York.

[180] *Canadian Archives, Report* (1905), II, Appendix A, Part III, 133.

[181] *Ibid.*, II, 82–3.

[182] Minutes of the Council, January 26, 1756, *Nova Scotia Doc.*, I, 294.

[183] *Canadian Archives, Report* (1905), II, Appendix A, Part III, p. 83; Pascal Poirier, *op. cit.*, pp. 142–3.

[184] *Ibid.*

With the idea in mind of securing a reimbursement of all expenses, both selectmen and overseers of the poor were called upon by the law in question to keep an exact account of all money paid out on behalf of the Acadians, which should be transmitted to the office of the Provincial Secretary "in order to ascertain the sum advanced by this Government for the Service and Safety of the Province of Nova Scotia. . . ." [185] A month later — with the coming of additional large numbers of exiles between December 26 and January 15 — it seemed important to establish the principle that the receiving and entertaining of inhabitants of Nova Scotia in the towns "shall not be construed or understood to be an admission of them as town Inhabitants." Not only was a resolution to this effect passed by the Assembly on January 23, but the individual towns were assured at the same time that the cost of maintaining these people would not fall upon the town but would be deemed a province charge, and as such, as has been indicated, the taxpayers were led to anticipate that they would be free of financial responsibility for it.[186]

But the attitude of the Massachusetts Bay Assembly must not be misunderstood. In addressing it on February 13 Governor Shirley said:

> "With respect to the French Inhabitants sent hither from Nova Scotia you seem to think yourselves that it was a necessary measure. . . ."

He then went on to state that he did not believe that Governor Lawrence had any apprehensions that their coming would occasion any considerable charge to the province or would be a disagreeable thing. He admitted his own regret that the care of them was likely to prove so burdensome and then concluded with a word of hope:

> "You have a good deal of encouragement to depend on it that his Majesty will not suffer any unreasonable Burthen to lye upon any of the colonies. I will make full representation of the state of this affair and in such manner as I hope you will receive a favourable answer." [187]

The statute of December 30 proved in practice to be inadequate in many respects to meet the situation. The Neutrals in most instances were without any useful employment. Therefore a new law was pro-

---

[185] Ibid.
[186] Ibid., p. 85.
[187] Shirley's Address to the Assembly, February 13, 1756, Nova Scotia Doc., I, 295–6.

mulgated on March 1 that required the selectmen and overseers of the poor to provide the exiles not only with implements of husbandry, and those for weaving, spinning, and other handicraft work according to the capacity of the individual, but also houses for those families whose heads would undertake to support them. The local magistrates were likewise required, as provided by the earlier law, to give support to those incapable of making a living.[188] Even this legislation, it was found, required clarification. Some of the exiles, with the passing of winter, it would seem, were taken into the service of masters of vessels engaged in either the fisheries or the coasting trade; more of them, it would appear, were inclined to wander about — perhaps in search of relatives or friends, or just to visit with their fellow Frenchmen. This appeared to open up the possibility of "many Inconveniences and Mischiefs," with the result that on April 15 the Assembly passed an act that provided that no person under penalty of ten pounds should ship any late inhabitant of Nova Scotia, and after May 1757 no Frenchman or Frenchwoman should be permitted to leave the bounds of the town to which he or she had been assigned unless with the written permission of one of the selectmen of the town or of the master to whom he or she was indentured. Those who for the second time were found guilty of violating this regulation were to forfeit up to ten shillings and to be publicly whipped up to ten stripes.[189]

That the Massachusetts Bay authorities both provincial and local had taken the problem of the control of the Neutrals vigorously in hand is quite evident.[190] In fact, two days before the enactment of the statute of April 15 the policy of indenturing the children of these unfortunates led to a combined petition, signed by nine heads of families living in six towns, protesting vigorously against the taking away of their children:

---

[188] Canadian Archives, Report (1905), II, Appendix A, Part III, p. 86. The act was to be in force until June 20, 1757 "and no longer." By a supplemental law the towns were again expressly relieved of financial responsibility for the support of those unable to make a living, who would, as provided by the statute of December 30, become a charge against the provincial treasury.

[189] Ibid., II, 87–8. That the tendency of the exiles to wander without permission was not sufficiently checked is indicated by an act passed on August 30 of the same year (1757) that provided three hours in the stocks for the first offence and for the second not exceeding ten stripes "on the naked Back" (ibid., II, 89).

[190] For local aspects of the story see Sara S. Griffin, "The Acadian Exiles," Lowell Historical Society, Contributions, Vol. II, No. 1, pp. 89–107, and G. F. Dow, "The French in Topsfield," Topsfield Historical Collections, 1909.

"It is an outrage on nature itself. Had we the power to choose we would prefer to give up our bodies and souls rather than be separated from our children." [191]

Upon considering it, the Provincial Council sought to prevent the selectmen of towns from binding out the children except in cases of necessity, in which instances it would be obligatory to secure the permission of two justices of the peace of the county in which the children were dwelling. The House of Representatives, however, refused to concur in this merciful measure, with the result that the practice continued.[192] That there was harshness displayed in some cases seems to be indicated by petitions presented to the Governor and Assembly involving the indenture of certain young men.[193] One receives the impression in studying the records, however, that the provincial government was watchful to abate the more serious abuses of the system and on occasion ordered the reunion of families thus separated. Yet even with the families intact there was continued misery among these exiles; they were likewise shifted about a good deal from town to town.[194] How widely the Acadians were dispersed throughout the province is indicated by the fact that as many as ninety-seven towns were required to receive them.[195]

Among those communities that were accused of treating the exiles rather harshly or neglecting them in their misery, according to petitions signed by heads of families, were Hanover, Watertown, Scituate, Wilmington, Methuen, and Lancaster.[196] In each instance the charges seem to have been investigated by the Provincial Council,

---

[191] Canadian Archives, Report (1905), II, Appendix A, Part III, p. 88.

[192] Ibid., II, 89.

[193] See, for example, petitions of April 26, May 4, October 7, 1756; and of January 6 and February 22, 1757 (ibid., II, 103, 107, 109).

[194] The shifting of the French Neutrals may be illustrated by reviewing briefly Salem's experience. On January 15, 1756 the Legoy family of twelve, assigned to this town, appeared; other exiles subsequently either were sent to this seaport or wandered there, so that in June they had increased to thirty-two. Alarmed at this movement, the selectmen in October petitioned the Assembly that all the French people residing there be removed inland for safe keeping; the following January this petition was renewed. In February the Assembly ordered the removal of seven of them to Hopkinton, five to Southborough, eight to Tewksbury, and twelve to Sturbridge (J. B. Felt, Annals of Salem, II, 413).

[195] Pascal Poirier, op. cit., pp. 142–3.

[196] For these petitions see Canadian Archives, Report (1905), II, Appendix E, pp. 103, 107, 109–10, 116, 118. Yet these charges of undue harshness were generally denied. Local historians have defended their towns. For example, A. P. Marvin, in his History of Lancaster, says (p. 252): "These unhappy exiles were kindly treated by our people. . . ."

and where proof existed of bad treatment by the selectmen or others
a remedy was provided.[197] It should be made clear that the infirm
among them, all those incapable of earning a livelihood, were, as a
rule, at best given no more indulgence than was tendered to those
in like circumstances who were inhabitants of the town and who had
fallen on evil days. Yet here and there in the records of that period
there does gleam through the prosaic pages rays of kindliness [198] and
even some toleration for their religion. Their great friend Thomas
Hutchinson, while indicating in his *History* that the public practice
of Roman Catholicism was not tolerated, remarked that

> "no exception was taken to their prayers in their families, in their
> own way, which, I believe, they practiced in general, and sometimes
> they assembled several families together; but the people would upon
> no terms have consented to the publick exercise of religious worship
> by Roman Catholick priests." [199]

While the experience of the Acadians in Massachusetts was far
from happy, as is quite clear, yet they experienced little brutality
from the authorities or the inhabitants — nothing compared to that
exercised toward the Huguenots in France. In the main, families
seem to have been kept together and conditions were such that the
members of these tended to increase rather than to diminish.[200] Most
of those who were able-bodied found it possible apparently to secure
a living that removed them from serious want and the category of
mere objects of charity. Governor Bernard, writing to the Board of

---

[197] While some of the complaints were dismissed as groundless, that there continued to be some abuses in the handling of the Neutrals is evident from the resolution
passed on June 14, 1758 that the selectmen of the towns should assist the able-bodied
among this group to secure employment and "take care that they are not defrauded" (*Canadian Archives, Report* [1905], II, Appendix E, p. 120).

[198] For kind treatment of Acadians in Sudbury see quotations from the records in
A. S. Hudson's *History of Sudbury* (pp. 97–8). For example, Sudbury had the charge of
eighteen Acadians for a period, and in its record of expenditures among the items relating
to the care bestowed upon them one reads, under date of December 11, 1755, of medicines
and medical attention for the "French young woman"; under date of March 22, 1756 was
recorded a doctor's visit "for the old Gentleman who fell off the house"; and under date of
May 1756: "To medicine and attendance for the old Gentleman, the whole month of
May and his wife greatest part of the time, himself when dangerously sick of a fever, violent coughs, and [they] are still remaining in a low languishing condition."

[199] *History of Massachusetts Bay*, pp. 41–2. Hutchinson in continuing his remarks
relative to Roman Catholic priests says: "A law remained unrepealed, that it is to be
hoped it would never have been executed, which made it a capital offense in such persons
to come within the province."

[200] *Canadian Archives, Report* (1905), II, Appendix E, p. 95.

Trade on August 13, 1763, showed a high appreciation of them and of their self-reliance, and he doubtless reflected the general point of view of the province:

> "I know so much of the industry and frugality of these people that I have been very desirous that they should not be lost to British America." [201]

According to a report presented to the General Assembly in June 1766, at the time of the great movement to Canada,

> "several Towns in the Province who had French Neutrals Assigned Them in the general distribution of them have for some Time past been wholly Freed from any Charges on their Account and other Towns Remain at Considerable Charges. . . ." [202]

With respect to public charity, it may be said that between the fall of 1755 and the summer of 1763 the province paid out for the relief of those incapable of supporting themselves and their dependents the sum of £9,563 sterling. [203]

Therefore, taking into consideration all the circumstances — including the determination of some of the towns not to be imposed upon in carrying an unfair burden of their support, and the misconduct of a few selectmen — the record of Massachusetts Bay in its dealings with the Acadians was not a bad one. Nevertheless, when in the month of September 1762 five additional shiploads of these exiles, numbering some fifteen hundred, who had hitherto managed to escape deportation from Nova Scotia, appeared at the port of Boston, the authorities flatly refused to permit them to land. As a result they were returned to the peninsula and for some time kept under guard in the eastern settled portion. [204] One reason assigned for this refusal was that the province had received no reimbursement for the charges of maintaining those already there. [205] Another was that some of the colonies to the southward had, it was felt, either actually or virtually freed themselves of all responsibility for the care of any of the exiles, leaving an unfair burden upon those colo-

---

[201] Quoted by J. G. Palfrey in his *History of New England*, II, 226.

[202] *Canadian Archives, Report* (1905), II Appendix E, 99 and 130.

[203] In some instances whole families were in this category. For example, Braintree was responsible for twenty-one Acadians; of this number but two were fully capable of working (*ibid.*, Appendix J, 243).

[204] Lauvrière, *op. cit.*, II, 128.

[205] J. B. Felt, *Annals of Salem*, II, 413.

nies that had co-operated with Nova Scotia in attempting to deal with a grave problem.

The end of hostilities between Great Britain and France in 1763 saw the Massachusetts Bay Acadians still devotedly loyal to France and to Louis XV, whom they regarded as their King. As in the case of most of those sent to other colonies, they were eager to embrace the offer of the Duc de Nivernais to be carried to France.[206] To accomplish this they applied to Francis Bernard, who had succeeded to the office of Governor. Bernard transmitted this request to the Earl of Halifax, who replied in September that these people were on the same footing as His Majesty's other Catholic subjects in America, and therefore he disapproved of the negotiation that was going on with the Duc de Nivernais. Nor was he happy over the suggestion to collect them all in a body and settle them with a priest on any part of the "eastern shore." [207] However, in October he and other members of the Board of Trade were prepared to signify that the exiles were at liberty to go where they pleased and at the same time made clear that the French Minister had declared that he had no intention of sending transports to carry them away.[208] Before their letter had reached Massachusetts Bay almost three hundred of the exiles had already left for the French colony of St. Domingue in the West Indies.[209] Three hundred more were planning to follow when, with the advice of the Council, Bernard issued a proclamation forbidding this, which brought from the Acadians a strong complaint. Writing of this protest the Governor said:

> "They added that if I detained them ever so long I could never make them English, and I really believe them."

He went on to say however:

> "There is a considerable body of Acadians living near this town (Boston), who, I understand, do not intend to go." [210]

---

[206] A list of heads of families, involving over a thousand persons desiring to go to France, has been preserved (*Canadian Archives, Report* [1905], II, Appendix F, pp. 134–7).

[207] Quoted in J. G. Palfrey, *op. cit.*, II, 226.

[208] *Ibid.*

[209] *Ibid.* Comte d'Estaing, Governor of the Windward Islands, issued a proclamation that all Acadians living in New England who would communicate with John Hanson, New York merchant, would be given transportation to St. Domingue and there receive land and provisions until they could earn their own living (*ibid.*, II, 227).

[210] *Ibid.*, II, 226–7.

It appears, that, in spite of the prohibition, the following year at least one hundred of the exiles followed their compatriots to the West Indies.[211] Moreover, a very considerable number, perhaps even before the migration to St. Domingue, moved across the country to Lake Champlain and followed the course of the Richelieu into Canada.[212]

The great migration out of Massachusetts Bay, however, was not to come until 1766. It may be noted that with the re-establishment of peace the rather rigid regulation of the exiles within the province was relaxed. There was a general movement of them, as a result, to the port towns such as Salem and particularly Boston, where to support their families, now "greatly increased," they turned to the fisheries and town labour; yet, even so, in January 1766 they petitioned the Governor and Council to assist them in getting work and the following month, when the Assembly had not acted upon their memorial, offered another petition that they all might be carried to Canada and supported there for a year with provisions.[213] This appeal was warmly recommended to the legislature by Governor Bernard, who declared in his message:

> "Ever since I have been Governor of this Province I have had great compassion for this People, as every one must who has considered that it was by the exigencies of War rather than any fault of their own that they were removed from a State of ease and affluence and brought into poverty and dependence. . . ." [214]

On February 18 the House of Representatives, ignoring the Governor's message and having in mind the undesirable concentration of Acadians in Boston, resolved that unless they would return to the towns to which they had been assigned, the house rent and provisions they were receiving from the province should be withdrawn. The Council, however, refused to concur, with the result that most of the Acadians continued in the seaports. Both houses, nevertheless, were now in favor of the proposed movement of the exiles to Canada and requested Bernard to write to Governor Murray at Quebec to secure his approval of their coming. This was done and two of the exiles were sent to bring Murray's answer. The latter replied on April 28

211 J. B. Felt, Annals of Salem, II, 413.
212 A. G. Doughty, The Acadian Exiles, p. 157.
213 Canadian Archives, Report (1905), II, Appendix E, pp. 94–5.
214 Ibid., II, 95.

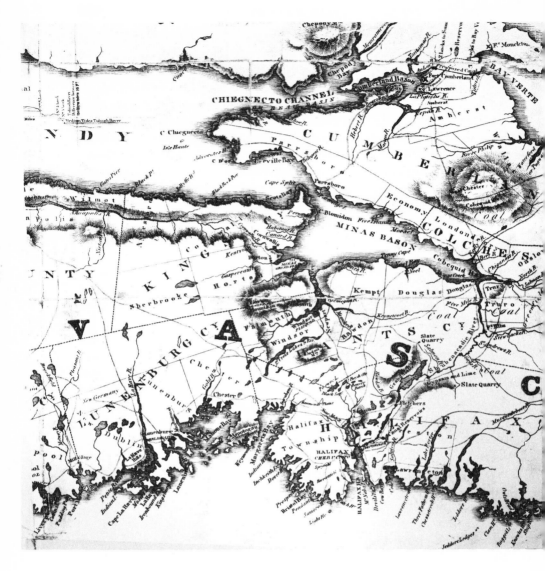

A portion of Nova Scotia in 1829, showing the results of the New England colonization of the peninsula.

(From T. E. Haliburton's *An Historical and Statistical Account of Nova Scotia.*)

that he thought it would be a good thing for the British Empire in general and the province of Quebec in particular to have these people settled there upon the same footing as His Majesty's "New Canadian subjects" and would therefore not hesitate to receive them — but on condition that they take the oath of allegiance, which they hitherto had refused.[215] On June 2 seven hundred and twenty of those in Boston and one hundred and forty in Salem, and also others elsewhere, at last, after so many misfortunes, made their full submission to the King and agreed, as those who expected to be good subjects, to take the required oath.[216] They were now free to go. Some of them were able to secure vessels and left Massachusetts Bay by water for Quebec.[217] Yet for most of them it was really not the province of Quebec that they sought, but the region of their former habitats about the Bay of Fundy. There were, however, no ships available to carry them nor had they been invited back to Nova Scotia by the local government. But what were these obstacles when weighted against them was the prospect of returning to the country of their nativity?

Therefore all those who were fit to march set forth early in the summer and moved slowly along the Atlantic coast with what they could convey. Passing through the Maine wilderness and that of New Brunswick, the great band of pilgrims finally reached the region of their old abodes — a weary journey that took some four months.[218] But everything was changed. New England people were now occupying their confiscated lands; New England houses and communities with New England names had taken the place of things that so long had characterized their country. Yes, old Acadia had passed away forever!

The returning exiles found that already steps had been taken by a royal order in council for a resettlement in Nova Scotia of former Neutrals who had taken an oath so framed by Governor Wilmot that there would now be no "equivocation, mental restriction or reservation whatsoever." [219] Each head of a family was provided with a minimum of forty acres of unsettled land, with ten additional acres for each member of the family; these lands, however, were so lo-

---

[215] Ibid., II, 96.

[216] Ibid., II, 96–8.

[217] Ibid., II, 99–100.

[218] A. G. Doughty, op. cit., pp. 157–8.

[219] For this oath see the Canadian Archives, Report (1905), II, Appendix J., p. 214; for the royal permission to resettle in Nova Scotia, ibid., p. 211.

cated as to prevent the occupants as much as possible from "having any intercourse with the Islands of Miquelon and St. Peter" (Saint-Pierre) — the last remnants of territory remaining to France of her once great empire in North America.[220] In line with this policy, most of those who made the long trek from Massachusetts Bay, after taking the required oaths, were allotted lands along the lower eastern shore of the Bay of Fundy within what are now the counties of Digby and Yarmouth. There they once again built their own villages, once again drained the salt marshes, and at last in undisturbed peace could farm and fish and sail the seas — for they had become His Majesty's loyal subjects and were under his full protection. Yet, preserving their language, their religion, their ancient customs, and their former simplicity of life, they have remained since that day a people apart, forming what one who has written sympathetically of their long travail has called "a hermit community." [221]

Before this chapter is brought to a close the point must be emphasized that those Acadians sent to the British continental colonies represent only a portion of those involved in the great dispersion. Many hundreds of the Neutrals, by hiding in the deep woods, were able to elude for years the soldiers who from time to time sought to round them up for deportation. Again, several thousands of those living within the peninsula succeeded between 1750 and 1757 in going either to Cape Breton or to Isle St. Jean (Prince Edward Island), with part of their herds and flocks; it seemed that in these places they could at last be safe from molestation from the British authorities.[222] In fact, to ensure this they gave their best efforts to strengthen the French cause.

But the capture of the great fortress of Louisbourg in 1758 brought with it the surrender of the two French islands. Once again these expatriates found themselves within the power of the representatives of His Britannic Majesty. In view of their record of disobedience and disloyalty and of the fact that they had taken an oath of allegiance to Louis XV, the British determined to treat them as French prisoners of war. As a result some thirty-four hundred of them, according to estimates, were deported from Isle St. Jean alone — mostly to

---

[220] *Ibid.*, p. 213.

[221] A. G. Doughty, *op. cit.*, p. 158.

[222] In 1752 Isle St. Jean had 2,223 habitants, most of them drawn from the peninsula; in 1758, according to Boscawen, its population numbered four thousand, but according to the Bishop of Quebec, six thousand (Earnest Martin, *Les Exiles Acadiens en France*, pp. 23–4).

France in flag of truce ships.[223] In 1759 the port of Saint-Malo in Brittany received over eleven hundred habitants from these two islands; [224] and to other French ports — to Le Havre, Cherbourg, Morlaix, Nantes, La Rochelle, and Rochefort — likewise came loaded transports in 1758 and 1759 flying the white flag; in the latter year and in 1760 Acadians living in southern Nova Scotia about Pubnico Harbour and those from the St. John country across the Bay of Fundy were also carried to France.[225]

Nor did the refugees from the peninsula who to the number of some thirteen hundred [226] had sought out Miramichi Bay and the Restigoushe, which flows into Chaleur Bay, fare any better. Many of these had been in arms at Beaubassin against the English and when they became established in this region busied themselves, it was charged, in "fitting out Piratical Vessels to cruize on His Majesty's subjects." [227] But Captain Frederick McKenzie, who commanded at Fort Cumberland, led an expedition to their haunts, surprised some seven hundred of them on Chaleur Bay and took them prisoner, and scattered the rest.[228]

At the same time there were in addition some two hundred and forty more Acadian prisoners at Fort Cumberland and four hundred and forty-five at Halifax.[229] The disposition of these people was a grave problem. For the government appeared to discourage the policy of sending more of them to France. One thing seemed clear to the Nova Scotia government: that by and large the prisoners were fanatically loyal to Louis XV and to the same degree were disloyal to the King who had a right to their allegiance, born as they had been, or at least reared from a tender age, within his dominion. It was equally clear that in this frame of mind they could never be useful to the province. Therefore in the summer of 1762 the experiment was tried of loading the prisoners into five ships and sending them to Boston to be disposed of as General Amherst, the commander-in-chief of the forces in America, should see fit. But the general was in New York, and when the transports arrived in Massachusetts Bay the authorities, as was stated earlier in the chapter, refused to permit

---

223 *Ibid.*, pp. 25–6.
224 *Ibid.*
225 *Ibid.*, p. 29.
226 *Canadian Archives, Report* (1905), II, Appendix L, p. 256.
227 Lieutenant Governor Belcher to the Board of Trade, April 16, 1761, *ibid.*, p. 261.
228 *Ibid.*, p. 257.
229 *Ibid.*, p. 256.

them to land their passengers and directed the ships to turn back to Nova Scotia,[230] thus blasting the hopes of Lieutenant Governor Belcher, who was praying that the province be "freed from so inveterate an enemy." [231] In fact, many of the Acadians had thrown away all disguise and boldly declared in 1764 in a petition asking to be sent to France that

> "they never did, nor ever would acknowledge any other Sovereign than the King of France." [232]

Some of these determined people kept their word and went to the French West Indies. Others changed their minds — as did the Massachusetts Bay exiles.

It should now be pointed out that the Acadians exiled to Virginia, who, as has been noted, had been transshipped to England by the provincial authorities in 1756, were given an opportunity in 1763, with the coming of peace, to determine whether or not they should return to America as loyal British subjects, after having taken the unqualified oaths, or be sent to France to join the two thousand other exiles. Their lot in England had not been a happy one. First neglected and then at last treated as prisoners of war, they were retained in the seaports of Liverpool, Southampton, Bristol and Penryn, except for some eighty who were placed on board British privateers; their number also was reduced during the seven years of confinement from over twelve hundred who landed to less than nine hundred.[233] Therefore, after some hesitation and in view of assurances of very liberal treatment given by the Duc de Nivernais, French Ambassador in London, they all decided to accept allegiance to the French King and were transferred to France.

It is to be regretted that the story of the sufferings and wanderings of all those who had at last returned to the country of their ancestors did not now have a happy termination. For disillusionment was to be added to their already cumulated trials and burdens. What the King's Minister Choiseul had in mind for them was to use them to salvage the tropical or semitropical remnants of the French Empire — to send them to the fever-stricken coasts of Guiana or to the Wind-

---

[230] *Nova Scotia Documents*, I, 325.

[231] *Ibid.*, I, 235–7.

[232] Petition of May 1764, *Canadian Archives, Report* (1905), II, Appendix L, p. 258.

[233] *Ibid.*, Appendix G, p. 151. This number also included, it is quite clear, those who found their way to England from South Carolina and probably from other colonies in small numbers.

ward Islands of the West Indies. When most of them refused to go, an almost endless series of schemes was evolved for settling them either in the interior of France or in Corsica. But the truth was they had tasted the freedom of America and most of them refused to consider the idea of becoming mere French peasants as their forefathers had been, even with the promises of special immunities and privileges. It is true that some fifteen hundred of them for a period participated in a bold but unsuccessful experiment to apply in the neighbourhood of Châtellerault in the province of Poitou certain of the teachings of the French physiocrats.[234] But the largest concentration of these refugees, in the neighbourhood of Saint-Malo, remained violently opposed to any of these schemes.[235]

Perhaps the Saint-Malo group realized more fully than did the other exiles what they had sacrificed in loyalty to the French King. For of all peoples in the world of that day, before the period of their expulsion from Nova Scotia, the Acadians were perhaps the most fortunate. Their lands were rich in yield; their herds and flocks grazing in the lush meadows were sleek and numerous; the waters of the bay or the basin, as the case was, afforded them an abundance of fish; they lived without obligation to any government, free of taxes, free of other burdens, such as military service, customarily borne by people living on the land: even free to have priests sent from France. They were indeed feared and courted rather than pitied by the government of the province of Nova Scotia when noticed at all, for their very numbers and their wealth made them formidable to the weak and impoverished British colony. This they were not unaware of and used repeatedly to their own advantage. Now all was changed. As objects of charity they lived in poverty on a pittance granted by His Most Christian Majesty. And for what? these exiles of Saint-Malo may have queried. They not only refused to go to Poitou, but proudly were led to speak as well as to think of themselves as a distinct "nation" and were in consequence bitterly upbraided by the King's representative for presuming that they could place themselves now outside the bounds of French nationality.[236] Having repeatedly refused

---

[234] The plan called for some fifteen hundred of the Acadians to cultivate the land and somewhat over a thousand to engage in handicraft (ibid., Appendix G, pp. 146–8). This experiment is fully set forth in Earnest Martin's Les Exiles Acadiens en France au XVIII° siècle, Part II.

[235] Ibid., p. 110.

[236] In 1773 in addressing Lemoyne, who wanted them to go to Poitou, they said: "You have, sir, submitted [your propositions] to the leaders of our nation" (ibid.).

obedience to George II, they again as repeatedly refused it to Louis XV. It is therefore perhaps not surprising that with the hope of regaining their former paradise some five hundred of them in 1767 should at last have secretly joined in a remarkable plea to George III in which they repudiated every former position they had so zealously taken as against his predecessor. In this they declared that they

> "throw themselves humbly at the feet of your Majesty. . . . As suppliants they venture to make clear to your Majesty that, deceived by the French missionaries, they had the unhappiness to become suspect by the British government; as a consequence they were made prisoners of war and thereafter transported to France. For a long time, Sir, they have not ceased to sigh for a return to their native country, they consider themselves as subjects of your King and their greatest desire is to live under his laws and to give him proof of their unbreachable fidelity. May it please your Majesty to extend his favour to old settlers who only aspire now to bind themselves to his service by the oath of fidelity and devotion which they burn to offer to him." [237]

The plan, of which the memorial was but a part, envisioned the flight not only of the five hundred but it was expected of as many more from Saint-Malo to the island of Jersey, the inhabitants of which had already agreed to aid them in their escape from France. Two of their number moreover, as was emphasized in an earlier chapter, secretly carried the memorial to London, where they succeeded in getting in touch with the former Frenchman Thomas Pichon, who may have earlier made their acquaintance while he was stationed on Isle Royale or at Beauséjour. Pichon agreed to aid them and early in 1768 wrote a forceful letter on their behalf to Pownall, Secretary to the Board of Trade.[238] In this he indicated that through the arrangements that the refugees had made with the people of Jersey they expected to leave France in the month of March so as to be enabled, if possible, to return early that year to their native land.

But the five hundred, it is quite evident, were faced with obstacles in their contemplated flight from France back to their native land. The desire to facilitate this plan, as was earlier indicated, appears to afford the most satisfactory explanation for the shifting of Pichon's place of residence from London to Jersey at this period. For the Brit-

---

[237] *Canadian Archives, Report* (1905), II, Appendix J, p. 251.
[238] This letter is printed in *ibid.*, pp. 250–1.

ish government had agreed not only to offer the expatriates homes in the region north and west of the peninsula of Nova Scotia where in 1784 was erected the Province of New Brunswick but, we are told, to provide them with everything to do so.[239] In the course of what seems to have been prolonged negotiations between the disaffected Saint-Malo group and Pichon and those associated with him on the island of Jersey, a letter coming from the island fell by some mischance into the hands of the French Minister of the Marine in 1772. This made clear the nature of the plans. As a result the Minister ordered a close watch on all the shipping of both Jersey and Guernsey so as to cut off all contacts between France and these islands.[240] How many people succeeded in circumventing the French authorities and fleeing is uncertain. It is clear, nevertheless, that one group of thirty-two found it possible to reach Jersey the following year and presumably were returned to the region of the Bay of Fundy in accordance with the promise of His Majesty's government.[241] But even before the plans for flight to the Channel Islands were exposed, the majority of the Acadians at Saint-Malo had turned their attention to the possibilities of Louisiana. When the King's Minister, Choiseul, insisted early in 1772 that they form a settlement on the island of Corsica, the heads of one hundred and thirteen families insisted even more strongly that they and their families be carried to the Spanish New World province, where already two hundred and thirty families of their old compatriots were established.[242]

In 1773 the Saint-Malo Acadian refugees numbered somewhat over seventeen hundred out of a total of twenty-five hundred in France that were receiving royal support.[243] This Brittany group had but one idea in mind: to return to the New World by some hook or crook. When the achievement of this objective by way of the Channel Islands — and also by way of pledging allegiance to the British Crown — was blocked by the French authorities, permission was asked to go to the French island of Miquelon in the Gulf of St. Lawrence or to Louisiana, now under Spanish control.[244] But they met with no encouragement. Most of them were therefore obliged to continue in France, as objects of charity. With the termination of the

[239] Earnest Martin, op. cit., p. 97.
[240] Ibid., p. 90.
[241] Ibid., p. 97.
[242] Ibid., p. 86.
[243] Ibid., p. 105.
[244] Ibid., p. 110.

hostilities of the American Revolution, and as little reconciled with their lot in 1784 as in 1764, they renewed their appeals to go to the New World.

The French government for its part — after so many times refusing to permit the exiles after their arrival to pass under the domination of a foreign power — was, in view of the increasing financial disorganization of France and the desperate need of funds to stave off bankruptcy, at last reconciled to the idea of their departure, which would also bring to an end royal contributions for their support.[245] However, in securing permission in 1784 to leave, it was understood that they were to go only to settle the lands of the allies of France in the late war and not to strengthen her enemies. They were therefore permitted to make a choice of "Louisiana, Mississippi, Spanish Florida, or a region of the continent of Boston (*ou une contrée du continent de Boston*) to pass the remainder of their days."[246] Those concentrated at Nantes on the Loire — or at least a shipload of them — chose to leave in that year in a Spanish vessel for Louisiana to join the other exiles who had already reached that province.[247] But those of Saint-Malo apparently still thought of the old haunts; and in choosing the "continent of Boston," must have realized that they would not be so far removed at worst and in close proximity at best to the Bay of Fundy. The explanation that they offered to the French government for their preference, however, stressed the fact that by going to "Boston" — where they would engage in such work as each of them could do and thus relieve the King of a financial burden — they would be able to reclaim to the Catholic faith many of tender years who had been carried from Acadia there and reared and instructed according to the rites of the Anglican sect.[248] It is not clear that they came to Boston or, if they did, that they found many of their own people who in their youth had been won over to Anglicanism or to any of the faiths that may more truly be called Protestant.

There was a tendency, as has been indicated, for the Acadians

---

[245] In a "*Mémoire of the Arcadians living in Nantes*" to the Comptroller of Finance, M. Joli de Fleury, prepared in 1781, it was pointed out that there were between twelve and thirteen hundred exiles at this port and that there was due them from the royal treasury up to 1778, on the basis of a grant of six sols a day, the sum of 186,000 livres; and when the grant was reduced in that year to three sols a day, the sum of 62,000 livres (Benjamin Franklin Papers, II, 156, Hist. Soc. of Pa.).

[246] *Canadian Archives, Report* (1905), II, Appendix G, p. 168.

[247] *Ibid.*, p. 162.

[248] *Ibid.*, pp. 162, 168.

wherever they went, even in their earlier enforced exile as well as in their later voluntary wanderings, to find a way to other French-speaking people of the New World — whether in the West Indies, where life for them was insupportable, or in the appealing, broad expanses of Louisiana or of Canada, where sheltered havens finally awaited them. But wherever they established themselves in numbers they remained, as they had become, a distinct people, as sharply distinguished from the Louisiana French Creoles as from the French-speaking Canadians. Their great and tragic dispersion — the subject of a now extensive literature in the form of poem, fiction, and history — will continue to hold the attention of the student and also of the general reader and will arouse, it may be hoped, a sympathetic attitude on the part of mankind toward all uprooted peoples; it could also be hoped that others in a like situation, as this chapter is being written, might meet so kind a fate as these exiles at length received in Louisiana and in Canada — a final reward for their mournful wanderings.

But great as was the blow that fell upon the inhabitants of old Acadia, their dispersion constituted, it should be emphasized, an even greater blow to the imperial ambitions of France in the New World. Even the French physiocrats, the most opposed of any group in France to imperialistic adventure, gave expression in the person of the Marquis de Mirabeau in 1756 to the national aspiration and determination to reclaim Acadia and the Acadians when he declared:

"But, Acadia, fortunate is that minister who will sign the treaty for her restitution!" [249]

Early the following year the French Minister of War, the Marshal Duc de Belle-Isle, writing to Vaudreuil and Montcalm, affirmed:

"We can never make a solid peace with England unless we have Acadia." [250]

But the reconquest of Acadia with the thousands of friendly inhabitants dwelling there with abundant supplies to provision a French army was one thing; a devastated country, devoid of settlers, was quite another. The great problem in logistics of the new military situation now presented, with the Acadian dispersion, was not lost upon the French military experts in Canada. For example, the mili-

---

[249] L'Ami des hommes, p. 541; Earnest Martin, op. cit., p. 3.
[250] Emile Lauvrière, op. cit., II, 57.

tary engineer Michel Alain de Lotbinière (Lobbinière, Lothbinère) in a letter to the Minister of the Marine dated November 2,
1756, after the fall of Beauséjour and the Acadian dispersion, wrote
respecting the plan for this vitally important military move:

> "Besides, attention is to be directed to the fact, that the absolute con-
> quest of this country is meditated; and not to Beauséjour which will
> be always a burthen to us, and which we shall never be able to re-
> tain so long as we possess it alone. The English have deprived us of
> a great advantage by removing the French families that were settled
> there on their different plantations; thus we would have to make new
> settlements." [251]

Never with the resources at their command could the French leaders
now solve this problem — an essential step for the realization of their
larger strategy with respect not only to the peninsula but to their
New World empire. The failure to do so was to spell the ultimate
doom of the citadel of Louisbourg. And with its fall the way was
open to the British to pierce the heart of New France.

But we must now turn from America to observe developments in
Europe that were destined to exert a profound influence upon the
course of the Anglo-French New World conflict.

---

[251] Translation in *N. Y. Col. Doc.*, X, 496.

CHAPTER XI

Britain and Her Continental "System"

OR THE PURPOSES of this study it is important to place in a clear
light the relations of Great Britain with other leading Euro
pean states during the period between the Peace of Aix-la-
Chapelle and the beginning of the Continental Seven Years' War in
1756 and to analyse at least some of the problems that affected those
relations and had a bearing upon the final alignment of the powers
in the tremendous struggle that was to have so profound an influence
upon the future of the British Empire and of all English-speaking
people.

Europe at the period under consideration was a conglomeration of
major and minor sovereignties, some three hundred in number.[1] The
leading states were France, Spain, and Portugal in the west; Sardinia and the Kingdom of the Two Cicilies in the south; the Otto-
man Empire in the southeast; the great Russian Empire and the
Kingdom of Poland in the east; and Sweden, Denmark, including
Norway, and the United Provinces or Holland in the north. In central Europe there were to be found the dynastic empire of the Habsburgs, which included the Archduchy of Austria, the Kingdoms of
Bohemia and Hungary, the Duchy of Brabant, the County of Flanders — the last two administered under the name of the Austrian
Netherlands — and other possessions in Germany and Italy; Brandenburg, the Elector of which was the King of Prussia and also the ruler

---

[1] Were one to count among the independent states the possessions of the free knights
of the Holy Roman German Empire the number would be over eighteen hundred.

of newly acquired Silesia and of a number of smaller states scattered about Germany; Saxony, the Elector of which was King of Poland; Hanover, the Elector of which was the King of Great Britain and Ireland; and, finally, the Electorate of Bavaria. Sandwiched in among these major German states were others of scarcely less importance, both lay and ecclesiastical, jostling others of no importance at all — innumerable principalities and non-principalities, states without cities and city-states. Theoretically Germany and northern Italy were embraced within the Holy Roman German Empire and theoretically the ruler of this Empire enjoyed certain rights and exercised certain powers truly imperial in nature. After the Treaty of Westphalia in 1648, however, all that really remained to the person given by election the imperial honour were certain outward and very formal trappings of a throne that at one time had bade fair to be a powerful agency for German unification but now became purely symbolic of a political ideal that had failed. In the eighteenth century the leading German states therefore conducted their foreign relations and developed their foreign policies in accordance with their individual needs and aspirations, and frequently these were in conflict with those of the person occupying the imperial throne, who after 1740 was Maria Theresa. Such briefly was Europe in the eighteenth century and such was Germany within the heart of Europe.

During the period under survey the relations of Great Britain particularly with Hanover, with Holland and Austria in connection with the operations of the so-called "System," with Russia, and with Prussia respectively, among the states enumerated above, are of such significance in their bearing on this study as to demand somewhat detailed consideration, which will be presented in the order just given. Before this, however, it would be well to make certain observations upon particular British characteristics of the eighteenth century that affected the diplomatic situation.

The people of Great Britain, while of European stock, did not by and large look to the Continent in the eighteenth century except for trade, for travel, fashion, and finery, and for inspiration in the arts. With a culture that was basically European but that had separated itself from both the prevailing ecclesiastical systems of the mainland and the Continental systems of jurisprudence; with an exuberant agriculture, industry, and commerce; with a chain of prosperous colonies yearly growing in importance; with commercial interests of vast scope embracing the then known world, the national outlook was in some respects peculiarly insular and non-metropolitan, and in other respects certainly metropolitan and almost global — a people passionately fond of rural life had become the core of a vast and dynamic empire. But geographically and dynastically Britain was bound to the Continent; her government was also bound to it by treaties. Two assets she possessed that gave her importance in the eyes of all European potentates great and small: her navy, which in size had outdistanced by far its nearest rival, and her unchallengeable financial position, that had come about as the result of the progressive development of her varied economic resources during the first half of the eighteenth century through the unleashing of the energies of the nation — a development fostered by a government now securely dominated by great landowners, industrial entrepreneurs, and city merchants rather than by idle courtiers or professional soldiers. But hand in hand with these assets in any game of power politics there went two serious drawbacks in seeking Continental allies: the lack of a professional standing army commensurate with the Kingdom's wealth and influence in world affairs, and the lack of a government that could act decisively in the field of international commitments without too much regard for local public opinion and popular demand. While Louis XV of France, Frederick II of Prussia, Maria Theresa of Austria, and Elizabeth of Russia could each — after having won the support of a small circle of powerful court aristocrats and generals — by the nod of the head embark his or her nation upon a certain course of action that seemed desirable and thereby set great armies into motion, George II was compelled to rely constantly upon the advice of his ministers as to how far his people would permit him to go; nor did he have an army to command, outside of a few scattered, depleted regiments. Writhing under constitutional restrictions unknown in other great European states, the British King with a German mentality could testily declare to Lord Holderness, who begged him to return to London from Hanover in the summer of 1755: "There are sufficient kings in England."

These two defects that Britain laboured under as a state in the European system — if defects they really were — stemmed from the same source: the determination of the English people in the eighteenth century — after experiencing in the seventeenth the invasion of the sanctity of their homes by the troopers of Charles I, the inquisitorial supervision of the major generals of Cromwell, and the ominous hovering about London and Westminster of the mercenaries of James

II encamped at Hounslow Heath — that never again would a professional army stand between them and the enjoyment of the liberties
and immunities of their Common Law and never again would a ruler
arrogate to himself the claim to interpret the constitution of the realm
in such a manner as to place himself above it. On the contrary, the
armed forces and the King were now bound securely by those restrictions that Parliament alone was competent to make, embodying as it
did after 1689 the sovereignty of the nation. Yet this statement standing alone is inadequate to clarify the real position occupied by George
II. When his father came from Hanover to accept the throne, he did
so as the direct descendant of an English King. Stripped as that
throne had been of certain great and sovereign powers by the Glorious Revolution and its aftermath — with its results embodied in the
Bill of Rights and the Act of Settlement — one may be sure that had
the throne likewise been stripped of all the honour and dignity that
had appertained to it for so many centuries, neither of the first two
Hanoverians would have been interested in occupying it. In agreeing
to ascend it they each in turn conferred a great favour upon the nation, which otherwise would have been sorely embarrassed. Therefore, while it is true that, at least from the beginning of the eighteenth century, the Great Seal, the once mighty weapon of English
royal prerogative, could be used no longer in derogation of the will
of Parliament and, in fact, only in harmony with the broad purposes
and intentions of that ancient High Court, the King's position was
one of the greatest honour and influence — lawyers continued to
speak of his "prerogatives" and still do. George II not only was consulted *pro forma* by his ministers with respect to national policy but
himself made decisions that bound the latter so long as they held
office — which was still within his gift. The limit of ministerial com-
pliance with the will of the reigning monarch could only be measured, as a rule, by the limit that Parliament, in control of the purse
and the armed forces, set. This, in the middle of the eighteenth century, was by no means narrow — and for very good reasons. The
Whigs, who controlled the Commons as well as the House of Lords,
historically were great friends of Parliament and great enemies of
the royal prerogative as wielded by the Stuarts, but they were at all
times deeply devoted to the institutions of monarchy and as deeply
committed after 1714 to the maintenance of the Hanoverian dynasty.
George, when checked, could by the merest threat of retiring permanently to Hanover give the leaders of this party cold chills. That

A portion of *An Accurate Map of the North West Part of Germany.*

(By Eman. Bowen [1756], indicating the possessions of the elector of Hanover.)

he never carried this threat into action evidenced the fact that the King was not unaware of the advantages of his restricted throne, and, even if grudgingly, accepted the fact that what he was as Elector of Hanover he could never hope to be as King of Great Britain. Thus there was created and maintained something of a formal balance between the older royal and the newer parliamentary authority, between the reality of the past and that of the present. Such was the constitution of Great Britain in 1754 and such are its chief characteristics even today, in spite of its historical evolution.

Great Britain and Hanover were bound together only by a so-called personal union. Each therefore maintained its own distinct government and laws, its ministerial council, its treasury, and its armed forces. Thus George combined in his person the inherited kingship of Great Britain and Ireland, the Arch-Treasurership of the Holy Roman Empire,[2] the Electorship of Brunswick-Lüneburg (generally referred to as that of Hanover), and the ducal titles of Calenberg with Hanover the capital, of Lüneburg-Zell with Lüneburg the capital, of Verden with the town of the same name the capital, of Bremen — but not the free city — with Stade the capital, and of Saxe-Lauenberg with Ratzburg the capital; he also had claims to the Duchy of East Friesland. The first four of these diminutive duchies[3] lay between the Weser and the Elbe and the fifth, to the east of the latter stream. Small as these were they did not constitute a solid block of possessions; in the case of Calenberg, the lower portion of the Duchy, containing the city of Göttingen — where George II in 1734 founded the University of Georgia Augusta and in 1751 a royal society of science — was quite separated from the other two main portions of it by the Duchy of Brunswick-Wolfenbüttel and also by the Bishopric of Hildesheim, each quite independent of it at the time. The intertwining of the indescribably complicated interests of various German princes is also illustrated by the condition of the

---

[2] In 1692 the title of Standard-Bearer of the Empire was conferred upon Ernest, grandfather of George II, by Emperor Leopold; but in 1709 the Duke of Württemberg took this title and Elector George received the title of Arch-Treasurer of the Holy Roman Empire.

[3] "The duchy of Hanover, also called Calenberg, from a castle that was formerly the residence of the prince, is bounded on the north by Lunenberg-Zell; on the east by the dutchy of Brunswic-Wolfenbuttle, and the bishopric of Hildescheim; on the south by Grubenhagen, which Moll calls Brunswic-Luxenburg; and on the west by the county of Schwenburg; extending thirty-three miles from north to south, and eighteen from east to west" (D. Fenning, J. Collyer, and others, A New System of Geography or A General Description of the World [1765], II, 202).

County of Schauenburg just west of the Weser — some thirty miles in length and twenty in depth. It was shared by the Elector of Hanover, the Landgrave of Hesse-Cassel, and the Count of Schauenburg-Lippe.

But these tiny principalities controlled by George were not to be despised. Not only did they provide him with annual revenues from their silver, iron, copper, and salt mines, from taxes on merchandise, inns, cattle, and other sources, computed to range from four hundred thousand to seven hundred thousand pounds, but they could furnish him on demand without difficulty an army of between thirty and forty thousand men. They also provided him with numerous satisfactions that he could not find in England. Within his electorate he was among his own people and the real master of them. It must not be forgotten that at the time he arrived in England with his father in 1714 he had spent from the day of his birth over thirty years among his fellow Hanoverians; his tastes and habits of life were by that time firmly fixed — they were German.

On the Leine, within his walled and fortified city of Hanover, was George's palace, partially rebuilt with great magnificence after the fire of 1741. There the government offices of the electorate were to be found; there the Elector met his privy council and his commissioners of war; there also were the electoral opera house and the theatre for the French comedians, in which concerts and plays were given weekly or biweekly throughout the winter; there an open table in the banquet hall was kept even when George was absent in England, where his chief administrators were regularly dined — reminding one at least in this respect of the old German institution of the *comitatus*. Attached to the palace was the church of the Electors, where Henry the Lion after his journey into the East in 1171 had placed a treasure of great value consisting of relics, gold and silver plate, and gems and where were to be found the memorials of the ancestors of the Elector. Then in the summer there was George's palace of Herrenhausen, only two miles distant from Hanover, built by his grandfather in 1670 at the same time that Louis XIV was embellishing Versailles. Here were doubtless the most magnificent gardens in all Germany and one of the finest orangeries in all Europe; here beautiful cascades, fountains, and basins stretching off in the distance delighted the eye; here the famous *jet d'eau*, built in 1716 by Benson that forced the water some seventy feet into the air and that, according to one commentator, "perhaps exceeds anything of the kind in the whole world "; here also a sylvan theatre adorned with statues and "cut out in green seats," with arbours and summer dwellings for the actors. Pray, what more could any mortal demand than George enjoyed in Hanover?

One may therefore understand why the King-Elector always felt himself to be rather an exile in London even among British people who paid court to him: there he dwelt at rather shabby St. James's when living in the city; there the real business of the Kingdom was transacted at the Cockpit or elsewhere than at the royal residence; there the ministers were concerned not only with immediate and familiar things but only too often with those far removed from the royal presence and interest — it might be by thousands of miles, and identified with utterly strange places — and there a Parliament sat in which Commoners had from time to time dared to speak contemptuously of Hanover. One may also understand why George was, above all things, determined so long as he was King to see that British foreign policy should never fail to take into consideration the welfare of his personal possessions and why he refused for many years to admit to his presence or favour William Pitt, who at the beginning of the War of the Austrian Succession, in opposing Carteret's policy of taking into British pay Hanoverian troops, had in the House of Commons referred to Hanover as a "despicable electorate."

However much Englishmen would have preferred in the past to ignore political developments on the Continent, they had not been able to do so — nor could they do so in the middle of the eighteenth century. In fact, long before the personal union of Britain and Hanover, even before the days of the Norman Conquest, the people had been made to realize that what went on directly across the narrow English Channel, as well as across the wider North Sea, might have a most vital bearing on their lives. Conquered by the Danes and then in 1066 by the Normans, centuries after these events Britons watched with apprehension any development on the Continent that might lead to a repetition of the experience. Especially did they watch developments in the Low Countries, and have done so down to our own day. Under Elizabeth they rejoiced at the revolt of the Netherlanders against Philip of Spain's despotic rule. But only the northern Protestant provinces persisted in resisting His Most Catholic Majesty and, in winning their independence, became the United Netherlands; for the southern Catholic provinces submitted again to the rule of the Spanish monarchs. But it is important to point out in connection with this study of the diplomatic background of the war that was to be ignited in Europe in 1756 that the peace that came with this reunion of Flanders and Brabant with Spain was bought with a great price that had to be paid for two centuries to come. Antwerp, the chief city and the most important commercial centre of Europe in the middle of the sixteenth century, not only had to endure the shattering Spanish Fury of 1576 but in the Treaty of Münster (or, as it is frequently called, Westphalia), signed in 1648, which brought to a close the Thirty Years' War, lost all its earlier significance. Spain, to receive in other respects an advantageous peace settlement, met the insistent demands of the Dutch for an open acknowledgment of their absolute independence from her and for the closing of the Scheldt River to all navigation — a stream that took the largest ocean-going ships and that had made Antwerp one of the wonders of the world and the heiress of great Venice. The river, once closed, remained so, except for brief intervals, until 1814.

The people of the United Netherlands even after 1648 had to face new threats to their independence. These now came from Louis XIV. It is therefore not surprising that after the unsuccessful attempts of the *Grand Monarque* to conquer Holland, and after the French armies that had overrun Flanders and Brabant in the course of the War of the Spanish Succession had been driven out by the troops of the Grand Alliance directed by the towering military genius of Marlborough, the Dutch should have demanded not only that the Scheldt remain closed but that they should be given the right to garrison the principal fortresses along the dreaded French border within what had been the Spanish, and had now become the Austrian, Netherlands as a result of the Treaty of Rastatt, signed in 1714, between the Empire and France. Britain, in view of a solemn pledge to support these demands given most reluctantly to Holland in 1709 in the midst of the war and even in face of the strong opposition to such commitments on the part of British merchants with large financial interests in some of the cities of Flanders, now firmly supported the Dutch, who had on their part pledged to help guarantee the Protestant succession in England in favour of the house of Hanover.[4]

---

[4] Townshend, a Whig, had in 1709 negotiated the treaty with the Dutch providing for English support of the continued closing of the Scheldt and the garrisoning of the barrier forts; in 1712 the Tory Party, in control of the Commons, voted that the treaty contained "several articles destructive to the trade and interest of Great Britain" and that

The year of the Treaty of Rastatt saw the Hanoverian succession installed in Great Britain. George I, whose family had been traditionally loyal to the Emperor and the Habsburg dynasty and who himself for a time had commanded the imperial forces in Germany in the war, desired to reconstruct the alliance between Britain, Emperor Charles VI, and the United Netherlands that had gone on the rocks in 1712 on account of the bad faith displayed by the Tory ministry toward the British allies as a result of a movement toward isolationism; and his views were heartily supported by the new Whig ministers. There was urgency. France was seeking to evade an article in the Peace of Utrecht that provided for the dismantling of Dunkirk, which the British had much at heart, by building a new war port at Mardyk, near by. Moreover, Emperor Charles, now lord of Flanders and Brabant, was strongly opposing the Dutch demand respecting the Barrier fortresses. Charles, however, at last agreed to accept his loyal supporter George as mediator between the Empire and Holland. As a result of complicated negotiations,[5] in the midst of which the British envoy in Vienna made clear that it was feared in England that the Emperor was engaged in far-reaching arrangements with France, Charles was led to sign with Holland the famous Barrier Treaty at Antwerp on November 15, 1715, and this agreement, in view of the pledge of 1709, was guaranteed by Britain. Thus were the former allies once more bound together by defensive arrangements.

According to the terms of the Barrier Treaty, Holland alone was given the right to provide garrisons for Namur, Tournay, Ypres, and other strong places facing the French border, using either her own troops or such as the Emperor had no reason to suspect; the governors of the Barrier towns, while nominated by the Emperor, were expected to take an oath of fidelity to the States General and another oath to maintain the fortresses for the house of Austria; further, within the Austrian Netherlands between thirty and thirty-four thousand men were to be kept under arms at the common expense of the two powers, Holland paying annually into the Barrier Office at Ypres three fifths of the total charge, amounting to four hundred thousand crowns, and the Emperor the remainder.

those who advised its ratification were "enemies to the Queen and Kingdom" (I. S. Leadam, *History of England from the Accession of Anne to the Death of George II*, p. 194). The Whigs, however, returned to power in 1714.

[5] William Coxe, *History of the House of Austria*, II, 22-5.

Thus the Emperor theoretically came into full possession of the Spanish Netherlands as the result of the formal agreement between the Empire and France. The truth, however, is that the latter did not really possess them to give. Indeed, the army of the Grand Alliance, made up not only of imperial troops but of British, Dutch, Northern Germans, and Danes under command of Marlborough and largely kept in the field by England, had driven the French troops out of them and before and after the peace they were still garrisoned by the Dutch. In other words, when Charles VI, much against his desires, signed the Barrier Treaty of 1715, it was certainly in recognition of the fact that Austria had acquired the Spanish Netherlands under conditions that gave her something far short of full sovereignty over them. This fact should be kept in mind in view of later developments.

The close of the War of the Spanish Succession saw the disappearance of Holland as one of the great states of Europe. In fact, she hovered on the edge of national bankruptcy, in spite of the wealth drawn from her Far East possessions, from her fisheries, and from her many domestic industries; for she faced the problem of servicing an immense debt accumulated in the course of her wars, and taxation had reached the limit of endurance for her people.[6] She also disappeared as a naval power that needed to be reckoned with; for her navy, composed of not more than thirty ships, was, when not laid up for repairs, largely engaged in convoy duty with her merchant ships sailing to the Far East or in protecting her Mediterranean trade from the Barbary corsairs. Vulnerable from attack by land, even with the protection of the dikes that could be cut, the limited resources that could be devoted to defence were largely concentrated upon the support of a few mercenary regiments and of the troops of her seven sovereign states or in otherwise buying protection from other states.

In the final analysis the chief security of the United Netherlands before 1754 had come from the existence of what has been called the "System." Its historical basis is of interest. Between the Treaty of Münster (1648) and 1674 England and Holland had fought three wars involving commercial and colonial supremacy. These wars had

---

6 "The inability of the States [the United Provinces], labouring under the load of an immense inextricable debt & exposed to a defenceless Barrier, and the impracticability of the Court of Vienna in not coming into reasonable means for the security of the Dutch, will render them entirely useless at a great emergency . . ." (Horatio Walpole, former British Ambassador at The Hague, to Newcastle, May 18, 1754, B.M., Add. Mss., 32,735: 285-9).

witnessed the final eclipse of the latter by her rival. The year 1677, however, saw the marriage of William of Orange to Mary, daughter of the Duke of York, and the year following this the conclusion of a defensive alliance directed against France by the representatives of the two states and involving the control of the Barrier towns of the Spanish Netherlands. Here was the beginning of the "System." The core of this in the eyes of Englishmen, stated in simple terms, was the idea that any aggressive power must be kept from the Low Countries. The War of the Spanish Succession involved not only this principle of state action but one even more vital: that France must not be permitted to dominate Europe and the New World by taking over Spain and her possessions. The "System" was therefore expanded — in the creation of the Grand Alliance in 1701 — to include the concept that the Austrian Habsburgs must be supported as against the French Bourbons — making for an exemplification of the principle of an effective "balance." Again in 1714 it was enlarged when George I became King, to include the concept that Hanover must, whenever necessary, be protected.

The year following George's accession Louis XIV died, leaving a great-grandson of four as heir to the throne of France. Philip Duke of Orléans now became Regent. Under his regency and that of his successor, the Duc de Bourbon, up until the year 1730 there was, in contrast to the earlier bitter antagonism, a close understanding between France and Great Britain, and the "System" was, as a result, pretty well in abeyance, with Britain and Holland openly opposing on more than one occasion the designs of Austria. Indeed, one may say that whenever the "System" possessed effectiveness it was largely the result of the moral influence and material resources that Great Britain contributed to it. When her two associates developed differences, she had to compose them, if possible. If compelled to make a choice between Holland and the Empire, she supported, as a rule and also as a matter of self-interest, the former, but in such a way as not to alienate the latter too seriously.

For example, in 1722 Emperor Charles had sought, by issuing letters patent to the Ostend East India Company, to put aside Article V of the Treaty of Münster, which forbade the people of the Spanish Netherlands to trade with the East Indies — considered in 1648, the year of the treaty, a part of possessions of the Spanish Habsburgs, since they then still claimed Portugal and its Empire. Great Britain supported Holland in upholding the binding power of the treaty;

each of the Maritime Powers had a flourishing East India Company and neither wanted another rival. But, to secure the suppression of the Ostend Company in 1731, the two were obliged to guarantee the Pragmatic Sanction promulgated by Emperor Charles VI to protect the imperial rights of his daughter Maria Theresa. This guarantee was honoured in 1743 when Britain organized and largely subsidized the so-called "pragmatic army" — composed of Austrians, Dutch, Hessians, Hanoverians, and British under the direct command of King George II — to defend Austria and her possessions against the claimant to the imperial throne, Charles Albert of Bavaria, and his ally, Louis XV of France. For these last-named powers were now determined to overthrow the Sanction and to dethrone Maria Theresa, who had come to the throne in 1740 upon the death of her father.

While George II, with the outbreak of the War of the Austrian Succession, had hoped to reconstruct the Grand Alliance of 1701 by including Frederick II of Prussia, the latter had attacked the Empress-Queen by invading Silesia. George therefore had to content himself with a treaty signed in 1742 with Frederick mutually guaranteeing the territories of the two and thus protecting Hanover from attack by Prussia, then allied to France. At first Great Britain played the role of auxiliary to Austria in the war just as France was an auxiliary to Bavaria, and this was true when the Battle of Dettingen was fought; but in 1744, with an open declaration of war between these two powers, they became principals in the so-called Second War of the Austrian Succession. Bavaria under its new ruler accepted the Sanction, and Frederick dropped out in 1745 as the result of the Treaty of Dresden, signed with the Empress-Queen, which followed the Convention of Hanover between him and George, again providing a mutual guarantee of territories and thus leaving France in the lurch. Austria, also at war with Spain over disputed Italian claims, was supported in Italy by Sardinia and also by the British fleet, for the Anglo-Spanish war that began in 1739 and had been languidly fought was now merged in the larger conflict.

The declaration of war between England and France in 1744 saw the outbreak of hostilities in America and in India; it also saw a French army under command of Marshal Saxe enter the Austrian Netherlands, defended by the Duke of Cumberland, now the commander-in-chief of the British, Dutch, and Imperial forces. After the defeat of the allies at Fontenoy in 1745, Tournay fell and then

Ghent, in spite of Cumberland's efforts to relieve the latter. With the Jacobite insurrection in Scotland, the British contingents were rushed back to England to combat Prince Charles. Saxe now had to face only the feeble Dutch and Imperial resistance. Crushing all opposition, he occupied in turn Oudenard and Ostend before the close of the year's campaign, and very early the following year his troops began to advance again. Brussels fell; then followed the surrender one after another of Louvain, Mons, Antwerp, Charleroi, Namur, and Liége, in spite of the presence once more of British troops. Again the Austrian Netherlands were at the feet of France. Only Maestricht in Dutch Brabant was left to cover Holland, and even a token surrender of this was provided for in the Treaty of Aix-la-Chapelle, signed in 1748.

Once more France by treaty was compelled to give up her conquests in the Netherlands, and the Empress-Queen, in spite of protests, was compelled to reconsign the Barrier fortresses to the weak protection of the Dutch. But the point to be noted is that when the Netherlands were returned to Austria at the end of the war, it only came about as the result, on the one hand, of the unwillingness of the British ministers to see France in continued possession of them and, on the other hand, of their willingness to make the very genuine sacrifice, in the face of colonial protests, of surrendering Cape Breton Island with the great fortress of Louisbourg. Therefore when Maria Theresa received them back it was under these peculiar circumstances and also with the same conditions and limitations of sovereignty under which she and her father, Charles VI, had held them previously.

The restoration of quiet in Europe with the ratification of the peace terms in 1748 thus saw again the survival of the "System," badly shaken as it was. However, the events of the war had indicated very clearly that to preserve it Great Britain would not assume unlimited liabilities in Europe — that she would not, for example, protect the eastern possessions of her ally the Empress-Queen from Prussia. Indeed, the two conventions entered into by George II and Frederick — that of Westminster in 1742 and that of Hanover in 1745 — were clear notice to the world that while the British would fight any great power attempting by aggression to lay hands on the Low Countries, they could not be concerned over the fate of Silesia in connection with the claims and counter-claims to it set forth by

Austria and Prussia respectively — reminding one of the attitude
of the Chamberlain government in connection with the German-
Czechoslovakian crisis preceding the present World War.

Frederick, however, would have been fought without hesitation,
it is well to bear in mind, had he invaded either Hanover or Holland,
or the Austrian Netherlands, in the treacherous manner in which
he had Silesia. His ability to do so, at least with respect to Hanover,
was very great, should the notion enter his head — striking as he
could have from his own possessions lying both east and west of the
Electorate. Happily, he had other objectives and, moreover, was
wary of bringing Russia down upon his back while assaulting Hanover. For Britain had abundant means of setting in motion against
him the forces of the Czarina Elizabeth, whose government was actually in the hands of her powerful Chancellor Bestuzhev, a statesman bitterly anti-Prussian as well as bitterly anti-French. It may be
noted that in 1746 the Chancellor had offered to send a hundred
thousand men into the field against the enemies of Austria and crush
all resistance in a year if the two Maritime Powers would provide a
subsidy of six million pounds; this offer, however, had been refused.
Nevertheless, late in the following year — as the result of the continued victories of Marshal Saxe in the Netherlands and the consequent danger to Holland — the subsidy treaty of St. Petersburg was
signed and ratified. This provided that Russia should concentrate on
the Courland frontier facing the Kingdom of Prussia, as a purely
precautionary measure, an "observation army" of thirty thousand
men and should send another army of equal strength under Prince
Repnin to the Rhine to operate against France, with Great Britain
paying the expense of the army of observation and sharing with Holland the expense of the army coming to the assistance of the latter.[7]
The approach of these troops undoubtedly was a factor that led
France to agree to an armistice, in spite of the victorious sweep of
Marshal Saxe's army.

Maria Theresa, it can be said, therefore, preserved the Netherlands not because she could defend them from France but because
of the "System" and, more specifically, because of the sacrifices of
Great Britain. So long as the Habsburgs and Bourbons continued
their traditional rivalry this would hold true in the future as it had
been in the past. But dependence on the "System" placed the Em-

---

[7] R. N. Bain, "Russia under Anne and Elizabeth," Cambridge Modern History, VI,
317–18.

press in a disadvantageous position; for she could not really be mistress in what she regarded as her own house. This she bitterly resented. Could she arrive at a complete understanding with France so that she had a strong friend rather than a dangerous enemy over the border of the Netherlands, one also allied to her other enemy Prussia, all this would be changed.

Indeed, France was regarded in 1748 as possessing not only the finest army in Europe, of some two hundred thousand regulars, but in Marshal Saxe the best strategist.[8] In spite of her weakness on the seas she was, in fact, regarded as the world's leading military power. With Louis XV as an ally, therefore, the Empress-Queen felt she could confidently look forward to continued security in the Netherlands; she could look forward, moreover, to eliminating the Dutch permanently from the Barrier fortresses; and, what was of even greater importance, she could have at hand the means of rescuing Silesia from the grasp of Frederick. But to turn an implacable and traditional enemy into a friend demanded management. This was provided by Wenzel Anton Kaunitz-Reitberg, Count of Kaunitz and later Prince Kaunitz. By his shrewdness France was to be led to exchange a tremendously virile ally for one that could in her hour of need bring little support to bear against a rival, Great Britain, far more dangerous than Austria had ever been to her. As the result of this motivation in favour of a new international alignment having its source in Vienna the "System" was to disappear.

Kaunitz had ably represented Austria at Brussels from 1744 to 1748, where Charles of Lorraine was administering for Maria Theresa, and at the Congress of Aix-la-Chapelle, where he had shown great resistance to the Dutch demands respecting their joint claim to the Netherlands. After this, with his growing reputation at court he began implanting in the minds of his associates there the idea that Prussia was the real enemy of his country and that the traditional alliance with the Maritime Powers must therefore be exchanged for one with France. All this had of course the blessing of the Empress-Queen, whose Council of State, however, was still dominated by devotees of the "System." Appointed as Ambassador to the court of Versailles in 1751, the following year Kaunitz took up his work in France

---

8 There seems to have taken place in 1748 some reduction in the number of French regulars. "We are now very well informed that there will be a reform in the King's troops of 200,000 men, and that only 180,000 will be kept on foot" (Paris Advices, November 25, 1748, *Maryland Gazette*, April 26, 1749).

after the most careful preparation. His very coming after proper delay was such as to impress Louis XV and his entourage. Entering Paris in September, he presented an almost regal appearance. William Mildmay, the British commissaire, gives a description of the procession, consisting of

> ". . . five state coaches with the richest Embroidery & Harness I ever saw, these were preceded by 6 Running footmen, or pages, 20 Grooms with Sumpter Horses & thirty livery servants. . . ." [9]

Mildmay some two weeks later wrote:

> "I cannot help reflecting how little of the Imperial treasure is spent in our city [London], from whence such large Subsidies [to Austria] are granted; the very house the Ambassadour here hires to live in amounts to £1200 pds. Sterling a year for its rent without furniture, a Sum perhaps equal to what the Imperial Resident spends in England for all articles together." [10]

With such an introduction, the Austrian Ambassador was able, under cover of the most solid and open assurances to Great Britain that his country was indelibly committed to the maintenance of the "System," to work for its liquidation. His residence in France, nevertheless, was of short duration; for in 1753, after having quietly laid the foundation for the reversal of the Austria alliances, he was recalled to Vienna to assume the office of Chancellor and leadership in the affairs of state. It would probably not be correct to state that the policies he now introduced were anti-British in the same sense that they were anti-Prussian and pro-French. It would seem that what he sought above all things was to isolate Prussia. Russia had come into an agreement with Austria. Were France to follow suit and Britain and Hanover at least to remain quite neutral, Austria would have little to worry about in coming to grips with Frederick. But Britain and France were themselves slowly but surely drifting into hostilities again. Were the choice of an ally between the two possible, France rather than Britain would now, it seemed quite clear, be of greater value to Austria, provided she could be led to renounce her acknowledgment of Frederick's claims to Silesia and break her alliance with him.

---

[9] William Mildmay to the Earl of Fitzwalter, August 29, 1752, Mildmay Private Correspondence, Clements Library.

[10] Mildmay to Fitzwalter, September 19, 1752, Mildmay Private Correspondence.

Under the Kaunitz plan large French armies, leaving the Netherlands in tranquillity, could strike at Frederick's possessions about the Rhine and move eastward through friendly country such as Saxony against Brandenburg; at the same time Russia could move westward against Prussia proper; this would give Austria in the midst of a threefold movement the utmost freedom to concentrate upon driving Frederick out of Silesia. After the completion of these tasks the allies could converge upon Berlin. But in preferring France to Britain for these reasons the Chancellor certainly had no desire either to drive Austria's traditional ally into the arms of Prussia or to permit France to feel that in embracing Austria she was making any sacrifice in the interests of Maria Theresa. On the contrary, she must be made to feel that she herself had achieved an important diplomatic victory in securing the friendship of the Empress-Queen, whatever might thereafter be the fate of her understanding with Frederick.

With the gradual closing of the old breach with France the attitude of Austria toward the maintenance of the "System" progressively hardened. But the British ministry — not fully aware of Kaunitz's secret moves — saw the great importance of supporting it, with war looming in America. While France, at least potentially, was much weaker in the New World than was Britain, it seemed that the chief danger to the latter lay in the ability of the armies of Louis XV to strike at Hanover through the Austrian Netherlands and Holland and thereby secure compensation for losses that might be sustained in North America.[11] Therefore this inviting avenue, in the eyes of Newcastle and his associates in the ministry, must remain closed to France, and Austria and Holland within the "System" must help to see that this was done.

But difficulties loomed before the British in revitalizing the "System," and for reasons that they did not suspect. Certain facts, however, were clear. Kaunitz, when acting as the Austrian plenipotentiary at Aix-la-Chapelle and after learning that peace preliminaries had been signed between France and the Maritime Powers without consulting his country, had heatedly declared that the Barrier Treaty had been abrogated. He had also rejected the demand of the Dutch that France should deliver the Barrier fortresses to Holland and Austria as joint sovereigns of them. Yet Maria Theresa had not been prepared to break with Great Britain in 1748 nor had the latter been

---

[11] Richard Waddington, *Louis XV et le Renversement des Alliances*, p. 126.

prepared to see the "System" shattered beyond repair. Once again, therefore, the British had held the balance between the unfriendly allies. Bentinck, the Dutch plenipotentiary, and Kaunitz had been brought to make mutual concessions whereby it had been agreed that the Empress-Queen would recognize the old right of the Dutch to garrison the Barrier fortresses while preserving her own "sovereignty" over them [12] — whatever in practice that meant.

One issue had still remained between Austria and Holland, an issue too difficult to resolve even with the British envoys, the Earl of Sandwich and Sir Thomas Robinson, using all of their tact. The Dutch had insisted that Austria should continue the subsidy payments covering garrison duty and pay the subsidy arrears; Kaunitz had as vigorously insisted that those payments relating to the past should be cancelled and those relating to the future should cease because the Barrier forts were no longer defensible. This problem of subsidy payments had therefore been left to subsequent negotiation.[13] As to the issue involving subsidy payments to Austria by the British, the latter had taken the position that the sum still due to the Empress-Queen, amounting to one hundred thousand pounds, should not be demanded because of her failure to supply the number of troops agreed upon. Kaunitz, however, had made clear that Austria would not ratify any peace treaty unless this was done. The British ministry, after a good deal of expostulation against the justice of this demand, had finally given way. Austria thereupon had acceded to the treaty. The "System," badly shaken, it is true, had therefore, as was previously indicated, emerged from the peace negotiations still a fact, with the right of the Dutch to preserve watch over the Barrier towns; but the claim of the Maritime Powers, as set forth by the Earl of Holderness, that the Netherlands, "Conquered with their blood and treasure, were delivered to the House of Austria as a deposit on the condition of defending those territories against the French," [14] had been rejected by Kaunitz; just as had Kaunitz's counter-claim that the people of the Netherlands no longer were bound by the trade restrictions that had arisen from the international agreements of 1648, 1715, and 1731 been rejected by the British and Dutch.

The situation in 1754 respecting the Low Countries, in the eyes

---

12 William Coxe, op. cit., II, 355.
13 Ibid., II, 356.
14 Holderness to Keith, April 26, 1754, ibid., II, 372.

of the British ministry, may be summarized in the words of New-castle:

". . . Our negotiations with our friends will give us as much trouble as those with other powers. The affair of the Barrier is still where it was, the Dutch pressing one way, with whom we join and shall do so in the strongest manner, and the Court of Vienna hitherto doing nothing, but sometimes giving fair words which end in nothing. The point in dispute between us is this. The Austrians look upon themselves as unconditional Sovereign of the Low Countries and therefore at liberty to lay what burthens they please upon our Trade, and further assert that without that liberty, they shall not be able to raise money enough in all the Austrian Netherlands, to pay the Dutch subsidy. To this we constantly insist that that Sovereignty is limited by the Barrier Treaty, that Flanders is, in some respects, to be looked upon as a Country in common between the House of Austria and the Maritime Powers; and is considered as such by the Grand Alliance of 1701, was, upon that foot, conquered by the arms of the allies, and given up upon conditions by the Maritime Powers, to the Emperor Charles the Sixth. They pretend they want the money to pay their Troops. We insist (and with justice) that they keep more Troops, vizt. 24,000 men in Flanders, than by the Barrier Treaty they ought to do, and therefore those Troops should not be paid by the Subsidy due and stipulated for the Dutch. In short, nothing has been wanting or shall be omitted that may bring the Court of Vienna to reason upon this head. But as partial as I am to them I must own that that is not always to be done." [15]

It must be re-emphasized that the "System," from the point of view of both the Dutch and the British, embodied the fundamental conception that the two maritime nations must possess guarantees that the Netherlands would remain free not only of French control but also of the absolute control of any great power. Enemy Spain for that reason had been curbed in 1648 as had been allied Austria in 1715. Therefore no matter how strongly Kaunitz might insist that Maria Theresa, their faithful friend, must be permitted to protect the Lowlands with her own troops, he was met with equal insistence that this protection must be, as it had been in the past, a matter of joint arrangement. Nor was he more successful in demanding that the old restrictions of trade that the Netherlands laboured under should be removed. That either he or the Empress-Queen in making this latter demand was thinking primarily in terms of the welfare of these pos-

[15] Newcastle to Horatio Walpole, May 14, 1754, B.M., Add. Mss., 32,735: 268–72.

sessions may be questioned; the repeated efforts to exchange them for Bavaria indicate the absence of any deep attachment to them.[16] On the other hand, both Kaunitz and Maria Theresa were certainly by 1754 secretly committed not only to the idea of an internal re-organization of the Empire but to that of its external reorientation — with the Netherlands sinking more and more into the background as their plans evolved, until it was tentatively agreed that they should be exchanged, as will be noted, for northern Italian possessions.

The inhabitants of the Austrian Netherlands certainly laboured under very real disadvantages and discouragements. Their unhappy situation was the result broadly of historical development and more specifically of the grave decision that their ancestors made in the sixteenth century: that the principle of religious orthodoxy and uniformity, as against religious toleration, was more important to them than that of political independence. For, turning their backs upon the Dutch, their comrades in arms in revolt, they had been led, as has been indicated, to acknowledge allegiance to Philip II and thus had accepted a subordinate place within his Empire in preference to a status of perfect equality in an independent Netherlands state such as William the Silent was at the time seeking to erect. Thereafter for some two centuries and a half they were to remain shackled to some great European state. In fact — without considering the period of temporary domination from 1792 to 1812 of Revolutionary France in the Lowlands — not until their enforced union with Holland in 1814, by no means one of political equality, were they destined to see the effective reopening of the Scheldt for commerce and at last to find themselves once again in a position of at least commercial equality with their northern neighbours of the dikes; and not until 1831, with their successful revolt, were they to attain a really independent position commercially as well as politically as a result of the decision of the London Conference of that year. Then it was that they were, significantly, given as their King, Leopold of Saxe-Coburg, closely related to the English royal family.

It would hardly be fruitful to pass in review all the proposals advanced by Kaunitz and the counter-proposals of the British Cabinet Council during the two years before the final collapse in 1756 of the Anglo-Austrian alliance and the "System." [17] In the midst of a be-

---

[16] Henri and Jacques Pirenne, "Belgium," Encyclopædia Britannica (14th ed.).

[17] For a very detailed and fairly satisfactory account of this see Richard Waddington's Louis XV et le Renversement des Alliances; of particular value are the extended quotations from the correspondence and memorials of leading statesmen.

wildering series of moves, now forward and now backward, in this diplomatic chess game with London, Kaunitz, perhaps the most astute but not the most far-seeing statesman of the eighteenth century, was, it is clear, skilfully preparing for the creation of a new Austrian "System" and for a declaration of independence from those who had been the most consistent and determined supporters of the Habsburg Empire, but who did not hesitate on occasion to remind him and the Empress-Queen of the extent to which both the British and the Dutch people had made sacrifices in giving aid.

In November 1754 Robert Keith, British Ambassador at Vienna, reported that the Chancellor refused to renew the entente so long as the Netherlands were under commercial restrictions.[18] Early the following year Newcastle indicated to Keith, in way of reply, that upon Kaunitz would rest the responsibility, if through his stubbornness the alliance of the house of Austria with the Maritime Powers was terminated.[19] In March Keith was able to send more satisfying assurances regarding Austrian intentions. He now found the court desirous of new discussions while still insisting on a treaty of commerce favourable to the Netherlands. Kaunitz, he was convinced, was as little pro-French and pro-Prussian as possible.[20] In that same month Count Colloredo, the Austrian Ambassador in London, submitted a *mémoire* embodying a plan for the reciprocal guarantee of the possessions of the three powers. This would commit Britain to support not only in the Netherlands ten thousand English troops and, with the aid of the Dutch, eighteen thousand Hessians, Saxons, and Bavarians, but also, on the borders of the Kingdom of Prussia, sixty thousand Russians. Prussia, not France, was the enemy to be most feared by all, according to the Austrian *mémoire*:

> "It is therefore the King of Prussia who confuses all measures and who as a result exposes England and Holland to the greatest dangers in engaging the attention of the forces of the Empress." [21]

While the British ministry welcomed this renewal of interest in the alliance, it could not consider the sending of its own troops, precious few in number, to the Continent for barrack duty nor could it contemplate the great charges involved in subsidizing such numbers of other troops. It did agree in April, however, to maintain four-

---

18 *Ibid.*, p. 128.
19 *Ibid.*
20 *Ibid.*
21 *Ibid.*

teen thousand Hessians, Saxons, and Bavarians in support of the "System" if Austria would guarantee to protect Hanover.[22]

It was at this juncture of affairs in the spring of 1755, with Boscawen under orders to strike at the French fleet, that the King determined to go to the Continent in order to place Hanover and the Netherlands, if possible, in a position to parry a likely blow from France. The Earl of Holderness, it was agreed, should join him. Holderness, arriving in Brussels on May 2, reported to Newcastle the situation respecting the defences of the Netherlands — a situation that might have led to suspicions as to the nature of the relationships developing between Maria Theresa and Louis XV. The borders of that international dependency were, he found, almost undefended; of the twelve thousand Austrian troops now maintained within Flanders and Brabant — but half the number maintained the preceding year — at least half of them were in Luxembourg; the frontier fortresses left in ruins by the French were still in ruins; also the Dutch had seen fit to concentrate most of their troops at one point, Namur, leaving other places quite exposed. In going to The Hague he soon discovered that even the friends of the "System" within the Dutch government were in a discouraged frame of mind. They were now quite prepared, in fact, to turn over to Austrian protection most of the Barrier towns, since they had become persuaded that Holland's own forces and resources would hardly be able to protect her own borders. Indeed, they sought to be relieved of all the old commitments under the "System," as well as those of recent date.

The Dutch, it is now clear, were taking steps to retire into a position of strict neutrality with respect to the conflict between England and France; this they conceived they could afford to do in the light of the cordial relations developing between France and Austria, which meant quiet within Flanders and Brabant so long as these relations continued. Thus sheltered, they doubtless hoped to be able to recuperate their strength. But to do so they had to be rid of their international financial as well as military obligations. In 1750, for example, as an insurance policy for the safety of Hanover and of the Netherlands, Great Britain had signed a subsidy treaty with the Elector of Bavaria which had also been subscribed to by Holland and Austria. This provided that he was to receive an annual payment of £40,000, one half of which would be contributed by Parliament

---

[22] *Ibid.*, pp. 130–1

and the remainder shared equally by the Dutch States General and the Empress-Queen.[23] The following year another subsidy treaty had been signed with the Elector of Saxony providing for the payment by Parliament of £32,000 and by the States General of £16,000.[24] In each instance the recipient of the subsidy had agreed not only to furnish six thousand soldiers to aid the Maritime Powers in case the latter were attacked but also to vote for King George's choice as King of the Romans in the next imperial election, which was Joseph, the eldest son of Maria Theresa.[25] The financial obligations as embodied in these treaties the Dutch, as has been indicated, now sought to avoid.[26]

As to the question of the imperial election, Elector George was deeply apprehensive that should Francis, the husband of Maria Theresa, die before the selection of a successor to the Empress-Queen, war again would break out over the imperial succession. He therefore had visualized the election of Joseph as necessary to the maintenance of the "System." But with all his efforts he could never count on more than five out of eight required votes in the electoral college,[27] with Prussia (Brandenburg) leading the opposition to the election, supported by the Elector of the Palatinate and the Archbishop of Cologne, who also had a vote. In fact, in order to secure the election of Joseph at this time it became clear to the government of Austria that so many demands in the way of concessions would be made upon it by those possessing votes that it would not be possible to meet them, and consequently it lost interest in the election — preferring to secure the future of the reigning house by means that it was not prepared to disclose to the British ministers. The British also lost interest in the election.[28]

One thing, however, was evident: that neither Holland nor Austria

---

[23] Journals of the House of Commons, XXVI, 24-5.

[24] Ibid., XXVI, 371-2.

[25] Coxe, op. cit., II, 368-9.

[26] Waddington, op. cit., p. 133.

[27] He could count on the votes of Hanover, Bohemia, and Mainz; after the subsidy treaties also on those of Bavaria and Saxony (Coxe, op. cit., II, 368-9).

[28] Newcastle, in writing to Keene on April 28, 1755, pointed out that nothing had been done to renew the subsidy treaties with Bavaria and Saxony, although these powers were anxious for a renewal: "We have given no Answer to their Proposals, And whenever we do, And if finally, with Holland, We should agree to renew these Treaties, I do assure you, that it is not, in the least, with a View to the Election of a King of the Romans" (B.M., Add. Mss., 32,854: 299).

would support Great Britain in the New World conflict with France. Kaunitz made that abundantly clear to Keith in the spring of 1755 respecting the attitude of the Empress-Queen. The Chancellor insisted that the old equilibrium in Europe had been overturned by the rise of Prussia and that this state, although less powerful, was not less dangerous than was France to the peace of Europe. Only when the proposed British-Russian treaty had been signed would Austria, he indicated, feel free to send any large body of troops to the Netherlands.[29] When Holderness wrote from Hanover to the British Ambassador at Vienna expressing hope of the prompt conclusion of a Russian negotiation but at the same time making clear that the King insisted that Austria should send without delay some thirty or thirty-five thousand troops to the Low Countries, this demand was deeply resented at the imperial court. In the reply penned by Kaunitz and handed to Keith it was declared that "if the armies of the Empress were in the pay of Great Britain they could not be disposed of more decisively." [30]

Still the Chancellor continued his proposals — proposals that he must have realized would never be accepted. He declared that thirty thousand Austrian troops might be sent — provided that Great Britain would support twenty thousand more, and Holland eight thousand, likewise to be stationed in the Netherlands, and also provided that George would make clear not only how far as Elector of Hanover he would go to support the Empress but also to what extent as King of England he was prepared to enter into subsidy treaties, in addition to the treaty with Russia (providing for a Russian army) that he hoped to conclude; and, finally by what means he would assure Austria that the King of Sardinia would not move against her in Italy.[31] All this, in the eyes of the British taxpayer, would have opened up an unfathomable abyss into which the treasures of the country would have to be poured. No minister could have gone before Parliament with such a set of proposals. In fact, Holderness, still in Hanover, by the early summer of 1755 was becoming convinced that Austria was not acting in good faith. In writing to Keith he asked to be informed as to the nature of the instructions given to Count Stahremberg, who took Kaunitz's place at Paris, and as to the character of the conversations the Austrian was having with the French

---

[29] Waddington, op. cit., p. 134.
[30] Précis of the Verbal Response given to Keith (ibid., p. 136).
[31] Ibid., p. 138.

Minister Rouillé; he did not hesitate to add that other courts as well had come to suspect Austria's duplicity.[32]

Whatever else may be said about British diplomacy at this period, it cannot be charged that the government was not sincerely devoted to the maintenance of the "System" and of the most intimate relations with the imperial court. King George, it must be re-emphasized, was a man of fixed ideas, devoted to traditional attitudes. The thought of breaking with the Habsburgs, who had received from the Electors of Hanover such a measure of devotion over so long a period of time, seems never to have entered his mind before the summer of 1755. Therefore, even when his British Minister, Holderness, had given up all hope of maintaining the Austrian defensive alliance, he encouraged his Hanoverian ministers, Münchhausen and Steinberg, to draw up an elaborate plan for the defence of Hanover, the Netherlands, and Austria against any attack on the part of France and Prussia. This envisaged the signing of the Anglo-Russian subsidy agreement that would provide a Russian army ready to move; the organization of a second large army to be furnished principally by Austria, Saxony (Poland), and Hanover and the posting of it in Germany so that it could come to the aid of any one of these states or their possessions if attacked; finally, the concentration in the Netherlands of a third army made up, on the one hand, of eighteen thousand British, Hessians, and Bavarians in the pay of Parliament and, on the other, of an equal number of troops to be furnished by states of the Empire, such as Württemberg, to which, under the circumstances, Austria would doubtless add at least twenty-four thousand.[33]

This comprehensive Hanoverian plan of Continental defence, sent to Newcastle in July, produced consternation within the British Cabinet Council, for, like the Kaunitz proposals forwarded in the spring, it involved vast expenditures for subsidies, and English public opinion was reacting strongly against the idea; the plan also seemed to subordinate the American crisis to Continental power politics. William Pitt in the preceding war had voiced his violent opposition to the payment of subsidies to European rulers for their support and was still strongly opposed to them. Also, when George at this period carried to completion a treaty with the Landgrave of Hesse-Cassel for the maintenance of eight thousand troops in British pay and the

---

[32] *Ibid.*, p. 139.
[33] *Ibid.*, pp. 141–2.

Council of Regency in London endorsed it, the Chancellor of the Exchequer, the Honourable Henry Bilson Legge, refused upon constitutional grounds to sign the necessary warrants to implement it.[34] The Hanoverian project was therefore consigned to oblivion with that of Kaunitz.

Reference has repeatedly been made to the negotiations for an Anglo-Russian treaty. This seemed to be of vast immediate importance to Austria and also to Hanover and of indirect importance to Great Britain for the purpose of holding Frederick of Prussia in check should he, in support of France, move against the allies embraced within the "System." [35] But during the first half of the year 1755 slow progress was made in the direction of consummating it. Elizabeth was uncertain at this moment how far she wanted to commit Russia; and Chancellor Bestuzhev, while agreeable to the idea, sought to squeeze the last advantages from such a treaty for his country — and also for himself. In the spring it was determined to recall the British envoy at Moscow, Guy Dickens, who was neither in the best of health, over-energetic, nor popular with the Great Chancellor, and put in his place, with the rank of Ambassador, Sir Charles Hanbury Williams,[36] who was at least energetic and who, incidentally, at the time bore no love for Frederick of Prussia. At first the latter was not more successful than was Dickens in getting the Russian court to agree to a proper pact. He was authorized by Holderness in June, however, to raise the amount of the annual subsidies Great Britain was willing to pay; this, with liberal distribution of money to those in the Russian court who were prepared to oppose any pact unless thus personally favoured, led in September, after the expenditure of so much effort, to the signing of a four-year defensive alliance.[37]

---

[34] I. S. Leadam, op. cit., pp. 436–7.

[35] Newcastle, referring to the court of St. Petersburg, said in 1754: "It is and must be a material Court, as that Court will be better able to keep Prussia quiet, than all the rest of Europe besides" (Newcastle to Horatio Walpole, June 29, 1754, B.M., Add. Mss., 32,735: 397–8).

[36] Williams was born a Hanbury but took the name of his godfather with his inheritance. In 1747 he was in Dresden, in 1750 in Berlin, but returned to Dresden after Frederick refused to communicate with him; in 1752 we find him in Poland and in 1753 in Vienna. He was a man of considerable ability but had a faculty for antagonizing influential people and cannot be compared in achievement to Keene at Madrid. His career has been most competently dealt with by D. B. Horn in his Sir Charles Hanbury Williams and European Diplomacy, 1747–1758.

[37] Ibid., pp. 186–92.

The Anglo-Russian treaty provided that Russia would supply a corps of fifty-five thousand men that would be held available to proceed immediately to support either the states of the King of England or those of his allies if they were attacked; some naval assistance was also guaranteed, consisting of a fleet of galleys in the Baltic. For this support Great Britain agreed in case of war to send a fleet into the Baltic and to obtain from the King of Poland, who was also the Elector of Saxony, free passage for the Muscovite army through Polish territory; Great Britain also agreed to pay each year in time of peace £100,000 for the support of the corps and with the outbreak of hostilities at the rate of £500,000 as soon as the Russian army passed beyond its own borders. Finally, the treaty contained a separate and secret article that provided for

> "an engagement to communicate with one another confidentially and faithfully everything that could have relation to any negociation with the common enemy." [38]

Williams, it is well to point out, was deeply committed to the principles of the "System" and felt that his achievement would be hailed at home as a triumph.[39] But, to his chagrin, by the time that his treaty reached London for final ratification, opposition to it and to any subsidy treaty had come to the point where it could not be easily ratified. Newcastle, however, was strongly in favour of implementing it and thought that it was designed to prevent the hostilities with France from becoming a European war. Writing in November to Sir George Lyttelton, who was about to take Legge's place as Chancellor of the Exchequer, he stressed the efforts that he and Hardwicke had put forth to guard against such an eventuality. Then turning to the dislike of subsidies, he declared:

> "But this is not a Reason, why a Measure which has been in Negotiation for above Two Years, had been approved by all the King's Ministers, & even spoken of in the House of Commons with Approbation, which is the Case of the present Treaty with Russia (which we receiv'd Yesterday sign'd, in the Manner, which had been proposed,)

---

[38] For the treaty see Waddington, *op. cit.*, pp. 152–3.

[39] Williams may well have felt that he had made a good bargain. The Russian soldiers were good fighters and he had brought into British service fifty-four thousand of them at a maximum cost per year of £500,000; whereas it was estimated in 1755 that it cost annually £628,315 to support only 18,857 British troops (*New-York Mercury*, December 22, 1755).

why such a Measure calculated for preventing a War upon the Continent, should now be rejected, or contemn'd. . . ." [40]

In taking this position Newcastle, it is important to note, was favourable to the treaty not because he was now so much concerned over the possibility of an attack on Hanover by Frederick but because of the possibility of using the Russian army for the protection of Hanover against France. In fact, with the progressive deterioration in British relations with Austria, conversations with the Prussian King, as will be emphasized later, had taken place during the summer, looking to a declaration of neutrality on his part in connection with the Anglo-French war. As a result, these conversations had progressed so far that early in October Newcastle, unaware that a treaty had already been signed, had written to Williams that the wording of the proposed convention when framed in London had rested upon a supposition that Hanover might be subject to an attack by Frederick, who at the time that the Ambassador had received his appointment and instructions had logically been considered the enemy both of the electorate and of Great Britain as well as of Russia; this was no longer true, Williams was notified, and it would therefore be necessary for him to revise the text. However, it was too late to do so. The Ambassador was thereupon compelled to make clear that the expression "l'ennemi commune," which in the minds of the Russians had meant Prussia, now meant France. This was far from satisfactory to Moscow. Nevertheless, while sharp words were exchanged between the two courts and the treaty was never ratified, the relations between Russia and Great Britain in the Continental Seven Years' War remained, although short of friendship, with the two countries fighting on opposite sides, at no time openly hostile. Prussia remained the great enemy of Russia, and France that of Great Britain. [41]

---

[40] B.M., Add. Mss., 32,860: 273–4.

[41] Chancellor Bestuzhev, it is clear, did not want to break with a power capable of rendering him personal favours. Grand Duchess Catherine was also in need of money and sought financial aid of England. As a result in July 1756 the Chancellor was granted a pension, and £10,000 was bestowed upon Catherine. But the influence of the two at the Russian court waned. On December 31, 1756 Russia acceded to the Austro-French treaty. Not until 1758 was Bestuzhev, however, placed under arrest on a charge of conspiring with Catherine to recall from the field the Russian army operating against Prussia (Historical Manuscript Commission, Third Report, pp. 126–7; D. B. Horn, op. cit., pp. 280–3).

CHAPTER XII

The Rivals Find New Friends

T HE STRENUOUS EFFORTS of the government of Great Britain to maintain the "System" involving Hanover, Holland, and the Habsburg Empire have been surveyed, as have the tortuous negotiations for the purpose of implementing a subsidy treaty with Russia that would bring that power fully into line with British Continental policy. The reversal of alliances, as embodied in the Convention of Westminster between Great Britain and Prussia early in 1756 and the Convention of Versailles between France and Austria in the late spring of that year, must yet be considered. Before taking up the history of the Anglo-Prussian *rapprochement*, however, it would be well to set forth briefly the course of Anglo-French diplomacy in the early months of 1755 and also British political developments of an internal nature brought about by the issue of the subsidy treaties.

With respect to France's relations with Great Britain in the spring of 1755, it may be pointed out that although the Duc de Mirepoix was persuaded early in May, as has been shown in an earlier chapter, that Admiral Boscawen had sailed to America with secret orders to attack the French fleet, and was given leave by Rouillé to remain in London or to return to France as he saw fit, he decided to remain and even rented a new establishment near St. James's Square, which caused Newcastle to remark that it "does not look as if He intended soon to leave England."[1] This may not be attributed solely to his guilelessness. There was desperate need for France to stave off open hostilities until she had brought her navy up to desired strength and had won support in Europe. With Prussia cool and with Spain fa-

---

[1] Newcastle to Holderness, May 16, 1755, B.M., Add. Mss., 32,854: 544.

vouring a strict neutrality, she was indeed isolated for the moment. With her navy too weak to face the enemy and with most of her great military force unavailable to employ against it, she was in a paradoxical situation. Crying out to the world that Great Britain was planning aggressions in North America against her, it did seem to be inconsistent, to say the least, to proceed, as the Foreign Office recommended, to attack those Continental neighbours who had in no way directly menaced her, who, on the contrary, had shown most peaceful inclinations, and whose only fault had been ties of friendship with the English.[2]

Therefore it is not surprising that Mirepoix should, with nonchalance, on May 10, six days after expressing his fears to Rouillé that Boscawen would attack the French fleet, secure an interview with Newcastle to ask him if it would be agreeable to His Majesty King George if François de Bussy were appointed to attend the latter in Hanover as the representative of His Most Christian Majesty. To this Newcastle replied with equal nonchalance that

> ". . . the Person of Mon^r Bussy would neither be agreeable or disagreeable to the King."[3]

To the Duke this diplomatic gesture of the French Foreign Office was simply an effort to indicate that France had at present no thought of giving disturbance to any part of His Majesty's dominions "either here or in Germany or even of Entering upon Hostile measures in the Empire."[4]

Newcastle himself proceeded likewise to maintain the same outwardly friendly attitude toward the French court that he had previously shown. In June he sent to the Marquise de Pompadour a supply of his favourite beer.[5] It well may be that he still had some faint

---

[2] Information as to proposals for attacks upon France's neighbours and opposition to these proposals was sent at this time by the secret service in Paris to Colonel Yorke at The Hague (B.M., Add. Ms., 32,853: 221–3).

[3] Newcastle to Holderness, May 16, 1755, B.M., Add. Mss., 32,854: 544.

[4] *Ibid.* De Bussy, it may be pointed out, was, while earlier in London, in British pay. Writing very privately to Holderness about the Frenchman, Newcastle says: "My Letter to the King is singley upon Bussy's Subject, who was formerly in our Pay when He was in England. I wrote to His Maj^ty to know His Thoughts, & Pleasure upon it, Whether if Bussy should come to Hanover, he should endeavour to revive this Correspondence, And how, & by Whose Means, to do it" (B.M., Add. Mss., 32,855: 1). In 1761 de Bussy was sent to England to negotiate with Pitt as to the means of putting an end to the war.

[5] Mirepoix to the Duchesse de Mirepoix, June 2, 1755, Waddington, *Louis XV et le Renversement des Alliances,* p. 99.

hopes that His Most Christian Majesty, through the Pompadour's influence, would not see fit to consider the British plans to eject the French from their encroachments in America a provocation for a European war. Likewise, between the latter part of April, when Mirepoix had written: "There is no longer any hope of reconciliation," [6] and July 15, there continued to be exchanges of futile memorials regarding the disputed points in America, each side maintaining resolutely its position without yielding any important particular.[7] No clearer indication of the real attitude of the British ministry regarding the French demands can doubtless be found than are contained in Robinson's plain-spoken letter to the British Ambassador at Madrid, Keene, under date of April 28:

> "Your Ex[cy] will find that the Plans and Sentiments of France truly analysed, & examined, are in Effect no more than if they had Spoke out & said, 'Lay down Your Arms & leave Us in Possession of what We have usurped, till, by tiring you out with a negotiation of two years, we can obtain Confirmation of our Exhorbitant Pretensions by a Treaty; or if you can not do this, by way of Preliminary, give us immediately a Communication through your Seas, & through the Heart of Your Countries from Europe to Quebec. Give us as much as we shall ask of your antient Colonies of New England & New York, to make new Limits for Canada on the south side of the River St. Laurence; acknowledge the Sovereignty of France to the Lakes, which belong to your own Subjects, the five Nations, & in the new Limits which we demand for Canada along the South Shore of those Lakes; include not only the very soil upon which these Indians are settled, but grant Us likewise that immense Extent of Country between the Ohio and the Oubache [Wabash], without which the Communication of Canada with Louisiana, cannot be maintained. Give Us what we have no right to; Leave Neuter what is Your own between the Ohio & the Apalachian Mountains. Grant us this, & we will treat upon the rest. But if you do not grant it previously, & in Form, we will not treat at all.' " [8]

On July 15 the news of Boscawen's attack on the French ships reached London; by that time it had already reached Paris.[9] According to the Spanish Ambassador in London, Rouillé wrote to Mire-

---

[6] Mirepoix to Rouillé, April 25, *ibid.*, pp. 92–3.

[7] This is especially well treated in Max Savelle's *The Diplomatic History of the Canadian Boundary, 1749–1763*, pp. 72–6.

[8] B.M., Add. Mss., 32,854: 291.

[9] B.M., Add. Mss., 32,857: 233.

poix ordering him home and at the same time indicating that he had sent orders to all the French ministers in the foreign courts that the King of France "would be fully revenged, for the insolent piracies of this nation and the duplicity of its ministers." [10] Newcastle in writing to Holderness enclosed a copy of the above statement, furnished by Abreu. Commenting on the French Foreign Minister's charges of piracy and falsity on the part of the British, the Duke wrote:

> "For which [charges], I may aver, there is not the least Foundation. And it is the most impudent thing to publish Such Falsities." [11]

Thus, as a result of the news from America, Mirepoix was recalled from London and de Bussy from Hanover.[12] One might therefore have anticipated an immediate declaration of war. Why was this not forthcoming? Why was it finally left to Great Britain, a year after Boscawen sailed, to declare that a state of war existed?

As has already been emphasized, France's record in North America and in the Neutral Islands was not one of good faith or reasonableness: she had committed herself to acts of violence against the British in well-established places, and behind the barrage of her ministers' angry words there must have been a realization that no nation, especially no great nation, could be expected to receive such treatment without retaliation. Again, she was appealing to Europe as a victim of British greed. A declaration of war would not help her. Only peaceful nations that had not offended her would be within reach of her great armies. Moreover, in declaring war there was grave danger not only that the seas would be swept of her commerce, as in the last war, unless her fleet could protect it, as it would not be in a position to do before the spring of 1756,[13] but also that she might lose some of her New World possessions in spite of the arrival in Canada of the large reinforcements. These dangers, it was felt, however, might be risked were Spain now to tie her fortunes once again to those of France in launching concentrated attacks against the British possessions. On July 18 therefore a courier hurried from the

---

[10] Newcastle to Holderness, July 22, 1755, B.M., Add. Mss., 32,857: 295.

[11] *Ibid.*

[12] B.M., Add. Mss., 32,857: 310. De Bussy was, in fact, just beginning his work at Hanover (*ibid.*).

[13] An unnamed person — apparently a Frenchman in British pay — writes at this period from Paris: "As to sea forces, we must depend on those we have out already; only eight others preparing which will not be ready till Christmas . . . but it is resolved to have wherewith all to make a figure next Spring" (B.M., Add. Mss., 32,857: 233).

French court to Madrid with the news of Boscawen's hostile acts and with an urgent request for aid. An unnamed writer at Compiègne declared in a communication written on July 26, that

> "nothing but the coolness from that Quarter [Madrid], hinders us here from entering into immediate action of what was long resolved & you as long advised off [of]." [14]

But the French Ambassador, the Duc de Duras, met with no success in passing over the heads of the Spanish ministers, strongly committed to neutrality, and making an impassioned appeal directly to King Ferdinand and Queen Barbara.

Thus France in her isolation and naval weakness was impelled to limit herself at the time to empty threats -- in answer not only to the British attack on the French navy but to the capture of the French forts in region of the Bay of Fundy. The British Cabinet Council, on the other hand, now quite reconciled to a war, requested Robinson to prepare commissions of marque and reprisal and also, significantly, to draw up a declaration of war — doubtless a declaration intended as a reply to one expected at any moment from France. He proceeded with these tasks. [15]

But declaration or no declaration, hostilities were now proceeding between the two great powers on the sea and in North America. It seemed that with France reluctant to invade her unoffending Continental neighbours, the struggle would leave the rest of Europe undisturbed. For British opinion was also stoutly opposed to being concerned in another Continental war. [16] The estimated expense of supporting government without such involvement was about five and a half million pounds, taking into account the vast needs of the navy and those of the military forces in North America. Newcastle thought it would actually run even much above this. [17] Nevertheless, the British ministers came to the decision at the end of July "to assist in the defence of His Majesty's German Dominions," in case these were attacked. [18] They also agreed that the best way to guard against such

---

[14] Enclosed in Hatton's letter to Newcastle of August 8, 1755, B.M., Add. Mss., 32,858: 53.

[15] Robinson to Newcastle, August 15, 1755, B.M., Add. Mss., 32,858: 171.

[16] The great merchant financier Sir John Barnard strongly advised Newcastle in the summer of 1755 not to become involved on the Continent even in the defence of Hanover. He also thought that the nation could not stand another levy of six million pounds (B.M., Add. Mss., 32,857: 45).

[17] Newcastle to Holderness, July 29, 1755, B.M., Add. Mss., 32,857: 405–6.

[18] Newcastle to Holderness, August 1, 1755, B.M., Add. Mss., 32,857: 500.

attack on the part either of France or of her ally Prussia and to prevent a Continental war was to support the subsidy policy that King George had so much at heart. But the problem of carrying this subsidy policy through the House of Commons deeply concerned them in view of the opposition to it on the part of such popular leaders as Pitt. In August Hardwicke spoke to Pitt to enlist his support, without results. Pitt agreed to support a war in America and on the seas, but not subsidies; yet he did admit that England had some obligations respecting Hanover. In September Newcastle conferred with him and indicated that in spite of the King's previous opposition to him, George was now prepared to admit him to a Cabinet post, providing that he would co-operate on the subsidy question. The utmost concession that Pitt would make was an agreement to support the Hesse-Cassel treaty, and only in view of the fact that the King's honour was involved in its ratification.[19] Pitt, although ambitious to establish his own leadership, also opposed the position taken by the King — in support of Newcastle — that he would "have no minister at the head of the house of commons,"[20] and therefore refused on both of these grounds to accept the proffered advance.

As a result, to strengthen the ministry in the House, especially after Legge, as Chancellor of the Exchequer, had refused to sign the warrants to implement the Hesse-Cassel treaty, Newcastle was led to persuade the King to do what he had previously been unwilling to do: to give to Henry Fox, who was Secretary at War, the post of Secretary of State for the Southern Department and with it "not only the lead but the power of the house of commons" — which implied more than met the eye. This change took place at the beginning of the new session of Parliament in November. At the opening on the 13th, with the speech from the throne in support of the subsidy policy, a debate took place in which Pitt denounced what he felt was the subordination of the interests of Great Britain to those of Hanover. To him the subsidy treaties were designed with this idea in mind.[21]

---

[19] Hardwicke to Newcastle, August 9, 1755, B.M., Add. Mss., 32,858: 74. Pitt's argument followed very closely that of Sir John Barnard of the preceding month; for Newcastle's conversation with Pitt see B.M., Add. Mss., 32,858: 408.

[20] I. S. Leadam, *Political History of England, 1702–1760*, p. 437.

[21] Before the session of Parliament the Cabinet Council met on November 11 to map out its strategy. At this meeting the proposed speech from the throne and also the proposed address were read and a discussion took place. Robinson declared that "however paradoxical It might appear he would maintain that the Russian Treaty was calculated for the security of our American Colonies" (B.M., Add. Mss., 32,860: 440).

However, on a division of the House, Hillsborough's motion pledging

> "to assist His Majesty against insults and attacks that may be made upon any of His Majesty's dominions, though not belonging to the Crown of Great Britain," [22]

was carried by 311 to 105. Pitt and others were thereupon dismissed from their posts, and the ministry was now free to employ the subsidy policy to protect the national interests, which, it had now been determined, included the Continental interests of the King.

As has already been made clear, the diplomatic situation on the Continent was shifting so rapidly that the subsidy treaty that had been signed between Great Britain and Russia was never implemented, because of the unwillingness of the court at St. Petersburg to accept the interpretation that its forces might be used against France but not against Prussia. Newcastle by the summer of 1755 had indeed begun to console himself that since Austria would not co-operate in maintaining the "System," conversations with Frederick's representatives were pointing to the possibility of an entente with Prussia whereby the latter power would observe a strict neutrality in connection with the Anglo-French war — something that could be, it was felt, an even more efficacious guarantee of the safety of Hanover than the Russian alliance, and, after all, appeared less costly.[23] These ideas were submitted to George in Hanover by Holderness. The King was still infatuated with the plan to energize the "System" drawn up by his Hanoverian ministers (reference to which has been made in the preceding chapter), and Holderness, in writing to Newcastle, declared that he himself trembled at the thought of abandoning the old Continental arrangements. Never would he believe, he affirmed, that any advantages that might be derived in America could possibly compensate for the danger of seeing France occupy the Netherlands, including Ostend and perhaps also Flushing.[24] Yet three days later he wrote to Ambassador Keith at Vienna informing him that it was no longer worth while to attempt to refute the false arguments con-

---

[22] *The Parliamentary History of England*, XV, 541. "Lord Hillsborough said that he would move the address as approved of by this meeting [of the Cabinet Council]; that to him It appeared that the *Dominions* in the speech meant British Dominions and that the Commons in their address out of zeal and Duty to the King declared that they would support the Hanover Dominion and in that sense he should openly move it" (West's account of the meeting of November 11, 1755, B.M., Add. Mss., 32,860: 440).

[23] Waddington, *op. cit.*, p. 146.

[24] Holderness to Newcastle, August 3, 1755, *ibid.*, pp. 146–7.

tained in the last Austrian proposals submitted in June and also expressed fear of Austrian duplicity.[25] All negotiations with Austria
thereupon ceased and increasing attention was now paid to Prussia.

The truth is that Austria had come to question the value of her
connections with Great Britain, which could not be used to protect
her central European interests. To Maria Theresa and her Chancellor these were now held to be infinitely more important than the
Netherlands, and to restore some and to preserve others from seizure
now seemed to require the dismemberment if not the destruction of
Prussia as the disturber of central Europe and the distribution of portions of this Kingdom among Austria, Russia, Saxony, and Denmark.
France might therefore have the Austrian Netherlands for her aid in
this great design framed by Kaunitz, although ultimately she might
have to return Lorraine to Austria.[26]

Thus far little has been said of Prussia and her King. Frederick
had come out of the Silesian wars with great prestige as a warrior
and yet with a reputation for unreliability. His sudden, unprovoked
invasion of Silesia, his desertion of France, his ally, were matters of
concern even within his own family.[27] Yet he was still theoretically
tied to France by a defensive alliance that was not to terminate until
the month of June 1756; further, he had his grudges against Elector

---

[25] *Ibid.*, p. 148. For the Austrian proposals see Chapter XI of this volume.

[26] Walter L. Dorn, *Competition for Empire, 1740–1763*, pp. 296–9.

[27] In 1753 Frederick's brother, Prince Henry, drew up a "Memoir on His Prussian
Majesty's Present Situation." In this he referred to the King's desertion of the French-
Bavarian alliances, "which [desertion] had profited nothing save to alienate the hearts" of
his allies and to "make distrustful those who saw themselves obliged to deal" with him
(Charles V. Easum, *Prince Henry of Prussia, Brother of Frederick the Great*, p. 31). The
court of Berlin, at least from the year 1737, had been the recipient of some fairly substantial sums of money sent secretly from France and with the knowledge of His Most Christian Majesty alone: in 1737 it was 100,000 livres; in 1738, 200,000 livres; in 1739, 100,-
000 livres; in 1740, the sum is uncertain, with 300,000 livres allotted to "several Princes
and states of the Empire." In 1741 the sum of 2,000,000 livres was "sent to Vienna and
to Berlin over the affairs of the Austrian Succession"; in addition, in that year a further
sum of 200,000 livres was given to M. de Belle-Isle to transmit as a subsidy to Berlin; in
1742 Cardinal Fleury sent 100,000 there; in 1743 the same amount was sent; in 1744 it
was 600,000 livres, "over and beyond the subsidy of six million" that France paid; in 1745
it was 300,000 livres; in 1746 the same sum; in 1747, 100,000 livres; in 1748, 300,000;
and in 1749, 500,000 livres ("*Mémoire concernant les affaires étrangères, depuis l'année
1724 jusques et compris 1750*, Affaires Secrètes Étrangères, 1716–1750." This rare manuscript prepared in the French Treasury as a report in 1750 is to be found in the Trinity
College Library, Dublin, Ms. K. 2.6: 896). But money did not buy gratitude in the face of
self-interest.

George of Hanover over the matter of conflicting claims to East Friesland [28] and against the same individual as King George of England for the seizure by his navy, during the recent war, of Prussian ships carrying contraband. When his ships were not returned at the conclusion of hostilities, he impounded in 1752 the last instalment due to British investors, amounting to £250,000, on the Silesian loan that had been floated in 1735 by Charles VI.[29] What is more, he did not like George as an individual. For these and other reasons he felt strongly drawn to France with the development of the Anglo-French crisis in America and did not hesitate to offer advice to the French on the proper method of procedure. In the spring of 1755, speaking to the Chevalier de la Touche, French Ambassador in Berlin, respecting this crisis, he declared, according to the latter:

> "Do you know, Sir, what I would do under the present circumstances were I the King of France? The moment that war would break out or that the English would commit any hostilities against France, I would march a considerable corps of troops into Westphalia in order to send it into the Electorate of Hanover: this is the surest way to make that —— sing!" [30]

When this conversation was reported to Rouillé, he, while refusing the advice, thought it would be opportune to suggest to Frederick — in view of the latter's lack of scruple about attacking other powers be-

---

[28] The claim of the Elector of Hanover to East Friesland dated from 1691 when "a brotherhood and an hereditary union" was entered into between the head of the house of Brunswick-Lüneburg and Prince Christian Eberhard; the claim of Frederick of Prussia was "in consequence of the expectancy granted to the House of Brandenburg by Emperor Leopold in 1694." When Frederick in 1744, upon the death of Prince Charles Edward of East Friesland, took possession of the country, Elector George made known to the regency of it his claims and also made proper declarations to Aulic Council of the Empire in opposition to those of the King of Prussia. For an interesting description of East Friesland at this period see D. Fenning, J. Collyer, and others, A New System of Geography, II, 257.

[29] S. L. Leadam, op. cit., p. 427.

[30] The epithet used by Frederick in paying his compliments to his uncle, George II, was not such as de la Touche felt free to repeat (Waddington, op. cit., pp. 163–4). Sir Richard Lodge in his thoughtful study Great Britain and Prussia in the Eighteenth Century says (p. 83) that Frederick in the spring of 1755 offered to France a Prussian occupation of Hanover and cites as his authority Frederick's letter to Knyphausen of April 5, 1755 (Politische Correspondenz Friedrich's des Grossen [ed. Droysen, Duncker, and Sybel], XI, 106–7). It seems to be clear that what he was suggesting was a sudden attack on Hanover by a corps of French troops, in harmony with his recommendation to de la Touche cited above.

fore they had acted so as to give occasion for such procedure — that he himself might be disposed to deliver an attack against Hanover.[31] But the Prussian King, always alert to the implications of any act involving the international scene, declined the invitation to go out for any such booty under existing conditions; for he clearly foresaw that he would inevitably bring down on his shoulders, in addition to Hanover, likewise Austria, Russia, Great Britain, and even a host of German states in the pay of the last.[32] Rather, he had his eye, it is quite clear, not on Hanover, or on the bishopric of Hildesheim, which he coveted, but on Saxony as his next victim — and a less dangerous one.[33]

As the weeks passed into months, with France, as Frederick viewed the situation, still apparently floundering about with no plan to hold Great Britain in check, he became impatient, especially over the fact that his advice had not been followed.[34] Never bound by any but momentary ties that might seem convenient for his purposes at the time, in the late spring of 1755 he apparently suddenly decided to seek a reconciliation with King George, who was resentful of the fact that his nephew was still holding East Friesland, to which he felt that he himself had a much better claim. Using a visit to his Rhenish provinces as an excuse, the Prussian King therefore sought an interview with his uncle at Hanover. The latter, however, was not disposed to see him, in spite of the pleadings of his Hanoverian ministers.[35] The intermediaries employed by Frederick in making the request were Prince Ferdinand of Brunswick, who held a command in his army, and his brother Karl, the reigning Duke of that principality.

It was soon after this incident and doubtless growing out of it that efforts were made to detach the Duke of Brunswick from his subsidy treaty with France, whereby he was obliged to maintain an army

[31] Rouillé's suggestion of a Prussian attack on Hanover was forwarded to Frederick by his Ambassador in Paris, Baron Knyphausen, in a letter dated April 25, 1755 (*Politische Correspondenz*, XI, 144).

[32] This apprehension of Frederick's was fully indicated in his letter to Knyphausen of May 6, 1755 (*ibid.*).

[33] In 1752 Frederick during an illness that seemed to threaten to terminate his activities drew up a last will and testament. In this he made clear to his successor the desirability, first of all, of conquering Saxony; after this he should seize West Prussia from the Poles, and from Sweden the part of Pomerania that the latter held (Emil Daniels, "The Seven Years' War," *Cambridge Modern History*, VI, 251, and G. B. Volz, *Die politischen Testamente Friedrichs des Grossen*, pp. 59–65).

[34] Frederick to Knyphausen, August 2, 1755, *Politische Correspondenz*, XI, 231.

[35] Newcastle to Holderness, June 6, 1755, and Holderness to Newcastle, June 7 and 18, 1755, Waddington, *op. cit.*, p. 199.

corps of four thousand men that would be at the disposal of Frederick of Prussia. The suggestion was made to him — apparently by the court of Hanover rather than by the British Minister Holderness [36] — that were he to give up his present treaty and enter into another with Elector George, he might anticipate securing an annual subsidy of £200,000 and even a marriage alliance with the house of Hanover by the union of one of his daughters and the Prince of Wales, the future George III. The offer itself was most flattering and did not fail to make a proper impression upon Duke Karl. But he realized that he could make no move without the permission of Frederick, for, with his principality lying on the borders of Brandenburg, he was little more than the latter's satellite; moreover, the Duchess was Frederick's sister. Therefore he also turned for assistance to his brother Ferdinand, who on June 27 wrote to the King of Prussia on his behalf. Frederick replied almost immediately that if peace continued, nothing could be more advantageous than such a marriage and the securing of such a large subsidy, but that the Duke was still bound by his previous commitments.[37] The same day, in spite of this apparent encouragement, Frederick wrote to Knyphausen in Paris instructing him to warn Rouillé of the proposal and to inform him also that the British had secured in France by some means a copy of the Franco-Brunswick subsidy treaty.[38] He continued his role of confidant of Brunswick, however, under injunction that this fact should be kept secret. In August he made clear to the Duke that no steps should be taken regarding the renewal and increase of the French subsidy until it was clear how the Hanoverian negotiation was proceeding.[39] That same day Prince Ferdinand forwarded to him certain propositions from Münchhausen, President of the Council of Hanover, which contained a cautious request that in case France attacked the German possessions of King George on account of the disturbances in America, Brunswick would dispose the King of Prussia not to prevent his Britannic Majesty from taking all possible measures to defend these.[40] Two days later Frederick wrote to Knyphausen to recommend to Rouillé that in negotiating with Denmark it was to be hoped that the King of Denmark would agree to join France in an invasion of Hanover. The Prussian King indicated that His most

---

36 Frederick to Knyphausen, July 1, 1755, *Politische Correspondenz*, XI, 192–3.
37 Frederick to Prince Ferdinand, July 1, 1755, *ibid.*, XI, 192–3.
38 Frederick to Knyphausen, July 1, 1755, *ibid.*, XI, 192–3.
39 Frederick to Brunswick, August 7, 1755, *ibid.*, XI, 237–8.
40 *Ibid.*, XI, 246–7.

Christian Majesty by sending thirty or forty thousand men by way of the Electorate of Cologne, the Archbishop of which was an ally of His Most Christian Majesty, could move directly into Hanover; France would also find Flanders without defence and in one campaign could get possession of the entire Netherlands. He added:

> "This country [the Austrian Netherlands] would serve at any time as the equivalent of Canada and, further, a combined French and Danish army that enters Hanover would soon force the King of England to turn to all imaginable expedients to hasten a peace. By such means France would shortly be able to end in Europe all the quarrels that she has with the English in America and secure such compensation in the peace that her gains would far surpass her losses." [41]

It was at this juncture that the Earl of Holderness appeared in Brunswick from Hanover to incline the Duke by direct conference to use his influence with Frederick to keep hostilities that had begun in America from spreading to Germany. Frederick, after being apprised by the Duke of the substance of the interview,[42] wrote to him that the quarrel between the two crowns over uncultivated American lands was "not worth the candle and that the great armaments involved were much more valuable than the disputed regions." [43] He attached a communication to be handed to Holderness in which he suggested that he himself and the Queen of Hungary might well be charged to mediate the differences between the two powers; this he felt was the only efficacious method by means of which European peace would be maintained.[44] However, in a separate letter to the Duke, Frederick made clear

> "under seal of the most inviolable secrecy — that Britain and her allies would never extort from me the declaration [of neutrality] that they presume themselves able to do."

The King also added that George of England

> "has a very hot fear for his Electorate and I begin to suspect that he is not satisfied with the court of Vienna, otherwise he would never be addressing me." [45]

---

[41] Frederick to Knyphausen, August 9, 1755, *ibid.*, XI, 244.

[42] *Ibid.*, XI, 252.

[43] Letter of August 12, 1755, *ibid.*, XI, 253.

[44] Holderness to Newcastle, August 20, 1755, B.M., Add. Mss., 32,858: 225.

[45] Frederick to the Duke of Brunswick, August 12, 1755, *Politische Correspondenz*, XI, 254–5.

But Frederick was soon to be impelled to make a dramatic change in his attitude toward Great Britain. Early in August rumours came from England and Holland of the signing of the subsidy treaty between Great Britain and Russia, which would bring sixty thousand Russians into the service of the former for a period of ten years. This disturbed him profoundly.[46] In writing to Knyphausen on August 19 he warned him that rumour also had it that Russian auxiliaries would be sent by sea to Lübeck and would then march by way of Hanover into the Netherlands and that Rouillé should be placed on his guard to take whatever steps were needed.[47] Four days later the Duke of Brunswick sent him a statement prepared by Holderness that made clear that the King of Prussia had heard only one side of the American difficulties and that emphasized the desire of the King of England to accommodate all of the outstanding issues between his court and that of Prussia.[48] This brought from Frederick a reply to his brother-in-law on the 25th that nothing was so important as to gain time, and therefore the Duke should assure the British Minister that the King of Prussia was so busy with troop manœuvres and with a trip to Silesia that he had little leisure for other matters at the moment.[49] Then came Michell's dispatch from London written on the 12th. He declared that he had been assured in London that Great Britain had reached an accord not only with Russia, but also with Bavaria; further, that things were now moving favourably for a reestablishment of the British ententes with Austria and Saxony. What is more, the Prussian chargé d'affaires assured the King in the same communication that although these treaties would involve great expense, Great Britain, far from being exhausted by a war of ten years — that is, from 1739 to 1748 — still had great resources; that the interest on the debt had been lowered, and that in place of a debt of one hundred and eighty million pounds, as Frederick had believed, it was not more than eighty million pounds and was being steadily reduced.[50]

From this time on, one notes a decided change in the tone of the King of Prussia's correspondence with his envoy in Paris. Britain's

---

[46] Frederick to his chargé d'affaires in London, Abraham Ludwig Michell, to von der Hellen at The Hague, to Klinggräffen in Vienna, to Maltzahn at Dresden, and to Knyphausen in Paris, all of August 19, 1755, *ibid.*, XI, 264–7.

[47] *Ibid.*

[48] *Ibid.*, XI, 272.

[49] Frederick to Knyphausen, August 30, 1755, *ibid.*, XI, 281–3.

[50] *Ibid.*, XI, 283.

"prodigious passion" to make war was contrasted with French vacil-
lation. He assured Knyphausen that France could not depend upon
a Saxon alliance and that the Elector of Saxony, who was also King
of Poland, could not possibly prevent a Russian army from marching
right through that country — never could the Poles stop a Russian
army; what was more, the Russian-Polish Convention of Varscovie
of 1744 compelled Poland to permit such a passage.[51] At the same
time he instructed von der Hellen at The Hague that should rumours
arise in Holland that England was extending a hand so that Prussia
would remain neutral in the Anglo-French hostilities, he would assure everyone that "there was nothing to it at all." [52]

By September 1 Frederick had begun to clarify his ideas and was
at last prepared to write to the Duke of Brunswick that his treaty
with France would end in the spring, which would give him freedom
then to act in conformity with his interests and his convenience. He
therefore instructed the Duke to continue to negotiate with Great
Britain on his behalf and indicated that should Frederick receive
from the King of England reasonable proposals, it might be possible
to attain the proposed end respecting the neutrality of the Hanoverian states.[53] The King also at this juncture informed Knyphausen
that his proposed mediation between France and Great Britain
would be impossible, for the British ministry would not accept it and
was of the opinion that England need take only a step "to crush
France completely" and had ordered Hawke to attack the French
squadrons and merchant ships.[54]

Frederick's coolness toward France now gradually became very
evident. He deeply resented the continued French efforts to conclude
an alliance with Saxony,[55] which he had his eyes upon; and in spite of
Knyphausen's optimistic reports of the rosy picture of the public
finances of France,[56] he was much more impressed with the news
that French financiers who had been in Holland and sought to secure
large loans for the French government in Amsterdam at six and even
at eight per cent had failed.[57] In fact, he was led to doubt seriously

[51] Frederick to Knyphausen, August 30, 1775, ibid., XI, 281–3.
[52] Ibid., XI, 283.
[53] Ibid., XI, 287.
[54] Frederick to Knyphausen, September 10, 1755, ibid., XI, 292–3.
[55] Ibid., XI, 288.
[56] Knyphausen reported on September 12 that the Farmers-General of France had
loaned to the government sixty million livres at four per cent (ibid., XI, 312).
[57] Frederick to Knyphausen, September 23, 1755, ibid., XI, 313.

France's financial stability and was well aware that Madame de Pompadour had invested immense sums in British securities, estimated as high as thirty or forty million livres.[58] He now began taking to task his representative in Paris for favouring France rather than England:

> "You must not take offence when I tell you very frankly that on this occasion I find you French to your very fingernails — since you prefer the conduct of the French up to the present to that of the English." [59]

He was also thoroughly disgusted with the way the French court took the British naval reprisals and pointed out to Knyphausen that

> "the terribly weak conduct of the French toward England, in spite of all the insults that the latter has offered, has turned all Europe against them. There is, in fact, scarcely such an example in history." [60]

His resentment, moreover, kept rising over the continued attempts of France to bind Saxony to herself, which he declared to his Ambassador would be not only of no utility to her "but indeed very prejudicial to our affairs"; and if she persisted, he would certainly never renew the Franco-Prussian treaty.[61] He also was led to contrast reports of conditions in France with those in England. According to these, the situation of the people in Provence was deplorable; in other provinces they were

> "crushed and ruined by the farmers of taxes, the troops in the most pitiable condition, the soldier hungry and dressed in rags, the officer badly paid and in despair, and, as for recruits, boys from twelve to fifteen years of age — indeed, all in the last desolation without prospects of remedy. See the hideous picture given by reasonable and impartial people!" [62]

Finally, by the middle of November he began having deep suspicions that France was arriving at a secret agreement with Austria.[63] That he might find himself in a most precarious situation, surrounded by enemies, was also indicated by a letter he wrote to Knyphausen on November 22 when he declared that he had learned in the most authentic manner that the Russian treaty had been concluded with England and that the sixty or seventy thousand Russian troops in

---

58 *Ibid.*, XI, 381, 410–11.
59 Frederick to Knyphausen, September 17, 1755, *ibid.*, XI, 306.
60 Frederick to Knyphausen, October 4, 1755, *ibid.*, XI, 323.
61 Frederick to Knyphausen, October 18, 1755, *ibid.*, XI, 343.
62 Frederick to Knyphausen, November 8, 1755, *ibid.*, XI, 373.
63 Frederick to Klinggräffen at Vienna, November 15, 1755, *ibid.*, XI, 377.

Livonia were to be placed under command of the Austrian General Lacy, whom the Empress-Queen was sending to Russia.[64]

Early in August the court of France had decided to send to Berlin, to take the place of de la Touche, the Duc de Nivernais, one of France's most enlightened statesmen and one also strongly favoured by the Marquise de Pompadour. Frederick had expressed his willingness to receive him and the proposals that he would bring. But there were unaccountable delays before the new Ambassador finally left Paris. Late in November the Prussian King wrote to Brunswick expressing his anxiety that letters from the British ministry that would consummate the Anglo-Prussian entente should arrive before Nivernais put in his appearance.[65] Yet when his Paris envoy informed him that there were suspicions in Paris that England was seeking to draw Prussia from her French alliance, he sent Knyphausen on December 2 a dispatch directing him to assure Rouillé that as to his permitting himself to be drawn into taking the side of England,

> "all such rumours that have come to him [Rouillé] were only the malignant and fabricated insinuations of my enemies. It is they not I who seek to bring about disunity with France; but there is not a word of truth in what they say." [66]

On the same day he wrote to Duke Karl of Brunswick, who had sent him a copy of a letter received from Holderness indicating the resolve of the British government not to use the Russian troops in Germany except in case the King's states within it were attacked. He indicated in his communication that the Duke should reply to the British Minister that he had found nothing in the letter that needed to be brought to the attention of the King of Prussia and ended his note by cautioning his brother-in-law in carrying on the negotiation with Great Britain "not to exhibit the least eagerness neither in your affair [that of the proposed marriage alliance] nor in mine." [67]

Meanwhile Michell in London forwarded to Frederick a copy of the proposed Anglo-Russian treaty which was given to him by Holderness for this purpose. With it came definite proposals from His Majesty's government that it was prepared not only to renew in the most precise manner all acts of guarantee given in the past

---

[64] *Ibid.*, XI, 388.
[65] Frederick to the Duke of Brunswick, November 24, 1755, *ibid.*, XI, 398.
[66] *Ibid.*, XI, 409.
[67] *Ibid.*, XI, 414.

to Prussia but to bind itself even more closely to the Prussian government.[68] This led Frederick to reply that he would receive with pleasure the propositions that the ministry had prepared for him. He also made clear to Michell that the affair of the seizure of the Prussian vessels in the late war was in reality only a "*bagatelle*," but might in time become a stumbling-block (*pierre d'achoppement*); and that the insignificant commerce of the Prussian merchants ought not in the present war to be disturbed, or at least the British government should make clear to him what it regarded as contraband.[69] He also expressed his contempt of the French ministry two days later in communicating with Knyphausen. It was carrying on, he declared, "just as though it had been deprived of reason, common sense, and everything!" [70]

The Comte de Broglie's continued activities in Saxony, it is clear, had deeply angered the King and he frankly admitted at this period to Brunswick — however he might in writing to Michell stress his desire for tranquillity in Germany — that he saw himself obliged to use "effective reprisals" against the Saxons.[71] But first, before moving against that principality, he realized that he must protect himself against a possible great coalition of powers that might hurl itself against him; for reports continued to reach him of Austrian and Russian military preparations.[72] Nevertheless, by the latter part of December the basis for an understanding with Great Britain had become so firm that he felt free to write to Maltzahn in Dresden that he had reasons why the malice of the Russian Chancellor Bestuzhev and the others plotting against him, although "enormous and without example," no longer caused him anxiety.[73] He now felt that he must be prepared to include in the number of potential enemies even his own ally France. The invasion of Hanover by French armies to strike at the British King's possessions would be, he was convinced, the signal for fifty thousand Austrians to enter Saxony on their way to Brandenburg and another army of the same size to

---

[68] Michell to Frederick, November 28, 1755, *ibid.*, XI, 418.

[69] Frederick to Michell, December 7, 1755, *ibid.*, 418–19. For a discussion of the points involved in seizure of the Prussian ships see Sir Ernest Satow, *Frederick the Great and the Silesian Loan*, pp. 65–7; Richard Pares, *Colonial Blockade and Neutral Rights*, pp. 93, 150, 154.

[70] *Politische Correspondenz*, XI, 426.

[71] *Ibid.*, XI, 432.

[72] Frederick to Knyphausen, December 16, 1755, *ibid.*, XI, 434.

[73] Frederick to Maltzahn, December 23, 1755, *ibid.*, XI, 446.

enter Silesia, while sixty thousand Russians would fall upon East Prussia.[74] He therefore on January 4 sent secret instructions and full powers to Michell in London to conclude a treaty; [75] he also on the same day addressed a very friendly letter to King George referring to the ties of blood that united them, which would now be fortified by other engagements.[76]

The Convention of Westminster, signed on January 16, 1756, pledged Great Britain and Prussia to enter into a sincere friendship. Neither party was to attack or invade the territories of the other; on the contrary, each was to use all efforts to prevent her own allies from making any move against the possessions of the other; further, should any "foreign" power, under whatever pretext, attempt to violate the tranquillity of Germany,[77] the high contracting parties agreed to unite their forces to oppose it. Again the specific guarantees of the Treaty of Westminster of 1742 and that of Hanover of 1745, together with Frederick's guarantee of 1746, were renewed; and, finally, a secret clause provided that this convention should not be extended to cover the Austrian Netherlands.[78] The outstanding causes of friction arising out of the preceding war were likewise liquidated, but outside the terms of the treaty.[79]

While Great Britain and Prussia had not by the Convention of Westminster become allies, Prussia had now placed herself squarely athwart the entrance into Germany of her own ally and, by agreeing to use force against France to that end, if need be, had destroyed the basis for continued co-operation with her. But His Most Christian Majesty, not to be outdone, had already just as secretly begun that *rapprochement* with the hereditary enemy of his own country that was to result in May in a convention of neutrality between France and Austria comparable to that of Westminster. Superficially, all things thereupon pointed to the limitation of hostilities between Great Britain and France and to the likelihood that Europe — outside of Minorca, which the French Crown was planning to take away

---

[74] Frederick to Knyphausen, January 3, 1756, *ibid.*, XII, 8–9.

[75] *Ibid.*, XII, 12–16.

[76] *Ibid.*, XII, 17.

[77] The British text used the term "*Empire Germanique*"; but Frederick, who did not want to guarantee the Netherlands to Austria, insisted that the term "*Allemagne*" be used (*ibid.*, XII, 14). The treaty, it will be noted, did not expressly forbid Frederick's contemplated attack upon Saxony — a project kept hidden from the British.

[78] *Ibid.*, XII, 15–16.

[79] Great Britain paid £20,000 for the seizure of the Prussian ships and Frederick released the money owing to British creditors of the Silesian debt.

from her rival — could be spared the anguish of war. But Frederick was to will otherwise, doubtless feeling he had won the required security to carry out his greatly desired conquest of Saxony and his determination to shatter forever Maria Theresa's hopes of recovering Silesia. This he did in one of his characteristic unexpected attacks, even in the face of British warnings. But in taking this fatal step he carried Europe into one of the bitterest struggles in its history and soon found himself face to face with a vast coalition of powers determined now once and for all to put an end to the predatory Prussian state.

Just before the signing of the Convention of Westminster by Michell in the name of Frederick with the authorization of the latter, the Duc de Nivernais, the new French Ambassador, appeared in Berlin.[80] On January 14 took place his first interview with the Prussian King who, doubtless to disarm him, immediately opened up the matter of the Anglo-Prussian correspondence. Frederick assured Nivernais that there was nothing in it repugnant to his engagements with France — everything could really be shown and even published. Thereupon he turned to the American crisis and the operations that France could undertake against England. With this lead, it appears that Nivernais, his mind now relieved and following out his instructions, laid bare all of the French plans.[81]

France, he indicated, desired to confine herself to a colonial and maritime war with Great Britain. Any serious failure at sea, however, would force her to transfer the theatre of hostilities to Europe. Under these circumstances she would be compelled to appeal to the powers friendly to her enemy as cosignatories of the Treaty of Aix-la-Chapelle and to demand their assistance against this disturber of the public tranquillity. Should a negative response be forthcoming, she would then be justified in invading their territories. The means to be employed and steps to be taken would involve an arrangement

---

[80] Nivernais left Paris on December 22 and arrived in Berlin apparently on January 13.

[81] Waddington, op. cit., p. 250. Frederick already had secured a copy of Nivernais's instructions through the efforts of Knyphausen. It seems that M. de Bussy had been entrusted by the French Foreign Office with the responsibility of putting them in final shape. De Bussy, previously in British pay while in London and also apparently during his short sojourn in Hanover before he was recalled upon the receipt in Paris of the news of Boscawen's attack on the French convoy, had now succumbed, it would seem, to the temptation of German gold (ibid., p. 239). The only difference in the instructions that Nivernais brought from the earlier draught obtained by Knyphausen was that the former failed to mention the French offer to Prussia of certain of the so-called Neutral Islands of the West Indies.

with Prussia. Assuming that the latter would co-operate against Hanover, she would, as a reward, be guaranteed the continued possession of East Friesland, which the King-Elector George also claimed. Stress was put upon the menace of a Russian corps that would doubtless be sent to Hanover, the efforts of the pro-French party in Poland to prevent the passing of Russian troops through that country, the possibility of securing the maritime aid of Sweden and Denmark, and the continued subsidization of the Elector of Cologne and the Elector of the Palatinate, the Duke of Brunswick, the Duke of Württemberg, and other princes, who thereby through French gold made available for Frederick twenty thousand troops. The French Ambassador was also provided with papers to indicate to Frederick that France had a mobile force of foot troops amounting to 236 battalions, embodying almost 150,000 soldiers, not including those in Canada; she also had 214 squadrons of cavalry, numbering 30,000 men and, besides, 3,800 artillerymen with artillery; in addition, she had at fortified places and in reserve 107 battalions of militia, numbering 53,000 men, which number could be easily increased. As to the fleet, thanks to new construction, she was hoping to bring it up to eighty or even one hundred ships of the line, supported by a considerable number of frigates; and, with respect to the financing of the war, she could assure Frederick that, in addition to her ordinary revenues amounting to one hundred and fifteen million livres, she had on hand, as the result of advances of the Farmer General of the revenues and of her men of finance, an additional one hundred million livres.[82] During the interview Frederick threw such a spell over Nivernais that after it had terminated, the latter felt free to write to Rouillé that the King of Prussia

"would appear to feel that our enemies are his and his are ours."[83]

It was not until January 22 that the French Ambassador was made aware that an Anglo-Prussian treaty was "about to be signed"; then it was that he expressed his astonishment to Frederick and added, according to his letter to Rouillé,

"that I found something malodorous about this proceeding and that I saw in it little glory or utility for him" (Frederick).[84]

---

82 *Ibid.,* pp. 246–7.
83 Nivernais to Rouillé, January 17, 1756, *ibid.,* p. 250.
84 Nivernais to Rouillé, January 22, 1756, *ibid.,* pp. 252–3.

Frederick, however, still assured Nivernais of his deep friendship for France and said that the understanding related solely to Germany; the dangers that surrounded him now required this measure of security. He also asserted, what was not true, that in the spring of the preceding year he would have joined France in an assault on Hanover, but that the signing of the Anglo-Russian treaty had changed everything. He also expressed himself with remarkable frankness, according to the Ambassador, on the binding effect of any treaty:

> "As to the convention with England, it is only for momentary purposes; whenever interest would demand he could easily find a pretext for terminating it; that he knew what his interest was and whatever he actually did was dictated for the moment and only for the moment." [85]

Once again the magic of Frederick's presence and sturdy assertions of the depth of his devotion to France restored Nivernais's confidence in him so that the two even consulted together later upon Belle-Isle's project for the invasion of England, and Frederick pointed out the territorial objectives that seemed to be most vulnerable.[86] It is therefore not surprising that Nivernais, clothed with full powers, lent himself to framing a new treaty with Prussia which provided a guarantee of Silesia on the one hand, and, on the other, that ten thousand Prussian troops were to come to the aid of France in case she was attacked. Frederick, now deeply suspicious of France's negotiations with Austria, evidently wanted to test her, as well as to keep up the illusion of his strong commitment to her real interests. This new treaty, signed on February 27, at least might bring her into the open. It was sent by courier to Paris just at the time when Rouillé had sent another courier to Berlin suggesting pointedly to Nivernais that he might well return to Paris by urging the state of his health. When this did not have a proper effect upon the infatuated Ambassador, a second letter, written on March 13, was sent, such that it could not be ignored.[87] In responding to his recall he was still deeply convinced that Frederick was sincere in all that he had said. Unhappily, he did not know what really was going on in Frederick's mind and he therefore accepted gratefully the many courtesies heaped upon him on his departure from Berlin.

---

[85] Ibid.

[86] Nivernais to Rouillé, January 31, 1756, ibid., p. 256.

[87] Ibid., p. 262.

As early as February 14 the Prussian King had written to Michell in London to inquire what measures England was taking to prevent an invasion that the French would probably attempt against her; further, he gave his chargé-d'affaires permission to reveal to Lord Holderness that news had been received that the court of France, as the result of a grudge against Prussia over the question of the treaty with Great Britain, was now dallying with Vienna and was suspected of having formed secret ties with the court there. Michell should therefore ask the British Secretary of State whether it would not be necessary, should this prove to be true, for England to take measures to preserve the European balance of power and especially to prevent the court of St. Petersburg from being won over by France and Austria. In this connection Frederick wrote:

> "Further, — and this is to the last degree confidential when I suggest to you the following: that you sound out for my sole direction, whether, should I find it proper to make a strict defensive alliance with England for six, ten, or a dozen years, you believe the British ministry would agree to it and would be able to include in it both Russia and the Republic of Holland." [88]

The British government, however, was well satisfied with its present arrangement with Frederick and was not disposed therefore to go farther at the time — committed as it was to the idea of confining the war with France to the colonies and to the high seas; it was, moreover, still deeply suspicious of the Prussian King and desired no closer relations with him.[89]

Returning now to the recall of Nivernais from Berlin by the French ministry, the question may be raised: What prompted this move? The answer seems to lie not only in resentment that Frederick should have negotiated and signed behind its back the Westminster Convention but in the growing conviction, promoted by such men as the Abbé de Bernis, who possessed great ascendency at Versailles, that

---

[88] *Politische Correspondenz*, XII, 109–10.

[89] Waddington (*op. cit.*, p. 277) points that only toward the end of 1757 — with Hanover overrun by the French and with Prussia faced by a tremendous coalition of great powers and overwhelming resources — was the British government, then under the masterful leadership of Pitt, led to turn its back on the latter's cardinal policy of non-interference on the Continent and to favour a subsidy treaty with Frederick. He also makes clear the deep suspicion that both Newcastle and Holderness had of Frederick before the fall of the Newcastle ministry.

Austria should be considered no longer a traditional enemy but, on the contrary, a new-found friend. Austria, as has been stressed in the preceding chapter, was, under the leadership of Kaunitz, looking for a new orientation to take the place of the old Anglo-Dutch alliance, one that would further the ambition of Maria Theresa to recover Silesia, an ambition that the Maritime Powers were unwilling to support. Throughout the year 1755 her Ambassador in Paris, Count Stahremberg, sought in vain to undermine French confidence in Frederick. Nevertheless, as the result of the news of the Anglo-Russian treaty late in December the government of Louis XV made certain proposals to the Count that seemed designed to prevent Anglo-French hostilities from spreading to Europe. These embodied the following features: France and Austria should establish an entente whereby the former would agree to respect the Netherlands and all other Austrian possessions, and the latter to forbid the Russians — or any other troops in British pay, such as the Hessians — from operating in Germany; that if such troops attempted to do so in spite of the interdiction, French troops would thereupon be accorded free entry to repulse the aggression.[90]

But Austria was not prepared to sacrifice her friendship with Russia, as she would be obliged to do, while leaving France still allied to Prussia. She nevertheless, in a reply framed on January 23, showed how little her old relations with Great Britain meant by applauding the French ultimatum to the latter demanding the unconditional restoration of ships captured by the British navy, and also approved of the idea, if Great Britain refused to restore them, of branding the British as aggressors; she also indicated her satisfaction that France was not seeking the aid of Prussia against either England or Hanover — as France, however, had previously done secretly — and her willingness to come to a mutual guarantee of territories in Europe.[91] Stahremberg was, moreover, instructed to secure from the French ministry a secret pledge that should Austria enter into an entente with France, the latter would agree not to undertake any enterprise against Hanover — something that, under the circumstances, would otherwise bring upon the head of Maria Theresa the wrath of other German states.

Then came the news of the Convention of Westminster, and on

---

[90] For the text see Waddington, op. cit., pp. 301–2.
[91] A. von Arneth, Geschichte Maria Theresas, IV, 409–15.

February 4 a majority of the French Council of State at a formal meeting expressed the view that there should be no renewal of an alliance with Prussia.[92] Yet the Council was not yet ready to enter into any offensive arrangement with Austria against her, as was made clear to Stahremberg. As a result Kaunitz late in March submitted an elaborate rescript looking toward at least a firm Franco-Austrian defensive alliance. But there were delays in Paris. De Bernis became ill and had other troubles.[93] It was not until May 1 that France was prepared to agree to this. Then she signed the Versailles Convention. Under the terms of this each of the powers not only promised to respect the possessions of the other, but, each, in the "treaty of union and defensive friendship" embodied in it, gave a guarantee of the reciprocal defence of the possessions of the other in Europe "against the attacks of whatsoever power that it might be" — excepting from this only the present conflict of France with Great Britain. Further, each agreed — if the exercise of good offices were not sufficient to achieve the end just stated — to aid the other with a corps of twenty-four thousand men or in lieu of this to extend financial assistance at the choice of the party attacked. Finally, in a secret convention of five articles this agreement of mutual aid was made more specific by one of these articles; another article provided for the admission to the concert of the Emperor, as Grand Duke of Tuscany, the Kings of Spain and Naples, and the infant Philippe, Duke of Parma, and any other prince who appeared desirable; a third forbade either party to renew or to conclude any treaty with a third power without the consent of the other.[94]

By this defensive treaty France on the one hand not only signed a self-denying ordinance against any enterprise hostile to the Netherlands but agreed to come to the aid of Austria should she be attacked by Prussia; but, on the other hand, Austria was freed of any responsibility for aid to France against Great Britain. This convention was visualized by the French ministers as a guarantee of the peace of Europe while they waged their war against Great Britain on and across the seas. But again they did not take sufficiently into account the King of Prussia. In fact, as Waddington insists, they did not dream that Frederick, the ruler of only five million people, would without French support suddenly hurl his armies against Austria and

---

[92] Waddington, op. cit., p. 311.
[93] Mémoires de Bernis, I, 263.
[94] Waddington, op. cit., pp. 332–4.

defy Russia.[95] Rather, they seem to have thought of the happy effects of this treaty: the turning over of most of the Netherlands to young Philippe in exchange for his duchies in Italy and the increase of French territory in Flanders — effects never destined to come to pass.

[95] *Ibid.*, p. 338.

CHAPTER XIII

The Loss of Minorca

THE MINISTERS OF George II, desiring no closer ties with Frederick of Prussia after securing in the Convention of Westminster the safety of Hanover, resisted the latter's suggestions of a defensive alliance similar to that ultimately signed by France and Austria. On the other hand, they continued, but without success, their efforts to bring Russia to accept their own view of the implications of the subsidy treaty that had been signed with her in the fall of 1755 so that Russian forces might be concentrated in the Netherlands should France seek to strike at Great Britain by that avenue. For the Anglo-Prussian convention had, as has been stressed in the preceding chapter, expressly excluded Flanders and Brabant from the area to be preserved from "foreign" interference. Moreover, with the coming of the new year reports continued to reach London of the concentration of great bodies of French troops about the Channel ports and of French plans for direct invasion — although war had not been formally declared. Unprepared to meet such an attack on land, prudence pointed to the necessity of bringing to England Continental troops in British pay. As a result, eight thousand Hessians and twelve thousand Hanoverians made their appearance. Holland was also called upon to fulfil her engagement to send a contingent, but pleaded inability to do so.

Beyond the problem of meeting an anticipated invasion of England there was that of sending reinforcements of regular troops to America. For no matter how firmly the tradition has been implanted in the minds of later generations of Americans that in this grave crisis in North American affairs they themselves were fully capable of dealing with it without gratuitous assistance or even advice from the mother country, that was certainly not the attitude of the colonials in 1755 and 1756, as has been made clear in the introductory chapter; for the colonials seemed to be unanimous on one point, at least, however much they might differ on others: that to save the situation they must have powerful support from England.[1] During the early months of 1756 the Cabinet Council, therefore, was busy with plans for sending this aid. It was also obliged to deal with an ultimatum sent by the French government relating to the seizure by the royal navy of a great quantity of French shipping as a reprisal for French aggressions against the colonies.

As to these seizures, in September 1755 a list of seventy French vessels captured and carried to British ports was published.[2] In October it was reported that the French agent in London had sent to his court a list of one hundred and ten ships valued at £400,000 secured by the fleet;[3] somewhat later in the month officers of the fleet calculated the value of the French ships taken — doubtless with the cargoes included — to amount to six million pounds.[4] At the end of October a London correspondent writing to New York stated that

> "we have near 170 French ships in our Harbours, their Value considerable; and to this Day the French have not taken one English Vessel, since the capture of the *Blanford* Man of War [which was immediately released];[5] this astonishes all Europe to see how patiently they bear every Thing. As for the Merchants of France they are most ruin'd, owing to so many Ships we have taken, and so valuable. . . . Our Court is doing every Thing they can to make them declare [war] first."[6]

But when the French government early in 1756 sent a sharp note to the British, indicating that, unless the ships were immediately re-

---

[1] This point is emphasized by Stanley M. Pargellis in his *Lord Loudoun in North America* (p. 39).

[2] *Gentleman's Magazine*, September 15, 1755.

[3] London advices, October 4, *New-York Mercury*, November 27, 1755.

[4] London advices, October 9, *ibid.*

[5] The *Blanford*, a small frigate, bound for South Carolina with William Henry Lyttelton, the new Governor, on board, was overhauled by a ship in M. du Guay's fleet and, having been forced to strike her colours, was carried to Brest. This seems to have been as a reprisal for the capture of the two French warships by Boscawen. No sooner was the French government notified of this, however, than orders were sent to set at liberty immediately the *Blanford* and also Governor Lyttelton (Massones from Paris to d'Abreu in London, September 10, 1755, B.M., Add. Mss., 32,859: 51; see also secret dispatch from Ostend of the same date, B.M., Add. Mss., 32,859: 45).

[6] *Boston Weekly News-Letter*, January 22, 1756.

leased, it would consider a state of war existed, and the Cabinet Council, after proper consideration, refused to release them until a proper settlement of the North American disputes had been arranged, still there was no declaration of war — although, as was indicated, the people of England were fully expecting an attempted invasion of the island. To Frederick France seemed to be drifting aimlessly and weakly at this juncture, and this has also been affirmed by French historians. There is, of course, abundance of evidence that there was hesitation on the part of the French court and divergence within the Council of State as to particular means to be employed to attain the desired ends, but the ends were undoubtedly fairly clear and so were most of the means, but not all.

France knew her potential strength, but knew that she could not act with advantage before well along in the spring of 1756. In estimating the advantages that she enjoyed, as the new year dawned, in facing Great Britain in what was destined to be a supreme test of strength, there was, first, her very large army of some two hundred thousand men as over against the mere remnants of one possessed by her rival — in all not more than thirty thousand troops in the British Isles.[7] Again, her fighting ships were, all in all, superior to Great Britain's ships of the same class, because of superior naval construction. France, moreover, still held the great keys to the North American continent, in spite of the loss of Beauséjour; she still seemed to hold the key to India with de Bussy and his army still the dominating factors in the Deccan. If she could not at the moment send her navy out to do battle with the British on account of numerical inferiority, she could use the speedy ships without too much hazard to carry reinforcements to Canada and elsewhere to consolidate her vital positions. Further, it is clear that once her navy was prepared to act effectively, with her vast ground forces she might find the opportunity to move across the narrow Channel with good prospects of assaulting England and of dictating in London the terms of peace — terms that would doom the British colonials to a strictly subordinate and even minor role in New World affairs for all time to come. Were this opportunity not forthcoming, at least from her advantageous position she could fall with overwhelming strength upon British Minorca in the Mediterranean; and with this bargaining point and with the expectation of recovering Gibraltar she might hope to bring Spain, in spite of the pro-British influence of General Wall, Spanish Foreign

---

[7] Waddington, op. cit., p. 438.

Minister, again to implement the Bourbon Family Compact — should the British not then be reasonable and agree to a proper settlement of differences, particularly those relating to North America.

Happily, France had in Machault, who had become Minister of the Marine in 1754, a man of great energy. Anticipating grave eventualities from the Anglo-French border conflicts in the New World, he had set to work immediately to strengthen the French navy. For there existed at the time, as has been indicated, a decided disparity between it and the royal navy of Great Britain. At the time of the beginning of hostilities between the two countries the latter comprehended, according to common report, over one hundred and sixty ships manned by over forty-five thousand sailors.[8] Of these about a hundred were so-called ships of the line, each armed with from fifty to one hundred cannon, and the remainder were frigates carrying from thirty-two to forty cannon. As against this, the French had to offer but sixty ships of the line and thirty-one frigates, and many of each class were not fit for service.[9] During the first year of Machault's administration of the navy he had succeeded in placing a majority of them in good condition; further, during the same period he had added fifteen more ships either by rushing to completion those on the stocks or by purchase abroad,[10] and also had begun the construction of many new ships. According to a report that was prepared toward the end of 1755 for the use of the Duc de Nivernais in Berlin, France was anticipating having soon between eighty and one hundred ships of the line[11] which would give her, in view of superior construction, approximate equality with Great Britain in first-class fighting ships. According to confidential information secured by Newcastle from the Continent some months later, the French fleet had by that time assumed such proportions that, should it be joined by the Spanish fleet, through a change in policy at Madrid, he feared that

8 New-York Mercury, December 22, 1755. According to figures given by W. C. B. Tunstall (Admiral Byng and the Loss of Minorca) the number of ships of the line possessed by Great Britain in 1755 was only seventy-seven. Of these but twenty-four were in home ports, with the remainder either cruising or convoying or in American, Far Eastern, or Mediterranean waters.

9 Henri Martin, Histoire de France, XV, 481. According to a British secret service report sent in December 1754 to Robinson, there were at Brest forty-four ships, twenty-two fit for service; at Rochefort twenty-two ships, of which nine were called "very fine"; at Toulon thirty-four ships, sixteen of these ships of the line; in addition, a number of ships were in course of construction (Shelburne Papers, 36: 104, Clements Library).

10 Henri Martin, op. cit., XV, 481.

11 Waddington, op. cit., p. 246.

the British navy would have arrayed against it decided numerical superiority.[12]

In the spring of 1756 Machault's preparations were so far advanced that he was ready to send three squadrons to the New World. One proceeded to the Lesser Antilles and another into the waters about St. Domingue; while a third, composed of six ships of the line, sailed to Canada carrying two additional battalions to reinforce the troops there. He also was ready early in April to send a squadron into the Mediterranean to undertake France's first aggressive move against Great Britain in the Old World.

When the British Cabinet Council refused the French demand for the return of the captured ships, it fully anticipated reprisals. The danger to Great Britain from a French invasion seemed very real.[13] Reports continued to come from the Continent that one hundred and eighteen battalions, each equal in strength to the British regiment as then constituted, and twenty-eight cavalry squadrons were being concentrated in the neighbourhood of the Channel coast and that orders had been given for the collection of six hundred transports of all kinds for ferrying them across the narrow waters under protection of warships whenever a favourable moment was presented. As there were no land forces in England that could possibly resist such a powerful thrust should the French army once get a footing, and as the American crisis demanded stripping the defences of some of the precious few regiments of regulars that made up these, every precaution had to be taken to guard the approaches. This, therefore, became the chief preoccupation of George Lord Anson, who since 1749 had occupied the posts of Vice Admiral of Great Britain, Lieutenant of the Admiralty, and Lieutenant of the Navies and Seas of His Majesty's Kingdom of Great Britain. Boscawen with his squadron had been ordered home the preceding fall from Nova Scotia; the

---

[12] Newcastle to the Duke of Devonshire, June 2, 1756, B.M., Add. Mss., 32,862: 6.

[13] While many contemporary and later writers have made great sport of the Newcastle ministry's apprehensions of an attempted invasion of England by the French, it is certain that Frederick of Prussia thought the danger was very great in the spring of 1756 and in warning the British Minister at Berlin, Andrew Mitchell, of French plans for such a move strongly advised, in the words of Mitchell, that "we could not be too much on our guard." In this connection the King expressed the hope "that neither the service of America, neither the defence of Minorca nor any project whatever would incline us to dégarnir our coasts by sending out too many ships of war" (Mitchell to Holderness, May 27, 1756, Politische Correspondenz, XII, 357–8). As was emphasized in the preceding chapter, the Duc de Nivernais, the French Ambassador, had indicated to Frederick in confidence early in 1756 how France was expecting to launch a successful attack against England.

Mediterranean squadron, a powerful task force during the late war, had been stripped so as to leave its commander, Commodore George Edgcumbe, with but four ships of between sixty and forty guns, three frigates of twenty-two guns, and a fourteen-gun sloop. Feverish efforts were also now made to recondition the ships that during the fall and into December had either cruised in fair and foul weather off the French coast to intercept de la Motte's fleet returning from the New World or had scoured the seas in search of French merchantmen as well as warships.

In face of this concentration of sea power about England in the spring of 1756, which seemed to make a direct assault upon her too dangerous to carry out Belle-Isle's project of invasion, the French ministry determined to strike where the enemy was weakest — in the Mediterranean and against Minorca, an island that had been a British possession since the conclusion of the War of the Spanish Succession. The circumstances could hardly have been more favourable for such a plan. The Governor of Minorca, Lord Tyrawley, and the four regimental colonels were then in England "being otherwise employed in his Majesty's Service"; [14] the Lieutenant Governor, General William Blakenay, eighty-four years of age and enfeebled with gout, had at his command only some four battalions of infantry, a company of artillery, and a detachment of engineers — scarcely more than twenty-eight hundred effectives, although the number was theoretically thirty-three hundred. Early in March, therefore, active preparations for the capture of the island took place at Toulon and at Marseille.

The Duc de Richelieu, placed in command of the expedition, was given twenty-five battalions of infantry and one of artillery — in all fifteen thousand men — and a siege train; he was also provided with a galaxy of high officers — two lieutenant generals, five brigadier generals (maréchaux de camp), and twelve brigadiers.[15] These forces, embarked on over one hundred and seventy vessels, moved out of Toulon on April 10 under protection of twelve ships of the line commanded by the Marquis de la Galissonière, one of the most capable and energetic men in the French navy, whose activities in Canada and in France have come under review in the last two volumes of this series. On the 18th the armada arrived at the small harbour and town of Ciudadela (called by the French Citadella) on the western point of Minorca. Richelieu, under orders framed by Min-

---

14 W. C. B. Tunstall, op. cit., pp. 97–8.
15 Waddington, op. cit., p. 440.

ister of War d'Argenson, was to compel the British garrison to surrender, after which it was to be permitted to go to Gibraltar; he was also to destroy the citadel of St. Philip's Castle, erected by the enemy at Port Mahon, and then was to return with his forces to France. These orders were subsequently revised in favour of the retention of Minorca and the strengthening of its chief fortress.[16]

The island — only some thirty miles in length and some fifteen in breadth, and of rugged formation in the northern and central portions — was colonized in turn by the Greeks, the Carthaginians, the Vandals, the Moors, the Catalonians, and the Aragonese. As a consequence its population, except for the more educated people, spoke a mongrel language composed of a mixture of Spanish, Latin, French, Greek, and Arabic words and phrases. In the year 1232 it had been subjected to the authority of the house of Aragon and remained under Spanish control until the English conquest of 1708, which was confirmed by the Treaty of Utrecht. While it produced salt, wine, fish, honey, wax, capers, and other commodities, most of the necessities of life had to be imported and its principal commerce in the middle of the eighteenth century was with the Barbary states of northern Africa. To supply the needs of the population of some twenty-seven thousand easy-going, poetical people, still, as earlier, dextrous with their slings,[17] between twenty and thirty ships of from one hundred to one hundred and twenty tons' burden were employed, which at that period were likely to be foreign vessels because of discriminatory tariffs against British importers at Tunis.[18] The island was therefore of little direct economic importance to Great Britain and was retained for strategical reasons, as well as for the facilities that the splendid harbour of Port Mahon offered to ships engaged in the Mediterranean trade. Across the island, connecting Ciudadela on the southwest coast with the capital, Port Mahon, on the northeast stretched a fine military road constructed immediately after the Peace of Utrecht by Brigadier General Richard Kane. This seemed

---

[16] Ibid., p. 441.

[17] The name Balearic (Balearides) attached to the islands of Majorca and Minorca by the Greeks signified the islands of slingers.

[18] These discriminatory tariffs were laid on British imports in 1735 by Tunis when the British government was slow in recognizing the authority of the reigning Bey. As a result, the corn and other produce of Tunis came to Minorca in foreign vessels, which led the merchants of Port Mahon to petition Governor Blakeney in 1750 to forbid under penalty those dwelling on the island to freight any foreign vessel in the Barbary trade (Board of Trade Journal, under date July 10, 1750; see also the testimony of the British consul at Tripoli, a Mr. White, before the Board under date October 11, ibid.).

to come as a godsend to the French in moving their forces eastward against the British garrison, which had concentrated at St. Philip's Castle; but before retiring to that strong place, detachments had so wrecked the road, which passed over mountainous country, that the siege train had to be sent to Fornelles on the northern coast of the island to be brought against the citadel.

Early in the year warnings had been sent to the government at home by the British consuls and others as to the designs of the French against the island, and these warnings kept coming. Keene at Madrid, writing in February, was also convinced of an imminent attack. As a result, on March 9 the so-called Secret Committee of the Cabinet Council came to the decision to send as strong a squadron as could be spared to support the Minorca garrison. By that time there was a growing sense of confidence that the British fleet concentrated in and about home waters would be more than a match for any force that the French might gather from Brest and Rochefort to support their transports in crossing the Channel. The man selected for the command of the relief was Vice Admiral of the Red [19] John Byng, son of Viscount Torrington, the hero of the naval battle of Cape Passaro in 1718, who had proved himself in many other engagements. Byng had as a lad entered the navy and served his first apprenticeship under his father. Not until he had been in the service for twenty-seven years did he pass beyond the rank of captain; then in 1745 he became Rear Admiral of the Blue; in 1747 he was second in command of the Mediterranean fleet of thirty ships under Admiral Medley and at that period was promoted to Vice Admiral of the Blue and soon after, upon the death of Medley, succeeded to the command of the fleet and the following year reached the rank of Vice Admiral of the Red, but one rank under that held by Anson. In the summer of 1755 he had been placed in charge of the Western Squadron, with Rear Admiral Temple West as second in command, and ordered to prey upon French commerce; and he succeeded so well that his fleet accounted for some three hundred prizes. The engagement of some of his ships under West with the French ship of the line *Espérance*, returning to France from Louisbourg *en flûte*, has already been related.

---

[19] The following were the ranks in the British navy: Admiral of the Fleet, Admirals of the White, Admirals of the Blue, Vice Admirals of the Red, Vice Admirals of the White, Vice Admirals of the Blue, Rear Admirals of the Red, Rear Admirals of the White, and Rear Admirals of the Blue. For those holding these ranks in 1755 see the "London Advices," July 1, 1755, *Boston Weekly News-Letter*, January 29, 1756.

Byng was not a popular officer; he was austere and a strict disci-
plinarian; [20] he nevertheless had gained a reputation as a very efficient if not a brilliant commander. On receiving his new assignment
he was also given an added mark of confidence by promotion to the
highest rank of active flag officers — that of Admiral of the Blue,
thereupon taking his place with Anson, previously his only superior
fitted for sea service. [21]

The Western Squadron that was ordered to the relief of Minorca
consisted of ten ships of the line headed by the *Ramillies*, a ninety-
gun vessel, as flagship, with the others ranging from the *Culloden*, a
seventy-four, to the *Defiance* and *Kingston*, both sixties. The fleet had
returned in November, after long months at sea, fouled and battered,
and after being cleaned and repaired had been sent out in February
for duty under Osborne and then early in March under Hawke. When
Byng reached Portsmouth on March 20, he found all but one of the
ships in the harbour, but they were undermanned by seven hundred
men. There were delays in getting this complement and other delays
by reason of orders of the Admiralty to send out immediately a fleet
from Portsmouth to blockade a French convoy at Cherbourg. The
Admiral was also ordered to give his marines to other ships and take
on board a regiment of fusiliers and also the officers belonging to the
Minorca garrison. In spite of all his exertions, by April 1 he was still
unprepared to sail since he was well over three hundred men short of
his complement, including even hospital cases; and many of the new
recruits came unprovided with clothes and bedding. [22] However, by
April 7 he finally sailed, in spite of the fact that two of his ships were
drawing water and four were still undermanned. [23] Nor was he given,
as requested, a frigate to repeat signals. Misfortune dogged his steps.
His ships had to battle their way in heavy weather the whole distance
to Gibraltar, where he finally arrived on May 2. There he found Edgecumbe with his little squadron and there he conferred with General
Thomas Fowke, Governor of Gibraltar, who had received confusing
orders from Lord Barrington, Secretary at War, respecting the aid
he should give to the admiral.

By the time the relief fleet had come, news had reached the Rock
that Minorca had been invaded by a large French army and that only

---

[20] See Tunstall (*op. cit.*, Chapter II) for many facts regarding Byng and his earlier
activities.

[21] *Ibid.*, p. 49.

[22] *Ibid.*, p. 53.

[23] *Ibid.*, pp. 55–6.

(From John Armstrong's *The History of the Island of Minorca*, 1756.)

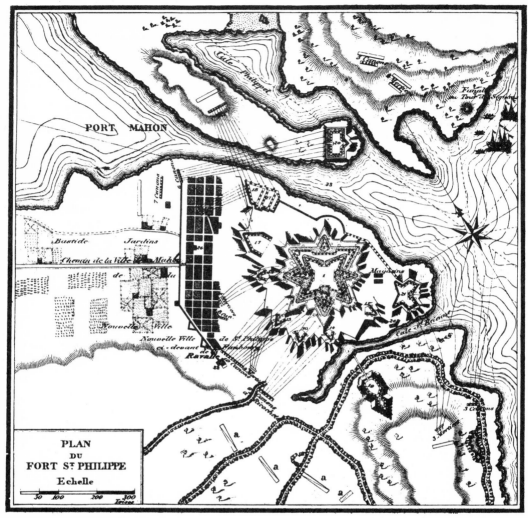

The siege of Fort St. Philip in 1755, indicating the position of the French artillery brought to bear on the fortifications.

(From Richard Waddington's *Louis XV et le Renversement des Alliances.*)

St. Philip's Castle was holding out. Governor Fowke, before meeting with Byng, held a council of war with his officers and those of the land forces that had come with the fleet. This council arrived at the conclusion that it would be dangerous to deplete Gibraltar's force of but twenty-seven hundred men in order to attempt to throw a relief into St. Philip's, which seemed to be doomed, and that the only men who should be spared from the garrison were a detachment that would permit the manning of Edgcumbe's fleet so that it could join the admiral's.[24] In doing so, it took the responsibility of disobeying orders that, while confusing, did seem to require the furnishing of one of the four battalions stationed there. When Byng at last appeared before Fowke, the latter reported the decision and yet agreed to furnish the battalion if Byng insisted. The admiral was faced with a hard decision. Were he to demand the men for the purpose of attempting to throw a relief into St. Philip's, he would be flying in the face of the unanimous decision of the army that the attempt was hopeless and that Gibraltar should not be weakened at this critical juncture. If, however, he did not press his demand, he would be facing possible criticism at home that he had not done his utmost to bring aid to the besieged garrison on the island. He chose to forgo the demand, doubtless feeling, on the one hand, that if he scored a resounding naval victory over the French fleet the garrison would hold out and the besiegers would find themselves cut off from all relief, and, on the other hand, that if he made the demand and Gibraltar, stripped of its defenders, fell, he would be obliged to face even more serious criticism at home.

Byng's one thought now was to prepare to meet the enemy in the element where he was at home. Time was pressing and he took only three days to refit — there was no time to clean and recondition Edgcumbe's fouled ships or his own. But before sailing on his fateful mission he wrote a letter to the Admiralty under date of May 4 presenting the great difficulties that faced him. In this he frankly questioned the utility — in view of the French strength — of throwing the small force available into the Castle, which must almost inevitably "fall into the enemies' hands." He indicated his determination to give to General Blakeney every bit of assistance within his power, however, and then stated: "If I should fail in the relief of Port Mahon, I shall look on the security and protection of Gibraltar as my next object. . . ." Before closing his letter he bluntly showed that

[24] Ibid., pp. 71–3.

he was faced by still other great handicaps in carrying out his assignment in the Mediterranean. At Gibraltar, he declared, "the careening wharfs, storehouses, huts, etc., are entirely decayed"; and many of his own ships as well as those of Edgecumbe's squadron were foul and some badly in need of repairing.[25]

Sailing from Gibraltar in the face of a strong head wind, he did not come into the region of Majorca until May 15. There two French frigates sighted him and sped away to carry the news of his coming to de la Galissonière. Continuing on in the direction of Port Mahon, he detached a forty-gun ship and two frigates to do their utmost to communicate with General Blakeney in the Castle. When only three miles from this objective the ships were becalmed. There was also delay at the fort in getting a boat ready to move out to communicate with the British fleet, with the result that before contact could be established between the besieged and the relief expedition, the French fleet appeared on the horizon off Port Mahon. De la Galissonière was ready to receive Byng.

Out of the maze of bitter controversy that followed the naval battle of Minorca certain facts emerge. De la Galissonière's squadron of twelve ships of the line was perhaps the best-conditioned battle fleet of its size that the French had ever possessed down to the period in question. The crews had been submitted by their commander to a long and rigorous course of preparation in the Mediterranean in gunnery, manœuvring, and signalling. For months during the spring and summer of 1754 de la Galissonière had exercised his fleet — a task apparently far more important in the eyes of the French ministers than that in which he was supposed to be engaged at the time as one of the two commissaries representing France on the Anglo-French commission for arriving at an amicable understanding respecting the New World disputes.[26] The crews were therefore highly trained, healthy, and, what is of equal importance, full of confidence in their ships and in their commander. This confidence was not misplaced. In fire-power the French flagship the *Foudroyant* was in a class by

25 For this letter see *ibid.*, pp. 84–6.

26 "On Friday Galissonière came to take leave being about to depart for Toulon to command the Ships of War Shortly to sail from that Port. He said that Silhouette would remain in Paris to proceed upon such Instructions we might receive. He said that he would be absent five or six months" (Mildmay and de Cosné to Robinson, April 17, 1754, Mildmay Papers, Clements Library). On September 25, the two British commissaries informed Robinson that news had reached Paris that Galissonière had returned to Toulon and would be expected in Paris in a few days (*ibid.*).

herself. Listed as an eighty-gun ship, she carried in reality eighty-four guns. Further, in contrast to the *Ramillies*, the British flagship, and to the other four most powerful ships that Byng commanded, all of which carried a lower battery of only thirty-two-pounders, she carried one of fifty-two-pounders. Moreover, four of her sister ships carried lower batteries of forty-two-pounders, and the seven others of thirty-six-pounders.[27] In weight of metal, therefore, the British fleet was hopelessly outclassed by its rival; it was equally outclassed in fire range, in speed, and in manœuvrability. Finally, in contrast to the poor condition of most of Byng's fleet — in long service on the turbulent Atlantic and badly in need of a thorough overhauling, with many of the personnel stricken with illness — it was clean and gleaming in its fresh paint.[28]

When, with the appearance of the French fleet on the horizon, Byng ordered the signal to engage, he was face to face with one of the most serious problems that ever confronted a British naval officer. Bound on the one hand by his "Fighting Instructions," which could not be violated with impunity by any commander, he could not follow these without running the risk of seeing his fleet battered to pieces.[29] Although the British public had learned to expect victories of the royal navy and would not hear of defeats, yet the more competent men of the service, including Byng, doubtless shared the views of Lord Anson, who in 1744 had declared with reference to the fighting qualities of the French ships:

> "I have never seen or heard . . . that one of our ships, alone and singly opposed to one of the enemy's of equal force had taken her, and . . . I have been in almost every action and skirmish since 1718, and yet we are daily boasting of the prowess of our Fleet."[30]

---

[27] Tunstall, *op. cit.*, p. 103.

[28] The following ships made up Galissonière's fleet as listed in the fall of 1755, according to British advices: the *Foudroyant*, an eighty-gun ship, the *Guerrier, Couronne,* and *Redoutable,* all seventy-fours, the *Achille,* the *Triton,* the *Lion,* the *Sage, Orpheus, Content* and *Hercule,* all sixty-fours, and, finally, the *Fier,* a fifty (London Advices, *Boston Weekly News-Letter,* January 15, 1756). This classification, however, may be considered a serious understatement of the actual armament of the ships. Moreover, as pointed out by a leading authority on the British navy, in the eighteenth century a French ship of fifty-two guns was the equal of a British seventy-two (H. W. Hodges, *Select Naval Documents,* p. 122).

[29] For an analysis of the Fighting Instructions see Julian S. Corbett, *England in the Seven Years' War,* I, 115–18.

[30] Quoted by W. L. Dorn, *Competition for Empire, 1740–1763,* p. 105. "I know not any one point more generally agreed upon amongst all who have opportunities of being

But now Byng was confronted by a force numerically almost as large as his own — thirteen British ships to twelve French — with the latter much better prepared to engage. Should he have given the signal for battle under the circumstances? It has been contended by serious students of naval action that, among the courses of action open to him, he should have avoided any engagement and rather should have blockaded Toulon, thus drawing off de la Galissonière, or should have landed the officers of the garrison and the fusiliers to bring relief to the beleaguered garrison, or should have engaged in what now would be called commando raiding tactics against the French land forces on Minorca.[31]

While there is much to be said in favour of the above views, it is hard to escape the conviction that under the circumstances no British naval commander of the eighteenth century would have dreamed of refusing to fight. Every alternative to this seems to present forbidding prospects in the days of sailing ships. To have gone on to blockade Toulon might well have resulted in the destruction or surrender of Byng's entire fleet, caught as it might have been between the fire of the shore batteries and de la Galissonière's fleet coming up in the rear. To have sent off the fusiliers, assuming that this was in reality practicable, would have made his fleet still more inferior to that of the French, who had apparently profited by the strong recommendation given to the Minister of the Marine the preceding year to increase the complements assigned to the fighting ships.[32] Finally, to have engaged in raiding tactics against the French army, while at the same time avoiding an engagement, called for not only convenient operating bases, but superior mobility with respect to the French fleet; it also called for clean ships instead of fouled ones, the hulls of which were likely to become at any moment infernos of death — a situation such as Boscawen the preceding year was face to face

informed," declared an unnamed member of Parliament in 1757, "than the French ships are in every respect preferable to ours; than that their metal is heavier, and that both their officers and men are at least as brave, and behave as well in action as ours . . ." (T. C. Hansard, *The Parliamentary History of England* . . . *to the year 1803*, XV, 786).

[31] These views are shared by such authorities as Corbett (*op. cit.*, I, pp. 111–12) and Tunstall (*op. cit.*, pp. 134–5).

[32] According to a report listing the strength of the French squadron at Toulon in the fall of 1755, the *Foudroyant* had a crew of seven hundred; the three seventy-fours, crews each of six hundred and fifty; the seven sixty-fours, crews each of five hundred and fifty, and the one fifty, a crew of four hundred and fifty (London Advices, October 24, 1755, *Boston Weekly News-Letter*, January 15, 1756). This meant that there were close to seven thousand men in the combined crews of the ships.

with before he got his ailing crews on land at Halifax. None of these conditions could be fulfilled with Gibraltar six hundred miles away.

The admiral of the French fleet was bound by certain instructions.[33] His mission was solely to guard the French forces, and any attacks upon the British merchant marine or navy were to be subordinated and only incidental to this. His duty therefore was to place his ships athwart any approach of a hostile fleet to the island where Richelieu was operating and to continue to shelter the ground forces. When Byng appeared and offered battle some seven leagues to the south of Port Mahon, de la Galissonière was thus bound by orders to manœuvre his ships with this fact in mind, and in consequence to ignore the ordinary rules of naval warfare in so far as striving for the weather gauge would permit the enemy to swing in between his fleet and Minorca.

It was not until the 20th that the two fleets came into contact with each other. Byng, with a full appreciation of his weakness, had determined that in coming to grips with the enemy he would avoid the risks of having his ships raked with the broadsides of the opposing line while bearing down upon it. By running in line of battle slightly beyond the enemy's line, then tacking, and then "lasking" — that is, approaching the latter's ships in a diagonal course — he could hope to avoid great risks, while temporarily enjoying an advantage in fire-power. Securing the weather gauge after some manœuvring — with his flagship moving third in the van — he continued along until his rear, under command of Temple West, was about to pass by the French van. It seemed that his brilliant strategy was unfolding. The two fleets at this juncture formed an angle of some thirty-three degrees with the French rear and the English van well out of firing range of each other. At this point de la Galissonière checked his own van so that it might not sail beyond the range of action, thus permitting the British to concentrate their strength on the French rear. As for Byng, after his van was well beyond the last of the French ships he gave the signal for all his ships to tack together — a manœuvre that now placed the admiral in the rear and Temple West's squadron in the van. He also signalled for the ships to take a lasking course in bearing down upon the enemy. The signal was misunderstood and Captain Andrews of the *Defiance,* in the new formation now leading

---

[33] These instructions were embodied in "*Mémoires* of the King to serve as an Instruction to the Marquis de la Gallissonière dated March 22, 1775" (Waddington, *op. cit.*, p. 441).

the van, bore directly down on the *Orphée,* the leading ship in the French van. Byng was furious. He again signalled for a lasking course, but the manœuvre was not carried out by West's squadron as anticipated, and when the red flag to engage was hoisted on the *Ramillies* the ships of the British van turned at almost right angles and bore directly down on the French line, which, in the leeward position moving under fairly full sail that gave additional range to its port broadsides, raked the rigging of the oncoming ships. The latter, unable to make use of their batteries, could return only an ineffective fire. Thus, in violation of all regulations, the British fleet was engaged in detail, with Byng's own squadron continuing to lask down toward the French, but at the time unable to support Temple West. What added to the confusion was that some of the ships in the British van became unmanageable, and as Byng with his squadron continued on his course, trying to preserve the line in harmony with the "Fighting Instructions" that bound him, he now bore down upon the crippled *Intrepid* and *Princess Louisa.* For a time there now existed a dangerous gap between the British van and the rear in the running fight, and Galissonière sought to separate the two squadrons. But Byng — after succeeding in driving one of the opposing French ships, the *Couronne,* out of line by fire from his flagship, now within fighting range — quickly proceeded to close the breach in the line, which was a matter of such supreme importance that all else had to be subordinated to it. As a result, firing ceased. Thus at five o'clock in the evening, with the French fleet driving ahead to the leeward in the direction of Minorca but little damaged and with the British *Intrepid, Defiance, Portland, Captain, Buckingham,* and *Princess Louisa* no longer fit for action, the historic engagement came to an end. Among the British killed was Captain Andrews of the *Defiance;* Captain Noel of the *Maria Louisa* was also fatally wounded. The sick, wounded, and dead of the crews totalled six hundred and twenty-eight, including seventy-one sick left at Gibraltar.[34] Tactically the engagement might be called a British victory, as Byng insisted; but, what is more important, strategically it was clearly a French victory.

The British admiral, on the one hand, had failed to relieve St.

---

[34] Tunstall, *op. cit.,* pp. 118–34. A. T. Mahan (*The Influence of Sea Power upon History, 1660–1783,* pp. 286–7) stresses the importance of Admiral Matthews's court-martial in 1744 in determining Byng's decisions in the course of the battle. Matthews in the Battle of Toulon against the French and Spanish fleets in that year violated the Fighting Instructions by leaving the line.

Philip's Castle as he had been ordered to do, while the French admiral, on the other, had successfully blocked the relief in line with his instructions. Moreover, the French squadron suffered little injury and the death of but thirty-eight men with only one hundred and seventy-five wounded.[35] It could easily have renewed the action, and would have, had Byng pressed again in the direction of Minorca; but the British *Intrepid* had been demasted and other ships were clearly unseaworthy and demanded attention, as has been indicated, and the crews were badly in need of hospitalization as well as recuperation. Good fortune had saved the British fleet to fight under more favourable conditions, and Byng assumed the responsibility, in calling a council of war on the 24th that included both naval and land officers, to frame a series of questions as to the course of action to be pursued. These clearly indicated his own best judgment that the attempt to relieve the besieged on Minorca should be suspended until reinforcements had arrived and that the fleet should therefore return to Gibraltar. His view that the Rock would be endangered should they again attack the French fleet without these reinforcements was unanimously supported by all the officers. In approving it little did they realize that they were thereby helping to seal the fate of the admiral.[36]

Byng has been exonerated of the charge of cowardice by historians, but has been heavily blamed for turning his back upon Minorca at this critical juncture.[37] As one distinguished naval historian has expressed it:

"It is obvious . . . that Byng had only to hold his ground till reinforcements could reach him, and he must have practically paralysed the siege. It required but a well-played game of hide-and-seek, and in this Byng, with his familiarity with the scene of action, should have been his adversary's equal." [38]

But does this view take sufficiently into consideration the actualities of the situation? Byng had no knowledge that Brodrick was coming to support him with four more ships of the line; his letter calling for reinforcements was written on May 25; but long before it reached England the news had arrived from French sources that the British

---

[35] Waddington, *op. cit.*, p. 449.

[36] For the five questions and unanimous answers to them see Tunstall, *op. cit.*, pp. 137–9.

[37] This is the view of Tunstall (*ibid.*, pp. 139–42); Corbett (*op. cit.*, II, 125–8), who wrote earlier, expresses a like view.

[38] *Ibid.*

fleet had failed to scatter its rival. The ministers, accepting the French version of the battle, determined to relieve Byng of his command and ordered Hawke to proceed immediately to Gibraltar in the speedy *Antelope*. Sailing on June 16 from Portsmouth, this vessel did not reach the Rock until July 3. Assuming that a reinforcing squadron had been sent in answer to Byng's appeal, delay of at least a week or more would have been involved in getting the proper complements of men and the supplies on board after his request had been received. It is therefore unlikely that such a relief could have reached Gibraltar under usual sailing conditions facing ships of the line until the latter part of July, and it might have been the early part of August, if not later, before it could have joined Byng, still playing hide-and-seek with the French fleet in the region of Minorca. This meant that his fleet, already foul when he left Gibraltar on May 5, would have continued operating for a period of three months without a base — had it still been in existence, which seems unlikely. Further, the above view does not seem to take sufficiently into account the larger strategy of the war, which was to become truly global in extent. This strategy demanded the careful balancing of objectives and the means and costs of realizing them. Important as Minorca, with its excellent naval base at Port Mahon, was in the eyes of the British, was it of sufficient importance to risk a British fleet faced with overwhelming odds against it, in view of the important role that the royal navy must play in the region of the Gulf of St. Lawrence, in the West Indies, and in the Far East as well as in the region of Gibraltar and off the western coast of France — with an empire at stake in North America rather than a small, rather barren island lying within an almost landlocked sea? In other words, was Minorca worth Byng's fleet? [39]

The trial of Admiral Byng by court-martial and his subsequent execution on the quarter-deck of the *Monarque* are undoubtedly

---

[39] Corbett makes the following statements on the fate of Byng that will, it would seem, hardly bear the test of critical analysis (*op. cit.*, I, 134): "It was for no mere tactical shortcoming that Byng died. It was for strategical incompetence, the failure to grasp the tremendous European issues that had fallen into his hands that could not be forgiven." The distinguished student of naval strategy, in fact, provides the best possible answer to this in another statement (*ibid.*, I, 135): "The eccentric attack on Minorca [by the French] involved a strategical error. As a naval position it had no relation to the object of the war. Its capture did little to improve the French position in regard to America, and, so long as we held Gibraltar, it in no way injured ours. . . . And thus in the end . . . the loss of the place soon proved to be a distinct advantage to us, and no attempt was made to recover it."

blots upon the records of both the Admiralty and the British ministry and equally so upon the honour of King George. The court proceedings were held during the fall of 1756 in the midst of great public excitement, with petitions coming from various parts of England demanding punishment for what was considered to be the cowardly behaviour of the admiral. When the naval officers who composed the court had completed their work of taking the testimony of witnesses, they drew up thirty-seven resolutions, all but one of which were agreed to unanimously. These had to do with Byng's actions previous to, during, and subsequent to the engagement. Among these was one to the effect that he did not do his utmost to relieve St. Philip's and another "that he 'appears' to fall under the Twelfth Article of War for not doing his utmost to take or destroy the enemy's ships and to assist and relieve his own." [40] This, the thirty-sixth, meant death unless the King saw fit to reprieve him, as was unanimously recommended by the court-martial.[41] But no reprieve came. Yet the other officers on board his flagship testified to his bravery and coolness during the engagement, his impatience to come to close action with the French, and his subsequent regret that he was not in a position to give chase to the enemy when it withdrew. It was also brought out that upon his return to Gibraltar he immediately set to work with great zeal to put his fleet in condition to meet the enemy on somewhat equal terms, now possible with the arrival of Brodrick at the Rock with four more ships of the line, which, unknown to him, had been sent out to strengthen him. Then, with the arrival of the *Antelope* with Hawke on board, came the news of his recall in disgrace.

Two reflections may be made upon Byng's attempt to relieve Minorca. The first is that had the admiral been less competent he would have been less apprehensive than he expressed himself to be in writing home as to his ability to succeed in his mission.[42] He knew the condition of his ships and he knew what he had to face in the Toulon fleet. The tremendous fighting ability that the crippled *Espé-*

---

[40] Tunstall, *op. cit.*, pp. 244–5.

[41] The examination of members of the court-martial in the House of Lords brings out the tragic misconception of the members regarding the connotation of the word "negligence" in the Articles of War (T. C. Hansard, *The Parliamentary History of England*, XV, 807–22).

[42] Anson, Byng's superior, unfortunately had no clear conception of the tremendous handicaps that would face Byng in the Mediterranean. Fox reported that the admiral had declared that he "took it upon himself that Byng's squadron could beat anything the French had" (quoted by I. S. Leadam in his *History of England from the Accession of*

rance had displayed when surrounded on the Atlantic the preceding fall by a group of his best ships of the line pouring their broadsides into her was doubtless not forgotten. His tactical arrangements for the engagement cannot be questioned with respect to soundness — in spite of the failure of his captains to carry out his orders for lack of signal practice involving the difficult manœuvre in question. If any tactical disposition of the fleet held out the slightest hope of success against de la Galissonière, it surely was the one adopted.[43] A less competent commander, bound hand and foot to carry out literally the Fighting Instructions, might well have sacrificed his entire fleet on May 20.

A second reflection is that in choosing a commander to carry out a distant mission, whether by sea or land, a wide range of discretion should be accorded him. It must be always assumed that if the mission is one of great importance, the best available person will be selected, and once his appointment has been made, he is entitled to every confidence and to full support when circumstances that cannot be fully anticipated may call for modifications of a general plan of operations. This has its application not only to Byng's mission but to that of Boscawen in the waters off Newfoundland and to that of Braddock in Virginia. In other words, the assumption must always be in favour of the judgment of the man in charge at the local scene of action rather than that of those far removed in time and space from the scene. Tested by this sound maxim, both the Admiralty and the ministry failed in their responsibility rather than Byng in his. But the public demanded that someone be punished for the loss of Minorca, and the admiral was chosen as the scapegoat. He met his death on March 14, 1757 before a firing squad, a truly brave man, in absolute serenity of mind, conscious that he had given his best, unhappily not enough, to serve worthily his country and his King.

Although the garrison at St. Philip's Castle succeeded in holding out until June 28, Great Britain did not await that event before de-

---

Anne to the Death of George II, p. 443). But after the engagement Byng, writing with complete frankness to Keene, realistically declared: "Between you and I, they are too strong for us" (*ibid.*).

43 Corbett, while condemning Byng for strategical incompetence, nevertheless speaks in high terms of the admiral's battle-orders involving the "lasking" of the fleet when moving down to the attack. In fact he goes so far as to say (*op. cit.,* I, 117): "His captains mistook his meaning, or the result might have been very different." Had the result been very different, however, would naval historians be likely to refer to Byng's strategical incompetence?

claring war upon France. This declaration came on May 18 after the news reached London that the French had invaded Minorca; the French declaration came on June 9. Whatever might be permitted to go on in the way of irregular hostilities beyond the "line of amity," such an occurrence as this could not be tolerated within the line.

CHAPTER XIV

The American Crisis Ushers In a World War

A s YET only two of the major European powers were at war. Only too soon, however, most of the Continent would be involved. The Convention of Versailles between France and Austria, signed on May 1, seemed but a measure to ensure the tranquillity of Europe, just as the Convention of Westminster was so considered by the British ministry. Kaunitz, however, wanted a more far-reaching understanding and Louis XV was still fascinated with the thought of securing most of the Netherlands for his son-in-law, Philippe of Parma, and a grant of the remainder of these lands to France; yet the government of France continued to refuse to consider the idea of an offensive war against Prussia in aid of Austria. On the other hand, the Austrian court was clear in its determination that these transfers of territory must not be made until Silesia had been recovered. Abbé de Bernis, with strong pro-Austrian leanings, now French Ambassador to the court of Vienna but remaining in France, and Count Stahremberg continued to negotiate; and the longer they continued, the more fully was de Bernis drawn to the Austrian position respecting Prussia. Early in July the priest gave to the Austrian envoy additional assurances of French support and, according to the latter, even pointed the way for bringing France fully to the side of Austria and Russia as against Prussia. His formula was simple:

> "Bring it about that the King of Prussia will give us plenty of subjects of complaint against him." [1]

---

[1] Stahremberg to Kaunitz, July 18, 1756, Waddington, op. cit., p. 469.

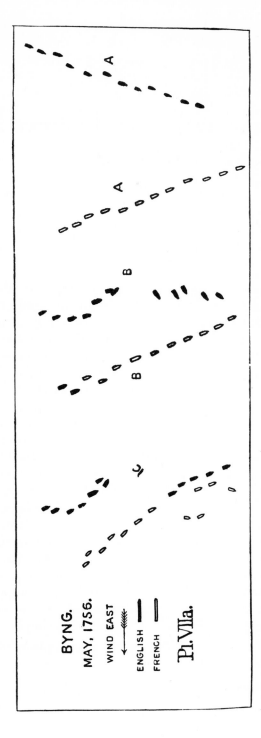

The three phases of the naval battle off Minorca. (A) As Byng approaches the French fleet. (B) When the British van, misunderstanding Byng's signal, moved to the attack. (C) The British van bearing the weight of the French superior fire-power.

(From A. T. Mahan, *The Influence of Sea Power upon History*, 1660–1783.)

Germany in the Middle of the Eighteenth Century. By T. Jeffrey.

By the latter part of August such progress had been made that the Count felt he was able to inform Kaunitz that the French court

"has made known to us without reserve that it is not only ready to enter into the views that we have presented to it but indeed desires to do so, and to such an extent that this appears to be the sincere termination [of the negotiations]." [2]

Still, it should be borne in mind that de Bernis, with all his facility, could not bind France to any aggressive alliance; evidence is also lacking that the French court, although desirous of expanding into the Netherlands and of rebuking Frederick for his bad conduct, was at all prepared to see Europe plunged into war on a grand scale. While certainly dallying with contingencies, it would not, as indicated, commit itself beyond a defensive alliance with Austria. It is equally clear that, in spite of Elizabeth's intense dislike of the King of Prussia and the tentative offer of her council earlier in the year to support Maria Theresa with eighty thousand troops to aid her to drive Frederick out of Silesia and Glatz, there existed no aggressive alliance between the courts of Vienna and St. Petersburg directed against him — only the old defensive alliance of 1746, made during the preceding war. In fact, Russia was actually not in a crusading mood; further, it was felt that she could not bring her strength to bear upon Prussia without heavy subsidies — and she certainly expected them — which Austria, accustomed to receiving substantial subsidies herself, could not provide. A great European war therefore doubtless seemed a rather remote contingency to most statesmen after the signing of the Westminster and Versailles conventions. But Frederick made it a reality.

Now fully prepared for another war and as fully assured that British gold would no longer bring down on him a Russian avalanche should he move, the King of Prussia determined by means of a quick and decisive war to accomplish two things: the absorption of Saxony and bringing home to Maria Theresa the folly of her dream of seeing the restoration of her province of Silesia and her county of Glatz. Without taking the British government into his confidence until the last moment when nothing could head him off and in complete violation of the spirit of the Convention of Westminster, if not its letter,[3]

---

[2] Stahremberg to Kaunitz, August 20, 1755, *ibid.*, p. 470.

[3] Sir Richard Lodge takes the position that Frederick's action was a clear breach of his obligations to Britain (*Great Britain and Prussia in the Eighteenth Century*, p. 95). While this action was certainly a gross violation of the spirit of the convention, still

he suddenly — and with the same disregard of every principle of political morality that had characterized his early movement into Silesia — invaded a peacefully inclined neighbouring state. For, in spite of the fact that the chief minister and statesman of Saxony, Count von Brühl, had long considered him a dangerous ruler who should be checked and had indicated as much in his correspondence, this state had refused to enter into any treaty directed toward curbing his ambitions. With almost unimaginable cunning Frederick first demanded the right of free and innocent passage through Saxony for his army. This was reluctantly granted by King Augustus. Once having moved across the border, he ordered the seizure of the public treasury and the public archives and the surrender of the Saxon army — all as necessary preliminaries to his entrance into Bohemia, where Maria Theresa had concentrated considerable forces, which he chose to regard as a provocative step on the part of the Empress-Queen, though she insisted the troops were there solely for precautionary reasons.

The inquiring student need not go beyond the tomes of the *Politische Correspondenz Friedrich's des Grossen* to see the extent to which Frederick was directly responsible for the suffering and devastation of the European Seven Years' War — and also the extent to which he relied upon indirection. On June 5, 1756 in a letter to von Klinggräffen, his Ambassador in Vienna, Frederick made clear that while he was convinced that Maria Theresa desired to embroil Europe he was equally convinced that neither France nor Russia would support her in her desires; Russia, he pointed out, liked subsidies which Austria could not supply, and the Great Chancellor, Bestuzhev, hated the French more than he loved the Austrians.[4] On the same day von Klinggräffen sent information from Vienna that the Russian court, deeply suspicious of France, would not break with England but would, on the contrary, abide by its engagements with her;[5] while two days later Knyphausen, Frederick's Ambassador in Paris, assured the King that the Versailles Convention was entered into largely for the purpose of stripping the French Minister of War, d'Argenson, of power.[6] Frederick was further assured on June 8 by

---

within its framework he could technically invade Saxony — as undoubtedly Frederick had in mind doing at the time that the treaty was signed although the British ministers were kept completely in the dark respecting his designs.

[4] *Politische Correspondenz*, XII, 383.

[5] *Ibid.*, XII, 414.

[6] *Ibid.*, XII, 424.

his chargé d'affaires in London, Michell, that the Russian Great Chancellor was still committed to the British interests. Thus Frederick's own understanding of Austria's isolation, were she to attempt to act aggressively, was supported by the assurances of these trusted representatives.

On June 16 von Klinggräffen wrote from Vienna that troops and artillery were moving into Bohemia;[7] two days later Frederick's Minister in Dresden, von Maltzahn, assured him from advices that he had received that Russia could not possibly take any effective military step during the year and that the King, if he saw fit, might therefore feel free to concentrate all his forces against Maria Theresa.[8] This information was reinforced by dispatches from Russia that indicated that troops moving into Livonia had been ordered back into the interior.[9] Frederick thereupon proceeded rapidly with military preparations. According to a letter written on June 23 to Holderness by Andrew Mitchell, the British Minister in Berlin, the Prussian King was completely ready for hostilities, with all orders for mobilization given.[10] The King himself two days later wrote to von Maltzahn warning him: "I begin to envisage war as inevitable,"[11] and the day after, he sent another warning to Klinggräffen to be ready to leave Vienna at any moment: "As for you, it will be necessary for you to have your foot in the stirrup."[12]

Alarmed at the Prussian hostile preparations, Lord Stormont, the British Minister at Dresden, on July 5 had a meeting with von Maltzahn, at which he expressed his fear that Frederick was about to make war and warned him that Great Britain would not support him in attacking Maria Theresa and that Russia would under these circumstances surely support the Empress-Queen as the result of her old defensive engagements, although also allied with Great Britain.[13] The King of Prussia, upon receiving von Maltzahn's report of the conference, on July 10 ordered his Minister to assure everyone at Dresden with whom he spoke that there was no need for alarm respecting any movement of Prussian troops.[14] On the same day

---

[7] Ibid., II, 464.
[8] Ibid., XII, 561.
[9] Ibid., XIII, 15.
[10] Ibid., XII, 447.
[11] Ibid., XII, 462.
[12] Ibid., XII, 464.
[13] Ibid., XIII, 47.
[14] Ibid., XIII.

von Klinggräffen wrote from Vienna that, in spite of all military preparations made by the Empress in Bohemia and Moravia, he was astonished at the prevailing pacific sentiments in Vienna and the equally prevalent opinion that these preparations were simply precautions in view of the fact that the King of Prussia had, it was said, already marked out four military concentration points (*camps*) in Silesia.[15]

On July 18, Frederick, fully determined to apply force against the Empress-Queen, sent orders to von Klinggräffen to demand an audience with her to ask her if she was moving troops into Bohemia and Moravia with the purpose of invading Prussia. The blunt note to Maria Theresa read: "I am asking the Empress if these warlike preparations are being made for the purpose of attacking me."[16] Fearing the outbreak of a Continental war, the British Minister in Berlin held a series of interviews with the King of Prussia on the 20th and 21st. At these conferences he pointed out that the movement of Prussian troops might well have caused the court of Vienna to send extraordinary succours into Bohemia and Moravia to prevent an invasion. In reply Frederick declared to him that the Austrians knew he had no such intentions and also tried to assure Mitchell that no additional soldiers had been sent to Silesia;[17] but Mitchell in writing to Holderness on the 23rd made clear that Frederick's troops were so quartered that in two weeks he could have ninety thousand of them concentrated in that province.[18] By the 30th Frederick had taken Mitchell sufficiently into his confidence to let him know that he had decided to strike at Austria late in August — assuring him that when the attack was delivered, France would be unable to move an army into Germany during the remainder of that year to operate against Hanover.[19] He might have added that it would likewise be too late for Russia to come to Austria's assistance.

Meanwhile on the 27th von Klinggräffen had his interview with Maria Theresa. In reply to Frederick's point-blank question whether she intended to attack him, she stated in writing that there was a crisis in the general affairs of Europe and in view of this fact she had judged it proper to take measures for her own security and that of

---

15 *Ibid.*, XIII, 90.
16 *Ibid.*, XIII, 90.
17 *Ibid.*, XIII, 99.
18 *Ibid.*
19 *Ibid.*, XIII, 123.

her allies — measures "that tended to the prejudice of no person." [20] Indeed, the day following this interview the Prussian Ambassador wrote to Berlin that even the subalterns in Vienna who were about to go to Bohemia were sure that nothing was contemplated by the Austrian court and that the purpose appeared to be to push His Prussian Majesty himself into some act of aggression.[21] When on August 2 the King of Prussia received the reply of the Empress he immediately ordered his Ambassador to secure a second interview, in which he should make clear that the King of Prussia insisted that, while neither the states of the Empress nor those of her allies were menaced, his own states were, and that it could not be questioned that the Empress at the beginning of the year had made an offensive alliance with the court of Russia directed against him.[22] Once more he demanded a categorical answer to his question. The same day Frederick gave specific orders to Field Marshal von Schwerin as to the conduct of hostilities.[23]

With preparations for war taking place on either side of the Austrian border King George, in his capacity as a German prince and acting through President of the Council of Hanover von Münchhausen, appealed to the court of Berlin on August 1 not to furnish the occasion to the court of Vienna to begin hostilities.[24] On August 6 the British Cabinet Council, equally fearful of Frederick's intentions, sent a special courier to Minister Mitchell in Berlin with a request to represent to the King the danger to the common cause if at the present moment he rushed to arms, and their desire that he would suspend every operation against the Empress if the latter gave him assurances that she had no evil designs against him.[25] On August 7, when von Klinggräffen demanded his second interview with the Empress, she requested that he put his inquiry in writing so that there would arise no misunderstanding; he thereupon wrote for permission to give to Maria Theresa the *mémoire* prepared by Frederick, which brought him a good scolding from his master for not immediately handing this document to the Empress. Significantly, the King, before waiting for a reply from Vienna, on August 21 informed von Maltzahn at Dresden that his troops were about to march into Sax-

[20] *Ibid.*, XIII, 163.
[21] *Ibid.*, XIII, 183.
[22] *Ibid.*, XIII, 164.
[23] *Ibid.*, XIII, 166.
[24] *Ibid.*, XIII, 188.
[25] *Ibid.*, XIII, 247.

ony and at the same time warned the Minister to act as though ignorant of everything connected with the Prussian movement — "pretend to know absolutely nothing about it." [26] In this connection it
should be pointed out that von Maltzahn had previously advised
Frederick that there was no evidence of any understanding between
the courts of Dresden and Vienna and that Saxony was totally unprepared for war.[27]

On August 20 Maria Theresa replied to the King of Prussia's
accusations contained in the *mémoire;* she again assured him that
the forces sent to Bohemia and Moravia threatened no one and further declared that the information given to the King of Prussia as to
the existence of an offensive alliance against him on the part of the
courts of Vienna and St. Petersburg as well as all the circumstances
and pretended stipulations of such an alliance were false and that
"such a treaty against His Prussian Majesty does not exist and has
never existed." [28] But nothing now would turn Frederick from his
designs. On August 26 he wrote to von Maltzahn to demand of King
Augustus a free passage through Saxony. This was reluctantly granted
on the 29th, and the next day he joined his troops to begin operations.

Frederick's aggressive move against Maria Theresa and his unexpected invasion of Saxony, together with the treacherous way in
which he turned his arms against that country, threw the British
ministry into alarmed confusion. King George was so outraged with
the conduct of the King of Prussia that he contemplated publishing a
disavowal of the act, but was finally held in check by his advisers.[29]
They realized that they were face to face with a *fait accompli* on the
part of their ally. In place of a Europe at peace — except for France
— as was hoped would result from the Convention of Westminster,
most of the Continent was now destined to be engulfed in one of its
most bloody struggles. Thus was to be added to the Great War for
the Empire, entering upon its third year, the European Seven Years'
War; yet in the case of the former the results, as has been indicated,

---

[26] *Ibid.,* XIII, 247.

[27] *Ibid.,* XIII, 261.

[28] *Ibid.,* XIII, 289.

[29] Under date of September 12, 1756 there is to be found the following memorandum
among the Newcastle Papers (quoted by Lodge, *op. cit.,* p. 96) : "To beg the King not to
publish, either in Vienna or Ratisbon, any disavowal of the King of Prussia's conduct in
attacking the Queen of Hungary or taking possession of Saxony. To observe a perfect si-
lence upon it."

were to be of tremendous historical significance, in contrast to the tragic futility of the latter. Frederick, it is true, saved Prussia from partition, if not from extinction, and retained possession of Silesia; but he failed in resorting to war to absorb Saxony and to make his state, as he had hoped to do, the unchallengeable dominator of the Germanies — over a century must still elapse before the latter objective would be realized by his successors.

As for Great Britain, the untoward events in Europe and also in America had their effects upon the stability of the Newcastle ministry and led to its fall before the end of 1756. The defeat of Braddock in 1755; the failure of Boscawen to capture the French fleet on its outward voyage to Canada and of Hawke to waylay it on its return to France; the outcry caused by Byng's inability to bring aid to besieged Minorca; the still louder outcry over the loss of the island; the deep national concern and foreboding with the news that Frederick had started a Continental war, which involved vast British commitments to Prussia; and the public shock that came when on September 30 information arrived from America that the colonials had lost their hold on Lake Ontario with the French capture of Forts Oswego and Ontario and the defending troops — all these events taken together seemed to indicate in the public mind that the war had up to the present been grossly mismanaged, and this shook the Cabinet Council to its foundations. William Pitt, closely in touch with the temper of the country, declared to Hardwicke in October that what he found fault with, stated broadly, was the "conduct of the war by sea and land." [30] The extreme incompetence of the Newcastle ministry at this juncture not only was charged by Pitt but has also been accepted as demonstrably true by most British historians. Nevertheless it may be said that when the Great Commoner took over the government, he found that the policies that he had so bitterly criticized when in the opposition were those that in the main he must follow to achieve victory — even in the matter of supporting Hanover and subsidizing other Continental states.

Newcastle saw as clearly as did Pitt the overshadowing importance of the American phase of the war, the necessity of crippling France on the seas, and the strict limitations that should be set upon diverting the resources of the Kingdom to the defence of Hanover. Perhaps even more clearly than Pitt he saw the importance of Gibraltar as a key to the larger strategy of sea power and never permitted

---

[30] B.M., Add. Mss., 35,870: 263.

himself as did Pitt in 1757 to dally with the idea of surrendering it for other advantages. To the credit of Newcastle it should also be pointed out — as an offset to the early disappointments and reverses in the Great War for the Empire — that during his administration the British had scored certain successes that would later bring unexpected returns. Before Pitt had come to power devastating blows had been struck at the French merchant marine — so serious, in fact, that to support her valuable West India possessions France was compelled to open freely the ports of these islands to neutral commerce, to which the British replied in the famous Navigation Rule of 1756. With the continuance of these blows her empire was destined to exhibit fatal weaknesses. Further, France had suffered a serious reverse in North America, the importance of which was out of all proportion to the number of troops involved on either side, in the loss of Fort Beauséjour on the Acadian isthmus — a fort equally vital for offensive as well as defensive strategy in North America. Lastly, by the removal of the Acadians from the critical area of military operations to the south of the entrance to the St. Lawrence after the fall of Beauséjour, France was deprived of the sorely needed support of many thousands of people bound to her by strong ties of nationality and religion. These Acadians not only had produced on their fertile farms large surpluses of food — commodities such as cereals and meat, so lacking in Canada and so difficult to transport from Europe and yet so vital to sustain the French fighting forces in Canada and on Cape Breton Island — but also before their exile had been in a position to make other equally important contributions to the French war effort in the New World.

In reality, therefore, in balancing the military advantages gained with the reverses sustained under Newcastle the war was not going too badly for the British Empire when Newcastle left office. At the same time the accession of Pitt to power may be considered an event of such importance in the history of the war itself and of the Empire that one is justified in referring to the period of his administration of affairs, brief as it was, as the epoch of Pitt. To a consideration of the momentous events of this epoch the next volume of this series will be devoted.

Index

Abenaki [Abnaki] Indians, with Dieskau attack the English, 170–1; conduct of, during the Battle of Lake George, 172; under the control of Le Loutre, 214

Abercromby, James, Major General, appointment of, as temporary commander-in-chief in North America, 192; the arrival of, at New York, 192; relieves Shirley of his command at Albany, 192; receives news of the danger to Oswego, 193; delays action until the arrival of Loudoun, 193; confers with Winslow over the issue of the use of regulars in the Crown Point campaign, 207

Acadia, the limits of, ceded to the British, 213–5; the reconquest of, a policy of the government of New France, 245; the importance of, to France, 343–4

Acadian refugees, the, behind the French forts, 246; the taking of an oath of allegiance by, 246; desire of, to return to their homes, in 1753, 246–7; terms offered, by the government of Nova Scotia, 247; unhappy situation of, 248; threatened by Le Loutre's Indians, 248; from Cape Breton Island return and take the oath, 249; the, deliver up their arms, 254; Monckton ordered to drive, from the country, 254

Acadians, the, do not live in "ancient" Acadia, 213–4; the number of fighting men among, 214; influence of the priests among, 214; the support of, in defence of Beauséjour, 229; request special protection from Vergor for armed support, 229; military aid rendered the French by, 229–30; lose desire to fight, 230–1; press Vergor to surrender, 231; special concessions for, asked by Vergor, 231–2; terms of surrender granted to, by Monckton, 232; arrest of leading, planning to continue resistance, 234; loyalty of, to France in 1713, 243–4; remain in Nova Scotia after the cession to Great Britain, 243–4; increase in numbers of, after 1713, 243–4; attempt of, to reconcile irreconcilable conceptions, 244; unique position of, within the British Empire, 244; deny that they are "natural-born subjects" of Great Britain, 244; limitations on land-holding for, 244–5; unauthorized appropriation of land by, 245; legal disabilities of, 245; demand of the Crown in 1749 of the oath of allegiance from, 245; the problem of permitting emigration into Canada of, 245–6; the support of the great body of, given to the French after 1750, 246; promise given to, by Nova Scotia government that they will not have to bear arms, 247–8; movement of, to assist at the French fort, 248; plan of Le Loutre to get all, behind the French lines, 248; passes to go to Fort Beauséjour refused to, 249; a memorial from, to the French King for lands in French Acadia, 250; Gov. Lawrence despairs of the loyalty of, 250–1; the Board of Trade advises Lawrence respecting, 251–2; Chief Justice Belcher's opinion on the rights of, who have refused the oath, 252; the expulsion of, envisioned by the Board of Trade, 253; warned as to conduct toward the French, 253; memorials of, in 1755, 254, 255, 258, 259–60; the deputies of, before, the Nova Scotia Council, 255–60; decision of the Council to exile, 256–7; the problem of the places of exile of, 260–1; Gov. Shirley advocates the exile of, in 1747, 261; devotion of, in 1764 to Louis XV, 263; decision of the Nova Scotia Council to distribute, among the other continental colonies, 263–4; confiscation of the landed property of, 264; stratagems of war against, 264; of Chignecto, the effort to collect at Fort Cumberland for exile, 265–6; the departure of, part of, 266; shipping arrangements for the exile of, 277–8; the numbers of, dispersed, 282; the petition of, sent to Pennsylvania, 283; the hatred of the English before the dispersion by, 284; the loyalty of, to their church and to the French nation, 284; the responsibility resting on, for their misfortunes, 284–5;

conditions in the colonies that receive, from Nova Scotia, 287; in Georgia, 287–92; in South Carolina, 292–7; in North Carolina, 297–9; in Virginia, 299–304; in Maryland, 304–9; in Pennsylvania, 237, 309–18; in New York, 319–21; in Connecticut, 321–4; in Massachusetts Bay, 324–35; return of, from Massachusetts Bay to Nova Scotia, 335–6; fate of, on Isle St. Jean and Isle Royale, 336–7; futile effort in 1762 to send more of, to Massachusetts Bay, 337–8; in England, 338; in France, 238–40, 338–42; final disposition of, 343; a great blow to the French Empire in the uprooting of, 343–4

Achille, the, French warship in the battle off Minorca, 409

Actif, the, French warship, activities of, in waters of the New World, 108, 114; eludes the British blockade, 121

Adams, Captain, report of, on the Rivière aux Canards settlement, 269

Adams, Captain, of the *Hannah*, carries Acadians to Pennsylvania, 277

Aix-la-Chapelle, the Peace of, France's record of bad faith after, 119; the Austrian Netherlands and, 357, 359, 361

Albany, New York, Braddock's beaten regulars, winter-quartered at, 133; Shirley on the bad effects of the intercourse between the people of, and the French Indians, 144; the neutrality between, and Canada, 144; French Indians trading at, warn of British plans, 154

Albany Commissioners, accusations against the, in 1755, 66

Albany Congress, liberal instructions for the Massachusetts Bay delegates to the, 130

Albemarle, William Anne Keppel, 2nd Earl of, British Ambassador in Paris, conference of, with Rouillé, 62–3

Alcide, the, French warship, the capture of, by the British, 111–2; why France did not declare war after the capture of, 118–9; Pichon on the capture of, 224; the prisoners from, and Pichon, 234–5

Alexander, William, secretary to General Shirley, assists in drawing up the plans for Fort Ontario, 157

Alexandria, Virginia, the governors' meeting at, in 1755, 71–2

Algonkin, the, French warship, in the New World, 114; sent up to Quebec for repairs, 115; departure of, for France, 120

American national tradition, *see* Chapter I

Amherst, Sir Jeffrey, commander-in-chief of

British forces in America, Acadians sent to, from Nova Scotia in 1762, 337

Andrews, Capt. Thomas, of H.M.S. *Defiance*, the battle off Minorca and, 411–2; the death of, 412

Anglo-Austrian relations, *see* Great Britain, George II, Kaunitz, Maria Theresa, Newcastle, the "System"

Anglo-Dutch relations, *see* England, Great Britain, Holderness, the "System," the United Netherlands

Anglo-French hostilities, *see* Beauséjour, Boscawen, *Espérance*, Lake George, Minorca, Oswego

Anglo-French negotiations, *see* Albemarle, France, Great Britain, Mirepoix, Newcastle, Rouillé

Anglo-Prussian relations, *see* Great Britain, Frederick II, George II, Holderness, Newcastle, Prussia

Anglo-Russian negotiations, *see* Bestuzhev, Great Britain, Elizabeth, Newcastle, Hanbury Williams

Annapolis, Maryland, Acadians at, 304–5, 308

Annapolis River, Nova Scotia, memorial and deputies of the Acadians of, before the Council, 258–9; the exile of the Acadians of, 267, 277, 280–1

Annapolis Royal (Port Royal), troops at, in 1754, 215; Acadians from, assist at Fort Beauséjour, 248; stirred up by the priest Daudin, 250; proposal to expel the English from, 250; the removal of the Acadians from, 267, 274, 277, 280–1

Anson, George, Lord, Admiral of the Fleet, 100; efforts of, to protect Great Britain from invasion, 402–3; on the fighting qualities of French warships, 409; failure of, to realize the nature of the task assigned to Byng, 415

Antelope, H.M.S., carries Hawke to Gibraltar, 414, 415

Antwerp, Flanders, the decline of, and the closing of the Scheldt, 352; the occupation of, by the French, 357

Apollon, the, French warship, eludes the British blockade, 121

Apthorp & Hancock, Boston merchants and shippers, unlimited credit upon, given to Monckton, 216; provide transports for removing the Acadians, 278; failure of, to provide adequate transports, 279

Aquilon, the, French warship, arrival of, at Louisbourg, 114; the blockade of, 123

Arch-Treasurership, the, of the Holy Roman Empire, George II and, 349

Armés en flûte, French warships sent to the New World, 104; the return of the ships, to France, 119–21

Arnold, Brigadier General Benedict, later expedition of, considered, 78, 153

Articles of War, the, and the provincial troops, 205; and the trial of Byng, 415

Artois, the battalion of, sent to Canada, 86; arrival of, at Louisbourg, 114

Ashford, Connecticut, Acadian exiles in, 323

Assassination, the question of, in connection with the death of Jumonville, 31–2

Aubry, Captain, later defeat of French forces under, 145

Augusta Court House, Virginia, mutiny of North Carolina troops at, 47

Augustus, III, King of Poland and Elector of Saxony (Frederick Augustus II), the granting to Frederick II the right of passage through Saxony by, 420

Aulac, Nova Scotia, the Acadians of, help defend Fort Beauséjour, 229

Austria, see Charles VI, Kaunitz, Holy Roman German Empire, Maria Theresa

Austrian Netherlands, the, the Treaty of Rastatt and, 352; the Barrier Treaty and, 353; the limitations of the authority of the Emperor over, 354; the occupation of, by France, 356–7; preserved to Maria Theresa by Great Britain, 358; the desire of Maria Theresa to exchange, 363–4; disadvantages faced by, for two centuries, 364; the Westminster Convention and, 390–1, 398; the Versailles Convention and, 396–7

Austro-Russian defensive alliance of 1746, the, and offensive war in 1756, 419

Bacon, the Rev. Thomas, of Oxford, Maryland, kind treatment of the Acadian exiles by, 305

Bagley, Lieut. Col. Jonathan, responsible for British shipping on Lake George, 207

Balfour, Mr., of Hampton, Virginia, notifies Dinwiddie of the arrival of Acadians in Virginia, 299; provides the exiles with food, 300

Baltimore, H.M.S., convoys the transports from Annapolis Royal to New England, 281

Baltimore, Maryland, Acadians at, 305, 306–7, 308

Bancroft, George, author of *History of the United States*, American national tradition and, 4, 10, 17; on the Acadian dispersion, 286

Banks, Capt. John, of the *Racehorse*, transports Acadians to Massachusetts Bay, 280; brings Acadian exiles to Boston, 326

Banyar, Goldsbrow, Deputy Secretary of the New York provincial Council, criticizes Johnson's activities, 165; on the lack of discipline of the army under Johnson, 175; aids in the undermining of General Shirley, 187

Barnard, Sir John, London financier, views of, on British taxation, 377

Barrier fortresses of the Austrian Netherlands, the Treaty of Antwerp and, 353; the desire of Maria Theresa to eliminate the Dutch control of, 359, 361; right of the Dutch to help defend the, recognized in 1748, 362; the Treaty of Aix-la-Chapelle and the, 357; the Dutch in 1755 no longer able to garrison the, 366

Barrier Treaty of 1715, the, guarantee of, by Great Britain, 353

Barrington, William Wildman, 2nd Viscount, Secretary at War, confused orders of, to General Fowke, 406–7

Bateau-men, the employment of, for his campaign by Shirley, 149; the desertion of many, 150; effect of shortage of, on the Fort Niagara campaign, 151; the disbanding of the companies of, by General Abercrombie, 202

Bateaux, the use of, on Lake Ontario, 149; contrast between the French and British, on Lake Ontario, 159; built by Connecticut too small for use on Lake George, 162

Bavaria, Electorate of, the Maritime Powers enter into a subsidy treaty with, in 1750, 366–7; the subsidy treaty with, not renewed in 1755, 367; the imperial election and, 367

Bay of Fundy, the strategic importance of, 216–7

Béarn, the battalion of, sent to Canada, 86, 100; ordered to Fort Niagara, 197; used against Oswego, 197–8

Beaubassin, the burning of, and Le Loutre, 246

Beauchamp, M., Piziquid merchant, aids Winslow and Murray with their addresses to the Acadians, 268

Beaujeu, Capt. Daniel Liénard de, appointment of, to attack Braddock, 91; brings the Indians to fight, 91; the death of, 94

Beaumont, Marie-Barbe Le Prince, Madame de, forms an alliance with Pichon, 237

Beauséjour, the burning of the village of, by the French, 228; see also Fort Beauséjour

Beausoleil (Brossard, dit Beausoleil) family, arrest of members of, 234

Becancour, Canada, British plans to capture, 87

Beef, furnished to Braddock in Maryland rejected, 76; demanded by Boscawen, for his crews, 276

Belcher, Gov. Jonathan, of New Jersey, attitude of, toward the Acadian exiles, 319

Belcher, Jonathan, Jr., Chief Justice and Lieutenant Governor of Nova Scotia, opinion of, respecting rights of the Acadians who refused the oath, 252; sends Acadians to Boston, 338

Belle Isle, the strait of, the French fleet traverses, 121

Belle-Isle, Charles Louis Auguste Fouquet, Maréchal, Duc de, on the importance of Acadia to France, 343; plan of, for invasion of England laid aside, 403

Benezet, Anthony, Philadelphia Quaker, kindness of, toward the Acadian exiles, 310–11, 314–5

Bentinck, Dutch plenipotentiary, makes concessions to Kaunitz in 1748, 362

Bernard, Francis, Governor of Massachusetts Bay, holds the Acadian exiles in high regard, 332, 334

Bernis, François-Joachim de Pierre de, Abbé, later Cardinal, French statesman, negotiations of, with Stahrremberg, 418–9

Bestuzhev (Bestuzheff), Alexis, Grand Chancellor of Russia, the War of the Austrian Succession and, 358; and the Maritime Powers, 358; the Anglo-Russian subsidy treaty of 1755 and, 370–2; the fall of, 372

Bic, the island of, St. Lawrence River, chosen as the concentration point for the fleet of de la Motte, 115, 120

Bigot, François, Intendant of New France, recommends that the Algonkin go to Quebec for repairs, 115; the treacherous conduct of, 225; advises Vergor to profit by his position, 233

Bizarre, the, French warship, activities of, in the waters of the New World, 108, 114; escape of, from Louisbourg, 122–4

Blakeney, Gen. William, Lieutenant Governor of Minorca, the defence of the island by, 403–4, 406–7, 416–7

Blanchard, Col. Joseph, of the New Hampshire regiment, in command at Fort Edward, 169–70

Blanford, H.M.S., capture of, and release of, by the French, 399

Blockade, British, of Cape Breton Island in 1755, 119–20, 122–3; of the port of Cherbourg in 1756, 406; the question of, of Minorca and Toulon in 1756, 410

Board of Trade, the denunciation of the fiscal legislation of North Carolina by, 47; finds it improper to continue Shirley in command, 187; recommends that a commander-in-chief be sent to America from England, 187; advice of, to Governor Lawrence respecting the Acadians, 251–2; permits the Acadian exiles in 1763 to go wherever they pleased, 333

Bobby Goodrich, the, carries Acadian exiles from Virginia to England, 303

Bohemia, the King of, and the imperial election, 367; the movement of Imperial troops into, 422

Boishébert, Charles Deschamps, Sieur de, commandant of the fort on the St. John, joined by Acadians exiled to South Carolina, 295; joined by the Annapolis River exiles who seize the Pembroke, 297–8

Bolton, Connecticut, Acadian exiles in, 323

Boscawen, Hon. Edward, Vice Admiral, sent in 1755 to cruise off Cape Breton Island, 103; activities of, in the New World, 109, 110–3, 116–7; the soundness of tactical movements of, considered, 117; how the French fleet escaped the blockade established by, 120; the tightening of the blockade of Louisbourg by, 123; the exile of the Acadians recommended by, 258; the demand of, for fresh meat for his ailing crews, 276; attitude in France after the news of the attack of, on the French fleet, 375–6

Boston, Massachusetts Bay, welcome given by, to General Shirley, 186; a concentration of Acadians at, 334; Acadians sent to, in 1762 refused admission, 337; the French government in 1784 permits the Acadians in France to go to, 342

Bourlamaque (Boulamaque, Bourlamarque), François Charles, Chevalier de, colonel, French military engineer, comes to Canada with Montcalm, 196

Bourbon, Duc de, the regency of, and the "System," 355

Bourgogne, the battalion of, to New France, 100; arrival of, at Louisbourg, 144

Bouville, Capt. de, of the Espérance, the great defence of the ship of, 124–6; rewarded by the French King, 126

Brabant, the reunion of, with Spain bought with a great price, 352

Braddock, Maj. Gen. Edward, early military experiences of, 57; qualifications of, for command in America, 57–8; instructions to, 58–9, 177; criticism of the instructions to, 59–60; British regiments assigned to, and their strengthening, 58, 63–4; the arrival of, in the New World, 64; the problem of securing provisions faced by, 65–6; attitude of, toward the Pennsylvania pacifists, 69; obliged to rely upon his "Private Instructions," 72; charges that he had been deceived as to the proper route to Fort Duquesne, 74–5; aided by Franklin, 75–6; strange treatment of, by inhabitants of Virginia, 76; adds Washington to his staff, 77; failure of Southern Indians to support, 77; denounces the bad conduct of Dinwiddie, 78; conference of, with the Pennsylvania Indians, 78; few Indians go with, 78; his great military feat, 78–9; secures sailors and heavy guns from the *Norwich*, 79; appraisal of his achievements during the march, 83–5; movement of army of, through the wilderness, 80–6; Contrecœur's comment upon the precautions taken by, 90; weakness of, for lack of Indian support, 93; sends support to Gage, 95; moves forward to support Burton, 95–6; failure of, to rally his soldiers, 96; mortally wounded, 96; the sending of troops to Americans under, not done secretly, 99; the death of, 127; the command of the army of, goes to Dunbar, 127; the effect of the defeat of, upon the Fort Niagara campaign, 150; orders and instructions given to, likewise given to General Shirley, 163; where Shirley failed success would doubtless have come to, 182–3

Braddock's Road, difficulties of terrain over, 80–6

Bradley, Capt. Housman, in command of the Royal Navy on Lake Ontario, admits French naval supremacy on the lake, 198

Bradstreet, Capt. John, later major, commands at Oswego, 1755, 149; report of, on the ruinous condition of Fort George, 153–4; warns the pro-French Indians against hostile actions at Oswego, 154; assists in drawing up plans for Fort Ontario, 157; warns of a concentration of French troops at Fort Niagara, 159; becomes lieutenant colonel, 184; arrival of, at Oswego with supplies, 184; placed in charge of supplies and bateau-men, by Shirley, 184; construction of boats by, 184; leads a great convoy to and from Oswego, 193; reports Oswego in danger,

193; requests the building of a fort at Three Rivers, 198; on the friction between the regular army and the New England volunteers involved in the Crown Point campaign, 206–7

Bragdon [Bragdton], Captain, of the *Prosperous*, takes Acadians to Virginia, 277, 300

Braintree, Massachusetts Bay, Acadians in, 332

Brandenburg, the Electorate of, the importance of, in 1755, 345–6; the Elector of, and the imperial election, 367; see also Frederick II, Prussia

Bréard, M., on the number of British troops at Oswego, 155–6

Bremen, the Archbishopric of, and George II, 349

Brest, France, the departure of the French fleets from, in 1755, 106

Breteuil, François Victoire le Tonnelier, Marquis de, French Minister of War, assists Pichon in France, 219

Briand, Jean Olivier, Bishop of Quebec, on the responsibility of the Acadians for their misfortunes, 284–5

Bristol, England, Acadians at, 338

British colonies, setting up of a common fund for the, opposed, 71–2; see Connecticut, Georgia, Maryland, Massachusetts Bay, New England, Newfoundland, New Jersey, New Hampshire, New York, North Carolina, Nova Scotia, Pennsylvania, Rhode Island, South Carolina, Virginia

British Empire, the Great War for the, Chapter I; see also British colonies, India, Minorca

British troops, Dinwiddie's desire for, 49; sent to Virginia, 58, 64, 99; conduct of, in the battle of the Monongahela, 96–7

Brodrick, Vice Admiral Thomas, sent to reinforce Byng, 413

Broglie, Charles François, Comte de, French Ambassador in Saxony, Frederick displeased with the activities of, 389

Brown, the Rev. Andrew, on the Acadian dispersion, 286

Brühl, Count Heinrich, Saxon statesman and chief minister, dislike of Frederick by, 420

Brunswick-Lüneburg, the Electorate of, and George II, 349

Brunswick-Wolfenbüttel, the Duchy of, helps to divide the Duchy of Calenberg, 349; activities of the Duke of, 382–5

Brussels, Austrian Netherlands, occupation of, by the French, 357

Buckingham, H.M.S., flagship of Temple West, and the capture of the *Espérance*, 125; damaged in action off Minorca, 412

Bujauld, Paul, a rebellious Acadian exile, treatment of, in Pennsylvania, 316

Bull, Lieut. Gov. William, of South Carolina, on the disposition of the Acadian exiles, 297

Burgoyne, Lieut. Gen. John, later expedition of, 78

Burgundy, the battalion of, sent to Canada, 86

Burnaby, English traveller, amazement of, at extravagance and luxurious form of living of the planters, 9

Burnet, William, Governor of New York, the building of a fort at Oswego by, 153

Burton, Lieut. Col. Ralph, reports on the difficulty of Braddock's route, 80–1; sent forward by Braddock to support Gage, 95; inability of the troops of, to carry out orders, 95–6; at the Albany council of war, agrees to the use of the 48th regiment against Crown Point, 204–5

Bussy, Abbé François de, French envoy in Hanover, 374; earlier career of, 374; return of, to France, 376; in the French Foreign Office, 391

Butte à Charles, Nova Scotia, the occupation of the, by the New England volunteers, 229

Byng, Admiral John, to relieve Minorca, 405; early career of, 405–6; difficulties faced by, 406–8; the naval battle off Minorca and, 408–14; trial and death of, 414–16

Cabinet Council of Great Britain, the determination of, to send assistance to the colonies, 55; the influence of Dinwiddie, upon the plans of, for defending North America, 60; and the problem of French reinforcements for New France, 101–3; decision of a committee of, to send a British fleet to the New World, 102–3; views of, on the military campaigns in the New World broaden, 179–80; grants a commission to Shirley as temporary commander-in-chief in North America, 181; the decision of, to displace Shirley in favour of Loudoun, 187; agrees in 1755 to help to defend Hanover, 377–8; decides to send a strong naval force to protect Minorca, 405

Cabot Strait, the British patrol of, 119

Cadaraqui, Canada, British do not claim, in 1755, 161; the Iroquoian claims to, 179; see also Fort Frontenac

Calenberg, the Duchy of, and George II, 349

Callender, Robert, Pennsylvania Indian trader, account by, of the pillaging of the Indians at Great Meadows, 41–2; failure of the Indians to support the English at Great Meadows reported by, 45

Callister, Henry, Oxford, Maryland, merchant, kind treatment of the Acadian exiles by, 305–6, 307

Calvert County, Maryland, petition from, against the Roman Catholics, 305

Campbell, Capt. John, of the *Providence*, brings Acadians to North Carolina, 299

Canada, a new plan for the conquest of, advanced by Shirley in 1755, 152–3; relation of Shirley's plan for the conquest of, to that carried out by Pitt, 152–3; permission given by Governor Murray for the Acadian exiles in Massachusetts Bay to settle in, 334–5

Canso fisheries, competition of the, with English Newfoundland fisheries, 16

Cape Breton Island, see Isle Royale

Cape Rosier, Canada, plan for the concentration of the French fleet off, 114

Captain, H.M.S., damaged in action off Minorca, 412

Carlisle, Pennsylvania, Dunbar ordered to protect, 133

Carlyle, Major John, of Virginia, commissary, failure of, to forward supplies to Washington, 33; and the North Carolina troops, 47

Carroll, Charles, of Maryland, the priest from the manor of, ministers to the Baltimore Acadian exiles, 307

Carteret, John, Lord (later Earl of Granville), policy of, respecting Hanoverian troops, 351

Castle Elizabeth, the island of Jersey, Le Loutre confined at, 239

Castleman's River, Braddock's Road, precautions observed by Gage at, 93

Catawba Indians, the aid of, sought by Virginia, 25; cordial relations of, with Shawnee and Delawares, 25; why Braddock did not get the support of, 65; held in dread by the Ohio Valley Indians, 93

Catawba Trail, description of, to the forks of the Ohio, 34

Catherine, Grand Duchess of Russia, secures financial aid from Britain, 372

Caughnawaga Indians [Christian Indians, French Mohawks], and Albany's neutrality in 1755, 66; charged with treachery by Dieskau, 170; conduct of, during the Battle of Lake George, 172

Cayuga Indians, at the Oswego conference with Shirley, 146

Chapman, Major Russell, later Lieutenant Colonel, of the 60th regiment, at the council of war held after Braddock's death, 133

Charles I, King of England, the development of constitutional limitations of power and, 247

Charles VI, Emperor of the Holy Roman German Empire, the Barrier fortresses and, 353

Charles Albert, of Bavaria, and the Pragmatic Sanction, 356

Charles Edward, Prince, the campaign in Northern Scotland against, 57, 357

Charles of Lorraine, administrator of the Austrian Netherlands, 359

Charleston, South Carolina, Acadians maintained by, 296

Châtellerault, France, Acadians sent to, 339

Chaudière River, Canada, Shirley's plan for sending troops down the, against Quebec, 152

Chauvreux, Abbé, of Grand Pré, the arrest of, 268; wise conduct of, 285

Cherbourg, France, Acadians carried to, in flags of truce, 337; the British blockade of, in 1756, 406

Cherokee Indians, the aid of, sought by Virginia, 25; cordial relations of, with the Shawnee and Delawares, 25; why Braddock did not get the support of, 64–5; friendly attitude of, toward the French in 1755, 77; missions of, against the Northern Indians, 93

Cherokee Trail, description of, to the forks of the Ohio, 34

Chickasaw Indians, the aid of, sought by Virginia, 25

Chignecto, the isthmus of, Nova Scotia, proposal to eject the French troops from, 216; the forts of, part of the vital protection for New France, 217; Shirley's plan in 1747 to colonize, 261; most of the inhabitants of, find refuge in the woods, 266

Choiseul, Etienne François, Duc de, French minister, the policy of, respecting the Acadians in France, 338–9, 341

Choiseul-Praslin, Captain, of the *Illustre*, on the undermanning of French warships, 104; eludes the British fleet, 115–6

Choueguen [Choueguin], see Oswego

Church, Captain, of the *Leopard*, takes Acadians to Maryland, 277; transports Acadians to Boston, 298

Ciudadela, Minorca, the seizure of, by the French, 403

Clarke, Capt. Thomas, of the New York Independent Company, becomes brevet Lieutenant Colonel, 33; the company of, while in New York, 46; illness of, in Virginia, 46

Clarke, William, author of *Observations on the late and present Conduct of the French*, his dedication to Shirley, 130–1

Claus, Daniel, assistant to Colonel Johnston, aids in the undermining of General Shirley, 187

Cleland, John, British scholar, the relations of, with Pichon, 237

Cobequid, Nova Scotia, the Acadians of, call for a revolt, 250; letters sent to Le Loutre from, 253; the burning of, ordered by Col. Monckton, 265; the inhabitants of, flee to the woods, 280

Cod fisheries, competition of the New England, with those of Newfoundland, 16; the threat to the, of New England by the loss of Nova Scotia, 217

Coldstream Guards, the, 57

Colleredo, Count, Austrian Ambassador in London, submits a plan of reciprocal guarantees, 365–6

Cologne, Electoral Archbishopric of, and the imperial election, 367; and French subsidies, 392

Colonial merchants, and trade with the enemy in 1755, 65

Colonies, British; see British colonies

Comette, the, French warship, the arrival of, at Louisbourg, 114; the escape of, from Louisbourg, 122

Commissioners, of the Northern colonies, the meeting of, after the Battle of Lake George, 176

Common Law, the, 3; liberties claimed under, 348

Common Sense, by Thomas Paine, 5–7

Connecticut, Colony of, the attitude of the people of, toward the laws of England, 8; the quota of troops from, for the Crown Point campaign, 142; New York secures a part of her quota from, in 1755, 163; Johnson asks reinforcements from, 165; desire of the people of, to give additional support to the Crown Point expedition, 166; the conduct of the troops from, under Johnson criticized, 175; commissioners from, meet at Albany after the Battle of Lake George,

176; Acadians sent to, 280; the Acadian exiles in, 321–4

Content, the, French warship, in the battle off Minorca, 409

Contraband trade, between Albany and Montreal, Shirley on the, 144; Indians engage in the, warn the French of English plans, 154

Contrecœur, Pierre Claude Pecaudy de, commander at Fort Duquesne, summons of, to Washington, 31; problems facing, at Fort Duquesne, 89; comment of, on the precautions taken by Braddock, 90; conferences with the Indians held by, 90–1

Convention of Hanover of 1745, the principle of limited British continental commitments and the, 357–8

Convention of Varscovie of 1744, the, between Russia and Poland, 366

Convention of Versailles of 1756, the, between France and Austria, 396–7; and the preservation of peace, 418

Convention of Westminster of 1755, the, between Great Britain and Russia, 390–1; and the preservation of peace, 418; see Treaty

Cook, Captain, of the Edward, difficulties faced by, in bringing Acadian exiles to Connecticut, 322

Cornwallis, Col. Edward, Governor of Nova Scotia, requires the oath of allegiance from the Acadians, 245

Corsica, the desire of the French government to send Acadians to settle in, 339, 341

Cotterell, Captain, Secretary of Nova Scotia, on the activities of Pichon in Pennsylvania, 237

Council of war, a, held by Washington at Wills Creek, 23; at Gist's Settlement, 35–6; held by Braddock on the march, 80; at Little Meadows, 82; at Salt Lick Creek, 85; held by Colonel Dunbar, 133; at Oswego, approves Shirley's plan to attack Fort Niagara, 158; opposes an attack on Fort Frontenac, 158; reverses its approval of the Niagara attack, 159; at the Great Carrying Place called by Johnson, asks for reinforcements, 165; at Lake George, on September 5, 168; on September 7, 168; and on September 9, 1755, 174; at New York, December 12, 1755, 177–9; at Albany, July 20, 1756, 193; at Oswego, on May 17, 198; on July 5, 199; and on August 14, 1756, 200; at Albany on May 25, 1756, 204; at Gibraltar, 407; called by Byng, 413

Couronne, the, French warship, in the battle off Minorca, 409; driven out of action by the Ramillies, 412

Court-martial, the, of Shirley in England contemplated, 189; of Vice Admiral Matthews, 412; of Admiral Byng, 414–5

Courville, Louis de, the King's notary, an account of the pillaging of the King's stores at Beauséjour by, 233

Craven, Major Charles, in command at the Great Carrying Place, receives news of the fall of Oswego, 195

Croghan, George, Indian trader, brings Indians to Braddock, 77; on the failure of Indian support for Braddock's army, 93

Cromwell, Oliver, the development of constitutional limitations of power and, 347

Crown Point, Fort St. Frédéric at, 13; British plan to move against, 59, 131; the attack on, agreed to at the Alexandria conference, 71, 130; the threat to, 89; Baron Dieskau sent to, 89; Shirley's plan for the campaign against, in 1755, 135–6; provincial levies for campaign against, 142–3; Col. Johnson approved to command the drive against, 137; conditions essential for the move against, 140–1; quotas of troops to be used against, 142–3; French reports of troops massed at Albany for attack against, 155; the strongest fort built on the French encroachments, 164; the strengthening of the fortifications of, in 1755, 167; project to capture, in 1756, 178; refusal of the more southern colonies to aid the campaign against, 185; strong support of the campaign against, by New England, 185–6; the plan of campaign against, changed by General Winslow, 204; the campaign against, thrown into confusion in 1756 with the displacing of Shirley, 205; Pichon seeks to win over officers at, 236

Culloden, the Battle of, and the Duke of Cumberland, 56

Culloden, H.M.S., in the battle off Minorca, 406

Cumberland, H.R.H., William Augustus, Duke of, Captain General, military experience of, 56; prestige of, 56; outlines strategy for New World campaign, 57; influence of, over George II, 57; commits Braddock to the Virginia route to Fort Duquesne, 74; project of, for the campaign of 1756 in North America, 180; Fort William Henry named in honour of, 174; favours in 1756 the sending of Loudoun to America as the new commander-in-chief, 187–8; would have Shirley brought to England as a prisoner, 189; as commander-in-chief of the pragmatic army, 356–7

Currency, of North Carolina, bad state of the, 47

Curtis, Captain, of the *Three Friends*, transports to Pennsylvania more Acadians than his quota, 279

Dagworthy, Capt. John, commander at Fort Cumberland, Maryland, and George Washington, 211

d'Argenson, Antoine René de Voyer, Marquis de Paulmy, Minister of War, orders of, respecting Minorca, 403–4; the Convention of Versailles and, 420

Daudin, Abbé Henri, stirs up the Acadians of Annapolis Royal and Piziquid, 250; threat to expel, 250; the arrest of, 268

Dauphin Royal, the, French warship, eludes the British fleet, 110–11, 113; sailing qualities of, 113; the escape of, from Louisbourg, 123–4

Davidson (Davison), John, Ohio Indian trader, report of, 31

Dawson, Dr. William, Virginia church commissary, on a committee to report on the Acadian exiles, 300

Declaration of war, why France did not issue a, upon news of Boscawen's attack, 118–9; British seizure of French shipping in 1755 fails to bring a, 309; the British and the French each issue a, in 1756, 416–7

Deffenseur, the, French warship, activities of, in the waters of the New World, 108, 114; great sailing qualities of, 113; the escape of, from Louisbourg, 123–4

Defiance, H.M.S., activities of, in Newfoundland waters, 112; in the battle off Minorca, 406, 412

de Lancey, Lt. Gov. James, of New York, 11; Shirley proposes a campaign against Crown Point to, 135; the coldness of, toward the project, 136; the instructions of, to Johnson, 138–9; dilatory procedure of, 141; opposition of, to Shirley's plan of campaign, 141–2; the attitude of, with respect to the New York-Massachusetts Bay land dispute, 143–4; the Albany contraband trade and the interests of the family of, 144; the views of, on the Crown Point and Niagara campaigns, 144; earlier opposition of Col. Johnson toward, 145; is now joined by Johnson in opposing Shirley, 145; dis-

placed as acting governor by the arrival of the Governor Hardy, 176; the undermining of General Shirley and, 187; the support of the Nova Scotia expedition by, 226

de Lancey, Oliver, Shirley refuses to give contracts for supplies to, 145

Delaware Indians, the defection of, 25; cordial relations of, with the Catawba and Cherokee, 25; take up the hatchet against the English, 33, 41; harass Washington's army, 45; make war upon Braddock's army, 78

Deligney (Des Lignerie, Des Ligneris, Lignery, Liniery) Marchand de, in the battle of the Monongahela, 91

Demler, George, placed in charge of the construction of Fort Ontario, 157; objections of, to the plan of the fort, 157

Denny, Gov. William, of Pennsylvania, the attitude of, toward the Acadian exiles, 313

Desenclaves (Deseuclaves) Abbé Jean Baptiste, Acadian priest, wise conduct of, 285

Desertion, of troops under Washington, 37; of North Carolina troops, 47; of troops of the Virginia regiment, 48; Dinwiddie's efforts to deal with, 52; of troops under Shirley, 151; of Acadians assisting in the defence of Fort Beauséjour, 230

d'Estaing, Count, Governor of the Windward Islands, invites the Acadian exiles in New England, 333

Detroit, the capture of, in 1756 proposed by Shirley, 160; the British do not claim, 161

Dianne, the, French warship, the first of the King's ships to sail through the strait of Belle Isle, 120

Dickens, Guy, British envoy to Russia, failure of, to sign a subsidy treaty, 370

Dieskau, Baron de, commander-in-chief of French forces in the New World, 86; sent to Crown Point, 89; leaves France for Canada, 100; the arrival of, 108; plan to place the troops to be used against Oswego under, changed, 156; order to, to move against the English in New York, 168; the Lake George campaign of, 168–74; becomes a prisoner, 173

Digby County, Nova Scotia, the returning Acadian exiles resettled within, 336

Diggs, Capt. Dudley, of H.M.S. *Nightingale*, separated from the transports with Acadian exiles, arrives in New York, 287

Dinwiddie, Gov. Robert, of Virginia, aid from the Southern Indians promised by, 25; unfortunate relations of, with the government of South Carolina, 25–6; futile Indian conference of, at Winchester, 27; the issue of soldiers' pay and, 29; rebukes Washington, 29–30; responsibility of, for the debacle at Great Meadows, 43; rebukes de Lancey for the condition of the New York Independent Companies, 46; notifies North Carolina that each colony must maintain its own troops, 46; gives financial credit to the North Carolina troops, 47; denounces the conduct of North Carolina, 47–8; plans on a second campaign against Fort Duquesne, 48; explanation by, of the failure of Washington's campaign, 48; proposals of, for British troops and American taxation, 49; displaced as commander-in-chief of the English colonial troops, 50; the plan of, to establish in Virginia Independent Companies, 51; the decision of, to deprive Washington of his colonelcy, 51; acceptance of Washington's resignation by, 52; and Sharpe fearful of a French attack at Wills Creek, 54; the responsibility of, for the Braddock plan of campaign, 59–60; efforts of, to gain support for the western campaign, 64; inability of, to fulfill his promises to Braddock, 65; denounces trade with the enemy, 65; the failure of, to bring the Southern Indians to support Braddock, 77; the bad conduct of, denounced by Braddock, 78; the views of, on the retreat of Dunbar's forces, 128; desires another attempt on Fort Duquesne in 1755, 132–3; the efforts of, to retrieve the Braddock defeat, 132–5; supports Washington for a commission, 135; recommends the displacing of Shirley as commander-in-chief, 180; the qualifications of, for commander-in-chief in North America compared with those of Shirley, 180–1; accuses the authorities of Georgia and South Carolina of aiding the return of the Acadian exiles, 289; refuses to receive Acadians sent from South Carolina, 296; the attitude of, toward Acadians brought to Virginia, 300–4

Dobbs, Gov. Arthur, of North Carolina, on the taxation of the people of England, 9; at the governors' conference in Williamsburg, 51; offers homes to Acadian exiles, 289

Dobbs, Capt. Edward Brice, of North Carolina, arrives at Fort Cumberland with troops, 75

Dolphin, the, transports to Maryland more Acadians than its quota, 279, 304

Dove, the, leaves Nova Scotia with Acadians for Connecticut, 280; the question of the arrival of, at New London, 322

Downwell, Captain, of the Seaflower, brings Acadian exiles to Boston, 325

Drucour, Chevalier de, Governor of Louisbourg, inability of, to send aid to Fort Beauséjour, 230; instructions of, as to support of the Indians at war with the English, 262

Duguay, see du Guay

Dulany, Daniel, of Maryland, on the difficulty of supporting the Acadian exiles, 306

Dumas (Dumars), Captain, in the battle of the Monongahela, 91–2; takes charge of the French forces, 94; failure of Pichon to win over, 235; subsequent career of, 236

Dunbar, Col. Thomas, decision to send the regiment of, to America, 58; difficulties facing the forces of, 85; blames Braddock for defeat of the army, 97; lack of qualifications of, 127–8; plans to go into winter quarters, 128; the dishonour of the retreat of, 128–9; the question of the independent command of, 129; orders of Shirley to, 132–3; decision of a war council called by, to leave Pennsylvania, 133; the subsequent career of, 134; at the New York council of war, 177–9

Dunkards, of Pennsylvania, and pacifism in 1755, 66–8

Dunkirk, France, the Treaty of Utrecht and, 353

Dunkirk, H.M.S., the sailing qualities of, 111; the capture of the Alcide by, 112; chases the returning French ships, 124

Dunning, Captain, of the Mary, takes Acadians to Virginia, 277, 300; brings Acadian exiles to New York, 319

Duquesne, Ange de Menneville, Marquis de, Governor General of New France, takes measures to protect Fort Duquesne, 35–6; orders from, as to reprisals for the killing of Jumonville, 36; welcomes the aid of the Shawnee on the Ohio, 88; sends to France an encouraging report on progress at Fort Duquesne, 88; orders given to, for aggressive action in America, 100; on the navigation of the St. Lawrence, 115; the return of, to France, 120

Duras, Duc de, French Ambassador at Madrid, the appeal of, to the Spanish King for aid to France, 377

Dutch, the mercantile policy of the, in the seventeenth century, 16; an oath of allegiance required of the, of New Netherlands, 244

Du Vivier, M., warning given of the attack against Annapolis Royal by, 259

Dwight, Timothy, on General Lyman, 174

East Friesland, the Duchy of, claims of George II to, 349; the rivalry over, 381

Eberhard, Prince Christian, of East Friesland, and the Hanoverian claims, 381

Edgecumbe, Commodore George, weak naval units of, in the Mediterranean, 403; reinforcements provided for the ships of, 407; bad condition of the ships of, 407, 408

Edward, the, brings Acadian exiles to Connecticut, 322

Elizabeth, the, transports Acadians to Maryland, 277; takes on board more than its quota of Acadians, 279; the arrival of, in Maryland, 304; brings Acadian exiles to Connecticut, 321–2

Elizabeth, Tzarina of Russia, a British subsidy treaty and, 370–2; the relations of, with Austria, 419; the need of subsidies by, before taking military action, 419; no offensive alliance existed in 1756 between Maria Theresa and, 424

Ellis, Gov. Henry, of Georgia, on the condition of the Acadians in Georgia, 290

Embuscade, the, Le Loutre captured on, 239

Endeavour, the, transports Acadians to Virginia, 277, 300

Enfield, Connecticut, Acadian exiles in, 323

England, the sending of Acadian exiles from Virginia to, 303; Acadians in, decide to become French subjects, 338; the historic interest of the people of, in the Low Countries, 351; see also Great Britain

English colonials, hemmed in by France in North America, 11; see also British colonies

Entreprenant, the, French flagship, sent to America, 107–8; the activities of, in the New World, 113–115; convoys the French ships armés en flûte out of the St. Lawrence, 120–1; the return of, to Brest, 121

Esnault, Marie, mother of Thomas Pichon, 218

Espérance, the, French warship, the arrival of, at Louisbourg, 114; the blockade of, 123; the escape of, from Louisbourg, 124–5; the great fight of, 125–6; the burning of, 126

Espérance, French packet boat, brings despatches to Bayonne, 126

Europe, the political organization of, in 1755, 345–6

Evans, Lewis, Pennsylvania map-maker and political controversialist, on the problem of slavery and defence in the southern colonies, 14–5; strongly favours the Virginia route to Fort Duquesne, 74; on the devastation of the Virginia frontiers, 134; on the desertion of soldiers in the Fort Niagara campaign, 151; calculates the time required for round trip between Schenectady and Oswego, 151; on the difference between the British and French batteaux used on Lake Ontario, 159; on the right of France to the lands north of the St. Lawrence, 179; author of A General Map of the Middle British Colonies, and of Analysis No. 1 (1755) and Analysis No. 2 (1756), 179

Experiment, the, brings Acadian exiles to New York, 319–20

Eyre, Captain, later Major, William, of Halkett's Regiment, military engineer, opinion of, regarding the colonial levies under Johnson, 165; plans for Fort Edward drawn up by, modified, 166; lays out a site for a fort at Lake George, 167; plans of, for Fort William Henry, 169; commands the artillery in the Battle of Lake George, 172; commended by General Johnson, 177; takes over the command of Fort William Henry from Winslow, 208

Fairfax, Col. George William, of Virginia, and the issue of officers' pay, 29

Fairfield, Connecticut, Acadian exiles in, 323

Farmer, Father, Philadelphia Roman Catholic priest, the Acadian exiles and, 318

Farmington, Connecticut, Acadian exiles in, 323

Faulker, Capt., of H.M.S. Lyme, follows the French fleet, 106

Ferdinand, Prince of Brunswick-Wolfenbüttel, in the army of Frederick II, an intermediary between the King of Prussia and George II, 382; an intermediary between his brother Duke Karl and Frederick II, 383

Fidelle, the, French warship, in the New World, 114

Fiedmont, Lieut. Jacau de, French military engineer, Pichon seeks to win over, 236; subsequent career of, 236

Fier, the, French warship in the battle off Minorca, 409

Fighting Instructions, the, and Admiral Byng, 409

Fitch, Thomas, Governor of Connecticut, at the New York council of war, 177–9

Flags of truce, carry Acadians to France, 337

Flanders, the reunion of, with Spain bought with a great price, 352; *see also* Austrian Netherlands, Spanish Netherlands

Fleury, Joly de, Comptroller-General of France, *mémoire* sent to, by the Acadians of Nantes, 342

Florida, the French government grants permission for the Acadians to go to, 342

Fontenoy, the battle of, and Braddock, 57; the defeat of the pragmatic army at, 356–7

Food supplies, scarcity of, for Washington's force, 33; the arrival of, at Great Meadows, 33; the sending of, to Canada from the English colonies, 65; the Braddock campaign and, 75; the defective character of, from Maryland, 76; the shortage of, at Fort Duquesne, 87–8; the raising of, about Fort Duquesne, 88; the delay in the arrival of, for the Niagara campaign, 159; the extreme shortage of, at Oswego, 183–4; the purchase of large quantities of, for Oswego, 184; the movement of, to Oswego, 184; Le Loutre purchases, for the refugee Acadians, 246

Forbes, Col. John, route followed by, to Fort Duquesne superior to the Braddock route, 73; the expedition of, against Fort Duquesne, 97

Forbes, Capt. Samuel, of the *Dove*, leaves Nova Scotia with Acadians for Connecticut, 280, 322

Ford, Capt. William, of the *Neptune*, transports to Virginia more Acadians than his quota, 278–9, 300

Forests, the character of the, in the region of the Monongahela, 34, 80

Forman, Capt. Zebad, of the *Dolphin*, transports to Maryland more Acadians than his quota, 279, 304

Fornelles, Minorca, the French use, in the invasion of Minorca, 405

Fort Beauséjour on the Acadian isthmus,

13; the British plan to move against, 59; the news of the capture of, reaches Vaudreuil, 89; the vital importance of, to New France, 217; the secrecy of the expedition against, 227; the sailing of the fleet to reduce, 228; the land movement from Fort Lawrence against, 228–9; plans for the defence of, 229–30; the siege of, 230–1; the terms of capitulation of, 231–2; factors in the fall of, 232–3; importance of the fall of, 234; the carrying of supplies from Nova Scotia to, forbidden, 249; the renaming of, Fort Cumberland, 265

Fort Bull, at the Great crossing, the French destruction of, 198

Fort Cumberland, Maryland, name given to the Wills Creek fort, 54; Braddock's Indian conference at, 78

Fort Cumberland, Nova Scotia, the renaming of Fort Beauséjour, 265–6; the collection of the Acadians at, 266; Acadians held prisoner at, in 1761, 337

Fort de Gaspereau, on Baye Verte, 212; the surrender of, to Col. Winslow, 233; the carrying of supplies out of the Acadian settlements to, forbidden, 249

Fort Duquesne, the middle colonies refuse to make a third drive against, 13; reinforcements reach, 33; the difficult route to, by way of Virginia, 59, 60, 73–4; the Shawnee bring scalps and prisoners to, 87; the number of troops at, fluctuate, 87–88; the completion of the fortifications at, 88; the production of food supplies at, 88; the campaign against, opposed by Colonel Johnson, 136; the campaign against, as the result of misrepresentation, 137; the project to capture, in 1756, 178; *see also* Braddock, Contrecœur

Fort Edward, New York, the building and naming of, 166; Dieskau moves against, and then turns to Lake George, 168–9; the grave danger to, 169; Captain M'Ginnis marches from, against the French, 173

Fort Edward on the Piziquid, Nova Scotia, the number of troops at, 215; Captain Murray commanding at, 249; Acadians ordered to bring in arms to, 253–4; Col. Winslow arrives at, 267; the Acadians of the Piziquid summoned to, 268, 273–4; a shortage of ships for transporting the exiled Acadians at, 278

Fort Frontenac, threatened by the British, 89; the use of armed sloops by forces at, 149; Shirley develops plans for the capture of, 151–2; the number of French troops concentrated at, 156; the Oswego council of war opposes an attack on, 158; the capture of, in 1756 proposed by Shirley at Oswego, 160–1; the New York council of war and the project to capture, 178–9; the concentration of French troops at, 196, 197; new entrenchments dug at, 197

Fort George, Oswego, the garrison of, increased, 149; Captain Bradstreet takes command of troops at, 149; the ruinous condition of, in 1755, 153–4; protection of, by the Six Nations before 1755, 154; the French troops ignore, 154; Shirley determines to strengthen, 156; Mackellar criticizes the plans for strengthening, 157–8; the weak defence of, 199–200; the destruction of, 200

Fort Halifax, on the Kennebec, French orders sent to destroy, 100; the construction of, by Gov. Shirley, 130; Shirley's plan for sending troops from, against Quebec, 152; the plan of, used by Shirley in constructing Fort Ontario, 157

Fort La Galeta, on the St. Lawrence, 149; the plan of Shirley to capture, 178

Fort Lawrence, Nova Scotia, warning given of an attack planned against, 214; weakness of the defences of, 215; arrival of the New England regiment at, 228; demand of the refugee Acadians for the lands at, 247; escape of some of the Acadians from, 266

Fort Le Bœuf, the establishment of, 22

Fort Lyman, see Fort Edward, New York

Fort Machault, the building of, at Venango, 88

Fort Michilimakinac, the capture of, in 1756 proposed by Shirley, 160

Fort Necessity, description of, 38; the defence of, 39–40; the destruction of, 44

Fort Niagara, British plan to move against, 59; the Earl of Halifax's would send British regiments against, 60; threatened by the British, 89; Shirley asked to command the expedition against, 131; a campaign against, favoured by Col. Johnson, 136; great importance of the move against, 141; Shirley opposed by de Lancey in plans for the campaign against, 141; the drive against, to aid the Crown Point campaign, 143; the number of troops to be used in campaign for the capture of, 143; de Lancey's views of the military requirements for the campaign against, 144; the inadequacy of the troops for the campaign against, 147–8; the

campaign against Crown Point should have been subordinated to that against, 148; the formidable obstacles to the capture of, 148–9; the protection of Oswego and, by the Six Nations, before 1755, 154; Vaudreuil on the importance of, to the French, 155; its weakness in 1755, 155; defended by Sieur de Villiers, 155; Duquesne recommends that the site of, be changed, 155; French detachments available for the protection of, 156; the fluctuation of the number of troops at, 158; a council of war supports the proposal to attack, 158; preparations for the attack on, stopped, 159; the project to capture, in 1756, 178; the chances of the success of the campaign against, had Braddock been in charge, 182–3; the failure of colonial support in 1756 for the campaign against, 185; the Béarn battalion sent to the defence of, 197

Fort on the St. John River, 13; threat to, 89

Fort Ontario, the plan of, based upon that of Fort Halifax, modified, 157; criticism of the plan of, by Demler and Mackellar, 157; the investment of, by the French, 198; the capture of, 199; the destruction of, 200

Fort Oswego, the beginnings of, 157–8; untenable nature of, 158; the provincial forces stationed at, strengthened, 199; the desertion of, by the colonials and the occupation of, by the French, 200; the destruction of, 200

Fort Pontchartrain, at Detroit, the capture of, in 1756 proposed by Shirley, 160

Fort Presqu'Isle, the securing of forage at, 88; the capture of, in 1756 proposed by Shirley, 160, 178

Fort Rouillé, Toronto, Canada, the capture of, in 1756 proposed by Shirley, 160

Fort St. Frédéric, see Crown Point

Fort St. Jean, Canada, military activities about, in 1755, 167

Fort Ticonderoga, Montcalm prepares for the defence of, 197; Chevalier de Lévis in charge of, 197; General Winslow plans the capture of, in 1756, 207; the expedition against, given up, 208

Fort William Henry, the capture of, 12; the killing of colonial defenders of, by the Indians, 42; the building of, 174; the naming of, 174

Fort Williams, the erection of, at the Mohawk-Wood Creek Great Carrying Place, 162–3; the burning of, by General Webb, 195

Fort Wood Creek, see Wood Creek Fort.

Fortress of Louisburg, on Cape Breton Island, the significance of, 13; see also Louisbourg

Foudroyant, the, French flagship, the powerful armament of, 408; complement on board, 410

Fougueux, H.M.S., former French warship, activities of, off Newfoundland, 113

Fowke, Gen. Thomas, Governor of Gibraltar, the orders to, 406; the decision of, regarding the support of Byng, 407

Fox, Henry, Secretary at War, financial estimates in supporting the colonies sought by, 61; succeeds Robinson as Secretary of State for the Southern Department, 188, 378; notifies Shirley that he is being displaced, 188; suspects Shirley, 189; rebukes Gov. Glen of South Carolina for permitting Acadian exiles to go to England, 294

France, Kingdom of, a record of bad faith by the government of, after the Peace of Aix-la-Chapelle, 119, 376; the government of, seeks to evade the Peace of Utrecht, 353; the War of the Austrian Succession and, 356–7; the Treaty of Aix-la-Chapelle and, 357; military standing of, in 1748, 359; plan of Maria Theresa to win over, 359–60; time required by, before open war with Great Britain, 373–4; seeks the aid of Spain in 1755, 376–7; the minister of, asks Prussia to attack Hanover, 381–2; efforts of the government of, to secure an alliance with Saxony, 387; the Convention of Westminster and, 390–1; the preparations of, for war with Great Britain, 391–2; the negotiations of the government of, with Austria, 394–6; the Versailles Convention and, 396–7; the advantages enjoyed by, in facing Great Britain in 1756, 400–1; the government of, plans to invade England, 402; blows struck against the power of, by the Newcastle ministry, 425–6; see also Louis XV, Mirepoix, Rouillé

Franklin, Benjamin, Deputy Postmaster General for America, aids Braddock to secure wagons, 75–6; opposes Gov. Morris, 191; views of, as to the respective abilities of Shirley and Loudoun, 191

Frazier (Fraser), John, Pennsylvania Indian trader, the house of, on the Monongahela, 92

Frederica, Georgia, Acadian exiles to be sent to, 288

Frederick II, King of Prussia, the autocratic powers of, 347; the invasion of Silesia by, 356; treaties signed by George II and, 356; the reputation of, for unreliability, 380–1; the basis of opposition of, to George II, 381; advises the French government how to deal with Britain, 381; unwilling to risk an attack against Hanover, 381–2; covets Hildesheim and plans to attack Saxony, 382; the growing dissatisfaction of, with France, 382; seeks a reconciliation with George II, 382; rebuffed by George II, 382; warns Rouillé of efforts to detach the House of Brunswick from France, 383; recommends that France and Denmark attack Hanover and Flanders, 383–4; the attitude of, toward Anglo-French rivalry in America, 384; offers to mediate between Great Britain and France, 384; effect upon, of news of the Anglo-Russian subsidy treaty, 385–6; resents France's interest in Saxony, 386–7; suspects France of duplicity, 387–8; reassures France, 388; is prepared to receive British proposals, 389; authorizes the signing of the Convention of Westminster in 1756, 390; the negotiations of, with Nivernais, 391–3; the attitude of, toward international ties, 393; desires a close alliance with Great Britain, Russia, and Holland, 394; warns Great Britain in 1756 of the dangers of a French invasion, 402; the determination of, to absorb Saxony and to defeat Austria, 419–20; the responsibility of, for the Seven Years' War, 420–5

French, the, in Canada, receive the support of most Indian tribes in 1754, 45

French "neutrals," see Acadians.

Fry, Col. Joshua, in charge of the Virginia volunteers, 28; at Winchester, 28; the death of, 32

Fry, Major, the difficulties experienced by, in carrying out orders to burn the Acadian settlements and collect the Acadians, 266

Gage, Lieut. Col. Thomas, clears the way for Braddock, 82; leads the forces over the Monongahela and back again, 92; precautions observed by, at Castleman's River, 94; the failure of, to take precautions before the Battle of the Monongahela, 94; the faulty orders of, 94; at the council of war held after Braddock's death, 133; agrees at the Albany council of war, to the use of British regulars with provincials, 204–5

Galerm (Galerme), Jean Baptiste, Acadian exile in Pennsylvania, the tribute of, to the people of the Province, 311; arrest of, 316

Galissonière (Gallissonière), Michael Rolland Barin, Comte de la, later Marquis, the inability of, to capture Oswego, 195; commands the French fleet in the Mediterranean, 403; the invasion of Minorca and, 403–4; condition of the fleet of, 408–9; the instructions binding, 411; the battle off Minorca and, 411–2

Gaspé Bay, Canada, French warships in, ordered out, 114–5

Gates, Capt. Horatio, of the New York Independent Company, at the Monongahela, 92

Gaudet, Claude, historian, on the Acadian exiles, 286

George I, King of Great Britain and Ireland, the efforts of, to recreate the Grand Alliance of 1701, 353

George II, King of Great Britain and Ireland, the loyalty of Massachusetts Bay and Rhode Island to, in 1750, 7; the opposition of, to sending troops to America, 55; the influence of Cumberland with, 57; asks funds in 1755 for increases in land and sea forces, 102; goes to Hanover, 103; the memorial of the Acadian exiles in Pennsylvania to, 314–5; limitations on the powers of, 348; the importance of the legal position of, in Great Britain, 348–9; the personal possessions of, in Europe, 349–50; Hanover offers attractions to, 350–1; the situation of, in Hanover contrasted with that in London, 351; the basis of the dislike of, for William Pitt, 351; the pragmatic army under command of, 356; the failure of, to reconstruct the Grand Alliance of 1701, 356; treaties signed by, with Frederick of Prussia, 356; the journey of, to Hanover in 1755, 366; the Austrian court resents the insistence of, that troops be sent to the Netherlands, 368; the devotion of, to the "System," 369, 379; signs a subsidy treaty with the Landgrave of Hesse-Cassel, 369–70; the desire of, to accommodate all issues with Prussia, 385; the death of Byng and, 415; the appeal of, to Frederick through Münchhausen, 423; the anger of, over the conduct of Frederick II, 424

George III, King of Great Britain and Ireland, the memorial of the Acadian exiles in Pennsylvania to, 317; the Acadians at Saint-Malo sent pledge of loyalty to, 340

George, Prince of Wales, later George III, the proposed marriage of, with the House of Brunswick-Wolfenbüttel, 383

Georgetown, Maryland, Acadians at, 308

Georgia, Province of, the Acadian exiles in, 287–92

Georgia Augusta, the University of, founded by George II at Göttingen, 439

German Flatts, New York, General Webb at, 194–5

Germans, the, of Pennsylvania, Shirley's charges against, 14; furnish wagons and horses for Braddock's expedition, 76

Germany, the political organization of, in 1755, 345–6

Ghent, Flanders, the capture of, by Saxe, 357

Gibraltar, as a bargaining point of France with Spain, 400–1; the problem of the defence of, and the support of Byng, 406–7; Dunbar becomes lieutenant governor of, 134; the attitude of Newcastle and Pitt respecting the surrender of, to Spain contrasted, 425–6

Girard, M., curé of Cobequid, taken into custody, 250

Gist, Christopher, Washington arrives at the settlement of, 34; the destruction of the settlement of, by the French, 44

Glazier, Adjutant General Beamsley, commended by General Johnson, 177

Glen, Gov. James, of South Carolina, views the Anglo-French struggle in North America as an "American affair," 20–1; has the responsibility for control of the Southern Indians, 25; the hostility of, toward the Virginia government, 25–6, 49; seeks a conference of Southern governors, 27; requests the return of the South Carolina Independent Company, 28; proposes the forming of a colonial confederacy, 49; not invited to the governors' conference, 50; the popularity of, in South Carolina, in 1755, 64; respecting the Ohio Valley campaign, 65; the qualifications of, for commander-in-chief in North America compared with those of Shirley, 181; rebuked by Secretary at War Fox, for permitting Acadians to go to England, 294; sends Acadians exiled to South Carolina to Virginia, 296

Gloucester, H.R.H. William, Duke of, Fort William Henry named in honour of, 174

Goodwin, Captain, of the Industry, takes Acadians to Virginia, 277, 300

Gorham, Lieutenant, at Piziquid, the Acadians seek to drive out, 250

Göttingen, Germany, the city of, and George II, 349

Grand Alliance of 1701, the War of the Spanish Succession and the, 352, 355; efforts of George I to recreate the, 353; the failure of George II to reconstruct the, 356

Grand Pré, Nova Scotia, an Acadian proposal to expel the English from, in 1753, 250; the massacre of the New England troops in 1747 at, 261; Winslow's activities at, in 1755, 267–80; the burning of, delayed, 280

Granger, Charle, Acadian, the possessions of, 273

Granville, John Carteret, 2nd Earl of, Lord President, the views of, on colonial assistance, 55; as a member of the Cabinet Council, decides to send out Boscawen, 101

Great Britain, Kingdom of, the determination of the people of, to protect the interests of the colonials, 17; the government of, sends financial aid to Virginia, 50; decision of, to give military aid to the colonies, 55–61; the government of, obliged to pay all expenses for the Braddock expedition in aid of the colonies, 73; the relations of, with Europe before 1756, 345, passim; the characteristics of the people of, 346–7; the limitations of the powers of the kings of, 347–8; the guarantee of the Barrier Treaty of 1715 by, 353; and the beginnings of the European "System," 355–6; the Ostend East Indian Company and, 355–6; the guarantee of the Pragmatic Sanction and, 356; and the pragmatic army, 356; the Treaty of Aix-la-Chapelle and, 357; the limited continental commitments of, 357; the ability of, to move Russia against Prussia, 358; the negotiations of, with Austria and Holland, 364–9; the devotion of the government of, to the "System" in 1755, 369; the sound financial position of, in 1755, 385; the danger of an invasion of, by French armies in 1756, 402; see also George II, Holderness, Newcastle, Robinson

Great Carrying Place, the Mohawk-Wood Creek, destruction of soldiers and stores at, in 1755, 147; forts built by Shirley at, 162–3; the shortening of the portage at, by Shirley, 184; the burning of the forts at, by General Webb, 195

Great Carrying Place, the Hudson River-Lake George, a strategic place, 139, 141; a magazine and fort built in 1755 at, 140, 165

Great Crossing of the Youghiogheny, the, Washington at, 29; Braddock at, 80

Great Meadows, Washington fortifies himself at, 30; Fort Necessity built at, 33; description of, 38; the engagement at, 39

Great Ogeehee River, Georgia, Acadian exiles to be sent to, 288

Great Savage Mountain, 80; the difficulty of traversing, faced by Braddock's army, 81

Great Seal, the, limitations on the use of, in the eighteenth century, 348

Greene, Gov. William, of Rhode Island, attitude of loyalty to George II expressed by, 7

Griffith, William, of Philadelphia, the remonstrance of, respecting the Acadian exiles, 314

Guay (Duguicy), Comte du, French admiral, the fleet under, to guard the French ships bound for France, 121; the capture of the Blanford by the ships of, 399

Guernsey, the island of, the French government seeks to keep the Saint-Malo Acadians from communicating with, 341

Guerrier, the, French warship in the battle off Minorca, 409

Guiana, South America, the French government desires to send Acadians to colonize, 338

Guienne, the battalion of, sent to Canada, 86, 100; at Fort Frontenac, 197; used against Oswego, 197–8

Guilford, Connecticut, Acadian exiles in, 323

Habsburgs, the, possession of, in 1755, 345; see also Charles VI, Maria Theresa

Haddam, Connecticut, Acadian exiles in, 323

Half-King, the, see Tanacharisson

Half Moon, New York, the camp of the provincial forces at, 207

Halifax, George Montagu Dunk, 2nd Earl of, President of the Board of Trade, plan of, for military operations in North America, 60; recommends that Shirley be displaced as commander-in-chief in North America and that Johnson be commissioned colonel of the Indians, 187; on the status of the Acadian exiles, 333

Halifax, Nova Scotia, the discovery of a French plan for the destruction of, 234–5; the Acadians unwilling to send supplies to, 246; deputies of the Acadians at, 255–60; Acadians held prisoner at, in 1761, 337

Halkett, Sir Peter, decision to send the regiment of, to America, 58; the regiment of, detached by Braddock to move forward, 82; the failure of, to carry out Braddock's orders, 95–6; the death of, in the Battle of the Monongahela, 96

Hampton, Virginia, Acadians exiled to South Carolina at, 295; Acadians exiled to Virginia left at, 300

Hancock, Thomas, Boston merchant and shipowner, offers to assume responsibility for the Pubnico Acadians, 298–9; see also, Apthorp & Hancock

Handfield, Major John, commander at Annapolis Royal, the removal of the Acadians from Annapolis River carried out by, 267, 274, 277, 280–1

Hangard, the, on the Redstone, the destruction of, by the French, 44

Hannah, the, transports Acadians to Pennsylvania, 277

Hanover, Electorate of, and its constituent parts, 349–50; the appeal of, to George II, 350–1; and the "System," 355; the imperial election and, 367; the British Cabinet Council agrees to help defend, 377–8; Parliament pledged to support, 379; Frederick II recommends that the French attack, 381; Frederick unwilling to risk an attack upon, 381–2; Russian troops available for the defence of, 385; Frederick willing to consider the neutrality of, 386; guarantees to, in the Convention of Westminster, 390

Hanover, Massachusetts Bay, Acadian exiles at, 330

Hanoverian Succession, the Dutch guarantee the, 352

Hanson, John, New York merchant, arranges to transport Acadian exiles in New England to St. Domingue, 333

Harding, Father, Philadelphia Roman Catholic priest, the Acadian exiles ministered to by, 318

Hardwicke, Philip Yorke, 1st Earl of, Lord High Chancellor, assists in the decision to send out Boscawen, 101; on Boscawen's failure to capture the French fleet, 117–8; the opposition of, to bring Shirley to England a prisoner, 189

Hardy, Sir Charles, Governor of New York, the arrival of, in New York, 176; attends a meeting of commissioners of the northern colonies in Albany, 176; at the New York council of war, December 12, 1755,

177–9; criticism of General Shirley by, 180; the policy of, toward the Acadian exiles, 320

Hartford, Connecticut, Acadian exiles in, 323

Hawke, Sir Edward, Vice Admiral, plan of the Lords Justices to send, to cruise against the French, 118; the capture of Abbé Le Loutre on board the Embuscade by, 239; cruises against the French, 406; takes over Byng's command, 414, 415

Hayes, Capt. William, of the Swallow, transports Acadians to Massachusetts Bay, 280, 326

Hazlum (Haslam), Captain, of the Swan, carries Acadians to Pennsylvania, 277

Helena, the, brings Acadian exiles to Boston, 326

Hendrick, Chief, Six Nations leader, objects to Johnson's plan of attack, 170

Henry, Prince, of Prussia, brother of King Frederick, on the general distrust of the King, 380

Herbert, François, Acadian, punishment of, for aiding at Grand Pré the escape of young Acadians, 277

Hercule, the, French warship in the battle off Minorca, 409

Héros, the, French warship, brings reinforcements to Canada in 1756, 196

Herrenhausen, Hanover, description of, in 1755, 350–1

Hesse-Cassel, Landgrave of, the Landgrave of, shares with George II the County of Schauenburg, 350; British subsidy treaty with, 369–70

Hildesheim, the Bishopric of, divides the Duchy of Calenberg, 349; Frederick of Prussia covets, 382

Hillsborough, Wills Hill, Viscount, asks support of Hanover in Parliament, 379

Hocquart, Captain, of the Alcide, activities of, in the waters of the Grand Banks, 110–2; the surrender of, 112; and the project to destroy Halifax, 235

Holburne, Rear Admiral Francis, a fleet under, sent to reinforce Boscawen, 109; the instructions to, 109; the arrival of, in the New World, 116; the blockade of Louisbourg and the St. Lawrence by, 117, 120; the fleet of, chases the returning French ships, 123–4

Holderness, Robert D'Arcy, 4th Earl of, Secretary of State for the Southern Department, promises aid to Virginia, 25; and the sending out of Boscawen, 101; joins the King in Hanover, 103; at the Hague in 1755, 366; suspects Austrian bad faith, 368–9; the devotion of, to the "System," 379; the efforts of, to persuade Frederick to keep the peace within Germany, 384; the negotiations of, in Brunswick, 384–5

Holland, *see* the United Netherlands

Holland, Lieut. Kitchen, commander at Oswego, warns the council of war against the use of English batteaux on Lake Ontario, 159

Holy Roman German Empire, the, characteristics of, in 1755, 346; *see also* Charles VI, Kaunitz, Maria Theresa

Hopkinton, Massachusetts Bay, Acadians ordered to, 330

Horses, for the Braddock expedition stolen by traders, 76; the poor quality of, furnished to Braddock, 81; Braddock's officers give up their extra, 81; the destruction of, in the Braddock expedition, 81

Howe, Capt. Richard, of the *Dunkirk*, the activities of, off the Grand Banks, 110–2

Huguenots, of South Carolina, the Acadian exiles face the, 292–3

Huron Indians, the support of the French at Fort Duquesne by, 90

Hutchinson, Thomas, member of the Massachusetts Bay Council, the kindness of, toward the Acadian exiles, 325–6; on the restrictions on Roman Catholics in the Province, 331

Illustre, the, French warship, in the New World, 114; the methods employed by, in eluding the British fleet, 115–6, 121; brings reinforcements to Canada in 1756, 196

Imperial election, the, Great Britain and, 367

Indentured labourers, Acadian exiles become, in Georgia, 291; in South Carolina, 295; in Maryland, 308; in Pennsylvania, 314; in New York, 320; in Connecticut, 323; in Massachusetts Bay, 329

Indentured servants, the enlistment of, bitterly resented in the middle colonies, 185

Independent Companies, the New York, Holderness promised to send two of, to aid Virginia, 25; ordered to Virginia, 29, 45; the condition of, upon arrival, 45; the low morale of, 45; the unwillingness of, to serve under provincial officers, 52; the return of, to New York, 133

Independent Company of South Carolina, promised by Holderness, to aid Virginia, 25; Glen demands the return of, 28; the

arrival of, in Virginia, 29; joins Washington's force at Great Meadows, 33; lack of co-operation between the officers of, and Washington, 33; at Mount Braddock, 35; the refusal of, to aid Washington in the retreat, 35; losses of, in the defence of Fort Necessity, 41

India, advantageous position of the French in, in 1756, 400

Indian trade, the disgraceful nature of, at Oswego, 154

Indian traders, of Pennsylvania, Braddock's low opinion of, 76

Indians, the need of, in frontier fighting, 25, 36, 45, 93, 145–6, 201; *see also*, Abenaki, Catawba, Caughnawaga, Cayaga, Cherokee, Chickasaw, Delaware, Huron, Michilimakinac, Micmac, Mingo, Missisauga, Norridgewalk, Oneida, Onondaga, Ottawa, Potawatomi, Seneca, Shawnee, Six Nations

Industry, the, transports Acadians to Virginia, 277, 300

Innes, Col. James, of North Carolina, leads the North Carolina troops to assist Virginia, 28; becomes commanding officer of the forces against Fort Duquesne, 32; the previous military training of, 32; the North Carolina regiment disbanded by, 47; plan to send, against Fort Duquesne, 48; refusal of the Independent Companies to obey, 48; the conference of, with Ohio Valley Indians, 53

Instructions, secret, given to Braddock, 58–59; "Private," to Braddock, 72; to Baron Dieskau, Duquesne, and Vaudreuil, 100; to Macnémara and de la Motte, 106, 107; secret, to Boscawen, 108–9; to Holburne, 109; Boscawen carries out faithfully his, 117; given to Major General Johnson, 138–9; Shirley receives the same, given to Braddock, 163; Shirley presents his, to the New York council of war, 177–8; the question of the violation of, 178–9; de la Galissonière bound by, 411

"Intercepted Letters," the, and General Shirley, 189

Intrepid, H.M.S., the battle off Minorca and, 412, 413

Ireland, soldiers on the establishment of, to be sent to America, 63

Iroquoian Confederation, *see* Six Nations

Iroquoian Indian lands, Fort Frontenac built on, 179

Isle St. Jean (Prince Edward Island), the Acadians seek asylum on, 252; the fate of the Acadians settled on, 336–7

Isle Royale (Cape Breton Island), the arrival of French reinforcements at, 114; the blockade of, in 1755, 230; the failure of the Acadians to move *en masse* to, 243; an asylum for Acadians, 252; fate of the Acadians settled on, 336–7

Jacob's Creek, see Salt Lick Creek
James II, King of England, the development of constitutional limitations of power and, 347–8
Japanese tradition, and emperor worship, 4
Jersey, the island of, the Acadians at Saint-Malo seek to escape to, 239–4, 340–1
Johnson, Col. William, later Sir William, of Mount Johnson, at the Alexandria conference, 71; Shirley recommends, to command against Crown Point, 71, 135; the opposition of, to the Fort Duquesne campaign, 136; given sole management of the Six Nations by Braddock, 137; becomes a major general and made commander of the Crown Point Expedition, 137; qualifications of, to lead against Crown Point, 138; the commission of, 138; the instructions to, from Shirley and de Lancey compared and contrasted, 138–9; plan of campaign of, 139–41; loss of interest in the Niagara campaign by, 141; encouraged by Shirley, 142; earlier opposition of, to de Lancey, 145; joins the de Lancey faction against Shirley, 145; refuses Indian support to Shirley, 145; denounces Lydius, 145; powers of, as superintendent of the Six Nations, 145–6; the sending of a belt against the Niagara campaign by, charged by Indians, 146; prepares his case against Shirley for the Board of Trade, 147; the insubordination of, 147; holds a large Indian conference at Mount Johnson, 163; the preparations of, for the Crown Point campaign, 163; the views of, on the strength of the fortifications at Crown Point, 164; the charges of, against Shirley, 165; the letter of, disapproved in the New York Assembly, 165; leads the advance to Lake George, 167; the activities of, at the Battle of Lake George, 171–4; wounded, 174; loses control of his army, 175; the desire of, to give up his military command, 175–6; the inability of the army of, to act, 176; the lack of confidence of, in the colonial officers, 176–7; the achievements of the campaign of 1755 under, 177; gives up his command, 177; the chief blame for the Shirley-Johnson feud rests upon, 182; harmonious agreement reached between Shirley and, 185; the part played by, in the undermining of General Shirley, 186–7; requested by Shirley to send Indian aid to Pennsylvania, 189; becomes a baronet, 190; receives a parliamentary grant, 190; granted a royal commission as superintendent of the Six Nations, 190; the failure of, to keep scouting parties out, 192; fears for the communications of Oswego, 192–3; the responsibility of, for turning the Six Nations away from the defence of Oswego, 201; the influence in 1756 of the friction between the New England officers and, 206

Johnston, Samuel, Deputy Paymaster of the Southern District of North America, payments of, to Shirley, 183
Joseph, Prince, of Austria, later Emperor, British hope to elect, King of the Romans, 367
Jumonville, Ensign Coulon de, leader of a French detachment, slain near Great Meadows, 31; the issue of the killing of, considered, 31–2

Kane, Brigadier General Richard, activities of, on Minorca, 404
Karl, Duke of Brunswick-Wolfenbüttel, acts as intermediary between the King of Prussia and George II, 382–6; efforts to persuade, to give up his subsidy treaty with France, 382–3; prospects of, for a marriage alliance with the House of Hanover, 383
Kaunitz, Wenzel Anton Kaunitz-Reitberg, Count of, later Prince of, desire of, for a reorientation of the Imperial foreign policy, 359; as Imperial Ambassador in France, 359–60; becomes Imperial Chancellor, 360; policies of, 360–6; states conditions under which the Empire will support the "System," 368
Keene, Sir Benjamin, British Ambassador at Madrid, warns of plans to invade Minorca, 405
Keith, Robert, British Ambassador at Vienna, negotiations of, to implement the "System," 365, 368
Kennebec River, Maine, Shirley leads a force up, 130; Fort Halifax built on, 130
Keppel, Augustus, Viscount, Commodore, later Rear Admiral, commander-in-chief of the British fleet in American waters, at the Alexandria conference, 71; on Indian aid for Braddock, 72; on the necessity of Great Britain paying for the Brad-

dock expedition, 73; loans sailors and heavy guns to Braddock, 79; the fleet of, joined to that of Boscawen, 109

Kilby, Christopher, provision contractor in North America for Loudoun, 195

King, Capt. John, of one of the New York Independent Companies, arrival of, at Oswego, with troops, 149

King's County, New York, Acadian exiles in, 320

Kingston, H.M.S., in the battle off Minorca, 406

Klinggräffen, Joachim Wilhelm von, Prussian Ambassador at Vienna, 420, movement of Imperial troops reported by, 421; warned to be prepared to leave Vienna, 421; reports peaceable sentiments in Vienna, 422; interviews Maria Theresa, 422–3; second interview of, with the Empress, 423–4

Knyphausen, Baron Dodo Heinrich of Inn and, Prussian Ambassador in Paris, called on to warn France of British moves, 383; to recommend a French-Danish attack on Hanover and Flanders, 383–4; accused by the King of Prussia with being pro-French, 387; views of, respecting the Versailles Convention, 420

La Coupe, Nova Scotia, the Acadians of, help to defend Fort Beauséjour, 229

Lake Champlain, Johnson's plan of campaign to seize control of, 139–40

Lake George, the naming of, by General Johnson, 167; storehouses erected on the shores of, 167; description of, 168; the Battle of, 170–4

Lake Ontario, the building of British naval vessels for, agreed to at the Alexandria conference, 71; the problems of the navigation of, 149; armed vessels of the French on, 149; construction of vessels on, 149–50; the first British vessels to float on, 150; Shirley's plan to dominate, 150–1; British ship-construction on, in 1756, 198–9; naval supremacy upon, held by the French, 198

Lake Sacrament, decision of Johnson to change the name of, to Lake George, 167

La Martinière, M., commandant of Fort Beauséjour, the incapacity of, 221; profits of, from his post, 221

Lancaster, Massachusetts Bay, Acadian exiles at, protest, 330

Land, unauthorized appropriation of, by the Acadians after 1713, 245; Acadians demand the return of, on which Fort Lawrence was built, 247; Acadians ask the French King for, 250; the Acadian claims to, and the refusal of the oath of allegiance, 251, 252; the forfeiture of all, belonging to the Acadians, 264

Landry (Landrée) François, an enumeration of the Acadians of Minas Basin prepared by, 273; notifies the Acadian exiles that they were to embark, 274

Landry, Pierre, Acadian, the possessions of, 273

Landy (Landry?), Jean, a rebellious Acadian exile, treatment of, in Pennsylvania, 316

Languedoc, the battalion of, sent to Canada, 86, 100; in the Battle of Lake George, 172

La Prairie, Canada, French military activities at, in 1755, 167

La Reine, the battalion of, sent to Canada, 86, 100; in the Battle of Lake George, 172–7

La Rochelle, France, Acadians carried to, in flags of truce, 337

La Sarre, the battalion of, brought to Canada by Montcalm, 196; at Fort Frontenac, 197; used against Oswego, 197

Lauvrière, Prof. Emile, historian, on the Acadian dispersion, 286

Lawrence, Gov. Charles, of Nova Scotia, the plan of, for an attack against Beauséjour approved at the Alexandria conference, 72; correspondence with Shirley over plans to capture the French forts, 130; credits Shirley with the colonization off Nova Scotia, 130; on the binding power of the oath of fidelity upon the Acadians, 248–9; on the lack of loyalty of the Acadians, 250–1; on the French encroachments upon Nova Scotia, 214; difficulties faced by, in keeping order in Nova Scotia, 215; proposes to rid the province of French troops, 215; orders Monckton to drive the rebellious Acadians from the country, 254; the responsibility assumed by, for the exiling of all the Acadians, 271; the plans of, for settling the Acadian districts of Nova Scotia, 281–2; charged as the source of the unhappiness of the Acadians, 284; the standing of, in Nova Scotia, 284

Le Blanc, Charles, a rebellious Acadian exile, the treatment of, in Pennsylvania, 316

Le Blanc, Jr., Charles, the wealth amassed by, 318

Le Blanc, Réné, notary public in Minas Basin, co-operates with Col. Winslow, 274; the treatment of the family of, 283

Leffingwell, Captain, of the Pitt, carries

Acadian exiles from Connecticut to Canada, 324

Legge, Hon. Henry Bilson, Chancellor of the Exchequer, refuses to sign warrants for implementing the Hesse-Cassel subsidy treaty, 370; loses his post, 371

Legneris, M., later defeat of forces under, near Niagara, 145

Le Havre, France, Acadians carried to, in flags of truce, 337

Le Loutre, Jean Louis, Abbé, missionary to the Micmacs, the control of the Indians of Nova Scotia exercised by, 214; asks for the services of Pichon at Beauséjour, 221; the treacherous conduct of, 225; the correspondence of, copied by Pichon, 225; the decision of, to destroy the church and village of Beauséjour, 231; the spirit of determination of, 232; activities of, before returning to France, 239; seeks to influence the Acadians in France, 240; the death of, 240; contrast and comparison of Pichon and, 240–1; the destruction of Beaubassin and, 246; secures supplies for the refugee Acadians, 246; gets the refugee Acadians to take the oath to the French Crown, 246; holds the fate of the Acadians in his hands, 248; stirs up the Acadians, 253; correspondence between the Acadians and, cut off, 253; the killing of the English settlers by the Indians of, 257; opposes tranquillity in Nova Scotia after 1749, 262

Lemaire, Abbé, of Rivière aux Canards, Nova Scotia, the arrest of, 268

Lemoyne, M., seeks to get Acadians to go to Poitou, 339

Léopard, the, French warship, in the New World in 1755, 114, 115; eludes the British blockade, 121; brings reinforcements to Canada in 1756, 196

Leopard, the, transports Acadians to Maryland, 277; also to Boston, 298

Leopold, of Saxe-Coburg, as King of Belgium, 364

L'Équille, Capt. Frazer, of the Dianne, sails his ship through the Strait of Belle Isle, 120

Lévis-Leran, Gaston François, Chevalier de, brigadier, brought to Canada by Montcalm, 196; commands at Fort Ticonderoga, 197

Lewis, Captain, ordered to burn Acadian villages, 265

Liége, Flanders, the occupation of, by the French, 357

Ligonier, Sir John, later 1st Earl of, Lieutenant General of Ordnance, the estimate of the Duke of Cumberland by, 57; consulted by the Cabinet Council on the question of waylaying the French transports, 101

Lincoln, William, historian, on the Acadian dispersion, 286

Line of amity, the, the concept of, and European diplomacy, 100–1; and the sending of a French fleet to the New World, 105

Lion, the, French warship in the battle off Minorca, 409

Litchfield, Connecticut, Acadian exiles in, 323

Little Falls, Mohawk River, the portage at, 148–9

Littlehales, Lieutenant Colonel, in charge of the defence of Oswego, 200; the surrender of the forces of, 200; on the small loss of soldiers at Oswego, 200

Little Ogeehee River, Georgia, Acadian exiles to be sent to, 288

Little Shades of Death, Braddock's Road, 80

Liverpool, England, Acadians at, 338

Livingston Manor, the political effect of the dispute between Westenhook and, over lands, in 1755, 143

Livingston, Peter van Brugh, and Lewis Morris, Jr. contract supplies for Shirley, 184; the purchase of great quantities of supplies for Oswego by, 195

Livingston, William, probable author of Review of Military Operations in North America (1756), 132

Lloyd, Col. Edward, member of the Maryland Council, opposed to aiding the Acadian exiles, 306

London, the inhabitants of, support the actions of Boscawen, 119

Long Island, New York, Acadians on, 319–20

Long Run, Pennsylvania, the protection of Braddock's army at, 86; precautions observed at, 94

Lords Justices, the, decision of, to send Boscawen to America, 103; the decision of, to send out Vice Admiral Hawke, 118

Lorgeril, Chevalier de, captain of the Lys, the explanation of, for the delay of the French fleet at Brest, 106; on the separation of the French fleets, 107; on the beginning of the Anglo-French naval war, 112; the surrender of his ship by, 113

Lotbinière (Lobbinière, Lothbinère) Michel Alain de, French military engineer, the problem of the reconquest of Acadia as seen by, 344

Loudoun, John Campbell, 1st Earl of, the appointment of, as the new commander-in-chief in North America, 188; Benjamin Franklin's view of the achievements of, in America, 191; the arrival of, in New York, 193; finds the accounts of Shirley in confusion, 194; supports the decision of the council of war to send aid to Oswego, 194; the hostility of, toward Shirley, 194; authorizes Webb to destroy the forts at the Great Carrying Place, if necessary, 195; interviews Winslow and other provincial officers, 207-8; orders Winslow not to proceed against Ticonderoga, 208; the desire of, to embody the provincials with the regulars in New York, 208; the charges of, against Shirley considered, 209-10; receives the Vaudreuil correspondence from Pichon, 235; the attitude of, toward the rebellious Acadian exiles in Pennsylvania, 315-6

Louis XIV, King of France, the Dutch and, 352

Louis XV, King of France, the idealization of, by the Acadians, 263; the attitude of, toward the Acadians in 1764, 263; the intense loyalty of Acadians to, in 1764, 338; the autocratic powers of, 347

Louisbourg, Isle Royale, French fortress, helps to overawe New England, 13; the carrying of food supplies to, from the British colonies, 65; a British fleet in 1755 sent to cruise off, 102-3; the blockade of, by the British navy, 119, 122-3; French forces at, 214; the importance of, to New France, 217; the isolation of, with the surrender of the French forts in Nova Scotia, 233-4; the carrying of supplies out of Nova Scotia to, forbidden, 249

Louisiana, Province of, the friendly attitude of the Cherokee toward the government of, 77; the demand of an oath of allegiance from the inhabitants of, in 1803, 244; Acadian exiles from New York go to, 321; the Saint-Malo Acadians seek to go to, 341; the French government in 1784 grants permission for Acadians to go to, 342; Acadians from Nantes sail for, in 1784, 342

Low Countries, the revolt of the, only partially successful, 351-2; see also, Austrian Netherlands, Spanish Netherlands, United Netherlands

Lowes, Henry, of Somerset County, Maryland, aids the Acadian exiles, 305

Ludwell, Philip, of Virginia, on a committee, to secure information regarding the Acadian exiles, 300

Lüneburg-Zell, the Duchy of, and George II, 249

Lydius, Col. John Henry, interpreter and trader, the home of, selected as site for a fort, 140; accusations against by Johnson, 145; attempts to negotiate with the Six Nations for Shirley, 145; the connections of, with Susquehanna Company, 145-6; magazines erected at the home of, 164; and the "Intercepted Letters," 189

Lyman, Phineas, of Connecticut, the early career of, 164; made a major general in the Crown Point expedition, 164; leaves Albany for Hudson River-Lake George Great Carrying Place, 164; a fort named in honour of, 166; the plans for, to lead the advance changed, 166-7; the conduct of, during the Battle of Lake George, 174; the lack of confidence of General Johnson in, 176; movement of provincials under, 207; disbands the New England provincials at Albany, 208

Lyme, H.M.S., follows the French fleet, 106

Lys, the, French warship, 106; the capture of, 110-2; the sailing qualities of, 112; why France does not declare war after the capture of, 118-9; Pichon on the capture of, 224; the prisoners from, and Pichon, 234-5

Lyttelton, Sir George, later Lord, becomes Chancellor of the Exchequer, 371

Lyttelton, Gov. William Henry, of South Carolina, orders to, with reference to the Acadian exiles, 297; the capture and release of, by the French, 399

Machault, d'Arnouville, Jean Baptiste de, French Minister of the Marine, the success of, in building up the French Navy, 401-2

MacKay (McKay), Capt. James, of the South Carolina Independent Company, arrives at Great Meadows, 33; refuses to recognize Washington's command, 33; becomes brevet lieutenant colonel, 33; the arrival of, at Mount Braddock, 35; the defence of Fort Necessity by the troops of, 39-40; activities of, at Wills Creek, 42

Mackellar, Patrick, military engineer, criticizes the plans adopted to strengthen Oswego, 157-8, 193; charges of the concealment of the report of, by Shirley considered, 194; reports on the insecurity of the environs of Oswego, 198; the recommendations of, for the improvement of the defences of Oswego approved by Shirley, 198

Mackinac Island, the British do not claim, in 1755, 161

Macnémara, M. de., Lieutenant Général d'Armée Navalle, 105; orders for, 106–7; special instructions drawn up for, 107

Mainz, the Archbishop of, and the imperial election, 367

Maize, the growing of, at Fort Duquesne, 88

Maltzahn, Hans Dietrich von, Prussian Ambassador at Dresden, Saxony, assures Frederick regarding Russia, 421; warned that Frederick was to invade Saxony, 423–4

Mardyk, the French plan to fortify, 353

Maria Theresa, Empress of the Holy Roman German Empire, the position of, 346; the Pragmatic Sanction and, 356; the War of the Austrian Succession and, 356–7; the Austrian Netherlands preserved by Great Britain for, 358; the desires of, to reorient the Imperial foreign policy, 359; supports Kaunitz, 360–1; the dismemberment of Prussia desired by, 380; the ministers of, suspected of duplicity, 380; Frederick's note to, in 1756, 422; the reply of, to Frederick, 424; no offensive alliance between Elizabeth of Russia and, 424

Marlborough, John Churchill, 1st Duke of, and the War of the Spanish Succession, 352, 354

Marshall, Capt. Hubert, of the New York Independent Companies, 46

Mary, the, transports Acadians to Virginia, 277, 300

Mary, daughter of the Duke of York and later Queen, the marriage of, with William of Orange, 355

Maryland, Province of, the Assembly of, agrees to raise troops, 28; recruits a company for frontier defence, 54; the failure of, to provide Braddock with provisions and horses, 75; the ravishing of the frontiers of, 127; faces its greatest crisis in 1755, 134; the government of, unwilling to support a campaign against Fort Duquesne in 1756, 185; resentment within, over the enlistment of indentured servants, 185; no support from, for the Crown Point campaign, 186; Acadians sent to, 277, 279; the Acadian exiles in, 304–9

Massachusetts Bay, Province of, the loyalty of the Assembly of, to House of Hanover, 7; the disposition of the forces of, for the Crown Point and Niagara campaigns, 142; its quota of troops, 142; Johnson asks reinforcements from, 165; a vote of the Assembly of, to send additional men against Crown Point, 166; commissioners from, meet at Albany after the Battle of Lake George, 176; fine response of, to Shirley's appeals for military support, 181; the demand of the Assembly of, that the provincial troops in Nova Scotia be returned, 206; testimony of the Assembly of, to Shirley, 211; the government of, urges the exile of the Acadians, 271–2; Acadians sent to, 280; the treatment by, of the Acadian exiles sent to Georgia, 290; the Council of, permits the Pubnico Acadians to remain within the Providence, 298–9; the Acadian exiles in, 324–35

Matthews (Mathews), Vice-Admiral Thomas, the court-martial of, 412

Maurice, Jacques, a leader of the Acadians exiled to Georgia, 290

McDowell's Mill, Pa., Dunbar ordered to protect, 133

M'Ginnis (McGinnis), Captain, routs the French at Lake George, 173; mortally wounded, 174

McKenzie, Capt. Frederick, commander at Fort Cumberland, Nova Scotia, captures and scatters the Acadians living about Chaleur Bay, 337

Melançon, Philip, a rebellious Acadian exile, the treatment of, in Pennsylvania, 316

Memramcook, Nova Scotia, the Acadians of, help defend Fort Beauséjour, 229; orders by Monckton to burn, and collect the settlers, 266

Mennonites, the, of Pennsylvania, and pacifism in 1755, 66

Mercantilism, and the British empire in the eighteenth century, 16–7; a departure from the canons of, in colonizing Nova Scotia, 56

Mercer, Lieut. Col. James F., the arrival of, at Oswego, 151; as commander at Oswego, conditions facing, during the winter of 1755–1756, 183–4; problems confronting, in the defence of Oswego in the summer of 1756, 198–199; the death of, in the French attack on Fort George, 199–200

Mermaid, H.M.S., convoys the transports with Acadian exiles, 324

Methuen, Massachusetts Bay, Acadian exiles at, protest, 330

Michell, Abraham Ludwig, Prussian chargé d'affaires in London, informs Frederick of Britain's strong position, 385; authorized by Frederick to sign the Convention of Westminster, 390; informs Frederick of the pro-British leanings of the Russian court, 420–1

Michilimakinac Indians, support the French at Fort Duquesne, 90

Micmac Indians, under the control of Le Loutre, 214; Le Loutre reports the killing of an infinite number of English by, 257; French policy keeps, in the field against the English after 1749, 262–3

Middletown, Connecticut, Acadian exiles in, 323

Milbury, Captain, of the *Elizabeth*, takes Acadians to Maryland, 277, 304

Mildmay, William, a member of the Anglo-French Paris Commission, sends information of the movement of the French fleet, 104; the comment of, on the Kaunitz embassy to France, 360

Milton, Massachusetts Bay, Acadians in, 326

Minas Basin, Nova Scotia, Acadians from, assist at Fort Beauséjour, 248; letters sent to Le Loutre from, 253; a memorial from the Acadians of, 254; a second memorial from, 255; deputies from, summoned to Halifax, 255; deputies from, before the Council, 255–8; a third memorial and deputies from, 259–60; the activities of Col. Winslow about, 265–80

Mingo Indians, hostile conduct of, at Fort Necessity, 41; harass Washington's army, 45; make war upon Braddock's army, 78; the desire of, to attack Braddock, 91

Minorca, the island of, ability of France to invade, 400; Frederick II on the defence of, 402; the French invasion of, 403–5, 406–7; a description of, 404–5

Miquelon, the island of, Gulf of St. Lawrence, the Acadians and, 336; the Acadians at Saint-Malo seek to go to, 341

Mirabeau, Marquis de, on the importance of Acadia to France, 343

Miramichi Bay, Canada, Acadians settled about, scattered, 337

Mirepoix, Charles Pierre Gaston François de Levis, Duc de, French Ambassador in London, the "Intercepted Letters" addressed to, 189; remains in London after Boscawen sails, 373–4; the recall of, to France, 376

Missaquash River, Nova Scotia, the crossing of, under fire by the New England volunteers, 228

Missisauga Indians, support the French at Fort Duquesne, 91

Mississippi River, Acadians exiled to Maryland go to the regions about, 308

Mitchell, Andrew, British minister at Berlin, on Prussian preparations for war, 421, 422; informed by Frederick of approaching war, 422; ordered to warn Frederick of the danger of going to war, 423

Mohawk Indians, the capture of, in the battle of Lake George, 172

Mohawk River, difficulties of the navigation of, 148–9, 150, 151

Monarque, H.M.S., the execution of Byng on board, 414–5

Monckton, Col. Robert, leader of the New England expedition against Fort Beauséjour, 135; friction that develops between the New England officers and, 266; has unlimited financial credit in coming to Boston, 216; activities of, in Boston, 226; placed in command of the expedition to reduce Fort Beauséjour, 227; terms of surrender granted by, 232; secures the surrender of Fort Gaspereau, 233; ordered to drive the rebellious Acadians from Nova Scotia, 254

Monongahela, Battle of the, the failure of Indian support and, 93; the disaster of, 94–6; a court of inquiry into the British defeat in, 133–4

Montalais, Capt. de, of the *Dauphin Royal*, eludes the British fleet, 113; the vessel of, again escapes the British fleet, 124

Montcalm, Gorzon de Saint-Véran, Louis Joseph, Marquis de, the voyage of, to Louisbourg in 1755, 108; return of, from Louisbourg, 196; appointed to command the French troops in New France, 196; the arrival of, 196; early activities of, in Canada, 197; leads the expedition against Oswego, 197–8; attacks Forts Ontario and George, 199–200; the capture of Oswego brings great prestige to, among the Indians, 200

Montgomery, Gen. Richard, the capture of Montreal and the siege of Quebec by, in 1775, 153

Montour, Andrew, Indian interpreter, the failure of, to support Washington at Great Meadows, 45

Montreal, Canada, the trade relations between Albany and, 144; Shirley's plan for the conquest of, 152–3

Montrésor, James, British military engineer, receives report on the condition of the forts at Oswego, 193–4

Montreuil, Adjutant General de, on the value of French regular soldiers in American warfare, 197

Moravia, the movement of Imperial troops into, 422

Morlaix, France, Acadians carried to, in flags of truce, 337

Morris, Gov. Lewis, of New Jersey, on the freedom of the people from burdens, 8

Morris, Jr., Lewis, and Livingston, secure supplies for Shirley, 184

Morris, Gov. Robert Hunter, of Pennsylvania, considers the Anglo-French hostilities in 1754 an "American" affair, 20; the unhappy relations between the Assembly and, 69; in favour of the Virginia route to Fort Duquesne, 73; opens up a road from Shippensburg to the Youghiogheny River, 75; gets Indians for Braddock, 77; on the plans of the French in 1755, 134; at the New York council of war, 177–9; asks military aid from Shirley, 189; difficulties facing, in Pennsylvania, 190–1; the decision of the Proprietors to recall, 191; on the loss to America in the recall of Shirley, 191; the policy of, toward the Acadian exiles, 310

Mortier, Abraham, Deputy Paymaster for the Northern District of North America, payments of, to Shirley, 183

Mostyn, Rear Admiral, the exile of the Acadians and, 258

Motte (Mothe), Comte Dubois de la, commands a French fleet sent to Canada, 106; orders to, 106–7; activities of, off the Banks, 107–8; movement of, to the St. Lawrence, 114–5; the return of, to France with his ships, 120–1

Mount Braddock, Pennsylvania, Washington at, 34; the retreat from, 37; the destruction of the settlement at, by the French, 44

Mount Johnson, New York, a great Indian conference at, in 1755, 163

Münchhausen, Ph. Adolf, Hanoverian minister, plan of, for the defence of the "System," 369; appeals to Frederick in the name of George II not to go to war, 423

Murray, Captain, commander of Fort Edward, Piziquid, Nova Scotia, ordered to refuse passes to Acadians to go to Beauséjour, 249; called on to warn the Acadians as to their conduct, 253; on the insolence of the Acadians, 254; co-operates with Col. Winslow in removing the Acadians from Minas Basin, 267–78

Murray, General James, Governor of Canada, grants permission to the Acadian exiles in Massachusetts Bay to settle in Canada, 334–5

Murray, John, the affidavit of, against General Webb, 195

Murrow, Capt. Nathan, of the Ranger, transports Acadians to Virginia, 280

Muse, Lieut. Col. George, of Virginia, brings reinforcements to Washington, 33

Namur, Austrian Netherlands, and the Barrier Treaty, 353; the occupation of, by the French, 357; Dutch forces concentrated at, in 1755, 366

Nantes, France, Acadians carried to, in flags of truce, 337; the mémoire of the Acadians at, 342; Acadians go to Louisiana from, 342

Napier, Maj. Gen. Robert, Adjutant General, 74

Naval vessels, the building of, on Lake Ontario agreed to at the Alexandria conference, 71; the quality of French, 104; the construction of, on Lake Ontario, 150, 198; the reconditioning and construction of, in France, 401

Navigation Rule of 1756, the French Empire and the, 426

Navy, the British, blockades the French fleets in the New World in 1755, 119–20; the strength of, in 1755, 401; the concentration of, in the English Channel, 402; ranks of officers in, 405; see also Anson, Boscawen, Byng, Hawke, Holburne, Howe, Keppel, West

Navy, the French, the decision of the French ministers to risk, to send reinforcements to Canada, 103–5; the good qualities of the ships of, 104; elements of inferiority of, with respect to the British, 104–5; the building up of, 400–2; activities of, in the spring of 1756, 402; fighting quality of, 409–10; see also Bouville, Galissonière, Machault, Macnémara, Motte, Salvert

Neptune, the, transports to Virginia more than its quota of Acadians, 278–9, 300

Neverville, M. de, sent against Braddock's forces, 90

Newcastle, Thomas Pelham-Holles, 1st Duke of, Minister and First Lord of the Treasury, on the Anglo-French conflict in North America, 10; sees the necessity of coming to the support of the colonies, 55; the attitude of, toward Boscawen and Braddock, 57; anticipates grave developments in Europe, and America, 101–2; the confidence of, in the outcome of Boscawen's expedition, 110; the attitude of, on the failure of Boscawen in the New World, 118; his high regard of Shirley, 182; opposes in 1747 the exile of the Acadians, 261; on British foreign policy in 1754, 362–3; strongly supports the Anglo-Russian subsidy treaty, 371–2; the friendly attitude of, toward the French court, 374–5; the comment of, on Rouillé's charges against the British, 376; encourages an entente with Prussia, 379; factors involved in the fall of the ministry of, 425; the achievements of, as chief minister, 425–6

New England, hemmed in, by French forts, 13; the Crown Point campaign supported by, 135; the sending of large reinforcements from, after the Battle of Lake George, 176; the provincials of, refuse to serve with the British regulars, 205–7; the arrangements of the governments of, with reference to the Crown Point campaign, 206–7; the disbanding of the forces of, gathered for the Ticonderoga campaign, 208; Governor Lawrence asks for troops from, 216; the threat to, by the loss of Nova Scotia, 217; furnishes a regiment for the reduction of Fort Beauséjour, 227; a massacre of the troops of, at Grand Pré in 1747, 261; see also Connecticut, Massachusetts Bay, New Hampshire, Rhode Island

Newfoundland, activities of French and British fleets off the coast of, in 1755, 107–15

New France, the disadvantages of, with respect to the British colonies, 12; the unified Indian policy of, 45; food supplies for soldiers in, come from the British colonies, 65; powerful reinforcement sent to, from France, 100; great activity of the government of, in 1755, 167; the limits of, with respect to ancient Acadia, 213–4; the importance of the Bay of Fundy to, 216–7; a chain of forts to protect, 217; the surrender of the French forts in Nova Scotia a great blow to, 233–4; the reconquest of Acadia a policy of the government of, 245–6

New Hampshire, Province of, the quota of troops from, for the Crown Point campaign, 142; a regiment from, marches to join Johnson at the Great Carrying Place,

166; the troops of, at Fort Edward, 169–70; the opposition of the government of, to recruiting soldiers for the Beauséjour expedition, 227; the attitude of, toward receiving Acadian exiles, 324

New Haven, Connecticut, Acadian exiles in, 323

New Jersey, Province of, the Assembly of, indifferent to the frontier crisis, 54; the Crown Point campaign and, 135; the regiment from, to support the Fort Niagara campaign, 142; the troops of, without military experience, 143; movement of troops from, to Oswego, 150; the regiment of, to winter in 1755 on the lower Mohawk, 162; resentment within, over the enlistment of indentured servants, 185; no support from, for the Crown Point campaign, 186; the troops of, and the defence of Oswego, 199–200; Acadians exiled to Georgia arrive in, 289–90; the attitude of the Governor of, toward the Acadian exiles, 319

New London, Connecticut, Acadian exiles in, 322–3

New Milford, Connecticut, Acadian exiles in, 323

New Orleans, the fortifications of, a part of the protective system of New France, 217

Newton, Maryland, Acadians at, 308

New York, Province of, the military weakness of, in 1755, 13–4; the claim of the government of, to an exclusive jurisdiction over the Six Nations, 45; the condition of the Independent Companies of, sent to Virginia, 45–6; merchants of, and trade with the enemy, 65; the Independent Companies of, return from Virginia, 133; the responsibility of the government of, for delays in the Crown Point expedition, 142; the opposition of, to Shirley, 142–3; unwilling to assume proper burdens in the campaign, 142; quota of troops to be furnished by, 143; the influence of the land dispute with Massachusetts Bay upon the policies of the government of, 143; seeks to get its quota of troops from Connecticut, 144; commissioners of, meet in Albany after the Battle of Lake George, 176; the feud between Shirley and the authorities of, 182; resentment within, over the enlistment of indentured servants, 185; gives additional support for the Crown Point campaign, 186; the Acadian exiles sent to Georgia aided by the Governor of, 290; the Acadian exiles in, 319–21

Niagara River, the attack on the French fort on, agreed to at the Alexandria conference, 71; see also Fort Niagara

Niaouré Bay (Sackett's Harbor), New York, a French camp at, threatens Oswego, 197

Nightingale, H.M.S., brings Loudoun to the New World, 193; convoys transports, with Acadian exiles, 277; separated from its transports, 287

Nivernais, Duc de, French Ambassador in Berlin, later in London, memorials of the Acadian exiles to, 317, 324; offers to carry the Acadian exiles in Massachusetts Bay to France, 333; persuades the Acadians in England to become French subjects in 1763, 338; the negotiations of, with Frederick in 1756, 388, 391–3

Noel, Captain, of the H.M.S. Maria Louisa, fatally wounded in the action off Minorca, 412

Norfolk, Virginia, Acadians landed at, 300

Normanville (Normenville), M. de, sent against Braddock's army, 89–90

Norridgewalk Indians, Shirley's treaty conference with, 130

North America, Shirley on the French designs respecting, 11; British designs respecting, in 1755, 62

North Carolina, Province of, the Assembly of, agrees to send a regiment to Virginia, 25; support of the Ohio campaign voted by the Assembly of, 46; troops of, and the question of pay, 47; the inflation of the currency of, and the campaign, 47; the movement of the regiment from, to Virginia and its disbandment, 47; furnishes a company in 1755, and votes £5,000 in good money, 54, 75; Acadians to be sent to, from Annapolis Royal, 280; revolt in Boston of the Pubnico Acadians sent to, 281; offers homes to the Acadians exiled to Georgia, 289; Acadian exiles within, 297–9

Norwich, Connecticut, Acadian exiles in, 323

Norwich, H.M.S., the guns of, loaned to Braddock, 79

Nova Scotia, Province of, the colonization of, marks a new aspect of British colonialism, 17, 55–6; the New England expedition against the French forts in, launched by Shirley, 131–2; French forts in, in 1755, 212–3; French claims to, 213; the military strength of the French within, 214; forces under the control of the government of, 214–5; the problem of maintaining order in, 215; the proposal to eject the French from, 215–6; the threat to, by the French system of forts, 217; the "key" of the eastern British colonies, 217–8; the government of, meets the costs of the New England expedition against Fort Beauséjour, 227; the cession to Great Britain of, 243; weak authority of the government of, after 1713, 244; unauthorized appropriation of land within, by the Acadians, 245; the danger to, in permitting the Acadians to emigrate to Canada, 246; the government of, lays down terms for the return of the refugee Acadians, 247–8; assures the Acadians that they will not be obliged to bear arms, 247; a proclamation against carrying supplies without licence out of the limits of, issued, 249; the decision of the government of, to drive out the Acadians who had revolted, 254; the decision of, to compel all other Acadians to take the oath or to lose their property, 255–7; the colonization of, by the British government a costly experiment, 262; the value of exports from, and imports into, 262; the decision of the government of, to distribute the Acadians among the other continental colonies, 263–4; the return of the Acadian exiles from Massachusetts Bay to, 335; the New England colonization of, after 1763, 335; see also Acadia

Oath of allegiance, an, demanded of the Swedes on the Delaware by the Dutch, 244; demanded of the Dutch on the Hudson by the English, 244; refusal of the Acadians to take, 244; the Acadians returning to Nova Scotia take, 335; Acadians at Saint-Malo, France, ready in 1767 to take, to George III, 340

Oath of fidelity, an, the Acadians who took the oath of allegiance to the French Crown offer to take, to the British Crown, 247; lack of respect for, shown by the Acadians, 248; of 1727 still binds the Acadians, 248–9

Observations on the late and present Conduct of the French (1755), by William Clarke, 130

Ogilvie, Lieut. William, of the New York Independent Company, the testimony of, 46

Ohio Company, the, the efforts of, to build a fort at the forks of the Ohio, 10; the loss of the storehouse of, at Redstone Creek, 44

Ohio River Indians, the failure of, to attend the Winchester conference, 27; the support of the French by, 91

Old Dominion, the, see Virginia

Oneida Indians, declare that Johnson sent a message for them not to go to Oswego, 146

Oneida Lake, transportation on, 149

Onondaga Indians, a delegation of, at Oswego, reports that Johnson sent a belt to the Six Nations against the Niagara expedition, 146

Ontario, H.M.S., on Lake Ontario, prepared for an attack against Fort Niagara, 158

Opiniâtre, the, French warship, in the New World, 114; eludes the British blockade, 121

Orange County, New York, Acadian exiles in, 320

Ordnance Board, guns sent by, to Virginia, 23

Orme, Capt. Robert, aide-de-camp of Braddock, on support in America of the common fund, 71–2; on Braddock's orders in the Battle of the Monongahela, 95; asks for Shirley's directions after Braddock's defeat, 129

Orpheus, the, French warship in the battle off Minorca, 409

Osborne, Admiral Henry, the Western squadron under, 406

Ostend, Austrian Netherlands, the occupation of, by the French, 357

Ostend East India Company, the, the Treaty of Münster and, 355; the suppression of, and the guarantee of the Pragmatic Sanction, 356

Oswego, New York, a plan to strengthen, agreed to at the Alexandria conference, 71; inadequate attention paid to the defences of, 147–8; communication between Albany and, described, 148–9; the time required for a round trip between Schenectady and, 151; the significance of, as a trading center, 153; difficulties of providing a defence of, 152; the ruinous condition of the fort at, 153; the disgraceful management of the Indian trade at, 154; the protection of posts of Niagara and, by the Six Nations, before 1755, 154, 195; the French report a large concentration of British troops at, 155; the plan of the French to move against, from Fort Frontenac, 156; decision of Shirley to provide added fortifications for, 156–7; the erection of barracks at, 159; condition of the garrison at, during the winter of 1755–1756, 183–4; supplies move to, 184; the garrison of, reinforced, 184; the danger to the communications of, 192–3; report on the condition of the forts at, 193; the sending of a relief to, 194; news of the fall of, received by General Webb, 195; the insecurity of the environs of, 198; need to strengthen the forts at, in the spring of 1756, 198; Shirley orders the required work done on the forts of, 198; delay in the strengthening of, 199; number of troops at, at the time of the attack, 199; the fall and destruction of, 199–200; significance of the loss of, 200; the question of the ability of the English to hold, considered, 200–3; Loudoun charges Shirley with the responsibility for the loss of, 209

Oswego, H.M.S., on Lake Ontario, prepared for an attack against Fort Niagara, 158

Oswego River, New York, perils of navigation down, 149

Ottawa Indians, support the French at Fort Duquesne, 90

Ouekad (Westcock), Nova Scotia, the Acadians of, help defend Fort Beauséjour, 229

Oxford, H.M.S., fights the Espérance, 125

Oxford, Maryland, Acadians sent to, 304, 308

Pacifism, the defence of Pennsylvania in 1755 and, 66–8

Paine, Thomas, author of Common Sense, American national tradition and, 5–9, 19

Palatinate, Germany, the Elector of, and French subsidies, 392; the Elector of, and the imperial election, 397

Paris, Peace of (1763), 9, 18

Parker, Capt. John, of the New Jersey regiment, sends word of the fall of Oswego, 195

Parliament, of Great Britain, the voting of subsidies for colonial defence by, 60–1; the great powers of, 347–9; the support of Hanover endorsed by, 379

Parrington (Purrington), Captain, of the Sally and Molly, takes Acadians to Virginia, 277, 300

Patuxent River, Maryland, Acadians sent to the region of, 304

Pavy, Lieut. Lewis, of the New York Independent Company, testimony of, 46

Pembroke, the, destined for North Carolina from Nova Scotia, seized by the Acadian exiles, 281, 297–8

Pennsylvania, Province of, the Assembly of, indifferent to the frontier crisis, 54; and pacifism in 1755, 66–8; the merchants of, trade with the enemy, 65; the protection of, by Great Britain, 66–8; privileged position of, within the British Empire, 68–9; the problem of, of providing Braddock with flour, horses, and wagons, 75; the ravishing of the frontiers of, 127; the government of, refuses to support the Crown Point campaign, 135, 186; faces its greatest crisis in 1755, 132; the government of, unwilling to support a campaign against Fort Duquesne in 1756, 185; western defences for, built, 185; resentment within, over the enlistment of indentured servants, 185; the continuance of the ravages of Indians within, 189; Acadians sent to, 277, 279; the Acadian exiles in, 309–18

Penryn, England, Acadians at, 338

Pepperrell, Sir William, qualifications of, as commander-in-chief in North America compared with those of Shirley, 181; considered for the command of the Crown Point expedition, 203

Pepperrell Regiment, see Regiments, the 51st

Perth Amboy, New Jersey, Braddock's army concentrates at, after defeat, 133

Pélegrin, M., lieutenant of the port of Quebec, guides the French fleet through the Strait of Belle Isle, 121

Petitcodiac, Nova Scotia, the Acadians of, help defend Fort Beauséjour, 229; the desire of the inhabitants of, to continue to resist the English, 234; Monckton's orders to burn, and to collect the settlers of, 266

Peyrode, Chevalier de la, sent to observe Braddock's march, 90

Peyronie, Adjutant William, at Fort Necessity, 40

Philadelphia, the memorial of the mayor and council of, regarding the devastation of the Pennsylvania frontiers in 1755, 309–10; Acadians in, 314, 317–8

Philadelphia County, Pennsylvania, difficulties with the Acadian exiles within, 312–3

Philip, Duke of Orléans, the regency of, and the "System," 355

Philippe, Duke of Parma, son-in-law of Louis XV, the Versailles Convention and, 396; plans to secure the Austrian Netherlands for, 418

Phips, Lieut. Gov. Spencer, of Massachusetts Bay, recommends the exile of the Acadians, 272; asks New Hampshire to help care for the Acadian exiles, 324

Physiocrats, French, the experiment at Châtellerault and the, 339; the desire of, to reclaim Acadia, 343

Pichon, Jean, father of Thomas Pichon, 218

Pichon (Tyrrell), Thomas, French traitor, the attitude of, toward Captain Hocquart, 112; the warning of, of a projected attack against Fort Lawrence, 214; works to undermine the French position in Nova Scotia, 218; recommends an attack upon Fort Beauséjour, 218; early career of, 218–21; the activities of, at Beauséjour, 221, 225–6, 231; disillusioned with French policy in Nova Scotia, 221–3; author of Lettres et Mémoires pour servir à l'Histoire . . . de Cap-Breton, 222; accepts secret service with the British, 224; defence of the position of the British in North America by, 224; gives an account of the pillaging of the King's stores, 233; assists Monckton in securing the surrender of Fort Gaspereau, 233; brings about the arrest of resisting Acadians, 234; the efforts of, to influence the Acadians of Piziquid, 234; the activities of, in Halifax in guise of a prisoner, 234–5; seeks to win over French officers, 235–6; French suspicions of, 236; forms an alliance with Madame de Beaumont, 237; the activities of, in Pennsylvania, 237, 316; literary activities of, 237–8; efforts of, to aid the Acadians at Saint-Malo, France, 238–9, 340; the activities of, on the island of Jersey, 239–42, 340–1; contrast and comparison of Le Loutre and, 240–1; the death of, 341

Piercy, Capt. Francis, of the Ranger, transports to Maryland more Acadians than his quota, 279, 304

Pitt, William, the plan of, for the conquest of Canada follows closely that of Shirley, 153; the contemptuous attitude of, toward Hanover, 351; the aid of, sought by the Cabinet Council in 1755, 378; denounces the Continental policy of the government, 378–9; dismissed from office, 379; the hostility of, toward the Newcastle ministry, 425; a beneficiary of the Newcastle statesmanship, 425–6

Pitt, the, carries Acadian exiles from Connecticut to Canada, 324

Piziquid, Nova Scotia, Pichon seeks to influence the Acadians at, 234; Acadians from, go to work at Fort Beauséjour, 248;

disturbances among the Acadians at, 249–50; an Acadian proposal to expel the English from, 250; letters sent to Le Loutre from, 253; the inhabitants of, send a memorial to Lawrence, 254; a second memorial from, 255; a third memorial from, 259; the deputies from, imprisoned, 258, 260; see also Fort Edward

Plymouth, England, a British fleet sent to, to watch the French fleet, 102

Poitou, the Province of, France, Acadians sent to, 339

Poland, the Kingdom of, and the Electorate of Saxony in 1755, 346

Pomeroy, Seth, of Massachusetts Bay, serves under General Johnson, 176

Pompadour, Jeanne-Antoinette Poisson le Normand d'Etioles, Marquise de, Newcastle and, 374–5; invests great sums in British securities, 387

Pont à Buot, Nova Scotia, a French force dislodged at, 228; the Acadians of, help defend Fort Beauséjour, 229

Portland, H.M.S., damaged in action off Minorca, 412

Port Mahon, capital of Minorca, the French converge on, 404–5; the capture of St. Philip's Castle at, 416–7

Port Tobacco, Maryland, Acadians at, 308

Potawatomi Indians, the conduct of, at Fort Duquesne, 91

Pownall, Thomas, sent by Shirley to New York in behalf of the Crown Point expedition, 136; becomes Lieutenant Governor of New Jersey, 146; joins the faction against Shirley, 146–7; aids the mapmaker Lewis Evans in his attack on Shirley, 179; other activities of, in the undermining of General Shirley, 186–7, 188, 190; offered and refused the governorship of Pennsylvania, 190–1; becomes Shirley's successor in Massachusetts Bay, 191; the relations of, with Benjamin Franklin, 191; returns to New York on Loudoun's staff, 193

Pragmatic army, the, Great Britain and, 356–7

Pragmatic Sanction, the, the suppression of the Ostend East India Company and, 356; the War of the Austrian Succession and, 356–7

Preble, General, of Massachusetts Bay, seizes the Pubnico Acadians, 298

Prévost, Jacques, Commissaire Ordonnateur of Isle Royale, opposition of, to the policies of Comte de Raymond, 219–20

Prideaux, Brigadier General John, later expedition of, against Fort Niagara, 145

Prince Edward Island, see Isle St. Jean

Prince Frederick, the, transports Acadian exiles to Georgia, 288

Prince George County, Maryland, orders regarding the treatment of Acadian exiles within, 307

Princess Ann County, Maryland, Acadians in, 308

Princess Louisa, H.M.S., the battle off Minorca and, 412

Proby, Captain, of H.M.S. Syren, escorts the transports with Acadians exiled to South Carolina, 291

Prosperous, the, transports Acadians to Virginia, 277, 300

Providence, the, transports Acadians to North Carolina, 299

Provincial troops, see Connecticut, Maryland, Massachusetts Bay, New Hampshire, New Jersey, New York, North Carolina, Pennsylvania, Rhode Island, Virginia

Prussia, Kingdom of, the policy of Kaunitz toward, 360; subsidies received from France before 1750 by the King of, 380; the dismembering of, contemplated by Maria Theresa, 380; see also Brandenburg, Frederick II

Pubnico, Nova Scotia, the Acadians of, carried to Boston, 281; Acadian exiles from, refuse to go to North Carolina and remain in Massachusetts Bay, 298–9; inhabitants of, sent to France in flags of truce, 337

Putnam, Israel, of Connecticut, serves under General Johnson, 176

Quakers, the, of Pennsylvania, indifference of, to frontier developments, 24; and pacifism in 1755, 66–8

Quebec, Shirley's proposal of 1755 for the conquest of, 152; the plan to threaten, in 1756, 178

Queens County, New York, Acadian exiles in, 320

Racehorse, the, transports Acadians to Massachusetts Bay, 280, 326

Ramillies, H.M.S., Byng's flagship, 406; contrasted with the Foudroyant, 409; drives the Couronne out of action off Minorca, 412

Ramsack, Nova Scotia, the burning of, ordered by Col. Monckton, 265

Ranger, the, Capt. Nathan Murrow, transports Acadians to Virginia, 280, 301

Ranger, the, Capt. Piercy, transports to Maryland more Acadians than its quota, 279, 304

Ratzeburg, capital of Saxe-Lauenburg, George II and, 349

Raymond, Jean-Louis, Comte de, Governor of Isle Royale, brings Pichon to Isle Royale, 219; recommends Pichon for important offices, 219–20; suspects for a time Pichon, and then recommends him, 220; incites the Micmacs to attack the English in peace time, 221; the question of the treacherous conduct of, 225

Reade, James, assistant commissary at Fort Williams, brings relief to Oswego, 184

Redoutable, the, French warship in the battle off Minorca, 409

Redstone Creek, Washington plans to concentrate his force at, 23; Washington's troops work on a road to, 35; the destruction of the Ohio Company post on, 44

Regiments: 44th (Halkett's, Abercromby's), ordered to Virginia, 58; becomes part of a special task force, 82; goes to New York, 133; to participate in the Crown Point campaign, 204; 48th (Dunbar's, Webb's), ordered to Virginia, 58; guards Braddock supply train, 85; goes to New York, 133; to participate in the Crown Point campaign, 204; 50th (Shirley's), the plan to revive, 58; to be used against Fort Niagara, 131; remains at Oswego, 162; defends Oswego, 199; surrenders to the French, 200; 51st (Pepperrell's) the plan to revive, 58; to be used against Fort Niagara, 131; remains at Oswego, 162; defends Oswego, 199; surrenders to the French, 200

Regular army, the British, American national tradition and, 11–3; the relations of, with the provincials under Washington, 29, 33; with the provincials under Winslow, 204–8; the conduct of, in the Battle of the Monongahela, 95–8; the conduct of the officers of, after Braddock's defeat, 128–9

Regular army, the French, the discipline of, in the Battle of Lake George, 172; the chief reliance of the French in North America on, 197; well adapted to warfare in the wilderness, 201; the strength of, in France in 1756, 392

Remstreque, Nova Scotia, a French post at, 212

Repnin, Prince, of Russia, brings an army to the aid of the Maritime Powers, 358

Restigoushe River, Canada, Acadians living about, captured and scattered, 337

Review of Military Operations in North America (1756), on Shirley's activities in Europe, 130; on Shirley as a leader, 132; the authorship of, 132

Revolutionary War, the, American national tradition and, 4

Reynolds, Gov. John, of Georgia, the policy of, toward the Acadian exiles, 288–9

Rhode Island, Colony of, the quota of troops from, for the Crown Point campaign, 142

Richelieu, Maréchal, Duc de, the French invasion of Minorca under, 403–4

Richmond, Virginia, Acadians carried to, 300

Richmond County, New York, Acadian exiles in, 320

Rigaud, François-Pierre de, Governor of Trois Rivières, and the traitor Pichon, 234–5

Rigoville, M., sent with a party against Braddock's army, 90

Rivière aux Bœufs, the problem of low water in, 89

Rivière aux Canards, Nova Scotia, delay in transporting the Acadians of, 278–9; the burning of the settlements of, 279

Rivière Habitant, Nova Scotia, delay in embarking the Acadians of, 278–9; the burning of the settlements of, 279

Robinson, Sir Thomas, Secretary of State for the Southern Department, Shirley and Dinwiddie ask, that regular troops be sent to America, 13; the decision to send out Boscawen and, 101; the letter of, to Gov. Lawrence on the treatment of the Acadians, 270–1; at Aix-la-Chapelle, 362; expresses the British attitude toward French policy in 1755, 375

Rochefort, France, Acadians sent to, in flags of truce, 337

Rochibeau, Louis, of Annapolis River, on the services rendered by his family to the Annapolis garrison, 259

Rockwell, Captain, of the *Elizabeth*, brings Acadian exiles to Connecticut, 321–2

Roctoyade, M., sent with a party against Braddock's army, 90

Roman Catholics, the fear of, in the English colonies in 1755, 287, 291–3, 302, 331; in Maryland, the treatment of, 305, 308–9; in Pennsylvania, 318

Rouillé, Antoine-Louis, Comte de Jouy, conferences of, with the Earl of Albemarle, 62–3; the reactions of, to Boscawen's attack on the French fleet, 375–6; recommends that the King of Prussia attack Hanover, 381–2

Rowan, Pres. Matthew, of the North Carolina Council, and the Virginia campaign of 1754, 46; responsible for policy favouring the North Carolina soldiers, 48

Royal Roussillon, the battalion of, brought to Canada by Montcalm, 196

Rush, Dr. Benjamin, the influence of *Common Sense* according to, 5

Russia, Empire of, the ability of Great Britain to use, against Prussia, 358; the subsidy treaty of, with the Maritime Powers in 1747, 358; failure of Great Britain to implement the subsidy treaty with, 398; *see also*, Bestuzhev, Elizabeth

Rutherford, Capt. John, later Major, the opinion of, of the troops under Col. Dunbar, 128

Sackett's Harbor, New York, *see* Niaouré Bay

Sage, the, French warship in the battle off Minorca, 409

St. Clair, Sir John, Deputy Quartermaster General in America, considers the Pennsylvania route to Fort Duquesne, 73; contracts for provisions, wagons, and horses, 75; on the difficulties of the Braddock route, 80, 83; on Braddock, 84; the proposals of, at Salt Lick Creek overruled, 85; crosses the Monongahela, 92; the retrograde movement of the troops of, 95; blames Braddock for the defeat, 97; at the council of war held after Braddock's death, 133; at the New York council of war, 177–9

St. Domingue, French colony of, Acadian exiles from New York go to, 321; Acadian exiles from Connecticut go to, 324; Acadian exiles in Massachusetts Bay go to, 333

St. Germain, M., servant to Vergor, aids in the pillaging of the King's stores, 233

Saint-Helier, on the island of Jersey, Pichon's activities at, 239–42

St. John River, a French fort on, 212; plans of forts on, furnished the English by Pichon, 234; Acadian exiles carry the transport *Pembroke* to, 281, 297–8; Acadians in South Carolina find their way to, 295; Acadians from, sent to France in flags of truce, 337

St. Joseph Roman Catholic Church, Philadelphia, marriage records of, 318

St. Lawrence River, the French fleet in, 115, 119

Saint-Malo, France, Acadians carried to, in flags of truce, 337; the Acadians at, 238–40, 339–42

St. Philip's Castle, British stronghold constructed at Port Mahon on Minorca, 404; French orders respecting, 404; the siege of, 406–7; the failure of Byng to relieve, 412–3; the surrender of, 416–7

Saint-Pierre, the island of, the Acadians after 1763 not encouraged to have relations with the French on, 336

St. Philippe, the Parish of, Charleston, South Carolina, maintains Acadian exiles, 296

Salem, Massachusetts Bay, Acadians in, 330, 334

Sally and Molly, the, transports Acadians to Virginia, 277, 300

Salt Lick Creek, Pennsylvania, Braddock's council of war at, 85

Salvert, M. de., Rear Admiral, of the French fleet, orders of, 107; the comment of, on the speed of the French ships, 113; blockade of the fleet of, at Louisbourg, 122; the escape of the ship of, 123–4

Sandwich, John Montagu, 4th Earl of, at Aix-la-Chapelle, 362

Savannah, Georgia, the Acadian exiles at, 288, 290–1

Saxe, Maurice, Maréchal, Comte de, the War of the Austrian Succession and, 56, 356–7

Saxe-Lauenburg, the Duchy of, and George II, 349

Saxony, Electorate of, the personal union between Poland and, 346; the subsidy treaty of the Maritime Powers with, in 1751 not renewed in 1755, 367; the imperial election and, 367; Frederick of Prussia has his eyes on, 382; the effort on the part of France to bind, in an alliance, 387; decision of Frederick II to seize, 419–20; the lack of preparation for war by, 424; Frederick's entrance into, 424

Scatary, island of, Cape Breton, the British blockade of, 119

Schauenburg, the County of, George II and, 350

Schauenburg-Lippe, the Count of, shares with George II the County of Schauenburg, 350

Scheldt River, the closing of the, and the Treaty of Münster, 352; the opening of, in 1814, 364

Schenectady, New York, time required for a round trip between Oswego and, 151

Schuyler, Col. Peter, of the New Jersey regiment, to support the Fort Niagara campaign, 142; mounts the Mohawks with his troops, 150; the defence of Fort Oswego by, 199; becomes a French prisoner of war, 200

Schwerin, Field Marshal von, ordered by Frederick to prepare for hostilities, 423

Scituate, Massachusetts Bay, Acadian exiles critical of, 330

Scott, Capt. George, commander of Fort Lawrence, establishes relations with Pichon, 223–4; goes to Boston to get New England aid, 226; commands a battalion of New England volunteers against Fort Beauséjour, 227

Scurvy, at Oswego, 183–4; the crews of Boscawen's fleet ill with, 276

Seaflower, the, brings Acadian exiles to Boston, 325

Seneca Indians, confirm at Oswego that Johnson sent a belt against the Niagara campaign to the Six Nations, 146

Seven Years' War, the futility of the, 424–5; the beginnings of the, 396–7, 417, 418–25

Shades of Death, Braddock's Road, 80

Sharpe, Gov. Horatio, of Maryland, appointed commander-in-chief of the colonial troops, 50, 55; calls a governors' conference, 50; plans to lead an expedition against Fort Duquesne, 51; seeks to retain Washington's service, 52; the inability of, to secure horses for Braddock, 75; at the council of war held after Braddock's death, 133; at the New York council of war, December 12, 1755, 177–9; the qualifications of, as commander-in-chief in North America compared with those of Shirley, 181; the attitude of, toward the Acadian exiles, 307

Shawnee Indians, the defection of, 25; cordial relations between the Catawba, the Cherokee, and, 25; take up hatchet against the English, 33; harass Washington's army, 45; the hostile conduct of, at Fort Necessity, 41; make war upon Braddock's army, 78, 91; bring British scalps and prisoners to Fort Duquesne, 87

Shepody, Nova Scotia, a French post at, 212; Acadians of, help defend Fort Beauséjour, 229; orders to burn, and collect the settlers of, for exile, 266

Shippensburg, Pennsylvania, a road from, to the Youghiogheny River opened up, 75; Dunbar ordered to protect, 133

Shipping, the seizure of French, by the British navy, 399–400

Shirley, John, son of Gov. William Shirley, on the dishonour of Col. Dunbar's re-

treat, 128–9; on the living quarters at Oswego, 153

Shirley's Regiment, see Regiments, the 50th

Shirley, Gov. William, of Massachusetts Bay, on the French plans to control North America, 11; persuaded that Great Britain must come to the aid of the colonies, 21; at the Alexandria conference, 71–2; plans of, approved by Braddock, 72; agrees to lead the expedition against Fort Niagara, 72; the record of achievement of, in America before becoming commander-in-chief, 129–32; orders to Col. Dunbar, 132–3; directs blame against the officers for the defeat of Braddock, 133–4; proposals of, for the campaign against Crown Point, 135–6; favors William Johnson to command the northern forces against Crown Point, 135; strong support of the Crown Point campaign by, 137, 141–2; the instructions of, to Johnson, 138–9; makes insinuations against de Lancey, 142; encourages Johnson, 142; growing rift between the New York government and, 143–4; refuses to give contracts to Oliver de Lancey, 145; Johnson refuses Indian support to, 145–6; get some Six Nations support for his campaign, 146; Johnson prepares his case against, for the Board of Trade, 146–7; inadequacy of the forces under, 147–8; employment of batteau-men by, 149; difficulties confronting, en route to Oswego, 150; views of, on the prospect of the campaign, 150–1; the arrival of, at Oswego, 151; explains the slow movement of his troops to Oswego, 151; the plan to conquer Canada modified by, 152–3; decision of, to fortify more strongly Oswego, 156–7; determines to strike at Fort Niagara, 158; unable to carry out his plans, 159; proposes to take over all French western posts in 1756, 160; departs from orders given by the King, 160–1; determines to reduce Fort Frontenac, 161; leaves Oswego in 1755 for New York, 162; receives his commission as temporary commander-in-chief of the British forces in North America, 163; Johnson levies charges against, 165; achievements of the campaign of 1755 under, 177; the council of war held by, in New York, December 12, 1755, 177–9; attack on the policies of, by Lewis Evans, 179; Governor Hardy's criticism of, 180; the qualifications of, as commander-in-chief in America considered, 180–2; Newcastle's high opinion of, in

1755, 182; and the Niagara campaign, 182–3; and the conditions at Oswego, 183–4; measures taken by, for the support of Oswego, 184–5; harmonious agreement reached between Johnson and, 185; popularity of, in Massachusetts Bay, 185–6; secures additional support from New England for the Crown Point campaign of 1756, 186; the undermining of, by his enemies in America, 186–7; decision of the Cabinet Council to displace, 180, 187–8; notified by Fox of his recall, 188; the "Intercepted Letters" and, 189; Governor Morris requests aid of, 189; Gov. Morris's view of the leadership of, in America, 191; Benjamin Franklin's tribute to, 191; relieved of command by Abercromby, 192; the accounts of, in confusion, 192, 193–4; an army collected by, for the drive against Crown Point, 192; makes clear the dangers to Oswego, 192; meets with Loudoun in New York, 193; the charges of the concealment by, of the Mackellar report considered, 194; directs Mackellar to carry out plans for strengthening Oswego, 198; appoints Colonel Winslow to succeed Major General Johnson, 203; works out an agreement between the regular and the colonial troops for joint action against Crown Point, 204–5; the effect upon the Crown Point campaign of the displacing of, 205; on the friction in Nova Scotia between the regular army and the New England volunteers, 206; at the conference between Abercromby and Winslow, 207; charged by Loudoun with the responsibility of the loss of Oswego and insubordination of the New England provincials, 209; rebukes Winslow, 209; charged by Loudoun with raising parties against him, 209; the reply of, to Loudoun, 209–10; the victim of partisan politics, 210; the loss to America of the services of, 210–11; on the French claims to Nova Scotia, 213–4; fears an Indian attack upon the English on the Kennebec, 215–6; the support of the Nova Scotia expedition by, 226–7; on the importance of the capture of the French forts in Nova Scotia, 234; advocates the exile of the Acadians and settlement of their lands in 1747, 261; the policy of, toward the Acadian exiles, 326–8

Shirley, Capt. William, of H.M.S. *Mermaid*, on the difficulty of transporting the Acadian exiles southward, 324

Silesia, the desire of Maria Theresa to regain, 360, 361, 390, 418

Silesian loan, Frederick II and the, 381, 399

Sirenne, the, French warship, in the New World, 114–5

Six Nations, the, the Shirley-Johnson rift over the issue of the support of the Niagara campaign by, 145–6; a belt hostile to Niagara campaign sent to, by Johnson, 146; the protection of Oswego and Niagara by, before 1755, 154; members of, at Oswego approve an attack against Fort Niagara, but change their minds, 159; in conference at Mount Johnson, 163; large numbers of, come to support General Johnson, 167

Slaves, the fear of an insurrection of, in the southern colonies, 14–5; fear in South Carolina that the Acadians would stir up, 293; the Acadian exiles in Virginia tamper with, 303

Smith, Abraham, of Virginia, sent to the Southern Indians, 26; Glen's low opinion of, 26

Smith, Lieutenant Colonel, the retreat from Concord in 1775 and, 96

Snow Hill, Maryland, Acadians at, 308

Soldiers, the pay of, as an issue, 28–30; see also, provincial troops, Independent Companies, regulars

Somerset County, Maryland, Acadians sent to, 304–5

Southampton, England, Acadians at, 338

South Bay, New York, plans to cut a road between the Hudson and, 166; Dieskau at, 169; plans to construct a fort at, approved by a council of war, 204

Southborough, Massachusetts Bay, Acadians sent to, 330

South Carolina, Province of, the Assembly of, supports Glen's Indian policy, 26; favourable attitude of, toward intercolonial co-operation, 26–7; the government of, alone could control the Cherokee and Catawba, 27; the government of, refuses to co-operate with the northern colonies, 50; preparations of, for defence, 50; plans for a fort in the Cherokee country made by, 54; the support by, of the general common fund for the British colonies, 71–2; the Acadian exiles in, 292–7

Southern colonies, lack of co-operation between, in common affairs, 27; see also, Georgia, Maryland, North Carolina, South Carolina, Virginia

Southern Indians, the failure of, to attend the Winchester conference, 27; why there was no support from, for Braddock's campaign, 65; Braddock's instructions and, 70; the failure of, to support Braddock, 77; bad treatment of, by the Virginians, 78; see also Catawba, Cherokee, Chickasaw, Creek

Spain, France seeks the aid of, after Boscawen's attack on the French fleet in 1755, 376–7; the French hope of securing the support of, in 1756, 400–1

Spanish Netherlands, the Treaty of Rastatt and the disappearance of the, 352

Sparke, Major, at the council of war held after Braddock's death, 133

Squaw's Creek, Braddock's Road, Col. Dunbar at, 85

Stade, capital of the Archbishopric of, and George II, 349

Standard-Bearer of the Holy Roman Empire, the House of Hanover deprived of the title of, 349

Starhemberg, Count George Adam, Imperial Ambassador at Paris, Holderness seeks to find what instructions were given to, 368–9; the activities of, in Paris in 1756, 395, 418–9

Stark, John, of New Hampshire, serves under General Johnson, 176

Staten Island, New York, Acadian exiles on, 319–20

Steinberg, Herr von, Hanoverian minister, a plan for the defence of the "System" by, 369

Stephen, Captain Adam, an account by, of the reprehensible conduct of the South Carolina troops in Virginia, 35; account of the Battle of Great Meadows by, 39; account of the surrender of Fort Necessity by, 40–1

Stevens, Captain, of the Oxford, fights the Espérance, 125–6

Stewart, Mr., Norfolk, Virginia, merchant, provides food for the Acadian exiles, 300

Stewart's Crossing, Braddock's Road, 85

Stobo, Capt. Robert, becomes a hostage of the French at Fort Duquesne, 40; on the fear of the Catawba Indians by those of the Ohio Valley, 93

Stoddard, Captain, of the Experiment, difficulties faced by, in bringing Acadian exiles to New York, 319–20

Stone, Captain, of the Endeavour, brings Acadians to Virginia, 300

Stormont, David Murray, Viscount (later Earl of Mansfield), British Minister at Dresden, warns Prussia of the dangers of aggressive war, 421

Stout, Captain, of the Endeavour, takes Acadians to Virginia, 277

Stratford, Connecticut, Acadian exiles in, 323

Sturbridge, Massachusetts Bay, Acadians sent to, 330

Sudbury, Massachusetts Bay, kind treatment of the Acadian exiles by, 331

Suffolk County, New York, Acadian exiles in, 320

Surlaville, Michel Le Courtois, Sieur de, helps to draw up a mémoire on Fort Beauséjour, 218

Susquehanna Company, the appointment of Lydius by the, to negotiate with the Six Nations, 145–6

Swallow, the, transports Acadians to Massachusetts Bay, 280, 326

Swan, the, transports Acadians to Pennsylvania, 277

Swedes, the oath of allegiance demanded of, of New Sweden by the Dutch, 244

Syren, H.M.S., comes to Beaubassin with the transports, 266; arrives at the Savannah with Acadian exiles, 287; arrives at Charleston with Acadians, 291

"System," the British European, Chapter XI

Talbot County, Maryland, address from, regarding the Acadian exiles, 305–6

Tanacharisson, Mingo chief, the Half-King, report of, on movement of the French, 30; assists Washington against Jumonville, 31; differences between Washington and, 31; at the Mount Braddock Indian conference, 355

Tatamgouch, Nova Scotia, the burning of, ordered by Col. Monckton, 265

Taxation, in England and in North Carolina, 9

Tennessee River, the building of a fort on, by South Carolina, 65

Terriot, Charle, Acadian, the possessions of, 273

Tewksbury, Massachusetts Bay, Acadians sent to, 330

Thomas, George, Deputy Governor of Pennsylvania, and the pacifists, 67–8

Three Friends, transports to Pennsylvania more Acadians than its quota, 279

Ticonderoga, plan of Johnson to erect a British fort at, 140; the French concentrate at, 168; an English fort to be constructed at, 168; see also Fort Ticonderoga

Tolland, Connecticut, Acadian exiles in, 323

Tor Bay, Devonshire, England, the fleet ordered to concentrate at, 102

Torbay, H.M.S., flagship of Boscawen, 112

Toronto, Canada, the capture of, in 1756 proposed by Shirley, 160; the British do not lay claim to, 161

Torrington, George Byng, Viscount, naval victory of, at Cape Passaro, 405

Tory Party, the Dutch treaty of 1709 and the, in 1712, 352–3; the Grand Alliance and the, 353

Touche, Chevalier de la, French Ambassador at Berlin, Frederick II gives advice to, on action against Great Britain, 381

Tournay, Austrian Netherlands, the Barrier Treaty and, 353; the capture of, by Saxe, 356

Townshend, Charles, Viscount, and the closing of the Scheldt, 352

Trattles, Captain, of the Prince Frederick, brings Acadian exiles to Georgia, 288

Treason, the, of Thomas Pichon, Chapter VIII; the problem of, 225

Treaty, of Aix-la-Chapelle (1748), the conduct of the French after, 22; the situation of the French armies in the Austrian Netherlands at the time of, 357; of Münster (1648), the fate of Antwerp and the, 352; of Ryswick (1697), and the French claim to Cadaraqui, 179; of St. Petersburg (1748), between Russia and the Maritime Powers, 358; of Utrecht (1713), the Five Nations claim the land of the Eries before, 22; and the French claim to Cadaraqui, 179; the question of the good faith of France in signing, 222; of Westminster (1742), and limited British continental commitments, 357; of Westphalia (1648), the Holy Roman German Empire and, 346

Trent, Capt. William, Washington discharges the detachment led by, 28; troops of, dissatisfied with their pay, 28

Triton, the, French warship in the battle off Minorca, 409

Tulpehocken, Pennsylvania, the destruction of, 309

Tumblestones, Braddock's Road, 80

Turkey Foot, Pennsylvania, 75

Turtle Creek, dangers of the Braddock route via, 85

Tyrawley, Gen. James O'Hara, Lord, Governor of Minorca, in England when Minorca was invaded, 403

United Netherlands, the origins of, 351–2; threats to the independence of, 352; the closing of the Scheldt and, 352; the Bar-

rier Treaty of 1715 and, 353; disappears as a great power in 1714, 354–5; difficulties faced by, 354–5; the protection of, and the "System," 354; the Treaty of Aix-la-Chapelle and, 361–2; no longer care to garrison the barrier fortresses, 366; desire of, to withdraw from all international commitments, 366–7

Upper Marlboro Parish, Maryland, orders to the vestry of, respecting the Acadian exiles, 307; numbers of Acadians in, 308

Van Braam, Captain, sent to treat with the French at Great Meadows, 41; becomes a hostage of the French at Fort Duquesne, 41

Varin, Jean François Victor, commissary of the marine and intendant of Montreal, orders to, respecting supplies and batteaux for the back country, 87

Vaudreuil, Pierre François de Rigaud, Marquis de, Governor General of New France, problems facing, on his arrival at Quebec, 89; military plans of, altered, 89; instructions given to, 100; the voyage of, to the New World, 108; intelligence received by, respecting the British plans for campaigning, in 1755, 154–5; the weakness of Fort Niagara according to, 155; orders Dieskau to move against General Johnson, 168; criticizes the conduct of Baron Dieskau in the Battle of Lake George, 172; instructions to, respecting the limits of Acadia, 213; the correspondence of, turned over to the British by Pichon, 235

Venango, the building of Fort Machault at, 88

Verden, the Duchy of, and George II, 349

Vergor, Louis du Pont du Chambon de, commandant of Fort Beauséjour, profits secured by, from his post, 221; steps taken by, to resist the English attack, 229; grants special protection to Acadians resisting the English, 229; efforts of, to secure relief fail, 229–30; obliged to capitulate, 231; the pillaging of the King's stores by, 233

Village de la Baye Verte, a French post, 212

Villeray, M. de, commandant at Fort Gaspereau, the surrender of, 233

Villiers, Capt. Louis Coulon de, brother of Jumonville, sent to Fort Duquesne, 36; placed in command of the expedition against Washington, 36; at Mount Braddock, 37; defeats Washington at Great Meadows, 39–40; terms of surrender of

Washington prepared by, 40; restrains the Indians at Great Meadows, 42; the return of, in triumph to Fort Duquesne, 44; sent to guard Fort Niagara in 1755, 155; the camp of, at Niaouré Bay, threatens Oswego, 197

Vire, France, the place of nativity of Pichon, 218; the gift to, of the manuscripts and library of Pichon, 242

Virginia, Province of, the Assembly of, votes funds for frontier defence, 24; the indifference of the inhabitants of, to the fate of the frontier, 24; the volunteers of, and the issue of officers' pay, 28–30; the conduct of the regiment of, at Wills Creek, 48; a plan to provide Independent Companies for, 51–2; recruits secured in, only in face of desertion and riots, 53–54; the failure of, to provide Braddock with provisions and horses, 75; the troops of, and the Battle of the Monongahela, 96–7; the ravishing of the frontiers of, 127; faces its greatest crisis in 1755, 134; measures taken by, 134–5; the government of, unwilling to participate in a campaign in 1756 against Fort Duquesne, 185; defences for the frontiers of, constructed, 185; no support from, for the Crown Point campaign, 186; Acadians sent to, 277, 279, 280; and the Acadian exiles, 285, 299–304

Voluntown, Connecticut, Acadian exiles in, 323

Wagons, the great waste of, in Washington's march to Mount Braddock, 35; Franklin secures, for Braddock, from Pennsylvania, 75; the destruction of, in Braddock's expedition, 80

Waite, Lieut. John, on the weakness of Fort Lawrence, 215

Wall, General Richard, Spanish Foreign Minister, pro-British leanings of, 400–1

Walpole, Horace, on Braddock, 57

Walpole, Horatio, former British minister in Holland, 55

War, the concept of a limited, 100–1; why France did not issue a declaration of, in 1755, 118–9; a declaration of, in 1756 by both Great Britain and France, 416–7

War of the Spanish Succession, the fate of Antwerp and the, 352; and the principle of "balance," 355

War of the Austrian Succession, 356–7

Ward, Ensign Edward, surrenders the unfinished fort on the Ohio, 23; sent from Wills Creek to Williamsburg, 24

Washington, Lieut. Col. George, potential military leader, 10; Virginia volunteers led by, 10; moves against Fort Duquesne, 22–3; the decision of, to advance to Redstone Creek considered, 23; urges reinforcements, 23; the attitude of, toward the Virginia recruits, 24; looks in vain for Southern Indian support, 28; the issue of officers' pay and, 29; threatens to resign command, 29; rebuked by Dinwiddie, 29–30; fortifies himself at Great Meadows, 30; warned by the Half-King, 30; determines to strike the French detachment, 30; aided by Tanacharisson, defeats the French, 31; the question of the assassination of Jumonville by, considered, 31–2; decides to proceed toward Fort Duquesne, 33–4; at Mount Braddock, 34–5; the decision of, to retreat to Wills Creek, 35; the soldiers of, arrive at Fort Necessity, 35; decides to defend the fort, 35; the defence of Fort Necessity by, 39; the surrender of, 40; the retreat of, from Great Meadows, 41–2; activities of, at Wills Creek, 42; the immaturity of, as a military leader, 43; the failure of the Indians to support, at Great Meadows, 45; refuses to serve under proposed reorganization plan, 52; the unpopularity of, with regular officers, 53; distrusted by the Indians, 53, 77–8; becomes a member of Braddock's staff, 77; the loyalty of, to Braddock, 77; the illness of, on Braddock's expedition, 80; surrenders his horse to Braddock, 81; expects to arrive at Fort Duquesne, 82; advises Braddock to send forward a detachment, 82; the impatience of, with the slow movement of Braddock's army, 83; Braddock's solicitude for, 84; the advice of, upheld at the Salt Lick Creek conference, 85; rejoins Braddock, 85; on the conduct of the regular troops in the Battle of the Monongahela, 97; arguments in favour of the tactical views of, 97–8; the defence of Braddock by, 98; placed at the head of the Virginia forces, 134–5; a colonel's commission sought for, 134–5; the claims of, supported by Shirley, 211

Watertown, Massachusetts Bay, Acadian exiles criticize, 330

Watts, John, a member of the New York Provincial Council, assists in the undermining of General Shirley, 187

Webb, Col. Daniel, sent to America with the rank of major general, appointed temporary commander-in-chief in America, 188; ordered to take over Shirley's command, 192; ordered to relieve Oswego, 193; delay in the departure of, 194; receives news of the fall of Oswego, 195; destroys the forts at the Great Carrying Place, 195; relations of, with Alexander and Morris, 195; question of military leadership of, 202; at the conference between Abercromby and Winslow, 207

West, Rear Admiral Temple, receives the surrender of the *Espérance*, 125–6; the battle off Minorca and, 411–2

Westchester County, New York, Acadian exiles in, 319–20, 321

Westenhook, Massachusetts Bay, effects of the dispute between Livingston Manor and town of, over lands, in 1755, 143

Whaleboats, the use of, on Lake Ontario, 159, 160

Whigs, the attitude of, toward the Hanoverian kings, 348–9

Wicomico County, Maryland, Acadians sent to, 304

Willard, Captain, ordered by Monckton to burn Acadian villages, 265

William of Orange, the marriage of, with Mary, in 1677, 355

William the Silent, proposals of, for the Low Countries rejected by Flanders and Brabant, 364

Williams, Charles Hanbury, British Ambassador at St. Petersburg, earlier activities of, 370; the Russian subsidy treaty signed by, 370–2

Williams, Colonel Ephraim, of Massachusetts Bay, commands the forces sent against Dieskau, 170; the forces of, ambushed, 170–1; the death of, 173

Williamsburg, Virginia, the governors' conference at, 51–2

Wills Creek, Washington at, 23; the building of a fort at, 48

Wilmington, Massachusetts Bay, Acadian exiles criticize, 330

Wilmington, North Carolina, Acadians exiled to Georgia at, 289

Wilmot, Montague, Governor of Nova Scotia, administers the oaths to the returning Acadian exiles, 335

Winchester, Virginia, Indian conference at, 27

Windward Islands, West Indies, the French government desires to colonize the, by Acadians, 338–9

Winslow, John, of Massachusetts Bay, colonel and then major general, placed in command of the army organized to capture Crown Point, 192; appointed major general, in command of the Crown

Point expedition, 203–4; receives the hearty support of New England, 204; the embarrassing situation presented to, with the displacing of Shirley, 205; and the New England governments, 206; fruitless conferences between Abercromby, Loudoun and, over the Crown Point campaign, 207–8; turns over Fort William Henry to Major Eyre, and disbands the New England forces, 208; enlists troops for the attack against Fort Beauséjour, 227; had constructed Fort Halifax in 1754, 227; commands a battalion of New England volunteers, 227; accepts the surrender of and occupies Fort Gaspereau, 233; sent to Minas Basin to collect the Acadians, 266–7; instructions to, from the Nova Scotia Council, 267; the arrival of, at Grand Pré, 267–8; the maturing of the plans of, 268–9; the inhabitants of Minas Basin addressed by, 269–70; qualifications of, for the task, 272; treatment of the Acadians by, 273–80

Wolfe, General James, the views of, respecting Cumberland, 56

Woodbury, Connecticut, Acadian exiles in, 323

Wood Creek Fort, erected at the Mohawk-Wood Creek Great Carrying Place, 163; the burning of, by General Webb, 195

Wood Creek, New York, the great portage between the Mohawk River and, 149; the navigation down, to Oneida Lake, 149; the clearing of obstructions from, 184; the stopping of the navigation of, by General Webb, 195

Wooster, Captain, brings Acadian exiles to Connecticut, 322

Wraxall, Peter, secretary to General Johnson, description of Lake George by, 168: accounts of the Battle of Lake George by, 170–3; commended by Johnson, 177; assists in the undermining of General Shirley, 187

Württemberg, the Duke of, and French subsidies, 392

Yarmouth County, Nova Scotia, returning Acadian exiles resettled within, 336

York, H.R.H. Edward, Duke of, Fort Edward named in honour of, 166

Yorke, Colonel, part of the regiment of, sent to Newfoundland, 109

Youghiogheny River, the impossibility of using boats on, 30; a road from Philadelphia to, built, 75

Ypres, Austrian Netherlands, the Barrier Treaty and, 353

A NOTE ON THE TYPE

This book is set in Linotype Caledonia. Caledonia belongs to the family of printing types called "modern face" by printers — a term used to mark the change in style of type-letters that occurred about 1800. Caledonia is in the general neighborhood of Scotch Modern in design, but is more freely drawn than that letter.

The book was designed by W. A. Dwiggins, and composed by The Plimpton Press, Norwood, Massachusetts. Printed and bound by The Haddon Craftsmen, Inc., Scranton, Pennsylvania.